The Quest for
a Just World Order

Also of Interest

†Available in hardcover and paperback.

Westview Special Studies in International Relations

The Quest for a Just World Order
Samuel S. Kim

In response to a growing sense of dissatisfaction with the state of the world and the state of international relations research, Professor Kim has taken an alternative approach to the study of contemporary world politics. Specifically, he has adopted and expanded the cross-cultural, interdisciplinary, and transnational approach developed by the World Order Models Project (WOMP), an enterprise committed to the realization of peace, economic equality and well-being, social justice, and ecological balance.

Systemic in scope and interdisciplinary in methodology, *The Quest for a Just World Order* explains and projects the issues, patterns, and trends of world politics, giving special attention to the attitudinal, normative, behavioral, and institutional problems involved in the politics of system transformation. Professor Kim also attempts to remedy a number of problematic features of traditional approaches, including a value-neutral orientation; fragmentation and overspecialization; overemphasis on national actors, the superpowers, and stability; and the Hobbesian image of world politics.

Part 1 presents a conceptual framework for developing a normative theory of world order. Each of the four chapters in Part 2 examines a specific global crisis in depth, working within the framework laid out in Part 1. In Part 3 a variety of desirable and feasible transition strategies are proposed, and Professor Kim assesses the prospects for achieving a just and humane world order system by the end of this century.

Samuel S. Kim is a professor of political science at Monmouth College and senior fellow at the World Policy Institute (formerly the Institute for World Order). He is the author of *China, the United Nations, and World Order* (Princeton University Press, 1979), the coauthor (with Richard Falk) of *The War System: An Interdisciplinary Approach* (Westview Press, 1980), and the coeditor (with Richard Falk and Saul H. Mendlovitz) of *Toward a Just World Order* (Westview Press, 1982).

Written under the auspices of the
Center of International Studies
Princeton University

A list of other Center publications appears at the back of the book.

The Quest for
a Just World Order

Samuel S. Kim

Westview Press / Boulder, Colorado

Westview Special Studies in International Relations

Published in 1984 in the United States of America by
  Westview Press, Inc.
  5500 Central Avenue
  Boulder, Colorado 80301
  Frederick A. Praeger, President and Publisher

Library of Congress Cataloging in Publication Data
Kim, Samuel S., 1935–
  The quest for a just world order.
  (Westview special studies in international relations)
  Bibliography: p.
  Includes index.
  1. International organization. I. Title. II. Series.
JX1954.K47 1983   341.2   83-10327
ISBN 0-86531-365-2
ISBN 0-86531-433-0 (pbk.)

Printed and bound in the United States of America

10   9   8   7   6   5   4   3   2   1

To the Memory of My Mother

Contents

PART 2
THE STATE OF THE HUMAN CONDITION

PART 3
BUILDING AN ALTERNATIVE WORLD ORDER

Tables and Figures

Acknowledgments

It is somewhat embarrassing to admit that so many individuals and institutions have been implicated in so many ways in the conception and completion of this modest work. Unlike my other projects, the moral and intellectual rationale for this book came directly from Saul H. Mendlovitz, a true friend, formidable colleague, and indefatigable director of the World Order Models Project (WOMP) for all seasons and scholars. Without his persistent prodding and unflagging support, this project would not have seen the light of day.

Subsequently, the Institute for World Order (recently renamed the World Policy Institute) was willing to bet on a skeletal idea by granting me several senior research fellowships for 1980–1983. I am particularly grateful to Robert Johansen and Sherle Schwenninger for their moral, intellectual, and financial support of this project through the various stages of its odyssey to completion.

I owe my greatest intellectual debt to Richard Falk, whose ground-breaking scholarship and pioneering contributions to the development of world order studies are such that I should require another book, not a mere paragraph, to recount them. I feel fortunate to have been his partner on so many projects, most recently as coeditor of the *Studies on a Just World Order* series. Much of the book, especially Chapter 3, has been greatly influenced by values that brought us together in our common journey. Even though his direct participation in this project has been minimal, he, more than any other single scholar, has helped me along the seemingly endless and tortuous road to a just world order as friend, teacher, critic, and companion par excellence.

My tenure as Visiting Professor of Public and International Affairs at the Woodrow Wilson School, Princeton University, in 1979–1981, provided me with an ideal setting and an invaluable opportunity to try out some of the ideas and values embodied in the book. Many discussions with my students in various courses, especially those in Politics 336 (Introduction to World Order), had an important influence on the shaping of this book. I also owe special thanks to the Center of International Studies, Princeton University, and especially to its director Cyril Black, for two postdoctoral research fellowships in 1979–1981, without which the research and writing of this project would not have been possible. The following pages, I hope, justify the Center's casting its lot once again with this project. I gratefully acknowledge that this is my fourth book-length project to be included in the Center's list of sponsored research.

I am grateful to Samuel Magill (President), Eugene Rosi (Provost), and Kenneth Stunkel (Dean) of Monmouth College for their extraordinary patience and tolerance with a "phantom professor." Furthermore, they have been most accommodating to the claim on my time made by this and other projects by granting me released time from teaching during the academic years of 1981–1983. I also acknowledge with gratitude two faculty creativity grants from Monmouth College in 1981–1983 for the preparation of the manuscript in its final form.

At various stages of research and writing, I have had the benefit of critical comments and suggestions from friends and colleagues in the field of international relations and world order studies. For their advice and criticisms in the conceptual stage, even though I have been more resistant than responsive in some cases, I particularly would like to thank Cyril E. Black, Michael Doyle, Richard Falk, Jonathan Galloway, Leon Gordenker, Joseph Grieco, Manfred Halpern, Robert Johansen, Friedrich Kratochwil, Saul H. Mendlovitz, Ralph Pettman, Sherle Schwenninger, and Robert C. Tucker.

In the course of revising the manuscript for publication, five scholars played the role of coaxer by providing extensive and detailed written comments and criticisms for change. Sherle Schwenninger read an early draft of a bulky and unmanageable manuscript in its entirety and offered very helpful comments on practically every part of the book. For this thankless yeoman's service as well as for his unflagging encouragement throughout, I am most grateful. I would also like to express my deep gratitude to Louis René Beres, Robert Gilpin, Michael M'Gonigle, and Margaret Sprout, all first-rate scholars with international reputations, who gave unstintingly of their time, enthusiasm, and knowledge in reading parts of the manuscript and providing extensive written criticisms for revision.

I am grateful to numerous international civil servants in the functional sector of the United Nations system, especially those at WHO, UNCTAD, and UNEP, who have responded generously and promptly to my inquiries and requests for information and documents on specific issues or problems within their bailiwicks. I also extend my special thanks to the staff personnel of the Dag Hammarskjöld Library at UN Headquarters in New York for their invisible collaboration with my search for relevant documentary materials.

It has been a great pleasure to work with Westview Press in the production of this book. As always Lynne Rienner has shown an abiding interest and trust in my work and has joined hands with Lynn Arts in guiding this manuscript through the various stages of the production process. Holly Arrow gave generously but judiciously of her enormous editorial imagination and talents in making the book more readable and jargon-free than would otherwise have been the case.

Finally, without the forbearance and support of two loving ladies—my wife, Helen, and our daughter, Sonya—this project would never have come to fruition. By participating at every step of this adventure and by sharing its opportunity costs, they have shown me many concrete means and ways to pursue my quest for a more decent and humane world order.

To all the above-mentioned individuals and institutions, I am deeply indebted without, of course, in any way implicating them in the particular views and interpretations of the book. From many kinds of "realist" skeptics in the field of international relations I beg indulgence. This study will not be music to the defenders of mainstream realism, but it is not intended to be. Because the quest for a just world order is a protracted process without any foreseeable conclusion, I am reluctant to pronounce the project finished. Instead, it is presented as a commencement exercise of sorts in "normative social science," a small first step in the journey of many thousand miles toward a relevant utopia.

S.S.K.
Elberon, New Jersey

Introduction

> *It was the best of times, it was the worst of times, it was the age of wisdom, it was the age of foolishness, it was the epoch of belief, it was the epoch of incredulity, it was the season of Light, it was the season of Darkness, it was the spring of hope, it was the winter of despair.*
>
> —Charles Dickens, *A Tale of Two Cities* (1859)

Although written more than a century ago, Charles Dickens's statement seems even more appropriate now as a characterization of our time and our global human prospect. Indeed, we are experiencing one of the most transformative and contradictory processes in the history of mankind. On the one hand, science and technology, with their instant worldwide communications and their fast mobilization of people's expectations and capabilities, offer unprecedented possibilities of developing a truly planetary human identity and unprecedented prospects for the betterment of the human condition. The common human journey into a relevant utopia is no longer a dream—it is a clear and present possibility. On the other hand, science and technology, far from realizing their potential for human liberation and well-being, have become instruments of control and dominance at the service of a small minority of economic, political, military, and scientific/technocratic elites throughout the world.[1] Science and technology have also become expensive luxuries beyond the reach of an overwhelming majority of the human race. The North-South gap is even greater in research and development (R&D) than in income, as the developed countries preempt 97.1 percent (leaving the developing countries only 2.9 percent) of world R&D expenditure.[2]

The social situation in our time, no less than in Dickens's time, reflects an ongoing dialectical tension between actual and potential normative reality. A radical reorientation and restructuring of science and technology for global human interests and needs must begin by debunking the mythology that science and technology are or can be value-neutral. Science and technology are man-made instruments for some social purposes; as such, they can be used to either close or widen the gap between what is and what ought to be in the human condition.

The challenging task of world order studies is to become familiar with the contradictory forces of creativity and destruction that affect the struggle for human emancipation and to become more sensitive to the underlying currents moving to transform the present global structure of violence, inequity, exploitation, and oppression. The search for a just world order necessarily centers upon the mastery of these contending forces.

This book makes no pretense of having discovered the master key to a relevant utopia. A work of "concerned scholarship," it has been prodded by a growing sense of dissatisfaction with the present state of the world *and* with the dominant modes of international relations research. It is guided by alternative—and I believe more realistic—orientations in the analysis of global problematique in each of the four world order value domains as well as in the prescription of what might be achieved by way of positive, transformative response to the human predicament. Although my preoccupations and perceptions may unwittingly reflect the constraining influences of this time in history, I have consciously striven toward a transnational, cross-cultural search for a more humane and just world order.

In pursuit of this line of macroanalysis, the present study adopts and expands the "just world order approach" developed by the World Order Models Project (WOMP), a cross-cultural, interdisciplinary, and transnational research enterprise committed to the realization of peace, economic equity, social justice, and ecological balance. The approach I have employed may be summarized as transnational and cross-cultural in value preferences, systemic in scope, and interdisciplinary in methodology, giving special attention to the attitudinal, normative, behavioral, and structural problems involved in the politics of system transformation. The issues, patterns, and trends of world politics are described, evaluated, and projected, and strategies for bringing about an alternative world order system are suggested—all within this explicitly normative framework of world order studies. Although it draws upon recent findings in various disciplines of the behavioral and social sciences, this book is particularly sensitive to actor-oriented and structure-oriented perspectives in deciphering the changing social reality of world politics.

Inspired by E. F. Schumacher's book, *Small Is Beautiful: A Study of Economics as if People Mattered,*[3] the late Roy Preiswerk, former Director of the Institute of Development Studies and a member of the faculty at the Graduate Institute of International Studies in Geneva, Switzerland, issued a plea for humanist reorientation in a thought-provoking article entitled "Could We Study International Relations As If People Mattered?"[4] This book is a response to his challenge, proceeding on the assumption that we can and must study international relations as if people mattered. But how?

I have placed special emphasis on what might broadly be conceived of as "world order populism," paying greater attention to the voices of the oppressed. My conception of the oppressed is quite broad, encompassing the victims of repressive regimes as well as the victims of invisible oppression in all of its ecological, cultural, and nuclear forms. By heeding the voices of the oppressed I hope to be more in touch with actual political struggles and movements, acknowledging both the extent to which world order values can be promoted in a variety of social contexts and the degree to which system transformation is a protracted, phased process entailing struggle and action (as well as thought and contemplation) at every stage. World order populism also calls for remedying a number of problematic (antipeople) features in the dominant modes of contemporary international relations research.[5]

The Centrality of Values

At the outset I reject the widespread illusion that science is a value-free, objective enterprise. In his brilliant and devastating critique of "scientific" racism from the craniometry of the nineteenth century to the hereditarian theory of IQ in the twentieth century, Harvard paleontologist Stephen Jay Gould shows how the history of scientific views on race has mirrored social prejudices and movements. Before 1859, he reminds us, nearly all scientists were creationists. In our time, nothing has dramatized the myth of value-neutral science as much as Cyril Burt's documented fabrication of data on the IQ of identical twins. No matter how much quantification is used to objectify its appearance—notice craniometry was the leading numerical science of biological determinism in the nineteenth century—"science, since people must do it, is a socially embedded activity."[6]

As if to capture a share of scientific aura and mystique, the modern social scientist often succumbs to the allure of statistics and accepts the desirability and feasibility of separating "facts" and "values" into two independent domains. The dominant bias in social science research against employing a normative framework in defining and evaluating social reality (especially strong in the United States), is predicated on the assumption that a fact/value—and science/ideology—distinction is logically possible, theoretically necessary, and axiologically essential.[7] "Social science," we are told, "is not concerned with what people should do, or whether they are doing what they should do."[8] Of course, any claim to be value-free or value-neutral is a value judgment of sorts, as it serves, whether wittingly or not, the maintenance of status-quo values. "In many societies, those who agree with the established power and values stand a good chance of being considered as scientists, while those who disagree and demand social change are easily discredited by the label of 'ideologues.'"[9]

In reality, the decision to study a particular dimension of global reality (subject) in any particular way (methodology) is seldom motivated by an abstract, absolute commitment to follow the canons of scientific inquiry or to meet the most rigorous philosophy of science tests of theories. Rather, it is influenced by underlying assumptions and penultimate social purposes. The selection of one set of problems over another, the application of a particular methodology or model, and the evaluation of the performance of the political system for the specified problems all involve value assumptions and preferences.

The final validation for all models and theories and "the ultimate court of appeal for all intellectual instruments, whether they are assertions of preference or claims to know," one political theorist writes, "is application to the environment, testing against *purpose*."[10] The philosopher John Dewey put it more bluntly: "Anything that obscures the fundamentally moral nature of the social problem is harmful, no matter whether it proceeds from the side of physical or of psychological theory."[11] Human purposes and goals cannot be value-free.

Moreover, any attempted value-neutral approach in international relations research is plagued by interactions between the status and image of the actor and the values and perspective of the analyst. It has even been suggested that "the actor must have no physical characteristics, such as clothing, beard, long hair, color, stigmata, and the like, that could affect the labeling process apart from the act itself."[12] Likewise, a cross-cultural study of aggression has shown the meaninglessness of describing one culture as more or less aggressive than another, given the difficulty of establishing a value-free universal criterion of evaluation.[13] Contrary to the repeated claims, then, there is no such thing as value-free (read purposeless and perspectiveless) research in international relations.

At the same time, there is a need to be sensitive to twin dangers in the osmosis between values and facts. On the one hand, a "value-neutral" approach tends to be morally naive or deceptive, conceptionally elusive, and substantively trivial or irrelevant to policy. It risks being trapped in straitjacket empiricism and losing sight of the ultimate raison d'être of international relations research. On the other hand, a normative approach, unless it is checked and balanced by a measure of empirical rigor, can easily become an exercise in sentimental or utopian wishful thinking. It tends to be methodologically sloppy and empirically suspect, and it always faces the danger of falling prey to some parochial ideological cause.

This study is anchored in the assumption that normative and empirical approaches are dialectical and can be complementary. Empirical research (data generation and trend analysis) is no longer the exclusive bailiwick of scientists, just as normative research (value evaluation and analysis) is no longer the exclusive bailiwick of philosophers. It is as difficult to formulate and assert values without any historical or factual basis as it is to conduct empirical research without any social purpose or normative frame of reference. Anatol Rapoport has argued that the probability of an event is not "an objective property of the event but depends on the way that we define the context in which the event is to be considered" and that "probabilities which we assign to events become reflections of our preferences rather than of our knowledge."[14]

What is needed is not to commit the common error of separating functional from political, fact from value, and empirical from normative theory, but to attempt to integrate and synthesize all of them.[15] There is no such thing as pure (i.e., value-free and culture-free) scientific or social fact. On the other hand, facts don't speak for themselves nor add up to a theory. On the contrary, it is a theory that makes sense out of facts, and "the most creative theories are often imaginative visions imposed upon facts."[16] In *An American Dilemma,* a classic written almost four decades ago and perhaps the most influential social science work in altering public perceptions on race and ethnicity, Swedish sociologist Gunner Myrdal offers a most cogent methodological explanation on facts and valuations in social science, capturing the dialectics of empirical and normative theory:

> Scientific facts do not exist *per se,* waiting for scientists to discover them. A scientific fact is a construction abstracted out of a complex and interwoven reality by means of arbitrary definitions and classifications. . . . Scientific terms become value-loaded because society is made up of human beings following purposes. A "disinterested social science" is, from this viewpoint, pure nonsense. It never existed, and it never will exist. We can make our thinking strictly rational in spite of this, but only by facing the valuations, not by evading them.[17]

No doubt, a "normative-empirical" approach goes beyond the commonly accepted paradigms of international relations research. But the dominant paradigms no longer work. As James Rosenau, a leading international relations theorist, put it: "Our great strides in theory and research during the 1950s, 1960s and 1970s no longer correspond well to the world they were intended to describe."[18] Even realist scholar John Herz now concedes that "a planetary view of the world and its problems comes closest to realities" and that he has come to align himself "with such students of international relations as Richard Falk or Richard Barnet, or futurologists, not of the Hermann {sic} Kahn variety but of the Flechtheim (1980) type, who recognize the outdatedness of many traditional interpretations of power or national interest."[19] The process of paradigm deterioration and delegitimation currently underway calls for an alternative approach (see Chapter 3).

Witness the impact of scientistic pretension in economic studies as it shifted from value-based thinking in the nineteenth-century mode of classical political economy to misplaced and blind aping of the mechanistic methods of physics in the twentieth century.[20] Modern mainstream economics has acquired the reputation of a dismal science largely because so many of its theoreticians became committed, as Oscar Wilde once said, to knowing the price of everything and the value of nothing. Even worse is the habit of equating "value" and "price" by defining and measuring the value of everything, including human beings, in terms of a price the market system of supply and demand puts on it. This is one of the main sources of dehumanization and alienation in the capitalist world system. Moreover, the failure of economists to come up with plausible explanations and potent prescriptions for contemporary economic maladies challenges the legitimacy of "chair-bound" economic theorizing.[21]

The challenge in international relations research, I believe, is not to pursue the mirage of mindless and value-neutral empirical rigor, but to make one's values and assumptions explicit and to synthesize normative and empirical theory. As Harold and Margaret Sprout once said, a "perspective-*less* book" in international relations is the rarest item in any library, and the choice is not between a particular perspective and no perspective but rather between "an explicitly stated perspective and an implicit, concealed, or disguised perspective, bootlegged in by the back door, so to speak. Furthermore, in assessing a particular chosen perspective, the relevant question to ask is not whether it is right or wrong, but whether it contributes more than other perspectives to a better understanding of the subject in hand."[22]

A just world order approach to the study of international relations rests upon the centrality of values. Every choice of theory, model, or conceptual framework in world order research is an expression of value preferences. However, this approach goes beyond the mere assertion of world order values. As a system-transforming approach to world order, normative transformation is a key issue on the world order agenda. This means that we have to begin by transforming the concept of value. As Yoshikazu Sakamoto, a key participant in WOMP, points out, the concept of value that underlies social science research assumes that "worth is a function of scarcity; i.e. things have *social values* when they are desired by a large majority of society but are accessible to only a portion of the members of society at the expense of others." Instead, the WOMP concept of value is based on "the notion that worth is a function of equal or equitable distribution of social values and things become valuable when they are shared as equally or equitably as possible by all the members of society."[23]

Of course, the approach suggested here is more easily promised than performed, but we need to try an integrated, normative-empirical approach because our task is not merely to describe global reality as accurately as possible but more importantly to change it in accordance with value preferences. We favor operational definitions of values that give insight into the authoritative allocation of social costs and benefits among different social and political groups in the global system so as to assess progress in a given period of international history in realizing world order values.

World order studies is postulated by the synthesis of normative and empirical analysis. Although the central objective is clearly normative in striving toward the realization of values, world order practitioners argue that the main global problems cannot be effectively explained, let alone projected or controlled, without first generating a vast amount of reliable empirical and behavioral data through rigorous empirical research. World order studies also adopts a holistic, integrated approach to the human condition by conceptualizing and analyzing the global problematique as a set of interlocking processes and relationships between and among the seemingly discreet global problems.

In short, world order studies does not so much reject the behavioral and social sciences as it attempts to refine, expand, and synthesize a variety of concepts, paradigms, and theories from different social science and humanities disciplines. The purpose is to develop concepts and theory suited to the world order modelling process. World order studies is designed to do what Saul H. Mendlovitz calls "normative social research"[24] and to develop a normative global paradigm for the study of value-shaping and value-sharing processes in a world that is becoming both increasingly interconnected and increasingly fragmented.

An Interdisciplinary Approach

As long as inquiry is constrained by the overspecialized and compartmentalized boundaries of modern academia, one risks slicing the subject into a scientifically manageable size to fit it into the purview of a specialized, methodological microscope. What emerges is a highly fragmented—and distorted—image of social reality, a worm's-eye view that accepts and legitimizes the existing social order. There are many reasons for the current fragmentation and specialization in the pursuit of human knowledge: the quest for "orginality" (which starts with the writing of a doctoral dissertation); the division of the world into separate nation-states; the allure of behavioral reductionism; the safety and comfort of expertise in specialized turf; academic fiefdom-building; the fear of being labelled a generalist or dilettante; and the professional prospect of advancement in an age of specialization. The division of labor and specialization in the global production of knowledge thus precede division of labor and specialization in the global production of goods and services.

The salami approach inherent in inductive empiricism and positivistic social science is the easiest way to make an unwieldy subject manageable. But a world order vision of humanity, let alone a coherent theory and praxis for intervention in the world historical process, cannot be achieved by slicing up and breaking down the global problematique into smaller and smaller bits and pieces. As one proponent of an interdisciplinary approach put it:

> The vast problems of hunger, war, hatred, and injustice cannot be solved by passing them down a specialized assembly line of social analysis in the blind hope that after thousands of small adjustments the situation will improve. We have spent too much time devising ways of evading responsibility for dealing with complex social problems by claiming to be capable of dealing with only a very small part of the solution. Moreover, we need to be motivated by a sense of urgency, as analysts and as humans, we cannot continue to engage in mere mental puzzle-solving while ignoring the immediate effects of global problems on millions of people every day. We must learn quickly how to put things back together in effective new ways rather {than} continue to find new ways to take things apart.[25]

Once the logic of the "multiversity" rather than the logic of the reality itself dictates our pursuit of knowledge, global reality becomes atomized, fragmented, and annihilated. The quest for "objectivity" leads social scientists to seek "crackpot rigor" and entraps us in fragmentation, narrowing our conceptual and normative focus (because of nationalistic, cultural, class, or methodological biases) to the point where our version of reality becomes too limited, too retrospective, and obsolescent in a period of rapid change.

Fragmentation also works to desensitize us to the moral and ethical implications of our knowledge-seeking activities. The pursuit of value-free objectivity, whatever the motivation, easily leads to an incapacity to call a spade a spade. Without a value-specific frame of reference, objectivity in social science scholarship—commonly interpreted as a minimum use of value-laden expressions and a maximum use of abstract, often dehumanizing terms and objectifying numbers—can turn into a will-o'-the-wisp at best and a mask for disguising social reality at worst. The more we commit ourselves to the division of labor and specialization in the pursuit of knowledge, the more we atomize our image of social reality, the more we diffuse our sense of shame, and the more we disavow our share of moral responsibility in the social process. As I will show in Chapters 5 and 6, fragmentation and dehumanization are proceeding hand in hand in the global political economy and human rights areas.

To follow mechanically the trajectory laid out by the disciplinary autonomy of academe leads invariably to fragmentation. To acquire a more holistic and integrated conception of a global human identity, we need an interdisciplinary approach. The world is now constituted biologically, materially, ecologically, and spiritually in such a way as to make the unity of the human species the starting point for analysis and prescription. The notion of a global capitalist system that operates independent of constituent national societies—the central assumption of the world-system paradigm as developed by macrohistorical sociologists (Bergesen, Chase-Dunn, and Wallerstein)—captures one important dimension of the changing global reality.

An interdisciplinary approach does not necessarily reject the basic theories, models, and paradigms of various behavioral and social science disciplines. Instead, it seeks to redefine, reformulate, and reintegrate different theories about human behavior and social process. In this way, an interdisciplinary approach may help in the elusive process of building consensus on world order values.

The main task of an interdisciplinary approach is to enhance "world order realism" so as to bridge the gap between theory and practice, between empirical and normative, between the academic and the activist, and between the present and the future. The world-system approach, exemplified in Immanuel Wallerstein's work, offers an interdisciplinary model for macro-inquiry into the world historical process. Wallerstein refuses to accept cleavages in social science research along disciplinary lines, arguing instead "for an integral connection between historical social science and politics which is avowed and unashamed."[26]

World Order Realism

The mystique of "realism" exerts a powerful hold on human thought and action. Indeed, the secret to the tenacity of the existing social order lies in the monopolistic power of ruling elites to define the limits of the possible—and to create the illusion of permanence—in a self-fulfilling and self-serving way. Elitist definition of the possible often works to suppress people's *hope* and reinforce people's *fear* of social change.

Conversely, any social movement for system transformation rests upon the assumption of human capacity for change. No social and political movement for change can go far without first conquering the credo of historical inevitability. Accordingly, "realism" plays a key role in first defining and then contracting or expanding the limits of the possible. The ruling elites' resistance to social and political change stands in striking contrast to their unabashed support of technological change. System transformation is the art of the possible or the art of the impossible, depending on how "realism" is defined.

From the perspective of world order studies, realism as defined by the realist school of thought in international relations research is problematic in several respects. First, realism is often expressed as a disbelief that normative or potential views of reality (what ought to be or what will be) are meaningful or applicable to politics. In effect, mainstream realism is not so much an empirical/scientific description of "objective reality"— whatever that may mean—as it is an ideology designed to discredit those who challenge the existing social order and prescribe change. The repeated charge of utopianism against any system-transforming approach to world order performs a system-maintaining function.

Second, the concept of "power" in mainstream realism is excessively narrow and limited. This realism respects only material and physical power and is contemptuous of "normative power," or what the late Martin Luther King, Jr., called "soul force." It denies the existence of the world normative system. This conception has influenced both rightist and leftist dictators, including Joseph Stalin, who dismissed the "soul force" of the Pope by retorting, "How many divisions does he have?" This brand of realism can be traced back to Machiavelli, who in a self-serving way advised his prince: "A prince should therefore have no other aim or thought, nor take up any other thing for his study, but war and its organization and discipline, for that is the only art that is necessary to one who commands, and it is of such virtue that it not only maintains those who are born princes, but often enables men of private fortune to attain to that rank."[27]

The supreme irony here is not that Machiavelli failed as a moralist but that he failed as a realist. Blinded by a narrow, mechanical model of reality, he failed to recognize some of the great economic and social transformations of his own time. While the Turkish conquests, the shift of trade to the Atlantic and the New World, and the Reformation were transforming the political landscape of Italy, Machiavelli brilliantly showed a termite vision of reality preoccupied with praetorian power politics and its many details, ignoring what was happening to its normative foundations.[28]

Third, mainstream realism is postulated implicitly or explicitly on the Hobbesian image of human nature as *homo homini lupus*—man as a vicious and cruel wolf unto his fellows. In the Hobbesian state of nature characterized by a war of everybody against everybody else, human life is "solitary, nasty, brutish, and short." Hans Morgenthau, the most eloquent spokesman of the realist school, has echoed this Hobbesian assumption by arguing that "politics, like society in general, is governed by objective laws that have their roots in human nature" and that human nature "has not changed since the classical philosophies of China, India, and Greece endeavored to discover these laws."[29] Kenneth Waltz, another realist scholar, reformulates the logic of Hobbesian "realism" by asserting that "necessities do not create possibilities."[30] The realist credo and logic of realpolitik, accepted and advanced in varying degrees by such prominent international relations scholars as Aron, Bull, Gilpin, Kissinger, Morgenthau, Rosecrance, and Waltz, are anchored in this deterministic Hobbesian view of human nature (see Chapter 3). But both realities and necessities do change, and in our time change rather rapidly. As they change they redefine the limits of the possible.

Fourth and finally, mainstream realism emphasizes the past and present. If traditional utopian thought has tended to escape into the future from the present human predicament, traditional/mainstream realist thought has shown a retrospective, siege mentality, selectively invoking the tragedies of human history to legitimize its system-maintaining, "law and order" approach. The logic of mainstream realism is the notion—and I argue throughout the book that this notion defies reality—that humanity can muddle through by continuing on the present course. The present global structure of values, interests, and institutions is so well shielded by the mystique of such power-oriented, state-centric "realism" that even many modest system-reforming measures (e.g. UN peacekeeping and the New International Economic Order—NIEO) are often dismissed as "unrealistic."

My approach, or what may be called "world order realism," starts with the assumptions that social reality is amenable to multiple readings, that it is more complex and mysterious than many of us imagine, and that it is not—and cannot be—perceived in a value-free manner. Social reality has both empirical and normative dimensions; it reflects not only what people actually see but also, more importantly, what they want to see. This definition of social reality tends to have a self-fulfilling effect. As sociologist W. I. Thomas put it: "If men define situations as real, they are real in their consequences."[31]

Twenty years and probably more than twenty books later, there is still no agreement on the central mysteries of the Cuban Missile Crisis. Scholars and policymakers are reinterpreting the event—and redefining the reality—of the Cuban Missile Crisis, we are told, "to support particular views about the virtues of arms control, or the untrustworthiness of the Russians, or the need for nuclear parity, or the necessity for restoring superiority."[32]

We need to remind ourselves here that all great transformations in the course of human history have been propelled by the introduction of a totally new conception of reality, by an alternative world view that shifted the flow of world history. This dialectical conception of social reality helps us to see more clearly what we have to fear and what we have to hope, where we are today and where we want to be tomorrow, and how we need to build bridges and pathways to make the world order transition from here to there. The ultimate test of social science research lies in the extension of our power to see the outer limits and possibilities of social reality for human betterment.

System Transformation

The system-maintaining bias of social science research is reflected not only in its pretensions of value-neutrality but also in its neglect of social change or system transformation. Sociologist Talcott Parsons declared in 1951 that *"A general theory of the processes of change in social systems is not possible in the present state of knowledge."*[33] Political scientists have also neglected change, Samuel P. Huntington wrote in 1971, "because they focused their attention on states where change did not seem to be much of a problem."[34] Even the rise of the international system approach in the 1950s and 1960s did not change the picture dramatically. System stability was the underlying normative and methodological assumption of international system theory. As a result, the central issue has been what variables contribute in what ways to the stability or equilibrium of the state-centric international system, and not system-transforming forces and processes.

In 1980 and 1981, however, there was a major rejuvenation of "system change" in international relations research. In 1980, a collaborative project, entitled, *Change in the International System,* and the inaugural issue of the *International Political Science Review* (official journal of the International Political Science Association), devoted exclusively to "studies in systems transformation," were published.[35] In 1981, the official journal of the International Studies Association devoted an entire issue to "world system debates" pivoting around the Wallersteinian macrostructural, system-transforming approach to international relations.[36] In the same year, Robert Gilpin presented a most sophisticated realist grand theory of system change.[37]

Despite the differences in normative assumptions and methodological orientations, these publications may be accepted as the opening salvos of a debate on grand theorizing on system change in international relations research. Nonetheless, the center of gravity in this debate lies in enhancing descriptive and explanatory approaches to system change, not in formulating viable strategies for system change. This is necessary but not sufficient. "Merely descriptive, or even explanatory and predictive approaches will only describe, explain, and predict mankind's pathological development without any chance of contributing to change."[38]

As critics have repeatedly pointed out, world order studies has also failed to develop a credible theory of social change. Obviously, the de-

velopment of a sound theory and praxis of system transformation is one of the most central and elusive tasks in world order studies. The theoretical and practical utility of contemporary world order studies rests largely on the extent to which it facilitates the normative, holistic shaping of human destiny. Its exploration of preferred futures can provide a road map for formulating transition strategies and for envisaging a positive transformation of political life at all levels, from the personal and local to the collective and global. The search for relevant pathways to preferred world futures that are normatively desirable and politically feasible is an ongoing dialectical process joining inquiry of the past, present, and future (see Chapter 8).

This study attempts to define and elaborate the underlying assumptions, operational values and principles, images of preferred world futures, and transition strategies of a just world order approach to system transformation. It may suffice here to summarize the general methodology and orientation defined and applied in the book—especially in Chapters 2, 3, and 8—as an alternative, non-Machiavellian, non-Marxist, nonviolent, nondeterministic, and nonapocalyptic approach to system transformation. System transformation does not *ipso facto* mean political integration or centralization at the global level, much less world government. Rather, it means a fundamental change in the existing values, norms, and structure in such a way, and to such an extent, that a different configuration of actors with different orientations toward power, security, well-being, and governance emerge. This is what is meant by the quest for a just world order.

An Organizational Overview

The organization of the book needs only a brief explanation. Part 1 presents the historical background and conceptual framework for the development of a normative theory of world order. Chapter 2 gives a bird's-eye view of the transformation of international politics. Chapter 3 evaluates contending images and approaches to world order and proposes a normative, system-transformation theory of world order as an alternative approach to the study of world politics. Each of the four chapters in Part 2 first examines a special global crisis within the framework developed in Part 1, then examines the response of the present international system to the crisis, concluding with a world order assessment of the global problematique involved. Part 3 depicts both traditional and contemporary future studies, establishes a world order/future studies interface, designs possible and preferred scenarios of alternative world futures, and suggests a number of broad orientations and principles for the transition process.

Part 1

From International to
World Order Politics

The Transformation
of World Politics

Any movement for a new social order necessarily rests upon the assumption of human capacity for change. The quest for a just and humane world order draws its energy from the conquering human spirit that translates the impossible of today into the possible of tomorrow. How many of the great social transformations of history would have been possible without the mobilization of this spirit? How much human suffering and exploitation could have been lessened if the victims had conquered the illusion of their fate and the credo of inevitability? The "Great Leap Forward" mentality is always fraught with the danger of becoming an easy escape from the predicaments of the present, yet there is even greater danger in allowing ourselves to be immobilized by the tragedies of human history.

The present is always too preoccupied with its own worm's-eye view of reality, which sees the future as unrelated to present concerns and beyond our theoretical grasp and social control. The transformations of historical world orders may provide a concrete empirical baseline from which the more plausible scenarios of alternative futures can be projected and contrasted with the extrapolations of the present. Before we can diagnose the conditions of the present world order system (see Part 2) and prescribe preferred futures (see Part 3), we need to reflect upon the historical roots and heritage of our present predicament.

Without some historical/transformational perspective on elements of change and continuity, it would be easy to inflate the outer limits or possibilities for the creation of a just world order. In seeking a relevant utopia, we may do well to recall what Marx once said: "Men make their own history, but they do not make it just as they please; they do not make it under circumstances chosen by themselves, but under circumstances directly encountered, given, and transmitted from the past."[1]

Transformation

What is "transformation"? This holistic term is used widely by writers of varying normative and methodological persuasions to connote a variety of images and visions ranging from an instrumental value to a terminal value, from a quantitative change to a qualitative change, from a slow, incremental, linear change to a sudden, drastic, discontinuous change, and from a self-deterministic to an interventionary, guided flow of the world historical process. Since I take a system-*transforming* approach to world order, the logic and rationale of which will be elaborated in Chapter 3, there is a need to reexamine and reformulate various meanings of the term to establish an integrated conception of world order transformation.

Transformation is a *transcultural* concept that connotes a fundamental break from the past in human experience and the beginning of a new life, new direction, and new relationship. It is also a *transdisciplinary* concept involving a drastic reshaping of human relationship at all levels of social organization.[2] Every religion or culture has its own stories and mythos of transformation. The Bible is particularly rich in transformational metaphors and anecdotes. The Old Testament begins with a vivid description of universal transformation in terms of God's creation of the heavens and the earth (the Alpha of divine transformation) and the New Testament ends with St. John's chiliastic, if somewhat amorphous, revelation of the coming of Christ (the Omega of divine transformation), with many human spiritual transformations in between. In the Gandhian philosophy of conflict, transformation is embedded in the normative principle of satyagraha (truth force)—that nonviolence, love, and truth can provide the energy to transform political, social, and economic inequities of society.

Transformation is a *revolutionary* concept of sudden awakening against the injustices of the existing social order. Hence, every conservative polity has its own protective devices designed to arrest transformation as subversive of the established order. *The Doctrine of the Mean,* a Confucian canonical text that guided the socialization process of traditional China for centuries, gives the following normative rationale:

> While there are no stirrings of pleasure, anger, sorrow, or joy, the mind may be said to be in the state of EQUILIBRIUM. When those feelings have been stirred, and they act in their due degree, there ensues what may be called the state of HARMONY. This EQUILIBRIUM is the great root *from which grow all the human actings* in the world, and this HARMONY is the universal path *which they all should pursue.*
>
> Let the states of equilibrium and harmony exist in perfection, and a happy order will prevail throughout heaven and earth, and all things will be nourished and flourish.[3]

Our main concern centers on the kinds of relationships that would have to be altered if we are to have a more just and humane social order. In short, we see transformation as a way of alternative human development, one that helps us to re-vision our past, present, and future in terms of the betterment of human relationship. It is a concept that calls for new standards of capacity, performance, and justice in describing and explaining the development of human bondage across levels and cultures and in prescribing change. It is a concept congenial to diachronic analysis of the development of human relationship through time.

More specificallly, we are concerned with system transformation. But how can we tell if a system transformation has taken place? Transformation is a *diachronic* concept, implying that a change takes place through time. Thus we can say that one type of system has become another type of system at a subsequent time if the principal defining characteristics of the former have been fundamentally and irreversibly altered. For the purposes of world order inquiry, values, norms, and structure are the principal defining characteristics. We therefore define world order transformation as a series of long-term and largely irreversible changes and trends in the established values, norms, and structure of international society, resulting in a new pattern of relationship between its constituent units (actors).

System transformation entails a metamorphosis in basic values. Every great transition from one system to another throughout human history has been accompanied by a widening zone of incoherence in the image of social reality. The discrepancies between theory and practice of the existing social order translate into anomalies of the established "social paradigm." Social paradigm is here conceived of as a master epistemological conception of reality and truth, one that performs cognitive, evaluative, and prescriptive functions in our coming to terms with "social reality."[4] When anomalies and discrepancies accumulate, the dominant paradigm can no longer provide explanations—let alone answers—for the changing social reality. Like a bent lens or a broken mirror, the paradigm becomes dysfunctional, giving rise to a legitimacy crisis. Out of such incoherence emerges a challenge, an alternative social paradigm. "Every transformation of man, except that perhaps which produced neolithic culture," as Lewis Mumford observed, "has rested on a new metaphysical and ideological base; or rather, upon deeper stirrings and intuitions whose rationalized expression takes the form of a new picture of the cosmos and the nature of man."[5]

In the beginning, the structural anomalies of the dominant social paradigm (or contradictions in Marxist terms) may be largely latent and invisible, and those who haul them into the light of day are merely ridiculed. As the anomalies and contradictions accumulate and multiply, expanding the zone of incoherence, the consensus on social values and norms begins to dissipate. The social classes polarize between the conservative forces defending the existing order and the emerging revolutionary forces challenging the legitimacy of that order. In such a situation, any alternative paradigm is branded as heretical.

The sudden and unexpected intervention of great cataclysmic forces or events can create managerial crises for the existing paradigm, and these crises serve as triggers that suddenly push the transformational process beyond the point of no return (threshold phenomenon). The Industrial Revolution unleashed such catalysmic force, giving rise to "modernization" in Western Europe. In the nineteenth and twentieth centuries, observes one noted historian, the changes of modernization "have been extended to all other societies and have resulted in a worldwide transformation affecting all human relationships."[6] Global war has served as a discontinuous, autocatalytic agent in the transformation of the international system,[7] and social revolution has performed a similar function in the transformation of the nation-state in modern times.[8] In either case, a rigid and maladaptive value system plants the seeds of its own decay and disintegration. Every revolution or social transformation is preceded by the collapse of consensus on the legitimacy of the normative order.

Great paradigm shifts that result in a new form of human relationship drastically different from the inherited mode of social order have been rare, and this metamorphosis has always taken a long time to mature. In the course of hominid evolution, the transformation of each of the five main hominid species (*Australopithecus afarensis, Australopithecus africanus, Homo habilis, Homo erectus,* and *Homo sapiens*) took the same time span of about 750,000 years.[9] Mumford writes that there have been no more than a half-dozen great transformations since the time of primitive man. In a comparative and macrohistorical study of the dynamics of modernization, Cyril E. Black identifies only three "great revolutionary transformations." Modernization, or the great process of revolutionary change in the modern era, "is of the same order of magnitude as that from prehuman to human life and from primitive to civilized societies; it is the most dynamic of the great revolutionary transformations in the conduct of human affairs."[10]

Thanks to the revolutionary rates of growth in human population, technology, information, communication, and social expectations in modern times, the pace of the transformation process has been greatly accelerated. The maturation periods for the agricultural, industrial, and postindustrial transformations have been successively shortened from millennia to centuries to decades, as if to catch up with the accelerating rates of human population growth. The current transformation, according to John Platt, "is as enormous as 10 Industrial Revolutions and Protestant Reformations, all rolled into one and occurring within a single generation."[11] The changes in the international system have also increased in both rapidity and scope.[12]

Yet system transformation has defied predictability. As one distinguished developmental economist put it, "The process of social change is much the same today as it was 2,000 years ago. . . . We can tell how change will occur if it occurs; what we cannot foresee is what change is going to occur."[13] Based on our accumulated knowledge about the antecedent conditions, mechanisms, and outcomes of the great transformations in the past, we can argue that another world-historical transformation is currently underway, but we cannot predict when or how this ongoing transformation process will reach the critical turning point. Like an invisible iceberg suddenly surfacing for its own historical moment, the hidden force that underlies the transformation process explodes in an unpredictable way. Who could have predicted a few years before the French Revolution that it would take only a few months to demolish the entire edifice of the social order buttressed by the aristocracy, the church, and the army? The critical turning points for the Russian, Chinese, Cuban, Vietnamese, and Iranian revolutions have proved to be no more predictable even by the participants themselves.

System transformation at both national and international levels is in large measure shaped by an interplay between environmental factors and human choice and intervention. Like cancers that may take from one to several decades to develop, depending on individual physiological conditions as well as on the dose of initial or repeated exposure to carcinogens, the transformation process is subject to a complex interaction of variables endogenous and exogenous to the system. Paradoxically, the unpredictability of human choice and intervention in the politics of transformation is at once our worst fear and best hope in the elusive quest for a new world order. This point will be further elaborated in Part 3.

Another important reason that the reality and predictability of world order transformation is denied is the dominant elites' control and manipulation of the superstructure—the flow of knowledge, information, and news in the service of the existing normative order. Paralyzed by social anesthesia, many of us have been led to accept what is defined as "real" as inevitable and immutable, denying in the process our own capacity for transformation. Manfred Halpern suggests a way out of this sociopsychological trap:

> We are not required to live out only one story in our life. We may even change our name to signify our entrance into a different destiny. It is essential, if we are to know who we are, where we came from, and where we are going, to discover what our initial story is—our personal story as well as the story of our own society. Then we can come to understand it and to ask if it still makes sense to live this story, or to find another.[14]

Although the international system approach has emerged as one of the dominant approaches to the study of international relations in general and international conflicts and crises in particular, theorizing about system transformation still remains controversial and underdeveloped. There is no agreement on whether the crucial variables of system transformation are exogenous or endogenous, autoregressive or interactive, discrete or continuous, deterministic or stochastic.[15] Consider the disagreement between two leading system theorists on transformation rules or types. Maintaining that there are no transformation rules, Richard Rosecrance nonetheless identifies nine different international systems since 1750. On the other hand, Morton Kaplan argues that there are transformation rules that govern the transition from one system to another, positing six generic types of international systems.[16]

In theory, international systems analysis is congenial to world order inquiry because it claims to be concerned about describing and explaining (1) the boundaries of the system, (2) the component political units, (3) the structures of the system, (4) the patterns of interaction, and (5) the rules and norms governing the process of the system. In practice, however, a system-maintaining bias has been the underlying normative assumption of this approach. As a result, attention has been directed toward variables that contribute to systemic stability or equilibrium, not to system transformation processes.[17]

As noted in Chapter 1, there is currently underway a resurgence of grand theorizing on system change.[18] Both neo-Marxist world-system and realist schools agree on the structure of the international system as the most important determinant of system change, but they differ as to what constitutes the underlying dynamic of the structure. Neo-Marxist world-system theorists, using the method of contradiction analysis, see the class-based economic structure of the global political economy as the principal defining characteristic and the prime motor of system change. As Wallerstein puts it, "We take the defining characteristic of a social system to be the existence within it of a division of labor, such that the various sectors or areas within are dependent upon economic exchange with others for the smooth and continuous provisioning of the needs of the area. Such economic exchange can clearly exist without a common political structure and even more obviously without sharing the same culture."[19]

The political realists, using the method of equilibrium analysis, instead see the state-centric power structure as the defining characteristic and the most important determinant of system continuity and change. The realist theory of international system change, as elegantly expounded by Robert Gilpin, postulates "the law of uneven growth" (or "the differential growth of power") among state actors—as against "the law of uneven development" in Marxist theory—as altering the costs, benefits, and incentives for changing the international system. An international system is in a state of equilibrium as long as there is a balance between the existing structure and the distribution of power and as long as no state calculates it profitable to attempt to change the system. A disjuncture between the existing structure and the redistribution of power puts the system in a state of disequilibrium, and war has been and still is the basic means of equilibrating the international system. "In both bipolar and multipolar structures," as Gilpin says, "changes in relative power among the principal actors in the system are precursors of international political change."[20]

The use of the terms "change" and "transformation" as synonyms has somewhat obscured the normative and heuristic power of the transformation concept. The question of whether or how much change constitutes "fundamental change" (and therefore transformation) is more a conceptual than an empirical matter. The answer depends on the nature, magnitude, type, and durability of what is changed and its impact upon the relationship among system actors. An incremental change that leaves the central defining characteristics of the system largely intact does not constitute transformation. Nor does a sectoral change that affects one component of the system, since this is not likely to affect systemic outcomes to any significant degree.

Despite the ado about the Organization of Petroleum Exporting Countries' (OPEC) transformation of the international petroleum regime, for example, it can be argued that this sectoral change was not sufficient to alter the class or state structure of the present international system. Without significant changes in all the principal variables, an international system cannot be said to have been transformed. On the other hand, a dialectical change with a critical turning point that alters the basic values, norms, and structure of the system constitutes transformation. In short, I conceptualize world order transformation as a dialectical and discontinuous process entailing broad and fundamental changes in the defining characteristics of the international system (i.e., the values, norms, and structure).[21]

Without the notion of discontinuous, nonlinear change, it is difficult to separate change from transformation. Analogous to the law of momentum, a discontinuous change becomes an autocatalytic (self-reinforcing) change when it reaches a critical turning point, which can be identified by a sudden confluence of multiple processes of mutual interaction and mutual reinforcement that significantly alters the direction and properties of a given social system. First, incoherence gives rise to the clarification and simplification of social choice. Second, hitherto quiescent and disparate individuals and groups join forces in opposition, besieging the old order from without and betraying it from within. Finally, there is a sudden great leap in momentum as changes in all segments of the system begin to gather strength. What is required in a world order transformation is not a myriad of small, incremental linear changes, but only a few powerful autocatalytic changes in the principal defining characteristics of a social system.

The critical turning point can also be identified retroactively by observing the outcomes of a transformed system. What are the kinds of outcomes that can be accepted as manifest evidence of system transformation? Change in the composition of system actors, change in power structure, change in the norms of statecraft, and change in the pattern of system processes— the system cannot be said to have been transformed without some basic change in these key variables. We are now back to our earlier formulation of world order transformation as a fundamental, irreversible change in the normative and structural variables to the extent that a new pattern of relationships among the constituent units emerges.

Values, Norms, and Structure

This conceptualization of world order transformation is anchored in the assumption that human behavior, including the behavior of the state, is conditioned and shaped by the values, norms, and structure of a given society. The international system may also be conceived of as a sort of society with its own values, norms, and structure. As Hedley Bull put it, "A *society of states* (or international society) exists when a group of states, conscious of certain common interests and common values, form a society in the sense that they conceive themselves to be bound by a common set of rules in their relations with one another, and share in the working of common institutions."[22] Before we examine the degree of continuity and change in historical international systems, however, the basic terms—values, norms, and structure—used in our diachronic analysis need to be defined and elaborated.

Values

The most common meaning of value is that of value as a criterion that influences selective human behavior. That is, values provide evaluative standards of desirable and preferable human behavior. "A *value* is an enduring belief that a specific mode of conduct or end-state of existence is personally or socially preferable to an opposite or converse mode of conduct or end-state of existence."[23] Values are a frame of reference for all human behavior except a narrow band of the most rigidly instinctive motor behavior.

The means/ends distinction is also found in the distinction between two kinds of values—*instrumental* (means) and *terminal* (ends) values.[24] Values as empirical components of social process can be conceptualized and analyzed as dependent variables that change as other variables change, as independent variables that cause change in social attitude and behavior, and as intervening variables that lead to action when activated. Values provide epistemological paradigms that perform cognitive, evaluative, explanatory, and prescriptive functions for human selective behavior. Values help us to define the state of the world, to evaluate the meaning of the world so defined, to explain the human condition, and to prescribe a correct line of action.

This is not to suggest that values are the only determinant of human behavior. By providing people with definitions of social situations and standards of behavioral preference, however, values do represent one of the major factors in the evaluation and prediction of human relationship. In the political process of both domestic and international society, the important function of values is to lay a moral foundation of shared beliefs and standards and to give or withdraw legitimacy. A typology of international societies can be made based on kinds or types of value systems. In our time, the UN General Assembly is the most active global arena for the politics of collective legitimation and delegitimation.

A value in itself is neither good nor bad; it depends on what it does to one's value system. That is, this too is a value judgment! Witness the contrast between the Parsonian and Marxist views on values. Parsonian value theorists see society as a "moral community" with commonly shared values that legitimate the inequalities of social organization. They assert that, "whatever their origins, values are an independent variable contributing to, or detracting from, the organization and integration of a society."[25] In sharp contrast, Marx saw values as no more than the ideological rationale of the dominant class: "The ruling ideas of a period have always been nothing but the ideas of the ruling class. . . . In each epoch, the thoughts of the ruling class are the ruling thoughts; i.e., the class that is the ruling material power of society is at the same time its ruling intellectual power. The class that has the means of material production in its control, controls at the same time the means of intellectual production."[26]

How—and where—do we find empirical evidence of values in a multicultural international society? The task is difficult but not hopeless. A careful, systematic analysis of the state actors' policy pronouncements and policy performance in various normative domains of international relations and of progressive codification of some commonly shared values (e.g., the UN Charter) provides preliminary clues on the status of values in world politics. The relationship between the degree of value coherence and sharing and the extent of collective cooperative action provides a point of departure for a value-centered analysis. As will be shown in Chapters 5 and 8, several comprehensive global survey studies of human values provide additional empirical data on the value-shaping and value-realizing processes.

Norms

Norms refer to specific prescriptive or proscriptive rules of behavior for a particular role or for a particular situation. Norms are not the same as values. Values, as general moral and definitional criteria and symbols, can exist independently of any specific situations; norms are role-specific and context-specific modes of behavior. For example, the world order value of nonviolence can be translated and codified into a great number and variety of behavioral norms. As sociologist Robin Williams describes it, "The same value may be a point of reference for a great many specific norms; a particular norm may represent the simultaneous application of several separable values. . . . Values, as standards (criteria) for establishing what should be regarded as desirable, provide the grounds for accepting or rejecting particular norms."[27]

When norms are defined in general terms detached from specific issues and circumstances, as sometimes happens in world politics, they become practically indistinguishable from values. The interchangeable use of the terms "norms" and "values" in international relations literature suggests that the line between the two is not clearly drawn. Nonetheless, shaping of the norms takes place within a framework defined and legitimated by the value system of a society. The common political science definition of politics as the authoritative and legitimate allocation of values indicates that a society's value system guides what social roles and functions are to be legitimated by what kinds of norms.

Accordingly, international norms are defined here as those rules and standards of behavior appropriate to a particular role or situation and elaborated or codified in accordance with the value system of international society. International norms define the bounds of the permissible so as to establish a measure of regularity and predictability in international relations. In short, international norms define what the members of international society ought to and ought not to do toward each other and to the society as a whole in their mutual interactions.

Viewed in this way, the decentralization of international society does not suggest so much an absence of norms as an extraordinary burden upon norms as a behavioral control device. The normative burden of international society is closely connected to the degree of strength and unity values enjoy among its members. When values are insecure and incoherent—as in a period of revolutionary change—norms become more important, more controversial, and more subject to defiance.

There are several contending schools of thought on the status of norms in international relations. The Hobbesian realist school still makes the assumption that international life is almost normless—that states are condemned to anarchy and war and that there is no escape from the perennial struggle for power. A variation on this realist theme acknowledges the existence of international norms but argues that they are the servants, not the masters, of national interests.[28]

The functionalist school in sociology (from Durkheim to Parsons) takes social norms as "givens" in any social system, including the international system, and stresses the consensus-generating and order-maintaining functions of norms. "In most current sociological theory," as Talcott Parsons writes, "order is conceived as the existence of normative control over a range of the action of acting units, whether these be individuals or collectivities, so that, on the one hand, their action is kept within limits which are compatible with at least the minimum stability of the system as a whole and, on the other hand, there is a basis for at least certain types of concerted action when the occasion so requires."[29]

The conflict schools, in particular the Marxian schools, do not deny that in a period of revolutionary change, norms become more important, more controversial, and more defied, but they regard norms as a means for one dominant social class to legitimate its hegemonic status and class exploitation. "The proletariat seeks to transform the world according to its own world outlook," as Mao wrote in 1957, "so does the bourgeoisie."[30]

International norms vary greatly in scope of codification and degree of precision or effectiveness. They may appear in the form of written bilateral and multilateral treaties and agreements, unwritten international customs and usage, hortatory resolutions and declarations of international organizations and conferences, and even unilateral self-restraint.[31] A great majority of international norms are—or are supposed to be—self-enforcing. Even in domestic social order, law-enforcing mechanisms work only at the periphery of society. Otherwise the social system would collapse.

Nonetheless, the legality and efficacy of international norms remain in the limbo of unresolved tension because of the variety of norm-making instrumentalities and the absence of widely accepted means to interpret and enforce these norms. The central question for world order inquiry is not whether there are international norms but rather what kinds of norms are being developed by whom for whose benefit and with what social consequences. Every international order is anchored in a set of normative assumptions and principles, and international politics is a value-realizing, norm-setting process.

Structure

"Man is born free; and everywhere he is in chains." This opening line in Rousseau's *Social Contract* (1762) captures the discrepancy between the ideal normative reality and the actual structural reality in social order. International structure is here conceived of as the aggregate of those established social patterns and arrangements that give coherence (and continuity) to the interrelationships of the actors in international society. A structure is one of the defining characteristics of a social system, not the other way around. Without the existence of two or more units there can be no structure. Without interactions between the units there can be no structure. Without an established pattern of interactions it is impossible to delineate structure.

International structure reflects the composition and stratification of international society. The size and scope of interactions, a function of the number and type of actors participating in the social process, suggests an empirical image of international structure. The status ordering, or distribution of certain rights and responsibilities, conveys a normative image of international structure. International structure defines the role, position, and status of each member.

The concept of social structure rests on the assumption of recurring patterns of human behavior. Social structure has the tendency to persist long after its original raison d'être has vanished. In seeking the causes of social injustice, a structure-oriented approach shifts attention from "human nature" or the psychological attributes of the dominant actors or groups to the social structure that defines who gets what, when, and how. Viewed in this light social injustice is no more than structural violence. Different structures affect behavior differently. Status and influence are fungible, mutually reinforcing, and also tend to be self-perpetuating because those actors with high status, or what Johan Galtung calls "structural power,"[32] define the rules of the game. There can be no doubt that the drive for status has far-reaching behavioral consequences for world order. What is often referred to as a struggle for power among nations is a manifestation of the struggle to maintain, reform, or transform the social stratification that underpins any given world order system. Hence, structural transformation is more important and necessary than normative transformation, but also more difficult to achieve in the quest for a just world order. An international system cannot be said to have been transformed unless its structure has been fundamentally altered.

The structure-oriented perspective so influential in sociology literature is useful in the development of a world-order theory of system transformation. For C. Wright Mills, "historical change *is* change of social structures, of the relations among their component parts."[33] For Immanuel Wallerstein, who almost single-handedly initiated the world-system approach and has already generated "world system debates" among international relations scholars,[34] the "long" sixteenth century brought about not an empire but

a Eurocentric world economy, which evolved into the modern world system as it began to link an international division of labor between core and periphery to the development of strong and weak states.[35] Defining social revolutions as rapid, basic transformations of a society's state and class structures, Theda Skocpol applies a "nonvoluntarist, structural perspective" in her analysis of the causes and processes of social revolutionary transformations in France, Russia, and China with special attention to international and world historical, as well as intranational, structures and processes.[36]

Another useful application of the concept of social structure in the study of world politics is "imperialism," a general theory of relations between or among social groups, in particular nation-states and classes, in a hierarchical structure. Although scholars have used the word "imperialism" in many different ways and for many different purposes, it was the Scandinavian school of peace research that redefined imperialism in a manner congenial to world order studies. Johan Galtung's theory of imperialism represents a pioneering attempt to construct a morphology of international society by establishing functional-structural linkages between imperialism and underdevelopment. Galtung's principal concern (value premise) is not to deal with the causes of war as such but to conceptualize, explain, and counteract *inequality* as one of the major forms of structural violence embedded in contemporary imperialism.[37]

In a similar vein, Dieter Senghaas presents a macrostructural theory of contemporary society. Senghaas conceptualizes conflict formations in contemporary world politics as a function of new domination structures, not as the outbreak of random processes.[38] Applying a macrostructural analysis to global political economy, Helge Hveem describes and explains the global dominance system as the development of an international hierarchical division of labor by which new levels and centers of control and accumulation are developed, whereas the structural constants—verticality, inegality, and feudality—are retained.[39] To explain "the international events that move over and around us," Ralph Pettman develops his arguments in terms of the overall social structure of the contemporary world. His central thesis is that the social structures most characteristic of our age are those of state and class.[40]

The concept of social structure thus provides a general framework of inquiry for our discussion of the macrostructural/historical development of international systems since Westphalia. Our broader concern may be described as the "who, what, how, and why" of status politics—who gets structural power, for what purposes, and in what manner? Why does social inequity persist? The concept of polarization, when defined in a structural sense as a pattern of interactions among the sovereign states for the preservation or restoration of an approximate power equilibrium, is also useful to our understanding of the change and continuity of international structure. It may shed some light on the mechanisms for sustaining the general pattern of power and influence (or persisting forms of dominant/

subordinate relationships) among the actors comprising the system. The development of international institutions is another dimension of change in international structure.

Changes in International Systems

For a diachronic analysis, I focus on international norms and structure as causally dominant variables in shaping behavior of the actors and in maintaining, reforming, or transforming international society. The choice of an original reference point and the delineation of developmental stages are also necessary. There is general consensus that the Peace of Westphalia (1648) marked the critical turning point in the transition from the medieval to the modern system of international relations.[41] We therefore accept Westphalia as a starting point against which subsequent changes can be broadly described and evaluated for their overall impact on the evolution of international systems through four historical periods: the classical period (1648–1789); the "concert" period (1814–1914); the League period (1919–1939); and the postwar period (1945–present).

The Classical Period

International Norms. The Thirty Years' War (1618–1648) served as a catalytic force, accelerating the transformational process that began as early as the Great Interregnum (1254–1273). The imperial/papal hierarchical conception of medieval society, dominated by the image of an Eurocentric Christian commonwealth, gave way to a new conception of world order based on the coexistence of sovereign states. The Peace of Westphalia marked the starting point for the development of new norms applicable to the behavior of new sovereigns. It was a landmark juridical event in the history of international law—or, more accurately, of the European law of states. International law, as Richard Falk observes, "performed a critical role in providing a normative bridge between the spiritualist pretensions of the Middle Ages and the statist pretensions of the modern era."[42]

Out of the protracted period of fratricidal religious wars and the ruins of a medieval Christian world order emerged the Westphalian statist paradigm, a secular concept embracing the state as the source of societal values, the guardian of survival and security, and the promoter of human well-being. Territorial states became the sole and legitimate actors in the transformed international system. World order was no more than a pursuit of the raison d'état of new sovereigns. Only sovereign states could wage war or enter treaty or alliance relations with each other. The principle of state sovereignty provided the general framework from which evolved specific state practices on war/peace, commerce, and political competition in non-European realms (the seas and overseas territories). The codification of statist norms in the form of international law followed state practice, not the other way around. International law is here defined as the more formalized and codified set of rules, principles, procedures, and standards more or less approved and observed by the actors in international society in their relationships with each other.[43]

The key international norms that developed were those compatible with sovereignty. The concept of sovereignty quickly became a protective principle of "real estate" with three coercive faces—absolutist, exclusivist, and segregationist—or, as Luiz Alberto Bahia put it, "*the property of properties,*" producing "violent resistance to any attempt at unifying the human species."[44] Like a property that has acquired an absolute value to be protected or expanded at any cost, the logic of sovereignty extended to the moral and legal right to resort to war. The strong and absolutist state at this time, as Perry Anderson has shown, was no more than a reorganized and redeployed apparatus of royal power designed to clamp the peasant and plebeian masses back into their traditional position at the bottom of the social hierarchy.[45] Even jurisprudential debate among international legal scholars proceeded from this straitjacket framework, reinforcing and legitimizing the centrality of sovereignty as the cardinal norm of international relations. That Vattel was without serious peer in stature and influence around the turn of the nineteenth century was a direct consequence of his faithful codification of the statist paradigm in his *Law of Nations* (1758).[46]

A corollary of the principle of state sovereignty was the principle of state equality—or, as Vattel put it in his celebrated argument, "A dwarf is as much a man as a giant is, a small republic no less a sovereign state than the most powerful kingdom." This norm of equality, however, was more applicable to the status of Catholicism and Protestantism than to the status of states. The principle of state equality was limited to the Great Powers in Europe, as both small European states and non-European states were treated as pawns in international (European) politics. The antihegemony norm of the classical period, embodied in a "just balance of power" (*justum potentiae equilibrium*), applied only to the members of the exclusive club. This principle of geopolitical equilibrium replaced the principle of natural law as an operative norm of world order. In depicting France as seen through the eyes of two Persians in the *Persian Letters* (first published anonymously in Amsterdam in 1721), Montesquieu offers a devastating commentary on the international law of the classical period: "International law is better known in Europe than in Asia, yet it can be said that royal passions, the submissiveness of their subjects, and sycophantic writers have corrupted all its principles. In its present state, this branch of law is a science which explains to kings how far they can violate justice without damaging their own interests."[47]

The international norms of the classical period were wedded to the conservative principles of royal legitimacy and dynastic succession. The doctrine of sovereignty meant that the dynasties ruling the territorial states of Europe recognized each other as rightful, independent, and equal sovereigns. Indeed, this period represents a golden age of international stability maintained by the balance of power in geopolitics. In commerce the prevailing norm was mercantilism, designed not so much to promote the welfare of society as to aggrandize the power of the absolutist state. The slave trade was even elevated "to the level of international law when England obtained from Spain under the Peace of Utrecht a monopoly for the importation of slaves through a special agreement—the Asiento Convention—and transferred that monopoly to the South Sea Company."[48] What mitigated the severity of power struggle and established a measure of stability in this competitive system of multipolarity were the common values and social ties shared and strengthened through cultural and marital interchange between aristocratic classes, the common interest to contain revisionist revolutionary challengers, and the common understanding that destruction of one sovereign state would destroy the very foundation on which the survival of all of them rested.

International Structure. From the very beginning of the modern states system the recurring tension between the normative pretensions of state equality and the structural realities of state inequality emerged as a major world order problematique. As noted earlier, the unipolar/imperial conception of world order based on the solidarity of Christendom was discredited beyond redemption during the Thirty Years' War. The big fragments of the shattered imperial order were rearranged at Westphalia as a multipolar system of secular sovereign states. Theoretically, each state became "separate and equal" in the enjoyment of its new sovereign status. In practice, however, the Westphalian system developed its own structure of dominance and hierarchy.

The so-called modern world system of states during the classical period was Eurocentric; its principal actors and the patterns of interactions among them all pivoted around "Europe." This system embraced North America, the Caribbean, and India, but these areas constituted the Periphery of what was basically a Eurocentric interstate system. The intense competition for status and power was limited to the great powers in the Center with France, Great Britain, Austria, and Russia enjoying first-class positions while Spain, Sweden, the Netherlands, Turkey, and Prussia struggled to reach the top without really attaining it for any length of time. In short, the first phase of a Center-Periphery dichotomy had already begun during this period. Not only non-European areas but also numerous small states within Europe were all treated as "the commons" needed for territorial compensation in the maintenance of the European balance of power among the great powers. The partitions of Poland, for example, did not violate the existing norms nor disturb the structure, because Poland was regarded as being outside the European system (Poland was a "frontier-country," as Europe stopped at the Vistula).[49]

The structural imperative for status drive and power struggle is inherent in the coexistence of sovereign states. The very competitive character of the state system of modern Europe, observes one historian, "distinguishes it from the political life of all previous non-European civilizations of the world."[50] This structure incites the incessant pursuit of state interests, disguised in the name of maintaining the European balance of power. The criteria for status assessment, though still ambiguous, clearly shifted from an ideological (religious) to a secular state-centric framework—emphasizing a state's capacity and performance in military, political, diplomatic, commercial, and cultural fields in the exercise of its sovereignty. Conflicts over symbolic issues of diplomatic protocol and precedence became an integral part of interstate relations, and at least two wars (the First Anglo-Dutch war and the War of Jenkin's Ear) were partly caused by disputes of this kind.[51]

The absence of codified rules for diplomatic precedence generated at one and the same time pressures for status competition and social stratification. During much of the period, France was *prima inter pares*. Although Louis XIV's global ambitions were perceived as a destabilizing accretion of power by one sovereign and were fought all over the world by a balancing coalition of major powers, ending with the Treaty of Utrecht in 1713, France's preeminence in the fields of language, literature, art, education, manners, fashion, cuisine, gardening, interior decorations, and architecture was widely recognized and even emulated. French became the lingua franca of diplomatic and high societies, and Versailles served as an architectural model for the German princelings. Nonetheless, the Westphalian principle of state sovereignty and equality could not disguise the fact that the classical period was marked by constant quarreling over diplomatic precedence and rank, as the contestants could not find a common ground for classifying the sovereigns nor agree upon the merits of each claim. "The great states, even the lowliest baronry of the empire, quarreled over rank."[52]

The classical period is often characterized as a golden era of the balance of power system. The balance of power as a war deterrent did not always work, as evidenced in the outbreak of two major wars in the period 1740–1758, when there was an approximate power equilibrium between the major European powers. But the balance of power as a flexible, ad hoc alliance system worked relatively well in moderating the severity and consequences of war as well as in preventing the rise of a single imperial power. A common ideology of aristocratic and monarchical conservatism fearing social revolution from within, freedom and flexibility of foreign policy decisionmakers in shifting alliance partners, relative stability and predictability in military technology, and availability of frontier countries and territories to which power clashes could be shifted and cushioned— all of these led to a common conception of legitimacy for the balance of power as a system-maintaining and system-stabilizing device. Of course, what made the balance of power so congenial to the competitive struggle among the great powers was its legitimizing cover for the pursuit of state interests in the Periphery through territorial compensation. In short, the multipolar balance-of-power system of the classical period worked well not as a war-deterrent device or as an instrument of social equity but as a device to moderate great-power clashes and to establish a hegemonic stability in the Eurocentric states system.

Despite some practice of conciliation, mediation, arbitration, and "international" congress as an ad hoc system of communication and conflict resolution among the sovereigns, social integration in the system was low. The logic of the Westphalian conception of sovereignty triumphed over the need for international institutions. The pleas for world order reform through institutional change—William Penn (1693), the Abbe St. Pierre (1712), Rousseau (1761), Jeremy Bentham (between 1786 and 1789), and Kant (1795)[53]—were all dismissed as being incompatible with the reality of the states system. The structure of the classical period reflected the dominant mood of separation, not integration, and autarky, not interdependence, in both political and economic fields, tempered by the shared notion that an Eurocentric world order had to be maintained through alliance (balance-of-power) politics among the great powers.

The "Concert" Period

International Norms. The outbreak of the French Revolution and the rise of nationalism in its wake gradually undermined the normative foundations of such multinational states as Russia, Austria-Hungary, and Sweden-Norway. The Westphalian system of states was "updated" as a new wine was poured into old bottles. The social and nationalist revolutions did not challenge the statist paradigm as such but merely argued that the only legitimate basis for political organization was a distinct ethnic or linguistic group. As the legitimacy principle shifted from royalty to nationality, the state as a legal concept of political authority and the nation as a sociopsychological concept of group identity gradually merged in the form of the state-nation or nation-state.[54]

There was no thought of seeking popular consent about the transfer of sovereignty at the Congress of Vienna. But the Paris Treaty, which ended the Crimean War, recognized the principle of national self-determination by taking into account the wishes of the Walachia and Modavia populations in the remaking of the political map of Europe. By World War I, national self-determination had become a global norm, a rallying cry of nationalists in Europe as well as in Asia, although it took another world war for this norm to find wider expression and realization. Yet this development has not so much altered the Westphalian statist framework as it has expanded it to accommodate a wider use of the nationality principle in normative international politics. The right of each nationality to become an independent political actor and enter world politics on an equal footing has developed as a central principle of world order.

The higher conception of human dignity emanating from the French Revolution with its Declaration of the Rights of Man and of the Citizen (1789) and the American Revolution with its Bill of Rights (1791) began to affect the normative discourse of international relations. The freedom of religious expression embodied in these historical documents was a great step forward, shifting normative concerns from the principle of religious toleration in interstate relations to the more positive affirmation of individual religious freedom. Treaties gradually began to incorporate more and more provisions concerning international protection of religious minorities, and the principle of religious freedom stimulated the development of the doctrines of humanitarian intervention in customary international law.[55] In addition, the abolition of slavery and the slave trade received international moral support early in the nineteenth century, although almost a century passed before the General Act of the Brussels Conference of 1890, "the Magna Carta of the African slave trade," provided military, legislative, and economic measures for ending the slave trade.[56] Thus ended the absolutist doctrine of *state* sovereignty with the entry of normative concerns for *human* rights in the international relations of the nineteenth century.

The exclusive concern of the Westphalian norms for system-maintenance could not withstand the mounting pressure of technological change associated with industrialization and modernization. The latter half of the nineteenth century witnessed the rise of international governmental organizations (IGOs) and nongovernmental organizations (NGOs) with their own norms and rules. Lacking independent political power and authority, IGOs and NGOs devoted themselves to the creation of global norms in various functional domains. This marked the beginning of nonstate actors' participation in normative international politics, extending international law into the functional domain of "low politics." Compared to the postwar period, however, the impact of IGOs and NGOs on the development of international norms was rather modest in the nineteenth and first half of the twentieth centuries.

The prototype of modern multilateral diplomacy was already established at Westphalia, Vienna, and Paris, but it was not until the 1860s that the international conference emerged as a regular forum for making multilateral conventions concerning the conduct of states in specified subjects. The subjects covered by these conventions included the rules of diplomacy (rank, protocol, procedure, and privilege), the principles of maritime law, neutrality, blockade, and contraband, free navigation and international waterways, copyright and patents, and rules of warfare. The number of "nonpolitical" treaties began to multiply, reaching the total of 16,000 between 1815 and 1926.[57] An increasing use of the international conference as a treaty-making forum and the proliferation of "open treaties" (open to signature and ratification by latecomers) expanded the jurisdictional reach of international law.

Yet the sheer quantitative increase in treaty-making activities does not necessarily suggest a qualitative change in the fundamentals of the Westphalian norms. The international norms of the "century of peace" (1814–1914) reflected the exclusive concerns of a few powerful states acting as self-styled guardians of world order. The Concert of Europe rested on the assumption of a conservative consensus that world order could not be maintained without the exercise of the special rights and responsibilities of the great powers. Such a world order even among the key players could not be maintained for too long. In the last quarter of the nineteenth century the Concert norms of great-power behavior could not withstand the explosive force of imperialist nationalism. With the ascendancy of social

Darwinism as a dominant norm of international geopolitics—and Hobbes-
ianism, statism, nationalism, and racism all joining in the service of imperialist
rivalry—the transition from "formative" to "integral" nationalism was
completed and international society was headed toward conflict on a scale
never witnessed in human history. Each major player was armed with a
legitimizing shield for overseas expansion and exploitation—Britain's "White
Man's Burden," France's "Mission Civilisatrice," America's "Manifest Destiny," and so on.

   This social Darwinian ethos was particularly congenial to the deformation
of cultural and revolutionary nationalism (Herder, Fichte, and Mazzini)
into integral or totalitarian nationalism (Maurras, Glass, and Maxse) with
its constant stress on strife and glorification of war. Both conservatives
and liberals joined in the militant march of jingoistic nationalism and
colonialism to legitimize their status and gain popular domestic support.
The resulting consensus on the legitimacy of colonialism laid the normative
foundation of the international system. As Donald Puchala and Raymond
Hopkins put it:

> The legitimacy of colonization was collectively endorsed by the metropolitan
> governments and, after 1870, by overwhelming cross-sections of national
> populations—including Americans. It was this overriding sense of legitimacy,
> the convictions that imperialism and colonization were right, that all means
> toward colonial ends were justified, and that international management to
> preserve major-power imperialism was appropriate, that contributed to the
> durability of the system.[58]

   Even in the development of international law, this was the heyday of
the positivist school. By severing international law from the societal,
philosophical, and axiological considerations and by drawing an artificial
line between what the law "is" (empirical law) and what the law "ought"
to be (normative law), the positivist school made international law irrelevant
by reducing it to the codified agreements of state wills. At worst, international
law was turned into a legitimizing cover for the state practice of realpolitik.
International law was at this time rather ingenious in concocting a variety
of rationalizations for aggression—notice "Spinoza's famous metaphor about
the sovereign natural right of big fish to devour the small, or Treitschke's
declaration that 'pacifists would mutilate human nature.' "[59] Note here that
every piece of Asian and African territories taken through imperialistic
plundering was "legitimized" by unequal treaties and defended by the
doctrine of *pacta sunt servanda* (treaties must be obeyed).[60] Some two and
a half centuries after the Peace of Westphalia, statism has taken the more
virulent form of nation-statism.

   International Structure. Many of the contradictions embedded in the
contemporary international structure began to emerge during this period.
While a number of ceremonial (protocol) issues of the preceding period
had been clarified, the overall structure seems to have developed a kind
of "dual personality" as if to accommodate the conflicting pressures of the

time. If the nineteenth century saw the rise of nationalism as a revolutionary/ liberating ideology, it also saw this ideology turning into imperialist nationalism. If the nineteenth century was an age of global order maintained by the Concert of Europe, it also witnessed the beginning of the modern arms race inexorably leading to a global war. If the nineteenth century was an age of liberal democracy, it also witnessed imperialistic power play and plundering in the Periphery on an unprecedented scale. This period exposed the inherent injustice and instability of "world-order industry" managed by the great-power condominium.

The new international system that emerged after the Congress of Vienna (1815) was still Eurocentric. Of the twenty-three member states that comprised the system, all except the United States were European. Nonetheless, it was a global system in the sense that its established patterns of interaction now affected almost every corner of the world. The conflicts of the great powers were fought out in the Periphery of the international system, and London developed into the center of world banking and shipping. By 1914 the system's membership increased to forty-three—thanks to the collapse of the Spanish and Portuguese empires in the Western Hemisphere— with the following geographical breakdown: twenty from Europe; seventeen from Latin America; three from Asia (Japan, China, and Siam), one from Africa (Ethiopia); one from the Middle East (Persia); and one from North America (the United States).

For the first time in modern history an attempt was made at the Congress of Vienna to establish a formal structure of world order. Although many countries had participated in the twenty-year conflict just ended, only five great powers (Britain, France, Prussia, Russia, and Austria) arrogated a special managerial role in the shaping of a conservative world order. What emerged was a system of great-power hegemony known as the Concert of Europe, a prototype of the collective security system of the twentieth century, resting on the assumption that "world order" could only be maintained by the formal recognition and vigorous assertion of the special rights and responsibilities of the great powers. Although the Concert functioned effectively for less than a generation, the class system it adopted remained as an integral part of the international structure. Throughout the nineteenth century these five powers remained great powers, surrounded by some two dozen lesser powers. It was not until the turn of the century that two non-European countries joined their ranks after having effectively asserted military supremacy within their own regions: the United States in the Western Hemisphere and Japan in East Asia. England and France, which stood at the top of the social stratification of the international system, also served as "legitimizers" of diplomatic status of other members of the international system.[61]

The *Règlement sur le Rang entre les Agents Diplomatiques* of Vienna (1815), supplemented by the *Protocol* of Aix-la-Chapelle (1818), established new rules for diplomatic rank and precedence "in order to avoid the difficulties which have often arisen and which might occur again by reason of claims to precedence between various diplomatic agents."[62] The protracted ne-gotiations leading to the Peace Treaties of 1648 at Westphalia took no less than eight years due primarily to a lack of rules governing diplomatic ceremonial and etiquette. Yet status politics continued unabated. In fact, the status politics of this period took a more virulent form as status was redefined in *national* rather than in *personal* (monarchical) terms. Status competition extended to Asia and Africa as overseas colonies acquired status symbols as much as economic values. The Center managed to have a period of peace because the Periphery provided a safe frontier to absorb imperialist rivalry. "Prior to 1875 not one-tenth of Africa, the second largest continent, had been appropriated by European nations. By 1895 all but a tenth of it was appropriated."[63] From the Opium War down to the Treaty of Versailles, China lost some 4 million square kilometers of territories. Sun Yat-sen characterized China under the unequal treaty system as a "hypo-colony," a grade worse than a semicolony because of the multiple control and exploitation exercised by the imperial powers.[64]

Latecomers like Germany, Italy, Japan, and the United States also joined the race to claim the shrinking colonial pie. Where outright conquest and colonization was not possible or desirable, the great powers used such devices as the protectorate, the sphere of influence, suzerainty, and the open door. In Egypt, Western powers gradually took over control of the railways, the telegraphs, and the harbor of Alexandria. By 1880, 40 percent of all Egyptian revenues went to pay off the national debt.[65] In East Asia, Korea became another Poland. "Not one power but five pushed their way into Seoul—Chinese and Japanese troops; Russian, British, and American diplomats, together with Catholic and Protestant missionaries, all exerted their several influences in this hermit kingdom that lacked any tradition or experience of multi-state foreign relations."[66] It is of some historical significance that the U.S. diplomatic presence, which began in 1882 with the signing of a friendship and commerce treaty, was easily terminated in 1905 by a classical imperialistic deal (the Taft-Katsura agreement) under which Japan recognized dominant U.S. interests in the Philippines in return for U.S. recognition of Japan's dominant interests in Korea. When Japan annexed Korea five years later, the United States did not even bother to protest.

Rivalries in East Asia also launched a revolutionary/transformational process in China. Paradoxically, it was imperial Japan who acted as a catalytic agent for the birth of modern Chinese nationalism. By the turn of the century, the cumulative impact of the unequal treaty system, coupled with the rise of expansionistic Japan, had discredited the traditional Sinocentric world order beyond redemption. A new generation of young nationalists grew up with a vivid sense of nationalistic outrage and grievance. As they watched their nation being sliced up like a melon, they learned the lesson of global power politics. They became convinced of China's need to be strong and powerful enough to compete with imperialist powers on an equal footing, or even beat them at their own game. The impact of this legacy on the structure of future world order was only dimly perceived at the time.

As the colonial frontier disappeared, the status politics among the great powers turned back to Europe. Just as the British-French colonial rivalry was as much symbolic as substantive, so the German-British naval race was a contest for national "honor" as much as for national "security." Without the colonial frontier as a safety valve, the great-power rivalry changed from a "mixed-sum game" to a "zero-sum game." The changing structure of domestic politics deprived decisionmakers of any flexibility in shifting alliance partners.[67] The revolution in technology and transportation (and destructive capacity of weapons systems) made the power equilibrium more unpredictable and unstable than ever before, compelling nations to seek not a balance of power but a preponderance of power as a politically safer (but strategically destabilizing) course of action. Between 1890 and 1914, military expenditure rose by 384 percent in Germany, 284 percent in Austria-Hungary, 153 percent in France, 244 percent in Britain, 190 percent in Italy, and 304 percent in Russia.[68] The multipolar structure of balanced interactions became a bipolar structure of two competing alliance systems (the Triple Entente and the Triple Alliance), and it became increasingly difficult for geopolitics to avoid a collision course. At the beginning of World War I, some 84 percent of the world's land was controlled by colonial powers.[69]

The mounting pressure of technological changes associated with industrialization and modernization gave birth to a variety of international institutions. The Concert of Europe was one based on a system of periodic consultation. During its heyday the Concert did perform a variety of functions associated with contemporary international institutions: collective legitimization of new states, collective neutralization of certain areas, collective peacemaking and peacekeeping, collective enforcement of certain decisions, and collective rule-making.[70] However, the first big wave of international institution-building occurred in the last quarter of the nineteenth century. As late as 1854 the number of IGOs stood at two, but it reached thirty by the turn of the century and forty-nine by 1914. In spite of the rapid numerical growth, however, international institutions remained a marginal component of the international structure. In status politics involving national honor, national interest, and national glory, nationalism triumphed, drowning out any dissenting voice of internationalism.

The League Period

International Norms. The establishment of the League of Nations in the wake of World War I was the first organized attempt to restructure the normative foundation of world order. Prior to the League, international law regarded war as an unavoidable corollary of the sovereign rights of states. International law was concerned with such procedural issues as neutrality and the "humane and proper" conduct of war. However, the outbreak of the first global war brought about a resurgence of pacifist movements as well as an emphasis on "natural law" and "just war" concepts. Pacifists and legal scholars began to advance antisovereignty arguments and doctrines in their disjointed quest for a warless future. Two extra-European powers, the United States and the Soviet Union, also entered global politics with their own revisionist challenges. The Wilsonian normative claims to national self-determination—and to make the world safe for democracy— and the Soviet revolutionary challenge to Western imperialism and big-power condominium—to establish a new world order based on the solidarity of socialist internationalism—suggested that a transformation of the West-phalian norms was in the offing.

As it turned out, the change in international norms was more modest, incremental, and reformist than revolutionary or transformational during the interwar period. In spite of initial euphoria for the transformation of world politics, the League of Nations embraced the basic principles of the traditional multistate system. The independent sovereign states still remained the basic constituent units of international politics (and of the League of Nations), and the great powers still retained their special rights and responsibilities as the guardians of this new collective security system. War was regarded as produced by misunderstanding, accident, and personal crime rather than as the unavoidable outcome of the competitive system of sovereign states or an illegal act in violation of international law. A fifteen-member Commission on Responsibilities reported to the Paris Peace Conference: "A war of aggression may not be considered as an act directly contrary to positive law, or one which can be successfully brought before a tribunal."[71]

The Soviet Union and the United States both abandoned their initial revisionist challenges to the Westphalian norms and retreated into the cocoon of state sovereignty. The Marxist notion of the state as a coercive instrument of exploitation that would eventually wither away was trans-formed (or rather deformed) into the Stalinist notion of a garrison superstate. Statism became a protective shield against capitalist encirclement in foreign policy as well as a sword of socialist regimentation in domestic policy. The Soviet school of jurists, headed by E. B. Pashkanis, was purged in 1937 for its support of the "withering away" thesis, and a new school of jurisprudence headed by Andrei Vyshinsky began to expound and justify the Stalinist revisionism of the Marxist theory of the state.[72]

The American rejection of the Covenant of the League of Nations was a decisive defeat of Wilsonian liberal internationalism. As President-elect Warren Harding told his fellow citizens in his victory speech: "You just didn't want a surrender of the United States of America; you wanted America to go under American ideals. That's why you didn't care for the League, which is now deceased."[73]

Normative activities during the interwar period centered largely on improving and reforming pacific settlement procedures and further devel-oping and codifying international law. The Covenant outlawed only certain kinds of "resort to war," effectively resuscitating the old concept of just war in the form of "legitimate use of force." Still, the Covenant provisions on the inadmissiblity of resort to war under certain circumstances (Articles 12, 13, or 15) restricted the permissible parameters of state sovereignty in international relations. The Pact of Paris (better known as the Kellogg-Briand Pact, 1928) was another step forward in the progressive delegitimization of war. Sixty-two nations ratified the pact, pledging to settle all international conflicts, regardless of origin or nature, through peaceful means, and denouncing war as an instrument of national policy. Of course, the ease with which this multilateral pact was so quickly ratified *and* so quickly vitiated suggests that norms cannot bear the sole burden of maintaining a world order.

The Westphalian statist paradigm also faced functionalist challenges during the interwar period. The extension of international law into functional domains continued unchecked. As individual rights and responsibilities are recognized that transcend moral and legal obligations to territorial states, normative conflicts between the requirements of state sovereignty and the requirements of world order intensify. Functional IGOs with or without ties to the League continued to define new norms on such matters as the social welfare of workers, white slavery, narcotics and drug trade, and customs violations. By introducing the concept of individual responsibility for war crimes, the Versailles Treaty may be said to have opened the first chapter in the development of international criminal law, although like the Nuremberg and Tokyo trials, it was seriously plagued by the problem of victor's justice (and revenge).

The realist interpretation attributes the lack of normative progress in the interwar period to the absence of hegemony in world politics. "In the absence of rejuvenation by the old hegemony or the triumph of its successor or some other basis of governance," it is argued, "the pressing issues of world order (rules governing trade, the future of the international monetary system, a new regime for the oceans, etc.) remain unresolved. Progress toward the formulation of new rules and regimes for an international system to follow the Pax Americana has been slow or nonexistent."[4] The realists tend to ignore the fact that the League of Nations never enjoyed universal membership nor popularity in normative politics as the United Nations has. As shown in the mandate system, the founders of the League retained their colonial mentality. The principle of national self-determination seemed too noble a norm to apply to the "uncivilized" colonial peoples and territories in Asia and Africa. The mandate system merely transferred sovereignty from the vanquished to the victor and legitimized neocolonial annexation. Some six decades later, the people of Namibia (the former German colony entrusted to South Africa as a Mandate C territory) are still struggling to gain their independence, and the United States, France, and Great Britain are still shielding the pariah regime with their triple vetoes in the UN Security Council.[75]

International Structure. After the First World War there was a dramatic increase in the number of states admitted into the international system.

System membership jumped from forty-three in 1914 to sixty-one in 1920 (see Figure 2.1). The entry of many non-European states (mostly from Latin America) globalized the international system, although most of the new member states played a marginal role in world politics. System membership remained virtually unchanged in the next twenty years, however. The League of Nations was a complete failure on decolonization and expansion of system membership, in striking contrast with its successor, the United Nations.

The international system of the interwar period was an interregnum between the demise of British hegemony and the beginning of U.S. hegemony, which E. H. Carr characterized as the "twenty years' crisis."[76] Like the Congress of Vienna, the Paris Peace Conference was dominated by the great powers (the United States, Britain, France, Italy, and Japan), whose conception of world order under new condominial direction and control was embodied in the Covenant provision for permanent membership of five great powers in the nine-member Council (Article 4). This conception also miscarried as each of the great powers was more interested in the pursuit of its own national interests.

The novelty of including two non-European powers quickly dissipated as the United States refused to join and Japan withdrew from the League of Nations. The Soviet Union, clearly a great power by now, was at first excluded and eventually expelled from the League. When another great power, Italy, committed an act of aggression in 1936, the remaining two, France and Britain, were more concerned about wooing Mussolini as a counterweight to Hitler than about upholding the collective security system. If the Council of the League of Nations "was a significantly *revised* edition" of the Concert of Europe,[77] that revision never materialized in the actual workings of the League.

The old politics of status ordering and distribution among the self-styled guardians of world order did not go away during the interwar period; it remained in a state of anomaly. The rise of total ideologies made it impossible to establish new rules of the game on geopolitical equilibrium. The Allied intervention to crush the Bolshevik revolutionary regime in Soviet Russia, made on purely ideological grounds and not to preserve or restore an European equilibrium in the classical sense, was an opening salvo of ideological warfare among the two emerging superpowers in world politics.

The First World War added more dangerous twists to the old status politics among the great powers. With the collapse of the Austro-Hungarian empire, Austria permanently disappeared from the list of Great Powers. France and Britain, though victorious, were seriously wounded and determined to inflict maximum humiliation on Germany. Germany was defeated but not incapacitated for recovery and revanchism. The Soviet Union was too preoccupied with state-building and state-legitimizing to be of great significance to world politics during the first decade of this period. Still feeling insecure as a global power, Japan concentrated on building and

FIGURE 2.1
Number of Nations and IGOs in the International System in Successive Periods

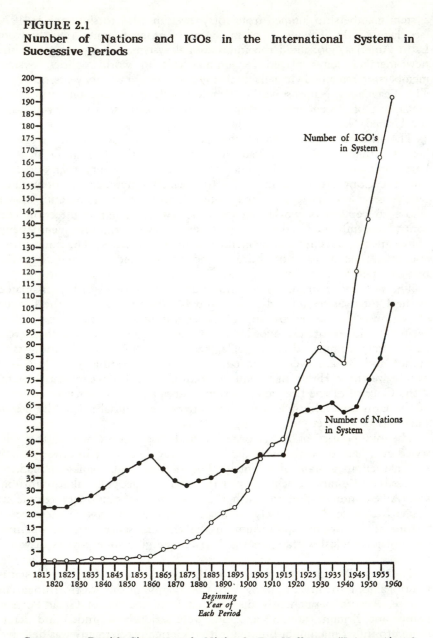

expanding regional hegemony in Asia rather than entangling herself in European alliance politics. The United States pursued a mixed policy of isolationism and interventionism, a curious mixture of a revived disengagement from European politics and a revised version of Manifest Destiny toward the Western Hemisphere and Asia.

The Washington Conference of 1922 sheds some light on the status ordering and distribution of the early interwar period. The Five-Power Treaty—often characterized as the only multilateral disarmament treaty prior to World War II—established a naval armaments ratio of 5-5-3-1.67-1.67 respectively for the United States, Britain, Japan, France and Italy, suspending the naval arms race. In structural terms, however, the treaty legitimized the rough approximations of then existing naval strengths among the great powers and the coexistence of three separate naval spheres of influence in the world: the Far East for Japan; the Western Hemisphere for the United States, and the North Sea eastward to Singapore for Britain. Yet this treaty of *unequal* ratio, preceded by the refusal of the Paris Peace Conference to grant racial equality and followed by the U.S. ban on Japanese immigration in 1924, aggravated the Japanese sense of inferior status. Taking advantage of the intensifying rivalries among European powers and of the truncated collective security system, Japan took the path of nationalistic aggrandizement in Asia.

Table 2.1 shows the changing distribution of military capabilities among the great powers. It also suggests that a global war serves as a catalytic agent in the transformation of international structure. The most important structural impact of the First World War was to weaken Europe as the center of the international system. The Second World War gave another big push to this structural transformation, as made evident in the table. The interwar period also witnessed a loose multipolar structure gradually giving way to a tight bipolar one as status politics among the great powers was pushed too far. In spite of its loose and somewhat incoherent multipolar structure, however, the international system retained its hierarchical feature with the great powers—five becoming seven with the entry of Germany and the Soviet Union—occupying the top of the social stratification.

The growth pattern of international institutions reflects the changing moods of the interwar period. As graphically shown in Figure 2.1, the number of IGOs increased from fifty-one in 1915 to seventy-two in 1920, reflecting the wartime spirit of cooperative internationalism among the allies, and peaked at eighty-nine in 1930. In the turbulent decade of the 1930s, when the "realism" of power politics replaced the "idealism" of international law and organization in academic inquiry, and jingoistic nationalism replaced cooperative internationalism, the number of IGOs dropped from eighty-nine to eighty-two. With congressional passage of the Smoot-Hawley Tariff Act (1930)—which imposed the highest rates on imports in U.S. history and helped to spread the U.S. depression worldwide—economic warfare had already preceded the outbreak of World War II. Fragmentation, autarky, and unilateralism—not integration, interdepen-

TABLE 2.1
Percentage of Total Combat Munitions Output of the Main Belligerents, 1938–1943*

Country	1938	1939	1940	1941	1942	1943
United States	6	4	7	14	30	40
Canada	0	0	0	1	2	2
Britain	6	10	18	19	15	13
U.S.S.R.	27	31	23	24	17	15
Total: Allied countries	39	45	48	58	64	70
Germany†	46	43	40	31	27	22
Italy	6	4	5	4	3	1
Japan	9	8	7	7	6	7
Total: Axis countries	61	55	52	42	36	30
Grand Total:	100	100	100	100	100	100

* Includes aircraft, army ground ordnance and signal equipment, naval vessels, and related equipment.
† Includes occupied territories.

Source: Klaus E. Knorr, *The War Potential of Nations*, Table, p. 34. Copyright (c) 1956 by Princeton University Press. Reproduced by permission of Princeton University Press.

dence, and multilateralism—dominated interactions between the nation-states in the 1930s.

The League of Nations symbolized the malaise and malfunctioning of the world order system in the interwar period, inviting the contempt of both topdogs and underdogs—aggressors and victims of aggression. It represented an institutionalized insult to colonial peoples in Asia and Africa through its mandate system, and the principle of national self-determination even failed to receive official normative support in the Covenant. Reacting in part to the League mandate system and in part to the Lytton Commission (which was too late and too little), the leaders of the Chinese Communist Party expressed one version of the underdogs' attitude in a telegram dated October 6, 1932:

> The Provisional Central Government of the Chinese Soviet Republic long ago told the popular masses of the whole country that the League of Nations is a League of Robbers by which the various imperialisms are dismembering China. The principal task of the Lytton Commission of Enquiry sent to China by the League was to prepare the dismemberment of China and the repression of all the revolutionary movements that have raised the flag of the Chinese Soviets.[78]

The Postwar Period

International Norms. The postwar international system witnessed a dramatic, if somewhat uneven, development of norms with two discernible cycles. The first big wave of activity occurred during the "reconstruction" period of 1944–1948 with the establishment or revamping of functional IGOs under the hegemonic leadership of the United States. Taking advantage of both its military, economic, and ideological supremacy and Soviet absence from most international regimes, the United States by and large succeeded in reformulating norms for the functional (specialized) agencies of the United Nations system, including the international monetary and financial institutions.

The second big wave came in the 1970s under the revisionist challenge of the Group of 77, the Third World caucus on development issues. Taking advantage of its overwhelming numerical majority, the Group of 77 turned the United Nations into the central arena for the politics of collective legitimation and delegitimation. Under the auspices of the United Nations some twenty global conferences were held in the 1970s to establish new norms or transform old ones on practically all of the problems and crises related to human well-being—environment, food, population, women, human settlement, water, the law of the sea, desertification, trade and commerce, science and technology, industrialization, employment, primary health, disarmament, and agrarian reform.

As specific international norms in different world order domains will be discussed in Part 2, we need to be concerned here with only a few notable features of the postwar development of normative politics. First of all, international norms have not only grown at an unprecedented rate but have also expanded into such hitherto uncovered domains as internal war, the human environment (including the nonterritorial realms of the open seas, outer space, and the weather), transfer of technology, and the transnational corporations (TNCs). This may be explained in part by the proliferation of international regimes in a world that is becoming increasingly interconnected, complex, and interdependent. The nation-state is being penetrated by all kinds of international norms.

By the 1970s, the United States' ideological hegemony had virtually collapsed in global normative politics. Figure 2.2 graphically shows the steady decline of U.S. influence in UN politics. The latter half of the 1970s (which the figure does not show) witnessed an even sharper decline in the U.S. normative position, with the United States often in a minority of one or two on many crucial issues in the UN General Assembly. Even in the Security Council, where the drama of high politics is played out, the U.S. normative hegemony collapsed in the 1970s as shown in its use of the veto.[79]

For the first time in the history of international politics the underdogs have come to exercise the dominant role in normative politics. Contemporary North-South politics has become a contest between two kinds of "power"— material power and normative power. *Material power* here refers to con-

FIGURE 2.2
The Position of the United States and the Soviet Union in
Relation to U.N. Majority

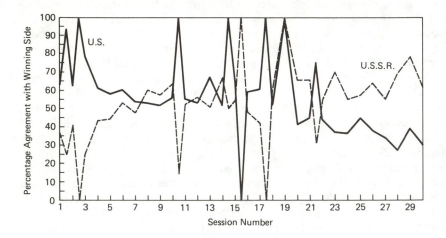

Source: Harold K. Jacobson, *Networks of Interdependence: International Organizations and the Global Political System* (New York: Alfred A. Knopf, 1979), p. 115. Reprinted with permission.

ventional national capabilities based on measurable economic, military, demographical, and technological factors, whereas *normative power* (a neglected dimension of power in international relations research) is the ability to define, control, and transform the agenda of global politics and to legitimate a new dominant paradigm. By exercising its aggregate voting power and its mobilized normative power, the Third World has indeed succeeded in transforming the agendas of most international organizations (the obvious exceptions being the international financial and monetary regimes). Third World normative politics in international organizations also works toward transforming traditional international norms.[80]

The year 1960 was a milestone in international normative politics. The newly independent states, having achieved a numerical majority in the state system, succeeded in passing the 1960 Declaration on the Granting of Independence to Colonial Territories and Peoples—General Assembly Resolution 1514 (XV). This was the Third World's initiation in global normative politics. Resolution 1514, re-cited ninety-five times in subsequent resolutions between the fifteenth (1960) and twenty-first (1966) sessions,[81] served well in the collective delegitimization of the colonial regime.

The 1970 Declaration of the Common Heritage of Mankind, another product of Third World initiative, was as radical a departure from the

Westphalian principle of state sovereignty in the traditional ocean regime as the principle of non-reciprocity and special and differential treatment for the developing countries is from the traditional norms of the General Agreement on Tariffs and Trade (GATT) trade regime. The Declaration on the Establishment of a New International Economic Order, a Programme of Action on the Establishment of a New International Economic Order, and the Charter of Economic Rights and Duties of States—the normative trinity of the NIEO—became a coherent and credible challenge to the legitimacy of the norms, rules, and procedures of all the postwar economic regimes molded in the image of *pax Americana.*

The resolutions of the General Assembly and the declarations of global conferences convened under its auspices have become the prominent form of norm-making in recent years. Excluded from playing any part in the making of international law, the Third World shifted its search for a normative order from the domain of international law to that of parliamentary diplomacy. The decision of the World Court in the *South West Africa* cases in 1966 merely confirmed Third World suspicions about the conservative bias of international law.

Of course, many states and many international lawyers have continued to deny any legislative status to General Assembly resolutions, except on internal budgetary decisions under Articles 17 and 19 of the Charter.[82] In recent years, however, an increasing number of legal scholars have challenged this formalistic interpretation.[83] They have rejected the artificially rigid demarcation line between binding and nonbinding norms, between treaty and custom, and between lawmaking and law-declaring activities in international organizations, calling attention to the discernible trend from consent to consensus in the decisionmaking process of international organizations.

Hence, General Assembly resolutions have been characterized as having the status of "quasi-legislative force," or of being "soft laws," "normes sauvages," or "legal custom," if they meet the following conditions: (1) they were formulated as behavioral norms for the member states or they employed the peremptory language of legal rights and obligations; (2) they were repeated with sufficient frequency and regularity;[84] and (3) they enjoyed consensus, if not unanimity. In short, norm-creating, and law-declaring expressions in General Assembly resolutions have the character of *opinio juris* and contribute to the development of customary international law.[85] Regardless of the merit of legal objections, the Third World has dominated global normative politics, drawing attention to the forces and ideas emanating from the hitherto forgotten two-thirds of humankind.

One must not, however, underestimate the tenacity of the Westphalian statist paradigm. The global normative politics of the 1970s highlighted the anomalies and contradictions of statism, sure signs that a transformational process is now underway, but the threshold or turning point has not yet been reached. Instead, global normative politics has evolved within the somewhat reformed framework of the statist paradigm. The present-day international legal system, as Burns H. Weston says, "is a system of law which has as its *raison d'être* the maintenance of the nation-state. It is a system which is maintained, for the most part, by and for States; as a result it tilts in favor of such nation-state imperatives as unrestricted domestic (or sovereignty) and monopoly control over the military instrument."[86]

Even "distributive justice," which has emerged as a central normative issue in global developmental politics, emphasizes *interstate* justice with little regard to universal *human* justice.

International Structure. World War II drastically altered the political/ functional map of the world, exposing the hidden contradictions and anomalies of the European colonial empires in Asia and Africa. The force of decolonization and transformation that the war unleashed proved irreversible, although resistance continued. Figure 2.1 shows the proliferation of national actors caused by decolonization. As measured by UN membership, the number of nation-states in the postwar system increased from 51 in 1945 to 98 in 1960 to 157 in 1982, with European countries now representing less than one-fifth of system membership. The demise of the Eurocentric international system is a salient structural change of the postwar period.

From the wreckage of the Eurocentric and multipolar international system rose a new global system comprised of two superpowers, a half-dozen exhausted middle powers (former great powers), small powers (ex-colonies), and minipowers (ex-minicolonies) plus an increasing number of nonstate actors (IGOs, NGOs, TNCs, etc.) and international regimes. As Bruce Russett writes, "The erosion of all other nations' unconditional viability is in effect what we mean by the transformation of the international system in the early postwar years."[87]

This postwar global system developed a Janus-faced personality. At the formal/superstructural level, the principle of state equality has received universal normative endorsement. Thanks to the revolution of rising intolerance for social inequality and to the coalition politics of the global underdogs (the Bandung Conference, the Non-Alignment Movement, and the Group of 77), the principle of interstate equality has also been institutionalized in the formal structure of status and influence in many international organizations. Yet at the level of deeper substructure, the disparities between the haves and the have-nots have become wider in the postwar period than at any time since Westphalia.

The postwar system has shifted somewhat from the state-centric to a mixed-actor structure. This shift has not so much eliminated the old hierarchical structure as it has changed the actors, the mechanisms, the types, and the forms of control and accumulation. The global production and distribution of values (i.e., attributes, resources, or capabilities) among actors has also blurred the conventional demarcation line between "high politics" and "low politics." The structural problems of war, inequity, injustice, and ecocide have become more interconnected than ever before in human history. Part 2 will more fully examine interaction patterns in each of the four world-order value domains. Here a synopsis of postwar structural characteristics of global geopolitics and geoeconomics will suffice.

The postwar superpower rivalry began in Europe and then shifted to the "safer" geopolitical periphery of the world. The successful communist revolution in China in 1949, followed by the outbreak of the Korean War in 1950, provided an excuse for the United States to globalize the East-West conflict through expanding networks of anticommunist military alliance systems. The superpower rivalry, or perhaps more accurately the U.S. attempt to maintain its global hegemony and the Soviet counterresponse, fragmented the international system into three contending blocs—Western, Eastern, and nonaligned. The postwar globalization of international politics was not so much a phenomenon of global social integration as it was a phenomenon of spreading superpower conflicts. In spite of some valiant attempts (such as Dag Hammarskjöld's "preventive diplomacy" halfheartedly institutionalized in UN peacekeeping), the firebreak between local and global conflicts has been difficult to maintain because of the global reach of the two superpowers.

Perhaps the most novel structural development of the postwar period was the reversal of the established pattern of the two preceding international systems. As noted earlier, the nineteenth-century international system managed to maintain its multipolar structure. It was not until the turn of the century that this multipolar structure began to regroup into two competing alliance systems. The interwar system was likewise a multipolar structure that eventually succumbed to bipolarization on the eve of World War II. The postwar system began with a bipolar structure, with the distribution of military capabilities heavily concentrated in Washington and Moscow, but has experienced a gradual relaxation of both bipolarity (i.e., an even distribution of military power in two centers) and a more dramatic decline of bipolarization (i.e., a process of alliance clusters around two centers).

The proportion of world military expenditures by the two superpowers reached the all-time high of 75.1 percent in 1953 and then began to decline to 61.9 percent in 1973 and to 58 percent in 1980. However, in the field of nuclear weapons the superpowers still hold 95 percent. Thus military bipolarity declined but has not yet been transformed into a multipolar structure. A more discernible and significant decline in bipolarization can be defined and measured in terms of interbloc hostility and intrabloc solidarity. Bipolarization was at its peak in 1948–1952, but declined to an insignificant level by 1972–1973.[88]

With the revival of Cold War II in the wake of the Soviet invasion of Afghanistan and the accelerated arms race, however, fresh attempts are being made by both superpowers to rejuvenate failing intrabloc solidarity. Whether this will reverse the downward bipolarization trend remains to be seen. China's rise as a global power in the 1970s has greatly complicated the structure of global geopolitics. Post-Mao Chinese global geopolitics has carefully cultivated the expectations that China is both capable and willing to play a decisive role of "balancer" in the central strategic equilibrium between the two superpowers. China seems to have succeeded in assuming

FIGURE 2.3
**World Military Expenditure 1908–1976 (Billion U.S. Dollars at
Constant 1973 Prices)**

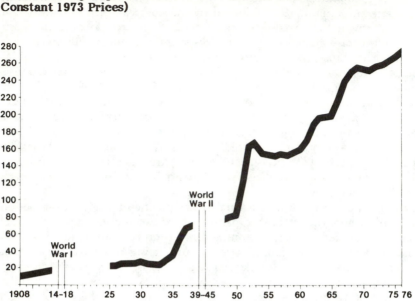

Source: Stockholm International Peace Research Institute,
World Armaments: The Nuclear Threat (Stockholm: SIPRI,
1977), p. 6. Reprinted with permission.

this global strategic role, inasmuch as both superpowers act as if China
has already become a key variable in their respective strategic thinking.[89]
    One structural consequence of this superpower rivalry is the globalization
of the war system. The contradiction between the superstructural delegitimization of war and the substructural globalization of war is intensifying.
The militarizing trend plotted by the rising curve in Figure 2.3 has been
accelerating since 1977, the cutoff point. In 1982, world military expenditure
reached the record amount of $600 billion, *matched* by the record number
(fifty-seven) of disarmament resolutions passed by the first part of the
Thirty-Seventh Session of the General Assembly.
    The widening absolute gap between rich and poor—and between formal
equality and actual inequality—has been most striking since the end of
World War II. At the beginning of the nineteenth century, the per capita
income ratio between the richest and poorest countries in the world was
only 2:1, compared to the present ratio of 80–100:1. In 1830, the gross
national product (GNP) ratio between the largest (Russia) and smallest
(Denmark) states in the international system was 41:1, compared to the
1970 ratio of 97,627:1 (between the United States and the Maldives). The

income ratio between "rich" countries of Western Europe and the rest of the world was roughly 2:1 in 1850, but this ratio increased to 10:1 by 1950 and 15:1 by 1960. By 2000, the gap is projected at 30:1 if present trends continue.[90]

The North-South dichotomy is a simplified abstraction of economic polarity in the present world economic system. Even the group politics in the UN Conference on Trade and Development (UNCTAD) does not perfectly fit into a bipolar structure because of the posture of calculated ambiguity assumed by China and the Soviet bloc countries (Group D). The problematic role and status of China and the Soviet group in NIEO politics had been brought to the fore in the controversial debate on the voting structure of a new commodity regime (see Chapter 5).

This voting structure catches one structural image of economic polarity. Another image is conveyed in the annual *World Development Report* of the World Bank, which divides system membership into five categories: low-income countries; middle-income countries; industrialized countries; capital-surplus oil exporters; and centrally planned economies. In a recent article, K.K.S. Dadzie, Director-General for Development and International Economic Cooperation for the United Nations, divided the countries of the world into seven categories: thirty-two rich nations; sixteen near-rich nations; sixteen upper-middle nations; twenty-nine lower-middle nations; thirty poor nations (I); twenty-three poor nations (II); and nineteen poor nations (III).[91]

Apart from conceptions based mostly on GNPs or per capita incomes, the underdog thesis that the production and distribution of economic values in the postwar period has been, and still is, controlled by the global dominance/dependence system is tenable. To sustain its oligopolistic position, the system has developed new forms of control and accumulation, with control devices and mechanisms more indirect, more diversified, more sophisticated, and more structural than the traditional direct on-the-spot control methods. The latter have become unacceptably inefficient and costly in economic, political, and normative terms. The former include the oligopolistic control and manipulation of technology, knowledge, patents, tariffs, trade, arms, food, capital, aid, entrepreneurship, and image-making— all that is needed in the global production and distribution of "goods" and "bads"—through direct (bilateral) as well as indirect penetration via local bridgeheads, transnational corporations, and even some international institutions. This global hierarchy works in the service of dominance relationships under world capitalist conditions, and the top level of the control is maintained through an alliance of the "technocapital" and political power.[92]

The rapid postwar growth of international institutions shown in Figure 2.1 should not be accepted uncritically as *prima facie* evidence of global social integration or species solidarity. Although many international institutions were no doubt established in response to the functional requirements of "complex interdependence," they have become an updated and revised extension of, not an alternative to, the Westphalian states system.

The postwar period has also witnessed an unprecedented rate of growth in global transactions, with human interconnectedness across national boundaries doubling every ten years.[93] Yet in a deeper sociopsychological sense, disintegration and fragmentation still seem to be the more dominant, if no longer the prime, forces. International, transnational, and global cooperative endeavors have grown at an unprecedented rate, to be sure, but national, ethnic, and tribal conflicts have also grown at an equally fast or even faster rate.[94]

Change and Continuity in World Politics

Since the inception of the modern states system at Westphalia, "security" has remained the predominant concern of actors in the changing international system. Yet the perennial search for security seems to bring only perennial insecurity. Each major war in modern world history has accentuated the sense of insecurity *and* the renewed quest for a better security system. In spite of all the normative and stuctural changes described in this chapter, however, security remains an elusive goal. How can we explain such a paradox? Is human security a utopian goal or a Sisyphean struggle?

The human security dilemma is embedded in the persistence and globalization of a narrow, retrospective, and reductionist notion of human security. The security managers of the states system have invariably defined security as a function of military strength and insecurity as a function of military weakness. All the principles of historical and contemporary international systems—the balance-of-power principle, the concert or collective security principle, the deterrence principle—are based implicitly or explicitly on the notion that security is a function of managing (or balancing) military power between the contending actors in the international system. The equation of world peace and U.S. military might has been the unquestioned and unquestionable creed for justifying the militarization of U.S. foreign policy in the postwar period.

Far from enhancing security, this Hobbesian *para bellum* doctrine has actually led to pervasive expectations of war, institutionalized preparations for war, and the militarization of social structures in the states system. Like an uncontrollable plague, this doctrine has spread to every corner of the world, fulfilling its own prophecy about anarchical society. This security dilemma reaches its most dangerous form in the nuclear deterrence doctrine. To be effective, deterrence must have credibility—a function of both capability and intent. Effective nuclear deterrence therefore requires a constant demonstration of the deterrer's capability and intent to use force. In short, the "delicate balance of terror" requires both a unilateral arms buildup to enhance credible capability and a periodic display of reckless behavior to enhance credible intention.

The postwar globalization of the war system suggests that the reductionist conception of security survives unchanged. Just as the overseas colonies provided both status and economic values, so today's superweapons convey both military and status values. The French and Chinese decisions to go nuclear were powerfully influenced by their acute sense of status incon-sistency. "India had to build a nuclear bomb," declared a high-ranking Indian military advisor recently, "not only to achieve military superiority over Pakistan *but also to insure that India would not be ignored by the United States.*"[95] This linkage of security and status through the politics of "quasi-proliferation" has become a survival weapon of sorts for the pariah states (Israel, South Africa, and Taiwan) in the contemporary international system.

War has not traditionally been an omnipresent condition of human affairs. More than half the nations (77 out of 144) that were at one time or another members of the international system between 1815 and 1965 managed to escape international war entirely.[96] The history of international relations until World War II suggests that great powers were the most war-prone and that the balance-of-power politics among contending nation-states led to conflict escalation. The great tragedy of our times is that the small nations have uncritically emulated this great-power style in their quest for security and status in world politics. The globalization of the security dilemma is symptomatic of the globalization of traditional great-power conceptions of security and status.

Of course, it has often been said that war in the twentieth century has become functionally obsolete, and there are hundreds of normative dec-larations to prove this axiom. War-makers no longer enjoy the certainty of victory and the decisiveness of outcome their nineteenth-century coun-terparts did. Yet the great enterprise of constructing a new world order system has become an integral part of settling scores and punishing the vanquished. A new postwar world order thus becomes an institutionalized expression of victor's justice, and its new security system reflects the trauma of the past and not an alternative blueprint for a warless future. Notice the current status of the Nuremberg principle of "crimes against humanity."

In a world order still dominated by the competitive system of nation-states, the normative delegitimization of war as an instrument of national policy may be a necessary but certainly not a sufficient condition for maintaining a humane world order. As long as human affairs are governed within the structural constraint of the competitive states system, an alter-native, nonmilitary conception of security is difficult to establish and even more difficult to implement. One empirical study of the global legal system has concluded that international norms "manifest a remarkable propensity for norm maintenance and endurance: many norms have a tendency to persist over time and to survive random or idiosyncratic systemic disruptions (i.e., major events such as total wars on a global scale) or macrostructural adjustments (such as the universalization of the system's composition)."[97]

This is not to underplay the importance of the normative and structural changes observed in the international system but to suggest that these changes have been insufficient to cope with the crises of human security generated by the exponential global trends in demographic explosion, weapons technology and spread, resource depletion, basic human needs and rights denial, and environmental degradation. To the extent that "system transformation" has occurred, it has come about more to avert the last disaster than to cope with the present danger. Every "world order planning" since Westphalia has been to avert the last great war. Every world order system has become an institutionalized expression of a negative, retrospective, and reactive mentality, a product of condominial consensus or compromise among the great powers embodying a corporate oligopolistic structure with an uneven distribution of values. Every world order system has been maintained or changed by the interactions of a few dominant actors, and has been designed more to manage interstate relations than to satisfy global human needs. Excepting the League period as somewhat anomic and abnormal, the longevity (and viability) of every world order system has become progressively shorter.

In comparing normative and structural changes in the history of modern international relations, it can be said that norms tend to be more volatile, more easily established or revised, and more easily neutralized or vitiated. Yet when a given norm recurs in global normative politics without disturbing the existing distribution of power, it does change the expectations and attitudes and eventually the behavior of the system actors. There is also a paradox here. In a multicultural world of independent/interdependent nation-states, norms are more important and more necessary precisely because of an absence of consensus on fundamental values, but at the same time more difficult to internalize precisely because of an absence of international socialization process.

On the other hand, structure tends to be more rigid, more resistant to change, and more easily manipulated for system maintenance. The development of NIEO politics to date suggests that the topdogs may acquiesce in the normative claims of the underdogs for socioeconomic justice, provided such claims are not embodied in any drastic way in the structure of power and influence. The Reagan administration refuses to make even such a normative concession. Its notion that the magic of economic growth and prosperity of developing countries lies in their normative conversion to "free enterprise" and private foreign investment is the most recent and crude strategy of structural conservatism in global geoeconomics.

Since the state (or nation-state) has been the dominant actor in world politics for several centuries, system transformation cannot be said to have occurred without a fundamental change in the status and function of the state in the global system. The questions concerning the status, function, role, and fate of the state have evoked contending responses and pervasive mixtures of descriptive and prescriptive analyses. Whether one takes system-maintaining, system-reforming, or system-transforming approaches to world order, the durability and role of the territorial state is one of most crucial and controversial issues. Since World War I, it has been subject to the contradictory internal and external pulls and pushes of state-enhancing and state-diminishing activities.

On the state-diminishing side are the rapid rise and proliferation of nonstate actors, nuclear weapons of global range, and transnational transactions. The rise of so many nonstate actors has certainly deprived the state of its exclusive status in international law and politics. In the functionalist image of a complex and interdependent world, the state is being bypassed in the global management, production, and distribution of goods and services. In the "world system" image of the capitalist world economy, the states, far from being autonomous, self-contained systems, are part of a global system of class formation. With the advent of the atomic weapon, declared (and later retracted) John Herz in 1957, "Whatever remained of the impermeability of states seems to have gone for good."[98] Likewise, Charles Kindleberger observed in 1969 that "the nation-state is just about through as an economic unit."[99] In an age of nuclear weapons, transnational corporations, and global production of goods and services, state sovereignty is seen as a paper tiger, easily penetrated or punctured. From this vantage point, the demise of the nation-state in a world of interdependence and interpenetration seems inevitable.

A variation on this theme holds that the state-centric realist paradigm has long since lost its descriptive, explanatory, and prescriptive power for the complex web of the global system. Drawing extensively upon the event/interaction data collected for the Nonstate Actor (NOSTAC) Project of Rutgers University, this approach to global politics has shown the far-ranging effects of such nonstate actors as terrorists, multinational corporations, and regional or international organizations in contemporary global politics. It has challenged the implicit assumptions of the state-centric paradigm about state homogeneity and state autonomy by showing actor and issue variation and diversity in global politics, accusing the state-centric realists of seeing only what they want to see and defining "reality" accordingly. As Mansbach and Vasquez put it: "Ultimately, the realists confuse alleged descriptions of rationality with prescriptions for rational behavior and impose an observer's version of such behavior upon a singularly uncongenial reality."[100]

Yet the state-enhancing view is not merely a phenomenon of selective perception on the part of the traditional state-centric "realists." It is also the phenomenon recognized—and targeted for varying prescriptions—by "world-order realists."[101] In spite of varying orientations, these "realists" generally agree that the universalization of the state system is a new reality of relatively recent origin, dating largely from the first two decades of the postwar period. They also agree that the globalization of the state system has actually outpaced the state-diminishing activities. The rise of nationalism, far from diminishing statism, has actually strengthened it by a nonviolent merger in some countries and by force in others. American Wilsonians, British liberals, Russian Stalinists, German socialists, Chinese communists, and Polish workers have all reverted to nation-statism.

The Third World's NIEO quest is linked to such statist principles as "permanent and inalienable resource sovereignty of each nation," "individual and collective self-reliance," "equality, mutual benefit, and mutual respect in international trade," and so on. The 1970 Common Heritage of Mankind

Declaration could not escape the pressures of statism and fragmentation. Twelve years later the United Nations Convention on the Law of the Sea finally emerged more as a triumph of statism than of globalism when it was adopted at UN Headquarters on April 30, 1982, by a vote of 130 in favor to 4 against, with 17 abstentions.[102] Even this "miracle" in having so skillfully balanced competing state interests is now placed in jeopardy because of new objections raised by the Reagan administration over U.S. "national" (read "mining") interests. Nonstate actors, such as the Palestine Liberation Organization (PLO) and the South West Africa People's Organization (SWAPO), are also struggling to achieve a statehood status in the international system.

The picture of proliferating IGOs is somewhat misleading as evidence of a state-diminishing development. Contrary to Mitrany's expectations, the postwar functional activities through the United Nations system have enhanced the state. The IGOs, instead of diminishing or replacing the state, have amplified the competitive states system in contemporary international society. The NGOs still struggle to penetrate the hard shell of international politics. As a result, political processes in international institutions are dominated by bargainings, negotiations, trade-offs, and compromises, balancing separate and competing state interests and demands. This may also explain the absence of any correlation between the rapid rise of IGOs and the incidence of wars in recent international history.[103] The state still plays a dominant role in the updated and revised mixed-actor framework of the contemporary global system.

The revolutionary changes of the postwar period have failed to *transform* the international political structure. What has really happened is not so much the demise or even diminishment of the state as the progressive delegitimization of the states system as a just and humane world order system. Martin Wight once remarked: "The principle that every individual requires the protection of a state which represents him in the international community, is a juristic expression of the belief in the sovereign state as the consummation of political experience and activity which has marked Western political thought since the Renaissance."[104] This principle of raison d'état has lost its appeal. The basic source of the human security problematique lies in the dynamics of a competitive states system less concerned with real human needs than with the status of security managers of the real estates abstracted and sanctified as "territorial nation-states."

Is a world historical transformation currently underway? An uncynical and unsentimental perspective has to acknowledge that the picture of the world is becoming more complicated and more confusing. Based on our concept of transformation, however, the Babel-like cacophony of conflicting and mutually unintelligible voices about the fate of the state is a sign of system transformation in progress. In a larger evolutionary and holistic sense, the state-enhancing activities may represent no more than the last heroic attempt of a dinosaur in a nuclear-ecological age.

We should not deny the power of the global dominance system with its self-repairing and self-regenerating capacity, but we must avoid exaggerating the power of the strong and underplaying the power of the weak in contemporary global politics. Great historical transformations are often wrought by those dismissed as marginal and powerless.

In our time, "the weak, not content to inherit the kingdom of heaven, seemed bent on conquering the earth as well."[105] In war, Algeria and Vietnam have already demonstrated that David can stalemate, or even beat, Goliath. For over two decades, Cuba has successfully defied the invasion, assassination attempts, and destabilization programs of her northern Colossus. In 1982, Vanuatu, a ministate in the South Pacific, caused a stir at U.S. Pacific Fleet Headquarters in Hawaii by barring a scheduled visit by two U.S. warships in the capital, Port Vila on Efate Island. This defiance, it was explained, was "in line with Vanuatu's policy, shared by all the island governments, of campaigning for a 'nuclear-free Pacific.'"[106] Despite conceptual and practical problems, the NIEO is a form of collective struggle by the weak against the strong in the global political economy.

The 1970s witnessed the widening concentric circle of global consciousness accompanied by the refusal to accept the inevitability and legitimacy of global war, poverty, injustice, genocide, and ecocide. In part, this new sense of transformation politics was translated into clarion calls for a *new* international economic order, a *new* world information order, a *new* international technological order, a *new* world food order, a *new* global ocean regime, and so on. The interchangeable use of the terms "international" and "world" (or "global") also suggests a dialectical tension between the forces of a new "world" order and of a new "international" order. The transformative forces for a struggle of this magnitude, once unleashed, can be halted or detracted but cannot be banned for good.

A crucial question remains. Will this world historical transformation come about through another cataclysmic global war as of yore, or can we intervene in time to shift it into a nonviolent and nonapocalyptical direction? We will return to this question in Part 3.

In Search of a World Order Theory

The Relevance of a World Order Theory

Theorizing has been neglected as a mode of inquiry in world order studies. How this affects our understanding of the shaping of global reality depends largely on our conception of the nature and functions of theory. If theory and praxis are dichotomized in the context of actual social engagement, the latter has greater priority. Given the human proclivity to theorize on almost every subject and given also the consensus that theory-building and policymaking remain disconnected in the field of international relations,[1] the case against joining the "faddish" search for a theory of world politics is persuasive. However, theoretical neglect affords little comfort to those who are convinced of the necessity for and feasibility of a world order theory.

The main purpose of this chapter is to explore the relevance of a world order theory. To what extent and in what sense can it be said that the construction of a theory for the pursuit of a more just and humane world order is both desirable and feasible? We begin with a set of assumptions. First we assume that theorizing has some redeeming intellectual *and* social value. Second, we assume that the important choice lies not so much in a theory/praxis dichotomy as in a particular conception and type of theory—a "theory of praxis," as it were. Third, we assume that there already exists in world order literature enough ground-breaking work to use as building blocks for world order theorizing. Fourth and finally, we assume that theory is a means, not an end; it is not an invention of some talismanic formula but a continuous, cumulative, and self-correcting process of improving our "road map" for the long journey into a preferred future. With these assumptions in mind, we will now briefly examine contending conceptions of international relations theory and then suggest the general contours of a world order theory in its own and comparative terms.

The content of some later sections of this chapter reflects my collaborative work with Richard Falk on *An Approach to World Order Studies and the World System*, WOMP Working Paper No. 22 (New York: Institute for World Order, 1982).

Theorizing in International Relations

It is both surprising and ironic that despite more than three decades of feverish "theoretical" activities, international studies still cannot claim any major theoretical breakthroughs. Nor is there any disciplinewide consensus on what constitutes a theoretical breakthrough or even on the feasibility of viable theories of international relations. In Kuhnian terms, the anomalies of the dominant paradigm—that is, the orthodox image of social reality subscribed to by the majority of theorists and practitioners in the discipline—are made increasingly evident, yet a critical paradigmatic shift has yet to occur.

Consider *Theoretical Aspects of International Relations*, a 1959 symposium volume of essays taking stock of the theoretical investigations of international relations in the 1950s. Although editor William T. R. Fox states at the outset that there is a "lack of an agreed framework for theoretical inquiry" because of the use of several different kinds of theories—normative, empirical, and scientific or rational—the dominance of the realist paradigm is clearly evident in the list of the contributors to that volume.[2] However, the triumph of "realism" (the state-centric model concerned primarily with the national interest defined in terms of "power") in the grand and deductive theorizing of the 1950s gave way to the triumph of "scientism" (where numbers and data became kingmakers) in the behavioral/classical debates of the 1960s.

The dominance of inductive empiricism was short-lived. The fallacies of value-neutral and atheoretical investigations so characteristic of the "scientific" approaches became increasingly evident. Before the 1960s were over, less than a decade after Robert Dahl issued a "presidential" declaration on the "epitaph for a monument to a successful {behavioral} revolt," David Easton, one of the pioneers of the behavioral revolution, issued another "presidential" call for a postbehavioral normative-empirical approach in political science.[3]

Dissatisfaction with the dominant empiricism of the 1960s gave rise not so much to a rejuvenated realist paradigm as to a variety of "neorealist" or "postrealist" approaches to the study of world politics in the 1970s. As noted in Chaper 2, the 1970s were years when practically all of the global problems and crises of human social, economic, and ecological well-being finally entered and, to a significant extent, transformed the agenda of global politics. As if to accommodate this changing reality, a dramatic upsurge of scholarly interest in the global political economy generated several contending approaches to the study of the interaction between politics and economics in the world. One scholar has even concluded that "*Power and Interdependence* {Keohane and Nye, 1977} may well become the *Politics Among Nations* of the 1970s."[4]

However, in the latter half of the 1970s, leading mainstream scholars of international relations like Stanley Hoffmann, James Rosenau, Morton Kaplan, and Kenneth Waltz all issued negative pronouncements on the theoretical status of international studies. Hoffmann was "more struck by the dead ends than by the breakthroughs."[5] International relations paradigms, according to Rosenau, are crumbling, undergoing a rapid process of "paradigm deterioration."[6] The "grand debate" on international relations theory between Kaplan and Waltz turned into an acrimonious, *ad hominem* exchange of volleys; it is revealing that in the end two leading international relations theorists could only agree on the barrenness of international relations theory.[7]

What I find deplorable is the resulting neglect of grand theorizing using broad, general conceptual schemes and frameworks in the normative tradition of international political philosophy. In the pursuit of "scientific methodology" and "empirical rigor"—the unwritten but widely acknowledged criteria for beauty contests in the mainstream of U.S. international relations research—more and more scholars have succumbed to conceptual fragmentation and inductive perfectionism. This fragmentation has produced many models and paradigms enjoying "crackpot rigor," but the gap between theory and practice continues to widen.

Raymond Aron's *Peace and War: A Theory of International Relations*, first published in French in 1962 and later translated into English in 1966, provides an apt illustration of the intellectual and normative confusion over the current state of international relations theory. Aron's book was greeted with a paean of praises by Bull, Hoffmann, Kissinger, and Morgenthau[8] not so much for any theoretical breakthroughs but because of the need of realists and traditionalists to put aside their minor intellectual quarrels in defense and legitimation of their common state-centric paradigm.[9] It is ironic that what Hoffmann characterized as "the most intellectually ambitious work that has ever been written about international relations" or what Bull has characterized as "surely the most profound work that any contemporary has written in the attempt 'to comprehend the implicit logic of relations among politically organized collectivities'" has had so little lasting impact upon international relations research.[10]

Various Meanings of Theory

The term "theory" has been used (and misused) for a variety of disparate analyses and orientations in international relations research. The late Charles O. Lerche, Jr., is reported to have said: "There is no more vicious theorist than the man who says, 'I have no theory; I just let the facts speak for themselves.'"[11] Used in this loose sense, theory can represent almost any kind of conceptual or analytical method or device, however underdeveloped or implicit. In the strict (philosophy of science) sense, theory is defined as a logically interrelated set of propositions and hypotheses that specify a causal relationship between one or more antecedent (independent) variables and a consequent (dependent) variable capable of explaining and predicting specified classes of phenomena. Most studies of international relations research fail to meet the requirements of this philosophy-of-science definition. But there is no reason why international relations research has to be conducted and evaluated according to such a rigid and overly rigorous conception of theory.

There are alternative, intermediate conceptions of theory. From the vantage point of developing a world order theory, the instrumental view of theory is most suggestive. Analogous to map-making, a theory conceived instrumentally helps us know where we are now and where we are going or ought to be going.[12] An instrument always presupposes a purpose, just as a means always presupposes an end; an instrumental theory is never judged by its veracity but only by its usefulness in performing its assigned functions or serving its desired end. This is what Oran Young calls a theory designed "to deal with the development of 'paradigms,' approaches to analysis, or conceptual frameworks."[13] It provides the criteria for separating the relevant from the irrelevant as well as for selecting, categorizing, ordering, simplifying, and integrating the "revelant" facts. It can also be used to generate relevant data. An instrumental theory, then, serves as a conceptual map that helps us make sense of a great melange of confusing and contradictory information. Even in "normal science," Thomas Kuhn reminds us, "all of the facts that could possibly pertain to the development of a given science are likely to seem equally relevant" in the absence of a paradigm.[14] I have adopted the instrumental view of theory as being most suitable to world order studies.

Common Theoretical Traps

Instrumental world order theory avoids three common theoretical traps. First, there is the trap of theory/praxis dichotomy. All solutions to practical problems—and all prescriptions for maladies—are based implicitly or explicitly on a theoretical foundation. Nothing can be as practical as a good (or advanced) theory. The inseparability of theory and praxis was one of the central and recurring themes in the epistemology of Mao Zedong, one of the most *practical* revolutionary theorists of the twentieth century. In his essay "On Practice," characterized in 1971 as providing the official "guiding principle for knowing and changing the world" in China's politics of transformation,[15] Mao argued that "Marxism emphasizes the importance of theory precisely and only because it can guide action."[16] The theory/praxis dichotomy applies only to the extremely underdeveloped and overdeveloped stages of theory-building, when a theory is still in its primitive stage, searching for a closer "fit," and when an outdated theory proves incapable of explaining a new reality.

Second is the trap of determinism characteristic of all monocausal theories of international relations. Both Machiavellanism and Marxism, though they differ in their underlying assumptions and normative orientations, suffer from deterministic interpretations of politics. The realist paradigm as a contemporary variant on Machiavellianism first reduces global reality to the single dimension of the struggle for "power" in the perennial state of anarchy and then imposes a deterministic interpretation on this immutable "reality." Like a photograph taken through a color filter, the "real" world seen through the prism of realist power-monism and power-determinism is always "nasty, brutish, and short."

How do we account for this realist determinism? For Morgenthau, two cardinal principles of a realist theory of international politics are that "politics, like society in general, is governed by objective laws that have their roots in human nature" and that human nature "has not changed since the classical philosophies of China, India, and Greece endeavored to discover these laws."[17] In a similar vein, Robert Gilpin concludes his grand theorizing on change and continuity in the international system with the argument that world politics "is still characterized by the struggle of political entities for power, prestige, and wealth in a condition of global anarchy."[18] There is a sense in which the realists fulfill their own prophecy. Seeing the worst in human nature and translating this view into global reality, the realists do contribute, wittingly or not, to the perpetuation of a Hobbesian environment of immutable power play. A world order theory must rest instead on an indeterministic assumption of social and historical process.

Third is the trap of value-neutral theorizing. The methodological premise, rampant in inductive empiricism, that values and facts can—and should— be treated as two independent domains feeds the prejudice of contemporary social science against employing a normative framework in defining and explaining social phenomena to be researched. In actuality, our choice to study a particular social or political reality in any particular way is seldom made in complete detachment from our implicit and unconscious biases. Rather it is influenced, in varying degrees, by our underlying assumptions and ultimate value orientations. The camel's nose of value judgment inevitably creeps into the tent of the "value-free" paradigm.

However difficult in actual execution, normative and empirical approaches are not inherently or necessarily incompatible. Anatol Rapoport reminds us that Galileo described not how bodies actually fall but how they *ought* to fall under idealized conditions.[19] A normative and policy-oriented scientific approach known as "peace research" was established on the assumption that it is both desirable and feasible to combine the strengths of traditional *normative* approach with modern *behavioral* approach.

As noted earlier, even David Easton issued a "revisionist" call for a postbehavioral revolution guided by a "Credo of Relevance" (that is, substance taking precedence over methodology). Easton was pleading for a normative-empirical approach to restore a measure of relevance in political science research. As editor of *International Organization* in 1975, Robert Keohane cited and accepted Easton's call, arguing "the need for a normative-empirical synthesis."[20] In rejecting the fallacy of a value-neutral approach, world order theorists affirm the centrality of values. At the same time, world order theory is receptive to the use of empirical tools whenever and wherever suitable to enhance our understanding of world politics as an authoritative and legitimate allocation of values.

The case for the relevance of a world order theory rests on the following conditions: (1) adoption of the instrumental view of theory; (2) avoidance of all of the common traps in theory building; (3) affirmation of the centrality of values (normative theory), using scientific tools when necessary or useful; and (4) acknowledgment that theory building is a continuous, cumulative, and self-correcting process. World order theory is a theory of human purpose and human action. It is also a nondeterministic theory of human possibility. It embodies a comprehensive and coherent body of core assumptions as points of departure, a general framework of inquiry, and a self-generating process to improve its paradigmatic potency.

Contending Images of "World Order"

The Rhetorical Uses of "World Order"

During the 1970s the term "world order" seems to have undergone a rhetorical renaissance in the vocabulary of U.S. foreign policy makers and global geostrategists. We might smugly delude ourselves that the concept of world order is finally working its way into the official thinking of U.S. foreign policy. In fact, however, this phenomenon poses the danger of a semantic (and conceptual) corruption of the term. By way of clarification, we note here three problematic uses of "world order."

First, the stress on "order" seems somewhat misleading for a theory built around "values." We do not use "order" as symbolized in the reactionary slogan "law and order." Instead, "world order" is used here descriptively and analytically—as an aggregate/empirical conception of values, norms, and structure that give shape and substance to world society at any given time and as a heuristic/normative framework for a systematic macroinquiry into the main principles, patterns, and processes of human interaction. A more accurate but somewhat cumbersome expression is a "just world order," suggestive of a new normative order embodying the values of peace, well-being, justice, and ecological integrity. Acknowledging that justice and order can be seen as mutually complementary or conflictive, this conception of world order is more normative than empirical, with greater emphasis on "just" than on "order."

Second is a perception of "world order" as a new globalizing ideology emanating from a superpower in hegemonic decline. The Third World is especially suspicious of "globalist" schemes for world order, fearing some cosmopolitan machination designed to erode its newborn national sovereignty on behalf of Western political, economic, and cultural interests. After all, the rich and the powerful have often disguised their hegemonic interests with legitimizing claims of maintaining social order. Many times through the long cycle of global politics, the predominant impulse to shape "world order" has been "an expression of a will to power, the urge to control and to dominate, to imprint a pattern on events."[21] When the term "world order" finds its way into the political language of Henry Kissinger, Richard Nixon, Zbigniew Brzezinski, Jimmy Carter, and Alexander Haig, for example, it gives credence to the suspicion that U.S. leaders are indeed manipulating the symbolism of world order to disguise the neo-imperial face of *pax Americana*. The rhetorical use of "world order" was particularly salient during the early inaugural phase of the Carter administration. In an address to foreign countries, President Carter said: "I want to assure you that the relations of the United States with the other countries and peoples of the world will be guided during my own Administration by our desire to shape a world order that is more responsive to human aspirations. The United States will meet its obligation to help create a stable, just, and peaceful world order."[22]

The third problem is that "world order" has been mistakenly identified with an apocalyptic/eschatological image of human future.[23] As a transition strategy, this alarmist approach is both necessary and risky. It is necessary for consciousness raising as an integral part of the system-transforming approach to world order. At the same time, it runs the risk of crying "wolf" too many times.

For most non-Western people the struggles for genuine political, economic, and cultural development at the national level still remain paramount. Their main "global" concerns are largely limited to arresting the hegemonic pressures of great power interventionism, multinational corporate penetration, or the manipulations of international financial and monetary institutions or Western-dominated global information networks. To be globally relevant, world order thinking must be as alert to neo-imperial perils as to the hazards of the arms race, the dynamics of population pressure, or the upsurge of international terrorism.

Despite these problems, "world order" remains symbolic of our central unifying concept and concern. Like imperialism, "world order" has already established its normative niche in international relations research. When correctly defined, world order can provide a comprehensive and integrated conception for our normative social research as well as for our social engagement as concerned citizens of this endangered planet. To seek another label after more than two decades of world order research can easily be perceived as an act of self-immolation. Besides, any successor or replacement term runs the risk of being a mere semantic escape.

During the 1970s contending world order images proliferated in the form of global models. Where does our world order theory fit in this confusing array of global model exercises? To further clarify the meaning of world order used throughout this book, we will first simplify, typologize, and then compare and contrast these contending images in contemporary world order thinking. Despite the differences in assumptions, methodologies, and prescriptions embodied in these contending world order (or global) models—which we sum up under the rubrics of "system maintenance," "system reform," and "system transformation"—they share several similarities.[24] First, they are all expressions of concern and anxiety about the state of a world in deep crisis. Second, most of these models take an international political economy approach, focusing on the production, distribution, and consumption of global resources. Third, they are all "future studies," projecting preferred and feasible futures based on different assumptions (see Chapter 8). Finally, their prescriptive or transition strategies, be they system maintaining, system reforming, or system transforming, tend to be linked to the structures of international society.

The System-Maintaining Image of World Order

In an age of hegemonic decline, world order rhetoric is invoked to legitimize the maintenance of the existing order. The main objective of intellectuals and policymakers who embrace the system-maintaining image of world order is defensive. They seek to prevent the breakdown of existing patterns of order and stability in a period of rapid change and disruption. The system maintainers are alert to the need for self-restraining behavior and for transnational cooperation, but have neither normative energy for reform nor any recognition that international stability requires major structural reforms. The system-maintenance view allows for only such marginal adaptions and accommodations as are perceived essential to preserve the stability of the status quo and its hierarchical/hegemonic structure of power and authority.

The Trilateral Commission, especially in its early phase (1973–1976), exemplifies this type of antivisionary approach.[25] Some of the early quantitative (computer) exercises of global modelling, as shown in Jay Forrester's *World Dynamics* (1971) and the Club of Rome's *The Limits to Growth* (1972), belong to this category as their preoccupation is to find the ways and means of maintaining or restoring "equilibrium" (computer language for stability) among the global subsystems.

In academia, Daniel Bell, Hedley Bull, and Stanley Hoffmann all seem to fit into this category. "The problem, then," writes Bell, "is to design effective international instruments—in the monetary, commodity, trade and technology areas—to effect the necessary transitions to a new international division of labor that can provide for economic and, perhaps, political *stability*."[26] Bull's system-maintaining image of world order is implied by his preference for "order" over "justice." He conceives order as a priority value as well as the condition for realizing other values—including the pursuit of justice. Bull champions the statist paradigm as being both necessary and sufficient for the maintenance of the international order.[27]

For Hoffmann, "world order" is always essential but elusive. He concurs with and accepts Bull's definition of world order "as the patterns or dispositions of human activity that sustain the elementary or primary goals of social life among mankind as a whole" at one point and then offers his own conception of "world order" as "nothing other than the set of processes and procedures, the global regime, that makes ethical foreign policy action possible."[28] Hoffmann's pursuit of this elusive "world order," which often takes the form of mainstream liberal analysis of U.S. foreign policy, turns into an endless intellectual search for "coherence" (or more brains and less muscle, as he put it in one analysis). There is little in his prolific work that can be linked to the system-reforming image of world order, and the system-transforming approach as represented by WOMP is condemned as "a kind of moral arrogance."[29]

The tenuous coalition between conservatives and liberals in the united-front strategy to maintain the existing world order is always susceptible to fracture with a change of power balance in domestic politics. With the election of Ronald Reagan, key members of the Committee on Present Danger—who can be characterized as "system-diminishers" in our typological scheme—replaced the Trilateralists as managers of the U.S. national security state, generating reactionary pressures for adjustment in the contending world order images. Two examples may suffice here. First, the Trilateral Commission has muted its earlier conception about how to manage turmoil and has succumbed for the moment to system-diminishing pressures. Second, the Council on Foreign Relations, whose system-reforming image of world order was reflected in its multivolume *1980s Project Studies*, has regressed in a system-diminishing direction. In 1981 the Council on Foreign Relations joined three other Western "think tanks" in proposing a number of united-front strategies to meet "enhanced Soviet military threats" and "an increasingly unstable and volatile Third World upon which it {the West} will depend more and more for its economic survival."[30]

The System-Reforming Image of World Order

Drawing upon the reform tradition of John Hobson, John Maynard Keynes, and David Mitrany, as modified and adapted to the problems and crises of the contemporary global political economy, system reformers seek a more efficient and equitable management of the global political economy through a series of institutional reforms. At no point does the system-reforming image seek to *transform* the statist paradigm in its quest for a more efficient, equitable, and lasting international order. Apart from occasional "world order" rhetoric, the most vocal supporters of this approach largely confine their reformist proposals to interstate social and political justice and interstate economic well-being. System reformers believe that they can have their cake and eat it too. They believe that greater international efficiency can be combined with greater international equity, greater international protection of national autonomy with greater international cooperation, greater international justice with greater international law and order. In short, system reformers affirm the functionalist belief that both North and South—and East and West—can indeed come together for joint cooperative management of "complex interdependence."

In the arena of global politics the prime mover for system reform is the Group of 77—the Third World caucus on global developmental stategy. Its views are expressed in the demands for the New International Economic Order, chiefly through UNCTAD or the UN General Assembly. To the extent that OPEC became a model as well as a supporter of the NIEO in the mid-1970s the system-reforming image of world order possessed serious leverage. Indeed, the formation of the Trilateral Commission can be seen as an effort to forge a system-maintaining countervailing response. More recently, however, OPEC has joined the system maintainers, uncoupling oil pricing policy from wider NIEO issues and reducing its official development aid (from 2.59 percent of GNP in 1975 to 1.36 percent of GNP in 1980).[31] As a result, the quest for the NIEO has been derailed from the track of structural reform. At the same time, the system reformers seem unable or unwilling to come to terms with the clear and continuing danger of nuclear destruction or even push hard to reform the discriminatory two-tier structure of the nonproliferation regime.

Of the contending global models, *RIO: Reshaping the International Order* and *North-South: A Program for Survival* are good examples of the system-reforming image of world order.[32] Prodded by the crisis of global inequalities and the failure of the present system to make an adequate response, both reports seek "an equitable international social and economic order" as the principal objective and suggest short-term and long-term reform proposals on a wide range of global developmental issues. Both reports advance a number of reform measures for strengthening the United Nations system in general and for restructuring international financial and monetary institutions in particular for a more efficient and equitable planning and management of the global economic system. Because both reports are firmly predicated on the primacy of the state system, "world order" modelling takes the form of muddling through by way of greater institutional reform and managerial efficiency.

In the community of scholars, the system-reforming image of world order is linked to the "complex interdependence" (or liberal internationalist) approach to the global political economy. Academic system reformers are "neorealists," skeptical of the utility or usability of force in global politics. Functionalists—neofunctionalists or "functionalists turned into regimists"— can be subsumed under this category. Although these scholars no longer accept the old functionalist separation of "high politics" and "low politics" or the transferability of supranational loyalty from transnational functional networks to the nation-states, the functionalist bias for scientific/techno-logical/managerial solutions still predominates. In fact, what used to be regarded as "low politics" has become "high politics" for the system reformers.

The authors of *Scientists and World Order* observe that "the world is evolving toward a model which gives increasing obeisance to the importance of scientific knowledge" and then conclude: "The claims to truth associated with science, if not objectively 'true,' have the function of being socially true and compelling because modern man has put himself in the position, by dint of his political values, of being unable to do otherwise, much as Bacon predicted."[33] Following this image of the science/world order nexus, Haas, Williams, and Babai use a narrow framework in separating world order models into three categories: the *rational* world order; the *pragmatic* world order; and the *skeptic* world order.[34]

Keohane and Nye, whose *Power and Interdependence* is perhaps the most influential work on regime research, while avoiding the trap of a narrow technocratic straitjacket nonetheless conclude with a rather mild functionalist plea "to orient the agencies {of U.S. Government} involved toward broader views of world order, rather than toward their narrowly defined problems."[35]

Thus the legitimacy and viability of the Westphalian statist system is not challenged; it needs to be reformed for more efficient management in an increasingly complex and interdependent world.

The System-Transforming Image of World Order

The belief that the Westphalian framework, dominated by interstate rivalries, can no longer meet the basic requirements of human decency and species survival in the nuclear-ecological age is central to the image of system-transformation. An image or model is system-transforming if it challenges the legitimacy and viability of the present international system and presents an alternative vision and structure that can be imposed on the ongoing world historical process. Antistatism is one test of this system-reforming image, although some allowance can be made for weak states, at least during a transition period, to neutralize the interventionary and penetrative pressures of strong states. A more positive test is a credible theory of system transformation accompanied by some specific transition steps or strategies needed for moving toward preferred world order systems.

The system-transforming image of world order is a preferred norm, not a working reality, in global politics. The Maoist image of world order came the closest to this norm. By casting its lot with the radical faction of the Third World in the struggle to break up the global dominance system, and by shifting from the conventional mode of power politics to a new style of politics as value-realizing and structure-transforming, Maoist China showed the potential of filling a leadership deficiency in "world-order politics." However, the normative and policy changes brought about by the post-Mao leadership since 1978 suggest a dramatic shift from the system-transforming to a system-maintaining trilateral direction. Nowhere is this shift more clearly demonstrated than in China's grand entry into the cockpit of the international financial and monetary institutions in 1980 and its immediate plunge into lobbying to increase its own shares and quotas.

Of course, Marxism has long represented the most powerful antisystemic force in the development of the world capitalist system. However, the status of Marxian theory today as a system-transforming approach to world order is problematic for several reasons. First, Marxist polity, as noted in Chapter 2, has purged itself of the normative principle of the "withering away of the state" in theory and practice, thus falling short of the test of antistatism. Second, although Marxism is still a powerful theory to explain the contradictions in capitalist society, its paradigmatic potency is considerably weakened by the inability to account for the rise of all kinds of contradictions in the socialist states, let alone intersocialist warfare. Third, Marxism, like Machiavellian realism, is a reductionist monocausal theory of economic determinism. Too many contradictions in the world today cannot be reduced as epiphenomenal of class conflicts. In short, Marxist theory has too narrow a value base to be qualified as a world order theory of system-transformation.

There is currently a crisis of faith in Marxism in China, Poland, and the Soviet Union as well as among Marxists outside the communist countries. Consider the extent to which world order values remain unrealized in the citadel of socialism, as summed up in Robert C. Tucker's depiction of the Soviet state today: "the swollen centralized state with superpower status in the world enforced by military might, the hierarchical system of power, the economic supermonopoly, the state and collective farm setup in the countryside, the foreign communist empire, the closed world of privilege for the nomenclature class."[36] The crisis among Marxists outside the communist world is acknowledged by no less a Marxist than Paul M. Sweezy:

> None of these 'socialist' societies behave as Marx—and I think most Marxists up until quite recently—thought they would. They have not eliminated classes except in a purely verbal sense; and, except in the period of the Cultural Revolution in China, they have not attempted to follow a course which could have the long-run effect of eliminating classes. The state has not disappeared—no one could expect it to, except in a still distant future— but on the contrary has become more and more the central and dominant institution of society. Each interprets proletarian internationalism to mean support of its own interests and policies as interpreted by itself. They go to war not only in self-defense but to impose their will on other countries— even ones that are also assumed to be socialist.[37]

The neo-Marxist "world system" approach, as exemplified in the work of Immanuel Wallerstein's historical investigations of the emergence of world capitalism, is another contending world order image that can be regarded as system-transforming. Wallerstein anticipates the eventual demise and replacement of the world capitalist system by "a socialist world-government" through Mao's continual class struggle.[38] A global socialist transformation will evolve out of the dynamics of national revolution at the periphery and semiperiphery. This dynamic process of transformation is believed to strengthen the position of socialist values and structures. Wallerstein has not yet specified a transition path, but he seems to envision a disintegration of the world capitalist system brought about by accelerating contradictions, on the one hand, and the coalition of the world's anti-systemic forces—or what he calls "real worldwide intermovement links"— on the other.[39]

While there are some parallel—and potentially complementary—formulations between the world system image and the system-transforming image of WOMP (the approach adopted and amplified in this book), several problematic features of the former need to be mentioned. As in Marxian theory, the world system image of system-transformation is grounded upon too narrow a value base. The WOMP approach relates "oppression" to a broader category of social reality than the adverse effects of the international division of labor, placing greater emphasis on what it means to be treated as "a nuclear guinea pig" or as ecologically expendable. This world order theory also clarifies the preferred future by postulating values rather than by conceiving of the oppressed as automatic bearers of the normative content of the politics of transformation. World order theorists are more concerned than world system theorists with mapping structural alternatives to either world government or statism. The world system approach is essentially a depiction of the rise and fall of capitalism as a world force in the aftermath of the breakdown of feudalism; the WOMP approach is more concerned about discerning challenges and devising responses in short-term as well as long-term time spans. In the remaining sections of this chapter, I will elaborate the principal characteristics and components of world order theory.

Human Nature and World Order

To date, the world order/human nature nexus has been left largely unexplored and unclarified. Implicit in the debates on world order lie contending images and assumptions about man and society, and different visions of the limits and possibilities of human behavior. The search for a viable theory of social change as an integral part of world order studies cannot go far without defining a credible conception of human nature.

Practically all of the significant traditional theories of world politics have been postulated either implicitly or explicitly on certain images of human nature. The dominant realist theory, for instance, can be traced to the Hobbesian image of man as *homo homini lupus*—a vicious and cruel animal with no compassion for his peers. This image of human nature—the first image in Kenneth Waltz's three-image typology of the theories of war— has been shared in varying degrees by St. Augustine, Luther, Malthus, Jonathan Swift, Dean Inge, Spinoza, Bismarck, Reinhold Niebuhr, and Hans Morgenthau in their attempts to explain societal defects or evils in terms of the allegedly innate nastiness of human nature.[40] Even the struggle for power among nations has been explained by some "realists" in terms of *animus dominandi*, the notion that *homo sapiens*, in his individual and collective capacities, acts like a beast of prey, driven by an insatiable lust for power.[41]

To a significant degree, then, our definition of "realism" and "utopianism" is preconditioned by our image of human nature. Consider world order implications of the popular cliché, "you can't change human nature." Such a credo of fatalism was embodied in the popular expression, "*meiyou fazi*," ("There is no way" or "Nothing you can do about it") in traditional China. For a long period in both Chinese and European history, Mao argued throughout his revolutionary transformation struggle, this fatalistic world view played a dominant role in human thought and action. Mao singled out as an example the traditional Chinese saying, "Heaven changeth not, likewise, the Tao changeth not."[42]

The logic of "realism," as shown earlier in Morgenthau's cardinal principles of political realism, is premised in the pessimistic and deterministic image of human nature. If human nature has not changed since time immemorial, as Morgenthau asserts, it follows that politics, which "is governed by objective laws that have their roots in human nature," has not changed either. It also follows that any quest for a *new* world order is no more than an utopian attempt to defy the "objective laws" of nature. As the Harvard paleontologist Stephen Jay Gould put it in his brilliant exposé of various versions of biological determinism and scientific racism: "After all, if the status quo is an extension of {human} nature, then any major change, if possible at all, must inflict an enormous cost—psychological for individuals, or economic for society—in forcing people into unnatural arrangements."[43]

Much of the current debates on "human nature" has evolved in the context of biological/ethological/psychological inquiries into the causes of human aggression. The study of human aggression has long been influenced by some metatheoretical assumptions and beliefs about the basic "nature" of man. The fears of Hobbesian realists and the hopes of Rousseauistic idealists have all made their way into descriptive, explanatory, and prescriptive analyses of aggression. For analytical convenience all contending images of human nature as expressed in these debates on human aggressive behavior can be divided into three theoretical schools: (1) aggression is a manifestation of an innate instinct (the instinctive theory); (2) aggression is an inborn reaction to frustration (the response-to-frustration theory); and (3) aggression is a learned social behavior responding to particular situations (the social-learning theory).

The Instinctive Theory

The instinctive theory as espoused by Konrad Lorenz and his followers has the following characteristics: (1) aggression is a phylogenetically programmed and ineradically instinctive behavior; (2) aggression is spontaneous (hydraulic model of energy motivation); (3) aggression is indispensable not only for the preservation of individuals and species in the service of evolutionary adaptation and survival but also for the mastery of creative human endeavors; (4) undischarged aggression leads to pathology; and (5) aggression cannot—and should not—be eliminated because catharsis serves as the only prescriptive remedy for human warfare in the nuclear age.

The instinctive theory of human behavior is plagued by numerous conceptual, methodological, and empirical weaknesses.[44] Yet the sweeping simplicity with which this theory has been presented by its proponents seem to have captured the malaise of our violence-afflicted times, attracting wide and uncritical acceptance by a large literate audience. The latest expression of this approach has been the "sociobiology" movement led by Edward O. Wilson.[45] Although sociobiology is more advanced in its theoretical construction and more prudent in its empirical generalization than Lorenzian theory, it still belongs to biological/instinctive determinism (the attribution of specific human behavior to the genetic programming in human nature), as evidenced in the following statement by Wilson: "Are human beings innately aggressive? This is a favorite question of college seminars and cocktail party conversations, and one that raises emotion in political ideologues of all stripes. The answer to it is yes."[46]

Is there any general human nature that explains the recurring phenom-enon of organized killing in human history? It may be reasonable to assume that the genetic endowment or biological potentiality of man plays an unspecified role in setting the outer limits of human behavior. But the instinctive image of human nature, which assumes such uniformity of human behavior in time and place, is inadequate in explaining why some people are so peaceful and others are so violent, or why the same people are peaceful and violent at different times under different situations.

The instinctive theory of aggression is conceptually flawed by its failure to take into account the role of perception (cognition) in human behavior. It disregards instrumental aggression, the most pervasive form of violence deeply embedded in the modern state system, in which privileged classes and groups commit indirect violence against social underdogs through the manipulation of social structures that stabilize unequal distribution of social goods. Given the prevalence of displaced aggression (scapegoating aggression) and the inherent tendency of aggression to move downward on the social and political ladder, this weakness is of great significance to world order studies.

Given the present conceptual and empirical status of instinctive/biological determinism, world order studies is unlikely to profit much from this particular image of human nature. The deterministic theory of human aggressive behavior both enhances the old Hobbesian theme that war is natural and inevitable and encourages the fatalistic sense of low efficacy—the "nothing much we can do about it" attitude. The pessimistic and deterministic image of human nature emanating from instinctive/biological determinism stands as an obstacle in the way of transforming our attitudes, beliefs, and values for a more just and humane world order.

Biological determinism, as Gould sums up, "is fundamentally a theory about limits."[47] It is a conservative theory of dominance designed to perpetuate the status quo and to lock up human future in the inherited (ascriptive) status of differential human "intelligence." It is a theory that discriminates and fragments (classifying and pigeonholing us all by race, sex, I.Q., brain size, class, or national origin) instead of enhancing human equality and species solidarity.

The instinctive theory of human aggression, often simplified as the "nature" theory as opposed to "nurture" theory, has far-reaching practical implications for social policy. The advocates of this brand of "human nature" theory had such a powerful influence on social policy in the United States in the early twentieth century that some state legislatures were persuaded to authorize the sterilization of those deemed "feebleminded, and in some cases, the mentally ill." By 1930 some thirty states had passed such legislation.[48]

One variant on the nature/nurture debates in the twentieth century has centered on race, class, and I.Q. with some prominent psychometricians faithfully mirroring the dominant prejudices of their time, class, or race. Notice, for example, the characterization of blacks in the 1911 edition of the *Encyclopaedia Britannica* (whose successive editions mirror in summary form general "scientific" consensus on race and ethnicity): "In certain . . . characteristics . . . the negro would appear to stand on a lower evolutionary plane than the white man, and to be more closely related to the highest anthropoids. . . . Mentally, the negro is inferior to the white."[49]

By applying extensive mental tests to recruits entering the United States Army in World War I, the Harvard psychologist Robert Yerkes reached predictable conclusions about people of Nordic European descent testing high and Latins, Slavs, Jews, and blacks testing low, providing the "scientifically" legitimizing basis for racist immigration policy.[50] A decade or so ago Arthur Jensen and Richard Herrnstein, relying on I.Q. studies, including those of Sir Cyril Burt on identical twins reared in different environments, repeated the same thesis that intelligence is predominantly inherited. For Jensen, compensatory education for the poor and minorities was doomed, while Herrnstein suggested a social evolution into a stratified caste system based on inherited levels of intelligence.[51]

The rush to fallacious racial inferences and judgments about I.Q. has been a persistent feature of the apostles of innate, hereditary, hierarchical intelligence in human beings. In the 1970s Sir Cyril Burt, the so-called pioneer, psychology's first knight, and author of (in)famous twin studies, who had enjoyed a lifetime of trust by psychologists, educators, and politicians, was exposed as a fraud, largely as a result of the skepticism of two U.S. scholars—D. D. Dorfman of the University of Iowa and Leon Kamin of Princeton University.[52] With the recent finding that Japanese pupils have an average I.Q. score that is eleven points higher than that of American counterparts—or that Asian-Americans, the majority of whom are Chinese, score about forty-five points above the national average in the math section of the Scholastic Aptitude Tests and about fifty-five points above the national math norm in the Graduate Record Exam[53]—the hereditary theory of I.Q. (a form of scientific racism) may easily suffer the fate of the nineteenth-century craniometry.

The Response-to-Frustration Theory

This theory of human aggression stands on sounder and firmer conceptual and empirical grounds than the instinctive theory. It also has greater potential in generating more policy-relevant hypotheses for describing, explaining, and predicting violent behavior at various systemic levels of human society.[54] In the original formulation of this theory, advanced by John Dollard and his associates (the so-called Yale school in aggression theory), it was proposed that "the occurence of aggressive behavior always presupposes the existence of frustration, and contrariwise, that the existence of frustration always leads to some form of aggression."[55] Dollard and his associates also linked their response-to-frustration theory with Marxian theory—specifically Lenin's argument that the state "is the product and the manifestation of the *irreconcilability* of class antagonisms"—by pointing out that in Marxist theory aggression is assumed to result from frustration and the state is invented to keep the frustrated workers from attacking the elite. As they put it, "An extremely important instrument of the ruling class which prevents the frustrated from expressing their aggression against their frustrators is the state."[56]

Does frustration ("an interference with the occurence of an instigated goal-response at its proper time in the behavior sequence") *always* lead to aggression? Recent research and experiment by Leonard Berkowitz and others have added some modifications and refinements to the original frustration-aggression hypothesis in three ways. First, frustration creates a *readiness* or predisposition (by arousing anger) toward aggressive acts. Second, aggressive responses do not occur even under such a state of readiness without aggression-evoking *cues*. That is, cues serve as mediating variables between frustration (independent variable) and aggression (dependent variable), revising the simple one-to-one relationship in the original formulation. A third revision of the frustration-aggression theory restricts the deterministic quality implied in the adverb "always" by adding *learning experience* as another mediating variable affecting the individual's definition of the situation.[57]

In spite of these revisions and modifications, the frustration theory poses several problems. The tendency to simplify and reduce the determinants of human aggression into a single cause has resulted in defining "frustration" in such broad terms as to make the concept almost circular, in which the cause (frustration) and the outcome (aggression) can each be cited as evidence of the other. Studies of monkeys and children have shown that frustration as well as such other nonfrustrating causal variables as rivalry for possession of a prized object, jealousy for the attention of an individual, and intrusion of a stranger in the group provide additional explanations of fighting.[58] Moreover, responses to frustration may take forms other than aggression, such as acceptance, submission, resignation, dependence, avoidance, alienation, and withdrawal.

The Social-Learning Theory

The social-learning theory of aggression shifts the locus of causal analysis from inner determinants (instincts, impulses, needs, and drives) to outer determinants (social contexts and targets) in advancing the proposition that human aggression is learned social behavior.[59] This theory implicitly repudiates the Hobbesian image of human nature. Based on the contrary assumption that man's basic nature is malleable and plastic, it argues with substantial empirical support that the so-called inner forces of human aggression cannot possibly account for the pronounced variation of a given behavior at different times and in different social situations.

The antideterminist image of human nature embodied in the social-learning theory is supported by ample experimental evidence that man's aggressive acts attributed inferentially to his inner stimuli can easily be changed in form and direction by varying external stimulus and reinforcement controls. This theory has gained considerable support in the modern behavioral sciences. For example, Bernard Berelson and Gary A. Steiner conclude their comprehensive survey of the behavioral science study of human behavior: "So behavioral science man is social man—social product, social producer, and social seeker—to a greater degree than philosophical man or religious man or political man or economic man or psychoanalytic man, or the man of common observation and common sense, for that matter."[60]

If the instinctive theory is about human classifications and limitations, the social-learning theory is about human adaptation and possibilities. The plastic and adaptive image of human nature embodied in the social-learning theory has been embraced in varying degrees by most theories of social change, including Marxism. For Marx men's social existence determines their consciousness, not vice versa. Still, in the Marxist vision of historical progress human transcendence will ultimately liberate itself from the constraints of bourgeois social existence in its exorable march toward humanity's communal (communist) utopia. For Mao the human mind is a virtual *tabula rasa*, clay in a potter's hand. Mao also believed in "man's *inherent unlimited* capacity for knowledge,"[61] although he may fall short of fulfilling this capacity in social practice.

The positive and plastic image of human nature as embodied in the social-learning theory goes a long way in clarifying the task of building a credible theory of social change. It provides a structure-oriented approach to the question of human behavior in social process; it also suggests the prescriptive possibility that learned behavior can be unlearned, a first step in laying the human behavioral foundation for a just world order.

Each of the three theories of human aggression sheds light on various dimensions of human behavior. The instinctive theory or biological determinism suggests inner limits of human behavior. The response-to-frustration theory suggests reciprocal interactions between inner and outer determinants of human behavior. The social-learning theory shows inner possibilities and outer (social) limitations of human behavior. However, we should be wary of attempting any major inductive leap from this grounding in individual behavior to higher levels of social organization. The question still remains as to how, in what ways, and to what extent the influence of individual human behavior is expressed (rather than modified) in the larger social and institutional contexts of world politics.

What about a "world order" image of human nature? The Hobbesian/ Lorenzian image of human nature is clearly incompatible with the antifatalist, antideterminist conception of human nature inherent in any system-transforming approach. The sanguine image of human nature embodied in the social-learning theory, while necessary and useful in the search for the outer possibilities of social transformation, has the danger of blurring, rather than balancing, empirical and normative realities. World order realism, in which the limits and possibilities of human behavior are constantly balanced, needs to draw upon and synthesize the response-to-frustration and social-learning theories to reach a basically positive and transcendental conception of humanity that also takes human biological potential and basic needs fully into account. In this connection, the concept of basic human needs as initially developed by Abraham Maslow and later modified and further differentiated by John and Magda McHale provides a most useful basis for fusing the positive and plastic image of human nature embodied in the social-learning theory with the necessary accounting of basic human needs and drives embodied in the response-to-frustration theory.[62]

Main Assumptions/Points of Departure

Explicitly or implicitly all political theories are based on certain epistemological and normative assumptions. These assumptions do not require proof for validation since they are *a priori* accepted as axiomatic. They do serve às points of departure for disciplined inquiry. The limits within which any political inquiry takes place are defined by the epistemological assumptions. The criteria of relevance and significance for choosing research paths are defined by the normative assumptions. Our world order approach starts with the prime assumption that the quest for a more just and humane world order—defined and monitored in terms of realizing world order values— is axiologically essential, intellectually feasible, and politically necessary. In short, the raison d'être of world order studies is grounded upon this assumption of desirability and feasibility. In this section we will briefly set forth several main assumptions marking the points of departure and defining the parameters of world order studies.

A Value-Centered Approach

Oscar Wilde's characterization of an economist as a man who knows the price of everything and the value of nothing provides a point of departure for a value-centered approach in world order studies. The inability and/or unwillingness to call a spade a spade is a professional disease that has afflicted a large number of mainstream social scientists. "The so-called disengaged scholar," Immanuel Wallerstein has pointed out, "has merely erected some barriers to the observation of his premises."[63] World order studies makes a conscious commitment to the definition and pursuit of the humanistic values of peace, economic well-being, social justice, and ecological harmony, rejecting any claim to a value-free or value-neutral approach as epistemologically untenable, intellectually misleading, and politically irresponsible.

In epistemological terms, the separation of empirical and normative theories is easier said than done. Consciously or not, our social action (or inaction) reflects a value judgment, "a choice among alternative outcomes, a selection of one outcome in preference to another in a given situation, or the application of a set of values to an empirical situation."[64] Values serve as explicit or implicit criteria for choice in human behavior (or in our theoretical model). Normative choice is inherent in every human action, and every human action has both direct and indirect, short-term and long-term consequences in the shaping of "social reality." Social reality necessarily embodies both empirical (the "is") and normative (the "ought") dimensions because it represents not only what we actually see but also, more importantly, what we want to see.

To the extent that empirical and normative theories are understood as mutually complementary, a value-centered approach can greatly improve our grasp of the global situation. World order values provide criteria of relevance and significance for what to look for and in what frame of reference. Politics, conceptualized as a value-realizing activity, serves as a coherent framework for this approach. We then ask: who gets what, how, and why in the value-realizing process in world society? What kinds of values are predominant in global politics? And why? In this way, a value-centered approach attempts to overcome the dehumanization of social science research and to reformulate the research agenda of global politics as if people really mattered. Of course, a value, like a structure, can be good or bad depending on how it does what to people; hence the use of the qualifier "world order" in reference to values.

A value-centered approach is not some utopian exercise of mixing empirical and normative images of world order or of leaping from the present predicament into the promised land. Instead, this approach is designed to answer the following set of related questions: What *is* the normative basis of the present world order system? What *ought to be* the normative basis of an alternative and preferred future world order system? How can we reconcile value conflicts and value trade-offs? Specifically, how can we relate world peace with world justice in our conceptual and operational scheme? To what extent are peace and justice conflicting or complementary? Which of the two values—world peace or world justice—should enjoy a "preferred position" or a "prior claim" and why? Here the role of knowledge is conceived as a socially purposive instrument for fusing the relationship among "feeling," "believing," "knowing," and "acting."

Methodology

Can there be a "world order methodology"? Given the centrality of values in world order studies, methodological concerns are secondary and instrumental. Still, all intellectual inquiries are grounded upon certain styles of thinking. World order methodology draws upon the following styles of thinking: *transcendental* thinking to overcome the constraints of social anesthesia; *diagnostic* thinking to decipher the causes and effects of system pathology; *prognostic* thinking to assess the trends of history; *prescriptive* thinking to suggest ways and means of system transformation; and *normative* thinking to connect "feeling," "believing," and "acting."

No single discipline or mode of analysis possesses the necessary wisdom and intellectual resources to singlehandedly lead world order studies. World order studies necessarily relies upon an interdisciplinary approach to integrate knowledge in the service of human values and needs. The interdisciplinary

approach of world order studies evolved from two antecedents: the mono-disciplinary approach of traditional international relations and the inter-disciplinary approach of peace research.

The study of war and peace was the central concern of traditional world order thinking, preempted largely by the students of international relations who jealously guarded the subject matter within the narrow boundaries of disciplinary autonomy. The peace research movement, which arose in the late 1950s and early 1960s out of a disenchantment with the intellectual self-isolation of traditional international relations, marked the next stage. Peace research differs from traditional international relations in the following respects: (1) it is more interdisciplinary (in fact, it served as a rendezvous point for various disciplines concerned with human conflict behavior); (2) it is more value-oriented, rejecting both the feasibility and desirability of value-neutral models; and (3) it is broader in its scope of inquiry, responding to the challenge of violence in any form anywhere; it probes the possibilities of dealing with conflicts in a comparative and interdisciplinary framework, moving up and down different levels ranging from international through intergroup to interpersonal and finally intrapersonal conflicts.

The interdisciplinary approach of world order studies—in which the value of peace is broadened and updated by relating it more closely with such other values as economic well-being, social and political justice, and ecological balance—is exemplified in WOMP, an outgrowth of peace research. World order studies does not reject the interdisciplinary approach of peace research. Instead it refines, expands, and synthesizes a loose juxtaposition of concepts, paradigms, and theories borrowed from various social science disciplines, formulating its own concepts and models suited to the futuristic orientation, the formulation of transition strategies, and the designing of preferred world order systems.

Specifically, the interdisciplinary approach is well-suited for utilizing two dominant perspectives on the global problematique: the actor-oriented perspective and the structure-oriented perspective.[65] As shown in our discussion of the transformation of world politics since Westphalia in Chapter 2, each perspective can capture a significant portion of the global reality. When these two perspectives are combined, however, they bring into focus practically all the problems (that is, both normative and structural variables) that world order studies needs to deal with.

System Pathology

The management of "power" as the crucial peace-maintaining or stability-enhancing variable is a common point of departure in mainstream theoretical approaches to world order—balance of power, collective security, and world government.[66] From this power-oriented perspective, social health or pathology in the world is judged by the extent to which the international system is capable of maintaining power equilibrium, preserving the existing order and preventing an outbreak of global conflagration. Our world order approach starts from a broader context of concern and anxiety about humanity in deep crisis.

This sense of concern and crisis rejects the power-oriented approach as insufficient and insensitive to the system pathology as manifested in structural violence as well as in physical violence. Although recognizing the crises of war, mass poverty, social injustice, and ecological hazards, world order realism refuses to accept the complacent notion that they are unfortunate but necessary and immutable evils that we have to live with—or that they can be ameliorated through prudential muddling or managerial fixes. The root causes of system pathology lie not so much in demographic pressure, resource scarcity, and stagflation (important as they are), as in the values and structures underpinning the global politics of planning, producing, distributing, and consuming the "goods" and "bads." We therefore seek consciously to put these symptoms of system pathology at the center of our intellectual agenda for diagnosis and prescription.

The Global/Local Nexus

World order inquiry presupposes two kinds of human bondage. In an objective sense, we are all citizens of one world, bonded by a shared legacy and a common destiny. This reality was vividly captured by the astronaut Frank Borman, on seeing Earth from Apollo 8: "We are one hunk of ground, water, air, clouds, floating around in space. From out there it really is 'one world.'" To ignore this reality is to ignore a hole in our lifeboat.

Yet how many of us can really claim to have embraced such a holistic world view of human destiny, feeling/thinking/acting as global citizens in our daily lives? In a subjective sense, we are still territorial prisoners within the caves of our own cultures and states. For most people in the Third World, the struggle to be free of colonial bondage and to be masters of their own national destiny has been, and continues to be, the predominant feature of their political experience. We can ignore this only at the risk of making world order inquiry largely irrelevant to the struggling masses in the global ghettoes.

How do we then establish a global/local connection in a mutually complementary manner? We have to proceed with the assumption that it is indeed possible "to think globally but act locally." As will be shown later in this chapter, world order studies has recently shifted its orientation to establish closer touch with the souls of the oppressed. Through a continuous dialogue between populist struggle and world order vision, one line of the global/local nexus is established. At the same time, it is necessary to impose a holistic world order vision to overcome the fragmentation of populist struggles—to transcend Marx's "rural idiocy," if you will—and to link together all antisystemic forces and movements as an integral part of the quest for a just world order. For the creation of a just world order, Saul H. Mendlovitz has recently proposed a fusion of "voices," "visions," and "transition."[67]

From an evolutionary holistic perspective, the statist structure of the world is transient and conditional, a subjective fragmentation of the objective planetary reality. This fragmentation arose at a given time in human history and is now being overlaid and overshadowed, if not completely superceded. Even such a planetary holism acknowledges the transient role of the state in preserving national autonomy and diversity in the world as now constituted, achieving national cohesion internally and safeguarding national autonomy against external actors and forces. Yet to retain statism with its present form and functions in some transformed world political system is a self-contradictory proposition.

In order to establish a global/local nexus on a viable basis, we need to know the reciprocal interactions and impacts of global politics at different systemic levels and the kinds of global problems and crises that exceed the separate capacities of individual states and the international system. This also entails giving due accord to nonstate actors, including those associated with intergovernmental arrangements (e.g., the United Nations, functional specialized agencies), transnational activities (transnational corporations, banks), and nongovernmental organizations (e.g., Red Cross, Amnesty International). As the world becomes more complex, confusing, and complicated, we need to assess the various activities of nonstate actors as well as of international networks and regimes constantly for their effects on the realization of world order values. Accordingly, the lines of the global/local nexus call for periodic review and redrawing.

System Transformation

Traditional world order images were largely apolitical, paying little attention to transition and eventual global transformation. The underlying assumptions rested on a rational appeal and argument designed to change elite beliefs and behavior. This topdog view of global reform has been recently supplanted by an underdog view based on the global potential of ongoing populist movements for social change. Hence, "the oppressed," to the extent that they are mobilized for global reform, become the social force capable of promoting a progressive realization of world order values. Given the dangers of nuclear war and ecological deterioration and the tenacity of present leaders regarding system maintenance, consciousness about system pathology and species survival expands at one and the same time.

No claim is being made here that mobilized movements among the oppressed are consistently or self-consciously dedicated to world order values. Their horizons are provincial at the moment, generally focused on radical change of the domestic authority structure. The world order approach contends, however, that these movements can have wider global implications. Indeed, it is becoming clearer that national revolution movements are often being derailed after their initial success, partly due to hostile pressures from the existing international system. Other movements, such as the growing West European movement against nuclear weapons and militarism, can only secure the grounds of their success by spreading everywhere and by adopting a global vision of transformation. Given the globalization of international relations, progressive radical changes at the national level are vulnerable to disruptive systemic reactions.

In the final analysis, a system-transforming approach to world order cannot remain viable for long without aligning itself with the flow of the world historical process. To capture the nature and direction of this world historical process at any given moment is an elusive task. Nonetheless, our approach contends that there are two competing trends—fragmentation/ integration, system breakdown/system transformation—engaged in a contest with an unpredictable outcome. As the signs of system pathology became increasingly visible, the zone of consciousness and the arena of social movement for human survival expands. It is unlikely that the 1980s will pass without a major nuclear and ecological disaster of some magnitude. If such a disaster occurs, the latent populist energies of those who feel victimized and oppressed could easily and quickly become an explosive force for system transformation. The sooner this challenge is met, world order inquiry presupposes, the more likely it is that violent change or traumatic system catastrophe can be obviated.

The General Framework of Inquiry

There is general agreement that world order inquiry "would have to use a much broader range of potential actors, including world institutions, transnational actors, international organizations, functional activities, regional arrangements, the nation-state, subnational movements, local communities and individuals."[68] Like the world-system approach, the world order approach self-consciously shies away from the straitjacket of the state-centric framework of inquiry.

The general framework of inquiry of world order studies is designed to perform several specific tasks of normative social research. Based on the methodological assumption that the transformation of global actors, values, and institutions needed for a preferred world order system is both necessary and possible, this approach requires (1) a diagnostic/prognostic task of describing present world order conditions and trends, (2) a modelling task of designing preferred futures, and (3) a prescriptive task of mapping transition strategies.

Systemic Trends and Capabilities

At the heart of this particular diagnostic and prognostic task lie two sets of inquiries. What is the "social health" or "social pathology" of the world system today? This is a matter of describing the degree to which world order values are distributed, realized or suppressed in empirical reality. There are several related tasks. We need to clarify emerging realities in relation to positive and negative trends bearing on prospects for world order values. We also need to extrapolate from the existing trends the possible world or worlds of the future. We emphasize the complex interplay between forces of destruction and creativity that are being set loose in the modern world political system. Out of this interplay, it is argued, we can begin to grasp the reasons for fear and hope at the present juncture in human history.

We follow world order realism in the analysis of the trends (the unfolding realities) by avoiding the sentimental exercise of wishful thinking, on one hand, and by rejecting the dominant paradigm of the realist school, on the other. Our ongoing search for the development of a credible conception of system transformation distinguishes contemporary world order thinking from traditional world order thinking. At the same time, we reject the "realist" image of world politics as being reductionistic and anachronistic. Seeing the worst in human nature and translating this one-dimensional view of human history into social policy, the realists do in a self-fulfilling manner lend a sense of inevitability and legitimacy to a Hobbesian world of interstate rivalry and competition.

The self-fulfilling prophecy of the realists seems to have made the functionalist pronouncements of the impending demise of the state premature and foolish. At the most visible level, the state has indeed demonstrated its staying power. It seems as if the state has acquired its own life impervious to class controls and interests, as it has progressively become more and more powerful in both liberal democratic and Marxist socialist polities. With the spread of the state system to Third World countries as the dominant form of authority structure, global statism seems to have now become an immutable part of international reality.

Although the resilience of the state is evident, at a deeper level an impending structural and legitimacy crisis is taking shape. Modern science and technology has brought about the functional demise of territorial impenetrability of the nation-state, an outmoded imperative that now remains protected by the legal paper tiger of state sovereignty. This global trend of human activities may be conceived as an interpenetrative process and structure through which "goods" (and "bads") are being planned, produced, distributed, and consumed in the present world system. If this perception of a new global reality is valid, the formal structure and the inner logic of the state are inconsistent with the requirements of world order politics.

In functional terms, many states have become increasingly dysfunctional in providing security from external threat, preserving human dignity, and promoting economic and ecological well-being. The nuclear arms race between the two superstates, far from making us secure, has made every human being a victim of fear, the fear of nuclear holocaust. In the Third World, too, there are many cases in which the state has degenerated into a neofascist instrument of oppression.[69] Even in the Marxist polities the state, instead of withering away as an instrument of class politics, has become a superstate with tentacles reaching into every domain of human thought and action.

Although the state system is still strong, the legitimacy crisis remains unresolved (and unresolvable), steadily eroding its structural, moral, and sociopsychological foundations. The extent to which the state's dominant role has been diluted can also be seen in the rapid rise in roles and numbers of nonstate actors. In the long run, the erosion of statist dominance in human affairs may be unavoidable.

Images of Possible and Preferred Futures

As a social and intellectual movement to catalyze thought and action toward shaping the future of human destiny in a more just and humane direction, world order studies is a species of future studies. The conceptual premise of world order modelling lies in the sociopsychological principle that may be reformulated as follows: what we feel, believe, think, expect or wish shapes not only our present behavior but also the kinds of futures we transmit and posterity inherits. This principle has found various formulations in social science research. Anatol Rapoport noted that "probabilities which we assign to events become reflections of our preferences rather than of our knowledge."[70] In a similar vein, Kenneth Boulding has written that our behavior depends on the image, which is defined as "the subjective knowledge structure" of any individual or organization consisting "not only of images of 'fact' but also images of 'value.'"[71]

The image often defines first; only then do we see "social reality." For centuries, slavery was "imagined" as an immutable part of the natural social order. Hence, it was utopian to advocate its abolition. It is clear that the image holds a powerful grip on how we define the outer limits and possibilities of social change. Our future does not have self-determination or self-realization. Everything we do or fail to do works its way into the shaping of our individual and collective future. Whether we realize it or not tomorrow is always present in images of today at all levels of social reality, from the individual to the state. The sense of the future is an aspect of the "is" (empirical reality) because of our social expectations that certain things or events are supposed to recur in a certain way and because we conform our behavior accordingly.

Many of the prominent global modelling exercises rely on computer technology and involve narrowing the scope of inquiry to a small number of quantifiable variables. Almost no attention is given to specific human wants or basic human needs, let alone to the psychological, cultural, and normative dimensions of the world in which we live. The Latin American World Model (developed as a Third World reaction to the Club of Rome projections) is a notable exception.[72]

Our world order modelling is not designed simply to manipulate quantitative data and variables or to seek a technocratic fix. As will be elaborated in Chapter 8, its principal aim is to highlight the value premises and values goals of each projected scenario of the future and to assess how each scenario facilitates the normative, holistic shaping of human destiny. Ours is a form of *soft modelling*, synthesizing and integrating the functions of exploratory and normative forecasting.

Contrary to some critics, the basic trust of the world order modelling is not apocalyptic or eschatological prophecy, but an exploration of preferred futures that can be used as a road map for formulating transition steps and envisaging a positive evolution of political life at all levels, from the personal and local to the collective and global. The search for preferred futures that satisfy the criteria of normative desirability and political feasibility is an ongoing dialectical process joining inquiry into past, present, and future.

Transition Politics

Transition politics is the multidimensional, multilateral, and multistep process of building relevant and reliable bridges connecting the present and our preferred future. The most elusive task in world order studies, it is greatly complicated by the lack of any credible (widely tested and validated) theory of system transformation. Although transition politics is accepted as a crucial link between the present world order system and a more just and humane world order system, our approach shies away from the search for one master key to the future. Given the contending images of preferred worlds and the uneven distribution and realization of world order values in different parts of the world, seeking a master key to utopia is misleading. Instead, a series of differentiated strategies keyed to existing circumstances and opportunities in various parts of the world seems the best way to proceed. The targets, actors, and arenas of transition politics should not be too rigidly specified or given too global an emphasis. In order to minimize the danger of acting locally without thinking globally, however, we propose some broad principles and orientations for world order transition in Chapter 8.

Our approach to transition politics also rests upon the centrality of values, understanding transition in terms of human intervention to shape the value-realizing process. At the same time, the world order values of peace, economic well-being, social justice, and ecological balance are not placed in abeyance pending the completion of the transition process; instead, those values apply to the *means* as well as the *ends* of transition politics. So many social and political revolutions have betrayed their own vision and devoured their own children due to an insensitivity to the mutually enhancing or corrupting effects of the relationship between means and ends. World order theorists seek a new conception of "revolution" that differs from "mere seizures of power, a way of circulating elites through bloody events, after which the same 'rotten things begin all over again.'"[73] We need operational definitions of values for use in assessing progress or regress during a given period in any of the four world order value domains.

The world order approach makes use of both actor-oriented and structure-oriented perspectives in the study of transition politics. Both are necessary for a broad understanding of how individuals and groups at different systemic levels and in different domains may successfully intervene in ongoing social, political, economic, and cultural processes to bring about social change. However, a credible politics of system transformation requires the conceptual and political inputs of those most victimized by the existing world order. Social change may be a luxury that only a few progressive or dissatisfied elites can be expected to work for, but it is an imperative for victims of the existing order who, becoming conscious of their suffering, develop the political will to reshape their destiny. The extent to which an individual or group perceives itself to be oppressed is a crucial element in consciousness-raising and mobilization during the transition process.

The Development of World Order Studies

In a critical appraisal of the promise and prospects of the world order modelling movement associated with WOMP, the late Harold Lasswell observed that "the agenda for coming basic revisions will be on a ten-year cycle, and the intervals will be adapted to the occurrence of major changes."[74] This assessment has proved on target. Because academic debates on contemporary world order studies have centered largely on WOMP, and because the world order theory employed in this book is closely associated with WOMP, it may be useful to briefly review how the WOMP approach has evolved. Three distinct stages of development can be depicted, although these shifts in conceptual focus and methodological orientation should not obscure certain common features that have remained since the inception of this academic enterprise.

The First Stage: A Law-Oriented and Institution-Building Approach

In the first stage (1961–1968), a group of concerned U.S. scholars largely devoted themselves to the task of establishing world order as a respectable academic undertaking. The general framework of inquiry was oriented toward law and institution-building. Within this framework primary attention was given to avoiding collective violence through the creation of a war prevention system constituted by a core of strengthened international institutions. In spite of the pronounced intention of studying war prevention in the spirit of social science, the primary focus of inquiry centered on international law and organization. The underlying assumption was that institutional centralization would come about through the consent of leading governments, which would realize that system change would serve their national interests better than the dangerous chaos of the decentralized and laissez-faire management of power in the nuclear age.

In effect, this law-oriented and institution-building approach anticipated the formation of some species of world government. The most comprehensive and rigorous example of this approach has remained *World Peace Through World Law*, conceived and written by two international lawyers, Grenville Clark and Louis B. Sohn.[75] Clark and Sohn proposed amending the UN Charter to transfer some functions, capabilities, and resources from national governments to a rearranged set of global institutions. The influence of the Clark/Sohn proposals on the development of world order studies during this first stage is evident in *The Strategy of World Order* series.[76] In the preface to the series, the editors noted: "It [*World Peace Through World*

Law} is not selected as an expression of the ideological preference of the editors so much as to provide a model, specified in some detail, of what an alternative international system might be like. Such a model of one future for the international system facilitates our understanding of international society as it exists and operates at present and informs us more clearly about the kind of changes that must be made to fulfill the objectives of war prevention."[77]

The world order approach at this first stage embodied a number of features that now seem dubious. First of all, it appealed to the enlightened self-interest of the privileged to take the initiative in transition politics, basing the appeal on the uncritical transference of liberal reform politics to the international scene. Second, this world order approach could not avoid the charge of wearing the mask "world order" to disguise the neo-imperial motive of *pax Americana.* Its conceptual origin, key participants, and pedagogical materials were all American. Its legal and structural design for world order reflects the rather unique historical experience of the United States with its largely successful transition from the relatively decentralized condition of "state" sovereignty under the Articles of Confederation to a "more perfect union" under a new federal system. Third, this world order approach betrayed the vestigial influence of the traditional definition of world order in terms of world law. This exercise in constitutional or legal engineering was a kind of intellectual utopianism through which world order scholars could escape the "messy and uncivilized" *political* struggles of forging an actual new order. Finally, this world order approach was conceptually inadequate as it defined world order largely in static terms of "order" and "war prevention." In short, the world order approach during the formative stage abstracted the question of system transformation in a manner unresponsive to the broader world-order agenda of the non-Western peoples of the world.

The Second Stage: Diverse Images of "Preferred Worlds" (WOMP I)

The establishment of WOMP in 1968 marks the initiation of the second stage (1968–1978) of world order studies. A sense of dissatisfaction with first stage efforts brought about a restructuring of the world order approach around the idea that a broader conception of world order inquiry called for the participation of representatives from the major cultures and ideologies of the world. In both a symbolic and substantive sense, WOMP represents a new cycle in the development of world order studies. The transnationalization process of world order studies through the active participation of non-American scholars of international stature has also broadened the value base of world order inquiry. The central focus on war prevention shifted to a more balanced normative framework with more or less equivalent emphasis on economic well-being, social justice, and peace, and somewhat less emphasis on ecological balance. As one Third World WOMP participant put it:

Non-Western participants in that project assaulted and challenged its Western ethnocentrism; "non-lawyers" enhanced and broadened its concerns and pushed it in the direction of political harmony and culture. Those concerned with socioeconomic justice drew attention to the fact that peace, unless rooted in socioeconomic justice, can be meaningless, stultifying, and perhaps repressive; the strong have always sought peace as a means of ensuring that their order would be unchallenged and undisturbed. The intrusion of concern for justice into world orderism was to profoundly change its thrust and essence. The hitherto legal emphasis of the movement was increasingly modified to be more self-consciously political.[78]

Based on this broadened normative framework, WOMP participants associated with principal regions or actors of the world (Latin America, Africa, Japan, Europe, Soviet Union, India, United States, with indirect representation for China and for the network of transnational actors) embarked on book-length formulations of their approach to world order. Because the values were stated in general terms and subject to a variety of interpretations, and because participants were free to propose additional values, this framework was pluralistic in its style of inquiry and substantive vision. This transnational collaborative research enterprise cut across cultures and world views to develop new ways of thinking about system transformation. It culminated in a series of six books under the umbrella title "Preferred Worlds for the 1990s."[79]

Although the *Preferred Worlds* series generated considerable interest and controversy in academic circles, including those outside the West,[80] its overall impact on collective ways of thinking, feeling, and acting has remained modest. The criticisms of WOMP, some justified and some not, covered the entire spectrum of intellectual discourse, including conceptual, methodological, empirical, and political objections. Mainstream international relations research, confined by its state-centric framework of inquiry, has tended to dismiss "world order" as naive, utopian, and diversionary.

On its own turf, WOMP has given insufficient attention to the transition problem. The *Preferred Worlds* series has not provided either a satisfactorily systematic or substantive treatment of transition politics by way of prescribing behavioral guidance for world order activists. In addition, WOMP was unable to achieve sustained, prominent participation of scholars from the Soviet Union, or more generally, from the communist world. Third World participation symbolized the transnationalization of world order inquiry without any corresponding cohesion in research purpose, modelling design, or an integrated world order vision. Instead, it entailed a constant questioning of WOMP's premises. Revealing in this respect, are the views of Rajni Kothari, a leading Indian scholar, who while evolving his own vision of "a just world," remains skeptical about "world order" enterprise, suspecting that it may be a carrier of Western hegemonic thinking, a species of cultural imperialism.[81]

Now that the second stage of world order studies (or WOMP I) is behind us, it is easy to see why and where it failed to live up to the promises set forth at its inception. First of all, generating a strong and cohesive political will toward normative goals of system transformation is difficult, if not impossible, in the current global conditions of fragmentation. The transnationalization of world order inquiry with the purpose of finding collective (and hopefully united) ways of thinking, feeling, and acting suggests the old Indian fable of the six blind beggars who encounter an elephant. Second, world order studies has not yet cracked the virtual monopoly of the realist school in defining what is real and feasible. Many influential specialists continue to reject the WOMP dual perception of system-deteriorating and system-transforming trends, and concentrate instead on improving the state system. Third, the repeated charge of utopianism cannot be convincingly dismissed unless WOMP articulates a transition politics to undergird its call for system transformation. These criticisms of WOMP, as noted earlier, ultimately direct attention to the question of "human nature." One inadequacy of WOMP I was its failure to base the future upon a coherent image of the plasticity of human nature.

The Third Stage: Struggle of the Oppressed (WOMP II)

The third stage of world order studies (WOMP II) began in 1978 with an increasing emphasis on the voices of the oppressed as the key basis for realizing world order values. In part, this new emphasis acknowledges that past approaches have been overly preoccupied with formal institutions and the tension between states and international organizations, and insufficiently concerned about social movements and the grassroots initiatives of the popular sector. The new approach builds its hopes for the future around various forms of "world order populism," adapted to diverse contexts and agendas.

This approach distinguishes between three intersecting systems of politics. The first consists of territorial actors: the state system and its supporting infrastructure of corporations, banks, and knowledge and news industries. The second is made up of international organizations, including the United Nations and regional international institutions; the third system consists of people acting individually and collectively (the popular sector) through voluntary social movements and associations of all kinds. This new stage in world order thinking is reflected in a number of recent WOMP projects, including a multivolume *Studies on a Just World Order* series.[82]

This synoptic sketch shows that the world order approach is neither static nor monolithic. Its continuing search for collective ways of thinking, feeling, and acting for a just world order is an ongoing process subject to periodic review and revision. Despite the shifts in focus and methodological orientation throughout the three stages of its development, certain core features give a measure of coherence to the world order approach: emphasis on system transformation; depiction of preferred world order systems; avowal of explicit values; concern about transition politics; and a holistic conception of global human interests and needs.

The Cutting Edge of World Order Inquiry

At the cutting edge of world order inquiry is the challenge of enhancing its relevance for disciplined inquiry into the global problematique and establishing a closer dialogue between the empirical reality of the present world order system and the preferred reality of alternative world order systems. Five broad areas of inquiry have recently emerged as the cutting edge of world order studies.[83]

A Struggle Notion of Social Change

A classic and influential formulation of a struggle notion of social change was embodied in The Communist Manifesto of 1848, which called upon the exploited of all countries to rise and rebel, for they "have nothing to lose but their chains." Can we reformulate and reapply this struggle notion in terms relevant to the present world system and compatible with world order values? Our contention is that system transformation takes place not through ivory-tower intellectual exercises but through the political struggles of oppressed peoples. The possibilities of system transformation depend on the extent to which the political consciousness of the oppressed is raised to the threshold of action and also on the extent to which political struggles in different parts of the world become oriented around the pursuit of world order values.

In this connection, Marxist theory seems too restrictive as it focuses too exclusively on one structural dimension of human oppression. The present world order system is oppressive in several respects. Adverse normative trends in recent years have also accentuated the contradictions in the world system. Some forms of oppression remain "invisible," not perceived as avoidable oppression by victims. The central manifestation of largely invisible oppression relates especially to the continuous threat to our lives, to our society and civilization, and even to our species in the form of catastrophic nuclear war. The enormity of the peril and our seeming helplessness to prevent it leads us to block out or numb our awareness of the danger. Other causes of failure or refusal to see the various forms of invisible oppression are too numerous to elaborate here.[84] A struggle notion of social change for world order studies should be able to identify oppressive structures of the present world order system and show their interconnections and global implications. This awareness could influence political consciousness and eventually help mobilize millions of people for the work of devising transition tactics and strategies to achieve alternative futures.

International Regimes and World Order

Although international regimes have been proliferating and various regime models have been advanced in recent years, the conceptual and normative relationships between the international political economy and world order approaches to the global problems remain largely unexplored. This has inspired the criticism that "world order and future studies were fundamentally flawed in terms of both theory and action" and the directive that scholars struggling to understand the basic dynamics of global politics should provide "both a description of central structures and processes at work in global politics and an explanation of why and how these structures and processes work the way they do."[85] In response, a world order inquiry into international regimes attempts to establish a linkage between the two by placing regime research in the world order theory and by formulating and exploring a number of normative questions.[86]

Specifically, this approach examines the global politics of "complex interdependence" by applying the "who," "what," and "how" of Lasswell's famous definition of politics. The question of "who governs in the world system" has become too inconclusive and unwieldy. A more appropriate question is "whose hands guide or govern international regimes in different issue areas?" International regimes may provide a specific setting and focus for examining systemwide conflicts and contradictions between the conservative forces defending the existing order and the emerging reformist or revolutionary forces struggling to create a new world order. What (and whose) norms and interests affect regime politics? What deeper social, political, and economic realities are embodied in international regimes? To what extent is a shared notion or competing notions of world order evident across the whole range of global institutions? What is the international regime/international organization nexus? What structural images of the future can we draw from regime politics? These are among the key questions that will be emphasized by the world order study of international regimes.

The regime approach to world order studies has advantages and disadvantages. By focusing on the formal and informal norms and the visible and invisible structures of power, this approach promises to give us a more "realistic" picture of world politics than traditional approaches that emphasize the potency of formalized rules and visible structures of power. The disadvantages of this approach lie in the conceptual elusiveness of "international regime," and in the tendency to take a fragmented and overspecialized approach that reproduces the technological division of labor and specialization and embodies a normative bias in favor of scientific/technocratic fixes.

In substantive terms, the world order approach to international regimes illustrates the normative power of the global underdogs and the material power of the global topdogs, defined and alluded to in Chapter 2. Our contention is that to fully tap the potential embedded in regime research, it is necessary to adopt a critical stance toward the prevalent "scientific/technocratic" style of thinking. A world order approach to international regimes, defined and applied in Part 2, places its emphasis on examining the response of the international system to the value-shaping and value-realizing processes.

Comparative Foreign Policy and World Order

State actors are the dominant participants in the present world order system. Their claim of legitimate dominance is based on both their competence to uphold national interests (especially territorial integrity and political independence) and their embodiment of statist values, including the consent of the governed, representation of the working people or their vanguard party, and the like. The performance of governmental actors in attaining professed goals and basic human values on a worldwide basis have rarely been systematically assessed. In 1976, Richard C. Snyder, Charles F. Hermann, and Harold D. Lasswell proposed a global monitoring system to appraise policy formulation and execution by major governmental actors in terms of their effects on "human dignity."[87] In recent years the world order approach has also begun to link comparative foreign policy and world order inquiry, as evidenced by several studies published between 1979 and 1981.[88]

In the background of comparative foreign policy analysis are some sructural questions. To what extent does the evolving structure of the world system constrain leadership at the state level? To what extent can imaginative leadership at the state level harmonize foreign policy goals with the promotion of people's interests and the realization of world order values? What attributes of statehood (e.g. scale, resource endowment, type of polity, etc.) condition relative world order performance? Is the evolving state system becoming more or less conducive to positive world order performance? Why? The normative and policy changes brought about by the post-Mao Chinese leadership under the impetus of the modernization politics at home and the new status drive abroad are particularly provocative in this context.[89]

Alternative Security Frameworks and Demilitarization

A central and continuous preoccupation of the world order approach is the war system. The early response advocated disarmament and international peacekeeping mechanisms and encouraged international and collective security systems over national and unilateral security systems. This approach has proved to be increasingly incompatible with the logic of state action and with the hierarchical nature of the state system.

In recent years the world order approach has begun reinterpreting the security problematique in more politically relevant and conceptually broader terms. It has emphasized the interlinked patterns of militarization that arise from the horizontal rivalries of the leading states, the vertical relations of powerful and weaker sectors of the world system and of various regional systems, and the domestic dominance patterns by which elites control the apparatus of government and the sources of wealth, prestige, and knowledge. Any countermovement must take account of all three dimensions.[90]

Prospects for demilitarization are not bright in the near future, with principal trends pointing to increasing militarization instead. There are some countertrends, including a growing anxiety at the grassroots level about the wisdom and legitimacy of nuclear-based security systems. Normative initiatives may be catalyzed to delegitimize all types of militarization. A global campaign for the prohibition of nuclear and other weapons of mass destruction deserves a high priority at this time. Scholarly research and political activity would be mutually reinforcing in this context.

We need to rethink "security" in an age of increasing perils and diminishing resources and opportunities. *Ruler's security* employs military and paramilitary means to secure a narrowly based hierarchy of privileges at home and more "power and prestige" abroad. *People's security* involves the protection of a broader category of social needs and conditions necessary for human dignity and self-realization, pursued in the least destructive manner.[91] People's security remains to be explored and instituted in a variety of local contexts and circumstances. The strategies of unarmed resistance, nonviolence, and neutralism may serve as desirable and feasible options in an age of guided missiles, rapidly deployable interventionary forces, and government units trained and equipped to administer torture routinely.

The Global Cultural Nexus

The world order approach has recently begun to reexamine the relevance of cultural factors. This is a departure from the initial stress on law and institutions as the building blocks of a new world order and the subsequent emphasis on economic development and national revolution. These earlier concerns have not been superceded, but now include the cultural grounds of politics and economics. The Iranian Revolution, despite its troubled path since 1978, has disclosed the dominance of nonmaterialistic concerns. The leaders of this revolution have consistently subordinated materialist considerations, confusing those who assume such priorities. However perverse and misguided, the Iranian Revolution is a quintessential defense of Iranian cultural and religious integrity, irrespective of conventional costs.

Locked in the cultural history of the world are many sacred images and myths that shape the path of human development for all societies and are organically connected with any eventual hope for demilitarization. These are elusive, controversial matters, but WOMP has formed a transnational group of scholars that seeks to bring these issues more clearly into the various dialogues about the future of world order. One early priority has been to demythologize the hegemonic claims of Western civilization and to engage other cultural traditions in a transcultural dialogue on "another development." The center (Western) model, with its rationalizations of "struggle for power," is not a rational model worthy of universal emulation. In fact, the center model is having a "legitimacy crisis" as it can no longer explain away the increasing signs and symptoms that the high technology path may lead to a dystopia of catastrophic system breakdown.

An appropriate world order quest must envision a future that draws on the richest traditions of the past, including the philosophic basis for planetary human identity that lies buried in every major world cultural tradition.[92] The world order approach is now seeking to clarify the various cultural traditions that influence the outlook and behavior of people located in different geopolitical and geoeconomic space. A more ambitious undertaking will be the search for sufficient transcultural common ground upon which to construct a global superstructure that encourages an idenfication with the human species without ignoring distinctive and different cultural and ethnic roots.

Part 2

The State of the Human Condition

Global Violence

The Epidemiology of Global Violence

The minimization of global violence in both a narrow (direct/physical) and broad (indirect/structural) sense is what a just and humane world order is all about. If we see this planet as a living system—and follow Plato's analogy of politics to medicine as the art of healing the soul and of helping the *body* politic—violence can be defined as a pathological force that destroys or diminishes life-sustaining and life-enhancing processes. Violence may be direct, killing swiftly through war, or indirect, killing slowly and invisibly through poverty, hunger, disease, and repression. Indirect violence (killing by installments, as it were) is as inhumane as direct violence from the victim's standpoint, yet it is generally a secondary concern in traditional world order thinking. Violence, like disease, is inherently antilife, and is antithetical to the establishment of a humane world order.

In our time war has increasingly become the tip of the iceberg, the most visible part of a militarized global system. War/peace needs to be more broadly understood in terms of the domestic and international structures and processes at work. This requires a normative theory of a "positive peace" free from structural violence. To define peace in the narrow traditional sense as the mere absence of war is to capture just one dimension of violence. Instead, I follow in this chapter what may be called an epidemiological model of world order.[1] Anchored in a broad and integrated definition of social health, this model is designed as a normative and analytical tool to sharpen our sensitivity to the determinants and distribution of violence as a life-destroying or life-diminishing pathological force at all levels of social organization.

"Health," the Constitution of the World Health Organization (WHO) aptly states, is "a state of complete physical, mental and social well-being and not merely the absence of disease or infirmity."[2] The Thirty-Second World Health Assembly of the WHO launched the "Global Strategy for Health for All by the Year 2000." Relying on the concept of countrywide primary health care systems as described in the 1978 Report and Declaration of Alma Ata (the WHO/UNICEF International Conference on Primary

TABLE 4.1
An Epidemiological Model of World Order

Health *(Value)*	*Disease* *(Violence)*	*Agent* *(Militarism)*	*Effect* *(Human Life)*
Peace	War	Arms race	Threatens human survival (life-destroying)
Economic Well–Being	Poverty	Resource Re-allocation	Threatens human needs (life-diminishing)
Social Justice	Injustice	Martial rule	Threatens human rights (life-devaluing)
Ecological Balance	Pollutants	Military activities	Threatens human safety (life-degrading)

Health Care was held at Alma Ata in the Soviet Union), the WHO's global strategy proposes concerted action in the health *and* related socioeconomic sectors.[3] On December 15, 1978, the UN General Assembly adopted by a recorded vote of 138-0-2 (the United States and Israel) a "Declaration on the Preparation of Societies for Life in Peace," which proclaimed, *inter alia*: "Every nation and every human being, regardless of race, conscience, language or sex, has *the inherent right to life in peace*."[4]

Given the pervasiveness and persistence of collective violence throughout the world, it is now possible to speak of a "global war system." The global war system is an all-embracing and mutually interlocking structure of normative, institutional, and behavioral variables, in which instruments of violence are the primary arbiters of social conflicts at all levels of human society. Viewed thus, it becomes difficult to disentangle violence from the economic, social, psychological, and cultural complex of interactions that shapes contemporary global politics.

Focusing on violence as a systemwide disease with militarism as an agent for its dissemination, in this chapter I follow the epidemiological model of world order shown in Table 4.1. My analysis is heuristic and diagnostic and proceeds on the basis of the following assumptions:

- Violence as a social (man-made) disease is not a natural or inevitable feature of the human condition; it is an avoidable evil.
- Violence as expressed in the modern arms race is a human problem; it cannot be explained as a necessary or unavoidable by-product of expanding technology beyond human control.

- Violence has multiple causes and consequences, domestic and international, internal (biological and psychological) and external (environmental). As with cancer, external environmental factors tend to be more potent and prevalent than internal biological factors.
- Violence is expressed in various forms ranging from direct killing to indirect killing.
- Violence has a structural "trickle-down" tendency, generally moving downward on the ladder of social stratification as an instrument of social control and dominance.
- Violence, like disease, hits hardest at weak, defenseless, and subordinate human groups in both domestic and international settings.
- Violence thrives in a weapons culture.
- Violence can be measured by the extent to which social norms and structures have become militarized.
- Violence tends to be self-destructive in the long run.

This chapter seeks (1) to depict the dynamics of global militarization, (2) to evaluate the epidemiological effects of global militarization, (3) to assess the response of the international system, and (4) to explain the contemporary security problematique.

The Dynamics of Global Militarization

Like a pandemic plague, collective violence has spread to every corner of the world, infecting both international and intranational political processes and structures during the "postwar" period. Of course, war has been a recurring plague in human struggles over the centuries. Prior to World War II, however, there was a sharper line of division between war and peace as well as a stronger tendency toward periodicity (war/peace cycles) in the international system's war experience. The great powers were the most war-prone; more than half the member nations of the international system managed to escape international warfare entirely.[5]

The postwar militarization is unprecedented in the magnitude and scope of its threats to basic human rights and values as well as in the multiplicity of its epidemiological consequences. This is the first time in human history that (1) a single person or a small group of war-makers holds a doomsday power to bring about a global catastrophe; (2) the arms race permeates the human environment (land, sea, air, jungles, deserts, and outer space); (3) the destructive force of weapons systems has reached a "megadeath" level, threatening to inflict irreversible damage to life-supporting ecosystems; and (4) global militarism and militarization dominates both great and small—and old and new—states.

The empirical dimensions of global militarization, such as global military spending, global nuclear stockpile, vertical proliferation, horizontal proliferation, military research and development (R&D), armed conflicts, foreign intervention, etc., are widely known.[6] But how can we account for the ongoing dynamics of military behavior evident in the empirical data? World order theorists reject the assumption that weapons technology has acquired a self-generating and self-sustaining momentum defying human control. This deterministic assumption is at best a recipe for social anesthesia that numbs our social consciousness and immobilizes our will. At worst, it disguises the links between social conflicts and armament dynamics at both intranational and international levels.

Ideological Dimensions

Contrary to Daniel Bell's declaration of "the end of ideology" about two decades ago, ideology plays as potent a role as ever in world politics. Militarism, whose origin can be traced back to state formation,[7] has now achieved the status of a global ideology. Contemporary militarism differs from its historical antecedents in its global reach, the immediacy of its impact, the degree of its structural penetration, and the magnitude of its lethal power. Militarism is defined here as a belief system that cherishes the romantic conception of war as indispensable for upholding state interests and considers organized violence a legitimate instrument for realizing social objectives or resolving conflicts. The military values of authoritarianism, centralization, hierarchy, regimentation, absolutism, ethnocentrism, chauvinism, secrecy, and jingoism can all function as disease agents in the superstructure of society. Like cancer, militarism is an aggregate term for a series of related diseases with different causes and consequences. Some germinate quickly, but most work like undiagnosed termites with gradual and cumulative effects.

Both Marxism and liberalism have a strong ideological bias against militarism. Yet, militarism has prospered in the Soviet Union and the United States. The world order explanation for this apparent paradox is that militarism and statism are symbiotic. As Yoshikazu Sakamoto and Richard Falk put it: "The modern state is permanently oriented around the demands and capabilities of its military sectors, even at times of ostensible peace."[8] Instead of being an instrument of man's exploitation of man (Marxism) or a servant to protect inalienable human rights (Lockean liberalism), the state has increasingly become a master of its own interests. Statism has outgrown both Marxism and liberalism with the result that two superstates in the world are also the two superpowers.

Superpower militarism can be differentiated from Third World militarism. The former surfaces in the exportation of repressive instruments and skills, covert and overt intervention, and the globalization of East/West conflict. Superpower militarism is not only an instrument of coercive diplomacy and but also a root cause of global militarism. Third World militarism is generally an instrument of repression in domestic policy and a status symbol in foreign policy. In both cases, however, the logic of statism (the "national security" syndrome) inexorably militarizes the political decision-making process. Militarism, like opium, is habit-forming.

That the United States currently has six times the number of nuclear weapons necessary to destroy the Soviet deterrent (and the Soviet Union has five times the necessary number)[9] or that recent technology and doctrine have been shifting from nuclear-war deterring to nuclear-war fighting does not necessarily suggest the failure of the system, as commonly assumed. It may instead indicate that the system is working as intended by the U.S. security managers. The thesis of Leslie Gelb and Richard Betts on U.S. Vietnam war policy can also be applied to U.S. strategic policy. As Gelb and Betts have put it: "The paradox is that the *foreign policy* failed, but the *domestic decisionmaking* system worked. . . . Vietnam was not an aberration of the decisionmaking system but a logical culmination of the principles that leaders brought with them into it."[10]

Presidential Directive 59, signed on July 25, 1980, acknowledged the doctrinal modifications, underway for the last two decades, that generated such destabilizing developments as missile accuracy, antisubmarine warfare, antisatellite warfare, and the command, control, communications, and intelligence (C^3I) system, all better suited to fight than to deter nuclear war. The normative assumption that nuclear weapons are an integral part of military power and that nuclear superiority is a usable political commodity was stated by Carter's national security advisor Zbigniew Brzezinski: "I don't consider nuclear superiority to be politically meaningless. . . . The *perception* by others or by oneself of someone else having 'strategic superiority' *can* influence political behavior. In other words, it has the potential for political exploitation even if in actual warfare situation the differences may be at best or at worst on the margin."[11]

President Reagan has gone far beyond PD 59, which redefined U.S. nuclear strategy in terms of attacks on specific military and political targets. The Reagan adminstration's overall nuclear strategy was expressed in a 125-page unpublished document called "Fiscal Year 1984–1988 Defense Guidance." As a blueprint for turning Cold War II (inaugurated by the Carter administration in January 1980) into an unrelenting war to the death, the document's main points include (1) acceptance of nuclear war fighting as a necessity in which the United States must be able to "prevail" over the Soviet Union even in a "protracted conflict period"; (2) a nuclear war strategy based on "decapitation," meaning attacks on Soviet political and military leadership and communications centers; (3) the need to devise plans for defeating the Soviet Union at any level of conflict from insurgencies to nuclear war; (4) the assertion that the United States and its allies should, in effect, declare economic and technical war on the Soviet Union; (5) special operations (guerrilla warfare, sabotage, and psychological warfare) for U.S. military needs; (6) the need to open up new areas of weaponry, especially in space, where it proposes the "prototype development of space-based weapons systems," including weapons to destroy Soviet satellites; and (7) measured military assistance to China in an effort to keep Soviet forces along the Sino-Soviet border tied down.[12]

Because of the secrecy blanket covering strategic debates in the Kremlin and because of the self-serving distortions of Western strategic planners, Soviet views on nuclear strategy are more difficult to ascertain. Nevertheless,

Soviet military writings and declarations have placed a greater emphasis on the deterrent strategy of massive retaliation than on the nuclear counterforce strategy of making nuclear war more "controllable," and more "fightable." As one Western analyst put it, "they {Soviets} reveal no trace of interest in the notions of intrawar bargaining, graduated escalation, and crisis management which play a heavy role in current U.S. strategic theorizing."[13] "Soviet military doctrine has been," the recently issued Soviet booklet entitled *Whence the Threat to Peace?* says, "and is based on the principle of retaliatory, that is, defensive actions."[14]

Whether Soviet emphasis on the deterrent strategy of massive retaliation will change with the improvement of their nuclear forces remains to be seen. To date, however, there is a discernible normative difference between Soviet and U.S. strategic posture, as shown in the responses of U.S. and Soviet leaders in 1981–1982. At the UN Second Special Session on Disarmament (SSOD-II) in June 1982, the Soviet Union pledged itself to the no-first-use principle, but the United States refused to follow suit.

In the domain of global normative politics, the legitimacy of war has suffered progressive erosion in recent decades. Aggressive war has been outlawed in a series of international agreements, including the League of Nations Covenant, the Kellogg-Briand Pact (1928), the United Nations Charter, and the consensus acceptance of an agreed Definition of Aggression in the 1974 UN General Assembly. The 1982 session of the General Assembly passed a record number (fifty-seven) of disarmament resolutions. Yet these normative declarations have had little impact on the armament dynamics. In fact, the trend curves for the number of UN disarmament resolutions and for world military expenditures have converged in recent years.[15]

Structural Dimensions

In a formal legal sense international society has no military sector beyond the miniscule quasi-military sector of UN peacekeeping forces. In 1981, for example, the world spent 2,300 times more for war-making activities than for international peace-keeping operations.[16] Yet there is a global military order in this formal state of "anarchy"; there is a centralization in this formal state of decentralized security management. The global military order has a hierarchical/dominant structure imposed by the great powers, and has a logic and rationale that parallels the Athenian argument for destroying Melos—that the powerful exact what they can, and the weak grant what they must (Thucydides' account). In the fragmented authority structure of international society, the strong become the self-styled guardians of "law and order."

In a sociological sense, the structural dimensions of militarization include the relative size, status, role, and influence of the military sector of the society. The superpowers play the dominant role in global military spending, military R&D, arms production, arms trade or transfer, and military training. Militarization—the extension of military influence throughout society to gain a dominant role in social, economic, cultural, and political processes—first occurred in the two superstates and progressively extended to more and more countries, just as vertical nuclear proliferation between the superpowers preceded and greatly stimulated horizontal proliferation. Global militarization has been an integral part of the globalization of superpower (East/West) conflict.

The linkage between local (Third World) and global (great power) militarization is made and sustained through arms trade and training. The number of Third World military personnel brought to the United States for military training was 346,600 for 1950–1980; the Soviet Union provided training to 27,700 for the period 1955–1979.[17] The transfer of military weapons and training, far from enhancing human security, resembles a hazardous narcotic trade, with unequal payoffs and penalties for most sellers and buyers. For some sellers the supposed payoffs are political (keeping a protégé regime in power), geopolitical (beefing up a front-line domino), and economic (reducing R&D and unit production costs of weapons systems). For the superpowers, geopolitical considerations predominate. The transfer of weapons and training is regarded as a means of sustaining dominant/dependent relations and continuing hegemonic rivalry.

The penalties for the seller are the threats of the buyer, a "tyranny of the weak" phenomenon. A dependent client state can raise its leverage by demonstrating its fragility, its unreliability, its unpredictability, or its mischief-making power. It can suck the dominant state into an unwanted conflict. Some specific hazards are the ready availability of alternative sellers (Sadat's switch); revolutionary nationalism (Iran); military coup d'état (Indonesia); expansionism (Israel); and parasitic dependency (South Korea). Yet the overall pattern of dominant/dependent relationships continues due to the common addiction to militarization which functions as an instrument of superpower hegemony and Third World regional hegemony (sub-imperialism) or domestic repression. In this kind of military and quasi-military relationship, the seller's leverage exceeds that of the buyer—the former makes the rules of the game and the latter's options are limited. The entry of some Third World countries (Israel, Brazil, and South Korea) into the global arms trade as arms exporters may not significantly alter this pattern.

The globalization of East-West superpower conflict has been the most powerful agent for the postwar militarization of social, political, economic, and cultural processes at different levels of governance. Global East-West conflict dynamics involve the control and manipulation of arms sale and transfer, the propagation of military culture by providing military training on the spot or at home, and covert and overt intervention. The recent crisis of resource scarcity has greatly exacerbated this conflict as the geopolitical rivalry is now being linked to and compounded by geoeconomic rivalry over strategic raw materials in the Third World. The Reagan administration guidance document cited above specifically directs U.S. armed forces to be ready to force their way into the Gulf, instead of waiting for an invitation from a friendly government as stated in the official policy pronouncements. With the globalization of superpower conflict, every local or indigenous conflict is in clear danger of escalation because "today almost any guerrilla or even opposition group can exploit East-West rivalry to some degree, and thereby draw upon external sources of supplies at early and most likely premature stages of conflict."[18]

There is a sense, then, in which war is being continuously fought in the modern form of structural intervention. The instruments of superpower rivalry mentioned above can all be subsumed under a broad definition "intervention." This form of war lacks formal acknowledgment (declaration of war) and direct visibility (body count), but, like traditional war, it uses or threatens to use force for political objectives. In a major study by the Brookings Institution of U.S. military intervention during the period January 1, 1946–October 31, 1975, the authors cite 215 incidents (compared to 115 for the Soviet Union) in which the United States utilized its armed forces for political objectives. "Favorable outcomes when the armed forces were used as a political instrument occurred most often," concludes the study, "when the objective of U.S. policymakers was to maintain the authority of a specific regime abroad."[19]

Social conflict is a breeding ground for militarization only if military force is conceived and used as a legitimate means of resolving social conflict. With the globalization of militarism, however, it thrives in any situation of social conflict. The growing militarization of authority structure is currently evidenced by some 54 military-dominated governments in the Third World with external support linkages.

The effects upon international trade are shown in the booming arms trade (now second only to oil in world trade) and in the linkage between oil and arms trade. A recent study has suggested that weapons have been used by the Western industrialized countries to recycle petrodollars from the OPEC countries.[20] Nature has not been exempt from militarization: the arms race has already expanded into all the dimensions of the environment, and military consumption of natural resources continues unabated.[21] Even the knowledge industry cannot claim immunity, as military R&D has penetrated all scientific disciplines—the natural, social, medical, and behavioral sciences.

The Epidemiological Effects of Global Militarization

The Nuremberg principle of "crimes against humanity" can be applied holistically to assess the effects of global militarization on human life. Conventional peace/world order thinking has focused too narrowly on the visible effects of warfare and thus has become an inadequate, and even misleading, response to the unconventional and multidimensional threats of contemporary global militarization to human life and health. Table 4.1 clarifies the linkage between and among the effects of violence on human life in four value domains. Given the scope and magnitude of its vertical and horizontal contagion, violence has become an assault on human survival, human needs, human rights, and human habitat. The main assumption in this epidemiological approach is that the wages of violence go beyond human casualties in war, including indirect, invisible effects (economic, social, and ecological warfare) on life-supporting and life-enhancing processes. The failure to see this pervasive violence as a common peril to humanity is in itself a major cause of growing violence.

Nowhere is the misuse of science and technology clearer than in the wide gap between our scientific knowledge of weapons systems and our prophylactic knowledge of the epidemiological effects of militarism on human beings. The so-called circular error probabilities (CEPs) of U.S. strategic nuclear missiles have been reduced from about 500 meters in 1972 to 220 meters (Minuteman III) in 1979—and to 91 meters with the planned MX missile system. This dramatic improvement in missile accuracy, coupled with the twofold collateral improvement in warhead yield, has increased the single-shot kill probability (against well-hardened Soviet missile silos) to 80 percent, enhancing the confidence of strategic planners that nuclear war is not only thinkable but also fightable with "surgical" precision.

Of course, in the dehumanizing jargon and euphemistic doubletalk of the military, the effects of weapons advancement on human beings are intentionally obscured or sanitized.[22] Much of what we now know about the physical, biological, and ecological consequences of nuclear war came to us not through deliberate scientific inquiry but by accident or by extrapolation from the effects of the Hiroshima and Nagasaki bombs. The impact of nuclear war on the life-protecting ozone was discovered inadvertently through ecological impact studies of supersonic transport (SST) aircraft in the mid-1970s, just as "Castle/Bravo," the largest nuclear weapon test ever conducted by the United States at Bikini Atoll on February 28, 1954, produced unexpected effects in the magnitude of explosive power (from the expected 8 million tons—7.2 million metric tons—of TNT to the actual 15 million tons—13.5 million metric tons—of TNT) and the scope of radioactive contamination (some 7,000 square miles—18,000 square kilometers— of the Pacific Ocean).[23] Even the National Academy of Sciences (NAS) 1975 study entitled *Long-Term Worldwide Effects of Multiple Nuclear-Weapons Detonations* is so problematic in its assumptions, methodology, and conclusion as to warrant its repudiation by the Federation of American Scientists as "the wrong form of the right question" fraught with "technological optimism."[24]

Life-Destroying Effects

In an epidemiological sense, war and disease are close allies in the merciless killing of human beings. Although war has not killed as many people as disease has in human history, it is nonetheless one of the major causes of death. The incidence of war has not increased in our times, yet war casualties in both absolute and relative terms have increased exponentially. According to Quincy Wright, at least 10 percent of deaths in modern civilization can be attributed directly or indirectly to war.[25] The war casualties for the seventeenth, eighteenth, and nineteenth centuries are estimated respectively at 3.7 million, 4.5 million, and 3.6 million but jumped to 22 million for the first quarter of the twentieth century alone. World War I and World War II inflicted 9.8 million and 51.2 million casualties respectively.[26]

Hiroshima symbolizes the dawn of the nuclear age, a beginning of the end for the age of "innocence." Overnight, the explosive power of a life-destroying bomb increased two thousand times! J. Robert Oppenheimer, who directed the Manhattan Project, is reported to have uttered a passage from the Bhagavad-Gita, the sacred book of the Hindus, on watching the first atomic test: "I am become Death, the Shatterer of Worlds!" Of course, not everybody perished in the ashes of Hiroshima and Nagasaki. Among those atomic bomb survivors (hibakusha), however, there still persists what the Yale psychohistorian Robert Jay Lifton calls a profound sense of "death in life." As Lifton put it: *The most striking psychological feature of this immediate experience was the sense of a sudden and absolute shift from normal existence to an overwhelming encounter with death.*"[27] The total breakdown of human life in Hiroshima and Nagasaki is graphically shown in Figure 4.1. Estimates of the human casualties in Hiroshima and Nagasiaki have varied. It was not until 1979—and late 1981 for the English edition—that the most thorough and comprehensive study of the effects of Hiroshima and Nagasaki became available. Commissioned by the cities of Hiroshima and Nagasaki and compiled by 34 Japanese medical, physical, and social scientists over three decades, Hiroshima and Nagasaki: The Physical, Medical, and Social Effects of the Atomic Bombings provides (in over 700 pages) a graphic and encyclopedic depiction of the destructive consequences of the two bombs (see Figure 4.1). Of the estimated population of 300,000 people in Hiroshima on August 6, 1945, the number of deaths following exposure to the bomb totaled 140,000 ($\pm 10,000$) by the end of 1945. Of the estimated population of 270,000 people in Nagasaki on August 9, 1945, some 73,884 ($\pm 10,000$) were dead by the year's end.[28]

The technology of human destruction has developed to such an extent that today a single nuclear warhead can deliver more destructive power than all the conventional explosives ever used in warfare since the invention of gunpowder. Table 4.2 sums up different estimates of human casualties in a strategic nuclear war. A nuclear detonation causes death or severe injury through several effects: air blast wave (eardrum rupture and hemorrhage of the lungs); thermal radiation (burn injuries to unprotected skin); fire (burn injuries or smoke inhalation); and nuclear radiation (radionuclides enter the human body through breathing, eating and drinking, causing bodily damage and genetic, developmental, and growth damage). Nuclear weapons differ from conventional weapons not only in the magnitude and severity of air blast, fire, and thermal effects but more significantly in their radiation (both initial and residual) fallout effects.[29] The destructive area of the Hiroshima bomb was only 3 square miles (7.8 km^2); it would be 50 square miles (130 km^2) with Minuteman III and 290 square miles (754 km^2) with MX missiles.

FIGURE 4.1
The Total Breakdown of Human Life in Hiroshima and Nagasaki

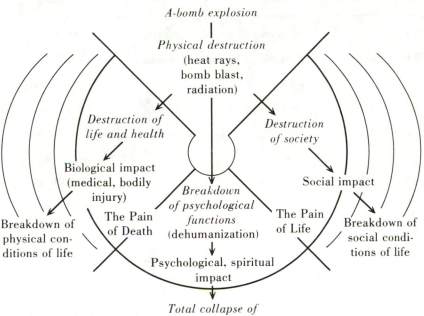

Source: From *Hiroshima and Nagasaki: The Physical, Medical, and Social Effects of the Atomic Bombings,* translated by Eisei Ishikawa and David L. Swain, Copyright (c) 1981 by Hiroshima City and Nagasaki City. Published in the United States by Basic Books, Inc., New York and reprinted by permission.

The estimates in Table 4.2 include only *local* (target zone) and *immediate* (usually within 30 days) effects; they do not include additional human casualties from latent and delayed effects of the fires, residual radiation fallout, collapse of social, medical, and economic support structures, and environmental damage. Although it is difficult to estimate casualties from these latent effects, it is reasonable to extrapolate from the Hiroshima/Nagasaki experience that postattack disease, starvation, and loss of will to live would claim as many casualties as the immediate blast. If we extrapolate from the Hiroshima casualties of 140,000 deaths from the immediate effects, the present global stockpile of nuclear weapons (approximately 20 billion

TABLE 4.2
Estimates of Immediate Casualties of Strategic Nuclear War

Explosive Power	Target	Casualties
13 kt[a]	Hiroshima (0.3 million population)	140,000[b]
22 kt	Nagasaki (0.27 million population)	74,000[b]
?	US ICBM silos	2-20 million
1 Mt (Air Burst)	Detroit (4 million population)	1.1 million
1 Mt (Air Burst)	Leningrad (4 million population)	2.2 million
10-20 Mt	New York City	5-10 million
20 Mt	San Francisco	2.8 million
100 x 1 Mt	US Population Centers	20 percent
1,000 x 1 Mt	US Population Centers	50 percent

[a]1,000 tons of TNT=1 kiloton (kt); 1,000 kt=1 megaton (Mt)
[b]Includes only deaths.

Sources: Adapted from The Committee for the Compilation of Materials on Damage Caused by the Atomic Bombs in Hiroshima and Nagasaki, *Hiroshima and Nagasaki: The Physical, Medical, and Social Effects of the Atomic Bombings,* translated by Eisei Ishikawa and David L. Swain (New York: Basic Books, Inc., 1981); H. Jack Geiger, "The Illusion of 'Survival'," *Bulletin of the Atomic Scientists* 37 (June/July 1981); United Nations, *Comprehensive Study on Nuclear Weapons,* UN Doc. A/35/392 (12 September 1981); U.S. Arms Control and Disarmament Agency, *Worldwide Effects of Nuclear War . . . Some Perspectives* (Washington, D.C.: U.S. Government Printing Office, 1975); U.S. Congress, Office of Technology Assessment, *The Effects of Nuclear War* (Washington, D.C.: U.S. Government Printing Office, 1979).

tons—18 billion metric tons—of TNT) is theoretically capable of destroying 224 billion human lives through immediate effects alone (1.6 million Hiroshima bombs × 140,000) or fifty-one times the present world population of 4.4 billion.

It is open to question whether a nuclear war between the superpowers can be controlled, limited, or restrained. Hence the terms "limited nuclear war," "tactical nuclear war," or "theatre nuclear war" are all misleading. Nonetheless, both weapons systems (the cruise missiles, neutron bombs, etc.) and military doctrines have been shifting in this direction as if a limited, controlled nuclear exchange in the European "theatre" is a rational and winnable scenario of conflict management. The employment of "tactical"

TABLE 4.3
Casualties in a Hypothetical Theatre Nuclear War

Weapons (all fission):	200 x 100 kt	1,500 x low yield	
Population Density, km^{-2}:	300	100	
Percentage of Surface Bursts:	50	10	

Civilian			*Approximate Total*
Immediate Effects	5 million	0.1-1 million	5-6 million
Early Fallout	0.7 million	0.02-0.05 million	0.7 million
Late Radiation	0.4 million	0.01 million	0.4 million
Total Civilian	6.1 million	0.1-1.1 million	6-7 million
Military			
All Causes			0.4 million

Source: United Nations, *Comprehensive Study on Nuclear Weapons*, UN Doc. A/35/392 (12 September 1980), p. 75.

nuclear weapons against military targets would produce considerable collateral (unintended and undesired) damage to surrounding civilian populations. As shown in Table 4.3, the ratio between civilian and military casualties in a hypothetical theatre nuclear war in Europe is 16:1.

It may be argued that the above description of the effects of nuclear war is a hypothetical and unrealistic doomsday exercise.[30] Even assuming that nuclear war will not break out in spite of the continuing vertical and horizontal proliferation in a conflict-ridden world, the ongoing process of researching, testing, manufacturing, deploying, servicing, and even simulating (strategic rehearsals) is susceptible to mechanical and human errors as well as sabotage, opening up more and more paths to nuclear catastrophe in world politics.[31] It has also been estimated that each kiloton fission exploded would lead to one death, and that "all past atmospheric tests could be equivalent to about 150,000 premature deaths worldwide, and approximately 90 percent of these would be expected to occur in the Northern Hemisphere."[32]

Of course, all war casualties since the end of World War II have resulted from the use of conventional weapons. "On a subject which must be of considerable importance to all humanity," as Ruth Leger Sivard points out in her latest annual survey, "official records are notoriously silent."[33] As a result, there are wide variations in the estimates of war fatalities maintained by private organizations and concerned scholars, ranging from 25 to 50 million deaths during the postwar period.[34] Perhaps the most cited source among peace researchers is the Hungarian scholar Istvan Kende, who estimates about 25 million dead from the 120 wars in the 32-year period

TABLE 4.4
**The Estimated Diversion of World Resources to Military Uses at or
Around 1980**

Type of resource	Unit of measurement	Estimate
Military expenditure	(a) Billions of dollars	510-630
	(b) Percentage of world GDP	4.9-5.3
Labour force	Millions	About 50
Military production	Billions of dollars	125-150
Use of land	Percentage of total surface	½-1
Expenditure on military science and technology	Percentage of total world expenditure on science and technology	20-25
Number of persons engaged in military research	(a) Thousands	400-500
	(b) Percentage of world scientists and research workers	20-25

Source: *Trade and Development Report, 1982* (New York: United Nations, 1982), p. 119.

between 1945 and 1976.[35] Sivard estimates for the 65 major wars during the 1960-1982 period a total of 10,700,000 deaths as "a partial accounting of the human cost which never appears in the world's official military expenditures."[36] Even if we accept Kende's calculation and ignore deaths resulting from latent or delayed effects, the epidemiological effects of the armed conflicts during the postwar period (until 1976) are equivalent to the explosions of 179 Hiroshima bombs.

Life-Diminishing Effects

It has been estimated that "structural violence, the violence of starvation and malnutrition, accounts annually for the death of upwards of 18 million people."[37] This amounts to the detonation of 129 Hiroshima bombs each year. Global militarization and global economic apartheid are not separate problems; they are two faces of the same process, and are functionally and structurally interconnected. Both the Johnson and Reagan administrations have shown in different ways that it is not possible, even for the richest country in the world, to have guns *and* butter. As for the Soviet Union, the Marxist ideal of "from each according to his abilities, to each according to his needs" seems to have been realized only in the arms race. In Western Europe, socialist President Francois Mitterand has categorically proclaimed: "We will not reduce by a single missile. Thinking that France might cut back on the number of its missiles—that's not even worth dreaming."[38]

Intranationally and internationally, militarization and structural violence are close partners in the allocation of financial, human, and natural resources. Table 4.4 shows the high cost and wastefulness of military spending. Even if we include the production of "waste" in defining and measuring "economic growth" as in mainstream econometrics, military outlays depress productivity, employment, and economic growth. Based on different macroeconomic models for different sets of countries, the most comprehensive UN study on the relationship between disarmament and development (completed in late 1981 by a group of governmental experts) shows a high correlation between military expenditures and low rates of economic growth.[39] Another study shows that for the period of 1960–1980, the slowest rates of growth among nine industrialized countries are found in the United Kingdom and the United States, which have the highest military-to-GNP ratio. Japan, with the lowest military-to-GNP ratio, has the best investment and manufacturing productivity record.[40]

There is a persistent myth that high military budgets protect the national economy against unemployment. In a major campaign to sell the Five-Year War Plan, Caspar W. Weinberger says that each $1 billion cut from the U.S. military budget means 35,000 fewer jobs. Far from contributing to general employment and economic well-being, however, military outlays reallocate resources to narrow, highly specialized, and capital/research intensive sectors of the economy. As the technology of lethal weapons becomes more advanced and sophisticated, the civilian spin-offs and job-creating potential of military outlays decline proportionately, as only the final assembly stage is labor-intensive. In a major industrial country, the employment differential between $1 billion spent on the military sector and the same amount on the public service sector is estimated at roughly 51,000 jobs.[41] Even U.S. government estimates have shown that $1 billion for the military creates 76,000 jobs; $1 billion for civilian programs creates 100,000 jobs (many more if allocated to labor-intensive projects) and $1 billion in tax cuts creates 112,000 new jobs.[42]

Military spending drains human resources from a life-enhancing to a life-diminishing direction. At least 50 million people are directly or indirectly engaged in military activities throughout the world today, including 25 million soldiers in the armed forces, 10 million in paramilitary forces, 4 million civilians in "defense" departments, a half million scientists and engineers in military R&D, and 5 million workers in the production of weapons and other specialized military equipment.[43] The intensity of military R&D, apart from its qualitative impact on the arms race, makes a priority claim on the world's qualified scientists. Their product is estimated to be twenty times as research-intensive as the average civil product. The number of draftsmen required for the design of a military aircraft today is generally of the order of 4,000 worker-years over a 7–10 year period, compared to about 170 worker-years over a 2–3 year period required for the design of the Halifax bomber on the eve of World War II.[44]

Currently world military R&D (estimated for 1980 at $35 billion or one-quarter of all R&D spending) "surpasses all public funds spent on research and development in the fields of energy, health, pollution control and agriculture combined, and amounts to at least six times the total

TABLE 4.5
Estimated Military Consumption of Selected Minerals As a Percentage of Total Consumption

Mineral	Percentage
Aluminium	6.3
Chromium	3.9
Copper	11.1
Fluorspar	6.0
Iron ore	5.1
Lead	8.1
Manganese	2.1
Mercury	4.5
Nickel	6.3
Petroleum	5.0-6.0
Platinum group	5.7
Silver	6.0
Tin	5.1
Tungsten	3.6
Uranium	..
Zinc	6.0

Source: *Trade and Development Report, 1982*
(New York: United Nations, 1982), p. 120.

research and development expenditures of all developing countries."[45] The resources devoted to medical research worldwide are only one-fifth of those devoted to military R&D. In the mid-1970s, more than one billion people in sixty-six developing countries lived in areas "where malaria is endemic, adding its effects to the other privations of poverty, inadequate nutrition, insanitary water supply, poor housing, and multiple infections, causing high prevalence of disease and high mortality, not least in the young, and undermining the capacities of the people in these communities to improve their lives, materially and socially."[46] The WHO spent $100 million (less than the cost of one strategic bomber) over ten years to completely eradicate smallpox. One UN study has identified that there are at least seventy-two possible alternative uses of military R&D capabilities for human development.[47]

The world's armed forces are major consumers of a variety of nonrenewable energy and raw-material reserves (see Table 4.5). Current U.S. military consumption of aluminum, copper, lead, and zinc is about 11–14 percent of total consumption, with titanium consumption as high as 40 percent. Extrapolating from U.S. data, world military consumption of liquid hydrocarbons (excluding petroleum products used in the production of weapons and equipment) is 700–750 million barrels annually, amounting to twice the annual consumption for the whole of Africa.[48]

The reallocation of resources from human needs to military demands is a "tragedy of the commons" in the Third World. With the flow of arms traffic comes the armament culture, and the life-diminishing effects of militarization intensify in rough proportion to a country's capacity to absorb such an unproductive, wasteful burden. The socioeconomic costs of arms imports include not only the purchase price of weapons systems but also maintenance, operational, and infrastructure expenses. To pay for these expensive and sophisticated modern weapons systems, countries must restructure their social and economic processes to raise export earnings. Cash crops replace food crops as part of the "export-oriented strategy." Ironically, the resulting neglect of agricultural development soon necessitates increased food imports as well, making a typical Third World country doubly dependent on life-destroying weapons and life-sustaining food.

Intranationally, resources are reallocated from the countryside to the town, from the civilian to the military sectors, and from the people to the powerholders. Internationally, resources are transferred from the Periphery to the Center through the creation of double dependency, offsetting the benefits of nonmilitary aid. Current world military expenditure is about fifteen to twenty times greater than the amount of official development assistance to the developing countries.[49]

Like the British opium trade with China in the nineteenth century, there is also the issue of unequal value here, with weapons (opium) flowing from the Center to the Periphery countries in exchange for raw materials (the drain of gold and silver). The net effect is that arms-importing developing countries are subsidizing a portion of the military R&D costs of arms-exporting developed countries. Social conflicts and contradictions exacerbated by the resource reallocative functions of militarization then increase the demand for weapons as an instrument of social control and dominance. The impoverished masses of the Third World have little chance of improving their lot as long as militarization persists.

Life-Devaluing Effects

Military rule and humane (nonviolent) governance are incompatible. The life-devaluing effects of the former are heavily concentrated in the Third World, where military-dominated regimes are the norm. The use of violence against the domestic population so characteristic of the military or military-dominated regimes in the Third World is, however, largely a transmitted disease. During the first major cycle of superpower conflicts (Cold War I), the United States poured military aid into newly emerging states willing to join its global anticommunist network, stimulating the rapid growth of large and sophisticated military establishments within otherwise underdeveloped states and provoking a Soviet countervailing response. With the shift from arms grants to arms sales in the mid-1960s, however, the military establishments in most Third World countries became parasites, hampering social and economic development and accentuating class conflicts. Faced with this crisis, the Cold War image of an absolute enemy has been revised and expanded to include the enemy within (dissident and opposition groups) to justify the parasitic claims and repressive rule of the military.[50]

The symbiotic relationship between Third World militarism and the persisting structure of global hierarchy are sustained through the arms trade and military training. During 1973-1978, the ten worst violators of human rights were the primary recipients of U.S. economic and military aid, receiving over $2 billion in economic aid and some $2.3 billion in military aid and credits; moreover, these countries were sold weapons in excess of $18 billion, and 17,723 of their military officers were trained in U.S. schools and programs. The protracted intervention in Iran—the CIA-engineered overthrow of Premier Mosaddeg, the establishment of SAVAK, and a succession of economic, technical and military missions culminating in the stationing of 41,000 Americans, including 25,000 weapons technicians at the time of the Islamic Revolution—tends to support the contention that the United States stands "at the supply end of the pipeline of repressive technology."[51]

Although the Soviet Union has lagged behind in almost every category of imperial geopolitics (the arms trade, covert and overt intervention, injection of mercenaries, training of foreign military officers, etc.) its role in the Third World to date is hardly congruent with its pronounced identification with the struggle of the masses. Its contribution to the minimization of human rights abuse is problematic. In a well-documented and well-reasoned study of militarization in Africa, Robin Luckham offers the following assessment:

> It can indeed be argued that the socialist countries have reinforced some of the more conservative tendencies of the African state-system; they have done so by preserving existing state structures, by encouraging repressive solutions to nationalities problems as in Ethiopia, and by sustaining State capitalism linked to the world economy in countries like Guinea, Algeria or Tanzania rather than supporting socialist transformation.[52]

Third World militarism/militarization is a recipe for the rule of violence. The reallocation of resources for military spending not only places a country on the path of dependent development (maldevelopment), but also exacerbates domestic class conflicts and contradictions. Any social and industrial disturbances must, however, be suppressed to restore "law and order," as suppressing dissent and maintaining social stability are imperative for the export-oriented strategy. Stability, or at least the image of stability, is necessary to enhance the country's credit worthiness to foreign bankers (to borrow more money to buy more weapons and pay off past debts) and to enhance investment attractiveness to multinationals. Safety, a function of political stability, together with the rate of returns and liquidity, is believed to be one of the three key incentives in attracting foreign investment.

The emergence of "free trade zones," uneven distribution of incomes, and the emergence of a marginal, "unproductive" labor force merely exacerbate social tension and political unrest. Of course, repression begets more resistance, setting in motion a vicious circle in which the distinction between violence as cause and violence as effect becomes blurred. In a militarized state with limited economic resources and a narrow industrial base, repressive rule becomes a way of life.

Life-Degrading Effects

The deterioration of the environment cannot be dismissed as the concern of sentimental bird-watchers and naturalists. Environmental damage vitally affects all human beings through its life-degrading effects on the air we breathe, the water we drink, the food we grow and eat, the land we live on, and the fish we catch in the ocean. The environmental consequences of military activities in our times defy historical comparison; their direct and indirect impact has been greatly magnified by the inexorable march of modern technology and the ongoing dynamics of global militarization.

Based on available studies as well as on the responses of forty-four governments to its survey of the environmental effects of the remnants of war, the United Nations Environmental Programme (UNEP) concluded in 1980: "Apart from great human suffering and an astronomical waste of resources, at least 12 of these {some 130 wars between 1945 and 1979} caused considerable environmental damage."[53] That UNEP's annual state of the environment report should now include the consequences of military activities is as novel as its graphic and documented description of what past wars have done to the human environment.

The remnants of World War II include considerable environmental damage. The war caused a short-term reduction of 38 percent in the agricultural productivity of ten nations due to the devastation of farmlands. Some three and a half decades later, the environmental remnants of World War II have not completely cleared up, as shown in the 1980 UNEP state of the environment report:

> The volume of munitions left behind in some of their territories by the Second World War is staggering. One Government reported that it had cleared 14,469,600 land mines, and that clearance was continuing at the rate of 300,000 to 400,000 a year. Many thousands of shells, bombs and other munitions had also had to be dealt with in various countries. The country most seriously affected reported that the remnants of war had killed 3,834 people, most of them children, and injured 8,384 others of whom 6,783 were children. For the past 5 years 30 to 40 people had been killed each year and 50 to 80 injured. Some 460 disposal personnel had been killed, and 655 injured. Other replies also indicated serious losses of life, and a cost of clearance running at tens or hundreds of thousands of dollars a year. Coastal States reported parallel difficulties with marine mines and with dumped ammunition and wrecked ships (some containing explosives).[54]

The demarcation line between "conventional" and "nuclear" weapons is constantly being redefined due to the rapid advancement of nonnuclear weapons of mass destruction (chemical, bacteriological, geophysical/environmental warfare, etc.) on the one hand, and the new development of "mininukes" and "quasi-proliferation" (Israel and South Africa) on the other. In a resolution adopted at the United Nations Conference on Desertification (1977), it was noted that chemical and bacteriological (biological) warfare was one of the factors contributing to desertification in certain parts of the world and that those factors were most seriously felt in developing countries.[55]

Bacteriological weapons could be used against human sources of food through the spread of persistent plant diseases or of infectious animal diseases. The epidemiological effects of possible bacteriological warfare through the introduction of new epidemic diseases can be compared to "megadeaths" on the scale of the medieval plagues. The terror of bacteriological warfare is so obvious and horrifying that it produced the one and only *disarmament* treaty since the end of World War II—the 1972 Biological Weapons Convention.

Chemical weapons can produce highly toxic immediate effects. Long-term ecological effects are much more difficult to estimate with precision, given the general neglect of this domain of scientific inquiry, but they include laterization (irreversible hardening) of the soil, permanent destruction of mangrove associations and attendant loss of aquatic protein resources, chemical deforestation in tropical areas with fragile soils (destruction of timber resources), depletion of soil nutrients by leaching of deforested areas, and invasion of herbicide-treated regions by bamboo and grasses.[56]

The long-term epidemiological effects of chemical warfare are equally difficult to estimate. The herbicide Agent Orange (2,4,5-T, extensively used by the United States in Vietnam and Laos) is believed to be linked to chronic health problems among thousands of U.S. Vietnam veterans, including liver damage, nervous disorders, birth defects in their children, and cancer. The veterans have as yet been unsuccessful in persuading their government to sponsor a broad-based epidemiological study of their health problems. It is not possible to estimate the extent of health damage suffered by the Vietnamese and Laotian populations as a result of their eating exposed vegetation and drinking contaminated water.[57]

Geophysical and environmental weapons are techniques and instruments designed to deliberately manipulate geophysical or environmental forces for hostile military purposes, through instigating fires and floods, rainfall modification, and ocean modification. As one spokesman for the U.S. Department of Defense explained it, geophysical or environmental warfare is aimed at giving the armed forces "the capability of modifying the environment, to their own advantage, or to the disadvantage of an enemy. We regard the weather as a weapon. Anything one can use to get his way is a weapon and the weather is as good a one as any."[58]

Although techniques such as the instigation of fires and floods have been used in past wars, including World War II, U.S. military conduct in Indochina again stands out as a negative example of contemporary warfare. Beginning in 1963 and continuing through the early 1970s, first the U.S.

Central Intelligence Agency and then the military carried out extensive attempts to manipulate the rainfall in Indochina, using silver iodide and lead iodide as the seeding agents. In addition, the United States repeatedly bombed agriculturally important dams, dikes, and seawalls, while publicly denying such attacks.[59]

Geophysical or environmental warfare is still in its technological infancy, but its enviromental impact could under certain circumstances be serious. For instance, rainmaking may seem innocuous, yet increased rainfall would greatly increase the incidence of various water-dependent diseases of wildlife, livestock, and humans. "Indeed, enhanced rainfall could in this and other ways trigger," concludes a SIPRI study, "a variety of more-or-less subtle imbalances in the ecosystems being thus tampered with, traceable to the resultant changes in reproductive, growth or mortality rates of some biota. . . . Thus, one can safely conclude that seemingly minor changes in precipitation (or in insolation or temperature) could bring about substantial and unexpected changes in the affected ecosystems, both natural and agricultural."[60]

The epidemiological effects of geophysical/environmental warfare would vary greatly depending on the techniques used, the location and duration of their use, and other related variables. Flood-making can cause enormous agricultural losses with corresponding human hardship. By improving habitat conditions for the vector insect, enhanced rainfall can also increase the spread of malaria in certain areas. Napalm and other incendiary weapons produce an exceptionally high proportion of deaths among their casualties compared with other weapons.

Nuclear weapons constitute the greatest threat to human life *and* the human environment. The immediate effects of nuclear weapon detonations have already been described, so our discussion here will consider the long-term ecological/epidemiological effects of nuclear weapons. Between 1945 and 1963, as many as 250,000 soldiers participated in the 293 U.S. atmospheric nuclear tests. The pools of poisonous nuclear wastes (transuranic wastes) generated by military reactors and weapons production are estimated at about 80 million gallons in the United States alone, and there is no safe means of disposal as it takes many thousands of years for these radioactive wastes to decay to a safe form. The long-term epidemiological effects of human exposure to the tests and by-product wastes are impossible to ascertain, but there is now growing fear about nuclear waste disposals in the United States.

To date the most comprehensive study of long-term physical and biological effects of nuclear war is the NAS report mentioned earlier. This 213-page report, reminiscent of Dr. Strangelove, serves as an example of how *not* to think about nuclear war. Based on a number of dubious normative and methodological assumptions, it arrives at the conclusion that the biosphere and the human species would survive an all-out nuclear war in which 10,000 megatons (or about one half of strategic arsenals in 1974–1975) are detonated.

The reliability of this report can be questioned on several grounds. First, it leaps to dogmatic conclusions from a limited (and untestable) empirical basis. Second, it lacks an integrated and synthesized vision of the long-term effect of nuclear war. Each category is isolated as an independent variable. One indisputable lesson we have learned from past nuclear tests (as well as from the Hiroshima and Nagasaki bombs) is "synergism," the combination of weapons effects producing a more severe result than the sum total of the injuries or damage in each individual category. Even the sponsor of the NAS study—the U.S. Arms Control and Disarmament Agency, a marginal institution that had largely preoccupied itself with technical studies for detecting possible violations of arms control treaties by the Soviet Union—could not hide its embarrassment and warned in its summary report that "we cannot rule out interactions with other phenomena, such as ozone depletion, which might produce utterly un-expected results."[61] Finally, the report employs an overly scientific and narrow definition of "human survival" in total isolation from the social, economic, and psychological consequences of an all-out nuclear war.

We need to ask: *Who* will survive an all-out nuclear war? The NAS study can only enhance the optimism and "psycho-logical" confidence of strategic nuclear game players that nuclear war will not be the end of the human race, certainly not for those who can find sanctuaries in doomsday underground shelters, doomsday air flights, or doomsday space shuttles during the transitional period (twenty to forty years?) from a nuclear to a postnuclear world order.[62]

International Response

The response of the international system to global militarization can be usefully evaluated by employing the concept of "international regimes." I follow Stephen Krasner's definition of international regimes "as principles, norms, rules, and decision-making procedures around which actor expec-tations converge in a given issue-area."[63] This definition is sufficiently flexible to encompass any set of patterned behavior and converging expectations within the framework of a specified international issue. "International security regimes" can be divided into three categories: the international arms trade regime; the international arms control regime; and the international dis-armament regime.[64]

The International Arms Trade Regime

Of the three regimes, the international (conventional) arms trade regime is the most anomic and the most prosperous. Like the traditional regime for the oceans, this laissez-faire regime is guided by the Westphalian logic of self-interest and self-help. The arms trade regime attracts a great variety of parochial or hegemonic interests for a number of reasons (ideological, geopolitical, economic, interest group, or constituency politics), all of which compete through the intermediaries of their national governments. National governments act as the "invisible hand" guiding this regime. The institutionalization of the arms trade regime, like the old colonial regime, is weak because major producers, sellers, and buyers are scattered throughout the world and because their business is conducted through so many overt and covert channels.

The distinction between private and public merchants has been blurred by the spread of the military-industrial-bureaucratic complex. As a result, official transfers of conventional arms (currently estimated at $35 billion a year) do not include the unrecorded channels and items of international arms proliferation, such as:

- Nuclear weapons;
- Gray-area trade in equipment such as computers and electronic machinery with military applications;
- Licensing arrangements for production of everything from small arms to weapons of mass destruction;
- Exports of plutonium, uranium, and nuclear reactors;
- Thefts from government arsenals;
- The remainders of past wars, including the estimated $5 billion in guns, vehicles, riot-control gases. etc., left in Vietnam by US forces;
- Training by the arms-exporting nations of thousands of foreign military personnel yearly in the use of the latest weapons of war;
- Black market trade in restricted items;
- Acquisition of equipment and production manuals through bribery and espionage; and
- Covert, officially-sanctioned movements of arms and supplies to guerrillas and insurrectionists.[65]

Like the old colonial regime, the international arms trade regime operates by a set of shared norms and informal rules designed primarily to serve the interests of the major producers/sellers. Headed by the United States and the Soviet Union (see Figure 4.2), the dominant actors of the arms trade regime decide who gets what weapons in what quantities at what prices. Regime norms become more specific and restrictive as we cross the firebreak between conventional and nuclear weapons. Consumers are assumed to be rational in their use of conventional weapons, but not with nuclear weapons. The arms traffic is regulated within the framework of military and geopolitical imperatives, as shown by the change of China's status from an embargoed to an actively sought customer in the Western arms trade, or by the Reagan administration's decision to sell AWACS electronic surveillance planes to Saudi Arabia.

The oligopolistic norm is deeply embedded in the present arms trade regime. The producers/sellers manage the regime in a self-serving and self-perpetuating manner by discouraging self-reliance in arms production on the part of their client states, by manipulating local or regional conflicts, by prodding their client states into regional arms races, and by exporting the phenomenon of "planned obsolescence" in weapons development. Because disarmament forces and movements in the world today are all

FIGURE 4.2
Share of the Major-Weapon Exporters and Importers, 1977–1980

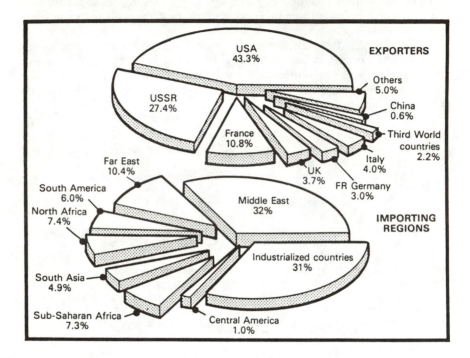

Source: Stockholm International Peace Research Institute, *World Armament and Disarmament: SIPRI Yearbook 1981* (Cambridge, Mass.:   Oelgeschlager, Gunn & Hain, 1981), p. xxi. Reprinted with permission.

concentrating what little energies they have on nuclear disarmament, the international arms trade regime grows unchecked and unchallenged.

The most serious but transient blow to the international arms trade regime—and perhaps the biggest single act of disarmament in our gen-eration—was struck by the Islamic Revolution in Iran when the new government cancelled some $15–20 billion worth of military contracts with the United States and $4 billion worth of contracts with the United Kingdom. President Carter's dispatch of Defense Secretary Brown and General Ernest Graves of the Defense Security Assistance Agency to find new arms customers was so successful that the Iranian cancellation was almost completely offset by new purchases.[66] In the international arms regime for conventional weapons, superpower *competition*, not *collaboration*, is the norm.

Based on the salient developments of the 1970s—and the trend for the 1980s seems even more ominous—it is difficult to avoid the conclusion that again the "system" worked well, making the arms traffic a major growth industry. The expotential increase in the volume of arms traffic, the qualitative upgrading of weapons sold (the U.S. sale of AWACS to Saudi Arabia is the latest example), the entry of the Third World into the arms market (Third World arms imports tripled in the 1970s, reaching about 75 percent of the global total), the increasing number of new manufacturers and suppliers (through the establishment of domestic arms industries in such Third World countries as Brazil, Israel, and South Korea), the shift from "aid" to "trade" in arms transfer, and the increasing structural linkage between arms and other strategic commodities (arms-for-oil, arms-for-ura-nium, arms-for-titanium, etc.)—all of these developments have accelerated the globalization of arms trade as an integral part of global militarization (see Figure 4.3).

The active participation of the Third World in the global arms trade has not only made more and more developing countries "drug-addicted and drug-dependent," but has also greatly weakened the normative power of the Non-Aligned Movement as a credible and effective force for disarmament in global politics. International response to the globalization of arms trade has been virtually nonexistent, with three *minor* exceptions. First, on November 4, 1977, the Security Council unanimously adopted Resolution 418, imposing a mandatory arms embargo on South Africa under Chapter VII of the UN Charter. The significance of this "historic event" (Secretary-General Kurt Waldheim's word) is more symbolic than substantive, however, for two reasons: South Africa as a pariah state is now well accustomed to receiving and ignoring such condemnations, and South Africa has already achieved near self-sufficiency in arms production. On the more crucial economic embargo, the United States, the United Kingdom and France have repeatedly shielded the pariah state with their triple vetoes.

Second, the Conventional Arms Transfer (CAT) talks between the United States and the Soviet Union, begun in December 1977, collapsed a year later after only four meetings. The United States saw CAT as a way of regulating Soviet behavior in the Third World; the Soviet Union saw it as a way of restraining possible U.S. arms sales to China. CAT could not get off first base even during the heyday of détente.[67]

Finally, there have been some multilateral *diplomatic* and *legal* attempts to deal with the *use* of "inhumane weapons" in recent years. The Diplomatic Conference on the Reaffirmation and Development of International Humanitarian Law Applicable in Armed Conflicts, held in Geneva between 1974 and 1977, produced two Additional Protocols to the Geneva Conventions of 1949, dealing almost exclusively with restrictions on "targetry" rather than on "weaponry."[68] In addition, the United Nations Conference on Prohibition or Restrictions of Use of Certain Conventional Weapons Which May Be Deemed To Be Excessively Injurious or to Have Indiscriminate

FIGURE 4.3
**Exports of Major Weapons to the Third World Compared with World
Trade, 1962–1980**

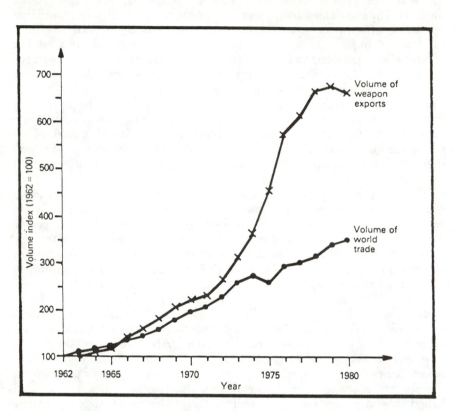

Source: Stockholm International Peace Research Institute, *World
Armaments and Disarmament: SIPRI Yearbook 1982* (London:
Taylor & Francis Ltd., 1982), p. xxvii. Reprinted with permission.

Effects, held at Geneva in 1979 and 1980, successfully concluded with the
adoption of the following instruments: (1) Convention on Prohibition or
Restrictions on the Use of Certain Conventional Weapons Which May
Be Deemed To Be Excessively Injurious or To Have Indiscriminate Effects;
(2) Protocol on Non-Detectable Fragments (Protocol I); (3) Protocol on
Prohibitions or Restrictions on the Use of Mines, Booby Traps and Other
Devices (Protocol II); and (4) Protocol on Prohibitions or Restrictions on
the Use of Incendiary Weapons (Protocol III). On April 10, 1981, the
convention and its three annexed protocols were opened for signature by
the member states.[69]

The SALT Arms Control Regime

The SALT security regime is unique. Its membership is limited to the two superpowers and its scope to strategic nuclear arms. In theory, it is an arms control regime, but in practice it has moved closer to an arms regime. It has evolved from dual necessity: the normative and structural imperatives of the two superpowers to play a zero-sum hegemonic game in a closed system for strategic armaments (two scorpions in a bottle), tempered by a mutual interest in avoiding nuclear suicide. The Cuban Missile Crisis intensified this sense of dual necessity, accelerating the nuclear arms race and nuclear arms control at the same time. The SALT regime evolved to reconcile the tension between the two conflicting imperatives.

The management of SALT has become as difficult as the stabilization of mutual deterrence. It was established on the shared assumption that the maintenance of international peace and security is a matter of *exclusive* superpower interaction entailing little accountability to other actors in the international system. Even a modest French proposal calling on the United Nations to *study* the establishment of an international satellite monitoring agency was rejected by both superpowers. In spite of approval by over 120 member states, the United States declared that the proposal is "not feasible, necessary or desirable" while the Soviet Union complained that such an agency would merely create "a wholly superficial appearance" of making progress in the control of arms.[70]

The SALT regime has defined its central tasks as (1) to redefine the parameters of bipolar conflict/cooperation interactions so as to minimize the uncertainty or unpredictability of an unregulated arms race; and (2) to institutionalize certain "fail-safe" devices and procedures to stabilize mutual expectations in a crisis. The regime has achieved a measure of stability in the conduct of coercive nuclear diplomacy during much of the 1970s, but has failed to arrest the nuclear arms race, which continues under newly defined rules—just as the Partial Test Ban Treaty of 1963 shifted (and stimulated) the nuclear arms race from the atmosphere to the underground. During the regime's tenure, the strategic nuclear warheads of the superpowers have actually tripled from about 5,500 in 1968 to about 17,400 in 1982 with a parallel growing sophistication of killing power, and this does not even include about 36,000 *tactical* nuclear weapons.[71]

The SALT regime stands on shaky grounds. Both partners refuse to accept the illegitimacy of nuclear weapons. Whether as a "bargaining chip" in negotiations or as a political/psychological instrument of imperial geopolitics, the utility of nuclear weapons is an unquestioned norm of their strategic behavior. The agreements of SALT I and SALT II (now miscarried) have projected the illusion of a controlled arms race in a rational framework of mutual restraint and understanding.

The quantitative ceilings embodied in these agreements are misleading because they exceed the existing capacities of both parties. In addition, they detract our attention away from the more dangerous shift from a quantitative to a qualitative arms race. The parallel with the Partial Test

Ban Treaty is striking. Just as the Test Ban Treaty pacified the public by moving nuclear testing underground, making it less visible and less objectionable, so has until recently the shift to a qualitative nuclear arms race that the SALT regime has legitimized and stimulated created the illusion of having capped the nuclear volcano. The peaceful antinuclear demonstrations that swept through Japan, Europe, and North America in 1981–1982 suggest that the illusion is breaking down.

The dynamics of military R&D (which is beyond the purview of the SALT regime) have brought about qualitative developments in nuclear warheads with improved *war-fighting* rather than *war-deterring* capabilities. The difficulties of controlling the Soviet-U.S. strategic nuclear arms race without first controlling the military R&D race are also demonstrated by the acceleration of the U.S.-Soviet space arms race *in spite of* the 1967 Outer Space Treaty, which declared outer space including the moon and other celestial bodies as "the province of all mankind" and which also prohibited signatory states from placing "in orbit around the Earth any objects carrying nuclear weapons or any other kinds of weapons of mass destruction, install such weapons on celestial bodies, or station such weapons in outer space in any other manner" (Article IV).[72] However, the Outer Space Treaty is generally interpreted as not proscribing certain important uses of outer space for military purposes, such as the use of the so-called Fractional Orbital Bombardment System (FOBS) and the use of satellites for the control and operation of strategic nuclear weapons. The Reagan adminstration's guidance document instructs the armed forces to proceed with space-based weapons systems: "The Department of Defense will plan, control, and operate national security shuttle missions. To maintain secure military space operations, the military space program will be conducted in such a manner as to diminish the enemy's knowledge and capability to discern specific missions among the population of national security satellites."[73]

Even within its limited frame of reference, the SALT regime has failed to check the destabilizing drift in superpower strategic behavior because, as the demise of SALT II suggests, the regime is hypersensitive to the pull of "invisible hands"—powerful domestic pressure groups with vested economic and ideological interests in perpetuating the arms race. Both opponents and proponents of SALT have committed the error of mixing the image and the reality of this strategic security regime, seeing it as a part of the solution rather than as a part of the problem.[74]

The Nonproliferation Regime

The Non-Proliferation Treaty (NPT)—signed in 1968 and entered into force in 1970—established a global nuclear security regime. In theory, it had the potential of becoming a disarmament regime; in practice it became an international arms control regime concerned merely with the expansion of nuclear club membership. It is somewhat surprising that the two superpowers took such an active role in both the General Assembly and the Geneva-based Eighteen-Nation Committee on Disarmament (ENDC) in the negotiations (1965–1968) leading to the establishment of the NPT regime. In fact, the USSR and the United States submitted a revised *joint* draft treaty to ENDC on March 11, 1968, and on March 14 the same draft treaty was submitted to the General Assembly. In short, the two superpowers (later joined by the United Kingdom) served as the chief architects for the establishment of the nonproliferation regime. It is worth noting here that the superpowers, especially the United States, that have shown nothing but contempt for the United Nations as a forum for disarmament deliberations and negotiations, used the world body as midwife for the birth of the nonproliferation regime.

The most serious problem of the NPT regime is the discrepancy between its reciprocal structure and its one-sided implementation. The regime established a simple bargain: the nuclear have-nots promised not to go nuclear (by signing and ratifying the treaty) in return for a promise from the nuclear powers "to pursue negotiations in good faith on effective measures relating to cessation of the nuclear arms race at an early date and to nuclear disarmament, and on a treaty on general and complete disarmament under strict and effective international control" (Article VI). In the General Assembly debate prior to the adoption of the NPT in 1968, Ambassador V. V. Kuznetsov of the Soviet Union declared that his government "is ready for such action."[75] Ambassador Arthur Goldberg of the United States declared: "My country believes that the permanent viability of this treaty will depend in large measure on our success in the further negotiations contemplated in article VI."[76]

The signatory nonnuclear weapon states (NNWS) have kept their half of the bargain, but the nuclear weapon states (NWS) that are parties to the treaty have not. At the time of the Second NPT Review Conference in 1980, for example, 114 states were parties (48 plus states were not) to the NPT.[77] Not a single NNWS party to the treaty has gone nuclear during the first decade of the regime, and three possible NNWS exceptions— India, Israel, and South Africa—have never signed the treaty. Meanwhile, the strategic arsenals of the superpowers have tripled.

The operational norms and procedures of the nonproliferation regime discriminate between nuclear haves and nuclear have-nots. It is difficult to explain logically why nuclear weapons are good or safe in the hands of the great powers but bad or unsafe in the hands of the small powers. The implicit pretensions of the nuclear haves for superior rationality in the control and regulation of nuclear weapons are empirically untenable. The superpowers have brought humankind to the precipice of a nuclear holocaust—there have been several close calls—while collaborating to propagate an arithmetic image of a nuclear world order and to shift the main burden of preventing nonproliferation to the nuclear have-nots. Yet the quasi-proliferation of India, Israel, and South Africa could not have come about—at least not as quickly as it did—without some indirect external "assistance."

India's nuclear test in 1974 was a public reminder that the nonproliferation regime could not remain effective or stable for long without some drastic changes. The regime's credibility is now at an all-time low among its NNWS members because of its one-sided concern with horizontal proliferation and its inability and unwillingness to check vertical proliferation. This legitimacy crisis was evident in the Second NPT Review Conference (1980), which could not even produce a hortatory declaration reaffirming the worth of the NPT. The conference highlighted the clashing strategies of nuclear world order. The nuclear have-nots insisted on linking nonproliferation to the larger question of restructuring the existing international order (especially in relation to the NIEO), while the nuclear haves and their allies attempted to narrow the dialogue to technical issues concerning the nuclear fuel cycle. The conflict between the image of a technical fix and the image of a restructured nuclear world order has shown the extent to which the normative foundation of the regime has been eroded.

The regime's effectiveness has also been seriously weakened by its inability to impose sanctions on nonsignatory states that defy its norms. In fact, the International Atomic Energy Agency (IAEA)—the regulatory arm of the regime—has been offering its technical and material assistance to developing countries regardless of whether a recipient nation is a party to the NPT. This absurdity was dramatized in 1981 when Israel—a member of the IAEA, but not party to the NPT—openly defied the IAEA and its safeguards regime by launching a surprise attack on the Tamuz reactor complex in Iraq. The irony here is that Israel, while refusing to place its own nuclear facilities under the regime's safeguards, destroyed Iraq's nuclear reactor, which had already been subject to the regime's safeguards. The *New York Times* characterized this as "an act of inexcusable and short-sighted aggression."[78] Yet only after this act of aggression did the IAEA, at its annual meeting in October 1981, adopt a resolution cutting off the $150,000 a year in technical aid that Israel would normally receive.

Another dubious aspect is the assumption that a clear separation between peaceful and military development of the atom can be—and should be—made and implemented. India's nuclear detonation in 1974 seriously undermined the validity of this assumption. More recently, the Reagan administration's proposals to use nuclear power facilities and fuel to make plutonium for nuclear weapons have further blurred the division between military and civilian nuclear programs. By the end of 1981, the nuclear industry had spread to 272 nuclear power reactors operating in 23 countries. In the coming years, according to 1981 IAEA report, 236 power reactors currently under construction are expected to come into service. Table 4.6 provides a list of countries and operating nuclear facilities completely immune from any multilateral *or* bilateral safeguards.

The unraveling of the nonproliferation regime may have already begun with regional nuclear rivalries in the Middle East (Israel vs. Iraq) and South Asia (India vs. Pakistan), with their possible catalytic chain effects on the Korean peninsula (South Korea vs. North Korea) and even on Latin

TABLE 4.6
Operating Nuclear Facilities Not Subject to IAEA or Bilateral Safeguards (as of December 31, 1980)[a]

Country	Facility	Indigenous or imported	First year of operation
Egypt	Inshas research reactor	Imported (USSR)[b]	1961
India	Apsara research reactor	Indigenous	1956
	Cirus research reactor	Imported (Canada/USA)[c]	1960
	Purnima research reactor	Indigenous	1972
	Fuel fabrication plant at Trombay	Indigenous	1960
	Fuel fabrication plant, CANDU-type of fuel elements, at the Nuclear Fuel Cycle complex, Hyderabad	Indigenous	1974
	Reprocessing plant at Trombay	Indigenous	1964
	Reprocessing plant at Tarapur	Indigenous	1977
Israel	Dimona research reactor	Imported (France/Norway)[d]	1963
	Reprocessing plant at Dimona	Indigenous (in co-operation with France)[e]	..
Pakistan	Fuel fabrication plant at Chashma	Indigenous (in co-operation with Belgium)[f]	1980
South Africa	Enrichment plant at Valindaba	Indigenous (in co-operation with FR Germany)[g]	1975
Spain	Vandellos power reactor	Operation in co-operation with France[h]	1972

[a] Significant nuclear activities outside the five nuclear weapon states recognized by the NPT. The list is based on the best information available to SIPRI.
[b] Egypt also has a small-scale reprocessing facility not subject to safeguards. Operability and current status is unknown. In view of Egypt's recent adherence to the NPT, all its nuclear activities will have to be safeguarded by the IAEA.
[c] The reactor is of Canadian origin; heavy water was supplied by the USA.
[d] French-supplied reactor running on heavy water from Norway.
[e] Assistance by Saint Gobain Techniques Nouvelles.
[f] Assistance at an early stage by Belgo-Nucléaire. In addition, Pakistan is about to establish significant reprocessing and enrichment capacities. The status of these programmes is unknown.
[g] Co-operation between STEAG (FR Germany) and UCOR (South Africa).
[h] Negotiations with the IAEA on safeguarding of this reactor were being held.

Source: Stockholm International Peace Research Institute, *World Armaments and Disarmament: SIPRI Yearbook 1981* (Cambridge, Mass.: Oelgeschlager, Gunn & Hain, 1981), p. 310. Reprinted with permission.

America (Brazil vs. Argentina). Although the United States has posed as a strict constructionist and hard-line enforcer of the NPT (especially vis-à-vis French and West German commercial deals involving South Korea, Brazil, and Iraq), powerful domestic pressure and the pull of geostrategic imperatives has caused a progressive downgrading of the nonproliferation goals.

The furious protest of Israeli and U.S. officials over the reported French nuclear deal with Iraq in the summer of 1980 were not without historical irony. In 1978, a top-secret CIA document (inadvertently released under the Freedom of Information Act) concluded that Israel had produced nuclear weapons as early as 1974. In a recent interview, Carl Duckett, Deputy Director for Science and Technology of the CIA from 1967 to 1976, confirmed the widely reported rumours that the Israelis "had fabricated nuclear weapons with 200 pounds of enriched uranium diverted from a nuclear processing plant of the Nuclear Materials and Equipment Corporation in Apollo, Pa."[79]

Yet the U.S. government has continued to shield the pariah state of the Middle East, maintaining a "know-nothing" posture. Israel's bombing of the Tamuz reactor brought only a token rebuke from the United States. In fact, the United States unsuccessfully opposed the IAEA resolution suspending the provision of any assistance to Israel under IAEA's technical assistance program, but succeeded in blocking another resolution calling for the suspension of Israel from the agency at the 1981 annual meeting. At the 1982 annual meeting, however, the United States withdrew its delegation from the final sessions in protest after the agency voted to withdraw Israel's credentials. Since then the Reagan administration has suspended an $8.5 million payment to the agency and has also withheld $300,000 of a $4.2 million voluntary contribution to its fund for technical assistance.[80]

Israel's "quasi-proliferation" suggests that nonproliferation norms can be defied with the backing of a superpower and shows that dramatic detonation is not the only route to achieving nuclear status. South Africa may easily follow Israel's quasi-proliferation path and emulate Israel's nuclear strategy of calculated concealment and preemptive strike.

In the case of India and Pakistan, the United States has followed the perceived imperatives of its geopolitical interests more closely than its own laws. The 1978 Nuclear Nonproliferation Act and the Symington Amendment prohibited the sale of nuclear fuel to countries that refuse to submit their facilities to international (IAEA) safeguards. They also required halting U.S. military aid to countries that appear to be developing the ability to make nuclear weapons. To beef up its receding geostrategic position in South Asia, the United States nevertheless decided in June 1980 to ship thirty-eight metric tons of enriched uranium fuel to India, reversing its protest against India's explosion of a nuclear device and in spite of India's refusal to place *all* of its nuclear facilities under the IAEA's inspection. From late 1980 to July 1982, as a former U.S. Ambassador to

India put it, "the course of Indo-U.S. nuclear relations, under the pall of the 1978 Nuclear Non-Proliferation Act, looked very much like a worst-case scenario. It illustrated mainly what American policy should *not* be: unilateral, retroactive, and tinged with self-righteousness."[81] In the wake of Mrs. Gandhi's visit to Washington in late July 1982, a new accommodation has been reached authorizing India to substitute French fuel for a U.S.-supplied Tarapur nuclear reactor. India has begun producing weapons-grade plutonium at a nuclear reprocessing plant near Bombay, U.S. government officials announced in February 1983, "but the operation is being monitored by international inspectors instructed to warn if the plutonium is diverted to military use."[82]

In the wake of the Soviet invasion of Afghanistan, the United States offered a six-year $3.2 billion economic and military aid program to Pakistan without even requesting assurances that Pakistan would not test a nuclear device[83]—a willing response to President Zia's geopolitical allurement, "We are a front-line state." In December 1982, the Senate Foreign Relations Committee received an administration briefing indicating that Pakistan's nuclear weapons program had continued unchecked and was further told "that China had helped Pakistan try to build a nuclear weapon and that Pakistan was now a year away from being able to produce fissionable material that could be used in a bomb."[84]

The Reagan administration has further softened its anti-proliferation posture by (1) easing restrictions on Brazil (a nonsignatory to the NPT) as a "special-case exemption" to permit it to purchase fuel for its nuclear reactor, (2) adopting a "more flexible policy" toward sales of nuclear materials to South Africa (a nonsignatory to the NPT), and (3) approving the sale of classified enrichment technology to a private consortium in Australia (a signatory to the NPT), technology previously denied to foreign governments.[85] In addition to reversing a thirty-year ban on the export of reprocessing technology, the Reagan administration has lifted the Ford and Carter ban on commercial reprocessing of plutonium in the United States.

These developments are symptomatic of deeper normative and structural maladies afflicting the nonproliferation regime, but do they not also carry a seed of regime transformation? The central thrust of mainstream regime research rejects both desirability and inevitability of nuclear proliferation, arguing that the world has witnessed a remarkable degree of nuclear stability and that our efforts should center on sustaining the current modest success of regime maintenance.[86] The world order approach argues instead that nonproliferation, unless firmly linked to a larger quest for normative transformation (a new conception of security), structural equity (vertical and horizontal nonproliferation), and demilitarization and denuclearization goals, is neither viable nor necessarily desirable.[87] Ali Mazrui has even suggested that the vaccination of "horizontal nuclear proliferation might be needed to cure the world of this nuclear malaise—a dose of the disease becomes part of the necessary cure."[88]

The International Peacekeeping Regime

The international peacekeeping regime that works through the Security Council and the General Assembly can be regarded as part of the international arms control regime. Its functional and geographical domain is theoretically broad and global, but in practice is specific and limited. Its modest peacekeeping operations may be of a military, paramilitary, or nonmilitary character. The regime's membership and normative orientation are oligopolistic, although the 1965 constitutional change (the amendments to Articles 23 and 27 of the UN Charter) and the shared responsibility of the General Assembly on financial matters have democratized the regime to a certain degree. It is a highly institutionalized regime, but its norms are informal.

The international peacekeeping regime is based on the following informal norms: (1) use the consensual (behind-the-scenes) decisionmaking process to see if major power agreement can be worked out on a given operation; (2) try merely to freeze local conflict but do not try to identify or punish aggressors; (3) structure an operation by politically impartial (neutral country participation) means; (4) use noncoercive and nonmandatory methods, requiring the consent of both the host and participating member states; (5) minimize great power involvement in the operation but maximize their managerial responsibilities; and (6) pass the financial responsibility to the General Assembly but keep the authorization control in the Security Council. Since the ONUC (United Nations Operations in the Congo) crisis in 1965, which brought the United Nations to the brink of the most serious political and financial crisis in its history, all the peacekeeping operations (UNFICYP—United Nations Peace-Keeping Force in Cyprus, UNEF-II—Second United Nations Emergency Force, UNDOF—United Nations Disengagement Observer Force, UNIFIL—United Nations Interim Force in Lebanon) have more or less followed these norms.[89]

The international peacekeeping regime is flawed on both normative and operational grounds. The realization of consensus is dependent on whether the Big Five, especially the two superpowers, will meet, or at least acquiesce in, competing demands placed on their behavior. To cooperate in peacekeeping, the superpowers must place their shared (conservative) community interest in arresting the globalization of local wars above their short-term geopolitical interest in exploiting local conflicts for strategic advantage. They must give moral, political, and even financial support to peacekeeping operations without interfering in the actual operation. In short, they are asked to give their consent without control, and their blessing without participation in the execution of peacekeeping missions. The peacekeeping regime has limited potential for realizing a "just peace" because it cannot operate without at least the tacit support of one superpower and the tacit acquiescence of the other.

The real danger is not that this peacekeeping regime will go out of business but that it will continue as a paper tiger, distracting UN concerns from the underlying structural causes of conflict throughout the world. In mid-1982 Israel's invading forces simply rolled through the zone of UNIFIL as if it were an invasion corridor. In August 1982 multilateral (French-Italian-American) forces outside the United Nations aegis were sent to Beirut to oversee the withdrawal of the PLO. Yet the Security Council has continued to extend the tenure of the largely impotent UNIFIL for another interim period of three months (in October 1982) and for another interim period of six months (in January 1983).[90]

The International Disarmament Regime

In a strict sense, there is no international or global *disarmament* regime today. However, the tenth Special Session on Disarmament (SSOD-I) of the UN General Assembly in 1978 succeeded in revamping and revitalizing the Disarmament Commission (the UN's *deliberative* body on disarmament) and the Committee on Disarmament (the UN's *negotiating* body on disarmament). These two organs can be grouped together as the international disarmament regime, but for analytical purposes I have singled out the Committee on Disarmament (CD) as the international negotiating regime on disarmament.

The Committee on Disarmament has a checkered institutional history.[91] Since 1962 it functioned in Geneva as a multilateral disarmament regime known as the Conference of the Eighteen-Nation Committee on Disarmament (ENDC), composed of five member states from NATO and the Warsaw blocs and eight other members. In 1969 the membership of ENDC was enlarged by seven states, and it became the Conference of the Committee on Disarmament (CCD). However, it was SSOD-I that served as the catalyst for regime transformation by initiating some major normative and structural changes for the CCD.

The structure of power under this new regime, now called the Committee on Disarmament, changed toward a more democratic and legitimizing framework. Membership has been enlarged to 40, bringing in more non-aligned countries. The Group of 21 is a coherent bloc in the regime representing the Non-Aligned Movement. Nonmember states can also take part in the committee's work and submit proposals on the questions under consideration, an important procedural innovation that gives virtually all UN members the opportunity to participate in the committee's work. Even NGOs can submit communications for circulation among its members. More significantly, the regime now has recently gained the participation of France and China. The hegemonic style of superpower chairmanship has been replaced by a more democratic rotational system. Normatively and structurally, this international disarmament regime comes very close to being the most ideal type that can be constructed within the framework of the existing state-centered world order. Unfortunately, this democratic structure makes the regime more legitimate but not more effective. The consensual mode of decisionmaking still gives *de facto* veto power to the nuclear weapons states.

The restructured regime for disarmament negotiations started its work in February 1979, immediately becoming embroiled in all kinds of disputes.

Even on the agenda-setting issue, the CD was sharply divided. A compromise now provides a global agenda as the framework for official norm-making activities in ten issue areas.[92]

The absence of genuine progress on any substantive disarmament issue calls into question the viability of the CD. In the 1981 report to the General Assembly on the work of its second annual session in 1980, the Committee reported:

> The Committee did not have an opportunity to attempt to reconcile the different points of view as regard the approach, machinery and basis for multilateral negotiations on nuclear disarmament. . . . It was emphasized that the Committee on Disarmament provided the most appropriate forum for multilateral negotiations relating to nuclear disarmament. On the other hand it was also emphasized that, without prejudice to the responsibilities of the Committee on Disarmament, all problems of a bilateral and regional character, were first of all within the competence of the States directly concerned.[93]

Moreover, the members of CD could not agree on a draft comprehensive program of disarmament by the time SSOD-II began in June 1982. Nor could SSOD-II itself reach agreement, turning the draft program back to the CD for further work and resubmission to the General Assembly in 1983. The contrast between what was happening outside the conference halls of SSOD-II (a demonstration drawing 750,000 people) and what was not happening inside the conference halls of SSOD-II was revealing. SSOD-II failed to completely review implementation of the decisions and recommendations of SSOD-I; it failed to adopt a Comprehensive Program of Disarmament, which took four years of effort and was regarded by many to be its centerpiece; and it failed to seriously consider, let alone adopt, more than seventy proposals by member states.

This multilateral regime for disarmament negotiations is seriously hampered by the unwillingness of the superpowers to accept the democratic deliberation and resolution of disarmament issues. Taking advantage of the consensus system, they have so far made it difficult for the regime to get going. The superpowers could not even bring themselves to accept the illegitimacy of nuclear weapons.[94] This normative-behavioral posture stands in striking contrast with their eagerness to condemn bacteriological weapons as a most dangerous plague threatening humanity, and their willingness to sign and ratify the 1972 Biological Weapons Convention, the first and only genuine *disarmament* accord since the end of World War II. Nuclear weapons are considered an exclusive symbolic badge for great power status and a concomitant instrument of stewardship for international security, while biological weapons (poor countries' equivalent of nuclear weapons) are condemned as "repugnant to the conscience of mankind and that no effort should be spared to minimize this risk."[95] Paradoxically, this hegemonic posture defeats itself, stimulating more and more countries to take the nuclear path as the sure way to achieving a great power status or to having a voice in global security affairs.

The Security Problematique

The dawn of the nuclear age at Hiroshima and Nagasaki led Albert Einstein to warn us all: "The release of atomic energy has so changed everything that our former ways of thinking have been rendered obsolete. We therefore face catastrophe unheard of in former times. If mankind is to survive, then we need a completely new way of thinking."[96] This warning has become increasingly more compelling. We live in a period of transition characterized by exponentially increasing threats to human life and health and diminishing opportunities to stem the drift toward Armageddon.

Even without the outbreak of general war, global militarization inflicts unacceptable epidemiological consequences. Yet the tragic irony of our time persists: security is pursued in a manner that guarantees insecurity. "Peace" has become continuation of war by proxy. Herein lies the modern security problematique, a cluster of interwoven and interacting conceptual, normative, psychological, and structural variables that together sustain— and explain—the maladaptive human behavior of pursuing "peace" by preparing for war—*si vis pacem, para bellum!*

Security is still narrowly defined as a function of military power. This one-dimensional image of security confuses the power to kill with the power to win, as shown in the "body count mentality" of the U.S. military in Vietnam. Security is defined anachronistically, as if global reality had remained unchanged. This outdated view assumes that one nation's security can somehow be assured without regard to the security of other nations, or even by increasing the insecurity of other nations—a manifest impossibility. Yet this so-called realistic conception of national security is sanctified in the *para bellum* doctrine. Every U.S. presidential request for an increased military spending echoes this doctrine of national security. As Richard Nixon put it in his 1972 State of the World Message, "American [military] strength is the keystone in the structure of peace."[97]

The frequency of war before and since Hiroshima suggests that this doctrine stands on shaky experiential grounds. In his classic mathematical study of the causes and origins of war the late Lewis F. Richardson reformulated the *para bellum* doctrine in two forms—"to be armed either keeps a nation out of war or diminishes its losses"—and convincingly repudiated the doctrine through a statistical test. He has furthermore demonstrated that war eventually breaks out if armaments increase indefinitely.[98]

Security is still defined in parochial and laissez-faire terms, as if there were no connection between the state of the nation and the state of the planet. This condemns humanity to a multiplicity of mutually insecure states, a global system of collective insecurity. The epidemiological model of world order defines security in a broader—and more realistic—context of those geopolitical, social, economic, and environmental conditions endangering or negating human life and health. The epidemiological conception of germ warfare as a common plague to humanity (embodied in the Preamble of the 1972 Biological Weapons Convention) is extended to all weapons of mass destruction, especially nuclear weapons.

Since the end of World War II, the concept of security has been more nationalized, militarized, and globalized than ever before. Neither the U.S. debacle in Vietnam nor the Soviet quagmire in Afghanistan have inspired the development of an alternative conception of "security" in the United States and the Soviet Union. For the great powers, armaments still serve as an instrument of hegemonic rivalry and control; for the small powers they are an instrument of repression at home and a symbol of power and prestige in international relations.

Legitimizing the weapons culture calls for constant pacification propaganda. The horrifying reality of strategic nuclear weapons has been "disarmed" through the deliberate use of sanitized Pentagonese (MIRV, MARV, FOBS, ICBM, SLBM, ABM, etc.) and Orwellian doubletalk ("air support" for bombing in Vietnam, "Castle/Bravo" for the test at Bikini Atoll, "peacekeepers" for the MX missile system). This misleading language is symptomatic of the military values that underpin the normative foundation of the security problematique. Arms are even used as "peace dividends"— Israel and Egypt were promised $4.5 billion in military grants and loans from the United States for having signed the Camp David Peace Treaty.

Since the 1963 Partial Nuclear Test Ban Treaty, the threat of nuclear weapons has become invisible. Nuclear missiles buried in underground silos and underground nuclear tests cannot be seen, felt, tasted, or smelled. We have no special sense organ for detecting the odorless and colorless radioactivity released by nuclear tests and accidents or the growing deposits of radioactive strontium-90 nibbling at our bone marrow. One way to deal with the unpleasant reality of nuclear threat is simply to put it out of our minds, a typical reaction found among the mortally ill.[99]

This feeling of well-being "is based on a denial of the most important reality of our time," observes Jonathan Schell, "and therefore is itself a kind of sickness. A society that systematically shuts its eyes to an urgent peril to its physical survival, and fails to take any steps to save itself cannot be called psychologically well."[100] Robert Jay Lifton and Richard Falk write that "nuclearism"—defined as "psychological, political, and military dependence on nuclear weapons, the embrace of the weapons as a solution to a wide variety of human dilemmas, most ironically that of 'security'"—is "the disease."[101]

Besides denial and defensive avoidance, there is also the mechanism of adaptation and habituation. By living with the nuclear threat for over a generation, many of us have become desensitized to the possibility of nuclear holocaust. The refusal to feel threats that seem beyond our power to remove, or what Lifton calls "psychic numbing," reminds one of Alexander Pope's comment on vice: "A monster of such mien/as to be hated needs but to be seen/but seen too oft, familiar with her face, we first endure, then pity, then embrace." This psychic numbing is partly responsible for the recent shift toward making nuclear war more thinkable, more fightable, and more "winnable." The resultant expectations of nuclear war do not augur well, for, as social psychologist Gordon Allport put it: "The greatest menace to the world today are leaders in office who regard war as inevitable and thus prepare their people for armed conflict. For by regarding war as inevitable, it becomes inevitable. Expectations determine behavior."[102]

The structural problems of the security problematique are suggested by the workings of international security regimes. Ideally, international security regimes are established to solve transnational problems in a spirit of transnational cooperation. In fact, however, there is a built-in structural imperative for international regimes, especially international security regimes, to govern according to the norms and procedures defined by the logic of statism. International regimes are seen as extensions of state bureaucracies through which national interests, needs, or problems beyond state boundaries can be secured.

Democratic institutions such as the Disarmament Commission and the Committee on Disarmament tend to be minority or opposition regimes, struggling to have their normative claims heard. The creation or restructuring of a regime in a democratic direction risks the danger of impotence or irrelevance. Both superpowers often insist as a condition of participation that a regime acknowledge the importance of military capability in efficient and stable governance.

The 1970 Common Heritage of Mankind Declaration specifically asserted that "the sea-bed and ocean floor, and the subsoil thereof, beyond the limits of national jurisdiction, as well as the resources of the area" are the common heritage of mankind and as such "shall be reserved *exclusively for peaceful purposes*" (emphasis added), but the two superpowers succeeded in purging this humane and holistic principle at the Third United Nations Conference on the Law of the Sea (UNCLOS-III).[103] In fact, the U.S. position on UNCLOS-III was largely determined by the Department of Defense and military considerations, particularly an alarm at the tide of "creeping jurisdiction" of coastal states restricting the maneuverable area of military (naval and air) activities. These military considerations, according to a former member of the U.S. Delegation, have "consistently guided not only the thinking of U.S. Delegation heads, but also the allocation of their direct personnel negotiation effort."[104] In short, the structural problems of the security problematique arise because international security regimes have become part and parcel of the existing international hierarchy and therefore part of the problem.

Security has always been the central raison d'être of the state. There seems to be no easy escape from the race for military superiority as long as the militarized conception of security and the present structure of global politics remain unchanged. Governing structures in most sectors of the global system accept militarization as an immutable fact of international political life. The militarized state can hardly be content with a delicate balance of terror (MAD or mutual assured destruction), even if this were feasible, for the normative and structural pressures of "the national security syndrome" gravitate toward a preponderance of military power.

The epidemiological knowledge of global violence per se cannot protect us from its life-destroying, life-diminishing, life-devaluing, and life-degrading effects, but without it we cannot begin to think about the human predicament, let alone formulate transition strategies toward an alternative security system. The year 1981 witnessed the first stirrings of a prophylactic antinuclear movement at national, regional, and global levels as the *nongovernmental* groups of moral, medical, and ecological concerns started forming a broad grass-roots coalition for nuclear disarmament. At its 1982 annual conference, the British Labor Party adopted, by a vote of 4,927,000 to 1,975,000, a motion binding itself to the doctrine of nuclear disarmament. The Green Party of West Germany followed suit by convicting nuclear weapons as "a crime against humanity" in February 1983.

Of course such frenzied antinuclear activism could turn into fatalistic paralysis or withdrawal. How can we construct a blueprint of thought and action that will help us steer between the Scylla of panic and the Charybdis of paralysis? In Chapter 8 we will return to this question and suggest some prescriptive principles and processes that should guide world order transition to preferred world futures.

Global Inequities

God does not speak to an empty stomach or a sick body.

—Mahatma Gandhi

Saving or Transforming the System in Crisis?

The decade of the 1970s witnessed the first stirrings of individual and collective soul-searching about the human prospect. The alarming realities of the global predicament became visible to just about everybody. Practically all of the human/national development crises of the 1970s brought about a series of UN-sponsored single-issue global conferences, and to a significant extent they transformed the agenda of global politics. The flickerings of this global consciousness-raising process have also generated many contending schools of thought on the causes of the human development crisis and the conditions for a more equitable world economic order. Yet the progressively deepening mood of pessimism about the capacity of the world economic system to correct itself is captured in the changing titles of three celebrated international commission reports published respectively in 1969, 1976, and 1980—*Partners in Development, Reshaping the International Order,* and *North-South: A Program for Survival.*[1]

Despite the proliferation of "crisis syndrome," there is still no universal consensus about the nature of the crisis facing humanity. There is only a vague and generalized sense of alienation and malaise—a sense that the basic values ingrained in the human behavior and institutions of all religious, cultural, and political traditions have long since outlived their usefulness. There is also growing skepticism about the capacity of the present world order system to muddle through to the end of the century without a catastrophic crash landing. This sense of normative incoherence seems responsible for the pervasive crisis of confidence affecting political cultures throughout the world. Jeremy Rifkin eloquently argues that the entrophy principle (the second law of thermodynamics) "will preside as the ruling paradigm over the next period of history."[2] However, it is open to question whether humanity has as yet unshackled itself from old patterns of thought and behavior and begun a new journey into the twenty-first century.

The crisis of faith in Marxism (an anti-Center and antisystemic model) is hardly surprising, as one socialist state after another seems to conform to, rather than transform, the logic of the global political economy dominated by core capitalist powers. If you can't beat the capitalist allure of the international division of labor and the liberal principle of comparative advantage, why not join and take advantage of them? In spite of rhetorical lip service to individual and collective self-reliance, practically all Third World countries (even China and Tanzania) are preoccupied with "catching-up" to the Center model, at the very time the Center is having a serious internal legitimacy crisis of its own.

A series of summit conferences among the seven industrialized capitalist countries in recent years have shown that the geopolitical and corporate managers of Center capitalism cannot put their own economic acts together. The Trilateral Commission was not the only group anguishing over the governability of Western democracy and the manageability of the capitalist world economy, proposing a series of united-front (trilateral) as well as cooptation strategies to save a system in deep crisis. The vision of a reunified Trilateral world as the anchor of the global political economy has become increasingly problematic due more to an internal crisis (which was underestimated) than due to the external threat from the Third World (which was overestimated). Even the neoconservatives in the United States have attacked the Reagan administration for its alleged failure (a failure of will) to beef up U.S. military, political, and economic power—the tripod of U.S. hegemony during much of the postwar period—to make the world safe for U.S. interests.[3]

Whether one looks at the development problematique as an overcrowded lifeboat with limited carrying capacity calling for a "triage" solution (the "ecolade" view), or as a well-designed global factory temporarily marred by an internal quarrel among its corporate managers or by an illegal wildcat strike (the Trilateral view), or as a superluxury liner with a hidden feudal class structure and a vicious and self-perpetuating process of exchange of unequal values moving on a collision course (the *dependencia* view), there seems to be a generalized loss of confidence and control, a feeling that the postwar international economic system established at Bretton Woods and Havana is now afflicted with some fundamental malady whose effects are being experienced everywhere.

The sudden surge of interest in contending political economy models and paradigms in international relations research can be explained as a Johnny-come-lately catching-up process to overcome intellectual embarrassment and malaise caused by a lag between the changing global realities and the dominant lines of intellectual inquiry. In the latter half of the 1970s, prodded by the increasing interaction between international politics and international economics, by the proliferation of global models, and by the desire to bridge the gap between global social reality (phenomenon) and international relations theorizing (paradigm), three different approaches emerged as serious alternative models in international relations research:

(1) the "complex interdependence" model of political economy (Robert Keohane and Joseph Nye); (2) the "world-system" model of the capitalist world economy (Immanuel Wallerstein) and the "ecopolitics" model designed to refocus our inquiry on economic, ecological, energy, environmental, and ethical issues (Dennis Pirages).[4]

A world order approach to the international political economy relies upon two different but mutually complementary perspectives: the value-oriented and the structure-oriented perspective. Drawing its normative inspiration from the populist orientation of Schumacher and Preiswerk (see Chapter 1), this world order approach proceeds on the assumption that it is not only desirable but also possible to study the international political economy as if people mattered. The value-oriented perspective considers the question of what (and whose) values/goals shape human behavior in the production, distribution, and consumption of resources in international society. The resource allocation processes at both the international and intranational levels are analyzed in terms of the dominant values/goals of the principal social actors.

The structure-oriented perspective focuses instead on constraints and parameters within which resource allocation takes place. The constraints and parameters of social processes that restrict policy choices and outcomes are seen in terms of the socioeconomic positions of the actors and the patterns of relation and interaction between or among them. The value-oriented vision sees the development problematique in terms of a crisis of basic values; a structure-oriented perspective sees it in terms of a crisis of basic structures in the global political economy.

This chapter seeks: (1) to depict the human and national dimensions of global inequities; (2) to assess the strengths and weaknesses of two normative principles of distributive justice—the New International Economic Order (NIEO) and Basic Human Needs (BHN)—and to locate a world order interface between the two; (3) to evaluate the response of the international community at both the conceptual and functional levels; and (4) to explain the development problematique in terms of key conceptual, normative, and structural variables.

The Dimensions of Global Inequities

The Human Dimensions

Global Poverty. As a general rule, Gunnar Adler-Karlsson has reminded us, "where we have good statistics, there is no absolute poverty; where absolute poverty is common, we have no good statistics."[5] Even growth rates statistics, whether measured by GNP or per capita GNP, can be misleading about the *human* dimensions of global poverty. There is general consensus that the *number,* if not the *proportion,* of people living under conditions of absolute poverty in the Third World has actually increased in spite of the fact that the developing countries as a whole exceeded by almost 1 percent the average annual GNP growth target of 5 percent for the UN's Development Decade I (the 1960s) and fell slightly below the annual growth target of 6 percent for Development Decade II (the 1970s).

Even per capita GNP, widely cited as having a strong correlation with the extent of poverty, does not always or fully measure the conditions and quality of human life in a given country. When we juxtapose the PQLI—Physical Quality of Life Index, a composite index of life expectancy, infant mortality, and literacy computed on a scale of 0 to 100, designed and used by the Overseas Development Council[6]—and per capita GNP, we find some remarkable contrasts and deviations among the developing countries. In PQLI performance, those developing countries (China, Cuba, Sri Lanka, and Tanzania) that give priority to meeting basic human needs score well above the norm of their per capita GNPs, while high-growth developing countries (Brazil, Saudi Arabia), where the dividends of growth are creamed off by the richest, score well below the norm for their per capita GNPs. In 1980, Saudi Arabia was well above the norm of high-income countries in per capita income ($11,260) but stood below the norm (forty-three) of low-income countries in PQLI (thirty-five). Cuba reached the norm of high-income countries in its PQLI (ninety-three) (the highest among all the developing countries), even though its per capita GNP ($1,410) was only about one-sixth of the norm of the developed countries. To cite another remarkable example, Sri Lanka's per capita GNP in 1980 was only $270, one forty-second of Saudi Arabia's, but its PQLI stood at eighty, 2.3 times that of Saudi Arabia.[7]

The actual extent and dimensions of global poverty are difficult to measure. Poverty has a high correlation with low per capita income, but there is more involved. Nonetheless, the socioeconomic profile of the world's absolute poor can be generalized as follows:

- They live at the margin of "existence" without adequate access to such basic human needs as food, shelter, safe drinking water, primary health care, literacy, and remunerative employment;
- They have few assets (land, education, credit, employment, political power, etc.);
- They are chronically undernourished and chronically in poor health;
- They are economically "marginalized," having few links, if any, with the "modernization" process of their national economies;
- More than three-fourths of them live in rural areas, the rest in urban slums;
- A disproportionate number, about forty percent, are children under the age of ten;
- Most of them have, or live in, large families;
- As much as four-fifths of their income is spent on food;
- They have a low-life expectancy, as only five of every ten children born to poor parents survive to the age of forty;
- Most of them live in the Third World, with disproportionate concentrations in the Indian subcontinent, Southeast Asia, and sub-Saharan Africa.

TABLE 5.1
Estimated Numbers of People in Developing Market Economies Living in Poverty, 1972

Region	Total population	Seriously poor	Destitute	Seriously poor	Destitute
		(millions of people)		(percentage of population)	
Asia	1 196	853	499	71	42
Africa	345	239	134	69	39
Latin America	274	118	73	43	27
Total [1]	1 815	1 210	706	67	39

[1] Excluding developing countries in Europe and Oceania, with a total population of about 25 million.

Source: ILO, *Employment, Growth and Basic Needs: A One-World Problem* (New York: Praeger Publishers for the Overseas Development Council in cooperation with the International Labour Office, 1977), Table 2, p. 22.

Estimates of the number of people living in "absolute poverty" throughout the world vary from 780 million to 1 billion. "Taking as the cutoff a level of income based on detailed studies of poverty in India," the World Bank's *World Development Report, 1980* noted, "the number of people in absolute poverty in developing countries (excluding China and other centrally planned economies) is estimated at around 780 million."[8] On the other hand, the World Health Organization estimated in 1981 that "nearly one thousand million people are trapped in the vicious circle of poverty, malnutrition, disease, and despair that saps their energy, reduces their work capacity, and limits their ability to plan for the future."[9]

Seeing poverty in the world in both an absolute and relative sense, and taking various coefficients into account to avoid the distortions associated with exchange rate conversions to reflect more accurately "purchasing power parity," the International Labour Office assessed the distribution of the poor in developing market economies along two dimensions (see Table 5.1). Based on the assumption that a typical basket of goods consumed by the poor costing U.S.$1 in Western Europe could be obtained for 20 cents in Asia, 23 cents in Africa, and 36 cents in Latin America the first poverty line of the "seriously poor" is defined as equivalent to an annual income per head of U.S.$500 in Western Europe, U.S.$180 in Latin America, U.S.$115 in Africa, and U.S.$100 in Asia. The second poverty line of the "destitute" includes those with an income equivalent of U.S.$250 in Western Europe, U.S.$90 in Latin America, U.S.$59 in Africa, and U.S.$50 in Asia.

More significantly, the number of the "seriously poor" increased by 119 million and the number of the "destitute" by 43 million during the period 1963-1972.[10] No matter what measuring stick one uses, it is safe to conclude that for the one-fourth to one-fifth of humanity entrapped in the vicious and seemingly self-perpetuating cycle of poverty and powerlessness, the twentieth century has not yet arrived.

Poverty and Food. The root causes of global hunger are poverty and income inequality, not food scarcity or overpopulation. World grain production increased 2.3 times—from 631 million metric tons (mmt) to 1,432 mmt—between 1950 and 1980; per capita grain production increased from 251 kilograms to 324 kilograms during the same period. Increased production has been accompanied by increasing inequalities. If world grain production was distributed evenly, each person on earth would have some 3,000 calories a day—and this does not include the enormous quantities of meat, fish, vegetables, and fruits—well above the established Food and Agriculture Organization (FAO) minimum caloric standard (2,200). The early 1980s witnessed massive surplus food production in Western countries along with extremes of hunger and insufficient funds for food in developing countries.

Global estimates of the number of hungry or undernourished people vary depending on the nutritional standard and the distribution of food consumption in various countries. The latest—and most conservative— estimate from the FAO places the number of undernourished people at at least 430 million. This figure does not include estimates for China and is based on the numbers of people thought to be consuming 20 percent below the level needed to sustain life and a light amount of activity (1.2 times the Basal Metabolic Rate level for life sustenance).[11] Using a higher calorie level, World Bank economists estimated in 1973 that no less than 808 million people had a calorie intake lower than the recommended level.

By conservative estimates, then, more than 500 million people (roughly one out of every nine) suffer from hunger today, compared with 100-200 million (one out of every fourteen to twenty-five people) in the 1950s. The number of people who are chronically undernourished is as high as 1.3 billion. In terms of the patterns of global food consumption, there are today three separate and unequal worlds: the average per capita daily calorie consumption in the "first world" of developed countries is about 3,400 calories, about 2,400 in the "second world" of most developing countries, and only about 2,000 in the "third world" of the least developed countries.

Most global models, though based on divergent normative and methodological assumptions, reach the same conclusion that the fundamental obstacles to establishing a more equitable world food order are more political than economic. "The principal limits to sustained economic growth and accelerated development," concludes Wassily Leontief in his input-output global model for the future of the world economy, "are political, social and institutional in character rather than physical. No insurmountable physical barriers exist within the twentieth century to the accelerated development of the developing regions."[12] In spite of a projected decline in land-man ratios, *the Global 2000 Report* concluded: *"The world has the capacity, both physical and economic, to produce enough food to meet substantial increases in demand through 2000."*[13]

The population explosion is often used as a pseudoscientific Malthusian theory to explain (and rationalize) the poverty trap. This fashionable theory makes a cause out of a symptom. Poverty-stricken, landless, illiterate, and "marginal" peasants are caught in the sociopsychological trap of wanting more children to protect themselves against high rates of infant mortality, to provide themselves with more hands for agricultural field work, and to insure themselves with a family-based social security system for survival in old age. Eradicating absolute poverty and its concomitant poor health, inadequate and unsanitary water and shelter, illiteracy, and unemployment/ underemployment is the surest way to cap the demographic volcano. The population-poverty link is very strong in most empirical studies, and the root cause of the population explosion in the poorest developing countries therefore lies in the absence or failure of income redistribution and basic human needs policies.

That some 30 percent of the human population is sick from overconsumption while 60 percent is sick from underconsumption dramatizes the inequities of the poverty-prosperity link between as well as within the states in the existing world order. On the one hand, there is an international contradiction between *widespread malnourishment* (resulting from overconsumption of junk food) in the developed countries and *chronic undernourishment* (resulting from insufficient quantities of food to meet the minimal nutritional requirements) in the developing countries. The amount of food lost through simple waste or spoilage by warehouse managers, shopkeepers, and consumers in affluent societies has been estimated as high as 40 percent of all food in a given country.[14] On the other hand, there is an internal contradiction within many developing countries between overconsumption and underconsumption. The caloric consumption ratios between the poorest and the richest in Brazil stood at 1,240:4,290 and in the state of Maharashtra, India, at 940:3,150.[15]

Chronic world hunger as the silent killer of our time is a symptom of structural violence embedded in the domestic and international order. Like disease, this form of violence hits hardest at weak, defenseless, and subordinate human groups. The great majority of the victims of this structural violence— some 80 percent by World Bank estimates—are women and children. Estimates of the number of people killed each year by starvation vary greatly, ranging from 30 million (United Nations Children Fund—UNICEF) to 18.3 million (United Nations Development Programme—UNDP) to 15 million (Overseas Development Council—ODC).[16] The U.S. Presidential Commission on World Hunger concluded that "about one out of every four children in the developing world die before the age of five—mostly from nutrition-related causes."[17]

Growing evidence supports the hunger-caused linkage between the patterns of morbidity and mortality in developing countries. Nutritional deficiency is reported to be the principal cause of infant mortality and, coupled with premature births largely due to dietary deficiency among pregnant women, has been the underlying cause of some 57 percent of deaths among children in the age group one to five in Latin America. In Africa, about 50 percent of the pediatric problems have been attributed to protein and calorie deficiencies.[18] Chronic hunger has less dramatic epidemiological effects on human development: it slowly and silently diminishes physical/genetic, mental, and psychological development of the victims, predisposing them to have deformed or retarded babies, to be less energetic and productive in human activities, less able to learn in social and intellectual activities, and even less active in political activities. Roger Lewin, a leading British science author, estimated in 1975 that more than 300 million Third World children were risking permanent damage to their brains because of inadequate nutrition coupled with other kinds of environmental poverty.[19]

Poverty and Water. Water is the most essential—and in theory the most plentiful—life-sustaining resource on earth. To sustain an acceptable quality of human life requires about 30 cubic meters of water per person per year for indirect domestic consumption. The total requirement for water for all human development needs (residential, industrial, and agricultural) is estimated to be in the range of 350–450 cubic meters per person per year. The total quantity of fresh water in the world exceeds all conceivable requirements of the human population. For example, the global water supply of 9,000 cubic kilometers per year could easily support a world population of 20–25 billion—4.5 to 5.7 times the present world population. Yet global water famine persists in the midst of global water abundance.

As a vital resource, water is subject to social management and control. To be usable, water must be tapped, collected, stored, purified, allocated, distributed, and recycled through a social process. It is at this point that environmental *and* social (man-made) inequities intervene, making water less accessible. It has been estimated that rural peasants in the Malagasy Republic eke out an existence on less than 2 cubic meters of water on an annual per capita basis, for which they pay $20 per cubic meter; in contrast, their urban counterparts in the United States and other developed countries consume 180 cubic meters, for which they pay only $.10 to $.25 per cubic meter.[20] The average urban resident of Arizona—where, it is often said, water is really gold—consumes 160 gallons of water (conservatively) each day, compared to 0.8 gallons a day for the average inhabitant of the semi-arid regions of Africa.[21] Worldwide per capita consumption of piped water in the developing countries is estimated to be roughly one-twentieth that of the developed countries.

Estimates of the number of people without access to a safe water supply vary, ranging from 1 billion (the World Bank), to 1.2 billion (Gunnar Adler-Karlsson), to 2 billion (UNICEF). The most recent WHO estimate, prepared in connection with the *Global Strategy for Health for All by the Year 2000*, shows that as of 1980 some 69 percent of people in the "least developed countries" (195.3 million) and 49 percent of people in the "other developing countries" (1.77 billion) make a combined total of 1.97 billion people not covered by a safe water supply.[22] The launching of the International Drinking Water Supply and Sanitation Decade (1981–1990) has already generated some calculations including the number of 2 billion people to be reached with safe water supply to meet the goals of the Mar del Plata Programme of Action adopted at the 1977 UN Water Conference.[23] In short, about half of the world's people currently lack reasonable access to safe drinking water.

The water system in the Third World performs a "triage" function, deciding who is worth saving or worth abandoning. The epidemiological effects of the deprivation of this basic human need are seen in the widespread waterborne diseases—diarrhea, malaria, and schistosomiasis—that are believed to be the worst killers of children in many developing countries with acute water famine. It is estimated that each year as many as 25 million people die of diseases caused by contaminated water.

The future of the international political economy of water is fraught with conflicting claims and disputes. Of the 200 major river basins of the world, some 148 are shared by two countries and 52 by three to ten countries. Some of the multinational river basins that have already generated interstate disputes include the Plata (Brazil vs. Argentina), Jordan (Israel vs. Jordan), Euphrates (Syria vs. Iraq), Indus (Pakistan vs. India), Ganges (Bangladesh vs. India), and Ussuri (China vs. the Soviet Union). Given the widely projected increase in demand for water resources in the Third World, a peaceful resolution of interstate conflicts over the use of multinational river basins will surely add another heavy burden for the future world order to bear.

Poverty and Housing. Despite problems of definition and measurement, the available information clearly suggests that a housing shortage affects all regions of the world with the exception of Europe and North America. At the end of the 1960s the world total of about 800 million dwellings included 350 million that could be classified as "standard" and 450 million as "substandard." About four out of every five households in the developing countries were living in substandard accommodations in rural areas and in urban slums and squatter settlements. The proportions were reversed for the developed countries.[24]

The North-South gap in housing conditions continued to widen during the 1970s. Between 1969 and 1979, the percentage of standard dwellings increased from 82 to 92 in the developed countries, but decreased from 19 to 18 in the developing countries. The number of people without standard accommodations increased by 437 million (or 14 percent) during the last decade, and "a quarter of this new population settled in the ever-expanding urban slums and squatter areas, which more than doubled in population during the 1970s."[25] The worldwide urban housing shortage is estimated to be increasing at a rate of four to five million units annually.

This shortage is made worse by four negative trends. First, the rate of deterioration is greater than the rate of improvement in housing conditions.

Second, the rate of new demands created by rapid urbanization is greater than the rate of new construction. For every newly formed household obtaining a standard dwelling unit, three additional households settled for substandard accommodations. For each housing unit built in a city of Africa, it has been estimated, there are ten new families immigrating from the rural areas.[26] The third trend is evident in the slums and squatter settlements of the urban centers of developing countries, where population is "growing at a rate of 12 percent per year—double the population growth rate of the fastest growing urban centers."[27] The fourth trend is an increasing mismatch between the ability of low-income families to pay for housing and the cost of currently available dwelling units. It has been estimated that 50 percent of the urban and 80 percent of the rural population in developing countries "have few, if any, institutional channels through which to obtain financial assistance for housing."[28] One survey in the early 1970s showed that the cost of the cheapest standard housing units in a sample of six cities in developing countries ranged from $570 to $3,005 and that only between 21 and 43 percent of the urban households could afford to purchase any form of standard accommodation.[29]

The UN's mid-1970s worldwide housing survey concluded that "a much larger number of people and a larger proportion of the total population of most less developed countries now live in housing at densities and in conditions which present a serious hazard to health and safety and an obstacle to the fulfillment of decent family life than at the beginning of the past decade."[30] The number of squatters in Manila has recently risen to over 1.6 million, making up nearly one-third of the population.[31] In a recent study of deteriorating conditions in Third World countries, one observer has gone as far as to say that "the gigantic slums of Sao Paolo and Calcutta are already the greatest health hazards to have been seen since the black plague swept across medieval Europe, and many cities will hold 20 million or more ragged inhabitants by 1990."[32]

Poverty and Primary Health Care. In a general sense, human health has multiple causes and consequences, biological/genetic and environmental, social and economic. Nonetheless, socioeconomic (purchasing power and hygienic knowledge) and socioenvironmental (health environment) factors tend to be the chief determinants of health in any human society. The concept of primary health care embraces nutrition, environmental sanitation, basic preventive and curative services, health education, and community participation.

The epidemiological effects of the juxtaposition of poverty and plenty are shown in a variety of health and socioeconomic indicators. The development gap between the world's richest and poorest countries can be summed up as follows: infant mortality rate (per 1,000 live-born), 1:8.4 (19 to 160); life expectancy, 1.6:1 (72 years to 45 years); percentage of birth weight 2,500 grams (5.5 pounds) or more, 1.3:1 (93 percent to 70 percent); per capita per annum public expenditure on health, 143.5:1 ($244 to $1.7); in public expenditure on health as percentage of GNP, 3.9:1 (3.9 percent to 1.0 percent).[33]

In both nature and magnitude, the health problems of the Third World are different from those of the industrialized countries. In the former, chronic undernourishment and poor environmental sanitation are the major causes of specific diseases and deaths. Here mortality and morbidity patterns are dominated by such infectious and parasitic diseases as influenza, viral infection, bacillary dysentery, amoebiasis and other diarrheal diseases. According to UNICEF, some 17 million children died in 1981 from malnutrition and preventable diseases.[34] Moreover, some 1 billion people are in clear and continuous danger of contracting one of six tropical diseases—malaria, schistosomiasis, filariasis, trypanosomiasis, leischmaniasis and leprosy.

In contrast, health problems in the industrialized countries stem from strenuous life-style, unbalanced diet, overeating, alienation, habit-forming drugs, and even sexual promiscuity. The "civilization diseases"—cancer, cardiovascular diseases, mental illness, accidents—all compete as major killers in affluent societies. As of mid-1982, some 20 million people in the United States are reported to be suffering from a new form of incurable and sexually transmitted disease called "herpes."

There is a reciprocal impact between public delivery of social services and health care and the social policy of income redistribution. Of course, any increase in income means an increase in the purchasing power for health care service. Less widely recognized is the reverse impact of public expenditure on health. A recent study of member states of the Organization for Economic Cooperation and Development (OECD) has shown that income redistribution has significantly benefited from greater accessibility to, and use of, health care programs by lower-income groups, *provided* that the public sector assumes a substantially increased role in the provision and delivery of health care, including subsidization of costs to the poorest citizens.[35] A similar redistributive impact of public health expenditures has also been observed in Canada, Sweden, and the United Kingdom. In the United Kingdom, public health expenditure has produced a greater income redistributive effect than public expenditures on housing, family allowances, or education.[36]

Obviously, poverty at both the individual and national levels defines the outer limits of health care. But the expansion and redistribution of health services in the developing countries is also constrained by established patterns of resource reallocation. Intranationally, the reallocation of resources is evident in the migration of skilled health workers from rural areas to cities. In most countries of the world, about two-thirds of the population do not have reasonable access to any permanent form of health care. In most developing *and* developed countries, the overwhelming proportion of resources for the delivery of health service is concentrated in the large metropolitan areas. To highlight the extremes, there is only one physician to serve more than 200,000 people in the rural areas of some least developed countries, compared with one physician to serve only 300 people in the metropolitan areas of some developed countries. Worldwide, some 1.5 billion people have little or no access to medical services.

In addition, these human and financial resources are devoted to capital-intensive, technology-intensive medical service for a small minority of special patients at the neglect of basic health care for the masses. Despite the increasing recognition of, and lip service to, the importance of universal low-cost basic health care in the 1970s, primary and populist health care still remains more of a slogan than a social reality in most developing countries. China's extensive reliance on paramedical health workers, affectionately called "barefoot doctors" (*chijiao yisheng*), stands out as a model for emulation. Barefoot doctors provide an appropriate level of primary health care for almost a billion people at a cost of less than seven U.S. dollars per person per year.

Internationally, there is also a resource reallocative process at work. At one level is the "blood drain" of an extensive international traffic in human blood. The league of Red Cross Societies and members of some WHO Expert Advisory Panels discovered in 1975 that Western commercial firms were obtaining blood or plasma from paid donors in developing countries in order to produce blood derivatives for sale in their own countries or for export. This international traffic in human blood, which started in the mid-1960s in Central and South America, has spread to Asia and Africa as a profitable trade. One liter of plasma can be bought for U.S.$2 to $4 in "donor" developing countries and be sold for $20 to $40 in "recipient" developed countries.[37] This adds another dimension to the international division of labor and comparative advantage.

At another level is the better known "brain drain." A recent WHO study documented the magnitude, direction and determinants of the international migration of physicians and nurses.[38] Of the 140,000 migrant physicians in the early 1970s, some 57 percent originated from the developing countries. Between 1962 and 1972, for example, 48,242 Third world scientists and engineers and 25,042 physicians and surgeons emigrated to the United States.[39] In 1972 alone, the United States "imported" over 7,000 physicians, mostly from Third World countries. On the other hand, the developing countries as a whole received only 3 and 6 percent of the migrant physicians from developed and developing countries respectively.

Ironically, most of these Third World immigrant physicians, seduced by the life-styles of the rich countries, find themselves condemned as second-class doctors performing "primary health care" in county, municipal, and rural hospitals that the graduates of U.S. medical schools would avoid.

Poverty and Education. The right to education has been recognized as a universal norm in a variety of international covenants and UN resolutions. What does this "right" mean? Progress on education has been defined and measured in terms of two indices: the number of literate adults and the number of children enrolled in school at the primary and secondary levels. As for adult literacy, the *proportion* of illiterate adults in the world has gradually shrunk from 44 percent in 1950 to 39 percent in 1960 to 32 percent in 1970 to 29 percent in 1980. Yet the absolute *number* of adult illiterates has increased during the postwar period. This number stood at

750 million in 1970, rising to 800 million in 1977 (one-third of the world population), and is now expected to reach up to 865 million by 1985, with some 60 percent of illiterates being women, and with Africa, Latin America and to a lesser extent South Asia as the most problematic regions.[40]

The total number of student enrollments worldwide at the three main levels of education—primary, secondary, and higher—rose from about 489 million in 1970 to 557 million in 1975, an average annual increase of 2.6 percent. This rate was about equal to that registered during the 1965–1970 period but sharply lower than the 5 percent annual growth rate of the 1960–1965 period. Patterns and rates of growth differ for the three levels of education. The proportion of students enrolled in primary education increased worldwide from 66 percent in 1965 to 68 percent in 1970 to 72 percent in 1980, while the proportion of students enrolled in higher education rose from 5.5 percent in 1970 to 6.2 percent in 1975. The educational gap between regions is more striking—the student enrollment ratio at the third level between Africa and Northern America was 1:11.3 (1.6 percent to 18 percent) in 1975.[41]

Although the role of education in overcoming poverty is complex, there is now growing recognition that it is at the primary level, especially for female pupils, that education tends to be most retributive for the poor. Since people mired in the poverty trap have neither opportunity nor ability nor will to take advantage of and benefit from secondary and higher education, public expenditures on these levels tend to have a "trickle-up" redistributive effect, reallocating resources and benefits from poor to rich. Gunnar Myrdal maintains in this connection that monopoly of education "is—together with monopoly of ownership of land—the most fundamental basis of inequality, and it retains its hold more strongly in the poorer countries."[42]

On the other hand, it has been shown that the annual output of a farmer who had completed four years of primary school was on the average 13.2 percent higher than that of an unschooled farmer. A number of country-specific empirical studies conducted by the World Bank show that primary education, especially of female students, has a variety of favorable effects on the next generation's health, fertility, and education. Specifically, the World Bank's studies reached the following conclusions: (1) children of more educated mothers are less likely to die even allowing for differences in family income; (2) families of more educated mothers are likely to be better fed at any given income level; and (3) more educated women are apt to delay marriage, have greater chances of employment, and are more likely to know about and use contraceptives.[43]

In a more fundamental sense, mass education and minimum literacy is a necessary precondition for social and political transformation. Without widespread literacy it is difficult to overcome self-defeating fatalism and social anesthesia. Poverty, powerlessness, and illiteracy feed on each other. Poverty breeds poverty, just as powerlessness breeds powerlessness, for the very groups that are denied power are the most vulnerable to the loss of will and motivation needed to lift themselves by the bootstraps. To raise literacy is to raise the threshold of intolerance for oppression and exploitation.

Poverty and Employment. There is little doubt about the causal linkage between unemployment/underemployment and poverty. The crisis of global poverty is a function of the crisis of global unemployment. The ultimate value of any economic system can be measured not only by the efficiency principle of productivity but also by the equity principle of maximum participation of all people in the production, distribution, and consumption of goods and services. Employment is more than an income-producing means for livelihood; it is—or ought to be—a fuller participation in the economic and political life of the country. In theory (if not always in practice), employment can enhance an individual's sense of self-respect and self-fulfillment.

The world unemployment/underemployment crisis worsened considerably in the 1970s and early 1980s. After almost two decades of economic prosperity characterized by near-full employment and a high rate of economic growth, most of the developed market economies suddenly encountered a sharp rise in unemployment in the mid-1970s. For the developed market economies as a whole, the rate of unemployment increased from 2.8 percent of the total labor force during the 1962–1973 period to 5.1 percent in 1975, 6.2 percent in 1980 and up to 9.5 percent in 1982, affecting some 30 million workers. In the United States, the unemployment rate rose to a 40-year high of 10.8 percent in the latter half of 1982, affecting 12 million workers.

Hard economic times in developed market economy countries hit ethnic and other minorities the hardest. Blacks and other minorities in the United States and migrant workers in many European countries have substantially higher rates of unemployment than national averages. Black workers, who represent 10 percent of the labor force, suffer disproportionately—they account for 20 percent of the jobless, 22 percent of the long-term unemployed, and nearly 40 percent of those who have given up the job search. In West Germany, social hostility generated by unemployment has been directed not so much at the government as, in a widespread flurry of nationalism, toward foreign migrant workers.

The Third World faces a different kind of employment crisis. According to ILO estimates made in 1975, *unemployment* (defined and measured in terms of the number of persons without a job and actively seeking employment) in the Third World constituted 4.7 percent of the labor force (or about 33 million people). Unlike their counterparts in the developed countries, however, the jobless in the Third World do not have a social safety net (unemployment insurance, food stamps, and social welfare). On the other hand, *underemployment* (defined and measured in terms of persons in employment of less than normal duration who are seeking or would accept additional work, and persons with a job yielding inadequate income to meet basic needs) is a much more common problem than open and registered unemployment, affecting 35.7 percent of the labor force (or about 250 million people excluding China and other Asian centrally planned economies). In short, some 40.4 percent of the total labor force of the Third World (about 283 million people) of which 80 percent are rural, are unemployed and underemployed.[44] The danger of a world unemployment/underemployment crisis of global proportions, another Sword of Damocles hanging precariously over the present world order system, can also be seen in the projections that some 36 million people will enter the labor force every year from now to the end of the century and that the number of jobs needed to close the employment gap in the Third World will rise to 455 million by the year 2000.[45]

To a significant extent, the unemployment/underemployment crisis in the Third World is a by-product of growth strategies that have shifted from labor-intensive, small-scale industry and rural development to capital-intensive, export-oriented industrial development. Thanks to the growing globalization of the capitalist principle of division of labor and comparative advantage, and thanks also to the rise of transnational corporations, there is underway a commodification of labor within as well as between nation-states.

The Third World's catch-up process via its "export-oriented growth strategy" has destroyed self-sustaining agricultural employment in the countryside without providing alternative jobs for the displaced peasants immigrating into the urban slums and squatter settlements. These people become "marginalized" in the productive process of the global political economy. The "free trade zones" (FTZ) or similar sites (export processing zones, investment-promotion zones and in-bound industries), which are being set up by Third World countries to attract export-linked transnational investments, have limited employment-creating potential, direct or indirect. This is the conclusion of an ILO study on the employment effects of TNCs in the Third World.[46]

Internationally, the commodification process of labor is seen in the flow of migrant workers from developing countries into Western Europe and, more recently, into the Gulf states of the Middle East. From the early 1950s through the early 1970s more than 30 million foreign workers were admitted to Western Europe. During the heyday of this flow (the mid-1970s), immigrants accounted for almost 16 percent of the total population in Switzerland, 8 percent in France, 7 percent in the Federal Republic of Germany, and 6 percent in the United Kingdom.[47] In 1980, remittances from these international migrant workers yielded about $24 billion to the developing countries. In some cases, the percentage of workers' remittances compared to the country's merchandise exports was considerable: 175.4 percent for Jordan; 92.9 percent for Pakistan; 88.8 percent for Egypt; 60.5 percent for Portugal; and 59.6 percent for Upper Volta.[48]

With the rising unemployment rates in the developed market economies in the 1970s, however, the migrant workers become front-line dominos. Between 1973 and 1976, some 1.3 million migrant workers lost their jobs in Western Europe, 600,000 in the Federal Republic of Germany and 300,000 in France.[49] In the first half of 1982, the Reagan administration even launched "Project Jobs" raids, arresting some 5,635 illegal aliens (mostly Mexicans) to force them out of "decent-paying jobs" that could be held by unemployed U.S. citizens.

The National Dimensions

The Bretton Woods postwar economic order served the rich and industrialized capitalist countries well, while providing only first-aid measures for the poor countries during the first two and a half decades. The developed "Northern" countries had a vested interest in preserving the existing order and the developing "Southern" countries had no power to bring about structural change. Thanks to abundant raw materials and oil, bought at exploitatively cheap prices from the developing countries, the economic engine of the West and Japan experienced unparalleled growth and prosperity. Thus, the postwar economic order worked to perpetuate the established pattern of overdevelopment-underdevelopment, dominance-dependence, and Center-Periphery relationships.

In terms of global socioeconomic stratification, however, a major structural change occurred in the 1970s, with the rise of two kinds of "middle-class" countries—oil-exporting developing countries (OPEC) and middle-income or "newly industrializing countries" (NICs). The ascendancy of this "semi-Periphery" in the South has to be taken into account in any macrostructural analysis of the global political economy, lest the aggregate data of the developing countries (since the early 1970s) obscure the underlying structure of global inequities between the richest and poorest countries.

Although the General Assembly issued a call as early as 1971 that "the United Nations should evolve a concept of collective economic security,"[50] it was not until a few years later, when the unprecedented energy and food crises "united" the rich North and the poor South in a new partnership of economic misery, that a first step in the protracted and elusive journey called "New International Economic Order" or "North-South dialogue" began. In substance, if not in exact title, such calls had already been issued by the Group of 77 in the 1960s through UNCTAD. Yet the unprecedented stocktaking of the postwar economic order was launched only after "system crisis"—generated by the sudden transformation of the international petroleum regime in 1973 and the resultant deepening stagflation in the industrialized countries—began to hurt the North. If nothing else, the NIEO has transformed the agenda of global politics by highlighting the national dimensions of global inequities in access to capital, markets, resources, and technology.

The North-South Gap. Table 5.2 sums up some of the key social dimensions of the North-South development gap. However, the main issue of the North-South gap, as defined in the context of NIEO politics, lies in reforming the structural inequities of international economic life (regime transformation), with emphasis on international trade, transfer of real

TABLE 5.2
The Development Gap, by Groups of Countries

	Low-Income Countries	Lower Middle-Income Countries	Upper Middle-Income Countries	High-Income Countries	Developing Countries	Developed Countries
	(excl. China)					
Mid-1981 Population (millions)	2,188.6 1,203.6	454.5	712.4	1,134.1	3,400.5	1,089.1
Average Per Capita GNP (1980)	$255 $225	$566	$1,800	$8,222	$711	$8,262
Average PQLI[1]	58 43	56	68	93	60	94
Average Birth Rate (per 1,000)	30 39	38	34	16	32	15
Average Death Rate (per 1,000)	12 16	14	10	9	12	9
Average Life Expectancy (years)	59 51	53	62	72	59	72
Average Infant Mortality Rate (per 1,000 life births)	101 138	98	83	21	96	19
Average Literacy Rate	49% 36%	57%	67%	97%	54%	99%
Average Per Capita Education Expenditures	$9 $5	$15	$60	$373	$24	$376
Average Per Capita Military Expenditures	$15 $6	$24	$57	$310	$29	$306

[1]Each country's PQLI (Physical Quality of Life Index) is based on an average of life expectancy at age one, infant mortality, and literacy.

Source: Roger D. Hansen and Contributors, *U.S. Foreign Policy and the Third World: Agenda 1982* (New York: Praeger Publishers for the Overseas Development Council, 1982), p. 155. Reprinted with permission.

resources, reform of international financial and monetary institutions, science and technology, food and agriculture, collective self-reliance (cooperation among developing countries), and restructuring of the developmental sectors of the United Nations system. It is beyond the purview of this chapter to give a detailed description and analysis of each of these issues. Instead, I will focus on a set of three closely interrelated isues—international trade, commodities, and debts—showing the national dimensions of global inequities in the contemporary world economic system.

Trade. Thanks to the phenomenal decline of tariffs and the phenomenal rise in the volume of world trade (see Figure 5.1), more and more countries—rich and poor, developed and developing—have come to depend on international trade as an integral part of their economy. World trade escalated from $52 billion in 1948 to over $2 trillion in 1980. The economic behavior of the Center or core capitalist managers of the global political economy has a powerful modelling effect upon the developing countries—and centrally planned economies—caught up in a frantic development race.

The growing interdependence of core capitalist countries can be seen in the increasing ratios of exports to production (excluding services) between 1960 and 1979: for France, this ratio increased from 23.4 percent to 52.2 percent; West Germany, from 32.2 percent to 54.8 percent; Italy, from 27.6 percent to 60.3 percent; United Kingdom, from 38.5 percent to 74.9 percent; Japan, from 18.8 percent to 29.2 percent; Canada, from 42.9 percent to 87 percent; and even for the relatively self-sufficient United States, from 11.5 percent to 25.3 percent.[51]

The notion that a nation cannot catch up without capturing its share of the world markets has even affected the socialist states. The value of external trade with developed and developing market economies for the Soviet-bloc countries increased from $10.8 billion in 1969–1970 to $79.4 billion in 1981. During the first half of the 1970s, the East European countries' exports to and imports from the developed market-economy countries registered an average annual growth rate of over 23 percent.[52] Even China joined this game, as the post-Mao Chinese leadership shifted from the needs-oriented self-reliance model to the export-oriented growth model in its accelerated march to the promised land of modernity.[53]

Since many developing countries "survive" on one or two primary commodities for export earnings, their national economies are correspondingly more dependent upon international trade than the industrialized and diversified economies of the developed countries. Likewise their national economies are more sensitive and more vulnerable to external forces and policies beyond their control. Even in quantitative terms, the developing countries as a whole fared poorly during much of the postwar period. Although total volume of world trade was rising steadily until recently—at the average annual growth rate of 8.5 percent during the period 1962–1972—the Third World share steadily declined from 31.9 percent in 1950 to 21.5 percent in 1960 to 17.7 percent in 1970. The increase in the Third World's share from 17.7 percent in 1970 to 26.8 percent in 1980 was largely due to the rise of the middle-class countries mentioned earlier.[54]

FIGURE 5.1
Trends in Trade and Tariffs, 1928–1978

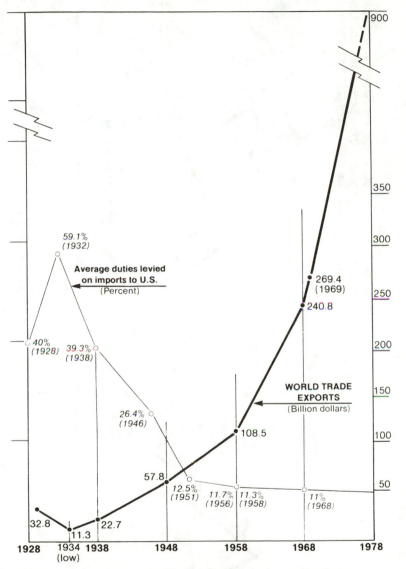

Note.—U.S. Export totals include military grant-aid and foreign merchandise.

Source: U.S. Department of State, *The Trade Debate*, Department of State Publication 8942 (Washington, D.C.: U.S. Government Printing Office, 1978), p. 6.

154

FIGURE 5.2

Changing Terms of Trade for Developed and Developing Countries, 1950–1971 (1950=100)

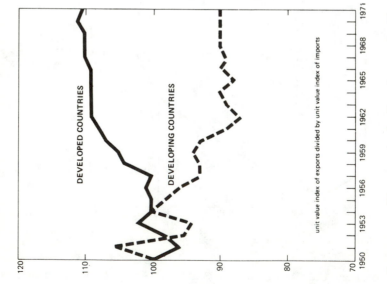

DEVELOPED COUNTRIES

DEVELOPING COUNTRIES

unit value index of exports divided by unit value index of imports

Source: *Finance and Development* 11 (March 1974), p. 14. Reprinted with permission.

FIGURE 5.3

Changing Terms of Trade for Developed Market Economies, Developing Market Economies, and Least Developed Countries, 1971–1980 (1969–71=100)

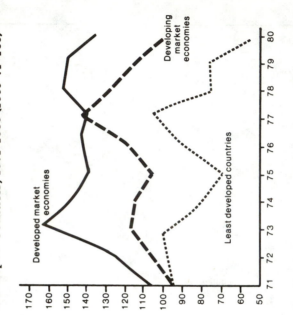

Developing market economies

Developed market economies

Least developed countries

Source: *State of Food and Agriculture 1981* as cited in *UN Chronicle* 20 (January 1983), Table B, p. 70.

The structural inequities underpinning the North-South trade gap can be seen more clearly in the progressive deterioration of the terms of trade for developing countries. Figure 5.2 and Figure 5.3 plot the changing terms of trade for developed and developing countries (and least developing countries) during the postwar period. The postwar history of oil pricing— which in real terms declined from the mid-1950s until the early 1970s, tripled in 1973–1974, declined by about 11 percent from 1974 to 1978, and doubled from 1978 to the first quarter of 1981[55]—suggests that the steady and long-term deterioration in the terms of trade for the exchange of primary commodities (excluding oil) for industrial products cannot be explained as a function of international market forces alone, an unavoidable by-product of the asymmetry between demands for the two types of goods.

The rules and decisionmaking mechanisms governing the world markets within which the exchange of goods takes place have been defined and manipulated by the industrialized countries as importers of primary commodities and exporters of manufactured goods. As a result, the developing countries have been subject to the discriminatory tariff and nontariff barriers of industrialized countries. Successive rounds of GATT negotiations have reduced the level of industrial tariffs to about 5 percent on a trade-weighted basis, but the goods the developing countries export—agricultural products, semiprocessed commodities, and labor-intensive consumer goods—have encountered tariff barriers two to four times higher than those for manufactured goods.

The developing countries were thus forced to sell their primary commodities and buy manufactured goods at prices designed advantageous to the industrialized countries. Between 1955 and 1963, it has been estimated, oil-importing developing countries increased their overall volume of exports at the average annual rate of 5 percent (still 3.5 percent below the worldwide average) only to see their import-purchasing power grow at the much lower annual rate of 2 percent because of deterioration in the terms of trade.[56]

The emergence of global stagflation in the 1970s in general and of major unemployment problems in OECD countries in particular has caused a crisis in the maintenance of the postwar liberal trade order. The average annual growth rate of world trade volume declined from 8.5 percent in 1962–1972 to 4.25 percent in 1973–1980; in 1980 and 1981 it dropped further, to 1.5 percent.[57] Despite, or perhaps because of, the conclusion of the Tokyo Round of Multilateral Trade Negotiations (MTN) in 1979, recent years have witnessed a creeping neoprotectionism, a chain-reaction process in which one developed country after another is pressured by a well-organized domestic group to institute a "nontariff" barrier in one sector, only to receive a retaliation in another sector. This neomercantilist policy stems from the inability or unwillingness of an affected domestic industry to make necessary structural adjustments; it can easily end by triggering a global beggar-thy-neighbor policy. The nontariff barriers to trade increased sharply in the latter half of the 1970s; they now extend to a wide range of sectors (steel, autos, fibers) affecting both North-North and North-South trade and cover as much as half of all trade.

The volatile terms of trade development for the Third World in the 1970s produced greatly varying results. Between 1973 and 1981 the average annual percentage change in the terms of trade was −1.5 percent for non-oil developing countries, +25 percent for oil-exporting developing countries, and −3.2 percent for low-income countries.[58] The data for non-oil developing countries are greatly skewed by the predominant role of the NICs in the Third World exportation of manufactures. South Korea, Taiwan, Singapore, and Hong Kong—the "Gang of Four" in the Asian political economy— account for more than 60 percent of the manufactured exports of all the developing countries. Yet the economies of the NICs are no less seriously affected by the current maladies in the global political economy—the stagflation in industrialized countries, the high energy costs, and the rising interest rates.

Having black gold (petroleum) is no panacea either. "For most of the oil-rich countries," observed Third World economist Jahangir Amuzegar before the onset of the recent "oil price war," "the tradition-shattering changes, the political uncertainties, the security risks, the economic bottle-necks, and the structural distortions are probably greater today than in the pre-1973 era."[59] With the steadily declining demand and price of oil in world markets since early 1981, the developmental dreams of such oil-exporters as Mexico and Nigeria have become debt nightmares.

Commodities. Given the overdependence of many Third World countries on one or a few primary commodities to supply the economic lifeblood of foreign exchange, it is hardly surprising that the commodities debate has become central to North-South dialogue. The developing countries as a whole (70 percent of the world's people) account for only about 9 percent of world manufactured output, and their exports come mostly (81.2 percent) from primary commodity products. Commodity exports affect a broad range of developing countries, while manufactured exports are disproportionately concentrated in a half-dozen NICs. Commodity problems highlight the predicament of the Third World in general and the poorest countries in particular in the contemporary global political economy.

The Third World's commodity problem is a textbook case for exposing the contradictions in the political economy of asymmetrical interdependence. Of course, the roots of this asymmetrical interdependence—what the Chinese used to call an interdependence "between a horseman and his mount"— lie in the colonial past. What is ironic is the passion and persistence with which Third World countries have cast their lot with this basically colonial political economy as a way to fuller integration in the capitalist world economy. There are several basic, interconnected problems that would make it difficult for the Third world to win this commodity game in the global political economy.

Overdependence *ipso facto* weakens bargaining power and magnifies vulnerability, especially for commodities in low or elastic demand and in high or substitutable supply. This generalized overdependence has made the Third World economies highly vulnerable to the vagaries of international commodity markets and the nonmarket manipulations of the TNCs. When world commodity prices drop, whether due to increasing supply from overproduction or to decreasing demand from recession in the industrialized countries, the developing countries must produce (and export) more to maintain the same level of exchange earnings.

This reactive behavior serves to further depress commodity prices—a tragedy, not a magic, of the marketplace. During the 1960–1971 period, the unit price of natural rubber declined from $16 to $8.50 as rubber exports rose from 1.9 to 2.8 mmt. In concrete terms, twenty-five tons of rubber could pay for at least six tractors in 1960, but only two tractors in 1974. The progressive deterioration of the terms of trade for commodities versus manufactures (see Figures 5.2 and 5.3) needs to be viewed in this light. In the 1970s the middle-income developing countries have accounted for almost 98 percent of the gain in the export-derived purchasing power of developing countries as a whole.[60] For the non-oil developing countries, however, 1982 was the fifth consecutive year of deterioration in the terms of trade, which dropped to 12–13 percent lower than in 1972.[61] Between 1980 and 1982, world commodity prices, excluding oil, have dropped by 35 percent to the lowest real levels in three decades. To buy a seven-ton truck in 1981, for example, Tanzania had to grow and export three times as much coffee (or cashew nuts), four times as much cotton, or ten times as much tobacco, as it took to buy the same truck in 1976.

Dependence on just one or a few primary commodities makes developing countries highly vulnerable to the boom-bust cycle caused by extreme and frequent price fluctuations in commodity markets. In the latter half of the 1970s, the prices of sugar, coffee, cocoa, and copper were the most volatile. Some examples of countries acquiring almost all of their export earnings from these volatile commodities include Zambia (94 percent from copper), Mauritius (90 percent from sugar), and Cuba (84 percent from sugar). The case of Zambia demonstrates the economic impact of high dependence on a single primary commodity. When the world copper price plummeted from $3,034 to $1,290 per metric ton, Zambia's purchasing power for imports (whose prices continued to rise) fell by 45 percent and the country's gross domestic product (GDP) fell by 15 percent; in comparison, the impact of the 1974 "oil shock," on the industrialized countries was equivalent to 2.5 percent of GNP.[62]

The dominant-dependent relationship in commodity trade is sustained through oligopolistic control of transnational corporations (TNCs). This modern form of global corporate power is constantly rigging and distorting market forces and mechanisms through its control over financing, processing, transportation, marketing, information, and distribution and through the exercise of its muscle in domestic politics as well. It is estimated that well over 50 percent of global trade is channeled and transacted through TNC intrafirm transfers, bypassing the market forces.

TNC power is even more pronounced in international commodity trade. In the 1950s and 1960s, small and medium-sized companies became endangered species through mergers, takeovers, and bankruptcies; by the end of the 1970s well over two-thirds of global commodity trade was dominated by a small group of very large multicommodity giants. A few examples may suffice: five TNCs controlled 75 percent of the world tea market; six TNCs controlled 50 percent of manganese ore capacity; three TNCs dominated 70–75 percent of the world banana market; six TNCs controlled over 70 percent of the world cocoa market; and six TNCs monopolized 85–90 percent of leaf tobacco.[63] The appeal to the marketplace is a rhetorical figleaf designed to disguise "invisible" oligopolistic hands manipulating supply and demand and controlling the allocation of costs and benefits in global commodity trade.

As a result, the benefits of cheap commodity prices are not passed on to consumers in the industrialized, commodity-importing countries. Some 90 percent of the actual earnings on commodity exports are siphoned off through the intermediary "services" of transnational corporations. The 1976 RIO Report concluded that "the final consumers in the industrialized countries pay over $200 billion for Third World commodities and the products derived directly from them," while "the poor nations receive only $30 billion."[64] A more recent UNDP study arrived at the same conclusion: of the estimated $350 billion that consumers in the industrialized world pay for the developing world's commodities, the latter receives only $35–40 billion in export earnings.[65]

Debts. In 1981–1982 the global political economy witnessed a proliferation of the "debt-bomb." In March 1981, Poland, with a debt of $27 billion, declared that it did not have the $2.5 billion due its creditors that year. In August 1982, Mexico announced that it could not come up with the interest on its debt of $80 billion. Brazil and Argentina followed suit with similar pronouncements. By early 1983 a $706 billion lien—representing $154 for every man, woman, and child on earth—is being held by Western private commercial banks, governments, and international financial institutions around the world against a group of developing *and* Soviet-bloc countries.[66]

There are several indicators for measuring the dimensions and severity of the debt burden. In terms of size and growth, the outstanding *long-term* external debt of the non-oil developing countries increased from $67.7 billion in 1970 to $505.2 billion in 1982 (see Table 5.3). The most dramatic change occurred in current account deficits of the non-oil developing countries (excluding China), which skyrocketed from $11.6 billion in 1973 to $99 billion in 1981.

Table 5.3 does not show the widespread and growing liquidity crisis in the seven members of the Council for Mutual Economic Assistance (COMECON)—Poland, Czechoslovakia, East Germany, Hungary, Rumania, Bulgaria, and the Soviet Union. The familiar "development disease" has spread and affected these socialist countries, which borrowed excessively in the latter half of the 1970s and early 1980s to finance imports of Western machinery and technology on which to build modern industries (that

TABLE 5.3
Long–Term External Debt of Non–Oil Developing Countries, 1973–82[1]

	1973	1974	1975	1976	1977	1978	1979	1980	1981	1982
Total outstanding debt of non-oil developing countries	**96.8**	**120.1**	**146.8**	**181.4**	**221.8**	**276.4**	**324.4**	**375.4**	**436.9**	**505.2**
By type of creditor										
Official creditors	48.3	58.2	67.9	82.2	98.2	117.4	133.3	155.5	175.6	199.5
Governments	35.7	42.6	48.5	57.5	67.4	79.6	88.9	102.1	114.3	128.1
International institutions	12.6	15.7	19.4	24.7	30.8	37.8	44.5	53.4	61.4	71.4
Private creditors	48.5	61.8	78.9	99.2	123.6	159.0	191.1	220.0	261.4	305.7
Unguaranteed debt	20.6	25.3	31.5	38.7	44.0	52.4	58.6	68.8	84.8	101.5
Guaranteed debt	27.9	36.5	47.4	60.5	79.6	106.6	132.5	151.2	176.5	204.2
Financial institutions	14.0	22.8	31.2	41.9	57.5	75.4	101.9	117.4	138.8	162.6
Other private creditors	13.9	13.8	16.2	18.6	22.1	31.2	30.6	33.8	37.7	41.6
By analytical group										
Net oil exporters	15.6	20.7	31.0	39.3	51.0	61.4	68.9	78.0	90.6	107.0
Net oil importers	81.2	99.4	115.8	142.0	170.8	214.9	255.6	297.4	346.3	398.2
Major exporters of manufactures	38.3	47.0	55.8	68.9	82.7	108.4	128.3	143.4	169.1	194.1
Low-income countries	21.6	25.8	29.1	34.3	40.7	47.3	53.4	62.3	70.6	79.7
Other net oil importers	21.3	26.6	30.9	38.9	47.4	59.2	73.8	91.7	106.6	124.3
By area										
Africa	13.1	15.9	19.9	24.2	31.7	38.7	44.7	49.2	56.0	66.0
Asia	27.0	31.5	36.7	43.9	53.0	62.9	71.6	85.6	102.8	121.4
Europe	11.6	14.0	16.2	20.8	25.4	33.5	44.0	54.2	60.2	67.2
Middle East	8.5	10.1	13.1	16.0	20.3	24.6	28.3	32.9	36.7	41.3
Western Hemisphere	36.6	48.5	60.9	76.5	91.4	116.7	135.8	153.4	181.2	209.3

[1] Excludes data for the People's Republic of China prior to 1977.

Source: *World Economic Outlook* (Washington, D.C.: International Monetary Fund, 1982), Table 30, p. 170.

would in turn pay for themselves through exports to the West). At the end of 1981, these seven "developed" countries owed more than $80 billion to Western governments and banks.

The dimensions of the debt burden can also be measured in terms of the value (cost) of debt service payments, debt-service ratio, ratio of external debt to exports of goods and services, and debt/GDP ratio. The *debt service payments* on the long-term external debt of non-oil developing countries—interest payments and amortizations—increased from $15.3 billion in 1973 to $107.8 billion in 1982. The *debt-service ratio* of non-oil developing countries—interest and amortization on long-term debt as a percentage of exports of goods and services—increased from 14 percent in 1973 to 22.3 percent in 1982. The *ratio of external debt to exports of goods and services* of non-oil developing countries increased from 88.7 percent in 1973 to 109.1 percent in 1982. And the *ratio of external debt to GDP* of non-oil developing countries increased from 16.6 percent in 1973 to 25.2 percent in 1982.[67]

The severity of the debt burden can also be seen in the increasing number of states accumulating arrears on current payments and the increasing number of states that have renegotiated debt over the years. The first indicator shows that the number of states has increased from three in 1974 to twenty-two in 1980 and thirty-two in 1981—and the amount in arrears has risen from about $500 million to $5.5 billion. The second indicator shows no less than sixteen debt renegotiations for nine countries (five for the first time) during the six-year period 1975–1980; in contrast, thirty renegotiations for eleven countries, involving total debt of about $7 billion, took place during the nineteen-year period 1956–1974.[68] Nine member states of IMF sought debt relief in 1981, the largest number of requests in any year since the inception of multilateral debt relief exercises in 1956, suggesting the extent and severity of the proliferating debt burden.

Although the debt burden has spread widely in recent years, the most salient feature of the international debt profile is still its concentration on both the debtor and creditor sides of the coin. On the creditor side, three-fourths of the developing countries' commercial debts are owed to about ten U.S. banks. On the debtor side, a half-dozen NICs (Brazil, Mexico, South Korea, Argentina) account for the lion's share of the total external debt of all developing countries. The modest size and rate of increase for the low-income developing countries' debt is accounted for by their heavier dependence on grants and concessional soft loans from multilateral agencies.

The debt crisis is a function of interaction between country-specific domestic variables and international systemic variables, a chicken-and-egg conundrum defying easy separation of causes and effects. A country's external debt represents a commitment/capability imbalance, an imbalance (debt) that can be greatly increased and exacerbated by unforeseen and unexpected systemic trends. For non-oil developing countries the dawn of an era of high energy and food prices necessitated high borrowing to relieve the crushing burden of high oil prices. In 1981, current account balances of oil-exporting developing countries (a surplus of $96 billion) and non-oil developing countries (a deficit of $97 billion) almost cancelled each other out.

The recycling of the petrodollar in the latter half of the 1970s has caused a dramatic shift in the flow of loans from public to private sources. Although the low-income oil-importing countries have continued to borrow from bilateral and multilateral official sources, the middle-income oil-importing countries have switched from official to private creditors. By 1980, private creditors accounted for almost three-quarters of the total outstanding debt. The greater reliance on private commercial borrowing has meant a hardening of the terms of the debt because loans extended by private creditors are of shorter maturities and higher interest rates than their official counterparts. Each percentage-point rise in interest rates adds an estimated $2 billion to the developing countries' annual debt bill. For the non-oil developing countries both amortization payments and interest charges have risen much faster than export earnings since the mid-1970s.

Under the combined pressures of the deteriorating terms of trade (for commodities) and the deteriorating terms of debt, more and more countries are falling into the debt trap, borrowing not for developmental purposes but to refinance past loans at ever-rising interest rates and ever-shortening debt maturities. This is reminiscent of the international politics of debt-management in the 1920s, when money merely shifted from one building to another in Washington, D.C., instead of being used for the reconstruction and rehabilitation of war-torn European economies.

The towering edifice of the international capital market stands on the sandy foundation of loans rolling over loans. Formal default has been avoided by simply postponing or rescheduling debt obligations. At the same time, the debt crisis has sharply increased the Third World's dependency on the World Bank and the IMF. The World Bank's lending increased from $3.4 billion in 1973 to $13 billion in 1982. Against the background of the global debt crisis, the World Bank reported in March 1983 the record earnings of $448 million in the first half of its fiscal year (July 1982–June 1983), or $200 million higher than its fiscal year 1981–1982.[69] The IMF responded to the debt crisis by increasing its quotas (lendable resources) by 47.4 percent, from $66 billion to $98.5 billion—with the full support of the Reagan administration. Thus the first major wave of the postwar global debt crisis was "managed" by sharply increasing the control and leverage of the international financial and monetary institutions and the dependency of the Third World.

Two Normative Principles of Distributive Justice

The question of justice is both elusive and essential in world politics. It is elusive because of the self-fulfilling pessimism about establishing transnational justice in a multicultural world. It is essential because an approximate consensus on social justice is a necessary, although by no means sufficient, condition for rectifying global inequities. The elusiveness of justice in world politics stems in part from the disagreement on the nature and dynamics of international society. Hedley Bull's argument that present world conditions allow only international justice to play a leading role, with a smaller role for human justice and no role for cosmopolitan justice—or Adda Bozeman's dismissal of any normative quest for a trans-culturally valid and viable world order system, given the tenacity of diverse and multicultural systems of public order throughout the world—is based on the static "realist" assumption about the immutable nature and conditions of politics beyond national borders.[70] The essentiality of justice arises in a context of growing social concern for human well-being in world politics today.

Although John Rawls's theory of justice stops at the water's edge, having little to say about interstate relations, it may be used as a point of departure.[71] Rawls sees "social justice" primarily in terms of "the basic structure of society, or more exactly, the way in which the major social institutions distribute fundamental rights and duties and determine the division of advantages from social cooperation."[72] From this premise Rawls presents two principles of justice: "First: each person is to have an equal right to the most extensive basic liberty compatible with a similar liberty for others. Second: social and economic inequities are to be arranged so that they are both (a) reasonably expected to be to everyone's advantage, and (b) attached to positions and offices open to all."[73] The quest for a more just and equitable world economic order can start with Rawls's second principle of distributive justice concerning how social and economic inequities in the world can be rearranged to maximize advantages and minimize disadvantage for the largest number of people—in Rawls's own words, "so that everyone benefits." Rawls's second principle does not require an exactly equal distribution of wealth and authority; it does require that all inequalities improve the prospects of the least advantaged.

As noted earlier, the multiple crises of the global political economy in the 1970s stimulated the mushrooming of a hundred schools of thought and contending global models. From the cacophonous symphony of global modelling we can easily discern two dominant themes (normative principles) of distributive justice around which all global models pivot—the NIEO principle and the Basic Human Needs (BHN) principle. In this section I will examine the defining characteristics and the problematic features of these two alternative principles and suggest a possible way of reconciling and linking the two principles for world order studies.

The NIEO Principle

The national dimensions of global inequities sketched out earlier in the chapter provided a backdrop for the official inauguration of the NIEO at the Sixth Special Session of the UN General Assembly in 1974. Although some of the principles, norms, demands, and strategies embodied in the NIEO had already been advanced by the Third World through UNCTAD and the Non-Aligned Movement in the 1960s and early 1970s, the General

Assembly provided the official imprimatur by passing three historical resolutions: a Declaration on the Establishment of a New International Economic Order; a Programme of Action on the Establishment of a New International Economic Order; and the Charter of Economic Rights and Duties of States.[74]

Together the three resolutions provide the conceptual and normative pillars, or "the foundations of the new international economic order," according to UNCTAD.[75] The declaration outlines seven broad principles of a general and declaratory nature; the programme of action is concerned with the structural problems of the world economic system as they affect the developing countries, and recommends specific reforms to deal with the immediate world economic crisis; and the charter adds to the declaration and programme a set of norms for the behavior of states in their international economic relations.

The Seventh Special Session of the General Assembly, which was originally scheduled to formulate the NIEO conceptual framework, instead spelled out broad implementation guidelines for all the appropriate organs and agencies of the United Nations system. Proceeding on the twin assumptions that the three historic documents had already established the conceptual foundations, and that the overall objective of the NIEO is to increase the capacity of developing countries, individually and collectively, to pursue their development, the resolution called for many specific policy measures bearing on trade, transfer of resources, reform of international financial and monetary institutions, science and technology, food and agriculture, cooperation among developing countries, and restructuring of the development sectors of the United Nations system.[76]

As a collective consensual package, the NIEO defies easy generalization. Nonetheless, all the grievances and demands embodied in the package—and the obstacles and oppositions put up by the political and corporate managers of the global political economy—can be reduced to one overall proposition: the transformation of international economic regimes that affect the transnational movement of goods and services. Economic regime transformation is believed to be a prerequisite to the enhancement of Third World economic well-being and political control. The NIEO sums up the Third World's concept of a more just and equitable world order in contemporary global politics. It may also be regarded as an internationalization of the Rawlsian second principle of transforming the existing international economic order to distribute the dividends of international socioeconomic cooperation more fairly and equally.

How can this be done? What are the specific strategies for transforming the international economic regimes? On this question the NIEO employs a strange mixture of *dependencia* theory in its diagnosis and of postwar liberal economics in its prescription. The logic of *dependencia* theory calls for a dissociative/delinkage strategy of self-reliance as a first step to the long-term transformation of the capitalist world economy. The logic of liberal economics calls for an associative/linkage strategy of integration into

the world economy based on the principle of the international division
of labor and comparative advantage.

The mainstream NIEO diagnosis closely follows the central argument
of Raul Prebisch, one of the pioneers of *dependencia* theory and the first
Secretary-General of UNCTAD, that the dominant-dependent, Center-
Periphery, and developed-underdeveloped relationship is sustained through
the exchange of unequal values and the long-term deterioration in terms
of trade for the Periphery. Although embracing this *dependencia* theory in
its diagnosis, the NIEO package proposes a hybrid collection of policy
options and strategies designed to overcome dependency and underdevelopment through more of the same. Although there is some ambivalence
between associative/linkage and dissociative/delinkage strategies, the dominant theme is a fuller integration of the developing countries into the
capitalist world economy—the growth-maximizing and trickle-down strategy
of development and modernization. The hidden assumption is that the
way to survive in the neo-Darwinian jungle of the global political economy,
dominated by capitalist robbers and barons, is to join and compete on an
improved footing, or even beat them at their own game.

The central demands of the NIEO—improving the terms of trade for
the primary commodities, increasing the transfer of resources and technology,
reforming international financial and monetary institutions, and greater
participatory democracy in the management of the global political economy—are all designed to reduce interstate inequalities in all key sectors
of the world economy. The aim is to enable the Third World to capture
its share of the world markets and its share of global resources and dividends.
The insertion of such dissociative norms as individual and collective self-
reliance and permanent and inalienable resource sovereignty of each nation
is due in part to the Chinese influence during the inauguration phase of
the NIEO.[77]

The dominance of linkage strategies in the NIEO has been made clear
by Gamani Corea, who as Secretary-General of UNCTAD played an
instrumental role in the formulation of the NIEO: "I am of the opinion
that the underlying desire, indeed demand, of all is that the countries of
the Third World be incorporated into the system of world-wide trade.
They do not any longer want to remain at the margin or outside of this
system. They want to belong to it and to participate in the decisions and
events that influence its development."[78] A content analysis of the NIEO
declaration also shows a predominance of associative/linkage norms and
concepts (cooperation, interdependence, etc.), compared with dissociative
norms and concepts (sovereignty, self-determination, self-reliance, etc.): the
former occur seventy-nine times and the latter occur only nineteen times.[79]

The NIEO thus approaches the problem of distributive justice at the
macro global level through a highly simplified bifurcation of humanity
into the developed Northern countries and the developing Southern
countries. It attempts to transform the principles, norms, rules, and decisionmaking mechanisms governing international economic regimes to enable

the South to improve its terms of trade and close the development gap. It assumes that the benefits and dividends of this growth strategy would trickle down within each developing country. The normative principle of distributive justice embodied in the NIEO is one of *interstate* justice. The NIEO does not challenge the state-centric paradigm but merely criticizes the existing (postwar) liberal economic order.

The NIEO as the normative principle of distributive justice runs into some serious moral and philosophical difficulties. Even if the principle of international redistributive justice is accepted, it cannot be expected to play a dominant role in a highly competitive system of sovereign states. Interstate justice, unless translated into human justice, is a legal abstraction devoid of moral weight. After all, the state is—or at least is supposed to be—a servant of human interests. In spite of rampant abuse of this philosophical axiom, there is universal normative consensus on the *instrumental* value of the state. For centuries the principles of justice in political and philosophical discourse have been concerned primarily with the treatment of individuals rather than states, the most conspicuous exception being the *jus ad bellum* and *jus in bello* debate.

The extent to which the principle of interstate redistributive justice can contribute to the enhancement of human dignity and justice or, in Rawlsian terms, to the improvement of the prospects of the worst-off is questionable. Although the evidence is far from conclusive, several recent studies show that the growth-maximizing strategy, unless accompanied by a social policy of distributive justice, generally contributes to growing income inequalities and, in some cases, absolute declines in the disposable incomes of the bottom 40 to 60 percentile of households. "Not only is there no automatic trickle-down of the benefits of development;" observes Irma Adelman, "on the contrary, the development process leads typically to a trickle-up in favor of the middle classes and the rich."[80] On the other hand, sufficient empirical evidence exists to show that the BHN strategy enhances rather than hinders increased economic productivity.[81]

Unless or until an empirical nexus between interstate and human justice is established, the NIEO's moral foundation is constantly eroded by the repeated argument of anti-NIEO reactionaries in the North that there is no compelling moral or political reason for asking the poor in the rich countries to give up their share of welfare pie to fatten the rich in the poor countries. Ali Mazrui offers a most cogent Third World rebuttal: "Those who claim that the workers of Detroit should not be forced to subsidize the ruling elite of Kenya or Zaire are, unfortunately, the same ones who would be alarmed by the ruling elites of Kenya and Zaire going socialist. Salvador Allende paid with his life not because he was getting too elitist but because he was trying to transcend economic elitism in Chile."[82]

Mazrui's argument goes a long way in cutting through the anti-NIEO cant, yet the unresolved political and moral problem of disjuncture between interstate and human justice remains. The transformation of socioeconomic structure at the global level, unaccompanied by the transformation of socioeconomic structure at the national level, can hardly go beyond a restructuring of status rankings among the state elites. Even Mahbub ul Haq, one of the most articulate and consistent Third World supporters of the NIEO, had to concede: "Many developing countries did not sufficiently realize that internal reforms were even more important than international reforms for the welfare of their people. Some of them started viewing the NIEO as a 'soft' option, as an alternative to hard decisions to restructure internal order. Lack of progress on the NIEO became an alibi for explaining a variety of economic sins at home."[83]

The BHN Principle

Rawls's second principle (also called the "difference principle"), is even more congenial to the BHN conception of distributive justice. Viewed from the perspective of the Rawlsian difference principle, the NIEO is a somewhat forced extension beyond the borders of national society. The BHN is instead safely on home turf with its principal concern for the absolute poverty (and concomitant basic human needs deficiencies) of the least advantaged. The Rawlsian difference principle may be reformulated as the normative principle of distributive justice primarily concerned with the basic human needs of the worst-off group within each human society.

Although the BHN is firmly rooted in all the great humanitarian and religious traditions, it was not until the 1970s that a BHN conception of distributive justice entered the agenda of global developmental politics. The term "basic human needs" strategy received worldwide currency in the wake of the 1976 ILO World Employment Conference. Yet a needs-based notion of socioeconomic justice had earlier been recognized and incorporated in a number of international human rights covenants. The Universal Declaration of Human Rights (adopted and proclaimed by the General Assembly on December 10, 1948) stipulates in Article 25: "Everyone has the right to a standard of living adequate for the health and well-being of himself and of his family, including food, clothing, housing and medical care and necessary social services, and the right to security in the event of unemployment, sickness disability, widowhood, old age or other lack of livelihood in circumstances beyond his control." The International Covenant on Economic, Social and Cultural Rights (adopted on December 16, 1966 and entered into force as of January 3, 1976) specifies and elaborates the key components of a needs-based conception of justice in the peremptory language of legal obligations. Article 11 stipulates: "The States Parties to the present Covenant recognize the right of everyone to an adequate standard of living for himself and his family, including adequate food, clothing and housing, and to the continuous improvement of living conditions."

In the early 1970s, the increasing recognition that the growth-maximizing strategy leaves absolute poverty untouched gave rise to the BHN as an alternative principle of distributive justice. Perhaps the most trenchant reformulation of "development" along BHN lines is found in the Cocoyoc Declaration, adopted by the expert participants (serving in their individual capacities) of the UNEP/UNCTAD Symposium On Pattern of Resource Use, Environment and Development Strategies held at Cocoyoc, Mexico, October 8–12, 1974.[84] The declaration rejects the notion of "growth first, justice in the distribution of benefits later." The whole purpose of development "should not be to develop things but to develop man." "Human beings have basic needs: food, shelter, clothing, health, education. Any process of growth that does not lead to their fulfillment—or, even worse, disrupts them—is a travesty of the idea of development." Yet the declaration goes beyond the satisfaction of basic needs, stating:

> There are other needs, other goals, and other values. Development includes freedom of expression and impression, the right to give and to receive ideas and stimulus. There is a deep social need to participate in shaping the basis of one's own existence, and to make some contribution to the fashioning of the world's future. Above all, development includes the right to work, by which we mean not simply having a job but finding self-realization in work, the right not to be alienated through production processes that use human beings simply as tools.[85]

Despite the *initial* IGO sponsorship of the symposium, the Cocoyoc Declaration may be regarded as a NGO product. As we will note in Chapter 7, the alternative, system-transforming vision and the strategy of self-reliance embodied in the declaration were vehemently attacked by Western governmental representatives in UNEP, revealing in the process the structural constraints and limits of interaction between IGOs and NGOs in contemporary global politics. The exact formulation of self-reliance in the declaration is worth noting: "The ideal we need is a harmonized cooperative world in which each part is a center, living at the expense of nobody else, in partnership with nature and in solidarity with future generations."[86]

Two other NGO system-transforming global models—*What Now—Another Development*, prepared in the fall of 1975 by the Dag Hammarskjöld Foundation, and *Catastrophe or New Society?* prepared by the Bariloche Foundation as a Latin American/Third World response to the Club of Rome's *Limits to Growth*—deserve to be mentioned for their contribution to the formulation of the BHN.

"The existing 'order' is coming apart and rightly so," the Dag Hammarskjöld report observes, "since it has failed to meet the needs of the vast majority of peoples and reserved its benefits for a privileged minority." The key to the process of struggle and transformation is "another development" of endogenous, self-reliant growth, which calls for the satisfaction of human needs, the strengthening of Third World capacity for self-reliant development, the reorientation of science and technology, and the transformation of existing social, economic and political structures in the world today.[87] Based on the assumption that another development "is geared to the satisfaction of needs, beginning with the eradication of poverty," the report identifies both material (survival) needs and nonmaterial (psychological and political) needs in mutually complementary terms, but argues at the same time that the two kinds of needs "form a hierarchy insofar as the satisfaction of survival needs obviously determines the possibility of satisfying the others."[88]

The Bariloche global model accepts the BHN as the normative principle of Third World development and then examines the possibility of satisfying the basic needs of the world's population without endangering the environment or exhausting natural and physical resources. Relying on mathematical models that set specific targets for food, housing, education, and health, the model concludes that sociopolitical obstacles, *not* the finiteness of resources, would present the major barriers to satisfying basic human needs. The alternative vision of the model can be realized only if the present global political economy is transformed into an egalitarian system: "The final goal is *an egalitarian society, at both the national and international levels.* Its basic principle is the recognition that each human being, simply because of his existence, has inalienable rights regarding the satisfaction of basic needs—nutrition, housing, health, education—that are essential for complete and active incorporation into his culture."[89]

The significance of the 1976 ILO World Employment Conference lies not so much in its formulation as in its catalytic role in making a needs-based conception of development the centerpiece of a global intergovernmental conference. Its concluding resolution states that the promotion of employment and the satisfaction of the basic needs of each country should receive top priority, and then divides "basic needs" into two categories: *personal needs,* defined in terms of minimum requirements of a family for private consumption (adequate food, shelter, clothing, household equipment), and *communal needs,* defined in terms of essential services for the community at large (safe drinking water, sanitation, public transport and health, educational and cultural facilities).[90]

Although there are a number of variations on the theme of the BHN, the dominant characteristics of this needs-based conception of distributive justice can be summarized as follows. The BHN redefines development in *human* terms. Economic growth is seen as a means to serve human interests, especially the basic needs of the poorest groups of people—not as an end in itself. The BHN defines development in terms of improving income-earning opportunities for the poor as well as establishing public social services (primary health care, primary education, employment) that reach the poor. The logic of the BHN calls for social transformation.

Table 5.4 sums up the defining and differentiating characteristics of the *dominant* NIEO and BHN principles in comparative terms. If the NIEO is the growth-maximizing strategy of development, the BHN is the poverty-minimizing (and basic needs-satisfying) strategy of development. If the NIEO follows the normative principle of interstate justice, attempting to transform sociopolitical structure at the international level, the BHN follows the normative principle of human justice, attempting to transform socio-

TABLE 5.4
Comparison between the NIEO and the BHN in Key Categories

CATEGORY	NIEO	BHN
Distributive Justice	Interstate	Human
Development Strategy	Maximizing Growth	Minimizing Poverty
Normative Targets	Terms of Trade; GNP Growth; Per Capita GNP Growth; Resource Transfer	Food; Shelter; Water; Primary Health Care; Education; Employment
Institutional Targets	International Structure	Domestic Structure (and International Structure)
Level of Analysis	Macro-level	Micro-level
Development Bias	Industrialization; Export-Oriented Growth	Rural Development; Self-Reliance
IGO Advocates	UNCTAD; Group of 77	ILO; World Bank; WHO
NGO Advocates	RIO; Brandt Commission	ODC; Bariloche Model; *What Now*; Cocoyoc Declaration
Problems	An Instrument of Status Drive; Uneven Distribution of Benefits	Anti-NIEO Diversionary Tactics; Co-optation Device; Pacifying Welfare Program
Linkage with the World Economy	Fuller Integration North-South Linkage	Delinkage; Individual and Collective Self-Reliance; South-South Trade

political structure at the intranational level. The dominant spirit and strategy of the NIEO is fuller integration of the developing countries into the world economy to overcome underdevelopment; the dominant spirit and strategy of the BHN is another development of endogenous self-reliance to break the bonds of external dependency. The NIEO sees developmental causation and consequence flowing downward; the BHN sees them flowing upward.

The main opposition to the BHN needs-based principle of distributive justice has come from the Group of 77 and from many Third World supporters of the NIEO. Far from being a moral or humanitarian principle of distributive justice, the BHN strategy is criticized as a morally deceptive alternative to triage or as a diversionary device to derail the NIEO from the track of regime transformation. In short, the BHN is regarded as a preemptive strike designed to demolish the NIEO and dampen the economic growth of the Third World.

Unfortunately, this attack is plausible for several reasons. Although a needs-based conception of distributive justice actually predates the official inauguration of the NIEO in 1974, an internationalization of the BHN *followed* the opening salvos of NIEO politics. Many people trace the official inauguration of the BHN principle to the 1976 ILO World Employment Conference. The BHN is also plagued with guilt-by-association, as many anti-NIEO system maintainers—the World Bank, the U.S. Congress, and OECD—have given their rhetorical blessing to the BHN strategy since the mid-1970s. However, neither the direction nor the levels of official development assistance (ODA), in the 1970s provide any substance to the Northern ideological support of the BHN.

In an age of rampant statism, the BHN principle of human justice strikes hard on the sensitive political nerves of Third World elites. A needs-based strategy of development, especially one advanced by the geopolitical and corporate managers of the global political economy, is perceived as a neocolonial Trojan Horse designed to legitimize the political intervention of hegemonic powers or of TNCs eager to expand their networks of global "interdependence," all contrary to the code of behavioral norms specified in the Charter of Economic Rights and Duties of States.

Actually, the NIEO/BHN conflict is not as severe as the dominant proponents of both have made it out to be. The dominant NIEO critique of the BHN is valid only when applied to the dominant but shallow version of the BHN advanced by system maintainers.[91] The most problematic feature of the latter is its apolitical functionalist posture, which rejects Kwame Nkrumah's famous advice: "Seek ye first the political kingdom." Unless informed and guided by the populist values of mass participation, self-reliance, and human dignity and equality, the BHN strategy risks becoming a cooptive pacification program or a self-perpetuating welfare program. To concentrate solely and exclusively on alleviating absolute poverty without system transformation may be morally and functionally appealing, but there is no historical and empirical reason to assume that necessary shifts in the redistribution of social goods can really come about—or be sustained for long—without transforming the distribution of ownership and the organization of production.

The Northern establishment versions of the BHN avoid the question of system change (except to pay lip service to necessary *domestic* reforms), but the two NGO system-transforming global models—the "another development" model of the Dag Hammarskjöld Foundation and the Bariloche model—come to terms with this central political issue, advocating system change at both the national and international levels as an integral part of the BHN development strategy. From a world order perspective, then, these two models of "another development," largely ignored or attacked by the mainstream proponents of the NIEO and the BHN, combine the desirable features of the two normative principles of distributive justice.

International Response

The quest for an alternative system-transforming model presupposes normative and structural anachronism in the present world order. It also presupposes the system's inability to enhance human dignity and justice and minimize global inequities. Such presuppositions are always informed by untestable values, to be sure, but they are also informed by emerging global realities that are amenable to analysis. In pursuit of such "normative inquiry," I will briefly examine the NIEO movement since its inception (1975-1982) as well as analyzing the performance of two international economic regimes as examples of systemic constraints and opportunities. The twin phenomena of globalization and specialization in the interstate movement of goods have rendered the question of "Who governs by what values within what setting?" more urgent but also more elusive.

Whatever Happened to the NIEO?

There is general agreement today among both the proponents and opponents that the NIEO is in disarray, if not already dead. Reflecting upon the collapse of the Eleventh Special Session of the UN General Assembly, convened in September 1980 to rejuvenate global negotiations for the NIEO, Mahbub ul Haq characterized NIEO politics as "this strange environment of formal motions without actual movement."[92] His argument is certainly justified if we measure NIEO progress ("actual movement") in terms of actual improvement of the economic status and conditions of the developing countries, especially non-oil developing countries. From 1975 (the year the NIEO shifted from its inaugural to its implementation phases) to 1981 (the latest year for available statistics), for example, the financial situation of all non-oil developing countries deteriorated as measured by all the key indicators of international economic life.

The Third World's NIEO politics is not, however, a complete failure. The Third World's most noticeable achievement in contemporary global politics, as noted in Chapter 2, is its discovery and exercise of normative power. By exercising its aggregate voting power and by mobilizing its normative power, the Third World has succeeded in transforming the agenda of all international organizations, forcing the North on the defensive. The significance of this hidden face of power was formulated by Peter Bachrach and Morton S. Baratz as follows:

> Of course power is exercised when A participates in the making of decisions that affect B. But power is also exercised when A devotes his energies to creating or reinforcing social and political values and institutional practices that limit the scope of the political process to public consideration of only those issues which are comparatively innocuous to A. To the extent that A succeeds in doing this, B is prevented, for all practical purposes, from bringing to the fore any issues that might in their resolution be seriously detrimental to A's set of preferences.[93]

Although a strong argument can be made that the Third World has indeed legitimized its NIEO claims by transforming the agenda of global development politics, the tangible fruits of NIEO politics measured in structural or institutional terms have been extremely meagre—the International Fund for Agricultural Development (IFAD) and a much diluted regime for ten core commodities. From the beginning, the hidden agenda of the NIEO was a restructuring of power relationships in the management of the global political economy. How can we account for the current disjuncture between normative progress and structural standstill in NIEO politics?

The NIEO can be defined dialectically as a conflict formation/resolution process at the global level, involving both the issues and the parties (actors). On the one hand is the South (the Third World) as the injured plaintiff challenging the existing normative order. On the other hand is the North (the First and Second Worlds), responding to this challenge. However, what really complicates the NIEO in both the inaugural (conceptual) and implementation (negotiating) phases is the further fragmentation of North-South polarity into five major global actors—the Group of 77, China, the United States, Western Europe/Japan, and the Soviet bloc, with each redefining the NIEO in its own image and changing economic interests. Whatever measure of consensus is achieved during the norm-setting phase runs into the familiar shoals and reefs of fragmentation and statism during negotiations.

As the chief architect of the postwar economic order and as its richest and most powerful participant, the United States rejected from the beginning the basic premise of the *new* economic order, regarding the NIEO as the product of a tyrannical majority in the United Nations. Responding to the passage of the NIEO Declaration and Programme of Action by consensus, U.S. representative John Scali stated: "We are—I must confess—disappointed that it was not possible to emerge from our deliberations with unanimous agreement on how these problems can best be solved. . . . We seriously question what value there is in adopting statements on difficult and controversial questions that represent the views of only one faction."[94]

In the wake of the NIEO inauguration phase, the U.S. government had some second thoughts. The forces of the neoconservative school, exemplified by *The Wall Street Journal* and *Commentary*, championed a major counter-offensive in "the New Cold War," while the liberals advised a united Trilateral strategy of case-by-case accommodation—actually a strategy of "divide and rule" or "divide and demolish"—to meet the "Threat from the Third World."[95] Bergsten's warning of the threat from the Third World—cartelization by primary commodity producers, takeovers of TNCs, and repudiation of debt obligations—seemed real enough in the mid-1970s, and the U.S. government accordingly assumed a conciliatory and accommodating posture at the 1975 Seventh Special Session to divide and diffuse this threat.

It soon became clear to U.S. policymakers that the threat from the Third World was only a paper tiger. Far from becoming a vanguard transformation model, OPEC refused to link oil to the NIEO, dealing a lethal blow to the Third World. The petrodollar surplus, instead of being used to create price support arrangements for other commodities, has actually been recycled or invested in European and U.S. commercial banks. In addition, Saudi Arabia became a *de facto* partner in Cold War II. With the unexpected convergence of geoeconomic and geopolitical interests between OPEC (or at least its most powerful member state) and core capitalism, the balance of power has decisively shifted from the system transformers to the system maintainers.

With the threat from the Third World thus divided and diffused—and with the twin threats of no growth and high unemployment in their own borders—the Trilateral countries in general and the United States in particular have hardened their anti-NIEO posture, as evidenced in the declarations of the annual economic summit conference of the seven Trilateral countries. The 1975 Rambouillet Declaration, drafted during the heyday of the NIEO, stressed the importance of continued economic growth and the need for North-South cooperation, but the 1978 Bonn Declaration quietly buried North-South relations. The 1980 Venice Declaration, although silent on the Brandt Commission report, advanced a new "divide and rule" formula, proposing that the burden of helping developing countries be equally shared by the trio of the OPEC, OECD, and industrialized communist countries.

The deadlock of the eleventh Special Session is another recent testimonial to the current disarray of NIEO politics. The North in general and the United States in particular has shifted the focus of NIEO politics from system transformation to partial and palliative accommodation. The session bogged down in conflict over the forum in which global negotiations should take place and over the mechanisms for implementing any eventual agreements. The Third World advocated an integrated and central approach through the United Nations, linking policy measures in several sectors; the United States, the United Kingdom, and West Germany insisted on a decentralized approach through the specialized agencies and on the continued compartmentalization of negotiations along sectoral lines.[96] This represents more than a procedural dispute. The bottom line of the successful Northern strategy was to shield the World Bank and IMF, the last stronghold of anti-NIEO resistance, from the "tyrannical majority" of the South. This hard-line strategy of system maintainance had already been adopted by the Carter administration, staffed by the "liberal Trilateralists."

The "support" of the OECD countries for the NIEO can be explained by enlightened self-interest. The large industrialized countries, especially West Germany and Great Britian, have given moral support to the NIEO while often taking refuge behind the stonewalling position of the United States,[97] but the small industrialized Nordic countries have firmly and consistently supported the Third World demands. In the negotiations on the Integrated Programme for Commodities, this support proved sufficient to isolate and outweigh the attempts of the other industrialized countries to block regime change.⁹⁸ However, the recycling of petrodollars to Western Europe for investment or arms purchases has adjusted the balance of OPEC/OECD interdependence with a corresponding dampening of European support for the NIEO. As the interfuture report (the original OECD report on global economic problems) states: "These countries have gradually come to realize that their own development depends upon the prosperity of the OECD countries."⁹⁹ Despite, or perhaps because of, the demise of U.S. ideological hegemony in international organizations, the United States still represents the most powerful obstacle to progress by the NIEO.

Whether speaking through its own representatives or through an appointed spokesperson of Group D (the Soviet bloc countries), the Soviet Union has refused to see NIEO in terms of North-South or rich-poor problems. In the Soviet image, the NIEO is basically a new manifestation of the old problem of Western colonialism. Soviet representatives have repeatedly cast the demands of the Third World in terms of a just and legitimate indemnity for Western colonial exploitation of the developing countries. Hence, the Soviet Union—and developed East European countries—cannot be expected to share any responsibility in the compensation process.

In short, the Soviet Union sees the NIEO as a phenomenon of West-South conflict, and has categorically rejected the 0.7 percent ODA target. It was in this vein that the Soviet Union tried—without success and with vigorous Chinese opposition—to strike the word "new" from the NIEO during the inaugural process at the Sixth Special Session of the General Assembly.¹⁰⁰ The Soviet Union was also invited but declined to participate in the Cancun Summit Conference in October 1981. Sensing the growing criticism of its passive, spectator role in NIEO politics, the Soviet bloc has bent its principled stand somewhat by agreeing to contribute 17 percent of the Common Fund's capital in return for only 8 percent of the total vote.¹⁰¹

For Third World countries the NIEO, at the highest conceptual level, was a mixture of moral appeal and revolutionary threat aimed at the structural inequities of the Bretton Woods economic order. Even though the quadrupling of oil prices seriously affected non-oil developing countries, the sudden transformation of the international petroleum regime through cartel formation represented a strategic model for self-assertion. Greater economic disparities among Third World countries themselves strengthened their collective solidarity against core capitalism for a fundamental structural reform in the global political economy.

As the NIEO was shifting from the normative to the negotiating phases, however, the unity of the Third World began to break down. With widening differences in income, growth, sectoral balance, and national development strategy, let alone their entanglement in regional and global geopolitical conflicts, the developing countries' united front in substantive negotiating terms has become increasingly difficult to sustain. OPEC's insistence upon disconnecting its oil pricing policy from the NIEO and the NICs' opposition to debt relief—to protect their creditworthiness and to keep the international arteries of their economic lifeblood open—are two conspicuous examples of fragmentation. At the 1981 Cancun Summit Conference, which was convened to reestablish the North-South dialogue but ended by revealing numerous anomalies and contradictions between and within the global blocs, Brazilian foreign minister Ramiro Elysio Sarairva Guerreiro stated: "The countries of the South have the greatest interest in preserving the stability of the Bretton Woods institutions."[102]

In 1977, Jagdish N. Bhagwati observed that "the developing countries now perceive their own economic and hence political power vis-à-vis the developed countries to be sufficiently substantial to warrant a strategy of effective 'trade unionism' to change the rules of the game and thereby to wrest a greater share of the world's wealth and income."[103] Let us accept this formulation and see what kinds of problems and handicaps have been plaguing the Group of 77 as a Southern trade union opposing Northern industrial management.

The dominant associative/linkage strategy of the NIEO package has diminished the leverage inherent in threatening succession from the global dominance/dependence system. The dissociation of OPEC's oil pricing policy from the NIEO struggle has also considerably weakened the bargaining power of the Southern union. In a sociopsychological sense, too, the cooptation of OPEC has caused a self-fulfilling sense of low efficacy. The increasing differentiation of the member states' economic interests has widened the fissure in the Third World, making it difficult for the Group of 77 to maintain collective unity on substantive issues.

All of this has deprived the Southern trade union of any credible threat to strike. As President Nyere has observed, "hunger-strikes are not the weapon of the starving."[104] The familiar frustrations and predicaments of the financially well-endowed (substantial strike funds) and politically powerful (many votes) trade unions in a time of depression and massive unemployment can also be applied to the problems plaguing the Group of 77 with the onset of worldwide recession in recent years. The Southern trade union has resorted to what Andre Gunder Frank calls "salami tactics."[105] In order to make its demands more palatable to the Northern management— and also in order to gain a measure of credibility—the Southern trade union has begun slicing the NIEO package up little by little, to the point where there is so little salami left that it might cut its own fingers. The NIEO commodity regime, as will be noted later, is a good example of "salami tactics."

Where does this leave China? During the Maoist era the NIEO was seen as part of an inexorable historical process, with the poor and the weak finally rising in a united struggle against the rich and the powerful. It is the Third World—and China has continued to identify itself as a socialist Third World country—that is playing the dominant role in destroying the old and creating the new international economic order; it is the superpowers who are defending the old economic order, persisting in colonialism, imperialism, and hegemony.[106]

During the post-Mao era, especially since the modernization drive was launched in 1978, China's rhetorical support of the NIEO has continued, though in a drastically revised and substantially muted tone.[107] Maoist China's unique principled stand on developmental issues in support of the global underdogs (the Third World) rather than in support of its own interests has been replaced by a more "realistic" redefinition of NIEO politics in terms compatible with the perceived requirements of national interests.

The two bête noires—global interdependence and division of labor and specialization—are no longer feared or attacked. Instead, they have now been redefined and functionally linked as integral parts of the modernization drive. A quantitative content analysis of the articles published in *Hongqi* {Red Flag} and *Beijing Review* between January 1977 and December 1981 shows the extent to which self-reliance has been rethought in all of its crucial dimensions: (1) the superiority of division of labor and specialization in production over an all-around, balanced, and self-reliant development; (2) the deepening and inevitable trend of international interdependence in world economic development; and (3) the downgrading of China's role in the transformation of the capitalist world economy.[108]

The triumph of Dengist "realism" in the post-Mao era leads to China's accepting—and adjusting to—systemic constraints and opportunities. China's tilt toward the Trilateral axis apparently represents an answer to the key foreign policy question of how to *maximize* external inputs—foreign capital, investment, joint ventures, technology, management techniques, concessional aid, most-favored-nation clauses, and preferential trade treatment under the Generalized System of Preferences (GSP)—and *minimize* defense costs by forming a broad united (Trilateral) front against the Soviet Union. One close observer of Chinese politics has argued that "the contemporary Chinese contradiction is just another ordinary consequence of the inevitable national egoism–global ethics contradiction which affects all nations" and "to end one's perceived victimization, one becomes complicitous with robbers."[109]

The Global Political Food Economy

The steady globalization of international relations in our century, especially since the end of World War II, is no less evident in the political economy of food. The transition from subsistence agriculture to a domestic division of labor and specialization, which started in the wake of the Industrial Revolution, has become global with the expansion of the capitalist world economy. The so-called global food regime is an integral part of this capitalist expansion, although it does have its own commodity-specific characteristics. The elusiveness of a more just and equitable world food order is embedded in this regime. The systemic limits of international response to world hunger can be determined by closely examining the dominant actors, values, and structures of the global food regime that affect the production, distribution, and consumption of food in the world economy.

The global food regime is managed by diffuse networks of private and public as well as national and international organizations. A U.S. Senate report on U.S. participation in the global politics of food listed no less than eighty-nine intergovernmental bodies involved in varying degrees with food issues.[110] The FAO is the most visible, but not the most central, organization in this complex of global food networks. In spite of its global scope and impact, the FAO lacks supranational authority or autonomous control over grain production, stockpiling, trade, or price. International food organizations merely serve as mediators between dominant producers and consumers. Theoretically, international food organizations can modify regime principles and norms—and this is true of IFAD and the World Food Council (WFC), two institutional offsprings of the 1974 World Food Conference—but more often they serve to legitimate the unilateral or bilateral policies and practices of the most powerful actors in the global food economy. The global food regime is a clearinghouse for domestic political food economies and domestic divisions of labor throughout the world.

On the other hand, transnational actors, especially multinational agribusiness corporations (the largest and most numerous are U.S. firms) often act as the "invisible" managers of the regime, playing key roles in the manipulation of supply and demand as well as in the movement of food in the world economy. The decision of the Reagan administration to lift the grain embargo against the Soviet Union in 1981—or, for that matter, its solo veto against adopting a voluntary code of conduct on the promotion of infant formulas—shows that agribusiness interests have sufficient muscle in domestic politics to override or modify the geopolitical and symbolic imperatives of state actors.

Unlike the international politics of arms trade, the food economy is not a focus of rivalry between the two superpowers. The United States has been and continues to be the single dominant actor in the global political economy of food. In 1981, for example, the United States exported about 40 percent of its harvest (163 mmt), earning a record $44.7 billion— sufficient to pay for more than half of its oil imports.

The discrepancy between patterns of global human needs and patterns of global food distribution can be explained by dominance/dependency structures at both national and international levels. It would take only about 36 mmt of grain to abolish world hunger. As Cheryl Christensen put it: "The grain fed to livestock in Western countries is over *six times* the 36 million metric tons needed to directly eliminate global hunger."[111] Yet as long as the skewed distribution of political power and economic wealth remains unchanged, all of the institutional and strategic changes adopted in the wake of the 1972–1974 world food crisis will have little effect.

The structural transformation of the global political economy of food is shown in Table 5.5. Two-thirds of the world's population today produces

TABLE 5.5

The Changing Structure of World Grain Trade: 1934–1938 to 1980 (Numbers in Million Metric Tons)

Region	1934-38	1948-52	1960	1970	1980
North America (U.S. and Canada)	+ 5	+23	+39	+56	+131
Latin America	+ 9	+ 1	0	+ 4	- 10
Western Europe	-24	-22	-25	-30	- 16
Eastern Europe and USSR	+ 5	0	0	0	- 46
Africa	+ 1	0	- 2	- 5	- 15
Asia	+ 2	- 6	-17	-37	- 63
Australia and New Zealand	+ 3	+ 3	+ 6	+12	+ 19

Note: Plus sign indicates net exports; minus sign, net imports.

Source: Lester R. Brown, "World Food Resources and Population: The Narrowing Margin," *Population Bulletin,* Vol. 36, No. 3 (Population Reference Bureau, Inc., Washington, D.C., 1981), Table 6. Reprinted with permission.

only one-third of the world's food, showing the extent of global "interdependence." As late as 1970, the Soviet Union was still a net food exporter, but by 1981 it was importing some 43 million metric tons of grain per year. More significantly, the three continents of the Third World moved from the self-sufficient position of surplus exporter to that of dependent importer.

The steady deterioration of the Third World's role in world food production can be partly explained by the two-step resource reallocation at both international and intranational levels. Just as double dependency causes the reallocation of resources from the Periphery to the Center, there is also a domestic transfer of resources from countryside to town, from civilian to miliary sectors, and from the poor majority to the minority powerholders. The low priority given to rural and agricultural development because of an export-oriented strategy is clearly shown in the distribution of national investment for different sectors. It has been estimated that less than 20 percent of national investment for development in poor countries goes to the agricultural sector. In the case of nine Latin American countries, less than 10 percent of all government expenditures have been assigned to agriculture.[112]

The deemphasis of agricultural development inevitably results in higher food imports—the other half of the familiar double dependency. Despite rampant hunger and undernourishment in the countryside, many Third World countries have also shifted from growing food crops for domestic consumption to cash crops (coffee, cocoa, sugar, jute, banana, etc.) for export to wealthy customers abroad. One study shows that approximately half of the agricultural land in Central America and the Caribbean was used to produce cattle and cash crops for export or for a domestic elite rather than basic staple foods in the mid-1970s.[113] Another study estimates that if the land used for cash crops were planted with cereals, it would eliminate all need for cereal imports in Africa and Latin America.[114] Ironically, it is not unusual "to find poor countries caught in a food emergency paying more per bushel to foreign traders than they pay to their own food producers at home."[115] If food crops have become weapons in global structural violence, cash crops have also become weapons in the domestic structural violence of many Third World countries.

Postwar developments have sharpened the Center-Periphery bifurcation in the global political economy of food. The Center, made up of geopolitical and corporate managers at home, their representatives in international food organizations, and TNCs governs the food regime; the food-importing Periphery (at times including the Soviet Union and China) is being governed by the principles and norms of the Center. The structural hallmark of the global food regime is what Thomas Nagel calls "radical inequality," a situation that "exists when the bottom level is one of direct needs, the top level one of great comfort or even luxury, and the total supply is large enough to raise the bottom above the level of extreme need without bringing significant deprivation to those above—specifically, without reducing most people to a place somewhat above the current bottom."[116]

In spite of its low degree of institutionalization, the principles and norms of the global food regime are biased toward those dominant in the production and distribution (exportation) of grain. There is no representation of the poor and the hungry in the global food regime. Instead, the pervasive influence of minority interests determines the allocation of burdens and costs in international food distribution. The dominant political forces that shape the norms of the food regime are unilateral or bilateral rather than supranational or multilateral. The food regime is guided by the U.S. image of a world food order, and is dominated by the corporate and geopolitical imperatives of *pax Americana* rather than the nutritional needs of the poor and the hungry.

Donald J. Puchala and Raymond F. Hopkins identified eight dominant norms in the global food regime: (1) respect for a free international market; (2) national absorption of adjustments imposed by international markets; (3) qualified acceptance of extramarket channels of food distribution; (4) avoidance of starvation; (5) the free flow of scientific and crop information; (6) low priority for national self-reliance; (7) national sovereignty and the illegitimacy of external penetration; and (8) low concern about chronic hunger.[117] If we compare these eight norms to four food values—equity, efficiency, security, and autonomy—it becomes clear that the dominant laissez-faire market orientation allows agricultural goods to move from those who produce and sell them to those who can afford to buy them. The world's hungry are concentrated in the Third World, but the Soviet Union, Japan, and China preempt the lion's share of global food imports. In 1980, South Korea and Taiwan—with a combined population of only 54 million—

imported more grain (9.4 mmt) than all of the low-income countries with their combined population of 1.3 billion.[118] The global food regime has a hierarchy of values, with market-guided "efficiency" on top. Needs-based and transformative "equity" and "autonomy" (self-reliance) came last, with "security" occupying an intermediate position.

The 1974 World Food Conference, held at the time of an unprecedented global food crisis, exposed the deficiencies of the global food regime in all key domains. Wheat prices had increased fourfold from 1972 to 1974, famine and starvation threatened in parts of Africa and Asia, and global grain reserves had declined drastically, falling from 102 days in 1960 to 40 days of the annual consumption requirement in 1974. The conference was also told that only 10 percent of all international aid funds had gone to agriculture during the three previous decades. The stage was set for taking stock of the existing world food order. Declaring that "every man, woman and child has the inalienable right to be free from hunger and malnutrition," the conference passed some twenty substantive resolutions to solve the food problem, including the creation of "world food security" through an, internationally coordinated system of grain reserves that would ensure "the availability at all times of adequate world supplies of basic food-stuffs particularly so as to avoid acute food shortages in the event of widespread crop failures, or other natural disasters, to sustain a steady expansion of food consumption in countries with low levels of per capita intake and offset fluctuations in production and prices."[119]

Not surprisingly, Bangladesh sponsored a proposal for a new World Food Security Council "with powers to intervene in emergencies concerning the world food situation and to take prompt, effective, and timely corrective measures."[120] This proposal was defeated by massive opposition from the OECD countries. In the time-honored tradition, the conference gave birth to two modest institutional offspring: the World Food Council (WFC) and the International Fund for Agricultural Development (IFAD). Acting upon the recommendation of the World Food Conference, the twenty-ninth Session of the General Assembly established a thirty-six-member WFC as an organ of the United Nations designed "to serve as a co-ordinating mechanism to provide over-all, integrated and continuing attention for the successful co-ordination and follow-up of policies concerning food production, nutrition, food security, food trade and food aid, as well as other related matters, by the agencies of the United Nations system."[121]

WFC regards itself as a prime mover in generating the overall political support needed to reverse the trend of growing food deficits and growing hunger in developing regions of the world. It emphasizes the need for structural change in the world food economy, arguing for increased food self-sufficiency within the context of rural and overall development. It challenges what it calls "a liberal food trade regime" in this manner: "In re ' ty, however, all the developed countries follow trade policies involving combinations of controls, taxes and subsidies to protect their domestic food markets."[122] Although the mandate and power of the WFC are unclear, it has assumed the posture of a counterregime, challenging the existing world food order as UNCTAD challenges the GATT-based international trade regime.

IFAD also grew out of the World Food Conference (Resolution XIII), although it was established by another UN-sponsored conference in mid-1976 and became operational in December 1977. WFC played a leading role in IFAD's establishment. Designed as a major new source of financial assistance for food production and agricultural development in the Third World, IFAD started its first period (1978–1980) of operation with special contributions from industrialized ($567 million), OPEC ($435.5 million), and other developing ($20 million) countries. IFAD's negotiations for a new programme (replenishment) of $1.5 billion for the following three years (1981–1983) have been plagued by disagreements over the proportionate shares of OECD and OPEC countries. It was not until January 1982 that an agreement for replenishment of $1.1 billion was reached, with the following distribution: $620 million by OECD countries; $450 million by OPEC countries; and $30 million by the non-oil developing countries. IFAD's governing and funding structure is unique; it is the only UN organization to which the member states of the OECD and OPEC contribute more or less equally but whose decisionmaking power is shared equally among OECD, OPEC, and non-oil developing countries.

Despite the pledge of the 1974 World Food Conference that "within a decade no child will go to bed hungry" and the establishment of WFC and IFAD, the changes of the last eight years have been marginal, designed more to stabilize than to transform the existing regime. Both in absolute numbers and as a percentage of total world population, there are more hungry people in the world today than in 1974. Per capita food production has actually declined in sixty-one developing countries in the 1970s. Observing that "the average African has 10% less food available to him today than 10 years ago," Edouard Saouma, Director-General of the FAO, issued a call in 1980 for a "new world food order."[123] The 66 percent of the FAO's budget spent on maintaining the organization's vast bureaucracy in Rome—only one-third goes to aid the world's needy—is conveniently ignored.

Little progress has been made on the proposed world food security system. In February 1979, negotiations to establish an international grain reserves system collapsed. No new movement is expected, as the Reagan administration is opposed to the concept of international food reserves. As a result, global food reserves against future disasters follow the vagaries of the climate, the fluctuations of the market, and the economic and geopolitical interests of the dominant food producers. As shown in Figure 5.4, the minimum safe level for global food stocks (17 to 18 percent of annual world consumption) was not maintained during most of the 1970s. Only the massive surpluses of Western countries in the early 1980s have pushed world cereal stocks above the minimum safe level, with no appreciable effect on the world's hungry people, however, who are bypassed in international food trade.

FIGURE 5.4
Fluctuations of World Cereal Stocks, 1971-1982

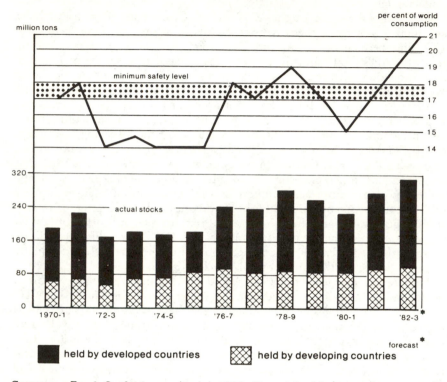

Source: *Food Outlook* as cited in *UN Chronicle* 20 (January 1983), Table A, p. 67.

The minimum food aid target of 10 million tons set by the World Food Conference has not been reached. The Food Aid Convention, signed in 1980 for a one-year period, was later renewed for two more years, although its commitments remained 2 million tons short of the target. Unilateralism and bilateralism remains dominant, with the proportion of total food aid channeled multilaterally actually declining from 17 percent in 1975 to less than 15 percent in 1977.[124] For low-income, food deficient countries, external food aid as a proportion of cereal imports has declined from 28 percent in 1976 to 18 percent in 1981-1982, at the very time when their need increased but their ability to pay decreased.[125]

The size and proportion of multilateral aid for the food sector—the IMF's addition of cereal-import needs as a condition for special help to meet balance-of-payments deficits and the World Bank's funding of food-storage and food-reserve programs, to cite two prominent examples—have increased in the last few years. Still, total food aid shipments of 8–10 mmt fall considerably short of the required 36 mmt to eliminate global hunger.

It was estimated at the time of the 1974 World Food Conference that some $5 billion (at 1972 prices) in annual financial aid was required to help developing countries achieve the agricultural growth rate target of 4 percent a year set for the Second United Nations Development Decade. This estimate, recalculated at $8.3 billion in 1975 prices, has been endorsed in various international meetings. Although official commitments to agriculture did rise from $3.5 billion in 1976 to $5.1 billion in 1978, they fell to $4.9 billion in 1980, 41 percent less than the estimated requirement. FAO's major study, *Agriculture: Toward 2000,* now estimates that the current $4.5–5 billion in aid to Third World agricultural development should be trebled in real terms by 1990 and quadrupled by 2000.

In sum, the structural imbalances and inequities and the growing dependency of developing countries on commercial imports, deplored by the World Food Conference in 1974, have remained largely unchanged. Regime norms have become more sensitive to the basic needs of the poor and rural and agricultural development, multilateral aid to rural development has increased, but the power structure and the managerial rules remain largely unaffected.

The transformation of the global food regime was not central to NIEO politics. Most Third World elites are uncomfortable with the BHN approach, and rich-poor gaps may indeed be wider within the developing countries than between developed and developing countries. The notion that Third World elites have failed to meet basic human needs at home and thus need external assistance leaves a basic moral and practical question unanswered. Can Third World leaders *legitimately* ask the rich North to establish a more just and humane social order without first or at least simultaneously working toward a more just social order within their own borders?

The Global Political Economy of Trade

During the 1950s and 1960s the unprecedented economic growth of core capitalist countries and the unprecedented expansion of international trade marched hand-in-hand. The resulting "demonstration effects" of the Center model for national development generated rising expectations and demands for the Third World. The belief in an export-oriented growth strategy as the only way to "catch up" has become the new religion of international development politics. The Third World's challenge to the postwar economic order was premised on the Center model of trade-development linkage, as symbolized in the creation of the United Nations Conference on Trade and Development (UNCTAD). It was Raul Prebisch, first Secretary-General of UNCTAD, who first advanced trade-based development as the central strategy for the Third World.[126] "All countries commit themselves to an open and expanding trade system to further progress in the liberalization of trade," declares the International Development Strategy for the Third UN Development Decade (1980s), "and to the promotion of structural adjustment which will facilitate the realization of the dynamic pattern of comparative advantage."[127]

The so-called open and liberal world trading order centered on GATT. The dominant principles, norms, rules, and procedures that define the parameters of world trade are coterminous with those of GATT; one could speak of the international trade regime as GATT-centered or GATT-based.[128] The identity of the international trade regime and GATT is demonstrated by UNCTAD's emergence as an alternative platform—an opposition regime, so to speak—for the Third World challenge to the postwar international trading order. Responding to the proposals of the United States, Japan, and the EEC to expand and liberalize international trade through GATT, Salvador Allende declared in his 1972 inaugural address before the third Session of UNCTAD: "The General Agreement on Tariffs and Trade has always been essentially concerned with the interests of the powerful countries; it has no reliable linkage with the United Nations and is not obliged to adhere to its principles, and its membership is at odds with the concept of universal participation."[129]

Since the enactment of the three historic NIEO resolutions and the omnibus resolution on NIEO implementation guidelines, UNCTAD has become the most active forum for the Third World's struggle to transform the GATT-based international trade regime. How viable is this strategy? What are the systemic constraints and opportunities for an effective international response to the repeated Third World demand to change the rules of the trade game?

The GATT-centered international trade regime has a dual personality. The official side is premised on the liberal norms of nondiscrimination, liberalization, and internationalism; the unofficial side is based on the neomercantilist norms of state interventionism, the principle of quid pro quo, and national interest "safeguards" and "escape clauses." The international trade regime has no supranational or independent authority; it acts as a mediator, balancing and reconciling the national/international normative contradictions of its principal actors.

The normative orientation of the regime at any particular time is generally shaped by the distribution of (trade) power among its member states and the associated domestic economic pressures. Even during the heyday of U.S. hegemony, when the regime was relatively more stable, effective, and liberal, there was no such thing as "free trade." Large numbers of national/international as well as economic/geostrategic constraints in the global trade economy led to state intervention or management through tariff and nontariff barriers. As a result, according to one estimate, about two-thirds of world trade is still managed by governments.[130] Free trade serves as a convenient smokescreen behind which "invisible" hands direct the movement of goods. The capitalist world economy may be characterized as a mixture of relatively more bounded trade in agricultural goods and relatively freer trade in manufactured goods.

The international trade regime has reflected the rise and decline of U.S. hegemony in international economic life. Supreme in all aspects of economic power, the United States played the most decisive role in regime creation and expansion. During much of the 1950s and 1960s, regime cohesiveness/ stability was maintained because the United States was able and willing to bear the costs of its hegemonic leadership. In order to keep the regime within the geostrategic bounds of *pax Americana,* for example, the United States not only played a crucial role in Japan's entry into the GATT, but was also willing to "give twice as much by way of scheduled concessions as she received, just as she had done to secure the general agreement in the first place in 1947."[131]

Moreover, the United States managed to persuade Canada, Denmark, Finland, Italy, Norway, and Sweden to make trade concessions to Japan in return for U.S. concessions to them.[132] Japan was regarded as the linchpin of U.S. strategic alliance networks in Asia and had to be kept in line with the U.S. economic embargo against China in the 1950s and 1960s. A revealing contrast is the more recent embrace of China as a *de facto* ally in restoring U.S. hegemony. Even official U.S. support of China's modernization drive is anchored in the hopeful, self-serving assumption that a stronger China would help halt the deteriorating geostrategic position of the United States in a world of rising Soviet challenge and rising Third World rebellion.[133]

By the early 1970s, however, U.S. hegemony as the dominant trading power has disappeared. The United States share of world exports declined from 32 percent in 1947 to 11 percent in 1974 (and to 10.9 percent in 1979). In manufactured exports, West Germany surpassed the United States in 1970 and Japan achieved parity in 1978.[134] Even in agricultural trade U.S. dominance is now challenged by the EEC countries. In the 1970s, the EEC's farm exports rose at a 16.9 percent annual rate, compared to 13.1 percent for the United States. Today, the power structure of the international trade regime rests precariously on the discordant trinity of Japan, Western Europe, and the United States.

As dramatized at the GATT-sponsored world trade conference in late 1982, the major threat of global protectionism emanates from the Big Three, not the Third World. By early 1983 the dispute has escalated to the point where it threatens to ignite a "farm-subsidy war" among the three core capitalists. Under the relentless pressures of well-organized farm groups at home, each is competing to shift the burdens of structural adjustment through neomercantilist protectionist policies. All three, especially the EEC and Japan, are fervent defenders of free trade in manufactured goods but consistently follow agricultural protectionism. The rhetoric of "free trade" cannot hide the fact that annual governmental agricultural subsidies in various forms amount to about $10 billion in Japan, $12.8 billion in the EEC, and $15.4 billion in the United States.[135]

Although tariffs have been cut deeply and progressively in GATT-sponsored multilateral negotiations (most recently in the Tokyo Round completed in 1979), tariff barriers have been replaced by "nontariff barriers," which now cover as much as half of world trade. Having lost its dominant position, the United States is no longer able or willing to bear disproportionate costs in maintaining the trade regime. The pressure the United States is exerting on Japan and the EEC to increase their military budgets and to liberalize their trade policies vis-à-vis the United States is not working because it is perceived as a desperate exercise of hegemonic leadership without the ability and willingness to bear the burden of leadership. The free-trade dogma, as France's Foreign Trade Minister, Michel Jobert, observed at the GATT-sponsored world trade conference in November 1982, is "the most subtle and most disguised form of protectionism—that of the absolute power of the strong over the weak."[136]

In spite of the decline of U.S. hegemony and the considerable stress of intense competition among the Big Three, the international trade regime has not collapsed. Nor has it been transformed. A recent study of the changes in the international regimes for petroleum, trade, and money for the 1967–1977 period concluded that "regime change was most pronounced during the decade in oil and least pronounced in trade in manufactured goods, with the international monetary regime occupying an intermediate position."[137] The changes and trends in the 1970s, as Charles Lipson also concluded, "are best understood as changes *within* the regime, not changes of the regime."[138]

As shown in Figure 5.1, overall trade did not fall in the 1970s. Even the recent drop in the growth rate of world trade caused by the recession and by protectionist measures cannot disguise the fact that trade in manufactures—the centerpiece of the international trade regime—has been growing at a faster rate than that of manufacturing output.[139] At the same time, the developed countries' "dependence" upon the Third World as a source of raw materials and as an export market grows unabated. U.S. materials dependency, defined and measured in terms of minerals and metals for which imports exceed 50 percent of domestic consumption, now extends to columbium, mica (sheet), strontium, titanium (Rutile), manganese, tantalum, cobalt, bauxite and alumina, platinum, chromium, tin, asbestos, nickel, potassium, cadmium, zinc, tungsten, mercury, and gold.[140]

More significantly, the volume of world trade (now over $2 trillion a year) has become increasingly dependent upon the ability of the developing countries to obtain loans to pay for manufactured imports. Every developed country exports from one-third to one-half of its manufactured exports to the developing countries. Almost half of U.S. exports now goes to the Third World, and some 500,000 U.S. jobs could be affected if this trade suffered a significant decline. As noted earlier, the ease with which the IMF arranged in February 1983 to increase its lendable resources also suggests that the dominant actors of the international trade regime cannot afford to let the dependent actors detonate the debt bomb.

Like the nuclear nonproliferation regime, the discriminatory structure of the GATT-based trade regime ensures that the benefits of the "open and liberal" trade system are heavily skewed in favor of its dominant industrialized states. Tariffs on most manufactured goods have been virtually eliminated through successive multinational trade negotiations, but there has been little progress in liberalizing agricultural trade. To change GATT's image as a "rich man's club" and thus to legitimize its status as the global open trade system, the United States and other industrialized countries have recently pursued a strategy of fuller integration of Third World countries into the GATT-based trade regime. It was in this spirit that a special treatment of the developing countries in the form of the Generalized System of Preferences (GSP) was accepted in 1971 as a ten-year GATT waiver and finally incorporated into the Tokyo Round "framework" agreement in 1979. "The generalized system of preferences," states the International Development Strategy for the Third United Nations Development Decade, "should be continued as an important long-term instrument for promoting trade and development co-operation and, in particular, for bringing about an increased share of developing countries in world trade."[141]

At face value, the GSP is a literal violation of the normative principle of nondiscrimination and an acceptance of the long-standing Third World demand for more favorable treatment on a nonreciprocal basis. Along with the normative significance of the GSP, however, its constraints and limitations must also be recognized. First the Tokyo Round "framework" agreement reduced the average worldwide duties on manufactured products by about 33 percent—the Third World accounted for only about 9 percent of world manufacturing output in 1977—while the average duties on developing countries' exports will decline by about 25 percent. It should also be noted that the level of tariffs rises in proportion to the level of commodity processing. Second, the scope of the GSP is greatly limited, as a number of "sensitive" items—such as shoes and textiles—have been excluded as harmful to domestic producers. Third, there are other escape clauses, such as the "competitive need" clause, under which the United States can remove individual commodities from the eligibility list when they achieve a 50 percent domestic market share or an overall quantitative ceiling (about $45.8 million per product in 1980).

Finally, a recent wave of protectionism in the wake of the Tokyo Round has erected numerous nontariff barriers, 70 percent of which fall on processed agricultural goods. These nontariff barriers include: (1) voluntary export restraints (VERs) that offer blanket protection to domestic industries in developed countries; (2) orderly marketing arrangements (OMAs), bilaterally negotiated agreements committing the exporting country to restricted exports; (3) custom valuation involving complex and diverse procedures designed as a means of indirect protection; (4) packaging and marketing requirements that raise the cost of imports; (5) import licensing schemes designed to restrict imports or discriminate in favor of certain suppliers; and (6) direct state subsidies to domestic industries (sometimes referred to as "microprotectionism") unable or unwilling to make necessary structural adjustments. In 1976, before the outbreak of the New Protectionism, only

13 percent of U.S. nonfuel merchandise imports from developing countries ($3.1 billion worth) was covered by the GSP.[142]

Of all the developing countries, only Argentina signed the *procès-verbal* in April 1979, which marked the end of the major part of the Tokyo Round. Subsequently, Third World countries have repeatedly complained in the General Assembly that the Tokyo Round virtually excluded the interests of developing countries, have issued calls for reforming the GATT trade regime, and pleaded for an end to tariff and nontariff barriers to Third World imports.[143]

The 1982 GATT World Trade Conference was distinguished by the U.S. drive to liberalize international trade in services—data processing, banking, insurance, engineering, motion pictures, even the franchising of hamburger restaurants—and by last-ditch bargaining sessions to forestall its collapse. The final compromise papers over basic differences and discords by mentioning trade in services as the next target for liberalization later in the decade. The United States merely won an agreement that GATT's eighty-eight signatories would exchange information and then review whether any multilateral action is "appropriate or desirable."[144]

The Global Political Economy of Commodities

From the beginning of NIEO politics, UNCTAD regarded its proposal for an "Integrated Programme for Commodities" (IPC) as the touchstone of future North-South cooperation. The original proposal had five key components: (1) establishing internationally-owned stocks covering a wide range of primary commodities; (2) establishing a Common Fund for the acquisition of buffer stocks; (3) arranging medium- to long-term commitments to buy and sell commodities at agreed prices; (4) setting up compensatory financing to producers to cover shortfalls in export earnings; and (5) promoting the processing of commodities within the developing countries themselves.

After four years of negotiations and controversies over the size and distribution of financial contributions, operational procedures, and the voting structure, an "Agreement for the Common Fund for Commodities" was adopted on June 27, 1980.[145] The Common Fund has two objectives: to serve as a key instrument in attaining the agreed objectives of the Integrated Programme for Commodities as embodied in Resolution 93 of UNCTAD-IV; and to facilitate the conclusion and functioning of international commodity agreements. The functions of the Common Fund are to contribute to the financing of international buffer stocks, to finance measures in the field of commodities other than stocking, and to promote coordination and consultation on global commodity issues. In carrying out these functions the Common Fund will have two accounts. The First Account of $400 million of directly contributed capital composed of a $1 million membership fee paid by each country and subscribed capital based on an "ability to pay," is designed as a sort of bank to help individual commodity organizations purchase buffer stocks of commodities. The Second

Account of $350 million, coming entirely from voluntary contributions, is designed to serve as an aid organization for commodity research, development and vertical diversification (local processing and marketing).

The Common Fund, as currently envisaged, is substantially scaled down from the original $6 billion that the UNCTAD secretariat originally estimated was needed to finance the buffer stocks of the ten "core" commodities (cocoa, coffee, copper, cotton, hard fibers, jute and jute products, rubber, sugar, tea, and tin). It may be characterized as a "pooling scheme" sought by the industrialized countries, giving up the original ideas of broad economic restructuring. As such, it is a breakthrough of sorts for the North and a defeat for the South. The compromise voting structure, which establishes a rough parity between North and South, may well prove to be a recipe for stalemating the decisionmaking process. Even this parity was considered insufficient to ensure Northern interests as the agreement embodied the use of a "qualified majority" (meaning at least two-thirds of all votes cast) and a "highly qualified majority" (meaning at least three-fourths of all votes cast) for the most important decisions.

This agreement exemplifies the Southern resort to "salami tactics." The Group of 77's consent to such a diluted commodity regime highlights the central dilemma of Southern trade unionism: how to translate the grandiose objective of system transformation into an effective and credible tactic in a specific issue area. There is a "desperation mentality" that a small slice is better than none when the commodity lifeboat is sinking. The overall index of primary commodity prices declined by 14.8 percent in 1981, the steepest annual decline during the entire postwar period, except during the 1975 recession (when prices dropped 18.2 percent). A 41 percent decline in sugar price, 22 percent decline in coffee price, and 17 percent decline in cocoa price all occurred in spite of support operations of the International Sugar Agreement (since May 1981), the International Coffee Agreement (since October 1980), and the Cocoa Buffer Stock (since September 1981).[146] The notion that the Common Fund can somehow stabilize commodity prices or improve the terms of commodity trade for the Third World deserves closer scrutiny in the light of increasing protectionism, recession in the North, high oil prices, and deteriorating debt service payments.

The commodity problems are parts of wider and more general structural problems of the global political economy. This becomes clear when we look at a standard list of so-called commodity problems: asymmetrical interdependence between producers and consumers; worldwide inflation and volatile exchange rates; wide fluctuations in prices; demand elasticities; intermediary role of transnational corporations; and relatively low prices. The UNCTAD secretariat estimates that TNCs monopolize the following portion of trade in primary commodities: cocoa (85 percent); bananas (70-75 percent); tea (85 percent); coffee (85-90 percent); sugar (60 percent); natural rubber (70-75 percent); cotton (85-90 percent); jute (85-90 percent); forest products (90 percent); and tobacco (85-90 percent).[147] The Common Fund conveniently papers over this reality.

The future of the Common Fund is uncertain. Apparently both producer and consumer countries have had second thoughts upon reassessing its advantages and disadvantages. The agreement was supposed to enter into force on March 31, 1982 if, by that date, at least ninety states whose total subscriptions of shares comprise not less than two-thirds of the directly contributed capital of the fund have ratified. On December 16, 1981, the General Assembly, finding that only fourteen states had ratified the agreement, passed a resolution prodding member states to ratify the agreement for its entry into force by the specified date. As of March 31, 1982, however, only twelve more states had ratified, falling far short of the Article 57 requirement. On June 3, 1982, UNCTAD decided to extend the ratification deadline to September 30, 1983. Many developing countries now insist that what has finally emerged is too diluted a version of the original scheme. Meanwhile, the Reagan administration is proselytizing "the magic of the market place" and private foreign investment as the salvation for Third World development. The future prospect of this commodity regime coming into force is as uncertain as that of the new global ocean regime.[148]

From the vantage point of the Third World, the postwar structure of world trade has not changed to any significant degree. With the exception of a half-dozen NICs, developing countries have failed to participate in the growing diversification of international trade. They are still dependent on commodity trade, which has always lagged far behind trade in manufactures during the postwar period. Their major trading partners have remained the same. Even the geographical distribution of their exports has remained practically unchanged in the last two decades with the following breakdown: 73 percent with the developed market economies; 4 to 5 percent with the centrally planned economies; and 22 percent among themselves (South-South trade).

The Development Problematique

If nothing else, the crisis of the capitalist world economy has further clarified dominant conservative and liberal images of world order. In the logic of conservative and neoconservative globalists, international inequality merely reflects some immutable reality of "natural" international order that cannot—and should not—be tampered with. Any egalitarian quest to alter this deeper social reality through redistribution is doomed to fail. "In a reversal of Rousseau's claim respecting individuals," writes Robert W. Tucker, "we may say that political collectivities are born unequal and that in consequence of their different natural endowments *they are destined to remain unequal.*"[149]

Yet the conservative "realists" nostalgically look backward to the halcyon days of gunboat diplomacy, constantly bewailing "a failure of nerve" to bear the military burden of U.S. hegemony, for "gunboats are as necessary for international order as police cars for domestic order."[150] The contradiction between the credo of inevitability and the imperialist quest for "natural" social order is clear for everyone to see. For the Machiavellian geostrategists concerned with a hegemonic world order, equality breeds chaos and "the inequality of states, though not a guarantee of international stability, at least makes stability possible."[151] For the liberal Trilateralists, the management of complex and delicate interdependence calls for coming to terms with the "threat power" of the Third World and therefore necessitates accommodation by globalizing the *embourgeoisement* (cooptation) strategy so effectively used in diffusing class conflict within core capitalist societies.[152]

The contemporary reality of global inequities is not so much a confirmation of the conservative assumption as it is a repudiation of the liberal-capitalist international order. The "trickle-down" promise embodied in international liberalism has miscarried, as global interdependence and global inequality proceed hand in hand. With the exception of a handful of client states, the integration of the Third World into the capitalist world economy seems to have contributed to its pauperization and peripheralization. What may appear to be the triumph of the conservative dystopia — as currently exemplified in Thatcherism and Reaganomics — is no more than a passing phase in the unravelling of the liberal-capitalist international order. International liberalism with its promises of efficiency and equity could no longer defend itself against the contradictory pulls of conservative stockholders demanding higher profits and radicalized workers demanding higher wages. The liberal vision of the promised land for everybody turned against itself.

Inequality has always been a part of international life, but neither conservatives nor liberals can or want to explain contemporary contradictions of this age-old social problem. Why has the per capita income gap between the richest and the poorest country widened from 2:1 at the beginning of the nineteenth century (the century of colonialism) to its current ratio of 80–100:1 (the century of decolonization)? Once every two or three years, we are told, "the developed economies generate additional wealth equal to or greater than the total wealth of the underdeveloped economies, and this additional wealth accrues to those societies which are already consuming twelve times as much as the other two thirds of humanity."[153] Indeed, it is this sharp and growing disjunction between the promise and the performance of the global political economy that is the most serious utopia/dysutopia contradiction of our time. Fernando Henrique Cardoso seems closer to the truth when he argues that the utopia of our century is materially possible but politically impossible.[154] Herein lies the development problematique.

At the conceptual level the development problematique is a crisis of model, the Center model of core capitalism. The allure of this model is twofold: it is sanctioned by the capitalist world economy with sufficient payoffs and penalties at its command; it is disseminated by the capitalist global knowledge industry as the only path to the promised land of "modernization." This Center model, perhaps best exemplified in *The Stages of Economic Growth: A Non-Communist Manifesto* by Walt W. Rostow, abstracts the general requirements of Third World development as the transition from one type of society (backward, underdeveloped, traditional, non-Western) into the other type of society (advanced, developed, modern, Western, capitalist, high-consumption).[155] This transition to "modernity" is supposed to come about through the diffusion of the Center model, through the diffusion of Western knowledge, capital, values, technology, and entrepreneurship from the developed core to the underdeveloped Periphery in the capitalist world system.

The widening discrepancy between the performance of the global political economy and the satisfaction of global human need suggests the extent to which the dehumanization of the social sciences has spread to the global politics of development. The Center model is potent precisely because it is believed to be the only viable model for modernization drive. As noted earlier, however, this drive inevitably entails resource reallocative processes at both the intranational and international levels. The Center model accounts for the widening Center-Periphery, urban-rural, and elite-mass gaps. The system-transforming models of "another development" break away from the Center model, providing an alternative conceptual framework.

The conceptual foundation of international economic regimes rests on scientific and technological determinism. The revolution in science and technology is assumed to have a positive value for building functional networks of international collaboration in the management of the global commons. This technological equivalent of war is the essence of the "pragmatic world order,"[156] based on the heroic functionalist assumption that science has indeed brought an end to ideology and a demise of the territorial state. This vision elevates science and technology to a value-free status, ignoring the question of how knowledge is obtained, for whose benefits, at what costs, and in what social and ideological setting.

Scientific and technocratic determinism is wedded to a fragmented paradigm for looking at global reality. Fragmentation has made regime creation or maintenance more feasible, to be sure, but also less congenial to the holistic modelling of a more equitable world order. The conflict between North and South over the decentralized approach through specialized agencies versus the centralized approach through the United Nations has highlighted what and whose interests would be served in a fragmented approach to the problems of the global political economy.

There is a sense in which the Third World's politics of collective legitimation and delegitimation in international organizations is working its way toward incremental transformation of the norms and principles governing international economic regimes. The 1960 Decolonization Declaration, the 1970 Declaration of the Common Heritage of Mankind, the 1974 NIEO Declaration, and the GSP all serve to remind us of the extent to which U.S. ideological hegemony has dissipated and of the extent to which the Third World has come to dominate global normative politics.

However, the central normative dilemma lies in the elusive role of the state for human well-being. Statism is rampant in all types of modern political systems, transcending ideological, geopolitical, and developmental divisions, and as long as statist norms remain dominant, there is no viable alternative organization that can promote general economic well-being or make and execute BHN policy. Even the delinkage and dissociative strategy of endogenous self-reliance cannot be carried out without the state. If the modern crimes against humanity have been committed in the name of the state, so have the remarkable achievements in meeting basic human needs in Cuba, China, and Sri Lanka occurred through state interventionism.

However, the state more often than not becomes a predator of urban-centered class interests, a tormentor of the dispossessed peasantry in domestic politics, and an instrument of status drive in international politics. The dehumanizing impact of this pursuit of status is seen in the treatment of human beings as commodities, whether expressed in the exportation of cheap labor abroad to earn foreign exchange or through the marginalization of displaced peasants in the production/accumulation process at home. Furthermore, recent global economic crises and setbacks have exposed the limits of the state's role as an efficient manager of political economy and as a reliable promoter of socioeconomic change.

Statism thus limits the outer possibilities of humane international economic regimes. Most economic regimes have implicit and explicit norms about the sanctity and inviolability of state territorial sovereignty. The phenomenon of "complex interdependence" has not seriously undermined the charter principle of nonintervention "in matters which are essentially within the domestic jurisdiction of any state." Because of the feudal structures of power in the global political economy, however, this norm has a selective and inequitable application. The powerful can defy it with impunity, while the territories of the poor and the weak are more easily penetrated for "interdependent" relationship.

The Third World's dominance in the global politics of collective legitimation and delegitimation has yet to transform the global political economy. As noted earlier, the recent changes and trends in the international regimes for food and trade amount to no more than adjustments of internal rules and procedures, not changes *of* the regimes. The structure of power and authority in international economic regimes remains largely unchanged. The transnational flows of weapons, goods, services, capital, labor, information, and technology are still guided by hegemonic hands. The North may acquiesce in the passage of hortatory declarations and resolutions for a new international economic order, but it remains adamantly opposed to the transformation of the power structure of any existing or new economic regime. As a result, the so-called restructuring exercise has become an exercise in bureaucratic gymnastics for the Third World.[157]

Systemic constraints for the establishment of an equitable economic order are more structural than normative. The NIEO principle of distributive justice cannot be realized without full participation of the poorest countries in the decisionmaking process at the global level. Likewise, the BHN principle of distributive justice cannot be realized without full participation of the worst-off group in the national decisionmaking process. Yet poverty remains synonymous with powerlessness at both national and global levels. Unless or until the poor, especially the dispossessed peasants and disenfranchised women, are allowed to fully participate in decisionmaking, governing processes in national and global political economies will continue to be dominated by bargainings, negotiations, trade-offs, and compromises among the metropolitan interests of dominant political actors, and will continue to function as if people did not matter.

It is revealing that statism has shifted its focus to the nonterritorial realms—the high seas, the Antarctic, weather, and outer space—the regulation of which does not threaten the sanctity of state sovereignty. Given a choice between unilateralism (or bilateralism or trilateralism) and multilateralism, statism often gravitates toward the former, as the case of persistent imbalance between bilateral and multilateral aid shows.

The competitive environment of the global political economy also leads the state in the direction of intense status drive. Since the dominant managers of international economic regimes tend to be the representatives of states or the representatives of special and powerful interest groups, especially TNCs, in partnership with their states, the logic of dominant actors dictates the movement of "goods" and "bads" across the state boundaries. The structural pressures of the state system tend to transform international economic regimes into extensions of state bureaucracies through which national interests and needs can be secured or the global commons managed in a fashion congenial to "balanced state interests" and "competitive collaboration." It is also this statist imperative that explains both international "humanitarian" response to visible natural disasters such as flood, earthquake, and famine as well as the inability and unwillingness of the international community to respond to state terrorism (chronic hunger and severe human rights abuse).

Fragmentation of global issues also inhibits the coordination of international economic regimes, limiting their potential as agents of system transformation. Once entrapped in a fragmented paradigm, we tend to lose sight of the larger normative and structural forces at work in the global political economy. A more comprehensive and long-range integration of information, data, and learning from separate fields and disciplines is needed to construct a more coherent body of "world order" knowledge if the fragmentation/dehumanization problem is to be overcome. Otherwise, each international economic regime will continue to act in accordance with its own fragmented image of global reality.

6
Global Human Rights

From Palestine to Iran, from Egypt to China and throughout all parts of the earth where there was civilisation, we had to carry the loads of stones to construct temples, palaces, and graves. Again in the name of charity, the representatives of the "gods" and the successors of the prophets began to loot us. Again, in the name of holy war, we were pushed into the battlefields. We had to sacrifice our innocent children for the "gods," temples, and idols![1]

—Ali Shariati

The most potent weapon in the hands of the oppressor is the mind of the oppressed. If one is free at heart, no man-made chains can bind one to servitude, but if one's mind is so manipulated and controlled by the oppressor as to make the oppressed believe that he is a liability to the white man, then there will be nothing the oppressed can do to scare his powerful masters.[2]

—Steve Biko

An Oppression/Liberation Dichotomy

"One picture," says an old Chinese proverb, "is worth more than ten thousand words." If we were to search for one model picture that captures all the anomalies, brutalities, and contradictions of international politics, Picasso's great painting *Guernica*—his trenchant condemnation of the dehumanization of Spanish fascism and the terror bombing of the city of Guernica—could be that one picture. *Guernica* sharpens our sensitivity to the sand heap of invisible bodies and bones crushed and buried at the foundations of repressive local and global governance.

There is something very old and very new in contemporary human rights politics. The contemporary pursuit of human rights is part of the age-old struggle for human emancipation, part of the ongoing historical process. This long struggle is marked by a series of revolutions against religious and secular tyranny—the Protestant Reformation, the American, French, Russian, Chinese, Cuban, and Iranian revolutions—that conquered the credo of inevitability. Each revolution has expanded the bounds of moral claims in politics. Each revolution in varying manners and degrees has contributed significantly to the broadening of the concept of human rights. Each revolution progressively raised the threshold of intolerance for inhumane governance. As a result, the human rights movement, which originated in the West in the wake of the Enlightenment, has spread to all parts of the world.

What makes the contemporary struggle for human liberation novel is its elusive and contradictory quality. Ours is the best *and* the worst of times for human rights. From the optimistic side, it can be said that the level of human consciousness has been significantly raised and the tenure of oppressive regimes has become shorter. In a world of increasing inter-dependence and instant communications, it is becoming more and more difficult for an oppressor to hide oppression, for the oppressed to be resigned to hopelessness, and for the rest of us to remain indifferent. The voices of the oppressed are becoming more and more difficult to silence, for the very act of silencing makes the voices more audible. Both Shariati and Biko were tormented and killed but their voices for the oppressed remain unstilled.

From the pessimistic—and perhaps more "realistic"—side of the situation, ours is indeed the worst of times for human rights. Never before in human history have there been such glaring gaps between rhetoric and reality, between norms and behavior, and between claims and capabilities. The recent revival and rhetorical celebration of human rights cannot obfuscate the extent to which state behavior has been dehumanized in the service of local oligarchies and tyrannies as well as of corporate and geopolitical interests. Hedly Bull captured an important dimension of international reality when he said that "international order is preserved by means which systematically affront the most basic and widely agreed principles of international justice."[3]

However, Bull's observation begs several important questions. To what extent and in what manner can it be said that "the most basic and widely agreed principles of international justice" merely reflect and codify the voices of the strong, rich, and articulate, ignoring the voices of the weak, poor, and inarticulate? To what extent and in what manner can it be said that the study of global human rights politics proceeds as if people mattered, heeding the voices of those who are either victims of oppression or who speak on behalf of the oppressed, i.e., the weak, poor, and inarticulate? To what extent does human rights politics ignore the structural deficiencies of the world economic and political systems that condition the behavior of state elites?

In pursuit of normative inquiry into global human rights politics, this chapter seeks: (1) to examine the evolution of human rights thinking; (2) to propose a world order model of universal human rights; (3) to describe the pattern of human rights abuses; (4) to evaluate the kinds and effectiveness of international response; and (5) to explain the human rights problematique.

The Evolution of Human Rights Thinking

Whether "universal" human rights exist at any given moment is rarely self-evident and always open to debate. What cannot be disputed is that there is no such thing as universal human rights whose validity has been accepted at all times, by all peoples, and in all places. Much like the closely connected concepts of justice, freedom, and equality, the concept of human rights has both evolutionary and revolutionary potential. In an open and democratic milieu, it is a dynamic concept, constantly evolving and expanding, seeking a closer interface between empirical and normative reality. In a closed and oppressive milieu, it is a revolutionary concept legitimizing the call for a new order. In short, the evolution of human rights thinking is a continuing process whose future is always open and unpredictable. It is seldom in a steady state.

The concept of human rights is a product of its time. It invariably reflects an evolutionary or revolutionary change of normative power in social and political processes. In order to have a better understanding of the dynamic process of human rights politics in the development of modern international relations—that is, in the authoritative shaping and sharing of human rights values—it is useful to evaluate the elements of change and continuity in terms of the "concept of three generations" advanced by the prominent French jurist Karel Vasak, Director of UNESCO's Division of Human Rights and Peace from 1976 to 1980.[4]

Throughout the history of modern international relations there have been three generations of human rights emanating from three competing schools of thought: the first generation of civil and political rights; the second generation of social, economic, and cultural rights; and the third generation of solidarity rights. Of course, the three generations of human rights is a simplified abstraction of the complex and confusing picture of human rights politics. It is also a heuristically useful model that shows the dominant school of thought at a given period as well as the changing patterns and trends in the development of human rights politics. Vasak has characterized the three generations of human rights as corresponding to the three normative components of the motto of the French revolution: *liberté*, *égalité*, and *fraternité*.[5]

The First Generation of Civil and Political Rights

The expression "human rights" is of relatively recent origin. It can be traced back to the "rights of man" (*droits de l'homme*) movement of the last quarter of the eighteenth century in Europe. The eighteenth-century social philosophers and political revolutionaries of Europe and America may be regarded as the founding fathers of the first generation of human rights. Although the notion of human dignity is embedded in all non-Western cultures and civilizations, the contemporary sense of human rights as entitlements that inhere in being born as a member of the human race is distinctively Western.

The ideas and principles embodied in the American Declaration of Independence, in the Virginia Bill of Rights of 1776, in the French Declaration of the Rights of Man and of the Citizen, and in the American Bill of Rights—thanks to the dominant position of Western Europe and the

United States in the development and codification of international norms—
have become the central model of human rights. "The American and
French revolutions," writes Louis Henkin, "and the declarations that
expressed the principles that inspired them, took 'natural rights' and made
them secular, rational, universal, individual, democratic, and radical."[6]

The first generation of human rights is impregnated with the Western
political philosophy of liberal individualism. Each human person, by virtue
of his/her membership in the human race, is supposedly endowed with,
and entitled to, certain natural and inalienable human rights such as "life,
liberty, and property" (Locke) or "life, liberty, and the pursuit of happiness"
(Jefferson). The essence of the concept of human rights in this Western
liberalism was negative "freedom from" rather than positive "rights to."
This essentially negative conception of human rights was also meshed with
the dominant social and economic doctrine of laissez-faire. In short, human
rights in the Western liberal tradition are more or less romanticized as a
triumph of Lockean-Hobbesian individualism over Hegelian statism.

The supreme worth of the individual has been the core value of liberal
constitutional democracy in the West. The moral and political strength of
the Western tradition of liberal democracy is attested to by the frequency
with which its key concepts and principles have been invoked to legitimize
revolutionary calls against oppressive rule and by the extent to which its
key concepts and principles have been constitutionalized as a protective
shield of individual citizens from the oppressive hand of political authority.
Richard Falk has argued that this represents the "comparative advantage"
of the liberal West.[7] Louis Henkin has observed on the power of the
Western liberal model: "What the United States (borrowing from its English
mother) and France planted and disseminated now decorates almost every
constitution of today's 150 states—old or new, conservative or liberal or
radical, capitalist or socialist or mixed, developed or less developed, or
underdeveloped."[8]

More significantly, the rights of individuals predominate in the International Bill of Rights—the Universal Declaration of Human Rights, the
International Covenant on Civil and Political Rights and Its Optional
Protocol, and the International Covenant on Economic, Social, and Cultural
Rights. The preamble of the declaration states that "recognition of the
inherent dignity and of the equal and inalienable rights of all members
of the human family is the foundation of freedom, justice and peace in
the world," while twenty out of the thirty articles are devoted to the
elaboration of individual civil and political rights. The preambles of the
two covenants are identical, repeating the above quote from the preamble
of the declaration and stating that "the equal and inalienable rights . . .
derive from the inherent dignity of the human person."[9]

The first generation of human rights is not without its "comparative
disadvantage." The expression "all Men are created equal" embodied in
the American Declaration of Independence—and "all men are equal by
nature and before law" embodied in the French Declaration of the Rights

of Man and of the Citizen—was misleading in theory and practice. It was only a half-truth that tended to obscure rather than clarify the relentless "pursuit of happiness" by some men against other men (and women). Until recently, the Western liberal individualistic conception of human rights provided little remedy against abuses of civil and political rights committed by social agents other than the government. Under the banner of liberal individualism, it is only state action of specific character ¬hat is proscribed. Individual or corporate invasion of individual civil and political rights, much less social, economic, and cultural rights, has generally remained beyond the purview of legal protection.

It is easy to see why and how liberal individualism can be used as a legitimizing instrument of structural violence in domestic and international politics. Freedom became the most powerful weapon to justify inequality. Freedom was not like a commons that became available to all in equal quantity. Much like money, the rich, the powerful, and the articulate had more know-how, more access, and more influence in the shaping and sharing of the first generation rights. As Marx once argued: "None of the so-called rights of man goes beyond the *egoistic* man. . . . Far from viewing man here in his *species-being,* his *species-life* rather appears to be an external framework limiting his original independence."[10] Kenneth Boulding revealed the embedded norm of Western liberal individualism—and in a sense confirmed the veracity of Ali Shariati's argument—when he said: "Without sharp inequalities, we would not have had the Parthenon or the cathedrals . . . or the great cultural achievements of any of the past civilizations."[11]

The sanctity of private property so deeply embedded in Western individual-corporate liberalism is uniquely inhospitable to the human rights of present *and* future generations, as it justifies the freedom to limitless material acquisition. Once the right to private property (the pursuit of happiness) is elevated to an inalienable status, it unavoidably accelerates the process of selective humanization (and selective dehumanization) in the wealth-accumulating process. This process, as Christian Bay has argued, extends "our traditional rights and liberties to corporations as if they were human beings."[12] On the other hand, private property rights and markets, having been placed on the same pedestal as human rights and freedoms, can easily become a threat to democracy.[13] The persistent "elitist" bias and insensitivity to the problematique of private property rights among the liberal advocates of human rights in the West have allowed this dehumanization to continue unexamined and unchecked.

In a legal sense, the inalienable rights of all men meant no more than the rights of citizens, and the correlative civil and political rights of citizens have been denied to many because of their "race, colour, sex, language, religion, political or other opinion, national or social origin, property, birth or other status" (Article 2 of the Universal Declaration of Human Rights). "We think [the people of the negro race} . . . are not included, and were not intended to be included," declared the majority of the U.S. Supreme Court in *Dred Scott* v. *Sanford* in 1857, "under the words 'citizens' in the

Constitution, and can therefore claim none of the rights and privileges which that instrument provides for and secures to citizens of the United States."[14]

That Alexis de Tocqueville, James Bryce, Harold Laski, and other European writers were so impressed by the strength of egalitarian thought and practice in American society sheds more light on the reality of the Old World than of the New World. Notice, for example, the recent British refusal to admit entry of certain East African Asians, even though they "were British passport holders, they were severely harassed by the anti-Asian policies of General Amin and they had members of their families resident in Britain."[15] If England was the cradle of parliamentary democracy, it has also been the chief propagator of white racism, which spread and germinated in a new, and in some cases a more virulent, form in the white settlement colonies of the United States, Canada, South Africa, Southern Rhodesia, New Zealand, and Australia. The immigration and naturalization laws and practices of these countries are full of racist norms and implications. That Western imperialism was legitimized under such "human rights" slogans as Manifest Destiny, the White Man's Burden, and Mission Civilisatrice requires no further elaboration. In a broader sense, "if the West has been the fountainhead of liberal constitutional democracy, it has also been the breeding ground of Fascism and Nazism."[16]

The moral credibility of Western liberal individualism has been greatly compromised by its self-styled champion, the United States. Unlike the other Western powers, the United States has been endemically prone to delude itself and others by disguising its imperial geopolitics in benign and altruistic slogans of human rights. While condemning the gunboat diplomacy of the other imperial powers in China in the nineteenth century, the United States seldom lost time claiming its share of victors' spoils through the most-favored-nation clause. At the turn of the century this Janus-faced policy was epitomized in the Open Door, a "me-too colonialism" legitimized as the protection of China's political and territorial integrity. President Wilson's championship for human rights as expressed in his call at Versailles for the right to national self-determination was no more credible than President Carter's revival of human rights as the centerpiece of U.S. foreign policy.

The long-standing, self-serving championship of universal human rights has significantly diluted the "comparative advantage" of liberal America. The liberal dilemmas and contradictions were brought to the fore in President John F. Kennedy's mixture of statist and globalist metaphors in his crusade for "freedom": "Ask not what your country can do for you, ask what you can do for your country" (statism at home); "Let every nation know, whether it wishes us well or ill, that we shall pay any price, bear any burden, meet any hardship, support any friend, oppose any foe to assure the survival and success of liberty. This much we pledge—and more" (globalism abroad). Some twenty years later prominent political scientist Samuel Huntington echoes the same theme: "The expansion of American power is not synonymous with the expansion of liberty, but a significant correlation exists between the rise and fall of American power in the world and the rise and fall of liberty and democracy in the world."[17]

Ironically, then, "liberty" is not only an instrument of liberation on the part of the oppressed but it can also become a legitimating instrument in the service of an unjust social order in domestic and international politics. In the course of heated and prolonged clash between Western and Third World delegates on the issue of individual human rights versus collective rights (or the rights of peoples) at a special UNESCO conference in December 1982, Amadou-Mahtar M'Bow, UNESCO's Director General, nicely captured both sides of this dialectic about the New World Information Order when he said: "If the {Western} media has the liberty to say what they like, then others {the Third World} have the right to judge what they say. What becomes of freedom when people claim to inform according to their own view and then refuse or seek to refuse to allow others to judge what they say? When this is the case, there is no liberty but the monopoly."[18]

Generally, the individual rights of the first generation were more formal than real, more procedural than substantive, more political than economic, and more civil than social. From a just and humane world order perspective, then, the most problematic feature of the first generation of human rights lies in its persistent abstraction of human rights in a manner irrelevant to the basic needs of humankind. Just as liberty often served as an ideological weapon to maintain an inegalitarian social order at home, liberty has also been turned into a propaganda weapon in the ongoing hegemonic rivalry between the two superpowers. In the domain of North-South relations, "liberty becomes an answer," as Fouad Ajami put it, "to the Third World's demand for global equity."[19]

Within the home turf, paradoxically enough, there is a crisis of faith and confidence in the Western model of democracy. Far from believing and acting as if democracy represents the "comparative advantage" of the West, the Trilateral Commission, representing the more liberal elements of ruling elites in the industrial democracies, has questioned the very governability of Western democracy in the face of the twin challenges from the Soviet Union and the Third World. The West in general and the United States in particular has taken freedom too far, we are told, and we must therefore limit the rights and liberties of citizens if "democracy" (liberal-guided democracy?) is to survive.[20]

The Second Generation of Economic, Social, and Cultural Rights

The human predicament arising out of the abuses and misuses of capitalist development provided a point of departure for the Marxist/socialist anti-thesis formulation of human rights in the nineteenth century. With the Russian Revolution of 1917, this philosophy found a home base. Out of this philosophical and political background emerged the second generation of economic, social, and cultural rights. Given the "minority" and "opposition" status of the Soviet Union in the normative domain of international politics, the internationalization of these rights was rather slow in coming. The economic, social, and cultural rights of the second generation received a secondary status in the Universal Declaration of Human Rights (Articles 22–29). With the massive entry of newly independent countries into the United Nations and the gradual ascendancy of the Third World as a dominant actor in UN politics, second generation rights have come of age. After nearly two decades of struggle, the economic, social, and cultural rights were legitimized when the General Assembly adopted (and opened for ratification) the International Covenant on Economic, Social, and Cultural Rights on December 16, 1966.

The defining characteristics of the second generation rights may be summarized briefly. First, they are *collective* rights, i.e., the rights of human beings in their various group and social roles and capacities. Second, they are *positive* rights, which to be achieved had to be demanded of the state. Third, they are social rights to *basic human needs*—the right to work, the right to education, etc. Fourth, they are rights to social *equality,* demanding an equitable participation in the authoritative shaping and sharing of human rights values. And finally, they are not human rights in the first generation sense of those inalienable rights that inhere in the nature of being a human person but human rights formulated and presented as affirmative *aspirations* of humanity, calling for state intervention in the allocation of resources. In comparison with the rights of the first generation, then, the rights of the second generation are more collective than individual, more social and economic than civil and political, more concrete than abstract, more positive than negative, more equality-oriented than liberty-oriented, and more substantive than procedural.

The establishment of a closer human rights/human needs interface is the most significant contribution of the second generation. For the masses of humanity, civil and political rights are practically meaningless in the absence of basic economic, social, and cultural rights and the minimum satisfaction of basic human needs. President Roosevelt's Four Freedoms— freedom from *want* and *fear* as well as freedom of speech and religion— nicely summed up the basic spirit of the second generation of human rights. By broadening people's social and economic rights and by linking them to civil and political rights, the Four Freedoms represented a revolution of sorts—a second Bill of Rights—in U.S. human rights thinking. Unfortunately, however, this new human rights thinking seems to have been cut off at the water's edge.

The human rights of the second generation are not without some theoretical and practical difficulties. The heroic assumption that the state can be trusted as a progressive agent of human welfare stands on shaky theoretical and empirical grounds. This assumption draws upon the most problematic feature of contemporary Marxist polity—the contradiction between the traditional conceptualization of the state as an instrument of class exploitation (hence the idealized theory of the withering away of the state) and the actual development of a bureaucratic, centralized, and militarized superstate. In his *The State and Revolution* (1917), Lenin argued forcefully that "The State is the product and the manifestation of the *irreconcilability* of class antagonisms. The State arises when, where, and to the extent that the class antagonisms *cannot* be objectively reconciled. And, conversely, the existence of the State proves that the class antagonisms *are* irreconcilable."[21]

In the contemporary international system still imbued with neo-Darwinian ethos, the state acquires its own "security" interests and myths. Once trapped in this competitive drive for security, power, and status, human interests are not abandoned; they are merely given low priority or shelved as long-term ends. The response-to-frustration school of thought in psychology has even suggested that the state serves as an instrument of the ruling class to prevent "the frustrated from expressing their aggression against their frustrators."[22]

Closely connected to the problem of the superstate is a means-end dichotomy implied in the second generation concept of human rights. More often than not the inconsistent and selective application of internationally legitimized human rights principles is rationalized as a necessary or unavoidable means in the long-run pursuit of human well-being. Although first and second generation rights are often claimed to be indivisible and interdependent, in practice it is often otherwise, as many Third World rulers justify their short-term suppression of civil and political rights in the name of long-term developmental imperatives. "Developmental fascism," argues Eqbal Ahmad, is one of the common characteristics of the neofascist state in the Third World.[23]

There is no empirical support for incompatibility between the two types of human rights. The world order approach rejects this means-end dichotomy. As noted in Chapter 3, the world order approach to transition politics rests upon the centrality of values, values that cannot be placed in abeyance pending the completion of the transition process. On the contrary, these values apply to the means as well as to the ends of transition politics. Both the Marxist and Machiavellian traditions have been insensitive to the procedural and substantive indivisibility of means and ends. We can never justify dysutopian means in the pursuit of utopian ends. In his trenchant critique of the utopian element in socialism, religious and social philosopher Martin Buber argued that the utopian socialist "refuses to believe that in our reliance on the future 'leap' we have to do now the direct opposite of what we are striving for; he believes rather that we must create here and now the space *now* possible for the thing for which we are striving, so that it may come to fulfillment *then*."[24] In short, there is— or ought to be—a transtemporal indivisibility of the first and second generation human rights.

Indeed, the insensitivity to the mutually enhancing or corrupting effects of the relationship between means and ends so evident in the actual practice of many Third World and socialist politics weakens the moral credibility of this contemporary approach. This is not to deny or minimize the enduring contributions of the Marxist theory and polity in the field of human rights: its revolutionary identification with, and struggle for, the oppressed and the exploited; its probing of the root causes of human rights abuses (structural violence); the admirable accomplishment in meeting the basic human needs of its own population as made evident in the PQLI performance of China, Cuba, and the Soviet Union; and the enlargement of the global human rights agenda in a manner more congenial to the struggling masses of humanity. Still, the Marxist approach as embodied in the second generation of human rights suffers from the problems of overcompensation—overreliance on economic rights; overreliance on collective rights; and overreliance on the "benign hand" of the state.[25]

This presents a perplexing practical question in the Third World. How can we balance the greater economic and social equity of socialist polities with the greater cultural and intellectual openness of capitalist nations? In a comparative analysis of the deep structural pressures toward oppressive governance in both socialist and capitalist Third World countries, Richard Falk concluded that "the costs of the transition to socialism seem higher in practice than those of the persistence of a capitalist social order, thereby offsetting to a significant extent the humanitarian structural advantage of socialism."[26] Yet capitalism as a whole is seen as inappropriate for the Third World because in failing to deal with mass poverty it creates a structural tendency for repressive rule. Given economic, social, demographic, ecological, and other structural constraints, a socialist human rights model is preferable, he argues, though not a sufficient precondition for the realization of human rights values.[27]

The Third Generation of Solidarity Rights

Almost every problem of global magnitude and concern has attracted a UN-sponsored global conference in the 1970s. The subject of human rights has the dubious distinction of being the only exception. The third generation of solidarity rights filled this gap by restructuring the debate on human rights in more holistic, planetary terms. Clearly, the Third World's successful decolonization revolution provides the background from which the third generation of human rights is struggling to be born. At this point, however, solidarity rights are still at a preliminary, norm-formulating stage.

The solidarity rights of the third generation include the right to peace, the right to development, the right to a healthy and ecologically balanced environment, and the right to share the common heritage of mankind. In a fundamental sense, this is an attempt to update, expand, and reformulate human rights in terms more compatible with the changing requirements of human solidarity in a contradictory world marked by increasing interdependence and fragmentation. In his inaugural lecture to the Tenth Study Session of the International Institute of Human Rights in July 1979, Karel

Vasak presented the defining characteristics of the solidarity rights of the third generation in the following terms:

> [the solidarity rights] are new in the aspirations they express, are new from the point of view of human rights in that they seek to infuse the human dimension into areas where it has all too often been missing, having been left to the State, or States. . . . [T]hey are new in that they may both be *invoked against* the State and *demanded* of it; but above all (and herein lies their essential characteristics) they can be realized only through the concerted efforts of all the actors on the social scene; the individual, the State, public and private bodies and the international community.[28]

The concept of the solidarity rights may be new, but its normative components are not. Hence, it may be more accurate to characterize the rights of the third generation as synthetic and synergetic ones, drawing upon, and interconnecting, various existing "rights" in a holistic framework of aspiring human solidarity. The most salient feature of solidarity rights lies in the expansion of human rights to embrace the whole planet. Solidarity rights can justly claim to be *universal* human rights, for they require the concerted efforts of all social forces and actors for their implementation. Each of the major components making up the solidarity rights deserves a brief mention.

The right to peace is not difficult to infer from various international norms, including the UN Charter. In the latter half of the 1970s the right to peace gained increasing support from various international organizations, NGOs, and human rights scholars. In its Resolution 5 (XXXII) in 1976, the UN Human Rights Commission declared: "Everyone has the right to live in conditions of international peace and security and fully to enjoy economic, social and cultural rights, and civil and political rights." The final report of the UNESCO Expert Meeting on Human Rights, Human Needs, and the Establishment of a New International Economic Order, held in June 1978, states: "By virtue of the proclamation contained in the United Nations Charter to the effect that human rights and freedoms shall be respected and the use of force prohibited, one of the basic rights of each individual is embodied in international law, namely, the right to peace."[29]

In its Declaration on the Preparation of Societies for Life in Peace, the General Assembly reaffirmed "the right of individuals, States and all mankind to life in peace" (in the preamble) and "Every nation and every human being, regardless of race, conscience, language or sex, has the inherent right to life in peace" (para. 1). This declaration was passed by a recorded vote of 138-0-2 as Resolution 33/73 on December 15, 1978, with only Israel and the United States dissenting. The Polish human rights scholar Adam Lopatka asserts that the right to peace embodied in the declaration "legalizes what had merely been a political and moral aspiration" and "constitutes a binding norm for UN organs and for organizations belonging to the UN family."[30]

The concept of "the right to development" was first formulated in 1972 by Keba M'Baye, who served as first President of the Supreme Court of Senegal, Vice-President of the International Institute of Human Rights, President of the International Commission of Jurists, and member of the UN Commission on Human Rights. M'Baye is currently serving a nine-year (1983–1991) term as a judge on the International Court of Justice.[31] On February 21, 1977, the Commission on Human Rights adopted a resolution—Resolution 4 (XXXIII), which M'Baye had sponsored—inviting the UN Secretary-General, in cooperation with UNESCO and the other competent specialized agencies, to undertake a study of "the international dimensions of the right to development as a human right in relations with other human rights based on international co-operation, including the right to peace, taking into account the requirements of the New International Economic Order and the fundamental human needs." What emerged two years later is a comprehensive (161-pages-long) report of the Secretary-General on the right to development as a human right.[32]

The right to development as a human right is a holistic idea which seeks to establish a closer interface between human rights and human development. The novelty lies not only in the linking of the two but also in the placement of individual and collective rights and needs in a mutually complementary framework. The right to development as a human right also acknowledges the individual and collective right to participate in the authoritative shaping and sharing of human rights and development values.[33]

Although the right to a healthy and balanced environment and the right to the common heritage of mankind are also included in the category of solidarity rights, their conceptual and operational linkage to human rights has not received full definition and elaboration. Suffice it here to say that the Declaration of the United Nations Conference on the Human Environment proclaims in its preamble that "Both aspects of man's environment, the natural and the man-made, are essential to his well-being and to the enjoyment of *basic human rights*—even the right to life itself."[34] The right to the common heritage of mankind—or the right to own, and benefit from, the common heritage of mankind—was first suggested in 1967 by Arvid Pardo in his capacity as the Maltese Ambassador to the United Nations,[35] and was almost unanimously endorsed by the General Assembly in its "Common Heritage of Mankind" Declaration in 1970.[36] This vague but revolutionary declaration affirmed, *inter alia,* that the area "beyond the limits of national jurisdiction, as well as the resources of the area, are the common heritage of mankind" and was embodied in the 1982 UN Convention on the Law of the Sea.

The right to a healthy and balanced environment and the right to the common heritage of mankind as new human rights embody both individual and collective dimensions. The collective dimension of the right to the common heritage of mankind, argues Hector Gros-Espiell, establishes the international community itself as a subject, i.e., a bearer of rights and obligations, of international law.[37] The individual dimension of the right to the common heritage of mankind, argues Stephen Marks, gives new meaning to individual rights "freely to participate in the cultural life of the community, to enjoy the arts and to share in scientific advancement and its benefits" (Article 27 of the Universal Declaration of Human Rights) by extending them to the international community as well.[38]

As will be shown in the next section, the solidarity rights of the third generation are more congenial than the first and second generation rights to our world order approach to human rights. The solidarity rights have embraced all four world order values in a synthetic and synergetic framework of human unity. They have embodied the participatory efforts of all social forces and actors in the authoritative shaping and sharing of human rights values. They strike a balance between the first and second generation rights in calling for state abstention as well as state action in different domains of human rights. The solidarity rights also imply the quest for a relevant utopia by projecting the notion of universal human community interests.

In spite of these strengths, solidarity rights represent no more than aspiring norms. At this point they enjoy the rather ambiguous status of international human rights norms. Even among strong advocates of global human rights, there is a kind of ideological fatigue in the unceasing elaboration and reformulation of new human rights at a time when the existing norms are systematically ignored and violated. There is also a sense in which normative exercise can serve as an easy escape from deeper structural realities of the state system. In short, the necessary conditions of universal hospitality needed to give full expression and implementation of the solidarity rights are still largely lacking in the prevailing system of world order.

A World Order/Human Rights Interface

It is possible to establish a world order/human rights interface based on the foregoing discussion. This is not to introduce a fourth generation of human rights but, for analytical and prescriptive purposes, to develop a human rights/human developmental model that is sensitive to world order assumptions, principles, and values. In doing so, I draw upon, but somewhat alter, the concepts, principles, assumptions, and approaches embodied in the three-generation evolution of human rights thinking. The establishment of a world order/human rights interface calls for the following tasks: (1) clarifying core assumptions and principles; (2) redefining "human rights"; (3) formulating the human rights/human needs nexus; and (4) establishing a world order hierarchy of human rights.

The Core Assumptions and Principles

The starting point for establishing a world order/human rights interface is a holistic and humanistic affirmation of the supreme value of human life and development. No matter how one defines "world order," it is a man-made order. The quality of world order and the quality of "human rights" are mutually enhancing or corrupting. Human rights when properly defined and effectively implemented become living norms of a just world order. In a negative sense, the deterioration of the existing world order means a corresponding increase in life-destroying, life-diminishing, life-devaluing, and life-degrading effects, and vice versa. In a positive sense, the protection and promotion of human life and its potential to becoming more fully human means a corresponding enhancement of a just and humane world order. The most basic task of a world order approach to global human rights politics is to define and reduce the large discrepancies between what *is* and what *ought to be* in the human condition.

Our image of human nature always influences how we define the outer limits and possibilities of resolving the discrepancies between empirical and normative human realities. What can then be said of a world order conception of human nature? Briefly summarized, it acknowledges the dual and plastic inner nature of human beings, a delicate and changing balance between human cruelty and human kindness, between the limits imposed by the necessity of basic biological needs and the possibilities of spiritual tran-scendance, and between deprivation-induced aggressive impulses and deeply embedded yearnings for the ultimate truth and unity of humanity.

More specifically, a world order/human rights interface is based on the following core assumptions and principles:

- Every human life, regardless of its location in social, territorial, and ethnic space, is of equal value and therefore entitled to equal protection;
- Each human life is an end itself and as such it cannot be devalued as a means to the rights of others;
- Each human person or group is entitled to democratic participation in the shaping and reshaping of human rights values;
- Each human person or group is entitled to equal benefit in the sharing of human rights values;
- Human rights are mutually interdependent and indivisible, but some rights are more basic and essential than others in human development;
- The affirmation of the supreme value of human life and dignity is the only way to reconcile the conflicts between cultural relativism and universal human rights norms.

The Meaning of "Human Rights"

As noted earlier, the postwar period witnessed a socialist and Third World revisionist challenge to the dominant Western liberal conception of human rights. Still, the Western concept of human rights, defined largely in legal procedural terms, enjoys a dominant status in the human rights debate. Even in the domain of international human rights politics the dominant modes and orientations of the 1950s and 1960s, as best exemplified in the West European human rights system with its elaborate adjudicative mechanisms, emphasized the establishment of international legal procedures to enhance respect for human dignity.

However, a legalistic conceptualization of human rights has some serious theoretical and practical difficulties. As the U.S. civil rights movement and the Soviet (Stalin) Constitution of 1936 have clearly shown, *having* human rights in a legal sense is not the same as *enjoying* human rights in an empirical sense. Most legal analyses do not go beyond standard-setting and norm-making activities, leaving the deep structure of the existing social order unexamined and unchallenged. In other words, legal protection is only one way, and certainly not the most effective way, of enhancing human dignity.[39]

A legalistic approach tends to encumber *universal* human rights with Western, middle-class, conservative norms and biases. It has been shown that a concern for human dignity is central to all non-Western cultural traditions, yet human rights in the Western legal sense are alien to Islamic, African, Chinese, and Indian approaches to human dignity.[40] Even in Western countries with well-established court systems, the status of law as an instrument of human rights and human dignity is problematic. Law is a powerful instrument in the hands of those who have money, power, influence, and knowledge, but it is a remote abstraction for the poor, the powerless, and the inarticulate. In a world torn by cultural relativism, fragmentation, and massive deprivation of basic human needs, to define universal human rights in terms of civil and political rights and duties is to make human rights irrelevant to the quest for a just and humane world order.

More seriously, a legalistic approach incurs the danger, willingly or unwillingly, of becoming an instrument of ideological manipulation in cold-war politics. Procedural violence to the human rights of a few prominent intellectuals in the Soviet Union receives wide condemnation and publicity in the United States, whereas substantive violence to the human rights of a hundred of thousands of people in "friendly regimes" can barely manage to receive token rebuke and publicity. Freedom House, a New York–based neoconservative organization, issues every January its annual "comparative study of freedom" report and map ranking of all the nation-states of the world on a descending scale from 1 (the "most free") to 7 (the "least free"). Looking at the world as though through Alice's Looking-Glass, this survey almost invariably comes up with a Humpty Dumpty definition of "freedom." "That South Africa can be deemed more 'free' than Tanzania," writes Fouad Ajami, "is testimony to the intellectual tyranny of form over substance."[41]

What should be the just world order conception of human rights? Based on the core assumptions and principles clarified earlier, we define "human rights" as follows: *Human rights are those claims and demands essential to the protection of human life and the enhancement of human dignity, which should therefore enjoy full social and political sanctions.* Substance is given more weight than form in this definition, since there is growing consensus on the substantive value of human life and dignity. The legitimacy of each human right is based on its indispensability first to the protection of human life and then to the realization of our being and becoming progressively more fully human, whatever form this may take in each cultural and political space. This definition therefore implies a hierarchy of human rights values linked with human growth and development.

A Human Needs/Human Rights Nexus

How can we implement the above definition in a manner appropriate to the quest for a just world order? My contention is that this can be done by establishing a closer nexus between human needs and human rights. A human needs/human rights nexus does not mean that the two categories are the same concepts. It is merely designed to seek a closer relationship between indispensable needs and actual rights. As Johan Galtung and Anders Wirak have suggested, human needs are located *inside* individual human beings, whereas human rights are located *between* them.[42]

The needs/rights nexus is a complicated and dynamic one, as some needs evolve into the status of socially sanctioned rights while other needs remain individual. On the other hand, some rights have no basis, or only a tenuous basis, in needs. One legal scholar has argued that the notion of need as a basis for entitlement is evolving into the central feature of the contemporary international law of development.[43] To conceptualize human rights in terms of human needs—and this is what the human needs/human rights nexus is all about—is to place the human rights debate more firmly at the center of the ongoing struggle of the oppressed and exploited for human emancipation.

There are several specific advantages in taking a needs-based approach to human rights. First of all, it has now been demonstrated in "health psychology" that the human being has basic specieswide needs that must be met in order to avoid "sickness and subjective ill-being." Health psychologist Abraham Maslow has observed that the deprivation of basic needs makes the human person yearn persistently for their gratification. Left ungratified, the deprived person sickens and withers. Maslow therefore used "basic needs" and "basic values" interchangeably.[44]

Second, there is growing empirical evidence in support of the concept of basic human needs. Findings from two separate global surveys provide examples. The picture that emerges from sociopsychologist Hadley Cantril's global survey of the patterning of human concerns is that the demands human beings everywhere impose on their society or political culture have a biologically built-in design that sooner or later must be accommodated. The universalized pattern of human concerns, Cantril concludes, entails first and foremost the satisfaction of survival needs and such other needs as physical and psychological security, the search to create new hopes and visions and to enlarge the range and quality of satisfactions, and the desire to experience one's own identity, integrity, and worthwhileness.[45] In more recent surveys sampling two-thirds of the world's population to measure their human needs and satisfactions, the Gallup International Research Institutes found that the main needs of the inhabitants of the major regions of the world "center about their economic welfare, their health, and family life." "One of our principal conclusions" says the report, "is that economic privation seems to affect the spirit as well as the body. Poverty adversely colors attitudes and perceptions. Although one probably could find isolated places in the world where the inhabitants are very poor but happy, this study failed to discover any area that met this test."[46]

In short, a human needs/human rights nexus overcomes to a significant extent the problem of formulating universal human rights norms against the background of prevalent cultural fragmentation. Third, this nexus avoids the legal and theoretical abstraction associated with the first-generation conception of human rights. Violations of civil and political rights are more difficult to monitor without imposing a culture-specific criterion. On the other hand, human rights as reformulated in terms of specieswide human needs are more specific and concrete, hence easier to measure and monitor as universally acceptable norms (life, health, well-being, etc.).

Finally, a human needs/human rights nexus minimizes the elitist (class) biases so prevalent in the human rights discourse and politics. "Until we endeavor to bring human need priorities into the picture, I submit," argues Christian Bay, "the natural preferences of jurists and philosophers for the wellbeing of members of their own class will tend to determine the prevailing views of the relative importance of rights—or even the difference between 'human rights' and 'so-called human rights.'"[47] A human needs/human rights nexus decisively shifts its main focus from the intellectual deprivation of middle-class elites in communist regimes to the basic human needs deprivation of the poor, weak, and inarticulate of the two-thirds of humanity concentrated in the Third World.

A World Order Hierarchy of Human Rights

To say that different categories of human rights are mutually interdependent and indivisible, as commonly and conveniently asserted in the UN debate, is not to say that they are or can be equal. Some human rights are inherently more essential than others to the enhancement of human dignity. The human rights essential to meeting *basic* needs cannot be placed on an equal footing with those rights essential to meeting *meta* needs. If we accept the proposition that human needs (both basic and meta) "are related to each other in a hierarchical and developmental way, in an order of strength and of priority,"[48] it is possible to construct a normative model of the typology and priority of human rights.

Christian Bay's analogy of reputable hospitals—that they do not treat all patients equally and that emergency wards and intensive care units give priority treatment to those who are most gravely injured or most seriously ill[49]—is most instructive in establishing a world order hierarchy of human rights values. A just world order approach to human rights therefore contends that the claims of the oppressed—those in the global poverty belt who are powerless to cry out—deserve preferred treatment as most seriously injured victims in the global system. Since women are so widely discriminated against and have such low and marginalized status in the development process of most communities throughout the world, they too deserve special treatment.

The Right to Human Life. This is an absolute, irrevocable, and nonderogable right that should enjoy the most preferred position in the hierarchy of human rights values. The loss of life cancels all other human rights. Violence, as noted in Chapter 4, is a pathological force that destroys or diminishes life-sustaining and life-enhancing processes. The normative significance of the right to peace as one of the solidarity rights lies in the fact that both negative peace (the absence of war) and positive peace (the absence of structural violence) are the greatest lifesavers in human affairs. The catchy slogan, "Better Dead Than Red"—there seems to be no counterpart slogan in the communist world—is symptomatic of pathology among the "freedom crusaders." The right to human life is essential to meeting survival needs that are transtemporal, transcultural, and transnational. The Biblical commandment "Thou Shalt Not Kill" should be the first and foremost principle of universal human rights.

The status of the right to human life in world politics is problematic. In one formulation or another, this right has received international legitimization in various parts of the International Bill of Rights as well as in the resolutions of the UN Commission on Human Rights and of the General Assembly. Yet the practical (behavioral) significance of this legitimation seems marginal for several reasons. The concept of the right to peace as a human right is relatively new and not without controversy. By repeatedly invoking the principle of interdependence and indivisibility between all human rights, the United Nations has failed to endow this right with the preferred position it deserves. In addition, the term "peace" has been subject to so many self-serving qualifications and reservations that it has become almost meaningless. Worse yet, it seems to serve as a symbolic instrument in the global politics of competitive legitimation and delegitimation devoid of any discernible impact on the actual strategic behavior of key global actors. As long as the deep structure of the war system remains untransformed, the right to peace or life, even when fully legitimized, can merely serve as a reminder of the discrepancies between normative claims and structural constraints.

The Right to Human Health. The right to human life really means the right to a healthy human life, and positive peace (the absence of structural violence) as distinct from the right to exist. Put differently, this right means an equal right *against* disease or an equal freedom *from* disease. Next to physical survival, therefore, health is the most basic human need throughout the world.[50] Without it the human person loses much of the quintessential quality of being human. Without it the human person cannot develop toward being and becoming more fully human. Without health life loses its meaning and value, and other human rights become academic. In mapping out its global strategy for health, WHO noted: "Most deaths in most developing countries result from infectious and parasitic diseases. These are closely related to prevailing social and economic conditions, and impede social and economic development."[51] The right to human health should be placed just below the right to human life in the hierarchy of human rights values.

The Right to Human Development. This right is a multidimensional one. It covers the largest domain of human needs/human rights, straddling both material basic needs and nonmaterial meta needs, individual and collective needs, and, in the parlance of UN human rights debates, economic, social, and cultural rights and civil and political rights. Recognizing a measure of complementarity between the two categories of rights forming the right to development, I still contend that the satisfaction of basic human needs deserves a prior claim since this constitutes the necessary, if not sufficient, condition for the realization of the nonmaterial meta needs (individual freedom needs and social identity needs).

The basic human needs—which, translated into entitlements, would include the right to adequate food, the right to safe water, the right to decent shelter, the right to education, and the right to work—are precisely the basic guarantees for human life and health. Their value and indispensability are so widely shared and so deeply felt in the inner nature of human beings everywhere that they have a legitimate claim to being a universal human right. Although there is no clear and concise definition of "the right to development," it has been contended that "almost all of the elements that constitute the right to development are the subject of existing declarations, resolutions, conventions or covenants."[52]

At the same time, the widespread phenomenon of "developmental fascism" warns of the danger of the prior claim of material needs being twisted into an excuse for oppressive rule. Unless or until the human factor reenters the development process as the main subject, not an object, unless or until the satisfaction of human material and nonmaterial needs are embodied as the primary purpose of the development process, and unless or until national development and human development are redefined in mutually complementary terms, however, developmental fascism will acquire its own self-sustaining momentum, claiming a heavy toll on human freedom.

The right to human development as a universal human right is then designed to seek a more humane interface between individual and national development so as to bring about the realization of the potentialities of the human person in harmony with the social process of his/her community. This redefines development in terms of a hierarchical expansion of human and social potentialities in a mutually complementary way. In short, development becomes a dynamic process of creating conditions conducive to the material, moral, and spiritual advancement of the whole human being in both individual and social capacities. Nonmaterial human needs such as individual freedom needs and social identity needs are part of this human development process. In order to ensure greater equality and social justice in the shaping and sharing of human rights values, the notion of popular participation has to be incorporated as an integral part of the right to human development. People must be allowed to participate in inscribing their own needs and dreams in shaping their own destiny. This is the meaning of the right to self-determination in the context of the human rights debate.

The Right to Human Environment. The right to a healthy and ecologically balanced environment is correlative to the rights to human life, human health, and human development. It is of vital concern to all human beings because of its organic linkage to the satisfaction of basic human needs. Even in a nonmaterial sense, the quality of human life is a function of the human environment. The right to a healthy environment is a solidarity right in so far as its implementation calls for the collective sharing of efforts and responsibilities of all human beings in their varying individual and social capacities. It is also a solidarity right in the sense of uniting the needs of present and future generations. The right to human environment is a holistic and normative answer to the clear and continuing danger of ecocide. As human dependence on environmental quality becomes increasingly evident, the status of the right to human environment as a human right will find a more secure place in the evolving international law of development.

The Pattern of Human Rights Abuses

If we apply the epidemiological model of world order developed in Chapter 4, every human right violation can be viewed as human injury. Human right injury differs from conventional human injury in the sense that it is, directly or indirectly, an injury inflicted by other human beings. It follows that a proper prescription cannot be made without a prior diagnosis of the causes and severity of injury. Yet the epidemiology of human right injury is in a "primitive" stage of conjecture. Unlike a good hospital, there is no accepted normative principle of priorities for giving preferred treatment to the most severely injured. There is no scientific procedure for measuring and monitoring the severity of human right injury. And, of course, there is no accepted principle or procedure for providing preventive or prescriptive health measures. In fact, for the victims and injured there is no court or hospital that they can turn to for help.

An undistorted delineation of the pattern, distribution, and severity of human rights violations throughout the world confronts the familiar problems of source and methodology.[53] Who collected data using what source(s)? Based on what normative and operational parameters of specification, at what levels of measurement, in what time scale, for what purpose, and for whom? Take, for example, the annual human rights report by the U.S. Department of State, entitled *Country Reports on Human Rights Practices*. Given the highly selective choice of value parameters, the use of a double standard in appraising "friends" and "foes," and the bureaucratic filtering process, this report cannot be used as reliable data for global or comparative assessment of the conditions of human rights violations throughout the world. It is designed to meet domestic political needs and functions, no more. Even the value parameters change or shift in response to the changing geopolitical rhythms of the power elites.

During the Carter administration the organization of the report followed three basic categories of human rights: (1) the right to be free from governmental violations of the integrity of the person; (2) the right to the fulfillment of vital needs such as food, shelter, health care, and education; and (3) the right to enjoy civil and political liberties. The first annual report of the Reagan administration (for the year 1981) has eliminated the second category of rights. The bottom line of the U.S. approach to human rights is also more clearly enunciated than under the Carter administration: "It is a significant service to the cause of human rights to limit the influence the USSR (together with its clients and proxies) can exert. A consistent and serious policy for human rights in the world must counter the USSR politically and bring Soviet bloc human rights violations to the attention of the world over and over again."[54]

Although there is no single unified global monitoring system, it is still possible to delineate in a preliminary way the general pattern and distribution of human rights violations based on a variety of NGO and IGO sources. The annual report of Amnesty International is useful and reliable on the status of the death penalty, torture, and political prisoners. The ODC's periodic comparative assessment of the PQLI performance, the UN's quad-rennial reports on the world social situation, and the ILO's documents and special studies can all be put to use in drawing up a global or comparative picture of the extent to which the right to human health and the right to human development are denied throughout the world. The periodic reports and documents released by the United Nations High Commissioner for Refugees (UNHCR) and such other NGOs as the United States Committee for Refugees are useful for tapping reliable data on this tragic dimension of the human predicament in Asia, Africa, and the Middle East. In addition, there are numerous journalistic and scholarly accounts of post-Holocaust genocidal massacres.

It is beyond the purpose and scope of this chapter to provide any comprehensive mapping of the pattern and distribution of human rights violations. Instead, we will give a synoptic sketch of three illustrative cases of gross human rights abuses—genocide, torture, and refugees. Each case reveals in its own way the pattern and distribution of human casualties inflicted by one human being or group against another human being or group throughout the world. Although basic human needs deprivation is an important illustrative case, it is not included here because its dimensions and distribution have been discussed already in Chapter 5. The global pattern of ecocide will be discussed in Chapter 7.

Genocide

For both etymological and political reasons the term "genocide" was given a narrow definition in the Convention on the Prevention and Punishment of the Crime of Genocide (also known simply as "the Genocide

Convention"), adopted by the General Assembly on December 9, 1948, and entered into force on January 12, 1961. Genocide, states Article 2 of the Convention, means "any of the following acts committed with intent to destroy, in whole or in part, a national, ethnical, racial or religious group, such as (a) killing members of the group; (b) causing serious bodily or mental harm to members of the group; (c) deliberately inflicting on the group conditions of life calculated to bring about its physical destruction in whole or in part; (d) imposing measures intended to prevent births within the group; and (e) forcibly transferring children of the group to another group."[55]

What is excluded from the above definition is the mass killing of a political group—political genocide. Nonetheless, the convention's definition provides the authoritative basis for sketching out the pattern of genocidal process in our times, a process of social pathology involving the mass murder of members of a specific national, ethnic, racial, or religious group. As Leo Kuper has shown in his authoritative study on the subject, the genocidal process occurs in many forms: "religious, racial, ethnic; on colonization and decolonization; in struggles for power or against defenceless groups, as scapegoats; against hunters and gatherers, and against assimilated urban populations; bureaucratic mechanized genocide, or more spontaneous and pre-industrial."[56]

There is no commonly accepted criterion for measuring and monitoring genocidal process. Any scientific or rigorous quantitative attempt is a choreographic exercise on the head of a pin. We can all agree that genocide is not an individual crime but a massive slaughter committed by one human group against another human group. But the question as to what constitutes a "massive slaughter" can be answered in absolute and relative terms only on the basis of the population of a given social group. In spite of wide variations in the estimates of the numbers of people killed in a given mass murder, however, no one is likely to deny that a genocide took place in Pakistan if only 1.2 million had been slaughtered as against the alternative higher estimate of 3 million. The total population of the Aché in the remote hinterland of Paraguay may be slightly over 1,000, but it would be difficult to avoid the charge of genocide if 50 percent of this small population were massacred.

Table 6.1 identifies seven different cases that may be regarded as genocide. This list is somewhat arbitrary due to the narrow definition of genocide adopted. It excludes such postwar political genocides as the Indonesian genocide against some half a million communists (actual or alleged) in 1965-1966, even though many of the victims were ethnic Chinese, and Idi Amin's reign of terror in 1971-1979 (which may have entailed the killing of 100,000-500,000 people from all kinds of social groups in Uganda). Pol Pot's revolutionary state terrorism in Cambodia (1975-1979), during which at least 300,000 people were killed, is excluded as coming closer to a political genocide. Moreover, the lag effects of a U.S. genocidal war that left large numbers of Cambodians ill, injured, and on the verge of starvation

TABLE 6.1
A Post-Holocaust List of Genocide

Country	Victims (Main Period)	Number of People Killed	Number of People Displaced	Regime Type of Perpetrators	Type of U.S. Support
Eastern Paraguay	Northern Ache (1962-72)	50% of Population	NA	Subfascist Military; DF	MED
Burundi	Hutu (1972)	122,000–500,000	80,000	Tribal Minority (Tutsi)	PAS
East Pakistan	Bengalis (Hindu) (1971)	1,247,000	10 million	Martial-Law	MED
Philippines (Mindanao Island)	Bangsa Moro (Muslim) (1972-80)	60,000	2.7 million (50% of Population)	Martial-Law DF	MED
Nigeria	Ibos (1966-70)	600,000–1,000,000	600,000	Military Junta	PAS
Indonesia (East Timor)	East Timorese (1975-80)	100,000–250,000	100,000–250,000	Military Junta; DF	MED
Brazil (Amazon Basin)	Indians (Various)	Various	NA	Neofascist Military; DF	MED

MED=Military, Economic, and Diplomatic; PAS=Passive Acquiescence and Silence; DF=Developmental Fascism; NA=Not Available.

Sources: Drawn from Richard Arens, ed., *Genocide in Paraguay* (Philadelphia: Temple University Press, 1976); Michael Bowen, Gary Freeman, and Kay Miller, *Passing By: The United States and Genocide in Burundi* (New York: Carnegie Endowment for International Peace, 1973); Kalyan Chaudhuri, *Genocide in Bangladesh* (Bombay: Orient Longman, 1972); Chomsky and Herman, *The Washington Connection and Third World Fascism*; Davis, *Victims of the Miracle*; James S. Dunn, *East Timor—from Portuguese Colonialism to Indonesian Incorporation* (Parliament of Australia, the Parliamentary Library, Legislative Research Service, 14 September 1977); Kuper, *Genocide*; Norman Lewis, "Genocide--From Fire and Sword to Arsenic and Bullets, Civilization Has Sent Six Million Indians to Extinction," *The Sunday Times* (London), February 23, 1969; *Genocide: A Documentary Report on the Conditions of Indian Peoples in Brazil* (Berkeley: INDIGENA and American Friends of Brazil, 1974); and Permanent Peoples' Tribunal, "Session on the Filipino People and the Bangsa Moro People," *Alternatives* 6 (Spring 1981): 599-619.

cannot be easily separated from "autogenocidal" process during the revolutionary reign of terror.[57]

On the other hand, the list includes the somewhat controversial Nigerian case based on the contention that an initial genocidal communal massacre against the Ibos was the trigger for the Biafran secession movement and the ensuing two and a half years of civil war, during which some 600,000 to 1,000,000 Easterners (Ibos) succumbed to battle, massacre, famine, and disease and some 600,000 became refugees. The plight of the Bangsa Moro People in the southern Philippine islands is virtually unknown in the West. Yet the developmental fascism of the Marcos regime has resulted in the deaths of some 60,000, the mass uprooting of some 2.7 million Bangsa Moro people from their native habitat, and their resettlement in "strategic settlements," a modern form of concentration camps.

The Brazilian case calls for clarification. The number of Brazilian Indians killed is not specified in the table because of the many different estimates based on different tribal groups in different periods. Following the release of the twenty-volume, 5,115-page government study of Indian policy (the Figueiredo Report) in March 1968 (possibly an unintended accident of domestic power struggle since it documents widespread corruption and the use of biological as well as conventional weapons against Indian tribes), numerous Western journalists and scholars have made follow-up investigations leading to the confirmation of a genocide. One report concluded that the population of the Brazilian Indians has been reduced from 3 million at the time of the white conquest to less than 100,000, while another study showed the reduction of the Indian population from 1 million in 1900 to less than 200,000 in 1957.[58] Anthropologist Shelton Davis, drawing upon all these investigations, reaches his own conclusion that official Brazilian policy of protecting Indian tribes became increasingly compromised between 1970 and 1974 and "a number of Indian tribes, such as the Parakanan and Kreen-Akarore, were uprooted and destroyed."[59]

From Table 6.1 it is possible to generalize about the social patterns and structures of genocidal process. Although these acts were all committed in the remote hinterlands of the Third World, all perpetrators and executioners (except in the two African cases) played their global role as neofascist clients or allies of the United States. This explains in part the complicity and/or "benign" silence on the part of the U.S. government and the "know nothing" posture of the U.S. mass media. The United States has yet to ratify the 1951 Convention on the Prevention and Punishment of the Crime of Genocide. In their two-volume work on the political economy of human rights, Noam Chomsky and Edward S. Herman offer a detailed and devastating exposé of "the Washington connection" of Third World fascism.[60]

Right-wing military dictatorship was a common, if not an exclusive, regime type in most cases, although this factor alone cannot explain genocidal outbreak. All seven countries were plural and heterogeneous societies marked by varying degrees of cultural, communal, and ethnic fragmentation. A neofascist regime with its absolutist Hegelian conception of the state and strong "developmental" drive is particularly prone to resort to official terror as an indispensable instrument of control and dominance.

There is an unholy alliance of sorts among genocidal process, modernizing process, and developmental process. In this connection, what the anthropologist Eric Wolf has said about the Paraguayan genocide against the

Aché is revealing and can also be applied to the generalized pattern of contemporary genocide:

> One thing is certain: the Aché are not alone in their dying. Hunters and gatherers like them have been dying and continue to die all along the internal margins of Latin America. Hundreds and thousands like them—in Peru, Brazil, Venezuela, Colombia—are driven daily from their former hunting territories to make room for incoming settlers and plantations, roads, airstrips, pipelines, oil wells. And this is hardly a new process, only the latest episode in the onward march of civilization. Wherever civilization advances, it spells the doom of the non-civilized. Out of the total range of human possibilities, civilization can tolerate only a few. In Latin America, this battle of the civilized against the non-civilized is fought by men who classify themselves as "men of reason" (*gente de razón*) against those who, bereft of that particular reason, can be classified with the animals. The Guarani-speaking Paraguayans who hunt the Aché, and the Aché, both speak varieties of the same language stock, Tupi-Guarani. But the Guarani-speaking settlers are men of reason, while the hunting and gathering Aché are in their terminology merely Guayaki, "rabid rats"; and rabid rats must be exterminated. As the Aché die, others inherit their land. The progress of civilization across the face of the earth is also a process of primary accumulation, of robbery in the name of reason. Nor is this process confined to Latin America. What goes on there now is but what went on in North America when the land was "discovered" and taken from its first occupants. It is only that in North America the process has been dignified by the passage of centuries: "dead men tell no tales."[61]

The neofascist regimes in Brazil, Indonesia, Paraguay, and the Philippines were all caught up in the modernization drive, and the "non-civilized natives"—the Amazon Indians, East Timorese, Aché Indians, and Bangsa Moro people—all stood in the way of "progress." The ideological impulse of developmental fascism called for clearing out all obstacles in the path of "civilization." In the Indonesian case, this "modernizing" impulse took the form of "expansionist genocide," conquering and subjugating the indigenous people in East Timor, a mixture of naked aggression and massive slaughter. In the Brazilian case, the genocidal and ecocidal processes proceeded hand in hand. In the Nigerian and Burundian cases, however, this "modernizing" impulse took the form of "atavistic communal genocide," designed to exterminate the Ibos and Hutus as the sources of autonomy or secession movements.

A virulent form of class conflict is manifest in all seven cases. The perception of challenge or threat to the dominant class in society served as the trip wire for setting the genocidal process in motion. This threat was a potential one in the Brazilian, Paraguayan, and Indonesian cases; it had already become an actual challenge in the remaining cases. The perception of threat moved inexorably toward its self-fulfilling prophecy. There is little doubt that external response to genocidal violence is also colored and shaped to a significant extent by preexisting ideological biases and class interests. An authoritarian social order cannot sustain itself long without believing in, and acting out, the mystique of a superior race, class, religion, or group.

Torture

Torture is defined by Amnesty International (AI) as "the systematic and deliberate infliction of acute pain in any form by one person on another, or on a third person, in order to accomplish the purpose of the former against the will of the latter."[62] Universal standards of protection against torture—and other cruel, inhuman, or degrading treatment or punishment— have been embodied in numerous international human rights declarations and conventions as well as in the constitutions and laws of more than fifty-five nations.[63] NGOs have also been active in promoting an international code of conduct to prevent torture. The Declaration of Tokyo adopted at the World Medical Association's Twenty-Ninth Assembly in October 1975, held in Tokyo, Japan, contained strict guidelines for medical doctors on the problems of torture, stating, *inter alia*, that "the doctor shall not countenance, condone or participate in the practice of torture."[64] Amnesty International, far and away the most influential human rights NGO on this subject, promoted codes of conduct for those professions most often in contact with victims of torture, in particular the Code of Conduct for Law Enforcement Officials adopted by the UN General Assembly on December 17, 1979 (Res. 34/169).

Universal human rights norms have clearly removed the stamp of legitimacy from torture, yet the recent trends are hardly encouraging. From the late eighteenth century to the early twentieth century torture seemed to be joining slavery as an historical anachronism. Yet in the mid-twentieth century torture has once again become a chillingly worldwide practice, not an aberration of a less civilized past or of a few police states. In opening AI's first International Conference on the Abolition of Torture, held in Paris in December 1973, Sean MacBride, then Chairman of the International Executive Committee of AI, stated:

> There is no doubt that the practice of torture has been on the increase in recent years. There is no doubt that its use has been more widespread. There is no doubt that it is practised with the direct or implied permission of a large number of governments, many of whom consider themselves civilized. There is no doubt that, like a contagious disease, it spreads from one country to another, and, in many cases, is deliberately imported by the armed services of one country and taught to the services of another country.[65]

Notice also the wide variety and combination of ancient and modern techniques used by many governments throughout the world. The latest annual AI report for the period May 1, 1980, to April 30, 1981, states: "Among the techniques reported during the year were: hanging people upside down and pouring water into their nostrils; electric shocks; beating the soles of the feet; smashing toes and fingers with a hammer; rape; forcing prisoners to eat live frogs and beetles; pushing people's heads into a bathtub filled with water, blood, vomit, excrement and food; deprivation of sleep; mock executions; and threats against relatives, including children. In some countries certain methods, such as flogging and amputation, were carried out in public."[66]

Torture is a particularly brutal and dehumanizing instrument of political control and dominance practiced in the hidden cells and chambers in many countries. Every now and then the grim details of torture surface. In an unusual and path-breaking decision in a case brought by the Filartiga family (the victim) against Pena (the perpetrator), announced on June 30, 1980, the U.S. Court of Appeals for the Second Circuit held in effect that torture, no matter where it is practiced, is a violation of international law and as such can be redressed in U.S. domestic courts. But what Irving R. Kaufman, a judge who wrote the opinion of the court, said about the political aspect of the case is worth quoting:

> On the night of March 29, 1976, the court documents charge, Paraguayan police officials awakened Dolly Filartiga, daughter of a political opponent of the military Government of Paraguay, and took her to the home of Americo Norberto Pena-Irala, Asuncion's inspector general of police. There she was shown the mutilated corpse of her 17-year-old brother, Joelito. He had been whipped, slashed and tortured with electrical devices. Dolly Filartiga fled from the house, and Pena followed her, allegedly shouting, "Here you have what you have been looking for for so long and what you deserve. Now shut up." The message, she felt, was clearly directed not at her but at her dissident father.[67]

Table 6.2 is a global profile of the practice of torture constructed on the basis of AI's qualitative country reports for 1981. This rather simplistic scheme is designed merely to show the worldwide spread of torture conditions, but it calls for several caveats. First, an exclusion of a country from the table does not necessarily mean that torture is not practiced there. It might mean an information gap or a temporary lull. Or it might mean that political genocide has preempted torture, as in the case of El Salvador, whose regular security forces are reported to have killed some 12,000 people in 1980 and another 16,000 in 1981. Second, the inclusion of a country in the table is based on AI's specific use of the word "torture" in each individual country report; the use of expressions such as "ill-treatment of prisoners," "poor prison conditions," and "imprisonment without trial" have been regarded either as too vague or insufficient for including that particular country. Third, the table is a summation of one year's report; it does not shed any diachronic perspective on the rise or decline of torture in a given country.

Finally, our initial attempt to use the U.S. Department of State's annual human rights report was abandoned because of the pervasive "double-think" and "double-talk" in individual country reports of favorite allies or clients (especially on South Africa, Israel, Somalia, Guatemala, and Paraguay).

TABLE 6.2
A Global Profile of Torture Practice in 1981

AFRICA	AMERICAS	ASIA	EUROPE	MIDDLE EAST & NORTH AFRICA
N=41	N=21	N=24	N=19	N=12
Benin	Argentina	Afghanistan	Spain	Bahrain
Comoros	Bolivia	Burma	Turkey	Iraq
Djibouti	Brazil	India		Libyan Arab Ja-
Ethiopia	Chile	South Korea		mahiriya
Ivory Coast	Colombia	Pakistan		Syria
Madagascar	Guatemala	Philippines		Tunisia
Mali	Haiti			
Mauritania	Honduras			
Namibia	Mexico			
Somalia	Paraguay			
South Africa	Peru			
Uganda	Uruguay			
Zaire				

Source: Adapted from *Amnesty International Report 1981* (London: Amnesty International Publications, 1981).

Nonetheless, it must also be added that AI is not completely free of its own ideological blind spot. For example, AI's country report on Israel almost self-consciously substitutes such expressions as "unnecessarily harsh methods" and "numerous allegations of police and army brutality" for "torture."[68]

Although torture is a worldwide phenomenon, its distribution is uneven. Torture is virtually nonexistent in Europe, North America, New Zealand, and Australia. The return of democracy in Greece in 1974 brought those who had committed torture during the seven years of military dictatorship (1967-1974) to the Athens Permanent Court Martial, and AI's *Torture in Greece: The First Torturers Trial 1975* (1977) is one of the most revealing—and moving—human rights commentaries of our troubled time. There are substantial numbers of political prisoners in the Soviet bloc, but credible allegations of torture are few and far between. Nonetheless, the Soviet practice of sending a select group of political dissidents to lunatic asylums in the disguise of "treatment" is a form of torture—and abuse of psychiatry for political oppression—and deserves condemnation.[69] As for the other regions of the world, torture is so rampant in Africa, Southeast Asia and Latin America that one may easily draw up a relationship between the "global genocidal belt" and the "global torture belt."

Jorge Dominguez suggests "a relationship between lower levels of torture (in frequency and intensity) and some institutionalized concern in the political system with suppressing torture" and "a relationship between higher levels of torture and conditions in which public discussions of torture are suppressed."[70] A UN study has also shown that torture is an instrument of apartheid.[71] Torture is an integral part of oppressive rule, to be sure, but it is also a function of the cult of violence. Just as torturers cannot dehumanize their victims without dehumanizing themselves, so any political culture that condones torture is also a sick and suicidal one.

Refugees

That so many people in so many parts of the world are being uprooted from their homelands and set adrift in the stormy seas of global politics is another tragic commentary of our time. Every refugee has his (or her) own story to tell, and this adds up to some 10 million stories of human catastrophe and suffering. However, it seems safe to generalize that any refugee is fleeing a clear and present danger to his human rights—the right to life, or the right to health, or the right to developmental freedoms. In breaking away from home, friends, family, and native environment, often abruptly and without possessions, in search of safety and freedom, the refugee often wakes up the next morning to find himself in a legal no-man's-land as a *de facto* stateless refugee or as an unwelcome and illegal alien in a foreign country.[72] Of course, many simply perish during the odyssey of traumatic transition.

Who is a refugee in the world today? Although formulated in the immediate postwar period for European refugees (and also in the context of Cold War I), the international community still follows the definition of a refugee provided in the 1951 Convention Relating to the Status of Refugees, as amended by the 1967 Protocol Relating to the Status of Refugees and as embodied in the Statute of the UNHCR—that is, any person who "owing to well-founded fear of being persecuted for reasons of race, religion, nationality, membership of a particular social group or political opinion, is outside the country of his nationality and is unable or, owing to such fear, is unwilling to avail himself of the protection of that country; or who, not having a nationality and being outside the country of his former habitual residence as a result of such events, is unable or, owing to such fear, is unwilling to return to it."[73]

The global dimensions of the refugee problem are suggested in Table 6.3, which provides a rough statistical breakdown of the distribution of refugees and "internally displaced" persons in 1981–1982. The table is an underestimation, for the figures include only those in "need of a permanent home," excluding those refugees who had already resettled. The 1980 survey, which used the same statistical procedures and UNHCR as the principal source but included 3 million "resettled" refugees, reported a global total of 16 million. The distinction between a refugee needing help and a resettled person is open to debate, but the 1980 total of 16 million may still serve as a more realistic global total for the world's political refugees.[74]

Although it is impossible to predict short-term trends and fluctuations for the flow of refugees, several long-term trends and patterns can be

TABLE 6.3
A Global Profile of Refugees, 1981–1982

	Refugees	Internally Displaced	Total
1981			
Africa	3,589,340	2,735,000	6,324,340
Asia	1,994,500	170,000	2,164,500
Europe	354,600		354,600
Latin America	189,600	50,000	239,600
Middle East	1,962,200	1,600,000	3,562,200
Global Total=	8,090,240	4,555,000	12,645,240
1982			
Africa	2,251,600	560,000	2,811,600
Asia	954,700	234,000	1,188,700
Europe	613,200		613,200
Latin America	388,700	183,000	571,700
North America	1,187,000		1,187,000
Middle East	4,637,200	250,000	4,887,200
Global Total=	10,032,400	1,227,000	11,259,400

Source: Adapted from U.S. Committee for Refugees, *1981 World Refugee Survey* (New York: U.S. Committee for Refugees, 1981) and *World Refugee Survey 1982* (New York: U.S. Committee for Refugees, 1982).

extrapolated from postwar developments to date. The refugee problem is no longer a local or regional problem. Its global nature is now clearly discernible. Some thirty-seven countries have acquired the dubious distinction as major refugee-producers located in every region of the world.[75] The spread and settlement or resettlement of refugees is global in scope. In spite of great fluctuation, the general trend of refugee flow is upward. When UNHCR won its first Nobel Peace Prize in 1954, for example, there were only 2.2 million refugees; this number had increased sevenfold by the end of 1981, when UNHCR won its second Nobel Peace Prize.

The refugee problem, once regarded as primarily a European phenomenon, has now become a worldwide Third World phenomenon. Once regarded as an unfortunate outcome of war, it has now become a permanent feature of the international social landscape, reflecting and revealing both direct violence (war) and the more deeply rooted structural violence. The cumulative and multiplier effects of so many violent conflicts and so many gross abuses of human rights make the refugee problem a global crisis.

Not surprisingly, the settlement or resettlement of refugees also follows the logic of competitive geopolitical and propagandistic gamesmanship rather than the logic of human needs or human solidarity.

However one defines a refugee, there is a general consensus that he or she is entitled to two basic human rights as a refugee: the right to *the principle of asylum* (also embodied in the Universal Declaration of Human Rights in Article 14, 1) and the right to *the principle of non-refoulement* (that he or she cannot be forcefully returned to the country or countries where he or she has well-founded reasons to fear persecution). However, the flight from intolerable economic misery cannot be invoked in claiming refugee status. There are three basic solutions to the refugee problem: (1) *repatriation* back to the homeland; (2) *settlement* in the country of first asylum; and (3) *resettlement*—the movement of refugees from the country of first asylum to another country of potentially permanent residence.

In spite of the protection of these rights, refugees suffer from a variety of threats (malnutrition, disease, and even death) during their journey to a "safe" haven. More often than not, they face the same or even worse threats to their basic human dignity in their host country. In a recent editorial, *Refugees*, UNHCR's newspaper, sums up the discouraging trends as follows:

> Those in search of asylum have been turned away or subjected to physical violence or even killed when attempting to enter a country of refuge. . . . Asylum seekers in boats continue to fall prey to pirates and to be subjected to the vilest of atrocities. Some reach the shore only to find that they are to be towed out and returned to the high seas. In other parts of the world, refugees are denied access to basic legal remedies in their efforts to obtain asylum or protection against arbitrary detention or forcible return to their country of origin. Elsewhere, refugees have been abducted and have disappeared without a trace.[76]

The settlement or resettlement process is subject to the class, racial, and geopolitical biases of host countries. If Soviet Jews have become first-class jet set refugees, preempting the lion's share of mass media coverage in the United States, the displaced and dispossessed in Africa remain largely ignored and forgotten as third-class refugees with no geopolitical or electoral clout. The U.S. treatment of the Haitian and Cuban "asylum seekers" in recent years is also revealing. About 5,000 Haitians, most of whom arrived by sea in dangerous boats, claimed that they were fleeing political repression in their homeland and seeking political asylum. But the U.S. government placed most of them in Federal detention camps as "economic refugees," while at the same time accepting and relocating nearly all of the 125,000 Cubans who fled by small boats to the United States in the spring of 1980, even though only a minority of them "met the conventional requirements for political asylum."[77]

In his survey analysis of human rights conditions in the Third World in the early 1970s, Rupert Emerson made two points about Africa. The first is that "Africa, in the years since most of its peoples achieved independence, has come to be the continent of refugees," and the second is that "the vast scale of this migration of fellow countrymen and fellow Africans is a sad commentary on the limitations of African solidarity and brotherhood."[78] Emerson was on target on his first point but somewhat off the mark on his second point. There is no doubt that since the early 1970s Africa has remained the continent with the most severe and crushing refugee burden. At the end of 1972, according to the 1973 report of the UNHCR, African refugees amounted to 1 million or more.[79] Today, African refugees and "internally displaced persons" represent a substantial portion of the global total (see Table 6.3). One out of every seventy-five inhabitants in Africa is a refugee.

However, despite ethnic and cultural fragmentation—there are some 800 distinct ethnic groups and more than 1,000 different languages in Africa—and despite the heaviest concentration of the poorest countries in the world, African countries have no peer in extending hospitality and generosity. Somalia hosts 1.5 million refugees from Ethiopia (90 percent of whom are women and children), one refugee to every three persons in the country. "Tanzania, like some other African nations, has set aside land for the permanent settlement of refugees who have come from neighboring states."[80]

Of course, such hospitality from an empty table has its limits, especially in hard times. The recent global economic recession has sharpened the perception of aliens, including refugees, as unwelcome competitors for limited economic opportunities, as tragically dramatized in the expulsion of over 2 million illegal aliens from Nigeria in early 1983, following the collapse of the oil boom in that country. To date, however, this expulsion policy has not spread to other African countries.

Although the refugee problem is choking the infrastructure and economic development of much of the continent, Africa is not asking the international community to resettle its refugee population—an enormously expensive and socially nonviable solution for the refugees and the host countries alike—but a fair and equitable sharing of the burden.

In contrast is the cold rejection of Indochinese refugees by the Association of Southeast Asian Nations (ASEAN) countries and Japan, the Asian members of "the free world." In July 1979, Thailand forcefully returned more than 40,000 Cambodian refugees back across the border, placing them in the cross fire between the Pol Pot and Heng Samrin forces. Of the 886,533 Indochinese refugees who have made "third-country resettlement" during the period 1975–July 1980, only 557 "resettled" in Japan and their conditions are so intolerable that they are now actively seeking resettlement elsewhere.

In a sense, Japan is worse than South Africa, for while resident Japanese businessmen in South Africa receive—and seem to enjoy—the absurd status as "honorary Caucasians," Koreans in Japan, notwithstanding their cultural and linguistic assimilation, remain socially and economically condemned as second-class citizens—another forgotten story of human rights abuse. It is little wonder, then, that Indochinese refugees in Japan assume their fate will be no better than that of the Korean minority in Japan.[81] No less an admirer of Japanese technocracy than Herman Kahn relates the following revealing anecdote:

> The Japanese do not think of themselves as being racist. I once brought surprise to a number of senior Americans and Japanese with whom I was having dinner by suggesting that in some ways Japan is the most racist nation in the world. One of them asked me to explain what I meant. I started, of course, with the obvious point that the Japanese, at least in comparison with other groups, are relatively pure racially. There are, so to speak, no blond Japanese, no red-haired Japanese, no blue-eyed Japanese. And the attitude of the Japanese toward miscegenation is very different from that of, say, the French or the Chinese. If somebody is born of a mixed marriage in France or China but grows up perfectly familiar with and skilled in the indigenous culture, he is largely accepted. That is not true in Japan. The children of mixed marriages are more or less permanently barred from participating fully and comfortably in the society. Those bars also hold against children born in Japan but of Korean or Chinese parentage. *One crucial point in the discussion was that the Japanese do not normally notice that they discriminate against these minorities, because the discrimination is so thorough that the issue usually does not arise* {my italics}. I asked the Japanese if they could imagine, for example, having a General of Korean parentage. They could not. I pointed out that it was perfectly possible in China.[82]

The imagery of "boat people" facing a life or death choice between sinking to hell and swimming to "freedom" has created a false impression that the global refugee problem is a "natural" disaster calling for humanitarian emergency aid. Aid is absolutely essential to alleviate the misery and suffering of the displaced, but the refugee problem is a man-made disaster rooted in both direct physical and indirect structural violence to human dignity. If it is natural for people to flee in the face of an imminent danger to life—Erich Fromm has called this the 'flight' instinct[83]—it is equally natural for people to return to their homelands once the original reason for their flight has been removed. Although refugee-producing situations vary from time to time and from place to place, the following success stories of repatriation in recent years[84] reveal some of the major causes and solutions of the refugee problem:

- The return of some 250,000 Algerian refugees from Morocco and Tunisia following Algeria's independence from France in 1962;
- The return of some 10 million Bengali refugees from India following East Pakistan's successful secession as the new state of Bangladesh in 1972;
- The return of 429,000 refugees to their homelands in Guinea-Bissau, Mozambique, and Angola following the transition of these former Portuguese territories to newly independent states in 1974–1976;

- As a result of negotiations between the Burmese and Bangladesh governments, some 200,000 Burmese Muslim refugees who had fled to Bangladesh were repatriated in 1978-1979;
- The return of some 100,000 Nicaraguan refugees from neighboring countries following the defeat of the Somoza regime in Nicaragua in 1979; and
- The return home of over 1 million refugees and internally displaced persons following the successful transformation of the white racist regime into the independent and multiracial state of Zimbabwe in 1980.

International Response

The protection of human rights was relegated to a marginal status in the development of international law during the pre–World War II era. The dominance of the state interest over the human interest remained the hallmark even in the normative domain of modern international relations (see Chapter 2). Notable exceptions include the abolition of slavery and the slave trade, the development of "humanitarianism" in the law of war, the promotion of international labor legislation, and the establishment of an international regime for the protection of minorities under the League of Nations. Both international law and practice, however, followed the statist logic of the Westphalian system that how each sovereign state mistreated its citizens was none of international business.

Out of the Holocaust evolved the revolutionary concept of "crimes against humanity" and the progressive erosion of the domestic jurisdiction defense in international law. The contrast between the preambles of the Covenant of the League of Nations and of the Charter of the United Nations in the field of human rights shows a great normative leap in the development of international concern and response. Whereas the former is silent, the latter proclaims "faith in fundamental human rights, in the dignity and worth of the human person, in the equal rights of men and women and of nations large and small." The embodiment of human rights principles and provisions in the UN Charter, followed by the adoption of the Universal Declaration of Human Rights in 1948, helped to place the concept of basic human dignity on the agenda of postwar international politics.

How, and in what manner, has this holistic concept of basic human dignity been applied during the postwar period? What may be called the United Nations system of human rights reflects the successes and failures of the postwar international system in this area. The UN system comes very close to being a global human rights regime, having developed and embodied the main attributes of an international regime in a given issue area—principles, norms, rules, and decisionmaking procedures providing the focal point for the actors' expectations and behavior.[85] The dynamics of human rights politics in international society can be understood in terms of two main types of activities in successive stages: the value-shaping process and the value-realizing process.[86]

The value-shaping process involves collective legitimation of certain moral claims based on basic human needs in the social process. Specifically, this legitimating process entails the first-stage translation of moral claims into general standards or general principles of human rights, usually in the form of declarations, and the second-stage translation of declarations into legal norms defining specific rights and obligations in the form of treaties and covenants.

The value-realizing process involves collective choice in the establishment of institutional machinery and procedures to implement human rights instruments. Human rights instruments, whether they take the form of declarations, covenants, or conventions, are effective only to the extent that they are implemented by the signatories acting either individually or collectively. To implement human rights instruments requires specific methods and procedures, such as periodic reporting systems, procedures for dealing with interstate and individual communications and complaints, as well as monitoring, supervising, and sanctioning mechanisms.

The Value-Shaping Process

Common methods employed by state actors in the value-shaping process include the preparation and adoption of multilateral declarations, covenants, coventions, or treaties relating either to human rights in general or to certain specific categories of human rights. The preparation and adoption of a declaration by the General Assembly, by a plenipotentiary global conference convened under the auspices of the General Assembly, or by a conference of specialized agencies of the United Nations system is a common practice by which certain needs become articulated and legitimated as general standards or general principles of human rights.

Between 1946 and 1981, the General Assembly adopted fifteen declarations dealing exclusively with human rights, and five more general declarations in which reference is made to the promotion and protection of human rights. In addition, UN-sponsored global conferences have adopted the following declarations concerning human rights: the Proclamation of Teheran (1968); the Declaration of the United Nations Conference on the Human Environment (1972); the Universal Declaration on the Eradication of Hunger and Malnutrition (1974); the Declaration of Mexico on the Equality of Men and Women and Their Contribution to Development and Peace (1975); and the Declaration on Equality of Opportunity and Treatment for Women Workers (1975).[87]

Although a declaration is normally adopted by the General Assembly in the form of a resolution, the main initiatives in this standard-setting process came from a variety of sources—the Secretary-General, member states individually or collectively, the General Assembly, the ECOSOC, the Commission on Human Rights, the Commission on the Status of Women, and the Sub-Commission on Prevention of Discrimination and

Protection of Minorities. According to a memorandum prepared by the UN Office of Legal Affairs and submitted to the Commission on Human Rights at its eighteenth session in 1962, a "declaration" in UN practice "is a solemn instrument resorted to only in very rare cases relating to matters of major and lasting importance where maximum compliance is expected." To the extent that the expectation of compliance is justified by state practice, the memo further notes, "a declaration may by custom become recognized as laying down rules binding upon States."[88] Likewise, Clyde Ferguson argues: "The erosion of this {positivist} concept has now reached the point that most lawyers at least assert that the Universal Declaration {of Human Rights} is, in and of itself, international law."[89]

However, the legal status of norm-creating and law-declaring activities of the General Assembly expressed through its declarations has always remained controversial. In actuality, the debate about the legislative or quasi-legislative status of declaratory resolutions is academic, since a typical declaration still needs to be translated into a more specific and concrete set of legal norms embodying specific rights and obligations. Unless the amorphous quality of a declaration is given a specific form and substance for the behavior of the states, it remains an instrument of competitive legitimation.

The drafting of the International Bill of Rights highlights the value-shaping process within the existing world order system. The Universal Declaration of Human Rights has exerted the most significant and far-reaching global influence in this value-shaping process. As a "common standard of achievement for all peoples and all nations," it became the most authoritative yardstick by which to measure the degree of compliance in the behavior of the member states. It served as the main catalyst and inspiration for the international legislative process in the field of human rights. Its provisions were repeatedly cited as the legitimizing authority in the decisionmaking of many international organizations. Its influence even extended to the creation of many new national constitutions and municipal laws.

The history of the International Bill of Rights also suggests a common practice of establishing a broad conceptual framework through a declaration, followed by normative specification and elaboration in the form of a multilateral convention. Besides the International Bill of Rights, the United Nations Declaration on the Elimination of All Forms of Racial Discrimination (1963) was followed by the International Convention on the Elimination of All Forms of Racial Discrimination. Currently, there is a treaty-making process underway to translate the 1959 Declaration of the Rights of the Child and the 1975 Declaration on the Protection of All Persons from Being Subjected to Torture and Other Cruel, Inhuman or Degrading Treatment or Punishment into multilateral human rights conventions.

Although the International Bill of Rights is normally defined restrictively as consisting of the Universal Declaration, the two covenants and the single protocol referred to above, it can also be broadly defined as encompassing the entire corpus of international human rights law, which contains (in addition to the Universal Declaration and the two covenants), some forty-seven documents.[90] Table 6.4 provides a list and the status of twenty-one main international human rights instruments as of July 1, 1982. As in the case of human rights declarations, there is no single unified formula, procedure, or time period for the treaty-making process. Each has its own birth place, its own politics of drafting and ratification, and its own degree of acceptability.

Given the centrality of the two covenants on human rights—notice that they have been termed "covenants," not "conventions," to signify their over-all importance—it may be useful to examine the making of the two covenants briefly. The entire process took almost three decades, with the first two decades (1947–1966) consumed in the politics of drafting and the last decade (1966–1976) in the politics of ratification.

This suggests that the shaping of human rights values entails an agonizingly slow process of working out an unending series of compromises on the principles, norms, and procedures to make a given convention or covenant acceptable to as many member states as possible. Next is the equally slow process of gaining signatures during the final ratification process. In the case of the International Bill of Rights, the complex nature of the two covenants, the East-West rivalry, and the membership explosion all played their parts in complicating and delaying the treaty-making process.

The postwar period witnessed an unprecedented growth and proliferation of international human rights instruments. This phenomenal growth has been necessitated by advancing science and technology, growing transnational networks of interactions, sharpening global consciousness of inhumanity, and rising popular demand for human dignity. All of these factors, coupled with the rise of the Third World as a global actor, have intensified global normative politics. The active participation in this global normative politics has also become an integral part of the status drive—an international beauty contest—that most governments cannot do without. Many governments have come to rely upon international legitimation as an important source of political legitimacy at home. In short, the postwar value-shaping process has drawn energy from both objective and subjective, practical and idealistic conditions of international society.

There still remains the question as to whether, and to what extent, this flurry of activity has shifted the balance of competing values from the state interest to the human interest. Our argument is that the value-shaping process has been allowed to proceed only as long as it does not seriously compromise the Westphalian statist principles and norms. Notice the pattern of selective adherence to the main international human rights instruments in Table 6.4. The Optional Protocol, which establishes and enables the Human Rights Committee to receive and consider communications from reported victims of human rights violations, has been ratified or acceded to by only twenty-eight states (as of November 30, 1982).

The ratification performance of the Big Five, especially of China, the Soviet Union, and the United States, merits a brief explanation. None of

TABLE 6.4
The Status of Multilateral Human Rights Treaties (as of July 1, 1982)

Treaty	DEF	TNSP	TNNR	PRC	France	UK	USA	USSR
(1)	1/3/76	73	10		X	X	S	X
(2)	3/23/76	70	11		X	Xa	S	X
(3)	3/23/76	27	7					
(4)	1/4/69	115	9	X	X	X	S	X
(5)	7/18/76	67	6					X
(6)	9/3/81	39	51	X	S	S	S	X
(7)	1/12/51	89	4		X	X	S	X
(8)	11/11/70	23	1					X
(9)	12/7/53	61	6		X	X	X	
(10)	12/7/55	46	0		X	X	X	
(11)	7/7/55	77	0		X	X	X	X
(12)	4/30/57	96	4		X	X	X	X
(13)	7/25/51	53	6		X			X
(14)	4/22/54	90	0	Xb	X	X		
(15)	10/4/67	89	0	Xb	X	X	X	
(16)	12/13/75	10	4		S	X		
(17)	6/6/60	32	8		X	X		
(18)	8/24/62	11	6		X			
(19)	8/11/58	54	8			X		X
(20)	7/7/54	90	4		X	X	X	X
(21)	12/9/64	31	8		S	X	S	
Total Number of Ratifications=				4	14	15	6	12
Total Number of Signatures Not Followed by Ratifications=				0	3	1	6	0

DEF=Date of Entry into Force; TNSP=Total Number of States Parties; TNNR=Total Number of Signatures Not Followed by Ratification; X=Ratification, accession, notification of succession, acceptance or definitive signature; S=Signature not yet followed by ratification.

a=Declaration recognizing the competence of the Human Rights Committee under Article 41 of the International Covenant on Civil and Political Rights

b=Acceded to subsequent to July 1, 1982.

(1) International Covenant on Economic, Social and Cultural Rights; (2) International Covenant on Civil and Political Rights; (3) Optional Protocol to the International Covenant on Civil and Political Rights; (4) International Convention on the Elimination of All Forms of Racial Discrimination; (5) International Convention on the Suppression and Punishment of the Crime of *Apartheid*; (6) Convention on the Elimination of All Forms of Discrimination against Women; (7) Convention on the Prevention and Punishment of the Crime of Genocide; (8) Convention on the Non-Applicability of Statutory Limitations to War Crimes and Crimes Against Humanity; (9) Slavery Convention of 1926; (10) 1953 Protocol Amending the 1926 Convention; (11)

the Big Five has signed or ratified the Optional Protocol. China, the worst holdout, has a variety of reasons for being so parsimonious in its treaty practice, the most important being its exclusion from the treaty-making process until 1971 and its excessive defensive claims of state sovereignty, an expression of a siege mentality that goes back to the traumatic period of unequal treaties.[91] The Soviet Union has ratified twelve conventions, suggesting not so much a renewed vigor in its commitment to carry out international human rights norms as its perception that the implementation procedures are incapable of penetrating through its domestic jurisdiction shield.[92]

This brings us to the ratification performance of the United States as the self-styled champion of global human rights. Of the twenty-one legally binding conventions, the United States has ratified the six least controversial and potent ones concerning slavery, refugees, and the political rights of women. Even though the United States was originally a strong proponent of an International Bill of Rights and even though the Covenant on Civil and Political Rights made its own liberal individualism the international norm, the Eisenhower administration, operating under the influence of the Dulles Doctrine, declared that it would not become a party to the proposed UN Covenants on Human Rights. This symbolized "U.S. unwillingness to be judged in front of the world by the very principles enshrined in its own Bill of Rights, particularly the principle of racial equality which was also reflected in the Covenant on Civil and Political Rights."[93]

There is some justification to the claim that the Carter administration placed human rights firmly on the agenda of global politics. By doing so, however, it also highlighted its own credibility problem. In order to deal with this problem, President Carter signed the two covenants, but not the Optional Protocol, in October 1977, and sent them to the U.S. Senate for advice and consent, where they have since languished. The refusal to sign the Optional Protocol is based on a fear that the private complaints procedure embodied therein would bring individual and group communications from Indians, Puerto Ricans, and others with long-standing

---

TABLE 6.4
The Status of Multilateral Human Rights Treaties (As of July 1, 1982) (continued)

Slavery Convention of 1926 as amended; (12) Supplementary Convention on the Abolition of Slavery, the Slave Trade, and Institutions and Practices Similar to Slavery; (13) Convention for the Suppression of the Traffic in Persons and of the Exploitation of the Prostitution of Others; (14) Convention Relating to the Status of Refugees; (15) Protocol relating to the Status of Refugees; (16) Convention on the Reduction of Statelessness; (17) Convention Relating to the Status of Stateless Persons; (18) Convention on the International Right of Correction; (19) Convention on the Nationality of Married Women; (20) Convention on the Political Rights of Women; and (21) Convention on Consent to Marriage, Minimum Age for Marriage and Registration of Marriages.

Source: Adapted from *Human Rights International Instruments, Signatures, Ratifications, Accessions, etc. 1 July 1982*, UN Doc. ST/HR/4/Rev.4 (New York: United Nations, 1982).

grievances. Moreover, the covenants, as submitted to the Senate, are saddled with many elaborate and anachronistic reservations, such as: "We are the United States but we are not Texas or Colorado, and therefore we cannot make them do anything; we will use our best efforts to tell them, please do not violate people's human rights, but you must recognize we are a federal system."[94]

Although the Reagan administration has shown no sign of pushing Senate action on the covenants, it finds no contradiction or embarrassment in invoking the authority of "internationally recognized human rights" as an instrument of its foreign (and domestic) policy. In July 1982, for example, the Reagan administration certified El Salvador as having complied with "internationally recognized human rights" as a statutory condition for continuing military aid.[95] This certification, albeit laced with many qualifications, is made in the face of the indiscriminate slaughter of unarmed civilians, as attested to by all independent witnesses (the American Civil Liberties Union, Americas Watch Committee, the Lawyers Committee for International Human Rights, the Council on Hemispheric Affairs, and the Washington Office on Latin America).[96]

The Value-Realizing Process

The United Nations Charter specifically obliges (in Article 55) that the world organization shall promote "universal respect for, and observance of, human rights and fundamental freedoms for all without distinction as to race, sex, language, or religion." The specific rules, procedures, and decisionmaking machinery for implementation provided in the human rights instruments referred to or developed by custom and usage all strive theoretically to fulfill this charter obligation. Yet the main weakness of the global human rights regime lies precisely in the wide, almost unbridgeable gap between normative claims and implementation capabilities. In fact, one of the defining characteristics of the global human rights regime is the enormous discrepancy between its human rights ideals and human rights realities.

Although the International Bill of Rights is now a juridical reality, the procedures established for its implementation are problematic. To make the International Bill of Rights acceptable to as many member states as possible, the implementation machinery was substantially weakened by optional and escape clauses. Yet adherence to the International Bill of Rights can hardly be characterized as universal. As of July 1, 1982, the ratification rate (measured in terms of percentage of the UN membership) of the International Covenant on Economic, Social and Cultural Rights, the International Covenant on Civil and Political Rights, and the Optional Protocol respectively stood at 47 percent, 45 percent, and 17 percent. There is no sign that this poor adherence rate will improve.

With the completion of the International Bill of Rights in 1966, the United Nations shifted gears from the treaty-making to the treaty-implementing phase. The outer limits and possibilities of the regime's implementation capability can be briefly summarized in three different sets of implementation procedures: (1) the procedures on periodic reporting; (2) the procedures for dealing with interstate complaints; and (3) the procedures on private individual communications and complaints.

The submission of reports to an international regime is a procedure of long standing that predates the United Nations. A variety of reporting requirements on human rights issues are specified in the UN Charter (Article 64) and several multilateral human rights treaties. The two covenants have detailed provisions on reporting. In May 1976, ECOSOC established a system of biennial reports for various parts of the Covenant on Economic, Social and Cultural Rights.[97] The Human Rights Committee (HRC), a newly established eighteen-member committee mandated to implement the International Covenant on Civil and Political Rights, has its own system of annual reports; the committee approved general guidelines regarding the form and content of reports at its second session in August 1977.[98]

All of these developments have merely produced a proliferation and multiplicity of competing reporting systems with no central cohesion and guidance. As noted earlier, there is no global monitoring system today, and even a meticulous compilation of all UN documents cannot be used as a reliable basis for a state-of-the-globe report on human rights conditions. Theoretically, HRC breaks a new path in implementation procedures for periodic reporting. Under Article 40 of the Covenant on Civil and Political Rights, for example, the states parties are required within one year of the entry into force of the covenant "to submit reports on the measures they have adopted which give effect to the rights recognized herein and on the progress made in the enjoyment of those rights" and thereafter whenever HRC so requests. Although some state parties have either failed to submit initial reports or have failed to submit additional information they had promised during the consideration of their initial reports, the record to date is better than expected as the great majority have fulfilled their reporting obligations, and HRC had examined as of its thirteenth session (July 1981) the initial reports of some forty-four state parties and nine supplementary reports.[99]

Of course, the key test of HRC's reporting system is not the exercise of bureaucratic gymnastics but the extent to which the system will help to reshape the domestic laws, regulations, administrative provisions, or even the judicial measures necessary to give effect to the provisions of the covenant. Viewed in this light, one cannot be too optimistic. The problematic states would still remain beyond the purview of the reporting system, limiting the committee to addressing a converted audience. That the states parties such as Canada, Sweden, and Senegal responded positively to a reexamination of their domestic legal systems in the course of their participation in HRC supports the argument about the limited implementation capability of the reporting procedures embodied in the committee.[100]

The central fact that the state is the perpetrator, not the victim, of human rights violations works against the establishment of viable implementation procedures for dealing with interstate complaints. More than a dozen multilateral human rights conventions provide for the submission of disputes between the parties to the International Court of Justice. Yet invariably these provisions are shackled by the consent principle, requiring a prior agreement of all the parties to the dispute for a third-party arbitration or conciliation.

The two covenants are instructive on this subject. The Covenant on Economic, Social and Cultural Rights has no provisions for dealing with interstate complaints. The Covenant on Civil and Political Rights has the *optional* provisions of Article 41 under which a state party to the Covenant "may at any time declare under this article that it recognizes the competence of the {Human Rights} Committee to receive and consider communications to the effect that a State Party claims that another State Party is not fulfilling its obligations under the present Covenant." Note here that the provisions of the optional Article 41 are further weakened by numerous qualifications and cumbersome multistage procedures requiring (1) that a complaining state party has to first of all bring the matter to the attention of the target state party through written communication; (2) that HRC shall hold closed meetings; (3) that HRC shall make available its "good offices" to the parties to the dispute with a view to a friendly resolution of the matter; and (4) that if no solution is reached HRC shall prepare a report limited to a brief statement of facts and the text of the written and oral submissions of the parties.

The provisions of this optional article can come into force when only ten States Parties to the Covenant have made their declarations recognizing the competence of HRC on this matter. In accordance with this requirement, the provisions of Article 41 entered into force on March 28, 1979. As of July 1, 1982, the governments of the following fourteen states had made their declarations: Austria, Canada, Denmark, Finland, Germany (Federal Republic), Iceland, Italy, the Netherlands, New Zealand, Norway, Senegal, Sri Lanka, Sweden, and the United Kingdom.[101]

Given the state-centric straightjacket surrounding the procedures for interstate complaints, it is difficult to see how HRC can serve as effective implementation machinery for handling interstate complaints. There are no unified or agreed methods for dealing with interstate human rights complaints. Nor is there any UN Court of Human Rights comparable to the European Court of Human Rights. This machinery is further weakened by denying any role to NGOs, the only viable parties that can act on behalf of the oppressed. The dominance of the state interest over the human interest in world politics also makes the enforcement of international human rights law both more necessary and more difficult to implement. Although it is still premature to give any definitive judgment about HRC's implementation capability, the built-in structural impediments are likely to immobilize the implementation machinery or to work more as a shield for state sovereignty than as a sword against violating states.

From its very inception, the United Nations through its Secretariat has been receiving each year thousands of private complaints and petitions alleging violations of human rights. Yet ECOSOC as the supervisory body has maintained that the Commission on Human Rights and the Commission on the Status of Women have no power to take any action concerning such complaints. Faced with the intensifying pressure and concern of the Third World with the colonial, racial, and apartheid dimensions of human rights in the 1960s, however, ECOSOC began to reverse the self-negating mandate through its Resolution 1235 (XLII) in 1967 and Resolution 1503 (XLVIII) in 1970. The former granted authority to its functional human rights bodies to examine information relevant to "gross violations of human rights and fundamental freedoms" as exemplified in South Africa, South West Africa (Namibia), and Southern Rhodesia. The latter set up a complex machinery authorized to screen and examine complaints from individuals and NGOs that "appear to reveal a consistent pattern of gross and reliably attested violations of human rights and fundamental freedoms."

The effectiveness of this new system of private complaints and communications has been spotty. Thanks to the Third World, it has been applied with some degree of consistency and vigor to the gross violations of human rights by the pariah states—Southern Rhodesia, South Africa, Israel, and Chile. But the use of cumbersome, long, and multistage procedure, coupled with the rule of confidentiality, has meant in effect only cases that would meet the requirements of political expediency and coalition in the commission at a given time can see the light of day.[102] For example, the Commission on Human Rights has recently applied the 1503 procedure with regard to Bolivia, Equatorial Guinea, Malawi, Republic of Korea, Uganda, Ethiopia, Indonesia, Paraguay, and Uruguay. Yet the rule of confidentiality has disconnected the commission from the international community and oppressed peoples. As a result, the commission's work has become a closet movement without the pressure of a world court of public opinion. At one point, even the Soviet representative Valerian Zorin complained that the confidentiality rule was being carried to the point of absurdity.[103]

With the coming into force of the Optional Protocol in 1976, another implementation machinery for handling private complaints has been added to the existing UN machinery. Under Article 1 of the Optional Protocol HRC is mandated to receive and consider communications from individuals (subject to the jurisdiction of a state party to the protocol) who claim to be victims of a violation by their state of any of the rights specified in the covenant. At its sixth (1977) and subsequent sessions HRC established working groups to consider the communications of the individual and the state party concerned under the Optional Protocol.[104]

However, this implementation system has also been weakened by more or less the same qualifications and restrictions as HRC's reporting system. This implementation net is not designed to catch big fish (gross violators). It seems destined to work as an international machinery of limited scope and jurisdiction among a minority of the state parties to scrutinize their domestic administrative and judicial imperfections.

A Critical Appraisal

From the preceding analysis we can draw the main conclusion, at once obvious and essential: there is a sharp discontinuity and discrepancy between the value-shaping and value-realizing capabilities of the present world order system.

We can argue, from the perspective of a world order optimist, that the thirty-year struggle, despite the gloomy predictions of the Cassandras, has finally made the International Bill of Rights a living political and juridical reality and that it now provides the core of universal human rights norms for rich and poor, for capitalist and socialist, and for developed and developing countries throughout the world. Given the statist and hegemonic constraints within which this struggle has taken place, it can also be argued, this is a miracle of sorts. The International Bill of Rights not only provides a common normative language of intellectual discourse but also serves as a concrete road map in our journey from here to there. We now have at least one specific example supporting this line of positive reasoning. An incipient human rights movement issued "Charter 77," drawing its legitimacy from the incorporation of the two covenants into the domestic laws of Czechoslovakia.[105]

Although the global human rights regime leaves much to be desired, it has had two effects. First, the regime has stimulated the rapid growth and proliferation of human rights NGOs throughout the world in the 1970s. Second, the regime has become the focal point for NGO activities.[106] With the introduction of the 1503 procedure, NGOs have one foot in the door to secretive UN human rights politics. The regime's failure to establish a global monitoring system or even an annual state-of-the-globe report on human rights conditions is partially compensated for by its informal reliance upon NGO documents such as Amnesty International's annual country reports. Despite the limited membership and jurisdiction, HRC also relies heavily on NGOs as an independent source of information, especially about non-European states. One member of HRC estimated that "the Committee would have been 50 percent less effective without NGO expertise."[107] The number of transnational human rights NGOs working in and around the UN-based human rights regime suggests that the statist shield of global human rights is not as impenetrable as many "realists" would have us believe.

Yet we cannot deny the unpleasant truth that the global human rights regime suffers from the general and endemic inability to fashion a timely response to gross human rights abuses. Of course, collective response of the international community can be formulated in a variety of ways, such as (1) condemnatory, delegitimizing resolutions, (2) commission of inquiry, (3) diplomatic sanctions (suspension or expulsion from international organization), (4) economic and military sanctions (arms and economic embargoes), and (5) humanitarian multilateral military intervention. Given the dubious historical record of "humanitarian intervention" and given also innumerable legal and geopolitical hazards and trip wires, military intervention is a questionable option except possibly in the case of genocide. Yet collective response by measures well short of military intervention was still found to be generally wanting.

Even in its bailiwick of collective legitimation and delegitimation, the United Nations has failed to extend the Nuremberg principle to the postwar perpetrators of "crimes against humanity." Each of the postwar genocides listed in Table 6.1 managed to escape collective sanctions. Ironically, the mass slaughter in East Pakistan, Uganda, and Kampuchea was brought to an end by invasions from India, Tanzania, and Vietnam. This has in turn brought about collective legitimation (by default) of the Pol Pot and Pakistani regimes and condemnations of Indian and Vietnamese invasion in the United Nations. Irrespective of the context and severity of human rights abuse in a given country, when the issue is presented as a contest between state and human interests, collective international response tends to close ranks in defense of the sanctity and inviolability of state sovereignty.

If the superpowers have lost their dominance in the value-shaping process, they still play a heavy hand in the value-realizing process. If the United States and the Soviet Union are locked in competitive imperial geopolitics, they are "united" in their conservative attempts to check the historical tide of antihegemonism. The common ideological denominator of their global human rights politics is the defense of what may be called "superstatism." Soviet superstatism means limiting UN activities to norm creating—except, of course, for a selective enforcement of human rights norms as applied to its ideological and geopolitical opponents. The Soviet Union has vigorously opposed all the proposals to beef up the implementation machinery—the establishment of a post of United Nations Commissioner for Human Rights, the strengthening of groups of experts or working groups not representing states, and the elevation of the Division of Human Rights to the status of a Centre for Human Rights to be headed by an Assistant Secretary-General—as "supranational" threats to the sacred principle of state sovereignty and the basic cooperative nature of international organization.[108]

The problematic ratification record of the United States on the International Bill of Rights is born of the womb of U.S. superstatism. Theoretically, the United States is more flexible and more committed to strengthening the UN implementation machinery. In practice, however, U.S. global human rights politics also follow the logic of hegemonic interests. While leading the Western effort to create a post of a UN High Commissioner for Human Rights (defeated by a coalition of communist, Caribbean, Arab and African countries), the United States is reported to have played a role in Secretary-General Javier Péres de Cuéllar's dismissal of Theo van Boven in early 1982. As a member of the Commission on Human Rights and later as director of the Division of Human Rights from 1977 to early 1982, van Boven has "offended the United States and others by drawing attention to the abuses of right-wing Latin American regimes."[109] Van Boven, a respected scholar on human rights issues, has served as a voice of the oppressed and has also advocated a more active participation of nonstate actors in UN politics of human rights.[110] That the first major decision of the new Secretary-General was to silence this articulate, courageous, and independent voice for the oppressed is another reminder of the statist and hegemonic constraints defining the outer limits of international response.

The Human Rights Problematique

The human rights problematique is caught in the abiding discrepancies and disjunctures between great hopes and great despondency, between universal human rights norms and omnipresent oppressive structures, and between growing popular demands for a share in shaping human dignity values and the ideological misappropriation of such values by a minority of dominant elites. The gap between what is and what ought to be is greater in the field of human rights than in any other domain of global politics.

Oppression is a function of governing structures and processes in domestic and international societies. Yet much of the prevailing approach has been preoccupied with surface symptoms rather than with structural causes. UNHCR's relief and resettlement operations, although essential for the immediate alleviation of human suffering, conveniently ignore the root causes of rule by violence. No doubt this "humanitarian" and apolitical approach assuages the moral conscience of the international community and assures its necessary financial and political support. Likewise, the regime's "promotional" activities, functioning in isolation from the struggle of the oppressed, create only the illusion of movement.

The human rights problematique cannot be overcome to any significant degree without transforming the existing world order system. The inner logic of the global human rights regime follows the interests of the dominant state actors. As the official report of the Fifth Assembly of the World Council of Churches states, "it is far more likely that the will and strength to end oppression come from those who bear the brunt of it in their own lives rather than from the privileged persons, groups, and nations."[111]

With the phenomenal growth and proliferation of our technological and military capabilities has come a steady, if silent, extension of oppressive forms of social reality. When human rights are understood as consisting of the right to human life, the right to human health, the right to human development, and the right to a balanced and stable environment, the zone of oppressive social reality expands far and wide. Deeply rooted conceptual, normative, and structural problems obstruct the quest for a more humane governance.

Conceptions of human rights reflect the prevailing intellectual and political currents of society at a given time. Despite considerable variance in different cultural and temporal zones, however, one imperative seems to spread like a global epidemic of our time—the imperative of "national security." Whether defined in terms of economic development, military buildup, or status drive, it always sides with abstract state interests over empirical human needs. "National security" is a blind spot, disguising the brutal, dehumanizing forms of social oppression and legitimizing the selective destruction of humanity.

At the core of this problematique lies the acceptance of dehumanization as a necessary evil for societal "progress." Dehumanization may be defined as the isolation of certain individuals or groups in society, defined as having unequal (subhuman) status, outside the prevailing moral and legal restraints of society. Racism is the most ubiquitous and virulent form of dehumanization. It is hardly surprising that the era of "race relations" and the era of European overseas colonialism developed hand in hand from the fifteenth century onward.

Dehumanization comes in many forms. The narrow definition of human identity in terms of a common race, a common culture, or a common language contributes to the tenacity of national chauvinism—the "our country or people right or wrong" syndrome. In social psychology this syndrome is termed the "mote-beam phenomenon," a cognitive process of overestimating in-group's virtues and out-group's vices. Ali Mazrui has argued that this dichotomy—expressed as native versus foreigner, friend versus foe, familiar versus strange, Orient versus Occident, East versus West, North versus South, developed versus developing countries—has become "an iron law of dualism, a persistent conceptualization of the world in terms of 'us' and 'them.'"[112]

Ironically, however, the heightened sense of ethnocentric security or solidarity engendered by this dualism has a self-destructive quality. Whatever measure of solidarity achieved in a given territorial space is more than offset by the intensification of intercultural, interracial, and international conflict. Until they are anchored more firmly in an inclusive sense of human brotherhood and human species solidarity, universal human rights will remain adrift in the vortex of global geopolitics. Given the intensification of transnational interactions, Charles Beitz has argued, it is no longer tenable to approach international relations as a Hobbesian state of nature with its prevailing beliefs about the confinement of moral obligations within the cocoon of each sovereign state.[113] The solidarity rights of the third generation, though still in a preliminary phase, are aimed at arresting this drift of international human rights norms.

Another conceptual problem stems from our willingness to accept structural violence as an integral part of domestic and foreign policy. The crimes of Hitler, Stalin, Pol Pot, and Amin are universally recognized and condemned because these tyrants were unwilling or unable to institutionalize their oppressive rule. Contrast the treatment of President McKinley and President Truman in U.S. diplomatic and military historiography. The former is derided for his moral agony and vacillation over extending the Manifest Destiny doctrine to the Philippines, but the latter is praised for showing courage (that is, for having no moral qualms) in his "genocidal" decision to destroy Hiroshima and Nagasaki. Dehumanization has developed to the point where we cannot recognize such obvious symptoms of social and leadership pathology.

In an age marked by slow economic growth, resource depletion, de-mographic explosion, and global stagflation, the value of natural resources is rising and the value of human life is declining. The neo-Darwinian perception of nasty and brutish social reality inexorably works its way toward the "triage" solution, a new form of dehumanization parading in the sheep's clothing of ecological sanity and survival. As increasing numbers of the world's population are perceived as irrelevant to the global production of goods and services, they also become marginalized (dehumanized) in the politics of global human rights.

Despite great advances in the progressive development and codification of international human rights legislation, some serious normative problems persist. First and foremost, traditional human rights norms are born and bred in the hard shell of state sovereignty. Note also the hypersensitivity of China, the Soviet Union, and the United States about initiating any institutional reform that would appear to endow the present human rights regime with a supranational authority. Human rights norms are relegated to the status of "soft" norms enjoying poor compliance and weak enforce-ment, which in turns strengthens the self-fulfilling cynicism that global human rights are utopian blueprints made only to be ignored. In the field of human rights, contempt begets contempt.

The old "realist" bifurcation of morality into private and public, domestic and international, also lingers. In a classical exposition of this argument, Reinhold Niebuhr argued elegantly, if somewhat unconvincingly, that, given the fundamental difference between the morality of individuals and the morality of collectives, group relations, including international relations, "must therefore always be predominantly political rather than ethical."[114] In a similar vein, contemporary liberal statists—Hedley Bull, Ernst Haas, and R. J. Vincent, to cite three notable examples—argue that the quest for international order is inherently at odds with the quest for universal human rights and that therefore the former should have a prior claim over the latter.[115] This system-maintaining approach is based on the arbitrary but traditional separation of politics and morality. It runs counter to the empirically more tenable, normatively more congenial notion of politics as an authoritative value-shaping and value-realizing process. At any rate, this "realist" posture, given its firm grips on both policymaking and mainstream international relations discourse, must be recognized as a serious normative constraint.

The main normative problem, then, lies in the persisting dominance of statist norms over humanist norms. As Immanuel Kant argued in the third article of *Perpetual Peace*, the parameters of universal human rights norms (the cosmopolitan or world law in the Kantian term) are severely limited by the conditions of a "universal hospitality."[116] Bounded universal hospitality may be seen as a function of the oppressive structures of governance in both domestic and international societies. As long as norm-making takes places within the setting of oppressive and unjust social structures, the protection of human rights is more likely to occur as a successful outcome (regime transformation) of struggle between opposed social forces in domestic society.

Given the global dominance/dependence system, however, domestic regime transformation always encounters external constraints, as exemplified by the Soviet role in Poland and Afghanistan and the U.S. role in Chile, South Korea, and El Salvador. Gernot Kohler has advanced the concept of "global apartheid," the macrostructure of extreme global inequality "in cultural, racial, social, political, economic, military and legal terms, as is South African apartheid."[117] The South African apartheid regime is continuously sustained by the support it receives from the outside world, principally the Western powers and Israel, precisely because it is part of the global nexus between the war system and the poverty system.[118]

Theoretically, the state is a double-edged sword that can cut either way on human rights—it can be a protector or a perpetrator. More often than not, however, state power is seized and abused by a dominant class minority, divorced from the general will of the people. When state power is brought into the struggle for power and prestige in the international scene, it rapidly loses its "humanity." Even in interstate cooperation, the domino principle encourages the solidarity of all Hegelian statists, for the failure of one state to uphold the sanctity and inviolability of its national and territorial integrity and unity becomes a threat to all. State interests are the basis for a lowest-common-denominator approach to global human rights politics.

The growth of superstatism in the United States and the Soviet Union suggests that the state, once locked in international rivalry, feels compelled to expand its domain of power and freedom. This expansion invariably comes about at the expense of human rights. Human rights, instead of limiting state power, are constantly being limited by state power. Yet a reversal of the *raison d'être* of the state intensifies violent social conflict, which in turns justifies further brutalization of political culture with its wholesale trampling of human rights.

In the foreseeable future, we are likely to witness the rise and fall of many repressive regimes, with a rather volatile impact on the status of human rights in national societies. The prospects of global transformation are less promising. The forces that generated global apartheid are so omnipotent and omnipresent that any struggle for human emancipation at the global level seems doomed. Steve Biko has reminded us, however, of the danger of allowing the oppressor—and the oppressive reality—to control and manipulate our world view into a self-immobilizing and self-fulfilling defeatism. Without being sentimental or utopian, a just world order approach rejects the credo of inevitability, seeking the voices of the oppressed as a way of articulating a praxis for human emancipation.

Global Human Environment

The survival of humanity demands that the condition of the natural environment and the needs of human beings be considered as interrelated parts of the same problem. This will require profound changes in our political, economic and social structures on the one hand and our individual life-styles on the other, with the aim not only of survival, but of survival with the maximum possibility of human fulfillment.

—The Dai Dong Declaration, 1972

Human Ecology and World Order

The quality of the human environment sets conditions for the quality of human life. An "ecocidal" process is "humanicide" in slow motion, gradually choking up the life-sustaining arteries of the man-nature relationship. Because "environmental epidemiology" is still in its infancy, however, we do not know the *when, how,* and *where* of the critical thresholds of irreversible environmental damage. An ingenious scientist, we are told, can "devise just as many new chemical products every year as it will take a whole lifetime of an industrial hygienist to investigate from the point of view of occupational health."[1] Nonetheless, there is growing evidence that many contemporary illnesses are environmentally induced and that the deterioration of the atmosphere, oceans, rivers, croplands, and forests can seriously damage the delicate, interconnected fabric of the ecosphere, rendering air unfit to breathe, water unfit to drink, food unfit to eat, and soil unfit to grow or live on.

Throughout history and prehistory, humans, like all other forms of life, have been bound to the ecological niche defined by the limits of the planet's life-support systems. The bounds of this biophysical environment have varied with the shifting balances of population, resources, technology, and man-made (social) environment. The normal limits of the ecosphere in a given territorial space can be—and have often been—extended by the intervention of science and technology. But we are inescapably earthbound. Even astronauts can take flight from the ancient human bond to the terrestrial ecosystem of air, water, and soil for only so long. Sooner or later they must return to mother earth. Extra-territorial ecological sanctuaries exist only in the perpetual utopian blueprints of technological Panglosses.

The present ecological crisis is unprecedented in scale, magnitude, intensity, and complexity. It threatens to change the basic biochemistry of the planet, with consequences we are only just beginning to understand. The biophysical environment, whose resilience has been taken for granted in modern industrial societies, seems to be approaching its breaking or collapsing point. The primitive did not overshoot, but the modern have. If "99.9999 percent of all the species that have ever arisen are now extinct,"[2] we may have to join Stanley Diamond "in search of the primitive"[3] to avoid fouling up the human nest in the nuclear-ecological age.

Human ecology—the overall pattern of relationship between a human community and its environment—defines and imposes several biophysical limits and constraints for human development. What are these biophysical limits and constraints? Ecologist Barry Commoner has formulated four basic laws of ecology, to be ignored at our own peril:

- The First Law of Ecology: Everything Is Connected to Everything Else (or the existence of the elaborate network of interconnections in the ecosphere);
- The Second Law of Ecology: Everything Must Go Somewhere (or what is excreted by one organism as waste is taken up by another as food);
- The Third Law of Ecology: Nature Knows Best (or that for every organic substance produced by a living organism, there exists in nature an enzyme capable of breaking that substance down); and
- The Fourth Law of Ecology: There Is No Such Thing as a Free Lunch (or because the global ecosystem is a connected whole, in which nothing can be gained or lost and which is not subject to over-all improvement, anything extracted from it by human effort must be replaced).[4]

Harold and Margaret Sprout, who have made a path-breaking contribution toward the development of an ecological perspective in the study of international relations, deplored a persistent tendency, especially strong in the United States, to think of "environment" in nonhuman terms by excluding from it "the wide variety of social conditions, intangible as well as tangible, which also environ individuals and populations."[5] The ecological crisis is much more than a crisis of external ecospheric limits, for it brings into focus—and challenges—the adaptability of basic values, institutions, and behavioral patterns of human society.

For centuries man-to-man exploitation and man-over-nature plundering have proceeded hand in hand. The "human conquest" of nature is also a conquest of some human groups over other human groups through the use and misuse of technology as a chief instrument of dominance. The noted historian William McNeill has suggested that "microparasites" (the insects, rodents, and one-cell creatures that compete with human beings for food) and "macroparasites" (human and social predators, especially the European military, state, and church systems and technology) are twin variables that have conditioned and shaped the course of man's ecohistorical development (or what he calls urban and commercial transmutation) in recent centuries:

> If microparasitism may be likened to a nether millstone, grinding away at human populations through time, human-to-human macroparasitism has been almost as universal—an upper millstone, pressing heavily upon the majority of the human race. Between them, the two forms of parasitism usually tended to keep the peasant majority of civilized populations close to bare subsistence by systematically withdrawing resources from their control.[6]

Curiously enough, it is only in the last decade—and especially since the energy crisis—that we have begun to engage in a collective dialogue over the penalties and punishments for ecological transgression. The dawning of an age of scarcity has highlighted the common dilemma of all humankind. Like a global epidemic, the ecological crisis is worst for the poor, the weak, and the defenseless. In the long run, however, it will punish us all—without regard to age, ideology, nationality, race, religon, or sex. The global logic of ecology translates one country's ecological negligence or transgression into every country's problem. The United States' "ecocidal war" in Indochina (the first full-fledged environmental warfare in modern history) and Brazil's silent "ecocidal" deforestation of the Amazon rain forest (which through its photosynthesis is providing a substantial portion of the world's annual production of oxygen)[7] can no more be justified or shielded by the principle of state sovereignty than the postwar genocides examined in the preceding chapter.

The Historical Roots of the Ecological Crisis

Essentially, the ecological crisis is a crisis of Center model core industrial capitalism, a dominant social paradigm (world view) that performed cognitive, evaluative, and prescriptive functions in the development of affluent societies in Western Europe, the United States, and Japan. Socially inequitable and ecologically suicidal, this Center model of modernization has brought about an era of abnormal abundance with its high-consumption life-style in core countries, but the ecological perils of this economic prosperity have just begun to surface.

The salient characteristics of the Center model may be briefly summarized. First, it is anchored in an anthropocentric world view. Derived largely from Christian theology and medieval Western political philosophy, this world view holds the anti-ecological assumption that nature is God's bounty to man for his pleasure and profit. Man shares with the Creator a role in transcending nature. Human progress has come to mean the capacity to *conquer* nature in the service of human (and national) material growth and expansion. "Nature, like the black man, came in the West to be regarded as subject to enslavement."[8] What emerges is a notion of man's perpetual progress exempt from the laws of ecology. In short, the anthropocentric world view has created the illusion of man's independence from nature, fostering an exceptionalist/exemptionalist mentality in human development.[9]

Second, the potency—and the danger—of the Center model stems from its ever-increasing reliance on energy-intensive machines as the chief engine for modernization. The essential distinction between the traditional and the modern, according to most theories of modernization, is the greater *control* which the latter have over their natural and social environment. Cyril Black defines modernization "as the process by which historically evolved institutions are adapted to the rapidly changing functions that reflect the unprecedented increase in man's knowledge, permitting control over his environment, that accompanied the scientific revolution."[10] Historian of science Lynn White has suggested that science (traditionally aristocratic, speculative, intellectual in content) and technology (traditionally low-class, empirical, action-oriented) suddenly merged in the mid-nineteenth century under the impetus of democratic culture, marking "the greatest event in human history since the invention of agriculture, and perhaps in nonhuman terrestrial history as well."[11] From this shotgun marriage the West (later emulated by Japan) rapidly translated science and technology into a powerful instrument of industrialization. The Center model is a model of ecological and social control and dominance par excellence. The "progress" imperative embodied in the model inexorably moves toward colonizing "wild" nature, "uncivilized" peoples, and "expendable" future.

Finally the Center model is a pre-ecological and prenuclear anachronism. As the state-centric, conflict-prone paradigm of power politics, it has long since lost touch with changing global realities. Its costs and risks, whether judged in political, economic, ecological, or moral terms, have become increasingly high. As a pre-ecological and prenuclear paradigm, the Center model cannot cope with the ecological crisis which, thanks to the steady march of bulldozer technology, has indeed become global. To apply the fourth law of ecology here, there is no such thing as ecological deficit-financing.

The ecological imperative of survival requires cooperation, not competition. In an age of relative resource scarcity and demographic explosion, there is no alternative to cooperative behavior for species solidarity and survival. Yet to cope with the rising expectations that the Center model generates, the dominant social class constantly transgresses against nature or against weaker peoples and countries in order to meet the requirements of exploitative patterns of production and consumption. Gradually, internal contradictions and anomalies grow and multiply, causing paradigm decay and transformation.

Despite the allure of the Center model with its emphasis on instant material gratification, its ethos of prosperity through constant growth and industrial expansion, and its promise of science and technology as the master key to modernity, the ecological laws of limits have finally caught up with the overdevelopment (maldevelopment) of this dominant Western paradigm. The model is no longer regarded as a reliable ecological guide through the end of this century, even for the Center's own welfare, as clearly delineated in *The Global 2000 Report to the President* (3 volumes), a comprehensive set of projections developed by U.S. government agencies on "what will happen to population, resources, and environment if present policies continue." The report depicts a depressing socioecological landscape in the year 2000: the world will be more crowded, more polluted, less equitable, more tension-filled and conflict-prone, less stable ecologically, and more vulnerable to irreversible disruption or disaster.[12]

At the very moment when the Center model is having a legitimacy crisis of its own, its influence has spread like a global epidemic, afflicting developing as well as socialist countries. The oligopolistic manipulation of the flow of information, knowledge, and technologies by Center countries serves to propagate the Center model. "So powerful has been this model of a high-consumption life-style," argues Rajni Kothari, "that it has undermined both the Liberal dream of expanding welfare for all and the Marxist dream of solidarity of the world proletariat ushering in an egalitarian, classless society."[13]

For years the Chinese model of self-reliant development served as an exception (an anti-Center model, as it were) that confirmed the *dependencia* thesis about the global political economy of core capitalism. Yet post-Mao China's new politics of modernization brought about many normative changes and policy shifts, all calling into question the domestic potency of the Chinese model, not to mention its transferability to the Third World.[14] The Center model is the principal trap standing in the way of "another development."

An Ecodevelopmental Order or an Eco-Imperial Order?

The demise of abnormal affluence and the return of resource scarcity fundamentally challenge the basic values, institutions, and behavioral patterns of the Center model. As noted in Chapter 5, the multiple crises of the 1970s served as chief catalyst for the development of contending global approaches and models. Not surprisingly, the quest for a new ecological order has not been immune from the search for a single escape route. Exemplified in the writings of the biologist Garrett Hardin,[15] the "lifeboat ethics" school represents the new wine of ecologism poured into the old bottle of class politics, a prescription from an eco-imperial order under the guise of saving our planetary lifeboat.

According to Hardin's "ecolate view of the human predicament," the world faces "the tragedy of the commons" under conditions of scarcity, an elegant and persuasive analogy first advanced in the nineteenth century by an English amateur mathematician named William Forster Lloyd in a little-known pamphlet, *Two Lectures on the Checks to Population* (1833). Hardin's 1968 article, "The Tragedy of the Commons," has become one of the most influential ecological essays of our time. Hardin sees a single threat to the sanctity of planetary carrying capacity—the demographic pressure of the multiplication of the world's poor.

Poverty can be shared, but not wealth, Hardin argues, and "freedom to breed will bring ruin to all." To avert the tragedy of the commons requires a regime of coercive police action to liquidate "excess hordes" in the global poverty belt. We will discuss the population problem later in the chapter. Suffice it to say here that Hardin has abstracted the concept of carrying capacity as an end (absolute value) and humans, especially the world's poor (his principal ecological eyesore), as only a means; the latter exists in the service of the former. He specifically rejects the sanctity of human life as counterproductive to the sanctity of carrying capacity.

From a world order perspective, Hardin's crusade against the world's poor as the only salvation for the global commons stands on shaky moral, ecological, logical, and empirical grounds.[16] His assault on the world's poor as the dead weight on the planetary carrying capacity is historically untenable. The real tragedy of the commons is not the lack of *ownership*, as Hardin suggests, but the lack of a living *community*.[17] Barry Commoner has rightly characterized Hardin's "ecolade" view as "faintly masked barbarism."[18]

The popular analogy is an overcrowded planetary lifeboat in which the overwhelming weight of too many people is threatening to ruin all. Even if we accept the lifeboat analogy, the ecological pressure of the world's poor majority is rather modest compared to the ecological pressure of the world's rich minority. In fact, one could as logically argue that the rich in affluent societies are not only carrying undue weight—per capita consumption of resources in the global poverty belt ranges from one-tenth to one-hundredth that in the global affluence belt—but also are drilling holes in the lifeboat through a variety of ecocidal activities.

A just world order approach broadens the concept of "crimes against humanity" by extending it to a variety of ecological transgressions in the concrete setting of contemporary global politics. What remains hidden behind the latter-day Malthusian arguments of the Third World's demographic threat are more fundamental questions concerning the integrity of the global commons or of a finite carrying capacity:

- In terms of the sanctity of the global commons, how do we explain the fact that a minority of twenty-five industrial states with 30 percent of the world's population is responsible for nearly 85 percent of the world consumption of nonrenewable energy resources?
- What is the logical or moral basis for defending the affluence of the United States against the world's poor when that affluence leads each American to pour more toxic wastes into rivers and oceans than a thousand poor Asians?
- Who suffers the most in the front line of ecological transgressions?
- Who is threatening to rupture the life-protecting ozone layer in the stratosphere?
- Who is releasing radioactive isotopes that silently poison the human environment in the course of researching, testing, manufacturing, and deploying nuclear weapons?

- Why is so much more money given to research on socially and ecologically destructive nuclear technology than on the development of renewable energy resources?
- Who subsidizes military R&D on environmental (geophysical) warfare, whose ecological outcomes are so unpredictable?

The root cause of the ecological crisis lies in the exploitative and unjust social structures of domestic and international societies. It follows that ecological stability and human well-being are mutually interrelated and complementary parts of another model of development (ecodevelopment). A just and humane eco-order should satisfy the following value requirements: socioeconomic justice; basic human rights; humane governance; and ecological safety. Clearly, then, a just world order/eco-order interface calls for the transformation of our basic social values and structures at both intranational and international levels on the one hand, and of our individual behavior and life-styles on the other.

Conceived in this way, human ecology is a natural partner in the quest for a just world order. As noted earlier, ecological balance is one of the four central world order values. Moreover, ecological thinking and world order thinking converge in their transnational and transdisciplinary framework of inquiry informed by values, holism, futurism, and humanism, and in their prescriptive commitment to social transformation for survival and solidarity with future generations.

There is one problematic area in a just world order/eco-order interface. Although committed in varying degrees to social and behavioral transformations, some ecologists tend to be too biased in favor of "conservation" and "preservation." Conserving nature can easily turn into conserving an unjust status quo; reducing excess ecological weight can easily turn into an "efficient" shoving of the weak, poor, and powerless. This may explain why such influential and sophisticated scholars as Robert Heilbroner and William Ophuls can do no better in the end than to prescribe authoritarian measures, modern-day Hobbesian regimes of ecological mandarins to maintain "ecological law and order."[19]

Although recognizing the outer limits of the ecosphere, a just world order approach at the same time holds that an alternative ecodevelopmental model can open up new possibilities for attaining *more human ends with less ecological means*. The real challenge is to seek an alternative path of human development that is ecologically sound, socially and economically just, politically democratic, and spiritually nourishing. As the Brazilian model clearly demonstrates, the ecological crisis now afflicts both developed and developing countries, but in each case it is to a significant extent a function of unjust social structures. A principal cause of the ecological crisis lies in the anti-ecological use of modern technology to exploit and consume scarce resources.

In a broader sense, then, there are two kinds of socioecological pollution: the pollution of overdevelopment (affluence) and the pollution of underdevelopment (poverty). The latter is also caused by unjust social structures, for peasants whose land has been preempted for cash crops end up cultivating marginal soil, contributing to further deforestation and soil erosion. Both forms of socioecological pollution are linked by the invisible hands of the global dominance/dependence system. As the Poona Declaration on the Perversion of Science and Technology put it, "To feed the insatiable demands of the machines of the industrial nations and the equally insatiable desire for foreign exchange among Third World elites hungry for imported luxuries and armaments, large areas are being mined and undermined, forests destroyed, fields flooded, rivers silted, and farmers and tenants displaced from independent sources of income and livelihood."[20]

Global Patterns and Trends

In this section I draw a global profile of the human environment. A profile is needed to appreciate the scale and magnitude of environmental impacts on human health and development as well as to evaluate the performance of the international community for the maintenance of a humane eco-order. The global environment can be divided into a complex set of separate but closely intertwined and interacting subsystems. I will briefly examine the condition of the atmosphere, marine, and terrestrial environments, on the one hand, and the environmental impacts of such human activities as population growth, resource use, and militarization, on the other. The former may be characterized as the *natural* environment and the latter as the *social* environment.

The Atmospheric Environment

Although human life and health depend on clean, breathable air, we have only recently become conscious of the extent to which anthropogenic pollutants can damage this vital resource. There is still a great deal of scientific uncertainty and controversy about what kinds of pollutants at what levels of exposure cause what types of human illness. At least seven common air pollutants—carbon monoxide, hydrocarbons, lead, nitrogen dioxide, ozone, particulates, and sulfur dioxide—have already been identified as hazardous to human health. The primary purpose of the 1970 Clean Air Act and its 1977 amendments, passed by the U.S. Congress, was to control these seven pollutants. Table 7.1 specifies their major sources, their characteristics, and their epidemiological effects.

Global emissions of anthropogenic sulfur dioxides grew at about 5 percent annually during the 1970s giving a total increase of 40–50 percent for the decade. By the end of the 1970s, global emissions of sulfur dioxides had reached 140–196 million short tons per year. Global emission projections for the future vary widely depending on the different assumptions of high or low growth scenarios, control or no control policies, high- or low-sulfur coals, and high or low use of coals as a main source of energy.[21] The reduction of atmospheric emissions through desulfurization processes is not a final answer, for the chemical-rich sludge that results from desulfurization

TABLE 7.1
Major Air Pollutants and Their Epidemiological Effects

Pollutant	Major Sources	Characteristics and Effects
Carbon Monoxide (CO)	Vehicle exhausts	Colorless, odorless poisonous gas. Replaces oxygen in red blood cells, causing dizziness, unconsciousness or death.
Hydrocarbons (HC)	Incomplete combustion of gasoline; evaporation of petroleum fuels, solvents and paints	Although some are poisonous, most are not. Reacts with NO_2 to form ozone, or smog.
Lead (Pb)	Anti-knock agents in gasoline	Accumulates in the bone and soft tissues. Affects blood-forming organs, kidneys and nervous system. Suspected of causing learning disabilities in young children.
Nitrogen Dioxide (NO_2)	Industrial processes, vehicle exhausts	Causes structural and chemical changes in the lungs. Lowers resistance to respiratory infections. Reacts in sunlight with hydrocarbons to produce smog. Contributes to acid rain.
Ozone (O_3)	Formed when HC and NO_2 react	Principal constituent of smog. Irritates mucous membranes, causing coughing, choking, impaired lung function. Aggravates chronic asthma and bronchitis.
Total Suspended Particulates (TSP)	Industrial plants, heating boilers, auto engines, dust	Larger visible types (soot, smoke or dust) can clog the lung sacs. Smaller invisible particles can pass into the bloodstream. Often carry carcinogens and toxic metals; impair visibility.
Sulfur Dioxide (SO_2)	Burning coal and oil, industrial processes	Corrosive, poisonous gas. Associated with coughs, colds, asthma and bronchitis. Contributes to acid rain.

Source: U.S. Environmental Protection Agency, reproduced in *Environment and Health* (Washington, D.C.: Congressional Quarterly, Inc., 1981), p. 21.

creates another environmental hazard. For some time in the future—barring the transition to an alternative energy strategy—the fate of air quality may depend to a significant extent on the contest between the less expensive but more polluting coal and the more expensive but less polluting oil as a chief source of energy.

Sulfur dioxide and its by-products can generate a variety of harmful effects on aquatic biota in the natural environment. Acid rain, a phenomenon of industrial air pollution created by the long-distance atmospheric transport and chemical change in transit of sulfur and nitrogen oxides, has caused increasing concern in recent years. Atmospheric transport over distances of 1,000 km and upwards is prevalent in Western Europe and eastern North America, causing the pH value of rainfall to decline from 5.7 to below 4.5, well into the acidic range, and disrupting the food chain in the lakes and streams of Norway, Sweden, southern Canada, and the Adirondack Mountains of New York.

Acid rain is seeded by tall smokestacks that improve local air quality by dispersing sulfur dioxides high upward and far outward. More than 200 smokestacks in the United States are reportedly between 122–366 meters in height. Great Britain's progress in controlling local air pollution, which depends heavily on tall smokestacks, has come at the expense of biotic resources in the rivers and lakes of southern Scandinavia.[22]

The recent developments in Scandinavia and North America do not augur well. All 1,500 lakes in a 13,000-square-kilometer area of southern Norway are damaged with a pH below 4.3; 70 percent of them have no fish. At least 5,000 lakes in Sweden are seriously ill, and the government is spending $40 million a year to counter rising acidity. On the other hand, some 3,000 lakes and 25,000 miles (40,000 km) of streams in the northeastern United States—and 23 percent of the lakes in the Adirondacks of New York—have become abnormally acidic, with sharply reduced fish populations. At least 140 Canadian lakes, mainly in Ontario, have lost their fish populations, and as many as 48,000 more lakes are in danger of losing their fish over the next decade.[23] If the current rates of sulfur and nitrogen oxides emissions continue unchecked, according to the U.S. National Academy of Sciences, the number of affected lakes is projected to more than double by 1990, expanding to larger and deeper lakes.[24]

According to a 1978 study, the economic costs of acid rain are estimated as follows: $5 billion in damages each year in the states east of the Mississippi River plus Minnesota; $2 billion in materials damages; $1.75 billion in reduced forest output; $1.0 billion in crop losses; and $0.25 billion arising from damages to aquatic life.[25] Sulfates also damage human lungs, exacerbating respiratory illnesses. After analyzing more than 2 million death certificates in the United States, Robert Mendelsohn and Guy Orcutt concluded that sulfates may account for up to 187,686 deaths a year in the United States. Even by conservative estimates, the authors further noted, sulfates account for more than 150,000 deaths annually.[26]

The ozone layer in the stratosphere, which protects life on Earth from an overdose of ultraviolet radiation, is now in danger of depletion by chemicals called chlorufluorocarbons (CFCs). CFCs are used as propellants in spray cans, as refrigerants, as solvents, and as foam-blowing agents, with North America, Western Europe, and Japan accounting for four-fifths of total global production. Between 1970 and 1979, ozone is estimated to have decreased at a rate of half a percent a year. The UNEP Co-ordinating Committee on the Ozone Layer estimated that continued releases of CFCs at the 1977 rate would eventually deplete the ozone layer by about 10 percent by the year 2050.[27] As noted in Chapter 4, the injection of a substantial quantity of nitrogen oxide into the stratosphere by an all-out nuclear war would result in 30–70 percent reductions in the ozone column in the Northern Hemisphere and 20–40 percent reductions in the Southern Hemisphere. It is generally estimated that a 1 percent depletion in ozone increases ultraviolet radiation by about 2 percent.

The known consequences of increased ultraviolet radiation include a greater incidence of skin cancers in humans, damage to microorganisms and individual cells in plants and animals with consequent effects on different ecosystems, and possible but yet undetermined effects on global climate. With modern jets flying as high as 45,000 to 55,000 feet (13.7 to 16.7 km), ozone, whose layer stretches from about 35,000 to 150,000 feet (10.7 to 45.7 km), is linked to eye, nose, and throat irritation as well as shortness of breath and even chest pain and nosebleeds among both passengers and crews. On October 6, 1981, a U.S. satellite (the Solar Mesosphere Explorer) was launched to conduct the first comprehensive global study of how nature and humans interact in the creation and destruction of ozone. Within three years, we are told, the results obtained from this satellite monitoring could establish a clear cause-and-effect relationship and provide a firm empirical basis for national and international actions.[28]

The increasing abundance of anthropogenic carbon dioxide (CO_2) in the atmosphere is of special ecological concern because of its potential for causing a warming of the global temperature through the so-called "greenhouse effect." The combustion of fossil fuels and deforestation are generally regarded as the main causes of increased CO_2 in the atmosphere. Today, the United States, Europe, and the Soviet Union together account for three-fourths of the CO_2 released. The CO_2 concentration in the atmosphere, between 265 and 290 parts per million (ppm) by volume before 1850, rose to 326 ppm in 1970 and 338 ppm in 1980. The 1979 World Climate Conference estimated that the amount of carbon dioxide in the atmosphere is increasing by about 4 percent every ten years. The projected increase in CO_2 concentration for A.D. 2150 to A.D. 2200 might lead to an increase in global mean air temperature of more than 6°C, concluded a 1977 study by the Geophysics Study Committee of the NAS, "comparable with the difference in temperature between the present and the warm Mesozoic climate of 70 million to 100 million years ago."[29]

A more recent major study conducted by a team of seven atmospheric physicists at the National Aeronautics and Space Administration (NASA) supports the more pessimistic predictions on this issue. The study finds that the warming predicted by various computer models of the greenhouse effect is consistent with global temperature readings since 1880, and it projects that the CO_2 concentration in the atmosphere will reach 600 ppm in the next century, *even if growth of fossil fuel use is slow*. Potential effects of the expected rise in global temperature would include the creation of drought-prone regions in North America and central Asia as part of a shifting of climatic zones, erosion of the western Antarctic ice sheet with a consequent worldwide rise in sea level, and the opening of the fabled Northwest Passage.[30]

The dilemma here is obvious. The greenhouse effect is a plausible hypothesis, not yet verified scientifically. Yet, it will certainly be too late to prevent this phenomenon by the time scientific proof comes our way. In the meantime, nearly all statistical studies of the effects of air pollution report that "they are most heavily borne by the poor, by children, by the aged and infirm; the most striking effects of air pollution on health seem to occur when the victim's health is already precarious."[31]

The Marine Environment

The ecological integrity and importance of the marine environment is not difficult to appreciate. The waters of the oceans represent 71 percent of the earth's surface and 97 percent of the earth's total water supply. Through evaporation, precipitation, and runoff, the oceans play a crucial role in determining the primary flows of solar energy and the distribution of the global temperature. To a significant extent, the macroenvironmental health of the entire planet is dependent on the environmental stability of the oceans.

The oceans represent the twin challenges of a common destiny or a common peril; they are endowed with enormous resources and have the claim of being a common heritage of mankind. The global fish catch alone is estimated to be worth more than $50 billion a year. The value of minerals under the sea is incalculable, but the figure of $3 trillion is often mentioned. The economic, political, and military stakes in the management of the oceans are so high that it took nearly a decade for the Third United Nations Conference on the Law of the Sea to complete the drafting of the 320-article Convention on the Law of the Sea in April 1982, whose prospects of final ratification or effective implementation remain clouded.

As shown in Table 7.2, the marine environment consists of coastal and oceanic ecosystems. The ecodevelopmental significance of the global marine environment lies in the fact that only 10 percent of the marine environment, representing the world's estuaries, coastal wetlands, reefs, and the many marginal seas over the continental shelves and slopes, produces 99 percent of total fish production. Marine pollutants are also concentrated in this biologically more productive and ecologically more sensitive area. For the moment, most developmental and demographic pressures affect the earth's coastal waters. Of the ten largest metropolitan areas of the world, seven are located in estuarine regions (New York, Tokyo, London, Shanghai, Buenos Aires, Osaka, and Los Angeles), and 60–80 percent of commercial marine species are dependent upon estuarine ecosystems during part or all of their life cycles.

The threat to the ecological stability of coastal waters emanates from two kinds of human activity: the injection of pollutants through river discharge, coastal outfalls, dumping, accidental spillage, and atmospheric transport, and the overexploitation of living marine resources. Many toxic waste pollutants, which include chemical substances that are carcinogenic, mutagenic, and teratogenic, pose real, if somewhat unspecified and under-

TABLE 7.2
Categories of Ocean Areas and Types of Pollution, with Effects on Uses and Their Duration

Types of Pollution	Effects on Uses and Pollution Trends	Duration of Effects
COASTAL WATERS		
(10 percent of total area; 99 percent of total fish production)		
Sewage; industrial wastes; litter; petroleum hydrocarbons	Living resources destroyed or rendered unusable; industrial uses of seawater adversely influenced; amenities reduced; recreational values diminished	Short-term; mainly during period of discharge
Synthetic organic chemicals; metals; radioactivity	Living resources decreased or rendered unusable	Long-term; metals and synthetic organic chemicals deposited in sediments may be released for a long time through normal leaching and/or dredging disturbance
OPEN OCEAN		
(90 percent of total area; 1 percent of total fish production)		
Synthetic organic chemicals; metals; petroleum hydrocarbons; radioactivity	Increasing concentrations in water and organisms may indicate dangerous trends	Long-term; duration depends on the residence time of pollutant

Source: Michael Waldichuk, *Global Marine Pollution: An Overview* (Paris: UNESCO, 1977), p. 12.

researched, hazards to human and marine life. Japan's Minamata Bay incident, involving mercury poisoning through human consumption of contaminated fish is a textbook Marine pollution case.

Given the military or economic imperatives behind marine pollution, and the time required for scientific detection and causal linkage, the marine environment cannot easily avoid being a dumping ground in the global production and disposal of "bads" and "wastes." In September 1982, the government of the Netherlands halted its fifteen-year practice of dumping radioactive waste materials into the Atlantic Oceans. A Japanese plan to begin dumping up to 100,000 curies of nuclear waste into the Pacific Basin encountered such strong opposition among Pacific island nations that it has temporarily been postponed. Still, Belgium, Britain, and Switzerland are currently disposing of their nuclear waste in the world's oceans.[32]

Faced with the refusal of state and local governments to permit the dumping of radioactive wastes on their land, the U.S. Environmental Protection Agency (EPA) has been preparing new rules to permit the dumping of radioactive wastes into the oceans. The United States Navy is also planning to dispose of retired nuclear submarines by scuttling them in the oceans. Even with its reactor core removed, each submarine would still contain an average of 50,000 curies of radioactivity.[33] If the United States lifts its twelve-year ban on the ocean dumping of radioactive materials, it could cause a chain reaction, dealing a death blow to the London Dumping Convention, the multilateral treaty that currently regulates the ocean dumping of radioactive waste materials.

Advances in fishing and processing technologies, growing demand for seafood, aggressive overexploitation, and the injection of toxic chemicals, fossil fuels, solid and sewage wastes, agricultural nutrients, and eroded sediments into the marine ecosystems have all contributed to the depletion, and in some cases, the extinction, of a number of marine species. Examples range from the oysters of Chesapeake Bay in the United States and the Arcachon Bay of France, to the mackerel of the Black and Azov seas, to the anchovy off the coast of Peru.

The total world fish catch for food and nonfood uses increased from 21 mmt in 1950 to 40 mmt in 1960, 68 mmt in 1970, and about 73 mmt in 1979. However, two important developments are hidden in these aggregate statistics; a steady and progressive decline of world fish production on a per capita basis (from 18.5 kilograms per person in 1970 to 16 kilograms per person in 1980) and the increasing conversion of world fish catch to fertilizer and fishmeal for animal feed.[34] Present harvesting methods run counter to the First Law of Ecology, considering only the effects on individual species without recognizing the need for assessing the impact on the full life cycles of many fisheries species in their mutual interdependency within the marine ecosystems.

Directly and indirectly, the open oceans receive substantial quantities of pollutants from coastal waters carried by currents, from the atmosphere, and from accidental oil spills, operational discharges, and intentional dumping. Thanks to the atmospheric explosions detonated by the Big Five, the world's oceans have received substantial amounts of radioactive materials, including two biologically active fission products—cesium-137 and strontium-90. By 1972, scientists had detected no less than fifty-two artificially produced radionuclides in the oceans.[35] Because of their vast size, great diluting and dispersing power, and relative stability, the environmental impact on oceanic ecosystems has been rather modest. The otherwise pessimistic Global 2000 Study projections see "no major impact on the earth's open oceans by the year 2000."[36] A four-year survey, "The Health of the Oceans," conducted by the Regional Seas Program of the United Nations Environmental Programme (UNEP) concluded that the wastes dumped into the oceans have not produced any significant effect on the health of the high seas and that the ocean is healthier in 1982 than it was in 1972, thanks to environmental laws in the most industrialized countries.[37]

Even the capacity of the open oceans to dilute and disintegrate pollutants has its limits. The sea's waters are believed to be regenerating themselves every eighty to one hundred years. Over an extended period of time, argues marine scientist Edward Goldberg, the unending introduction of pollutants into the open oceans could lead to a long-term buildup of toxic materials, causing widespread mortalities and morbidities in ocean organisms. Once such a condition is reached, there would be no turning back with any technological fix. "The great volume of the open ocean makes the removal of a toxic substance, identified by a catastrophic event, an endeavor beyond mankind's capabilities with the technologies of today or of the foreseeable future."[38] "Ironically," observes Peter Thacher, UNEP's deputy head and a main architect of the Mediterranean Action Plan, "the effort to protect the oceans may provide its greatest benefits on land."[39]

The Terrestrial Environment

The quantity and quality of cropland available for food production to meet the basic dietary needs of the human population is perhaps the most crucial ecodevelopmental issue. Soil is a basic resource essential for human well-being, but it can be depleted. Most projections take a pessimistic view of the changing balances between resources, environment, population, and development if the present patterns of production, distribution, and consumption continue unchanged. As Lester Brown put it, "civilization can survive the exhaustion of oil reserves, but not the continuing wholesale loss of topsoil."[40]

From the beginning of agriculture to the mid-twentieth century, increases in world agricultural output were made possible largely through the expansion of cultivated land. Since 1950, world agricultural output has more than doubled from increased yields on existing cropland through substitution of energy for human labor and land. However, this impressive increase "has entailed land abuse so severe that fully one-fifth and perhaps as much as one-third of the world's cropland is losing topsoil at a rate that is undermining its long-term productivity."[41]

Since only modest amounts of additional land can be brought into cultivation for agricultural production—probably no more than 10 percent by the year 2000—the ecodevelopmental integrity of cropland is of central importance to human development. Although there are considerable national and geographical variations in the patterns of soil depletion, a worldwide acceleration of land deterioration through desertification, deforestation, water logging, salinization, alkalinization, humus loss, urban, surburban, and industrial encroachment, and toxic waste dumping is clear. The present patterns and trends of land deterioration are likely to worsen without some fundamental structural and behavioral changes in domestic and international societies.

Desertification encompasses a variety of ecological changes that destroy the cover of vegetation and fertile soil in the earth's drier regions, rendering the land useless for crops, if not for human habitation. Desertification is a self-accelerating—and almost irreversible—process.[42] The most extensive desertification process occurred during the five-year Sudano-Sahelian drought (1968–1973). Aerial photographs taken in northern Sudan in 1975, when compared with 1958 maps, showed that the desertification process had proceeded southward by ninety to one hundred kilometers in the seventeen-year period (1958-1975).[43]

Currently, about one-third of the earth's total land area is threatened by desertification, including more than half of Africa. Present losses to creeping desert encroachment throughout the world are estimated at some 6 million hectares (60,000 square kilometers) per year: 3.2 million hectares of rangeland; 2.5 million hectares of rain-fed cropland; and 125,000 hectares of irrigated farmland. The areas currently undergoing desertification cover some 30 million square kilometers (23 percent of the earth's ice-free land area). Desertification results in an economic loss of over $26 billion per year. Unless present trends in land mismanagement are slowed or reversed, some scientists project that "fully one-third of today's arable land will be lost during the next 25 years, while the world's need for food will nearly double."[44]

According to several statistical analyses of climatological data prepared for the 1977 United Nations Conference on Desertification, the principal cause of desertification is land mismanagement (overgrazing, destructive cropping practices, and overcutting of forests), not a global climatic shift. The 1977 Conference also identified the use of chemical and biological weapons during wars as one of contributing factors in certain parts of the world.[45] Here again, the basic-needs strategy and ecological rehabilitation are mutually complementary. The transformation of domestic social structure needed for initiating and implementing the transition from cash crops for export back to food crops for basic needs is also needed for initiating and implementing the necessary antidesertification campaign.[46]

Most regions of the world in their natural condition would be forested. The forest coverage of the earth decreased from some 5 billion to 2.6 billion hectares during between 1950 and 1975, mostly in the Third World,

FIGURE 7.1
The State of Forest Resources in the Third World, 1980–1985

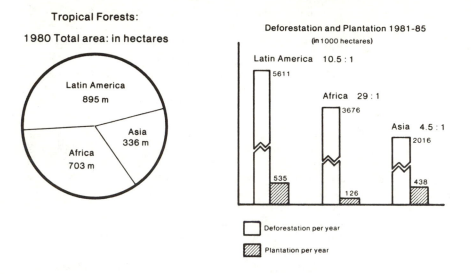

Tropical Forests:

1980 Total area: in hectares

Deforestation and Plantation 1981–85
(in 1000 hectares)

Latin America
895 m

Asia
336 m

Africa
703 m

Latin America   10.5 : 1
5611

Africa   29 : 1
3676

Asia   4.5 : 1
2016

535

126

438

☐ Deforestation per year

▨ Plantation per year

Source: *Tropical Forest Resources* (Rome: FAO 1982) as re-reproduced in *UN Chronicle* 20 (January 1983): 74.

where one-quarter of all humans dependent on firewood for fuel are concentrated.[47] In the most thorough survey of deforestation yet conducted, FAO and UNEP concluded that the total of 1,935 million hectares of closed and open tropical forests in 1980 were cleared at the rate of 11.3 million hectares a year in the early 1980s. As shown in Figure 7.1, the rate of deforestation outpaces that of new plantation by more than 10 to 1 in Latin America, 29 to 1 in Africa, and 4.5 to 1 in Asia. The ratio in the most crowded continent, Asia, has improved substantially due largely to a major replantation campaign in China. Each spring, on a set day, everybody in China, from high officials to schoolchildren, plants a tree, and in 1980 alone some 12,000-14,000 million trees were planted in China.[48]

The raping of forests has been particularly rampant in Brazil, Costa Rica, the Philippines, Burundi, the Ivory Coast, Burma, India, and Indonesia. By the end of the century, about 40 percent of the remaining forests of the developing countries will have been razed.[49] The expansion of agricultural frontiers into forested areas, local invasion for firewood and charcoal, and the multinational plundering of forest products—all of these forces can accelerate the deforestation process. Of course, destruction of forests also destroys the habitats of hundreds of species of bird, mammal, and plant life.

The heavy hand of social structures in domestic and international societies is at work behind global deforestation. A few illustrations will suffice. The U.S. government subsidizes the overcutting of its national forests and ships the logs to Japan. In Andean Latin Ameria, wealthy ranchers use the relatively level valley floors for grazing, forcing local peasants onto steep slopes to produce subsistence crops. In 1975, 7 percent of these landowners possessed some 93 percent of the arable land. The natural forest area of Brazil has been reduced from the original 5.2 million to less than 3.5 million square kilometers, and the Amazon region has lost 840,000 square kilometers of forests (about 24 percent of its original reserve). Daniel K. Ludwig, reportedly the richest man in the United States, purchased 202,350 hectares of the Amazon forest to establish a $400 million paper mill in the midst of the tropical jungle. The destruction of forests and pastures by commercial interests has forced tens of thousands of tribal people in the Bihar and Madhya Pradesh areas of India to flock to the cities in search of work, and finally led to tribal rage and revolt in 1982. A wood-chip operation in Papua, New Guinea, pays a royalty of $48 per hectare cleared, yet it costs $450 per hectare to replant denuded areas. One-third of the trees left behind after a timber operation by a transnational corporation in Indonesia are reported to have died, leaving the surrounding soil in bad condition.[50]

Since trees maintain soil structure by binding it together and by protecting it from the sun, the ecological consequences of deforestation are far-reaching: accelerated soil erosion; the silting of rivers, irrigation canals and dams, ruining freshwater sources; destabilized seasonal flooding; the extinction of many tropical plant and animal species; expanded desert encroachment; and increases in carbon dioxide levels. All of these ecological changes make it difficult for the global forest resources system to keep its ecological equilibrium at an optimal, sustainable yield. As shown in Table 7.3, deforestation slowly but steadily takes its insidious ecological toll on the planet's biological energy mechanisms. If present policies and trends continue, both forest cover and growing stocks of commercial wood in the Third World will decline 40 percent by the year 2000.

One-tenth of the world's total irrigated area, amounting to some 21 million hectares, is reported to be waterlogged. Each year some 125,000 hectares of irrigated land are lost to agricultural production due to waterlogging, salinization, and alkalinization. Waterlogging, salinization, and alkalinization occur mostly in arid regions where irrigation systems have inadequate underground drainage. A recent FAO-UNEP collaborative study found that 35 percent of the land area of North Africa was threatened from water erosion, 17 percent from wind erosion and 8 percent from salinization; comparable figures for the Near East were 22 percent for water, 12 percent for wind, and 1.4 percent for salinization.[51] When the water table rises to a level near the ground surface, the growth of deep-rooted crops is impaired. Soon, the excess water evaporates, bringing soil salts to the surface where they form a mineral crust. Reclaiming waterlogged and

TABLE 7.3
Estimates of World Forest Resources, 1978 and 2000

	Closed Forest *(millions of hectares)*		Growing Stock *(billions cu m overbark)*	
	1978	2000	1978	2000
U.S.S.R.	785	775	79	77
Europe	140	150	15	13
North America	470	464	58	55
Japan, Australia, New Zealand	69	68	4	4
Subtotal	1,464	1,457	156	149
Latin America	550	329	94	54
Africa	188	150	39	31
Asia and Pacific LDCs	361	181	38	19
Subtotal (LDCs)	1,099	660	171	104
Total (world)	2,563	2,117	327	253

	Growing Stock per Capita *(cu m biomass)*	
Industrial countries	142	114
LDCs	57	21
Global	76	40

Source: *The Global 2000 Report to the President*, Vol. II: *The Technical Report* (Washington, D.C.: Government Printing Office, 1980), p. 319.

degraded irrigated areas is a slow and prohibitively expensive process—costing as much as $650 per hectare.

Practically every country with a sizable irrigated area has waterlogging problems. Afghanistan, Argentina, Pakistan, Peru, and the United States chronically suffer from these problems. About 400,000 acres (160,000 hectares) of irrigated farmland in the San Joaquin Valley, one of the richest farm regions in the United States, are currently affected by high, brackish water tables that pose an increasingly serious threat to productivity. Some 1.1 million acres (.44 million ha) will ultimately become unproductive unless subsurface drainage systems are installed.[52]

Soil erosion and loss of soil organic matter can also be caused by certain cultivation practices. For example, land planted to corn-wheat-clover rotation loses an average 2.7 tons (2.4 metric tons) of topsoil per acre annually through erosion, whereas comparable land planted continuously to corn loses 19.7 tons (17.7 metric tons) annually. The United States, as the world's largest corn producer, is in special danger. To date, the problem of topsoil loss has been disguised by the extensive application of fertilizers, but progressive thinning of topsoil degrades the quality of cropland and reduces inherent soil productivity. The U.S. Department of Agriculture has recently reported that the inherent productivity of 34 percent of U.S. cropland is now falling because of the excessive loss of topsoil. The U.S. Soil Conservation Service has also concluded that topsoil losses should be cut in half in order to sustain crop production at present levels.[53]

General soil erosion and humus loss destabilize the organic matter that serves to retain soil structure and moisture. This breakdown of soil organic matter not only reduces agricultural productivity and but also increases carbon dioxide in the atmosphere. Rotation methods, fallow periods, and green manuring can reverse the thinning of topsoil. Unless current cultivation practices are altered, many croplands that are currently producing well will soon face serious soil problems.[54]

Under the impetus of industrialization, urbanization, suburbanization, and militarization, more and more land is being lost each year for agriculture. This has now become a worldwide phenomenon, as asphalt is rapidly replacing food as the *last* crop of our fertile soils. In the course of preparing a *World Conservation Strategy*, the International Union for Conservation of Nature and Natural Resources (IUCN) found that "at least 3,000 km² of prime farmland disappear every year under buildings and roads in developed countries alone" and "hundreds of millions of rural people in developing countries, including 500 million malnourished and 800 million destitute, are compelled to destroy the resources necessary to free them from starvation and poverty."[55] Urban and industrial developments, we are told, "are often located on some of a nation's, or the world's, *best* agricultural land—rich, irrigated, alluvial soils in gently sloping river valleys. Such lands lost to urban and industrial growth often involve taking lands out of production and therefore represent an *actual* loss of production as opposed to a *potential* loss."[56]

In the OECD countries as a whole, urban land area has been growing about twice as fast as the population. In Canada, half of the land lost to urbanization is coming from the best one-twentieth of its farmland. Of the 1–1.2 million hectares of agricultural land lost every year to highways, urban and other nonfarm uses in the United States, .4 million hectares are prime farmland. In Egypt, some 26,000 hectares of the best cropland along the Nile are taken up by roads, factories, and military installations. If present trends in urban and industrial expansion continue, the world's cities are projected to occupy an additional 54 million hectares of land by the year 2000.[57]

At the present time it is not possible to accurately measure the extent to which toxic wastes have poisoned the land and the health of peoples throughout the world. The problem is particularly acute in the United

States, where products connected with more than 70,000 chemicals are manufactured, and where the typical citizen wakes up each morning to learn of another ecological time bomb exploding in some part of the country. If *Torrey Canyon* signalled the beginning of a new age of marine pollution, Love Canal signalled the beginning of a new age of land pollution. As Eckardt C. Beck, EPA's administrator for water and waste management put it at the time of the dump site's first discovery in 1978, "We have learned that Love Canal was merely the first detonation of a string of chemical time bombs literally strewn across the nation."[58] Beck was right. On December 20, 1982, the EPA released a list of the 418 most dangerous toxic dump sites around the country. This may be the tip of the iceberg, as the EPA and various states are currently investigating over 14,000 sites where hazardous wastes are believed to have been improperly dumped in past decades. In early 1983, the number of sites suspected of deadly dioxin contamination in the state of Missouri alone has reached about 100.

The Second Law of Ecology—Everything Must Go Somewhere—is at work here. Once industry overcomes the initial hurdles and receives authorization to manufacture a new product, it is under virtually no constraints on the marketing, use, and final disposal of the product. Ironically, today's land pollution is partly a by-product of the relative "success" of the air and water pollution programs of the 1970s. Huge amounts of toxic materials removed from waterways and smokestacks were solidified and dumped in some 50,000 disposal sites scattered throughout the United States.

Nuclear wastes pose a special disposal problem. The United States has already accumulated about 291 million liters of high-level liquid waste through uranium and plutonium reprocessing. Wastes produced in the reprocessing of nuclear fuel and the production of nuclear weapons account for another 56,600 cubic meters. A recent survey has estimated that waste from commercial nuclear power plants will have increased from its current level of 2,943 cubic meters to more than nine times that amount by the year 2000.[59]

These toxic chemcials and nuclear wastes never remain inactive: they can explode through aging drums; they can seep through the ground, poisoning water supplies; they can seep into rivers and lakes, killing fish and wildlife; and they can find their way into animal feed and eventually into the human body. The greatest danger lies in their invisible and slow "ecocidal" process. Poisonous chemical substances may remain dormant in the human body for long periods, causing health problems as much as fifteen to forty years after initial exposure.[60]

The social process is also a factor in the disposal of harmful waste materials. With the increasing restrictions and difficulties of finding disposal sites at home, more and more U.S. corporations are looking to Third World countries as cheap dumping sites. At present it is not possible to estimate how much hazardous waste material is being "exported." What is unsafe to dispose of in developed countries is even more dangerous in developing countries, which have no facilities for the safe handling of hazardous waste.

The Social Environment

It is evident from the preceding discussion that practically all threats to the ecological stability of the natural environment originate from the social (man-made) environment. The centerpiece of contemporary ecological thinking is the concept of carrying capacity, which connotes the potentiality of an ecosystem to support or sustain a given amount of human pressure at a given rate of human consumption or waste. This concept can be used either to clarify or to obscure the real causes of the ecological crisis and to serve different class or national interests. Like the monocausal paradigm of original sin, ecological holism is susceptible to the notion that each and every human being is *equally* guilty of overconsumption and overpollution, a patently false assumption.

What happens to the human environment is not merely a linear, numerical function of expanding human populations, as some ecologists would have us believe. The ecological crisis is largely a result of certain authoritative patterns of global production, distribution, and consumption of the planet's resources. In short, this is a crisis of social values, structures, and behavior. The ecological crisis caused by the research, development, and employment of destructive, anti-ecological technology is indeed a crisis of contemporary political economy. The Third World's population explosion, although it undoubtedly claims its own ecological toll, is a symptom rather than a cause of the ecological crisis. To develop this line of argument, we need to look more closely at the twin ecological nemeses of overconsumption and overpollution in the larger systemic context of the global social environment. Environmentalists have greatly overstated the impact of human population on the one hand and greatly understated or ignored the impact of growing militarization on the other.

Ecology and Growing Population. There is now mounting evidence that a significant decline in fertility is under way in the Third World. The 1982 State of World Population Report prepared by the United Nations Fund for Population Activities (UNFPA) predicts that the annual growth rate of world population could come down to 1.5 percent (6.1 billion) by the end of the century (from 1.7 percent in 1980 and 2.0 percent in 1965). This represents a 20 percent reduction from the 7.5 billion that the birth and death rates of the 1950s would have produced had they continued to the end of the century. The 1974 World Population Conference catalyzed social consciousness raising in the developing countries on population questions. The number of developing countries with population programs increased from twenty-six in 1969 to fifty-nine in 1980.[61]

Of course, this decline in the growth rate is hardly grounds for complacency. The Third World's population is such that there will still be an annual increase of some 70–80 million people, for a cumulative population increase of almost 50 percent (1.5–1.6 billion) between 1980 and 2000. There can be no doubt that this absolute gain—despite the anticipated decline in the overall growth rate from 32.3 per 1,000 in 1980 to 25.7 in 2000—will tax the countries least capable of bearing this additional demographic burden.[62]

The ecological impact of the declining but still excessive rate of population growth is a complex and entangled question. Africa, with the highest rate of population growth, suffers from the ecological hazards of water pollution, desertification, deforestation, and urban sprawl, but it would be a mistake to say that population growth *causes* these problems. As elaborated in Chapter 5, the population-poverty link is very close in most empirical studies. Eradicating absolute poverty and its concomitant poor health, unsanitary water supplies, illiteracy, and unemployment/underemployment through a basic needs strategy of ecodevelopment is the surest way to cap the demographic volcano. In particular, high infant mortality is closely associated with high fertility, on the one hand, and declines in mortality and fertility rates are closely associated with improvement in primary education and primary health care, on the other. The socioeconomic status of women is an extremely important determinant of fertility rate and family size.

It may not be a coincidence that two developing countries with the biggest declines in birth rate—Cuba and China—have also shown the best performance in meeting basic human needs as measured by the PQLI in their respective income categories. Of all the developing countries, according to the 1982 State of World Population Report, Cuba showed the largest birth rate decline of 47 percent between 1965–1970 and 1975–1980, followed by China with a 34 percent decline in the same period.[63]

What the aggregate population statistical data and projections do not reveal is a highly skewed pattern of global resource consumption. Given the centrality of energy in national and global ecopolitics,[64] the established pattern of energy consumption serves as an apt example. Two revealing reminders are in order here. First, the rate of global energy consumption has been increasing at the annual rate of 4 percent in the last 100 years, as compared to the annual rate of 2 percent in global population growth during the same period. Second, and more significantly, per capita energy consumption in developing countries pales in comparison to per capita energy consumption in developed countries. Table 7.4 shows the patterns and trends in per capita global primary energy use for the period 1975–1990. The environmental impact of this skewed pattern of energy consumption is not difficult to infer.

Historically, as demographer Nathan Keyfitz demonstrates, the effects of affluence on resource consumption have been more pronounced than the effects of population increases. Today, the world's "middle-class person," he estimates, has five times as much impact on the material base as the poor person.[65] Even in such an affluent and throwaway society as the United States, where per capita energy consumption was 553 percent of

TABLE 7.4
Per Capita Global Primary Energy Use, Annually, 1975 and 1990

	1975		1990			
	10^6 Btu	Percent of World Average	10^6 Btu	Percent of World Average	Percent Increase (1975–90)	Average Annual Percent Increase
United States	332	553	422	586	27	1.6
Other industrialized countries	136	227	234	325	72	3.6
Less developed countries[a]	11	18	14	19	27	1.6
Centrally planned economies	58	97	65	90	12	0.8
World	60	100	72	100	20	1.2

[a]Since population projections were not made separately for the OPEC countries, those countries have been included here in LDC category.

Source: *The Global 2000 Report to the President*, Vol. II: *The Technical Report* (Washington D.C.: U.S. Government Printing Office, 1980), p. 347.

the world average in 1975 and projected to increase to 586 percent of the world average by 1990, population growth or decline does not provide a very reliable basis for a full and accurate environmental impact assessment. Barry Commoner's study of the relative effects of three factors on intensity of environmental pollution—population size, degree of affluence, and the tendency of the productive technology to pollute—in the United States since World War II reached the following conclusions:[66]

- The population factor accounts for 12 to 20 percent of the increases in total pollutant output since 1946;
- The affluence factor accounts for 1 to 5 percent of the total increase in pollutant output, except in the case of passenger travel, where it rises to about 40 percent of the total;
- The technology factor accounts for about 95 percent of total pollutant output, except in the case of passenger travel, where it accounts for about 40 percent of the total; and
- The chief reason for the environmental crisis that has engulfed the United States in recent years is not increased population or affluence but the sweeping transformation of productive technology since World War II.

Ecology and Growing Militarization. The environmental movement has, until recently, shied away from confronting the greatest environmental predator and polluter of the earth—the war system. However, with the nuclear arms race having already reached an advanced, pathological stage, there is now evidence that some environmental groups are finally breaking their self-imposed silence. In 1981, environmental groups constituted one of the core groups in the European antiwar movement that swept through the whole continent. In mid-1982, Friends of the Earth, a U.S.-based conservation group, issued a manifesto of sorts, declaring:

> Until recently we were content to work for our usual constituency: life in its miraculous diversity of forms. We have spoken for the trees and plants, the animals, the air and water, and for the land itself. We have argued that human well-being cannot be separated from the health of the natural world from which we all emerged. We have left it for others to argue about war. But the nuclear war contemplated by the U.S. and Russia would kill life of *all* kinds, indiscriminately, on a scale and for a length of time into the future that is so great that it qualifies as the major ecological issue of our time.[67]

The environmental impact of war is more serious in nature and more extensive in scope than generally recognized. Three basic reasons may be suggested. First, the environmental impact would not be confined to one phase, the execution phase, of modern warfare. Second, militarization has progressed so far and spread so widely that the war system has become a dominant political culture in both national and international societies. Third, it is not just nuclear weapons but other weapons systems as well (chemical and biological warfare, geophysical or environmental warfare) that can exact ecological punishments (see Chapter 4).

Unlike natural disasters, the environmental impact of war can be discerned in all three phases: the pre-eruption (preparatory) phase; the eruption (execution) phase; and the posteruption phase. It is in the pre-eruption phase that R&D for destructive technologies, testing and deployment of weapons systems, priority claims upon and exploitation of nonrenewable resources, and ideological campaigns combine in the war system. A draft environmental impact statement on the proposed MX missile system has concluded that the project "will produce rapid, large-scale changes in the character of the human environment of those deployed regions" and that the most significant potential effect is "lowering of the present ground water levels."[68] In a broader sense, the development of nuclear weapons systems entails (1) mining uranium and plutonium, (2) transporting nuclear materials, (3) releasing anthropogenic radiation into the oceans, air, and soil, and (4) dumping deadly nuclear wastes. All raise the levels of environmental and epidemiological hazards.

In the execution phase, the imperative of winning the war—or of avoiding defeat—is so paramount that ecological considerations can play at best a marginal role. The conduct of U.S. warfare in Indochina was unique in that it represented the first instance in the post-Hiroshima era when the human environment was singled out as a "legitimate" military target for deliberate and systematic attack. The extensive use of the chemical herbicides Agent Orange, Agent White, and Agent Blue against forest vegetation is well known and requires no elaboration here.[69] The United States also employed rainmaking as a form of weather modification warfare. Between March 1967 and July 1972, a total of 2,602 cloud seeding missions were flown over Laos, Cambodia, and North and South Vietnam, and 47,409 cannisters of silver and lead iodide were expended to bring about destructive landslides.[70]

In the posteruption phase, the ecological and epidemiological consequences of the first two phases begin to surface. The consequences of nuclear weapons tests include the pollution of the atmospheric, marine, and terrestrial environments as well as the death of some 4,500 sheep in Utah (in 1953) and the slow "ecocidal" suffering among GI guinea pigs (often called atomic soldiers or atomic veterans) who participated in the atmospheric nuclear tests in the 1950s. The founding of the National Association of Atomic Veterans symbolizes an epitaph to the monument of "successful" nuclear testing.[71] There is now a fresh outbreak of previously suppressed epidemiological evidence about the elevated incidence of leukemia among the populations of small towns in northern Arizona and southern Utah located downwind from the Nevada Test Site.

The nuclear chain links all three phases of war as well as the interrelations between war, energy, and environment. The Center is responsible for its invention, its romanticization, and its diffusion. China's entry into the nuclear club in 1964, India's nuclear detonation in 1974, and Israel's nuclear aggression against Iraq in 1981 all serve as public reminders that there is only one way to break the nuclear chain and to close this Pandora's box— the path of global denuclearization. As it becomes increasingly clear that nuclear power is the most costly—and the most dangerous—energy source, the switch to an alternative energy path becomes correspondingly more attractive.[72]

Societal Responses. Despite the recent proliferation of global models and projections, future patterns and trends of the global environment are difficult to predict with any high degree of confidence or reliability. One major difficulty is the unpredictability of societal responses to different environmental crises.[73] To highlight this difficulty and also to suggest contrasting styles and time lags of societal responses, I have selected three cases involving environmental crises in three different countries. Of course, I make no claim that these cases in any way constitute typical or representative samples.

The first case concerns China, the most populous country in the world. As a result of successive torrential rainstorms in the summer of 1981, China's longest river, Changjiang [Yangtze], encountered its highest flood peak since the founding of the People's Republic of China (PRC), leaving 753 people dead and 1.5 million people homeless in Sichuan Province. Until this crisis, it was claimed that the menace of flood, which for centuries had plagued the lower reaches of China's great rivers, had been brought under control and that the danger of two dyke breaches every three years had been permanently done away with.[74]

Most revealing in this recent crisis was China's societal response. Instead of accepting or rationalizing this as a *natural* disaster, Chinese ecopolitics concluded swiftly and decisively that this was largely a man-made disaster. Indiscriminate overcutting of forests, the blind opening up of wasteland, and the destruction of vegetation on the mountain slopes were singled out as chief culprits in undermining the ecological balance of the affected areas. On September 3, 1981, the *Renmin Ribao* (People's Daily), the most widely used outlet for disseminating the official norms of Chinese mobilization politics, began publishing a special series of ecological articles under the umbrella title "Draw Useful Lessons From the Sichuan Floods." The government immediately embarked on a *renewed* nationwide reforestation campaign to cover more than 20 percent of its nearly 3.7 million square miles (9.6 million km^2) with trees. How? All able-bodied Chinese eleven years of age and older are asked to plant three to five trees a year.[75]

Our second case occurred in Japan, the most efficient and productive economic superpower in the world. Japan's societal response to the Minamata Bay incident, as summarized in Table 7.5, provides a stark contrast with the Chinese approach. Of course, the nature of the crisis was quite different; some seventeen years passed between the time mercury-laden pollutants were first injected into the bay and the observation of neurological disorders among the fishermen and their families. However, we might well wonder why another decade and a half had to elapse between the discovery of

TABLE 7.5
Timetable of Societal Responses to Mercury Pollution of the Ocean, Minamata Bay, Japan, 1939–1973

Year		Years Elapsed Since Pollution Began
1939	Chemical production begins on the shores of Minamata Bay; the factory discharges spent catalysts containing mercury into the bay.	0
1953	Birds and cats in the bay area act oddly; the behavior disorder becomes known as "disease of the dancing cats."	14
1956	Neurological disorders observed among Minamata Bay fishermen and their families.	17
1959	High concentrations of mercury ascertained in bay fish and in dead patients; an independent study shows disease was methyl mercury poisoning and factory effluent the likely source.	20
1960	Chemical company denies relationship of mercury to the disease but finds new discharge sites for waste; several new cases break out at new site.	21
1961–64	Very small compensations paid by the chemical company to disease victims and to fishermen for loss of livelihood.	22–25
1965	A second outbreak occurs at Niigata, Japan, where an acetyldehyde factory discharges spent mercury catalysts into the river.	26
1967	Niigata patients initiate a civil action, presumed to be the first large civil suit brought against a polluter in Japan.	28
1971	Niigata District Court pronounces judgment against the Niigata factory; compensation awarded the 77 Niigata victims or their families.	32
1973	Kumamoto District Court finds Minamata Bay factory culpable and orders company to pay reasonable compensation to victims or their families.	34

Source: *The Global 2000 Report to the President, Vol. II: The Technical Report* (Washington, D.C.: U.S. Government Printing Office, 1980), Table 13-28, p. 318, based on Edward D. Goldberg, *The Health of the Oceans* (Paris: UNESCO, 1976), pp. 21–23; Paul R. Ehrlich, *et al. Ecoscience: Population, Resources, Environment* (San Francisco: W. H. Freeman Company, 1977), p. 574.

epidemiological effects in the victims and the court decision ordering the company to pay compensation to victims or their families.[76]

Despite its initial slowness, Japan has demonstrated the "comparative advantage" of its capacity for social learning adaptability. The polluter-must-pay principle is stronger in Japan than in any other industrialized country. Under a 1973 law, for example, 80 percent of compensation funds are paid by polluting industries, with the rest coming from taxes on motor vehicles. Faced with rising energy costs in 1974, Japan introduced some of the most stringent pollution control requirements to be found anywhere in the industrialized world. As a result, sulfur dioxide emissions fell by more than 50 percent between 1970 and 1975, and Japanese industry began to introduce new technology and renovate its polluting and wasteful old plants. This program paid off handsomely: Japanese pollution control technology is now selling extremely well worldwide, and Japanese industry is cleaner, more efficient, and more competitive than that of most industrialized countries.[77]

For our third case we turn to the United States, still the world's most powerful country, the center of Center countries dominating the contemporary global system. The U.S. ecological movement is also the most advanced and active in the world. In many ways, the actions of the United States, what happens or fails to happen in the United States, is still a powerful model for emulation elsewhere in the world. Against this backdrop, the deepening malaise of the nuclear power industry in the wake of the 1979 Three Mile Island accident provides a revealing commentary on U.S. societal response.

The nuclear power industry is slowly sinking under its own economic weight. In the forty months since the Three Mile Island accident, not a single new nuclear power reactor has been ordered; work on thirty-eight others has been cancelled. The uranium mining industry is now in a deep recession. A number of factors have contributed to the nuclear malaise, but they can all be translated into a "cost-profit" balance sheet for the nuclear power industry, as summarized below:[78]

- *The Safety Factor.* The industry's pet theory about the safety of nuclear power plants collapsed at Three Mile Island. Each year the number of newly detected safety problems increases. In October 1982, for example, the Nuclear Regulatory Commission pinpointed forty units that may eventually need modifications to guard against "thermal shock."
- *The Regulation Factor.* As more and more safety problems are discovered, and as old plants develop unexpected problems, the regulators discover even more potential safety problems, adding to safety and design requirements.
- *The Delay Factor.* Complying with new safety and design requirements inevitably delays the completion of a plant. Antinuclear groups may not succeed in preventing the completion of a nuclear power plant, but they can certainly *delay* its completion. The Shoreham Nuclear Power Station (Long Island, New York) is ten years late.

- *The Demand Factor.* The exponential rise in energy prices has substantially reduced the demand for electricity.
- *The Comparative Cost Factor.* The cost of building a nuclear power plant has risen twice as fast as the cost of building a coal-fired power station in the 1970s. A nuclear power plant is now estimated to cost 60 percent more than a comparable coal-fired plant fully equipped with the latest pollution-control devices. Shoreham's electricity will be three times as expensive as the electricity produced by oil-fired plants.
- *The Aging/Repair Cost Factor.* The industry's twenty-five-year history shows that nuclear power plants become progressively more prone to accidents as they age. Annual repair costs at a typical nuclear power plant rose from $21 million in 1978 to $90 million in 1982.
- *The Disposal Factor.* As people become more aware of the hazards of nuclear wastes, state and local governments are frequently forced to deny access to their land as dumpsites.
- *The Accident/Insurance Factor.* To date it has cost about $1 billion to clean up the Three Mile Island accident. No insurance company is likely to offer nuclear accident insurance *without* government guarantee, and this guarantee is far from assured. In fact, a recent decision of the U.S. Supreme Court upheld states' right to veto nuclear power plants on economic grounds.
- *The Legislative/Legal Factor.* In 1979 California imposed a moratorium on future nuclear power plant construction, citing the lack of a national program for the long-term storage of nuclear waste. Existing nuclear plants are threatened with unpredictable future costs or even shutdowns. In 1982, the House of Representatives voted for the first time to hold up additional funds for the Clinch River breeder reactor in Oak Ridge, Tenn. The Supreme Court's stunning 9-0 decision in April 1983, upholding the authority of states to veto construction of nuclear-power plants is another unexpected setback for the troubled nuclear industry as well as for the federal government.

All of these factors have helped to highlight the multiple hazards of nuclear power for the consuming public and the multiple hidden costs of nuclear energy for the profit-conscious investor. They have also raised the *uncertainty factor*, the nemesis of the U.S. Stock Market, to such an extent that nuclear power plants are no longer regarded as attractive, profitable, or safe investments.

Nonetheless, it is premature to write an obituary for the nuclear power industry. The twenty-four TNCs that control the nuclear industry possess the overwhelming corporate power to rejuvenate the mystique of U.S. preeminence in "nuclear power" by first linking the future of the nuclear power industry with the future of U.S. geopolitical hegemony in the world and then removing nuclear power from the economic pressures of the market place. In late 1982 the nuclear power industry expressed its disappointment with the Reagan administration—striking an ironic note, for the Reagan administration has a messianic zeal for nuclear power—and pronounced that it would spend $30–$40 million in 1983 in a major campaign to persuade the public that "nuclear power is a necessary element in our hopes to build a better America."[79]

International Response

From Stockholm to Nairobi

The first United Nations Conference on the Human Environment, held in Stockholm from June 5 to June 16, 1972, symbolized the official inauguration of global ecopolitics. Some 1,200 delegates from 113 countries, surrounded by 27,000 planetary citizens from all over the world, assembled to form a global charter on the human environment. On trial was the moral, intellectual, and institutional capacity of the international community to survive together and to cooperate in the face of clear and continuing ecological danger. The global ecological consciousness that converged in Stockholm confronted the existing postwar world order system with what Teilhard de Chardin once called "the cry of a world trembling with the desire for unity."[80]

In May 1982, the second UN conference on the global environment— officially called "Session of a Special Character of the Governing Council of the United Nations Environment Programme"—was held in Nairobi, Kenya, to commemorate the tenth anniversary of the first conference and to assess the measures taken to implement the declaration and action plan adopted at Stockholm. The Nairobi Declaration reaffirmed the principles of the Stockholm Declaration as providing "a basic code of environmental conduct for the years to come."[81] The development from Stockholm to Nairobi shows the outer limits and capabilities of the existing world order system to adapting to the changing human requirements of the ecological-nuclear era. The post-Stockholm development of global ecopolitics also shows the UN's potential in dealing with unanticipated dangers and opportunities.

What happened at Stockholm—and its final outcome—is open to contending interpretations.[82] Given the constraints of the international system, however, Stockholm can be viewed as a remarkable accomplishment. Stockholm established a path-breaking precedent for the global politics of consciousness-raising and norm-making through conference diplomacy in the 1970s and beyond. And Stockholm did, after all, succeed in producing a global compromise on the 26-principle declaration and 109-point action plan as well as on a new global regime of coordination on environmental affairs.

In a sense, Stockholm was an end, not a beginning, for the global environmental movement. This movement was largely responsible for the successful, if flawed, formulation of the global environmental charter. A number of forces contributed to the gathering momentum of this movement in the 1960s. Although the United Nations Charter did not provide any specific principles or provisions on the human environment, the mandates of such specialized agencies as WHO, WMO, (the World Meteorological Organization), UNESCO, FAO, IMCO, and ILO included a number of separate sectors of environmental concern. UNESCO's program on Man and the Biosphere (MAB) and WMO's Global Atmospheric Research Programme (GARP) are two notable examples of growing collaboration between specialized agencies and scientific NGOs on environmental or environment-related issues.

The environmental movement was galvanized in the 1960s by a number of ecodisasters. The *Torrey Canyon* disaster off the southern coast of England, which polluted over a hundred miles (some 160 km) of British and French beaches in Cornwall, Normandy, and Brittany; the deaths of birds caused by the unexpected side effects of dichloro-diphenyl-trichloro-ethane (DDT); the air pollution episodes in London and New York; the fatal instances of mercury poisoning in Japan; and acid rain in Nordic countries, to cite a few notable examples, have all energized and expanded the environmental movement, led by such world-renowed figures as Rachel Carson, Barbara Ward, Barry Commoner, and Margaret Mead. Even the U.S. space project helped to popularize an Apollo vision of one world. The picture of the earth taken from the Apollo spacecraft dramatized more vividly than anything in human history that ours is a small, beautiful planet without political and ideological borders; it only shows *natural* ecological boundaries of oceans, deserts, mountains, forests, and drifting clouds, all holding together one fragile biosphere adrift in space. "From out there," as the astronaut Frank Borman put it, "it really is 'one world' "[83]

The preparations for the conference took nearly four years. From December 1968, when the General Assembly adopted a Swedish draft resolution for the convocation of the conference, to June 1972, the behind-the-scenes preparation entailed a complex and continuing interaction between the twenty-seven-nation Preparatory Committee, a small but well-organized Conference Secretariat, headed by Maurice F. Strong, former president of the Canadian International Development Agency, panels of independent experts, and an Intergovernmental Working Group established to prepare the draft declaration on the basis of member states' replies to a questionnaire by the Secretary-General.

To a significant extent, the "success" of the Stockholm Conference can be attributed to Maurice Strong's extraordinary leadership. Widely admired for his singleminded tenacity and his uncanny talent for compromise, Strong realized from the outset that a global consensus depended upon winning the support of the Third World, where the word "environment" merely evoked skepticism. The Third World's perception was that the ecological crisis was no more than the rich man's mental disease, designed to divert the attention of the international community from the poor man's physical survival. To overcome this misconception, Strong travelled extensively in the developing countries from mid-1970 on. In addition, an important seminar involving an international panel of twenty-six experts was held at Founex, Switzerland in June 1971 to seek a closer interface between environment and development. The Founex Report did contribute to broadening the agenda and concept for the Stockholm Conference by redefining economic well-being and ecological balance in mutually complementary terms.[84]

If the Stockholm spirit of compromise produced a success, this was achieved by reasserting the imperatives of power politics, by separating global pollution, poverty, population, and politics from their underlying social, political, economic, and cultural structures, by institutionalizing the primacy of states in the new global environmental regime anchored in UNEP, and by sidestepping some of the central environmental issues of the time. This becomes all the clearer when we compare the Stockholm Declaration and the Dai Dong Declaration,[85] issued by the Dai Dong Independent Conference, also convened and held in Stockholm from June 1 to June 6, 1972, in the recognition that the official conference would be torn with irreconcilable conflicts. F. H. Knelman, an independent academic observer who was a delegate to the Dai Dong Independent Conference, forcefully argues that the style of ecopolitics within nations was no less operable among nations at the international level: "Tokenism, co-option, jurisdictional juggling, expiation by legislation, and the trade-off of unmentionables were all quite common." Yet in the end Knelman concedes that Stockholm was "a small but clear step toward the great global revolutionary change that is beginning."[86]

Ten years later, the spirit at Nairobi was more retrospective than prospective, more sobering than euphoric. The number of participating countries dropped from 113 at Stockholm to 105. Perhaps the most conspicuous change reflected at Nairobi was the role reversal between the rich and poor countries. Apparently, the developing countries learned the bitter ecological lesson the hard way. Ironically, while developing countries are becoming environmental enthusiasts, the industrialized countries, burdened by the intractable economic woes of stagflation, have retreated from their domestic and international environmental programs.

To what extent, and in what manner, can it be said that the present international system is capable of realizing the world order value of ecological balance? I will attempt to answer this question by examining three types of regime activities—the expansion of knowledge, the shaping of values, and implementation.

The Knowledge-Expanding Process

The expansion of the collective knowledge base in the field of global environmental affairs is a necessary, if insufficient condition for collective action. This assumption was embodied in "Earthwatch," the term used at the Stockholm Conference for the global environment assessment program, one of three functional components of the action plan. Earthwatch was conceived and designed as an internationally financed and coordinated knowledge system that would evaluate the changing interaction between man and the environment, identify significant environmental trends, monitor early signs of environmental hazards, and assess the condition of selected natural resources.

Earthwatch is a dynamic knowledge-expanding process whereby relevant problem areas are identified, available knowledge reviewed, further research conducted, and relevant data and information collected, analyzed, and evaluated to provide a firm scientific base for collective action. Three types of the knowledge expansion—research, information exchange, and monitoring—have been closely associated with UNEP.

Research. Regime-sponsored and coordinated research on the state of the global environment takes many forms at many different levels. The annual state of the environment report is a notable example, and is something the global human rights regime has yet to develop. The first three reports, for 1974, 1975, and 1976, discussed and evaluated a broad spectrum of environmental issues and problems. In 1976, the Governing Council of UNEP decided that the annual state of the environment report should be more selective—and that an analytical, comprehensive state of the environment report should be prepared every fifth year.

Table 7.6 provides an overview of the topics covered in the annual state of the environment reports for 1974–1981. The criteria for selective inclusion and treatment of topics since 1977 included (1) international importance, (2) new public and governmental interest or new scientific knowledge, (3) urgency, (4) insufficient attention from governments and the United Nations system, and (5) a close fit to the regime's bailiwick. Moreover, in preparation for the second United Nations Conference on the Global Environment, UNEP has published a number of comprehensive reports focusing on the positive and negative changes that occurred in the world environment in the decade following Stockholm.[87]

Most of the comprehensive research on specific sectors of the environment is carried out through collaborative work between specialized agencies and outside scientific NGOs. An example is the collaborative work of the International Council of Scientific Unions (ICSU) in GARP and MAB. Launched jointly by WMO and ICSU, GARP is one of the most significant research programs in the history of meterology.[88] Growing out of the 1968 Biosphere Conference organized by UNESCO and joined by FAO, WHO, ICSU, and IUCN, MAB is a program of intergovernmental and interdisciplinary environmental research. Organized around 14 themes, MAB involves some 500 research projects in more than 50 countries, including such categories as the structure and functioning of different levels of ecosystems, the pattern of interactions between various human activities and the biosphere, and the development of policy planning models. The execution of the MAB program depends entirely upon the national committee of each participating country.[89]

Information Storage and Exchange. The International Referral System for Sources of Environmental Information (INFOTERRA) grew out of recommendation 101 of the Stockholm Action Plan on the assumption that information exchange is of prime importance to national decisionmakers

TABLE 7.6
Topics Treated in the Annual State of the Environment Reports 1974–1981

Subject Area	Topic	Year
The atmosphere	Climatic changes and their causes	1974,* 1976, 1980
	Possible effects of ozone depletion	1977
The marine environment	Oceans	1975*
Freshwater environment	Water resources and quality	1974,* 1976
	Ground Water	1981
Land environment	Land resources	1974*
	Raw materials	1975*
	Firewood	1977
Food and agriculture	Food shortages, hunger, and losses of agricultural land	1974,* 1977, 1976
	Use of agricultural and agro-industrial residues	1978
	Resistance to pesticides	1979
Environment and health	Toxic substances and effects	1974,* 1976*
	Heavy metals and health	1980
	Cancer	1977
	Malaria	1978
	Schistosomiasis	1979
	Biological effects of ozone depletion	1977
	Chemicals in Food Chain	1981
Energy	Energy conservation	1975,* 1978
	Firewood	1977
Environmental pollution	Toxic substances	1974*
	Chemicals and the environment:	
	—possible effects of ozone depletion	1977
	—chemicals and the environment	1978
	Noise pollution	1979
Man and environment	Human stress and societal tension	1974*
	Outer limits	1975*
	Population	1975,* 1976*
	Tourism and environment	1979
	Transport and the environment	1980
	Environmental effects of military activity	1980
	The child and the environment	1980
Environmental management achievements	The approach to management	1974,* 1976
	Protection and improvement of the environment	1977
	Legal and institutional arrangement	1976*
	Environmental economics	1981

*Indicates brief treatment in early reports.

Source: UN Doc. UNEP/GC.10/3, pp. 3–4.

TABLE 7.7
Select Features of INFOTERRA, 1978–1980

Governing Council Session (UNEP)	Number of Participating Governments	Number of Countries with Sources Registered	Number of Registered Sources	System-Wide Queries Per Month
6th (1978)	87	48	5,000	150
7th (1979)	94	63	7,100	150
8th (1980)	107	68	7,800	200
Dec.31, 1980	112	76	8,400	350

Source: UN Doc. UNEP/GC.9/5, p. 13.

if they are to plan and devise environmentally sound development strategies. As subsequently conceived and developed by UNEP, INFOTERRA is a decentralized global network of environmental information systems. It does not provide any substantive environmental information; it merely acts as a global computerized switchboard collecting and disseminating *sources* of information. Its main functions include: (1) promoting greater international cooperation between institutions and governments in the collection, evaluation, and distribution of environmental information; (2) educating national developers on the need to incorporate available information on the environment in planning and programming processes; (3) assisting the development of national systems for the retrieval and processing of environmental information; and (4) developing the referral sevice itself, with the identification of more sources of information and with the expansion of "focal points" networks.

Table 7.7 sums up the key variables in the development of INFOTERRA during 1978-1980. By the end of 1981, 116 countries had joined the system, over 9,000 sources of environmental information were registered and over 9,700 referrals provided, and over 200 operatives in over 100 countries had been trained in information handling techniques. INFOTERRA has also helped in introducing environmental issues into many other international information systems.[90]

The description of an actual case may show how INFOTERRA works. The Beijing Municipal Institute for Labor Protection sent to the INFOTERRA National Focal Point in China the following inquiry: "Where can we obtain information on noise abatement in metropolitan areas?" A computer search produced twenty possible sources of information for this question. The inquirer obtained material that, in its own words, was "very helpful in solving the truly international problem of noise control" and that provided "useful information for setting up our own regulations." As a result, the municipal authorities reportedly established "standards for car

horns and redesigned the traffic flow, with many streets changed to one-
way traffic, all of which resulted in considerable reduction in traffic noise
levels."[91]

Monitoring. Another key component of UNEP's "assessment" process is
the Global Environmental Monitoring System (GEMS). The title is a
misnomer, for GEMS is not a full-fledged early warning system in an
operational sense. At this stage GEMS is no more than a collective and
coordinated research effort of the international community to acquire
through a variety of sectoral monitorings the data needed for a more
rational management of the environment. GEMS is still in the preliminary
research stage, although it is struggling to evolve into an operational system.

The Stockholm Action Plan was the main catalyst for UNEP's establishment in 1975 of a Programme Activity Centre for GEMS at UNEP
headquarters in Nairobi. The GEMS Centre coordinates international
environmental monitoring activities conducted throughout the United
Nations system. It does not itself conduct research, evaluate specific environmental problems, or operate any monitoring stations, but works
through the intermediary of the specialized agencies in its main role as
global coordinator and catalyst on environmental affairs.

UNEP's monitoring activities within GEMS fall into five closely linked
programs, each containing various monitoring networks with built-in provisions for training, technical assistance, and evaluation and review:[92]

- *Resource Monitoring.* Employing a combination of ground work, low-
  level reconnaissance flights, conventional aerial photography and
  Landsat imagery, a number of pilot monitoring projects have been
  conducted on tropical forest resources, soil degradation, and Sahelian
  pastoral ecosystems, in collaboration with FAO.
- *Climate-Related Monitoring.* Initiated in 1980, the UNEP/WMO climate-
  related monitoring project consists of eight projects: continuation and
  extension of current background air pollution monitoring activities;
  monitoring of the earth's heat budget; monitoring of the cryosphere;
  monitoring of physical and thermal ocean characteristics; monitoring
  of volcanic effects on the atmosphere; development of the use of
  meteorological satellites; investigations of historical and proxy data;
  and development of climatological data management systems. In
  addition, a world-wide inventory of glaciers (a UNEP/UNESCO
  project), has gathered a considerable amount of data on glacier surfaces
  and masses from forty-five countries and is now incorporated under
  the common umbrella of "climate-related monitoring."
- *Ocean Monitoring.* This is carried out by the Regional Seas Programme
  Activity Centre in cooperation with GEMS. Most activities are related
  to UNEP's action plans for individual regional seas. Attention is
  currently being given to the more difficult problem of open-ocean
  monitoring in collaboration with the Intergovernmental Oceano-
  graphic Commission.

- *Health-Related Monitoring.* This is concerned with environmental quality and the associated exposure of human and other targets to pollution. Five health-related monitoring projects are currently under way: air quality monitoring, global water quality monitoring, food and animal feed contamination monitoring, biological monitoring, and exposure-to-air-pollution monitoring.
- *Long-Range Transport of Pollutants.* This UNEP/WMO/ECE (Economic Commission for Europe) monitoring provides data on the deposition of pollutants (particularly sulphur oxides and their transformation products) in relation to the movement of air masses from the pollutant sources to distant targets in Europe. Samples are obtained from forty-two stations in twelve countries and studied by East and West European Centres located in Moscow and Norway.

Despite its "pragmatic" functional appeal, the knowledge-expanding process can be criticized for a variety of reasons. There is no empirical evidence to support the technocratic assumption that the global production and distribution of knowledge can be a value-neutral process. The present global environmental monitoring system, although evolving and expanding, is still too "sanitized" (exclusion of social parameters), and too "sectoralized" (coverage is limited to a small number of physical parameters within any given sector). Governments have to date refused to provide the data needed to monitor radioactive releases to the biosphere. As shown by the response of major global actors to the Cocoyoc Declaration, any attempt to broaden and extend ecological monitoring to socioeconomic parameters is effectively squelched. The existing approach therefore runs counter to the First Law of Ecology and the desired integrated, multidisciplinary approach.

Ideally, the expansion and distribution of knowledge should catalyze necessary action. In reality, however, states tend to be highly selective in their use of existing scientific knowledge, seeking only those findings that support existing policy preferences. In environmental science, facts and evidence are often contradictory, incomplete, and uncertain due to the slow and protracted maturation of ecological response. States often seize the weakest link in scientific knowledge as a pretext for inaction. The habitual response of Japan to commercial whaling in the International Whaling Commission (IWC) and the angry and punitive response of the Reagan administration to recent NAS reports on acid rain[93] are instructive examples.

The scientific determinism implicit in the knowledge-expanding process is particularly problematic in the complex, interrelated, and interdependent ecosystems. Nonlinearities, discontinuities, and apparent randomness in environmental processes constantly produce new, rare, and unexpected problems. Faced with this dilemma, many environmental scientists respond according to a self-serving axiom—define problems in such a manner that they are susceptible to easy solution. This means selecting sector-specific problems without too many "externalities" and "surprises." Of course, such sectoralized research and sweetened medicines are more palatable to the patients/clients, for they create the illusion that environmental problems are being solved.

The Value-Shaping Process

The value-shaping process in the domain of global ecopolitics follows the same common methods practiced in global human rights politics—the preparation and adoption of multilateral declarations, conventions, or treaties (see Chapter 6). The General Assembly plays the central supervisory role in this value-shaping process. With the creation of the global environmental regime, however, UNEP has become the global catalyst and coordinator on all environmental matters, including the shaping or reshaping of environmental values. What in UNEP jargon is misleadingly called "environmental management" actually refers to "goal setting and planning," in which environmental law serves as an integral part of sound environmental management.

The 1972 Stockholm Declaration on the Human Environment is to the human environment what the 1948 Universal Declaration of Human Rights is to human rights—a global charter of basic ecological principles and values. The preamble of the declaration notes "the need for a common outlook and for common principles to inspire and guide the peoples of the world in the preservation and enhancement of the human environment," and provides an overall framework for progressive development and codification of international environmental law.

As a product of global compromise and reconciliation between various contending values and interests, the Stockholm Declaration lacks conceptual clarity and internal consistency. Too many values and norms need further elaboration and evaluation, but this is unavoidable in drafting a multilateral declaration of this nature and magnitude. Before discussing the extent to which post-Stockholm developments have added further clarity and coherence, however, a number of notable features of the declaration merit brief mention.

First of all, the conceptual linkage between human rights and human environment is revealed in affirming the value of a safe and stable environment as a basic human right—even the right to life itself. The Maoist populist ethos prevailed over the Malthusian approach to population in the proclamation that "of all things in the world, people are the most precious." Inserted at China's insistence, this statement is a triumph of China's debut in multilateral conference diplomacy. The declaration conveniently ignores all of the social and structural causes of the ecological crisis except one, proclaiming that "man and his environment must be spared the effects of nuclear weapons and all other means of mass destruction." This statement was a major defeat for China and France.

The declaration's emphasis on the duty of all governments in protecting and improving the environment is another mark of Chinese influence. "The Chinese delegation was somehow able to persuade the other members of the Working Group not only to accept this [governmental] duty but also to put it most appropriately in the forefront of the Declaration. This was a striking accomplishment, though the language is more obscure than might have been desired, considering the importance of the principle involved."[94] Not surprisingly, the primacy of statism in its rights as well as in its responsibilities is also stressed throughout the Declaration.

Finally, two major threats to the universality of the Stockholm Declaration did not materialize. The initial fear that the Third World might not attend the conference was put to rest by broadening the agenda and by incorporating ecodevelopmental values in the declaration. The boycott of the Soviet Union and several East European countries over the status of the German Democratic Republic caused no permanent damage, as they later decided to participate in UNEP. The temporary absence of the Soviet Union was more than offset by China's debut as a participant in a UN-sponsored global conference at Stockholm. China largely succeeded in reformulating paragraphs 2, 4, 5, and 7 of the preamble in accordance with its own "Ten Cardinal Principles on Amending [the] 'Declaration on [the] Human Environment.'" China's major contribution to the declaration was to broaden and link the concept of environmental protection to improving the welfare of peoples, economic development, and the duties of all governments.[95]

Thanks to the successful conclusion of the Stockholm Conference, UN-sponsored global conferences have become a principal means of shaping values on functional issues in the 1970s. The scope and magnitude of the post-Stockholm value-shaping process can therefore be measured by the number of environmental or environment-related conferences and meetings. As shown in Table 7.8, some twenty global conferences and seminars were held in the decade after Stockholm. This table does not include annual sessions of the UNEP Governing Council.

As a rule, these global conferences and seminars reflect changing environmental conditions, changing societal values, and changing policy goals. Value shaping is a dynamic, ongoing process in which the international community is constantly prodded to seek a better interface between normative and empirical realities. The declarations, resolutions, decisions, and reports of these multilateral conferences and seminars tend to show the lowest common denominator of converging environmental perceptions among the key actors in global ecopolitics. Stockholm was a beginning for this ongoing value-shaping process.

At the highest level of conceptualization and legitimation, the principles of the Stockholm Declaration have been repeatedly reaffirmed as universally valid. Nonetheless, the environmental values embodied in the Stockholm Declaration in a confusing and disjointed form have received progressive reformulation and reordering. The Declaration took little account of the interrelations between various environmental sectors and values. The most noticeable post-Stockholm development may be seen in continuing attempts to seek a closer interface between various competing sectors and values. At its first session in 1973, for example, the Governing Council of UNEP singled out the theme of "environment and development" as a subject of

TABLE 7.8
List of Environment-Related Conferences and Meetings within the United Nations System, 1971-1982

Year	Conference Title	Place
1971	The Founex Panel of Experts on Development and Environment	Founex
1972	The United Nations Conference on the Human Environment	Stockholm
1973-82	The Third United Nations Conference on the Law of the Sea	Caracas Geneva New York
1974	The UNEP/UNCTAD Symposium on Patterns of Resource Use, Environment and Development Strategies	Cocoyoc
1974	The World Population Conference	Bucharest
1974	The World Food Conference	Rome
1975	The Second General Conference of UNIDO	Lima
1976	The Tripartite World Conference on Employment, Income Distribution and Social Progress, and the International Division of Labour	Geneva
1976	Habitat: United Nations Conference on Human Settlement	Vancouver
1977	The United Nations Water Conference	Mar del Plata
1977	The United Nations Conference on Desertification	Nairobi
1977	The UNEP/UNESCO Intergovernmental Conference on Environmental Education	Tbilisi
1978	The International Conference on Primary Health Care	Alma Ata
1978	The United Nations Conference on Technical Co-operation among Developing Countries	Buenos Aires
1979	The World Climate Conference	Geneva
1979	The World Conference on Agrarian Reform and Rural Development	Rome
1979	The United Nations Symposium on the Interrelations between Resources, Environment, Population and Development	Stockholm
1979	The High-level Meeting within the Framework of the ECE on the Protection of the Environment	Geneva
1980	The Third General Conference of UNIDO	New Delhi
1980	The World Conference of the United Nations Decade for Women	Copenhagen
1981	The United Nations Conference on New and Renewable Sources of Energy	Nairobi
1982	Session of a Special Character of the Governing Council of the United Nations Environment Programme	Nairobi

high priority in further refinement of its own thinking. The central theme in the post-Stockholm quest pivoted around the interrelations among people, resources, environment, and development. This theme received its most comprehensive treatment and formulation at the 1979 United Nations Symposium on the Interrelations between Resources, Environment, Population, and Development, held in Stockholm.[96]

There has been a discernible shift from a narrow, one-dimensional concept, focused primarily on sectoral approaches and pollution abatement strategies, to a broader understanding of the systemic character of sociocultural and economic interactions. The condition of the biophysical environment, so obviously a focal point in the years leading up to Stockholm, is no longer regarded as an independent sector but as part and parcel of a more systemic conception of the human environment. The practical implications of this conceptual and normative shift are two fold: (1) greater emphasis on a broader systemic approach, considering development strategies from the perspective of qualitative values and ethics rather than from that of quantitative economic growth; and (2) greater recognition of the important interconnections between the components and processes that support the life of the planet in development strategies.

In the international community the value-shaping process often culminates in a multilateral treaty or convention. These treaties may be accepted as authoritative crystallizations of shared community norms, expectations, and standards of what *should* be done in a given issue area. Besides having greater binding force than such unwritten norms, a treaty is supposed to give greater normative clarity and coherence to commonly shared values couched in the peremptory language of legal rights and obligations. Realizing that the international community's shared norms and expectations on proper environmental behavior are in an embryonic stage, the Stockholm Conference through its Action Plan even specified a number of areas for progressive development and codification of international environmental law, including the protection of species inhabiting international waters, a ten-year moratorium on commercial whaling, creation of river basin commissioners, and the protection of the marine environment against pollution.[97]

The Post-Stockholm progress in environmental law has been impressive but highly uneven. Over thirty international and regional agreements for the protection of the environment have been concluded since Stockholm, and fourteen of these have fulfilled specific recommendations of the Stockholm Action Plan. On the whole, good progress has been made in the area of international conservation conventions, with the notable exception of the ten-year moratorium on commercial whaling specifically recommended by the Stockholm Action Plan. Fair progress has also been made in the area of ocean dumping conventions.

The development of international environmental law on weather modification and natural resources shared by two or more states—including liability and compensation for the victims of transboundary pollution and other environmental damage—remains problematic. The 1979 Convention of Long-Range Transboundary Air Pollution, completed in Geneva under the auspices of the ECE, was signed by thirty-one of the commission's thirty-four member states, but only a handful have actually ratified it so far. The question of international liability for injurious consequences arising from acts not prohibited by existing international law is currently under review by the UN's International Law Commission.

After having reviewed the progress to date, the Meeting of Senior Government Officials Expert in Environmental Law (Montevideo, 1981) singled out three subject areas—marine pollution from land-based sources; protection of the stratospheric ozone layer; and transport, handling, and disposal of toxic substances—as deserving highest priority for the development of international environmental law. The other subject areas deserving early action in the field of environmental law included international cooperation in environmental emergencies, coastal zone management, transboundary air pollution, international trade in potentially harmful chemicals, protection of rivers and other inland waters against pollution, legal and administrative mechanisms for the prevention and redress of pollution damage, and environmental impact assessment.[98]

The making of international environmental law, as shown most dramatically in the Third United Nations Conference on the Law of the Sea, is a painfully complex, precarious, and protracted process. This is partly because the potential benefits and costs are so high, especially when regulating the use of global commons, and partly because of the difficulty of reconciling conflicting vested interests and traditional principles. The acceptance of the new and holistic principle of "common heritage of mankind," for example, does not make other competing principles—as state resource sovereignty and state responsibility—vanish; it merely sets the stage for hard bargaining to find some acceptable compromise between these conflicting international law principles.

As in global human rights legislation, the ratification process of translating a draft convention into a mandatory law is a slow and often elusive process. In the drafting of international oil pollution legislation through the Intergovernmental Maritime Consultative Organization (IMCO), for example, only six of nine international conventions have finally entered into force—and this after a hiatus of about six years each. Although many years have elapsed since their drafting, three additional agreements miscarried during the ratification process, failing to attain the status of international law.[99]

From a just world order perspective, the most problematic feature of the value-shaping process is its limited normative parameters. Operating as it does within the state-centric framework, the process allows the shaping or reshaping of values in a deliberately restrained and incremental fashion that never challenges the basic premises of the existing social order in domestic and international societies. The fate of the Cocoyoc Declaration is instructive. As discussed in Chapter 5, the Cocoyoc Declaration is a *system-transforming* ecodevelopmental model. "The problem today is not primarily one of absolute shortage but of economic and social maldistribution and misuse," concludes the declaration. "Mankind's predicament is rooted primarily in economic and social structures and behaviour within and between countries."[100] It follows that structural transformation in both domestic and international societies is a necessary precondition for an alternative ecodevelopment.

The Cocoyoc Declaration was immediately singled out for target practice by all major global actors. The Western countries responded in unison, reminding UNEP that it had no business concerning itself with the global political economy, let alone trying to transform it. The Soviet Union joined the cant, by harping on the declaration's putative logical inconsistencies and empirical inadequacies; the United States attacked the declaration for its castigation of the market mechanism, announcing that its pledged contributions to the UNEP Fund would be withheld. The declaration's criticism of domestic socioeconomic structures in the Third World was no less an indictment of Third World elites as part of the same global dominance system; the response of Third World representatives was no less vigorous than that of their First and Second World counterparts in condemming the Cocoyoc proposals.[101]

Clearly, the value-shaping process has its limits. New environmental values, norms, and regulations must coexist and compete with the old established values, norms, and rules guiding the states in a highly competitive world system. Still, it is possible to argue that the most notable accomplishment of the post-Stockholm developments lies in the universal legitimation of environmental issues. On the initiative of Zaire, the General Assembly adopted in 1980 a proposal on a "Draft World Charter for Nature" that affirms the urgency of safeguarding the balance of natural systems and of conserving the earth's habitat and resources.[102] The International Development Strategy for the Third United Nations Development Decade has also incorporated environmental concerns.[103] The adoption by nine multilateral development agencies, including the World Bank and UNDP, of principles for incorporating environmental factors in their development projects suggests that the value-shaping process has even penetrated the hard citadel of global money managers.

This universal legitimation has been made possible by the remarkable transformation of Third World thinking. The decision to establish UNEP headquarters in Nairobi, the first UN agency to seek its central "habitat" in the Third World, the progressive expansion and reformulation of the concept of environment, the advances in environmental science, and the global logic of the basic laws (and harsh penalties) of ecology—all of these factors have contributed to the full and active participation of the developing countries in global ecopolitics. From Stockholm to Nairobi, the number of states with environmental agencies or departments increased from about 10 to about 106 (including 70 developing countries), and the number of environmental NGOs from about 2,500 to about 15,230. Revealingly, about 60 percent of some 2,230 environmental NGOs in the developing countries were founded in the decade following Stockholm, compared to only 30 percent of some 13,000 environmental NGOs in the developed countries.[104]

There is now a conflict between the developed and the developing countries on the proper role of UNEP. The developed countries in general and the United States in particular have retreated from leadership positions, trying to minimize their contributions and to confine UNEP to informational and catalytic functions. Meanwhile the recently converted developing countries are pressing vigorously for a more active implementation role of UNEP in the protection of the human environment.

The Implementation Process

The collective shaping of values, whether through multilateral decla-rations, resolutions, decisions, or conventions, does not necessarily mean that things will be done in a certain prescribed manner. In a decentralized and voluntaristic system of sovereign states, the process of translating normative code into behavioral reality is always strewn with political and institutional hurdles and impediments. The Stockholm Conference at-tempted to mitigate this problem, though in a confusing and contradictory way. On the one hand, the conference was not content with the adoption of a universal environmental charter for self-implementation. It self-con-sciously specified an overall functional framework for institutional growth and adaptation as well as for progressive development and codification of international environmental law.

On the other hand, the governmental representatives at Stockholm in the end were faced with a choice between two institutional alternatives. A new regime within the United Nations system, responsible for initiating and implementing full-fledged, integrated multidisciplinary activities to meet changing environmental needs and challenges, was one possibility. The alternative regime, also in the United Nations system, would merely act as a global coordinator and catalyst on environmental affairs, but would not be operational in the sense of directly running programs where existing specialized agencies had already established jurisdiction. Although the initial controversy over the site of UNEP headquarters obscured this institutional problem, the General Assembly decided to establish a new environmental regime of the latter type with four principal components: a fifty-eight-member Governing Council; a small Secretariat; a voluntary Environment Fund; and an Environmental Co-ordination Board.[105]

As if to debunk the assumptions of the functionalist theory of world order, UNEP's implementation process has been plagued from the outset by the intrusion of larger systemic constraints. First of all, UNEP's role is in a state of flux subject to conflicting interpretations because the definition of global environmental problems changes in space and time. The developing countries have recently become liberal interpreters and advocates attempting to expand the outer limits of the possible, while the developed countries have retreated into the position of strict constructionists attempting to limit regime functions to a modest coordinating role.

At the operational level is the problem of making consensual political judgment about a proper scale of priorities. This problem caused such vehement controversy at the first and second sessions of the Governing Council as to threaten the very existence of UNEP. The disagreement is partly conceptual and partly financial. The regime's definition of practicality and priorities depends on the definition of its role and the resources available for carrying out its task. A small secretariat was clearly inadequate for implementing the grandiose action plan adopted at Stockholm. As shown in Table 7.9, the kinds and scope of UNEP activities are limited by the resources pledged by the member states. Since 1979, pledged

TABLE 7.9
Environment Fund Contributions and Expenditures 1973–1981
(in million US dollars)

| Year | Pledged Contributions | UN System | Fund Activities | |
			Other External Projects	Direct Implementation[a]
1973	11.80	0.11	0.09	0.16
1974	15.49	2.25	0.83	0.94
1975	18.41	7.42	2.50	3.22
1976	24.29	9.23	3.11	3.46
1977	28.48	11.74	3.87	5.66
1978	29.55	10.19	5.81	6.90
1979	31.98	10.94	7.43	8.67
1980	31.90	NA	NA	NA
1981	30.88	NA	NA	NA

[a]Including Programme Activity Centres.

NA=Not yet available.

Source: Adapted from UN Doc. UNEP/GC.10/INF.1, pp. 62–64.

contributions have actually declined even in *current* dollar terms, while inflation has greatly eroded their actual value. Within these twin constraints, however, the amount allocated to direct implementation has progessively and proportionately increased.

Faced with the political reality that it did not—and could not—have the capability to implement the Stockholm Action Plan, UNEP redefined its role in an ingenious way. As the recent UNEP report, "Review of Major Achievements in the Implementation of the Action Plan for the Human Environment," prepared for the 1982 Nairobi Conference, put it:

What UNEP had to do was develop a programme for implementation by the operational agencies of the United Nations, by other intergovernmental bodies and non-governmental organizations and by Governments, using disbursements from the Environment Fund to initiate necessary new activities and stimulate the needed expansion of others. Often, it also had to persuade Governments and co-operating agencies that the activities proposed were desirable and feasible.[106]

It is often charged that UN-sponsored global functional conferences create no more than a false consciousness, a flurry of superficial and short-lived concerns, some rhetorical documents devoid of substance, and almost no implementation. It is tempting to concur with such a simplistic—and cynical—interpretation of global ecopolitics. However, this interpretation rests on a mistaken notion of the nature and probabilities of "law enforcement" in social process. Even in domestic society, deeply ingrained values and behavioral habits are much more important than the legal mechanisms of law enforcement. It has even been suggested that "laws become difficult to enforce when less than 90 percent of the population will obey them voluntarily" and that "the greatest changes in society come about through changes in habits of compliance."[107]

Viewed in this light, UNEP has redefined its "implementation" role in more realistic terms. The "programmatic process" is central to this redefined role. The programmatic process involves defining problems as well as mapping means of solving them through a three-stage sequential procedure at three levels. The first level aims at providing a state-of-the-art review of environmental problems and of current efforts to solve them, in order to identify the gaps in knowledge and action. The second level aims at specifying and presenting to the world community the objectives and strategies needed to close the gaps. The third level aims at selecting for direct support from the Environment Fund a set of activities specified at the second level. Through this three-level process, projects can be undertaken by cooperating specialized agencies within the United Nations system, by other supporting NGOs, or by UNEP itself.

In short, UNEP has simultaneously assumed the roles of catalyst, coordinator, reviewer, and direct participant. It is generally agreed that UNEP has to date been most successful in its Regional Seas Programme. It is possible to argue that the functionalist theory has in part been validated in this particular instance, as functional representatives of hostile states—Israel and Syria, Egypt and Libya, Greece and Turkey, Morocco and Algeria—have all cooperated in the meetings of the Mediterranean Action Plan, working together with a common desire to control pollution.

Without overstating the potency of the implementation process at the global level, however, three main types of constraints can be recognized. The first and principal type concerns deep-rooted *political and systemic constraints* beyond the control of UNEP, such as the structure of global geopolitics, the role of national governments in planning and executing their own environmental policies, and the impact of world economic conditions. The second type concerns *bureaucratic and jurisdictional* constraints, i.e., the extent to which UNEP and the functional specialized agencies of the United Nations family can successfully resolve or mitigate their conflicts and effectively collaborate in the integrated, multidisciplinary planning and execution of global environmental programs.

The third type concerns *methodological and managerial constraints* that are susceptible to self-correction and self-steering. Based on one decade's experience in planning and implementing a variety of global environmental projects and programs, seven factors considered essential for successful programmatic process have been identified: (1) concretization; (2) collab-orative undertaking; (3) interdisciplinary planning and execution; (4) design flexibility to cope with uncertainty; (5) administrative simplicity; (6) feasible scheduling; and (7) adequate technical and financial support.[108]

The outer limits and possibilities of the implementation process at the international level may be seen in two contrasting international responses to the specific environmental issues of commercial whaling and desertification. Although the Stockholm call for a ten-year moratorium on commercial whaling was not immediately and fully implemented, three important decisions of the International Whaling Commission (IWC), the international regulatory regime for whales, constitute substantial progress toward halting the slaughter of marine mammals: (1) in 1979 the Indian Ocean north of 55°S was declared a sanctuary for whales, and the use of factory ships was prohibited except for taking minke whales; (2) in 1981 a ban on sperm whale hunting, with the exception of the North Pacific region, was passed with only Japan dissenting; and (3) in 1982 IWC decided by a vote of 25 to 7 (Brazil, Iceland, South Korea, Japan, Norway, Peru, and the Soviet Union), with 5 abstentions, to phase out *all* commercial whaling starting in 1982, with the deadline set for the 1985/86 season. The whaling quota was reduced from 46,000 in 1973 to 14,000 in 1982. Moreover, international trade in the oil, meat, and bones of three species of whale was outlawed in 1981 over the opposition of Japan, with the United States and the Soviet Union abstaining, when the delegates from sixty-seven countries added the sperm, sei, and fin whales to Appendix I of the Convention on International Trade in Endangered Species of Wild Fauna and Flora.[109]

There is no way to know whether these measures will be sufficient to prevent the extinction of the sperm, fin, and sei whales or to determine the extent of full compliance by the pro-whaling states. The response of the Soviet Union and Japan—the world's two major commercial whaling nations—is critical. For commercial and culinary reasons Japan remains adamantly resistant, although it has not yet withdrawn from IWC. The Japanese government announced on November 2, 1982, that it would file a formal complaint against the IWC's decision to end commercial whaling in three years.[110]

The Soviet response is more encouraging. In 1981, for example, Tass declared that "the end of whaling is one of the points of an extensive program for the protection of nature on the continent and in the coastal waters of the Pacific,"[111] although the full extent of Soviet changes in policy and practice remains unclear. It is significant, nonetheless, that IWC has been strengthened by the accession of most whaling nations, and seven more countries, including China and India, have recently joined, enhancing IWC's universalism and strengthening the conservationist bloc within the organization. Several of the member states that were engaged in commercial whaling in 1972 have already ceased their practice.

In sum, the expansion of IWC's membership, the sustained global campaign of conservationists against pro-whaling countries, in particular Japan and the Soviet Union, the high concentration of whaling interests and consumption in a few countries, the absence of U.S. obstruction, and the essentially normative character of international response requiring no financial commitment have all contributed to the recent progress in this field.

In contrast, international response to the Plan of Action to Combat Desertification adopted by the 1977 UN Conference on Desertification has been extremely limited and slow. The plan concentrates on those areas in Equatorial Africa, often far away from the main deserts, where the fight might still be won—but at the estimated annual cost of about $400 million. Despite strong General Assembly support, the Special Account to Combat Desertification established in 1978 remained empty until 1980, when Mexico made the first contribution of $100,000. Faced with this situation UNEP has been advancing the concept of automatic international taxation for financing the plan (e.g., an international tax on desert minerals).[112] In 1982, the member states of the United Nations spent more money on armaments in a mere six hours than they contributed over ten years to help UNEP implement its environmental programs.

The lack of financial resources to implement the Plan of Action to Combat Desertification is symptomatic of deeper problems. The governments in the risk areas are too preoccupied with the politics of survival to give a high priority to this problem. Governments elsewhere regard desertification as a basically African problem for Africans to solve. There is no global antidesertification grassroots movement, and scientific knowledge about the desertification process is incomplete, providing a convenient cover for international inaction. Above all, the spreading impact of the recent global recession has "desertified" this environmental issue for the time being.

Predictably, the major catalyst for international action to date has come from visible, dramatic ecodisasters, not from the slow and gradual knowledge-expanding and value-shaping processes. Just as Stockholm would not have been possible without the catalytic power of the preceding ecodisasters, the Plan of Action to Combat Desertification would have been impossible without the catalytic power of the Sahel drought/famine. In a thoroughgoing study of the international politics of marine pollution, Michael M'Gonigle and Mark Zacher concluded that IMCO has been extremely *dependent* on catastrophes such as the *Torrey Canyon* oil spill to catalyze political action: "Anything short of visible, immediate catastrophe is equivocal and invites an equivocal response."[113] Yet ecodisaster seems to lack *sustainable* catalytic power. As each disaster recedes from public consciousness, so does international response.

The Ecological Problematique

The manifest symptoms of the ecological crisis suggest that we live in a period of rapid change and paradigm decay. The signs of the critical turning point in system transformation, as discussed in Chapter 2, are becoming increasingly evident. The ecological crisis is a potentially powerful agent of social change; it constantly reminds us that the moment of truth is already here. In this unsettling situation, the real question is not *whether* but *how* the impending social change will come about. Will it come about through what Robert Heilbroner calls "convulsive change,"[114] "change forced upon us by external events rather than by conscious choice, by catastrophe rather than by calculation"?

The prospects for adaptive, nonviolent change depend on the extent to which existing societal values, norms, and institutions can be transformed—and in time—to take a development path in harmony with the basic laws of ecology. This clearly involves the adaptability of human behavior; but human behavior never functions in a social vacuum. It is bounded and guided by social values and structures. The central task of all social and intellectual efforts of our time should therefore be focused on correcting and steering system change in an adaptive, nonviolent way. This calls for a more "realistic" understanding of the inherent difficulties in effecting societal and structural changes and in creating new values, habits, life-styles, laws, and institutions. Herein lies the ecological problematique—the whole indivisible complex of conceptual, psychological, normative, and structural processes and problems that set the parameters of system transformation.

Historically, a new concept of "security" emerged only in the wake of a major, catastrophic war, during which established patterns of social values and behavior suffered profound disruption. Ecodisasters of rare, unexpected kinds in the 1950s and 1960s cried out for new concepts of "ecological aggression" and "ecological security." Conceptual response to this call came in a variety of forms in the 1970s. In 1970, biologist Arthur Galston raised the issue of ecocide for the first time at a Congressional Conference on War and National Responsibility when he said that "the willful and permanent destruction of environment in which a people can live in a manner of their own choosing" is no less a crime than genocide and hence "ought similarly to be considered a crime against humanity, to be designated by the term *ecocide*."[115] In 1973, Richard Falk proposed several draft legal instruments including a Proposed International Convention of the Crime of Ecocide.[116] In 1974, Norman Cousins broadened the concept of "crimes against humanity" by extending it to the human transgression of the life-protecting ozone in the stratosphere.[117]

Yet the concept of ecological security seems to have been virtually ignored, if not downright repudiated. One major difficulty lies in the inherent conflict between traditional economic principles and new ecological concepts. The economic virtues of optimal output, maximal growth, risk-taking, and high consumption run counter to the ecological virtues of simplicity, harmony, brevity, and frugality. Even in terms of social process economics and ecology clash; the former thrives on the dynamics of comparative advantage and competitive drive, the latter on the harmony of mutuality and indivisibility. We cannot have our ecological cake and eat it too.

The economic/ecological dichotomy can be illustrated in the cost-benefit analysis. Even the OECD secretariat has recently come up with an interesting cost-benefit analysis for its member states: pollution control expenditures amount to 1-2 percent of GNP and pollution damage ranges between 3 and 5 percent of GNP.[118] Likewise, the U.S. Council on Environmental Quality reminds us that in 1978 $21.4 billion in damages were avoided in the United States as a result of mandated reductions in air pollution at the cost of about $17 billion.[119] It costs $1,000 per barrel to clean up oil spills. Desertification constitutes an economic loss of over $26 billion per year. It has thus become clear in recent years that it is far cheaper to *prevent* than to *pay* for the tragic consequences of ecological mismanagement. In short, pollution does not pay—not if economics is allowed to work on the polluter-must-pay principle.

Of course, modern mainstream economics follows the inviolable principle of "optimality" by externalizing costs and internalizing benefits. The maintenance of the natural ecodevelopmental assets of air, water, soil, and plant and animal species is regarded as a "cost" to be minimized or externalized to the society as a whole. Given the modelling power of U.S. economic and environmental policy, three cases may be mentioned here as having global significance. First, the dominant U.S. approach to forest management follows a suicidal pattern of high cuts now and lower cuts later, inexorably moving toward shorter and shorter rotations to the point where the ecology *and* economy of the affected locality will collapse.[120] Second, the asbestos industry is now seeking protection in bankruptcy courts to internalize profits and externalize costs to the society. Finally, as part of the oft-stated objective of minimizing industry's environmental protection costs, the Reagan administration has drastically reinterpreted and diluted the existing environmental laws.[121]

These examples indicate which prevails in the conflict between economics and ecology, and with what social payoffs and penalties. The purpose of the producing economic system, as Lewis Mumford suggests, "is not primarily to satisfy human needs . . . but to multiply the number of needs,"[122] What is desirable here is a thoroughgoing rethinking, to establish a harmonious interface between human needs and human ecology. Deforestation, desertification, and degradation of cropland not only threaten the stability of terrestrial ecosystems, but also directly affect the societal capacity to meet basic human needs. If conventional economics and ecology seem mutually incompatible, the same cannot be said of the relationship between two world order values—basic human needs and human ecology.

The high priest of modern science and technology is part of the problem. In the pursuit of methodological rigor and empirical verification, modern science has largely divorced itself from moral philosophy. Instead of becoming part of the value-shaping and value-realizing processes, science has become an instrument of social control and dominance. The modern phenomenon of overspecialization also divides scientific inquiry into empirically man-ageable sectors and subsectors of the environment. This encourages the fragmentation of social reality and the sectoralized approach, all contrary to the First Law of Ecology. The post-Stockholm development has made it clear that the physical sectors of the biosphere cannot be isolated from the social and technological activities of human society.

To be sure, science has greatly reduced our level of ecological illiteracy. On balance, however, science has created more ecological problems than solutions. The genocidal/ecocidal logic of "modernity" has also uprooted many of the world's indigenous peoples who have mastered the art of ecological survival, but not political survival. As they join the list of endangered species, so does the rich and priceless repository of ecological knowledge they have accumulated in the evolutionary course of their adaptive and harmonious relationship with Nature.

The slow and cumulative nature of the ecological crisis poses a number of sociopsychological problems of risk/cost perception. To catalyze individual and public action, the ecological crisis has to be made more real, more visible, and more immediate. But how is it possible to have a *sustainable* social consciousness about the impending ecological catastrophe without crying wolf? Crying ecological wolf inevitably causes credibility problems. Crying too much can easily deaden our nerves and paralyze our political will. Crying too little can be too little and too late. It is not easy to find a balance. Besides, there is no way of knowing or proving whether the ecological wolf would actually show up on the predicted date at the predicted place or whether we will even recognize it when and if it comes.

In a sense, sharpening risk perception about the ecological crisis is comparable to warning about possible dangers of cigarette smoking to the healthy but addicted smoker. The immediate and experiential pleasure is too real and too irresistible; possible hazards and dangers seem remote and theoretical. This sociopsychological problem is defined as a "social trap," a situation in which short-term rewards and long-term punishments are all mixed up, calling for a behavioral choice. As John G. Cross and Melvin J. Guyer put it, "Just as an ordinary trap entices its prey with the offer of an attractive bait and then punishes it by capture, so the social situations which we include under the rubric "social traps" draw their victims into certain patterns of behavior with promises of immediate rewards and then confront them with consequences that the victims would rather avoid."[123]

The social trap runs counter to the Fourth Law of Ecology that there is no such thing as a free lunch. The free-lunch or free-ride syndrome stems from the inability or unwillingness of human individuals and groups to identify with the larger interests of the human community as well as with future generations. The costs of environmental policy are readily perceived as too immediate, too personal, and too demanding, while the benefits, which may be a decade or more away into the future, seem too remote, impersonal, and abstract. Of course, the cultural and political fragmentation of the human community is hardly conducive to overcoming global social traps. Another closely connected problem can be formulated as follows: the more unusual a projected ecological event or consequence, the more problematic it is to produce scientific proof, the harder it is to overcome our social traps.

Statism is a double-edged sword that can cut both ways—positive or negative, constructive or destructive, unifying or divisive on environmental affairs. In an ecological sense, the freedom of the market is a sure recipe to bring ruin to all. Yet socialism has its own social traps. In fact, the public sector of central government in all political systems has grown so rapidly and so widely in our time that its difference between capitalist and socialist polities amounts to only about 10 percent.[124] As the most authoritative arbiter of social conflicts and allocator of social values, the modern government can be a powerful catalyst or obstruction to social change.

Statism as the legitimator of the modern government can be said to have played a paradoxical role to date. Whether on its own initiative or under popular pressure, it has guided the value-shaping, institution-building, and value-sharing processes at domestic and international levels. A large portion of bureaucratic activity, as Murray Edelman once suggested,[125] is purely symbolic, intended to convey the *impression* of solving problems. No doubt statist activities in the field of environmental affairs, could have similar uses. At the same time, the state on its own or in partnership with the dominant social groups has been the main culprit and perpetrator of ecocidal transgressions.

This apparent contradiction can be explained by the social trap of "national interests." In an age of scarcity, ecological values have a serious comparative disadvantage in domestic and international politics. The established pattern of behavorial response, as depicted by Michael M'Gonigle and Mark Zacher in their study of the international politics of oil pollution, is suggestive. The wealthy industrialized capitalist countries of Western Europe, the United States and Japan—the prime consumers of global resources and the main polluters of the human environment—have dominated the politics of oil pollution control, but their policies and strategies are guided predominantly by national *economic* interests, not by ecological concerns. The minor influence of the Soviet bloc is a corollary of its *commercial and economic* isolation in the world economy. The weakness of the developing countries, on the other hand, follows from their *economic* dependence on the developed industrialized countries.[126]

In a fundamental sense, most ecological problems are outgrowths of pre-ecological (industrial) social structures. Inevitably, ecodevelopmental self-correction and self-steering are constrained by these anachronistic social structures. The common language of the knowledge-expanding, norm-making, and programmatic activities in the domain of global ecopolitics belies the invisible structural constraints imposed by the heavy hand of the dominant states. Global ecopolitics tries hard but seldom succeeds in escaping from the strategic and economic imperatives of international politics. This is the opposite of what functionalist theory predicted. In taking stock of the post-Stockholm development, UNEP repeatedly blames "the will of Government" as the primary cause for slow progress. But the very existence of states in an anarchical/hierarchical system can only generate the will to compete, conquer, and control. The hegemonic structure of global geopolitics is in absolute conflict with the requirements of a planetary eco-order.[127]

Ultimately, the quest for a decent environment is but one part of the quest for a more just and humane world order. Yet the quest to bring the social environment into harmony with the natural environment does not seem too promising without normative, structural, and behavioral transformations in both domestic and international societies. The transformations envisaged in this alternative ecodevelopmental path depend on the extent to which nonstate actors—dedicated private citizens, local and national groups, and transnational NGOs, all currently crying out for recognition at the edges of the power structure—can mobilize their renewable normative energies and political resources to form a broad-based, sustainable movement. The task is to translate into reality the motto, "think globally, act locally."

There is also a compelling need for some restructuring of our ecological thinking. The ecological crisis is a crisis of priorities in human development. The perspective of the victims deserves more attention than it has received in ecological literature. The poor in both rich and poor countries suffer most as they live in the most polluted areas. Even the holistic world order approach faces the clear and continuing danger of losing touch with the voice of the oppressed by abstracting—and diluting—the consequences of ecological transgressions in terms of the "tragedy of the commons" or escaping from the *present* plight of the wretched of the earth into the holistic ecological obligations to *future* generations.

Part 3

Building an Alternative
World Order

Alternative Future Images
and Transition Orientations

Behold! human beings living in a sort of underground den, which has a mouth open toward the light and reaching all across the den; they have been here from their childhood, and have their legs and necks chained so that they cannot move, and can only see before them; for the chains are arranged in such a manner as to prevent them from turning round their heads.
— Plato "Allegory of the Cave" *Republic*, VII

and you shall know the truth, and the truth shall make you free.
— *New Testament*, John VIII:32

The whole future of the Earth, as of religion, seems to me to depend on the awakening of our faith in the future.
— Pierre Teilhard de Chardin

Ultimately, the quest for a just world order is a collective, transnational struggle in which individuals and groups at different systemic levels join hands, actively participating in ongoing social, political, economic, and cultural processes that embrace all of humanity. A world order politics of system transformation calls for both conceptual and political inputs (voices, visions, and struggles) from those who are most victimized by the existing world order. The prospects of system transformation depend largely on the oppressed becoming conscious of their suffering and developing the political will to change the present human course.

This consciousness raising and mobilizing activity is a crucial and challenging element in world order transition from the present to an alternative world order system. The present is evenly split between the past and the future—it is a part of the immutable past as well as a part of the malleable future. How can we connect the unfinished part of the present to the clean slate of the future? How do we bridge the gap between empirical reality (the "is") and normative reality (the "ought")? In this concluding chapter I leap into the future—more accurately, I make a deductive leap from preferred alternative futures back to the present.

This is not an exercise in eschatological escapism from the present human predicament. Rather, it is a transformative act of planetary consciousness-raising, seeking alternative images and paths into the future. There is an element of faith in this journey, the assumption that human beings can transcend the bounds of their objective situation by shifting from present actualities to future potentialities. There is also an element of will in this journey—the past is closed but the future is always open to new visions and struggles.

One of the most elusive tasks of world order studies has been, and still is, to formulate a credible praxis of transition politics that would help us build relevant and reliable bridges between where we are now and where we want to be in the future. The theoretical and practical utility of world order modelling may be assessed by the extent to which it can translate the world order value structure into a series of preferred images and viable transition strategies, that is, the power to prevision, to design alternative world futures that are both desirable and feasible as well as to prescribe general transition principles and processes.

In pursuing this line of inquiry, I will evaluate the development of futuristic thinking from the utopian tradition to contemporary future studies, the interface between future and world order studies, the designing of possible and preferred scenarios of alternative world futures, and some broad orientational guides for the transition process.

The Utopian Tradition

The image of utopia as an alternative setting for human existence has long exerted a powerful fascination over the human imagination.[1] E. H. Carr gives a classic "realist" formulation by juxtaposing "utopia" and "reality" as fundamentally opposed—the former being "the inclination to ignore what was and what is in contemplation of what should be," and the latter "the inclination to deduce what should be from what was and what is." "The utopian," according to Carr, "believes in the possibility of more or less radically rejecting reality, and substituting his utopia for it by an act of will."[2] On the other hand, the concept of utopia as reflected in the writings of prominent contemporary futuristic thinkers—Lewis Mumford, Martin Buber, Mulford Sibley, Fred Polak, Elise Boulding, Johan Galtung, and Richard Falk—is one of previsioning a desirable social order. Instead of dichotomizing utopia and reality as antinomies, utopian thinking tends to conceptualize the flow of historical reality in terms of ongoing dialogue and feedback between the actual and the potential.

Plato's *Republic* marked the beginning of a long series of utopian visions of the Good Society that have engaged imaginative human minds over the centuries.[3] The common theme running through utopian thinking from Plato through More, Bacon, Rousseau, Kant, Owen, Marx, Buber, down to Skinner is a prevision of alternative human condition.[4] It is a radical redrawing of the bounds of human possibility. It is a radical re-visioning of the social order as an alternative human community where the gap between feeling, knowing, and acting disappears and where harmony between man and nature, between man and man, and between man and society reigns.

One of the earliest expressions of traditional utopian thinking in the West was also embodied in the ancient Chinese concept of *datong*—literally meaning the Great Harmony but actually conveying a utopian sense of perfect society or commonwealth—as expressed in the Chinese classic *Liji* [*The Book of Rites*]:

> When the Great Principle prevails, the world is a Commonwealth in which rulers are selected according to their wisdom and ability. Mutual confidence is promoted and good neighborliness cultivated. Hence, men do not regard as parents only their own parents, nor do they treat as children only their own children. Provision is secured for the aged till death, employment for the able-bodied, and the means of growing up for the young. Helpless, widows and widowers, orphans and the lonely, as well as the sick and the disabled, are well cared for. Men have their respective occupations and women their homes. They do not like to see wealth lying idle, yet they do not keep it for their own gratification. They despise indolence, yet they do not use their energies for their own benefit. In this way, selfish schemings are repressed, and robbers, thieves and other lawless men no longer exist, and there is no need for people to shut their outer doors. This is called the Great Harmony [*datong*].[5]

Utopian thought rejects fatalism and the credo of historical inevitability by holding up a normative beacon for alternative human development— what is not yet but might be brought to bear if the bounds of human potential were redefined and fully realized. Utopian thinking is *ipso facto* anti–status quo. "Conservative mentality as such," as Karl Mannheim put it, "has no utopia."[6] Every revolutionary movement has been energized by a belief in, and an appeal to, utopia. In Mao's "utopian" world view, for example, it is the conquering human spirit more than anything else that acts as the prime motive force of societal transformation. The conquering spirit translates the impossible into the realm of the possible. Indeed, Mao recalls Max Weber's paragon of a leader and hero: "Certainly all historical experience confirms the truth—that man would not have attained the possible unless time and again he had reached out for the impossible. But to do that a man must be a leader, and not only a leader but a hero as well, in a very sober sense of the word."[7]

The terrors of the twentieth century have had a chilling effect upon the utopian tradition. The rise of totalitarian ideology, the unrelenting march of hard technology, the explosive growth of human population, the outbreak of two global wars, and the spread of the weapons culture seriously ruptured our faith in a better future and our capacity to envision a relevant utopia. With the ascendancy of analytical methods in philosophic inquiry and of inductive empiricism in social science research, the normative and intellectual center of gravity in utopian thinking has also shifted from social and political philosophers to novelists and science fiction writers, making it somewhat less relevant to actual political struggles.

The demise of faith and hope caused the tormented futurism of the present in twentieth century utopian thought. The future, instead of becoming a source of hope, has become an object of fear ("future shock") to be avoided, as manifested in the new literary genre of dystopian (anti-utopian) novels. Eugene Zamiatin's *We*, written but not published in the Soviet Union just three years after the Revolution, marked the beginning of a flurry of dystopian writings. Among the best known are Aldous Huxley's *Brave New World* (1932) and George Orwell's *1984* (1949).

These dystopian novels have greatly overshadowed the humanist utopian contributions by B. F. Skinner, Paul and Percival Goodman, Theodore Roszak, Pierre Teilhard de Chardin, and Warren Wagar,[8] blurring the utopian/dystopian distinction in the twentieth-century human imagination. The decline in utopian thinking is a decline in what theologian Paul Tillich called "ultimate concern," and as such is deplored even by such conservative religious institutions as the Roman Catholic Church. In a major statement on social ethics issued in 1971, Pope Paul VI characterized utopia as a great social critic of the existing order which "provokes the forward looking imagination both to perceive in the present the disregarded possibility hidden within it, and to direct itself towards a fresh future; it thus sustains social dynamism by the confidence that it gives to the inventive powers of the human mind and heart."[9]

Despite wide variations in form and content, the utopian thinking that has evolved over the centuries still provides a rich source of insight to help unshackle our imagination from the credo of inevitability of human misery and to re-vision a more humane and just society. By affirming the possibility and desirability of alternative forms of human community, by stressing the mobilizing and liberating functions of faith, vision, and hope, and by defining values and facts in mutually complementary terms, the utopian tradition has made an important contribution to the dialectical synthesis of empirical and normative theory.

At the same time, the utopian tradition provides a problematic guide for mapping transition strategies of change. Perhaps it was this problematic linkage between the present and the future that led Marx to denounce utopianism with the assertion that "philosophers have only interpreted the world in various ways; the point is to change it."[10] Whether looking backward to the Garden of Eden or looking forward to the resurrection of a city of God, the present has always been an elusive link in the utopian vision. Utopian thinking has also tended to be excessively preoccupied with harmony as a central value, projecting an image of a hermit society that seeks to isolate itself from the systemic constraints of the external world. Witness the extent to which the value of harmony was idealized and legitimized in the service of the hierarchical social order in the traditional Sinocentric world order in East Asia.[11]

Moreover, the self-sustaining and self-repairing capacity of microcosmic island communities, as envisioned in so many utopias, remains an open question in a contemporary world afflicted by a multitude of systemwide crises. Although the final verdict on the viability of self-reliant development in China, Tanzania, and North Korea is not yet in, there can be no question about the short-term penalties of autocentric self-reliant development in the hostile environment of the global political economy. There also remains the difficult question of intercommunity relations, the elusive process of binding different peoples and communities together in larger wholes.[12] Any relevant utopian vision must address itself to the challenge of a cosmic order as well as to the struggle of the oppressed in our time.

The Development of Future Studies

The decline of utopian thinking and the accompanying dystopian sense of futurelessness were overtaken by a sudden explosion of future studies in the 1960s. Despite great diversity in assumptions, methodologies, and prescriptions, futures research had become a kind of global growth industry. This sudden and undisciplined growth can be explained by a convergence of several factors. First of all, man cannot live by the past alone; he also needs the future. In the latter half of the twentieth century, however, man also lives in a drastically changed environment of a highly complex and interdependent world with increasing perils and diminishing opportunities. Future studies can be said to be a belated recognition of and a response to this emerging sense of planetary crisis in prospective orientation and governability. The common concern and urgency about the consequences and implications of our interdependent world future has served as a powerful stimulant for the development of future studies.

Second, the mystical benchmark of the year 2000 has exerted a powerful magnetism in the development of futures studies. Self-consciously, many of the influential future projects bear the magical number 2000 in their titles.[13] Third, the Club of Rome played a pioneering role in creating a new species of future studies known as "global modelling." The World 2 and World 3 models, basis of the 1972 Club of Rome report, give so much attention to environmental factors that they may be characterized as ecological doomsday models. As products of the "industrial-academic complex," the Club of Rome global models also bear the imprimatur of high finance and "high methodology" (statistics, survey and sample techniques, and advanced computers). However, the influence of the Club of Rome's global modelling, both positive and negative, in the further development of global or world models as an integral part of futures studies cannot be gainsaid.[14]

Finally, military R&D has been the "invisible hand" in the development of future studies. The Manhattan Project of the United States during World War II was indeed a futures project on a grand scale, paving the path for the postwar development of "think tanks." The institutionalization of future studies in the United States can be said to have started in 1946, when General H. H. Arnold persuaded Douglas Aircraft to establish Project RAND (Reasearch and Development)—later renamed the RAND Corporation—to study alternative weapons systems. The impact of the RAND Corporation on the development of future studies is twofold: first, it pioneered such forecasting techniques as learning curves, gaming, model building, systems analysis, and Delphi method, as well as applying these techniques to a wide range of social issues; second, RAND researchers (Olaf Helmer and Herman Kahn, e.g.) have spread out to found a number of futuristic "think tanks."[15]

Systems of patronage generated by military R&D have been a pervasive and pernicious factor in the development of future studies. The source of financial support and patronage for institutionalized future research is roughly as follows: ninety-three organizations received almost all their support (80–100 percent) from national governments; thirty-seven almost all support (80–100 percent) from private business, including those internal to business itself; eight organizations showed 50–59 percent support from national government.[16] There is more than meets the eye here. Contrary to the carefully cultivated image of hard-nose realism, the military establishment tends to be the most avid consumer of "planned obsolescence" and practitioner of dystopian future thinking, as every new weapons system is based on an alternative image of future warfare. In a recent study called "Air Power Entering the 21st Century," designed to guide long-range planners, to cite one example, the U.S. Air Force advocates enhanced readiness to fight across the spectrum of conflict from guerrilla operations to nuclear exchange based on a projected image of warfare in the year 2000 and beyond.[17]

In methodological and substantive terms, contemporary futures studies defies any neat characterization. The competing nomenclatures[18] suggest contending images of the present and future world order, diverse modes of analysis, and contradictory projections and prescriptions. Instead of becoming a metadiscipline, synthesizing and integrating empirical and normative modes of inquiry in the various disciplines of the social sciences, future studies has generally followed the modern phenomenon of technical and methodological specialization.

Nonetheless, there is a discernible difference between European and U.S. orientations in future studies. Drawing upon the utopian tradition, humanist philosophy, and governmental practice of long-range socioeconomic planning, European scholars (Gaston Berger, Fred Polak, Robert Jungk, and Johan Galtung) are more self-consciously committed to normative futurology. On the other hand, the requirements of the military-industrial complex and the distribution of research contracts to a handful of influential "think tanks" have been the main driving force behind the development of future studies in the United States. Not surprisingly, then, mainstream U.S. futurists (Herman Kahn, Daniel Bell, Olaf Helmer, Theodore Gordon, Jay Forrester, and Dennis Meadows) have shown greater commitment to technocratic futurology.[19]

The contending images of the world's future embodied in various genres of futures studies can be highlighted by briefly reviewing a variety of typological and theoretical schemes used by a select group of futurists. In

The Next 200 Years: A Scenario for America and the World (1976), Herman Kahn and his associates at the Hudson Institute compare and contrast contending images or models of the future purely in terms of technological pessimism and optimism. The former category is subdivided into the "Convinced Neo-Malthusian" ("finite pie") and "Guarded Pessimist" ("uncertain pie") positions, while the latter category is subdivided into the "Guarded Optimist" ("growing pie") and "Technology-and-Growth Enthusiast" ("unlimited pie") positions.[20] In short, there are only two contrasting perspectives on the future.

Using liberalism, Marxism, and economic nationalism as the three dominant theories of the global political economy today, Robert Gilpin describes and evaluates the alternative futures, or what he calls "three models of the future," in terms of "the tendencies and assumptions" associated with each of the three models: the sovereignty-at-bay model; the *dependencia* model; and the mercantilist model.[21] In a similar vein, a group of scholars at the Science Policy Research Unit of the University of Sussex classify contending scenarios of world futures in terms of three "world views": conservative, reformist, and radical.[22] With some minor modifications and qualifications, both theoretical schemes can easily be interfaced with the system-maintaining, system-reforming, and system-transforming approaches to world order described in Chapter 3.

In an essay entitled "Religion, Futurism, and Models of Social Change," Elise Boulding starts with the observation that the imaging of the future has always been one of the major preoccupations of Judaism and Christianity. Yet the *current* millennarian fervor has been preempted by scientists instead of theologians. Boulding attempts to establish a dialogue between scientific and religious futurists by delineating four models of religious imaging of the future—the existential model, the radical-Christian-secularist model, the signals-of-transcendence model, and the sacration model—and to assess what eschatological and utopian elements in those models can be made relevant to contemporary future studies.[23]

In an essay written for the World Order Models Project, Richard Falk sets out seven images of the world's future with a number of variations, and challenges us to look at these images for their workability and potentiality for realizing world order values. In doing so he raises a central question of world order inquiry: who will hold power and authority in the future? At the same time, he challenges us to ponder whether incremental reforms of the present system are capable of providing the necessary change for realizing world order values. In projecting a range of future images from a corporate-dominated world system to world government, he delineates a variety of scenarios for alternative forms of global governance. He suggests but does not specify the nature of domestic authority structures in different regions of the world and their probable impact on the global polity.[24]

Unlike the hopes and fears aroused by the last millennial benchmark year 1000, our eschatology for the year 2000 and beyond is secular, centering on the questions of resources, population, ecology, technology, and social change. The most positive contribution contemporary futures studies has made lies in its popularization of the notion that the future is not providentially predetermined but rather a product of human choice and behavior. Theoretically, the identification of future dangers and opportunities as an integral part of future studies provides a more reliable basis for steering social systems in a desirable direction.

At the same time, mainstream future studies is fraught with methodological and normative hazards. Yehezkel Dror has called for "sharpening some of the required hard choices which must be taken by futurists if they want to prevent futures studies from becoming too many things to too great a diversity of persons, and thereby eventually degrading into becoming nothing at all."[25] The one-sided empirical approach, as exemplified in extrapolation techniques, can be a trap in a period of convulsive change marked by breaks in past patterns, discontinuous jumps, and even reversals of trends. Extrapolation, an intellectual exercise linking past, present, and future by projecting future trend curves based on our knowledge of historically important and recurring patterns, regularities, and relationships, can run the danger of venturing into the future by looking backward.

Paradoxically, it is not only generals who are busily preparing to fight the last war. Some prominent conservative futurists are actively preparing to repeat the past! This is the danger of prophecy through extrapolation. As Boulding put it: "What we have in the world today is exactly what everybody feared. For 30 years we have been mentally fearing that things might get worse. We have created the present out of our fears."[26]

The technical and scientific biases in mainstream future studies, plus governmental and corporate sponsorship and patronage, impose some constraints on future studies as a social instrument of human liberation. Mainstream future studies risks becoming a scientific instrument serving to rationalize and perpetuate the existing social order. Knowledge about the future—the new-fangled and sophisticated instruments of extrapolation, anticipation, prognostication, planning, and self-serving predictions—can never be value-neutral; it always serves certain values and interests at the expense of other values and interests. Can we study the future as if people mattered and as if it belonged to everybody?

A World Order Approach to the Study of the Future

Futuristic thinking is one of the hallmarks of world order studies. If the past and present are emphasized in traditional approaches to international relations, images of possible and preferred futures hold an equivalent position in world order studies. Out of the many contending, and often mutually contradictory, approaches in contemporary future studies, we need to establish a world order approach that is sensitive to its own assumptions, principles, values, goals, and prescriptions.

The central objective of a world order approach is to shift the course of the human journey in a more humane and just direction. As shown in

FIGURE 8.1
World Order Approach to Designing an Alternative Future

		WORLD ORDER VALUES			
STEPS	*TASKS*	*$*WOV_1$*	WOV_2	WOV_3	WOV_4
1	Clarification of Assumptions				
2	Diagnosis of the State of the World				
3	Exploratory Forecasting of Trends				
4	Normative Forecasting of Preferred Futures				
5	Mapping Transition Strategies				
6	Review and Evaluation				

$*WOV_1$=Maximization of Nonviolence
WOV_2=Maximization of Economic Well-Being
WOV_3=Maximization of Social Justice
WOV_4=Maximization of Ecological Balance

Figure 8.1, this requires an ongoing, dynamic process involving six separate but mutually interacting stages. The first stage calls for clarification of underlying assumptions, operational principles, and ultimate objectives of the whole enterprise. The second, third, and fourth stages are integral parts of the modelling process requiring diagnosis of the present state of the global (the actual), prognosis of positive and negative trends (the possible and the probable), and scenarios of preferred futures (the potential and the preferable). The fifth stage is the formulation of transition steps and strategies to bridge the gap between the empirical reality of the present and the normative reality of the future. The review and reassessment process of the sixth stage becomes both possible and necessary as the unknowable future unfolds, revealing its inner secrets and validating or invalidating the assumptions, principles, diagnoses, prognoses, and prescriptions. Chapters 4–7 dealt with the present state of the globe and the main trends and policy responses; my focus here is on providing a coherent way of thinking about the future and the transition to a peaceful, just world.

Underlying Assumptions

Arthur C. Clarke once observed: "Mathematics is only a tool, though an immensely powerful one. No equation, however impressive and complex, can arrive at the truth if the initial assumptions are incorrect."[27] Diametrically opposed forecasts can be, and have been, made by simply changing the assumptions of a given model. The famous Forrester-Meadows model is based on the questionable assumption that industrial growth and pollution increase at the same rate. By substituting the assumptions of technological optimists for the assumptions of technological pessimists embodied in the Forrester-Meadows model, however, Robert Boyd produced a computer model that forecasts extensive and sustainable worldwide industrial growth.[28]

The decision to study a particular global reality in a particular way is seldom guided by the absolute canons of scientific inquiry. Complete detachment from one's value premise and commitment is neither possible nor desirable. The initial assumptions underlying any model are unavoidably influenced by our penultimate goal, for values and assumptions are inseparable. We can never reach a preferred future unless our initial underlying assumptions are correct.

We reject the chiliastic, deterministic assumption that the future is preordained. Instead, our approach assumes that the future belongs to the realm of human choice and freedom. The poor, weak, and oppressed of the world have literally nothing but their power to hope, to envision, and to create an alternative future. Our present actions shape tomorrow's future. Whether we realize it or not, the future is always in the creation of the present and the present is always in the creation of the future.

The main determinants of the future are our purposive visions and goal-directed actions. If human choices are guided by values—the criteria by which we decide—the goal of human behavior is to improve the future for greater enhancement and sharing of values. Viktor Frankl, a survivor of the Nazi concentration camps, commented on the crucial role human purpose plays in the shaping of human destiny: "A person who has a *why* to live can bear with any *how*."[29]

The image of the future is a powerful shaper of human behavior, a driving force toward a self-fulfilling prophecy. The reciprocal relationship between human expectations and human behavior has found increasing empirical support in sociopsychological research. As social psychologist Gordon Allport put it: "The greatest menace to the world today are leaders in office who regard war as inevitable and thus prepare their people for armed conflict. For by regarding war as inevitable, it becomes inevitable. Expectations determine behavior."[30] The image that high school students have of their future, it has been discovered, plays a major role in determining their scholastic attitude and behavior. Likewise, parents' image of a child's future is found to be among "the best predictor variables for cognitive growth in pre-school among a disadvantaged population."[31]

We also find problematic the assumption of system continuity so prevalent in mainstream global models. In a period of systems crisis, we can no longer afford to plan for the future by assuming that the most positive or negative trends in present global reality will continue in more or less the same pattern or rate.

On the one hand, the predictions of *The Year 2000* assumed continuity of the "long-term multifold trend" and exponential extrapolation (to 2020) of economic and demographic trends. Based on this assumption, Kahn and Wiener predicted the coming of *la belle époque*. "The most crucial issue of our study is that economic trends will proceed more or less smoothly through the next thirty years and beyond," and "capacities for and commitment to economic development and control over our external and internal environment are increasingly seeming without foreseeble limit."[32] Herman Kahn's grandiose concept of a 20 × 20 world society is based on the unrealistically heroic assumption that U.S. hegemony and life-style will continue and spread so that 20 billion inhabitants will reach the promised land with an annual per capita income of $20,000. More recently Kahn and T. Mitchell Ford put it this way: "There's no reason why the world should not be able to support a population of 30 billion people with all the energy, raw materials and food they need *using only current technology*. With technological progress we should do even better."[33]

On the other hand, the hidden pitfall of the global computer model embodied in *The Limits to Growth* is the unreality of many undifferentiated and aggregate assumptions concerning population growth, consumption rate, and ecological deterioration at the global level. Reflecting neo-Malthusian assumptions, this model overstates the physical limits and constraints to human development while understating the human potential for behavioral and social change. Predictably, it has little to say about the problem of income redistribution under the policy of no growth or what is called "an equilibrium state." But it is curious that the authors of the doomsday model discount or ignore such discontinuous phenomena as global wars and epidemics.

Even the more carefully researched *Global 2000 Report* is based on the initial assumption of system continuity. Projections and prognostications based on the assumptions of system continuity see in the future more or less the same trends as the past with respect to economic growth, population growth, energy growth, food situation, water problems, and environmental stress.[34] Although the report was published in 1980 and 1981, some of its prognostications on social, economic, and environmental issues are already wide of the mark due to the unexpected and discontinuous downward turns in the world economy and the general decline in population in recent years.

Note what happens when the system-continuity assumption is replaced by a system-change assumption. The Latin American World Model—also called the Bariloche global model—rejects the extrapolative projection of the future based on past and present trends and policies. Instead, the model employs normative forecasting, making its initial assumption explicit with the following question: "How can global resources best be used to meet basic human needs for all people?" The Bariloche global model is based on the system-change assumption, seeks an egalitarian, nonexploitative, wisely managed world society that avoids environmental degradation, and comes up with a positive and cautiously optimistic set of projections for an alternative, basic-needs-oriented human development.

The contending models of the world's future are riddled with unstated, underlying assumptions about human nature and about the prime mover of social change. In general, pessimists tend to see the worst of all possible futures because of their negative image of human nature; optimists tend to see the best of all possible futures because of their positive image. In the grand debate on world futures, however, neo-Malthusian demographic pessimists and Kahnian technological optimists represent two extreme poles on the optimism/pessimism scale. In the image of the future held by technological Panglosses, system transformation is neither necessary nor likely; all the positive factors of technological advancement are assumed to accelerate the growth and distribution of the global pie. Human intervention has little meaning, for the future is seen as guided by the inexorable logic of technological progress and self-determination.

In the crystal ball of Robert Heilbroner, convulsive system change will be forced upon us by external ecodisasters rather than by our conscious choice or by our purposive image of the future, by system catastrophe rather than by human decision. For Heilbroner, "the answer to whether we can conceive of the future other than as a continuation of the darkness, cruelty, and disorder of the past seems to me to be no; and to the question of whether worse impends yes." Only authoritarian regimes will be able to cope with the (environmental) crisis of the human future because "the weakest part of the humanitarian outlook, both philosophically and pragmatically, has been its inability or unwillingness to come to grips with certain obdurate human characteristics."[35]

Our assumption and attitude may be characterized as "concerned optimism," a combination of pessimism about the present human condition but necessary, self-mobilizing optimism about the human capacity to create a preferred alternative future. Johan Galtung comes close to our initial assumption and attitude toward the study of the future when he says:

Man is somewhere between God and termite, and the future of human society takes shape according to principles somewhere between those underlying the Act of Genesis and termite society. Man has neither the freedom of God—His insight in sufficiency—nor is he condemned to the "freedom" of the slave, the termite—the insight in necessity. He is somewhere in between, and it is difficult to tell whether over time he becomes more like God or more termite like.[36]

Without exaggerating the possibilities of social change powered by "what ought to be" and the prospects of what the late Rene Dubos called "the *willed* future, which is largely brought about by deliberate choices—made by the free will,"[37] it must be noted that a world order approach is necessarily more optimistic than pessimistic. All human behavior tends to be self-defeating or self-fulfilling depending on its initial assumption and attitude. The crucial gap underlying pathogenic premises of the industrial-era paradigm is not between generations, writes futurist Willis Harman, "nor between liberals and conservatives, but between those who anticipate a continuation of present trends and those who insist that a drastic change must occur."[38] The collapse of hope for the future, warns futurist Edward Cornish, has brought about a sharp increase in suicides among young people: "During the 1970s, the suicide rate for 15 to 24-year-olds in the United States is *triple* the rate of the 1950s. Suicide now is the third major cause of death among the young (following accidents and homicides); among college students, only accidents still claim more lives than suicides."[39]

Self-defeating and self-denying pessimism has no place in world order studies. Guided by the Hobbesian image of man as *homo homini lupus*, pessimists tend to be more concerned with minimizing losses and maintaining the present social order—by authoritarian means if necessary. They look at the future backward (like the chained prisoners in Plato's allegorical cave), through the prism of historical tragedies and struggles.

Prospective Principles

Before we envision and design preferred alternative futures, we need explicit operational principles. Given the importance of attitudes, beliefs, and values in human behavior and in the shaping of human future, "image" (or "world view" or "dominant social paradigm") is an important prospective principle that helps link world order and future studies. In order to act, people must extract from the complexity of social reality a clear image of the world. Image as a cognitive principle has already become familiar in international relations research, as detailed in Chapter 3. Through cross-national survey research, we are now able to evaluate the nature and distribution of dominant elite and popular images of the future and to assess the limits and possibilities of altering current trends in world history.[40] Unless present images of the future are clearly delineated, there can be little basis for designing road maps for alternative futures.

The search for an alternative future must draw its normative vision and energy from "planetary holism," the unity and interconnectedness of global reality and the affirmation of a world order ethos that gives priority to the interests of mankind as a whole over the interests of its fragmented parts. For W. Warren Wager this holistic attempt to place mankind above all other loyalties will produce a "transvaluation of all values" and a "cosmopolis"—a universal city reflecting "the quintessence of a civilization, the gathering of all its vital human resources into a living organic city."[41] In a similar vein, the late Harold Lasswell conceptualized "world public order" and "cosmic process" in mutually complementary terms: "The need for a worldwide system of public order—a comprehensive plan of cooperation—is fearfully urgent. From the interplay of the study and practice of cooperation we may eventually move more wisely, if not more rapidly, toward fulfilling the as-yet-mysterious potentialities of the cosmic process."[42] Planetary holism serves as a guiding prospective principle for the enhancement of such a cosmic process.

The creation of an alternative world order system requires a clear sense of time. For our world order modelling purposes, the future may be divided into four time horizons, as shown in Figure 8.2: the immediate future, understood as the horizon of immediate concern and focus (the academic year, fiscal year, etc.); the middle-range future, or the horizon of a longer-term project or program (e.g., a four-year college career, the five-year economic plan in socialist countries, or the Reagan administration's five-year military plan); and the two long-term futures, the far horizons of dreamers, revolutionaries, and designers of system transformation. The fifty-year boom-to-bust cycle known as the Kondratieff long economic wave, often used in world-system literature, belongs to the outer reach of the long-term future.

As shown schematically in Figure 8.2, the immediate future has minimum possibilities and maximum limitations. The short-term limitations and long-term possibilities of social change reflected in Figure 8.2 were nicely captured by Mao's principle of protracted conflict—that the enemy must be despised strategically but respected tactically. This is a dilemma that every futurist must face. If he leaps into the future, he risks irrelevance and escapism from the present reality. If he accepts and adapts to the limitations of the immediate future, he risks losing or forgetting the system-transforming possibilities of a broader horizon.

Perhaps this dilemma is inherent in the tension between human imagination, which can easily transcend temporal and spatial bounds, and human behavior, which cannot. To cope with this dilemma, we need to remember several points. First, "social reality" has both empirical and normative dimensions. When reality is defined in a narrow horizon and a fragmented framework, it can become a worm's-eye view that accepts and legitimizes the status quo. Second, we need a constant but dialectical balance between empirical and normative dimensions as we transit the different time horizons of the future. Third, microdecisions made today follow the law of momentum, having a progressively larger impact on the future we will transmit and posterity will inherit. A 5 percent annual increase in world military spending may seem modest today, but it will effectively double world military spending in fourteen years.

Paradoxically, the most predictable quality of the human future is its unpredictability. The future is like clay in a potter's hand, and, like clay,

FIGURE 8.2
World Order Map of Alternative Paths to the Future

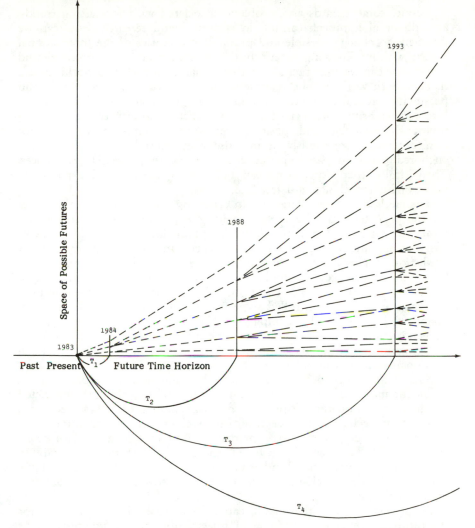

the future can be transformed or at least reshaped. From this we can deduce another prospective principle of futurism—the principle of indeterminacy and inventability. Out of the variety of alternatives, images, and decisions at our disposal today, a future with a particular form and shape will emerge. Because of the law of momentum, however, and because of the self-sustaining capacity of social system, the human future is likely to be a continuation of the present *unless* alternative images, policies, and plans actively intervene in the world historical process.

Prognosis of Trends

Despite some hazards and problems associated with forecasting trends, a world order approach cannot do without trend research. How can we intervene to change possible and probable trajectories of the international system without knowing recent historical trends and the forces behind them? How can we construct alternative scenarios of preferred world futures that are both workable and feasible without knowing the outer limits and possibilities revealed by the unfolding of global reality? How can we formulate transition strategies for system transformation without first iden-tifying the negative and positive trends that counteract or reinforce transformation? Consciously or unconsciously, most human decisions are anchored partly in past experience and partly in projected preferences. Theoretically, then, forecasting can help us to identify and expand the range of human choice and freedom.

The method we need to rely on in clarifying the gap between the actual (or the probable) and the preferable (or the potential) is *forecasting,* not *prediction.* As Nazli Choucri put it: "A prediction is generally made in terms of a point or event; a forecast is made in terms of alternatives. A prediction focuses upon one outcome; a forecast involves contingencies."[43] Given the unmanageable number of known variables, the magnitude of the unknowns, the volatile nature of political phenomena, the resistance of available data to controlled experiment, the elusiveness of values in quantitative analysis, the complex and mysterious interaction between exogenous and endogenous factors, and the pronounced tendency for random and discontinuous jumps in the international system, international relations research is unlikely to profit from prediction.

Since man's social behavior is powerfully influenced by expectations, a prediction may itself influence behavior, helping to bring about the predicted phenomenon through a self-fulfilling mechanism. Beneath every prediction, religious or secular, lies a deterministic eschatology. By encouraging a fatalistic sense of powerlessness, prediction functions as a kind of social anesthesia. To the extent that it fosters the credo of historical immutability and inevitability, prediction hinders rather than helps world order modelling; it erects a barrier to changing our orientation toward the creation of a better world future.

A forecast, on the other hand, can help us to be better prepared for the future by reducing the range of uncertainty about a given event or phenomenon. As a previsioning speculation about prospective situations, based on a knowledge of recurring patterns in the past and of the relationship between known variables, a forecast can help us to make contingency plans for alternative future events. When "exploratory forecasting" (extrapolation of various alternative trends) and "normative forecasting" (restructuring of preferred and probable futures) are used together, we are in a better position to invent what Betrand de Jouvenal calls "futuribles" (possible futures).

Yet forecasting, especially exploratory forecasting, has several hazards and traps. The most common and serious objection is that social forecasters tend to project their own conservative, technocratic, elitist, system-maintaining biases into the future. Ali Mazrui perceives a "caste factor" in social forecasting. The social forecaster, by reducing the range of conceivable alternative patterns and by thus projecting the immutability of the international stratification system, finds himself sharing a vested interest with Brahminic and bourgeois beneficiaries of the international status quo and its rigid system of global caste structure.[44] In Charles Hampden-Turner's view:

> The projection of present trends into the future represents a vote of temporary approval for such trends. Yet the trends themselves are the consequence of thousands of individual human decisions . . . the decision not to change direction (is) a decision. By concentrating upon the technical and material aspects of the trends, the impression is fostered that these things "are," like stars and planets around us, so that "realistic" men must humbly subordinate their minds to these physical "facts." . . .
> But these projections of existing trends are quite *unlike* the physical universe of dead objects. They are *cultural, political* and *social* choices. Men have the capacity to rebel against any trend at any time, in any place, by deciding to stop it, or alter its direction, or persuade others to do so . . . the shared expectation that the trend whose direction you oppose will *not* be continued in the future may be politically essential to any success in halting or redirecting it.[45]

The recent history of international relations is full of examples of failed predictions and failures to anticipate major events. A few cases may suffice. Ithiel de Sola Pool predicted in 1965 that "major fighting in Vietnam will peter out about 1967; and most objective observers will regard it as a substantial American victory."[46] In the grandiose long-term trend projection of *The Year 2000*, Kahn and Wiener failed to anticipate such major international events as the ecological movement, the oil crisis and the transformation of the international petroleum regime, or the global stagflation of the 1970s.

Even the relatively safe extrapolation of demographic, social, and technological trends can be quite misleading. By extending statistical curves of female premarital sexual behavior through the 1920s, Lewis F. Terman (the American pioneer of the intelligence test) reportedly predicted in the early 1930s that no girl born after 1940 would enter marriage a virgin. Another famous psychologist, John Watson, was quoted in 1927 as having said, on the basis of projected rates of change, that marriage as a social institution would no longer exist within fifty years. In the late 1940s nobody predicted the wide use of computers. The most extensive market research conducted at the time concluded that the world computer market would absorb no more than 1,000 computers by the year 2000.[47]

These examples underscore the hazard of single-scenario forecasting as well as the need to be sensitive to countervailing trends. Nonetheless, world order theorizing needs exploratory (descriptive) forecasting of global trends to establish empirically feasible parameters for various scenarios of alternative futures. I have selected for the following trend projection exercise the separate but interconnected domains of global war/peace and political economy, which respectively have received the least and most attention in future studies.

Global Military Trends

The global war system and military trends are almost completely ignored in exploratory forecasting.[48] There is a methodological rationale for excluding unpredictable, discontinuous events such as global nuclear war. However, this avoidance constitutes a normative blinder when thinking about possible and preferred futures. It amounts to continued acceptance of orthodox perspectives and presuppositions regarding deterrence. The logic of the assumption of system continuity, aptly summed up in the acronym MAD (Mutual Assured Destruction), is especially strong among futuristic strategic planners in the United States and the Soviet Union. It assumes that the present world order system can and should be maintained through an infinite process of balancing and counterbalancing more and better nuclear weapons.

All of the basic indicators of global military trends suggest an upward expansion. Whether measured in governmental expenditures, men under arms, R&D, or number of strategic nuclear warheads, the dominant military trend is unchecked growth and proliferation. If the historical trend curves of 1960–1981 continue at the same rate, writes Ruth Leger Sivard, "by the year 2000 national governments will have spent an additional $15 trillion (in today's prices) on military defense. Furthermore, by 2000 at least 8 million more men will be added to the regular armed forces; the value of arms traded will approach $100 billion a year; and the number of strategic nuclear warheads threatening human existence will be more than double the overkill of today."[49]

A state's budgetary process is a sensitive barometer of future orientation; it is also perhaps the most readily manipulable and unpredictable variable in the forecasting equation. Notice the current debate in the United States about President Reagan's five-year ($1.6 trillion) plan to rearm America, or the drastic retrenchment of military spending in the modernization drive of post-Mao China. In the final analysis, domestic factors may be more decisive (and more unpredictable) than external, systemic factors. The longer-term historical trend in global military spending may be a more reliable base from which to project future military trends.

In real terms, world military expenditures increased by a factor of 1.9 during the twenty-year period 1960–1980, representing an annual average growth rate of 3.2 percent. A wide variety of projections under different assumptions (growth rates) are possible, but I will present only three alternative scenarios. Scenario A (low scenario) represents the trend curve tapering off with an average annual rate of 2 percent; scenario B (medium scenario) represents the trend curve continuing at the same rate of 3.2 percent; and scenario C (high scenario) represents the trend curve rising with an average annual rate of 7 percent. Under the optimistic assumption embodied in scenario A, the projections of world military expenditures for 1990 and 2000 will be $U.S. 609.5 billion and $U.S. 742.9 billion in 1980 prices. Under scenario B, the projections for 1990 and 2000 will be $U.S. 685.5 billion and $U.S. 940 billion. The pessimistic assumption embodied in scenario C yields projections for 1990 and 2000 of $U.S. 983.5 billion and $1,934.7 billion. The actual development during the first two years of the 1980s is closer to the most pessimistic scenario C. In 1982, the global arms bill was $U.S. 600 billion, thus exceeding scenario C's annual rate of 7 percent.

Given the volatility of global geopolitics and the unpredictability of domestic budgetary politics, future trends of nuclear proliferation are even more difficult to project. To establish an empirical base for future projections in this field, we need to take into account not only historical trends but also the relative intensity of military R&D effort. There are today about 50,000 nuclear weapons in the world (30,000 for the United States and 17,400 for the Soviet Union). The *strategic* nuclear weapons of the two superpowers alone increased from 2,070 in 1962 to 8,200 in 1972 to 17,400 in 1982.[50] This historical growth rate does not convey the relative intensity and magnitude of the technological arms race of the 1960s and 1970s. In virtually all categories of major weapons systems, "a completely new model is introduced, on average, every 5 to 8 years and . . . the range of weapons in which this process occurs has also expanded continuously as technological developments have encouraged greater product differentiation or permitted greater functional specialization between weapons."[51]

It is widely believed in strategic circles that there will be about 75,000 nuclear weapons by 1990, as the United States currently plans to deploy about 17,000 more tactical and strategic nuclear weapons in the 1980s at an additional cost of some $300 billion. We may accept this as a medium scenario. The prospects of checking horizontal proliferation are none too reassuring. The world now has 279 operating power reactors and at least 323 research actors in 54 countries. The number of countries with nuclear reactors increased from 28 in 1960 to 48 in 1970 to 54 in 1982.[52] It is generally estimated that the global total of nuclear reactors—even if no new projects are started—will top 800 by 1989. The capability to acquire nuclear weapons has rapidly shifted from the technological to the political domain.

Unless or until these historical trends are reversed, the prospects of capping the nuclear arms race are getting dimmer and dimmer. Several studies have reported the increasing probability and destructiveness of nuclear war.[53] The "doomsday clock" on the cover of *The Bulletin of the Atomic Scientists*, a form of the Delphi technique in forecasting,[54] has moved from 12 minutes to "midnight" in 1972 (SALT I) to 9 minutes in 1974, 7 minutes in 1980, and 4 minutes in the December 1982 issue.

At the subnuclear level, the prospects for peace are even more dismal. With increasingly active participation of Third World countries in global arms trade, arms spending, and armed conflicts, there seems to be no immediate letup in the "statistics of deadly quarrels." Between 1960 and 1982 at least sixty-five major wars (deaths over 1,000) have been fought in forty-nine countries (representing approximately two-thirds of the world's population), causing some 10,700,000 deaths.[55] Without system transformation, this trend too is likely to continue unchecked.

Global Economic Trends

As if to underscore the economic and social costs of the growing military bill, all basic indicators of global economic trends have dropped in recent years. The world economy has moved through several phases since the end of World War II. The latter half of the 1940s and 1950s may be regarded as a period of (European and Japanese) recovery and rehabilitation under the hegemonic leadership of the United States. The 1960s represented relative stability and high growth as well as a beginning of the end of U.S. hegemony. After more than two decades of relative stability and high growth, the world economy entered into the 1970s to encounter unparalleled turmoil and instability—the collapse of the fixed exchange rates regime (1971), the food crisis (1972-1974), the energy crisis (1973-1974), the inauguration of NIEO politics (1974), and the demise of Soviet-U.S. detente (1979).

The current global economic trends, started in the latter half of the 1970s but accelerated with the 1980-82 recession, are characterized by greater instability, uncertainty, and malaise than at any other time during the entire postwar period. As the highly complex and interdependent world economic system seems unable or unwilling to come to grips with deepening recession (and rising unemployment), balance-of-payments disequilibria, and creeping protectionism, atavistic economic nationalism is growing.

All groups of countries are affected by the current difficulties, but developed market economies are more able to externalize and export these difficulties through tariff or nontariff barriers, exchange rates manipulation, and restrictive fiscal and monetary policies. Thanks to the deteriorating terms of trade, the declining volume of exports, the increasing interest rates, and the diminishing access to new private commercial loans to roll over old loans, developing countries suddenly discovered in late 1982 that they have at their disposal a remote control to a huge debt bomb hovering over the world banking system.

For exploratory forecasting of global socioeconomic trends, three recent studies by U.S. governmental agencies, the World Bank, and the Secretary-General of the United Nations provide a point of departure. Based on careful analysis of all global models including its own, *The Global 2000 Report* make the following prognostication: "Up to the turn of the century, all of the analyses, including the Government's, indicate more or less similar trends: continued economic growth in most areas, continued population growth everywhere, reduced energy growth, an increasingly tight and expensive food situation, increasing water problems, and growing environmental stress."[56]

Taking into account "likely developments in world trade and capital flows that enforce internal and external balance across all regions of the developing world," the World Bank's global model makes growth projections in the form of two alternative scenarios: the high case scenario and the low case scenario. The high case scenario is based on several optimistic (favorable) assumptions: (1) "the developing countries would benefit from higher levels of trade with the developed world, in both manufactured goods and primary products"; (2) "increases in aid and exports would help alleviate the problems of the least developed countries"; and (3) "oil exporters would be able to borrow to maintain the high imports which have helped them expand quickly." The high case scenario projects rapid recovery from the current recession followed by sustained growth of 4.3 percent a year for the remainder of the decade (1983–1990) through successful adjustment by the industrial economies to the current global stagflation.

The low case scenario is based on the pessimistic (unfavorable) set of assumptions. Under the low case scenario, the projected rate of growth for the remainder of the 1980s is 3.3 percent a year. Under either scenario, however, the projections for official development assistance as percentage of GNP (DAC—Development Assistance Committee of the OECD— countries) changes little: 0.33 percent under the low case scenario and 0.37 under the high case scenario.[57] Thus, the World Bank's global model relies almost exclusively on exploratory forecasting with normative components (official development assistance) having a marginal role.[58]

In contrast, *Long-Term Trends in Economic Development* (prepared by the Secretary-General and released in May 1982 at the request of the General Assembly), combines exploratory and normative forecasting in its three longer-term scenarios. The first scenario, called "a low world-growth scenario," is based on the assumption that the recent low-growth experience of the world economy during the latter part of the 1970s will continue. The second, a medium-growth scenario, is based on the assumption that the world economy will soon recover from its current slump and return to the average medium-growth historical trends of 1960–1980 (i.e., the 5.5 percent annual growth rate). The third scenario, called "the International Development Strategy scenario," is a species of normative forecasting, as its initial assumption is based on the attainment of the normative targets and goals of the International Development Strategy for the Third United Nations Development Decade.

The second scenario can be dispensed with, and I shall return to the third normative scenario later. Only the first low world-growth scenario deserves elaboration here.

To describe and evaluate the future performance of the world economy under the three alternative scenarios, the United Nations has developed "a global econometric framework," designed to highlight "the interrelations in the economy among such important factors as long-term determinants of productivity growth and resulting output growth, investment require- ments and saving potentials, export prospects and import needs, and international aid and other capital flows and their possible impact on growth."[59]

The most pessimistic low world-growth scenario postulates an international economic environment characterized by (1) more rampant protectionism attempting to minimize or avoid the necessary requirements of structural adjustments to the changing global economy, (2) less coordination and cooperation of macroeconomic policies among major trading economies, exacerbating the tensions created by growing interdependence, (3) less willingness on the part of the developed countries to open their markets to manufactured imports from the developing countries, and (4) less willingness on the part of the developed countries to provide concessional aid to the developing countries. The low world-growth scenario projects an over-all annual growth rate of 4.8 percent in the developing economies for the 1980s and 1990s, lower than the 5.5 percent annual growth rate experienced on average in the 1960s and 1970s. However, the projected growth rate of the low-income and least developed economies is only 3.5 percent or less, implying a less than 1 percent annual increase in their per capita product. The Secretary-General's report raises some serious implications for the low world-growth scenario:

> Under low-growth conditions the general expansion of the world economy that began after the Second World War will have come to an end. Any hope of even a modest beginning toward narrowing the gap in standards of living between the economically developed and developing areas of the world will be dashed. In all probability this economic decline would be accompanied by a deterioration in the political environment and the social situation as well, both within countries and between different blocks of countries.[60]

Designing Preferred World Futures

In designing preferred world futures the central question shifts from the domain of facts (the "is") to the domain of values (the "ought"). A preferred future is consciously transposed onto the present to discover or invent the elusive process by which alternative paths can be charted to redirect present trends toward the desired future. This cannot be done without first unshackling our imagination from the tyranny of the past and present, as many futuristic science fiction writers (H. G. Wells, Doris Lessing, Ursula LeGuin) have done in their depiction of a new shape of reality. Of course, this cannot be done without strong affirmation of, and commitment to, the centrality of values in social process.

Normative forecasting is a value-centered method specifically designed for this future-to-present process so as to make the preferred futures lead, not follow, probable futures. As in "liberation theology," there is a form of liberation, unshackling of our mind and heart from the straitjacket of short-term "realism." As A. Michael Washburn and Thomas E. Jones put it: "Normative forecasting of international relations could expand the range of 'oughts' (i.e., desirable goals), which has been circumscribed by the unnecessarily narrow range of *perceived* 'cans' (i.e., what is judged to be feasible in the realm of international relations)."[61] In this way, normative forecasting attempts to re-vision and re-create global reality. The principal aim of normative forecasting is to specify relevant utopias as preferred futures and to identify the conditions or paths likely to lead to them. Purpose and planning are so integral that normative forecasting is also known as the "normative forecasting/planning process."

In a sense every social forecast is normative, since it can exclude neither values nor assumptions. The Manhattan Project, the Marshall Plan, and the Apollo Project are often cited as successful examples of the normative forecasting/planning process. In the normative forecasting of world order studies, however, the underlying assumptions, operational principles, and ultimate values and goals are made explicit and operational. There can be no raison d'être of normative forecasting unless it is anchored in the assumption that no past and present trends are self-determining. On the contrary, our initial assumption is that every trend detected in exploratory forecasting is a product of past human action or nonaction and as such can be altered by human intervention. The master key to preferred world futures lies in some combination of utopian vision, animating faith, and willed commitment. Whether we recognize it or not, our individual or group behavior tends to be goal-directed. The search for hidden opportunities and positive factors buried dormant beneath the facade of the seemingly irresistible flow of historical trends is the central challenge in designing preferred world futures.

However, there are several unresolved dilemmas in the designing of preferred world futures. First, the future is everybody's business because it concerns everybody. Yet, there is a highly uneven participation in the making of the future. Like participatory democracy, participatory futurism is a desired norm, not a working reality. It has been widely accepted, concludes a comparative study of public images of the future, that the social future is for elites to project and prescribe and that it is for the masses to fight for the concrete issues today. Such notions "have penetrated deeply in the social consciousness, possibly so deep that they will not easily yield to a more systematic, more democratic distribution of future-consciousness."[62]

There are two contrasting and contradictory views on this dilemma. On the one hand, Arthur I. Waskow, reflecting the bottom-up perspective, has advocated a participatory strategy of gradual, grassroots construction of elements of a future design without the help, or even the permission or approval, of powerful elites.[63] Warren Wagar makes an equally persuasive argument in favor of forming "revolutionary elites," because "we cannot wait for the several popular masses to become so disenchanted with the status quo that the old orders collapse without a struggle."[64] The elites have the power, knowledge, and time to participate in the making of the future, but their images of the future tend to be self-serving, technocratic, and system-maintaining. The masses have the needs, potentials, and interests, but their level of future-consciousness is generally low and their normative energy is preempted in the struggle of the present, although it can be argued that the struggle itself is often waged with a vision of a preferred future and itself will have an impact on the future that emerges. Herein lies the challenge of participatory, democratic futurism: how to blend and balance the needs and interests of the masses, on the one hand, and the knowledge and expertise of professional futurists (elites), on the other. A small but steadily expanding transnational network of nondominant, non-state actors, currently working at the fringe of the international system on behalf of the poor, weak, and oppressed, can serve as the prime source of normative energy and political insight for participatory futurism and system transformation.

Second, it is necessary to extend the time horizon under which alternative world futures are previsioned and planned. This broadening of the time horizon is called for to (1) evaluate the longer-term consequences of our present actions and policies, (2) avoid being paralyzed by so many constraints and limitations—and so few opportunities and possibilities—in the immediate time horizon, and (3) discover more possibilities and paths that lie ahead in the long-term time horizon. Long-term futuristic modelling always runs the risk of implying that contemporary global problems and needs are less crucial. Every futurism invites the temptation to *escape* from the human predicament of the present. The dawning of a nuclear-ecological age has made John Maynard Keynes' aphorism, "In the long run we are all dead" even more compelling and relevant.

Third, normative forecasting generates its own self-serving tendency to overstate or exaggerate the possibilities and feasibilities—and to understate or even ignore the limitations and constraints—of system transformation. Indeed, the history of utopias is full of shattered expectations, dreams, and blueprints and hastily updated time tables for the coming of a better future. In the introduction to the second revised edition of *World Peace Through World Law*, published in 1960, coauthor Grenville Clark ventured "a reasoned prediction as follows: (a) that within about four to six years (by 1965–67) a comprehensive plan for total and universal disarmament and for the necessary world institutions to make, interpret and enforce world law in the field of war prevention will have been officially formulated and will have been submitted to all the nations for approval; and (b) that within four to six years thereafter (by 1969–71) such a plan will have been ratified by all or nearly all the nations, including all the major Powers, and will have come into force."[65] In an author's note added to the 1966 third enlarged edition, Clark admitted that his 1960 prediction "was too optimistic," but proceeded to say that he still retained "a reasonably optimistic view as to the prospects and, as of 1966, believe that such a plan will have been formulated by some important government or group of governments by 1980 and that within five years thereafter (by, say, 1985) such a plan will have been ratified by all or nearly all the nations, including all the major Powers."[66] Unless checked and balanced by exploratory forecasting, normative forecasting can easily turn into an exercise in sentimental, wishful thinking.

And finally, there is the design specificity question. How much and what kind of specificity should be given to a preferred future model? As shown in Chapter 3, the first stage in the development of world order studies was characterized by a law-oriented and institution-building approach. In a sense, this was an attempt to outdo *World Peace Through World Law* with the aim of producing a highly specific and delimited design in the form of a constitutional/institutional blueprint. In the second stage, however, the central focus shifted to a more balanced, broader normative framework as part of the transnationalization process of world order studies. As a result, specificity in the modelling process has come to be regarded as more harmful than helpful.

Richard Falk perceptively points out "the fallacy of premature specificity" as a static and rigid movement toward a terminal future model, suggesting that only "general principles of constitutional structure" can be used to overcome obstacles in the transitional processes.[67] This argument appears congruent with the functionalist orientation. The functionalists, in keeping with their "pragmatic" temperament, are skeptical of any grandiose or specific blueprints for the brave new world commonly envisioned in the utopian tradition. To design a structure at the outset is to rigidify the functional process of community building. The functionalists thus assume that forms and structures will vary according to their functions in the course of building transnational networks of cooperation and interdependence.

However, both the selection process and the feasibility of alternative world futures become problematic without some degree of specificity in a preferred future model. General normative principles can serve as criteria for the goal-setting and goal-specifying process for each of the four time horizons. In short, what is needed is an ongoing dialectical blending of specificity and flexibility in the normative forecasting/planning process to provide a reasonably flexible and specific guide for transition politics.[68]

Contending Scenarios for the Future

Most global future models and scenarios reflect conscious and subconscious projections of the modellers' dominant concerns, preferences, and interests. We are all prisoners of our own cultural and historical time and space. Wedded to present distributions of social, economic, and political resources in the world, professional futurists tend to project into the future their own system-maintaining or system-reforming perspectives. Why has global social forecasting become an almost exclusively Western preoccupation? Why has this social and intellectual enterprise been subsidized largely by the military and corporate systems of patronage? Why has this happened at a time of resource scarcity and of a crisis of faith in Western liberal democracy? Why has the Third World been so negative in its reaction to global modelling?

FIGURE 8.3
Normative Positions of Contending Global Forecasters or Modellers

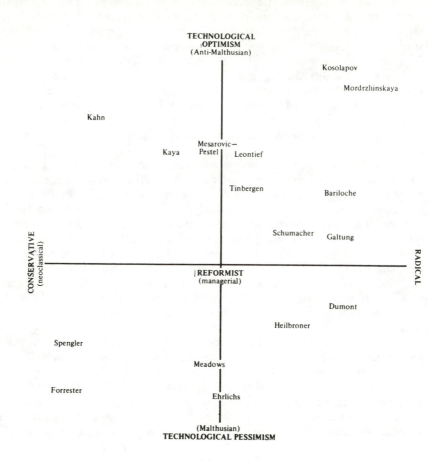

Source: *World Futures: The Great Debate,* edited by Christopher
Freeman and Marie Jahoda. New York: Universe Books, p. 246.
Reprinted with permission.

Part of the answer is suggested by the distinct future orientations of
major global actors as reflected in their respective mainstream future studies
or models. Figure 8.3 shows how each of the prominent "global" futurists
or modellers stands in terms of ideological (world view) and technological
orientations. (The area of the Bariloche-Schumacher-Galtung triangle, whose
basic element is an egalitarian ecodevelopment, comes closest to the normative
orientation of this book.) In a comprehensive survey analysis of the global

futures debates as revealed by the diverse global models in the period 1965–1976, Sam Coles concludes that each study or report reflects a strong national or regional interest:

> To some extent this {using the same words to express different ideas} is inevitable, given the complexity of the problems and the diverse national and disciplinary origins of the participants in the debate. The Bariloche group explicitly take up a stance favourable to the Third World in general, and to Latin America in particular. The report of the Japanese Club of Rome reflects a strong national interest when, for example, it criticises the doctrine of self-sufficiency, or "American and Australian Monroeism." . . . Throughout the debate Kahn champions the U.S.A. and Modrzhinskaya the U.S.S.R.[69]

Predictably, the dominant global models in the two superpowers share the technological-breakthrough mentality. Criticizing the majority of Western scientists who take a fatalistic view of global problems, two Soviet futurists characterize the Marxist scientific approach as "one of historical optimism and a belief in the *inevitable triumph* of reason and of modern social attitudes that will make it possible to solve existing global problems and those that may arise."[70] Both superpowers also champion their respective ideological systems, although the Soviet global models tend to be more normative than their U.S. counterparts by giving greater prominence to the abolition of all forms of social oppression and social inequality as the transition process toward a socialist world order.[71] It seems safe to conclude that the superpower hegemonic struggle has been extended to the global futures debate.

At almost every turn and corner in Japanese society, one cannot escape overwhelming evidence that this is indeed a country obsessed with high-tech advancement and adaptation to preserve its newborn economic prosperity and its comparative advantage in international trade. The dominant image of the future shared widely by the masses and elites alike may be characterized as "Kahnism" or "conservative-technological futurism." "Portopia '81," the biggest technological showcase since Osaka's Expo '70, dramatized Japan's self-made leadership in the transition from an industrialized to an electronic-based, fully computerized society. Computers and robots are pacesetters for Japan's drive toward the promised land (island?) of technological utopia. Technological optimism is extremely high in Japan's image of its own future.

Except for the grassroot movement against nuclear weapons, however, Japan's posture in global politics or in the shaping of the world's future is modest and mediatory. In the North-South dialogue, Japan has somewhat belatedly claimed a mediator role based on its dual identity as a member of the Asian group as well as a member of the OECD. Japan also tends to be optimistic about the prospects of the NIEO, but this optimism rests upon the twin pillars of its unwavering faith in international market mechanisms and the importance of domestic reforms within the developing countries themselves as preconditions for achieving international development strategy.[72] In general, as Yoshikazu Sakamoto and Hiroharu Seki concluded in their study, "the predominant stand taken by the Japanese elite in their relations to international politics is, instead of freely choosing an independent future course of action, to follow the general trends in world affairs. Adaptations to international environment parallels reconciliation with natural environment."[73]

The West European image of the future is difficult to generalize. In 1976 the OECD established a research project, known as *Interfutures*, to study "the future development of advanced industrial societies in harmony with that of the developing countries." The project was completed at the end of 1978, and the results were published in 1979 as *Facing the Future: Mastering the Probable and Managing the Unpredictable.* At the risk of some oversimplification, *Interfutures* may be used as a sample representation of the dominant (establishment) European image of the future.

Interfutures is a normative model with a system-maintaining orientation, although it does contain four computer-based scenarios. The efficient management of global economic interdependence is the most salient normative thrust of this global model. The global political economy is seen as locked in an irreversible process of progressive transformation, with expanding links and networks within and between the North, the East, and the South, but especially within the OECD area, the core of global interdependence. Like the United Nations World Model (Leontief in Figure 8.3), *Interfutures* sees the limits of growth more in terms of political, economic, and social than physical constraints. Yet *Interfutures* dismisses the notion that the OECD can return to the golden era of the high rates of economic growth.

The centerpiece of *Interfutures* is its self-serving, hierarchical management prescription for the future of the global political economy. To maintain the stability and efficiency of the world economy under rapidly changing conditions, *Interfutures* issues managerial prescriptions for concentric circles of multilateral cooperation. Highest priority is given to the imperative of the Big Seven (the United States, Canada, France, Italy, West Germany, the United Kingdom, and Japan) to put their geopolitical and geoeconomic acts together for a united managerial front, to be followed by increased cooperation among all the member states of the OECD. The NICs as the "middle class of an evolving world society" are seen as the key link to the Third World; as such they deserve top priority for fuller integration into the world economy. This completes the concentric circle of multilateral cooperation. The poor countries deserve increased aid but are denied any leadership role in the global political economy. The principal purpose of this concentric circle of multilateral cooperation should be to improve international market mechanisms. *Interfutures* concludes that "the only possible solution" is "to take the present system and progressively improve it until it is significantly transformed."[74]

Future-consciousness is not only unevenly distributed between the top-dogs and underdogs *within* the nations but also *between* the nations. Global modelling as an expression of future-consciousness in our time is no more equitably distributed than is global wealth between the rich and poor countries. The NIEO appears to come closest to embodying the Third World's image of the world's future. If this inference is correct, we can say that the Third World's image of the future is located somewhere between Leontief (the United Nations World Model) and Tinbergen (*Reshaping the International Order*, which accepts and amplifies most demands of the NIEO) in Figure 8.3.

It should also be noted in this connection that the Bariloche world model cannot be accepted as representing the Third World's establishment (governmental) position. Like the Cocoyoc Declaration, the Bariloche model is a radical (system-transforming) alternative to the diffusion of the Center model popular in the Third World in general and in Latin America in particular. (The military commander of the Neuquen district in Argentina gave the Bariloche group twenty-four hours to leave the country.) It is perhaps the best example of normative forecasting emanating from a Third World NGO in search of a relevant utopia, "an egalitarian society, at both the national and international levels" with "inalienable rights regarding the satisfaction of basic needs—nutrition, housing, health—that are essential for complete and active participation."[75]

The IDS (third) scenario can be accepted as representing the most recent Third World image of the world's future. Given the Third World's dominance in the normative domain of global development politics, this scenario, constructed at the request of the General Assembly, tends to reflect the dominant perspective of the Group of 77.

The IDS scenario is a good example of the normative forecasting/planning process at the United Nations. Its primary aim is "the attainment of the normative targets and goals of the International Development Strategy for the Third United Nations Development Decade" (the 1980s). The IDS scenario explicitly postulates growth rates for every developing country that are significantly higher than longer-term trends, changes in present resource use patterns, structural transformations, and international trade relationships as a means of restructuring contemporary world politics and as an integral part of the NIEO. The feasibility of the scenario is assumed to be contingent upon successful implementation of the IDS in all its important aspects.

This latest exercise gives one a sense of déjà vu, a sense of having already traversed the familiar economic trajectories charted in the system-reforming NIEO model. To cope with "projected external gaps," the IDS scenario in effect recommends that the developing countries should follow the NIC model by adopting "policies which increase capital productivity, encourage more capital inflows, substitute domestic products for imported ones and promote exports" and by moving "toward greater and more aggressive participation in world markets." The IDS scenario also stresses the importance of supplementing domestic reforms within the developing countries by "appropriate policies in the developed economies and by the international community." As for the special problems of the low-income and least developed economies, the IDS scenario assumes an increase in ODA supplemented by current proportions of OPEC aid and private capital market flows.[76]

Which Scenario for the Future?

How can the future of mankind be shaped more by human needs than by the structure of the existing international system characterized by the Soviet-U.S. arms race? Table 8.1 addresses this question by constructing three alternative scenarios of projected effects on per capita consumption in the year 2000. *The baseline scenario* assumes that the share of military outlays in GNPs and the geographical distribution of military industry would be roughly the same throughout the period 1970–2000; *the accelerated arms race scenario* assumes a doubling of the share of GNPs for military outlays by 2000; and *the disarmament scenario* assumes that the computer parity levels of the military spending of the United States and the Soviet Union will fall by one-third by 1990 and by a further one-third by 2000.

The process of previsioning and planning a more peaceful, equitable, and harmonious world future needs to be based on a synergetic systems approach. As suggested in Table 8.1, the problem of the global arms race and the problem of global poverty and underdevelopment are two dimensions of the same problem. Both world military spending and the Third World's outstanding debt stood at about $600 billion in 1982—problems that need to be solved together or not at all. Herein lie the dangers and opportunities of global interdependencies.

Table 8.2 presents a preliminary world order projection of a preferred world future. It includes a set of three alternative scenario projections of the military, economic, social, and environmental state of the world in the benchmark year 2000. Scenario A represents the maximum desirable goals—and scenario B the minimum necessary goals—to be achieved by 2000. Scenarios A and B are both constructed through a normative forecasting to realize world order values in alternative futures. Based on the historical trends of 1960–1980, scenario C postulates the medium-growth projections of trends in the select categories; the figures for C underscore the magnitude of the difficulties to be overcome in achieving the normative targets of scenarios A and B. Scenarios A and B constitute two sets of normative realities for the year 2000; accordingly, they suggest two alternative normative maps for redirecting the likely trends (scenario C) so as to bridge the gap between the actual (or the probable) and the preferable (or the potential) in our journey into the future.

This kind of goal setting is an integral part of world order modelling. A preferred future that is discontinuous with historical and extrapolated trends could not be achieved without first setting normative goals and targets to guide the transition process. The value-realizing process here proceeds from the desirable to the feasible to the probable. The principal aim is to make negative trends less feasible and positive trends more

TABLE 8.1
Projected Effects on Per Capita Consumption in 2000 of Three Alternative Scenarios

Region	Percentage Change		
	The Baseline Scenario	The Arms Race Scenario	The Disarmament Scenario
Arid Africa	− 33.3	− 42.3	+ 166.7
Asia, Centrally Planned Economies	+ 116.0	− 8.0	+ 2.9
Asia, Low Income	+ 2.1	− 13.4	+ 47.6
Asia, High Income	+ 266.9	− 4.1	+ 1.1
Latin America, Resource-Rich	+ 244.0	− 6.3	+ 7.5
Latin America, Medium Income	− 45.7	− 5.1	+ 21.3
North America	+ 67.8	− 12.6	+ 3.7
Oceania	+ 111.0	− 2.8	+ 0.7
Developing Oil Producers	+ 1,444.8	− 0.0	+ 0.0
Soviet Union and Eastern Europe	+ 200.9	− 19.3	+ 6.3
Southern Africa	+ 58.8	− 4.4	+ 1.4
Tropical Africa	+ 51.1	− 10.0	+ 65.8
Western Europe, High Income	+ 114.3	− 6.0	+ 1.2
Western Europe, Medium Income	+ 15.6	− 11.7	+ 7.1

Source: Adapted from *Study on the Relationship Between Disarmament and Development*, Report of the Secretary-General, UN Doc. A/36/356 (5 October 1981), pp. 106–107.

feasible. A global nuclear war is both feasible and probable; hence, the need to impose denuclearization as the normative goal. The normative targets specified under scenarios A and B in Table 8.2 can be catalyzed into "intervening variables" that would lead to discontinuous and countervailing trends toward the year 2000. To merely follow probable and feasible trajectories as shown in scenario C in the name of "realism" is a sure recipe for disaster.

TABLE 8.2
Projections of Three Alternative Scenarios for the Year 2000

CATEGORY	1980	Scenario C	Scenario B	Scenario A
World Military Expenditure (1980 prices in million dollars)	500,000	940,000[a]	1,000	Neglible[b]
Number of Soviet-American Strategic Nuclear Weapons	15,200	104,338[c]	400[d]	None
Global Arms Exports (1980 prices)	26.1	283.8[a]	0.5	Neglible[b]
Armed Forces (thousands)	24,642	32,527[a]	10,000	5,000[b]
Per Capita Income Gap Between Rich and Poor Countries	12:1	11-12:1[a]	5:1	1:1
Foreign Economic Aid (ODA As Percentage of GNP)	0.37	0.23[a]	1.5	3.0
Developing Countries' Outstanding Debt (billions of current dollars)	438.7	2,843[c]	20.0	10.0
Number of Absolute Poor (Per Capita Annual Income of Less Than $150 in 1975 prices; in millions)	825	975[c]	50	None
Number of World's Refugees (in millions)	12.6 (1981)	14.0[e]	1.0	None
Number of Repressive Regimes in the Third World	41	40-50?[f]	Neglible	None
Rate of World Population Growth (percentage)	1.72	1.5[g]	1.0	0.5
CO_2 Concentration in the Atmosphere (parts per million by volume)	338 ppm	363 ppm[c]	300 ppm	280 ppm
Desertification (thousand square kilometers)	7,992 (1977)	23,976[h]	10,000	8,000
Deforestation (World's Closed Forest in millions of hectares)	2,563 (1978)	2,117[h]	2,500	3,000

The Transition Process

In the final analysis, the transition to a peaceful, humane, just, and harmonious future is contingent upon far-reaching changes of an attitudinal, normative, structural, and behavioral character both within and between human societies. For example, scenario C in Table 8.2 is premised on the continuation of the political fragmentation of the earth and the state-centric international system. Scenarios A and B start with the opposite assumption that the permanence of political fragmentation and state sovereignty is illusory. Both scenarios anticipate a long-term, incremental transformation process, steadily eroding the authority and legitimacy of the state-centric international system and generating pressures toward a more cosmic politics of the planet earth.

Because of the telescoping impact of modern technology and growing global interdependence, there always exists a "transition" of one sort or another. However, our conception of transition is not a matter of the changing social landscape as the technological train moves from one station to the next. Instead, world order theorists mean by transition a series of normatively purposive and politically planned processes designed to change

---

TABLE 8.2 (continued)

EXPLANATORY NOTES:

Scenario A=The maximum desirable goals and targets for 2000 set by a normative forecasting.

Scenario B=The minimum desirable goals and targets for 2000 set by a normative forecasting.

Scenario C=The medium-growth exploratory forecasting based on the historical trends of 1960–1980 or 1970–1980 depending on the availability of data.

a=Exploratory forecasting based on the historical trend of 1960–1980.

b=Assuming the existence of some transnational security system and making some allowance for domestic police functions.

c=Exploratory forecasting based on the historical trend of 1970–1980.

d=Based on the assumption of finite mutual deterrence, which is believed to require only 200 nuclear warheads by each side sufficient to destroy about 100 of the opponent's cities.

e=This merely represents the annual average during the period 1961–1982, based on the annual survey of U.S. Committee on Refugees.

f=Based on Ruth Leger Sivard's estimations of the number of repressive regimes in the Third World in the 1980–1982 period.

g=The latest UN projection.

h=Based on the projections of *The Global 2000 Report to the President.*

the course of human development; we mean the processes of building relevant and reliable bridges and pathways to connect us to the preferred futures sketched out in Table 8.2.

Given the uneven distribution of world order values and political consciousness in different parts of the world, there can be no single, specific transition strategy. Instead, world order transition needs a differentiated structure and substance keyed to the local circumstances and opportunities, that is, multidimensional, multilateral, multiple-step transition strategies. There is some danger of leaving transition politics unconnected to the global bridge-building movement toward a just world order. With this danger of acting locally without thinking globally in mind, the strategies suggested below are not a rigid package of specific action plans but five "principled processes" of an overall world order transition.

A Nonviolent Revolutionary Process

As a non-Machiavellian and non-Marxist alternative to global transformation, our orientation shies away from managerial quick fixes of (liberal) reformist strategy as well as political-structural quick fixes of (Marxist) revolutionary strategy. The liberal reformist strategy of social change, concentrating on the injection of technocratic prescriptions into the established policies, practices, and institutions, merely alleviates symptomatic pains of system pathology in specific situations. Although this strategy can contribute to short-term crisis management, its long-term, systemic impact seems insufficient. The recent history of UN peacekeeping, arms control, and NIEO underscores the inherent limitations of the liberal reformist strategy as an agent of system transformation in world politics. The "reform measures" have proved to be no more than short-term palliatives, leaving the dominant values, structure, and behavior of the present international system more or less intact. The reformist strategy seriously underestimates the damage-limitation capacity of system maintainers to divert and detract the expressions of discontent through first-aid or cooptation measures. What is most needed is a revolutionary process calling for a radical shift from the present system to a new one.

At the same time, our orientation is generally skeptical of any revolutionary strategy of system transformation predicated on the putative potency of violence, although we do recognize that the struggles of the oppressed, even when violent, may be an unavoidable part of the political process of liberation in such places as Central America and South Africa, where all peaceful forms of struggles have been precluded. The commitment to the world order value of peace (defined in its direct, physical as well as in its indirect, structural sense) applies to the means and the ends of transition politics. There is a mutually enhancing or corrupting symbiotic relationship between means and ends in social process. As discussed in Chapter 6, the perpetrators of violence in its various modern forms cannot dehumanize their victims without dehumanizing themselves in the process.

The resort to revolutionary violence is a form of political-structural quick fix. The power to kill and destroy is not the same as the power to overcome and win, just as the power to capture the state apparatus is not the same as the power to transform social process. Yet the Marxist-Leninist strategy of social transformation is often premised on such mistaken equations of different kinds of power. When such a revolution succeeds in seizing the power of the state, a new class disguised in the name of "proletarian dictatorship" emerges to preside over a superstate—a case of violence-based power corrupting violence-based power. A just and humane social order cannot be established "by deliberately building it on the foundation of a refined application of the most dubious characteristics of the old society: elite domination, centralization, political violence, and manipulation of the supposedly incompetent 'masses.' "[77]

Given the enormously destructive power at the disposal of system maintainers today, any violent strategy of conflict cannot succeed without bringing in its wake intolerable levels of human suffering and social destruction. However, there is a third alternative—a nonviolent revolutionary praxis for the transition from value commitment to principled action. Both Mahatma Gandhi and Martin Luther King, Jr., have given concrete political expression to nonviolence. Although it is debatable whether nonviolence is the only viable transition strategy in every conflict situation (e.g., the liberation struggle in South Africa), Gandhi and King have demonstrated the feasibility and workability of the nonviolent strategy for social change in two different social contexts. For them, nonviolence served as a grand strategic guide for long-term normative and structural transformation as well as a tactical guide for everyday struggle. Far from implying passivity, submission, cowardice, or inaction, writes Gene Sharp in his careful study of the history of nonviolent action in a wide variety of historical and social situations, the nonviolent strategy is a positive reaffirmation of commitment to social change through various forms or methods of *nonviolent protest* (marches, pilgrimages, picketing, vigils, public meetings, etc.), *nonviolent noncooperation* (social boycotts, economic boycotts, strikes, civil disobedience), and *nonviolent intervention* (sit-ins, fasts, reverse strikes, nonviolent obstructions, nonviolent invasion, and parallel government).[78]

The key to nonviolent revolutionary praxis for transition politics is not winning political power but generating the political consciousness and mobilization required to challenge and transform an unjust social order rooted in violence. Following *satyagraha* (truth power) and relying on nonviolence, this revolutionary praxis seeks to bring the oppressor and the oppressed together in a confrontational pedagogy of truth seeking. When the truth is discovered, it liberates the oppressed and the oppressor alike. The Biblical statement of the truth as the liberating power is particularly compelling in the nonviolent strategy of conflict because the ultimate objective of the nonviolent revolutionary praxis for world order transition is human liberation.

The most potent and enduring process of social transformation comes about through changes in social behavior, but behavioral transformation is always a function of fundamental changes in social norms, values, and structure. The nonviolent revolutionary praxis for world order transition is therefore designed to directly confront and challenge the defenders of the status quo, especially their hegemonic power to define social reality and truth through their control and manipulation of the superstructure, the critical domain of the language, art, literature, imagination, and myth-making where we find the opening salvos of transformation struggle and where we become suddenly conscious of our individual and group role in the struggle.

A Linkage Process

World order transition has to be grounded in an ongoing dialectics between preferred futures and the unfolding present. This is a dialectical process of linking theory and practice, paradigm and praxis so as to seek creative space for an interface between normative and empirical reality. A reverse linkage process is needed here. Instead of allowing the present trends to continue unchecked, normative goals and targets of an alternative world future are imported and grafted onto the present as "intervening variables" to generate countervailing, discontinuous trends in an alternative direction. The linkage process is a trend-deflecting strategy.

The role of scholarship here is not passively relegated to describing and exploring probable trends; it is actively extended to linking probable and preferred futures in a creative dialogue. A viable transition strategy calls for connecting thinking, believing, feeling, and acting so as to bridge the gap between principle and practice.

Our social existential circumstances condition not only the level of social consciousness but also the structure and substance of our social struggle. The 1970s and early 1980s have already witnessed the rise of a multitude of social actors, groups, and organizations pursuing various world order goals in various arenas, all relevant to the linkage process of transition politics. The task here calls for identifying all progressive and humane forces for a global-local linkage. This represents one concrete way of building transnational networks for world order transition, one concrete expression of the global-local linkage—thinking globally and acting locally.

Far from ignoring or underestimating these locally anchored social movements as being irrelevant to world order transition, then, our task is to link fragmented parts together as building blocks for the global bridge-building and path-breaking process. This cannot be done without fostering a great measure of ideological tolerance and social experimentation for diverse transition strategies reflected in the seemingly disconnected and diverse social movements throughout the world.

The linkage process suggested here cannot go too far without some overriding conception of planetary *human* security.[79] In a word, the linkage process should work toward building a sense of species solidarity, an Apollo vision of common human destiny. In an objective sense, the global-local linkage is not a matter of invention; it is empirical reality. "Whether we like it or not," as Robert C. Johansen aptly put it, "in the nuclear-ecologically fragile age, all governments become 'my' government."[80] What is required here is the fostering of widespread public understanding of this new reality of the mutual interrelatedness of global and local problems and goals as well as of the local impacts of the global system's fundamental anomalies and contradictions. In this way, the linkage process would raise global consciousness among the diverse social movements and with it the prospect of global transformation.

Such a holistic—and realistic—conception of global reality, though considerably obscured and distorted by the dominant mythology of anachronistic sovereignty and narrow nationalism, is a precondition for world order transition. To catalyze and canalize the many possibilities embedded in global reality and to link embryonic grassroots social movements in various parts of the world are some of the crucial challenges of the transition process. Wittingly or not, human rights dissidents in China and the Soviet Union, the Solidarity Movement in Poland, the antinuclear movement in Japan and Europe, the Lokayan project in India,[81] liberation theology in Latin America, and the environmental movement in the United States, to cite only a few examples, have all taken concrete steps toward a better world future.

A Systemic, Synergic Process

World order transition is necessarily a systemic, synergic process in which positive or negative trends in one dimension effect changes in the other dimensions of world politics. As discussed earlier in the book, the threats to human survival, human needs, human rights, and human ecological safety all represent different dimensions of the global problematique (see Table 4.1). If this analysis is correct, it follows that world order transition for the demilitarization and developmental processes can also be defined in mutually complementary terms (see Table 8.1) and can be prescribed in symbiotic and synergic terms (see Table 8.2).

There is now growing realization of the systemic, interrelated nature of human problems, as shown in the social activism of religious and medical professions in the antinuclear movement that has swept through Europe, Japan, and North America in recent years and the 1982 antiwar manifesto of the Friends of the Earth. The solidarity rights of the third generation— the right to peace, the right to development, the right to a healthy and ecologically balanced environment, and the right to the common heritage of mankind—are another testimonial to this systemic, synergic process in transition politics.

These are concrete and pertinent examples we can use to conceive and plan world order transition. Conceptually, world order transition rejects any monocausal theory that traces the origin of all human injustice and suffering to a single source. Monocausal explanation makes the basic error of mistaking the part for the whole. "It is very rare, in studies of social change," as sociologist Wilbert E. Moore says, "that we come across a classically neat demonstration of a singular cause, producing a singular effect, under finitely specifiable and repeatable conditions."[82]

Clearly, one-dimensional change is not enough. In this connection, the debate as to the relative importance of normative as against structural transformation during world order transition is misleading, as system transformation proceeds on the basis of both normative and structural transformation. As suggested in Figure 8.1, our approach and prescription for world order transition are premised on a complex global reality and on the need to fully capture this reality through constant review and reassessment of all normative, structural, and behavioral variables of the human situation. This orientation is also helpful to minimize factional division and fragmentation among various movements for social change that are currently under way in different arenas of national and global politics.

A Coalition-Building Process

It is self-evident that world order transition cannot go too far without an active, cohesive, imaginative, and broad-based movement for system transformation. Most of the early world order reforms appealed to the enlightened self-interest of the power holders to take normative initiatives in transition politics toward a better world order based on the uncritical acceptance and transplantation of liberal reform politics to the international scene. A more realistic conception of transition has to be grounded in a power-sharing and coalition-building process first starting outside the governmental process and then working its way into all key decisionmaking points. This approach is based on the assumption that the main sources of normative energy and political mobilization lie in the dissatisfaction of those victims of the existing order with the political will to resist it, acting alone or in concert with other victims.

The awareness of our own "oppression" is a precondition to our engagement in the politics of change. The extent to which an individual or groups perceives itself to be oppressed determines the degree of commitment to social change. The ascendancy of Christianity in the Roman Empire suggests that it spread among the elites who were dissatisfied with the existing social order while "persons of lower status were greatly encouraged by recruits from the upper classes and found corroboration of their resentment against discrimination."[83] In a similar vein, Dankwart A. Rustow argues that political change is the product of dissatisfaction with the existing social order and that this discontent produces political action.[84] In *Injustice: The Social Bases of Obedience and Revolt*, Barrington Moore, Jr., argued persuasively that there is no guarantee of political and social changes without a very considerable surge of moral outrage.[85]

There has been a dramatic extension of oppressive forms of social reality in our time. This new reality opens up more creative space for world order transition. After being paralyzed for years by "psychic numbing," the process by which we deny the reality of the bomb in order to minimize cognitive dissonance or to stay sane, Robert Lifton reminds us, a kind of reality principle is finally working its way to spreading the "worldwide hunger for nuclear truth."[86] As this antinuclear consensus-forming and coalition-building process spreads and expands across nations, classes, and cultures, so does the base of transnational coalition-building process for world order transition.

The coalition-building process, as an integral part of world order transition, can move horizontally and vertically. The future global order, as Chadwick F. Alger suggests, can be served by the creation of symmetrical and responsive relationships between local communities and peoples in all parts of the world.[87] This is a horizontal movement in a global coalition-building process for world order transition. On the other hand, Rajni Kothari calls for the forging of a grand global coalition for change, spanning various regions and political systems and joining progressive governments and elites in the Third World and activist reformers and radical social movements in the North.[88] World order transition has to rely upon a creative dialogue and cooperation between dissatisfied elites and oppressed masses united in their common commitment to change the status quo.

The collapse of the student-led rebellions of the 1960s, which can be attributed largely to their violent tactics and their failure to broaden the mass base, serves as a lesson of ill-conceived, ill-planned, and ill-executed transition strategy. The central challenge of this coalition-building process for world order transition is to canalize embryonic beginnings of important transformative movements which have not yet reached mass—and global—proportions. In this way, the coalition-building process can redefine normative boundaries and widen the limits of the possible in the politics of system transformation.

A Protracted, Phased Process

In principle, if not always in practice, Mao was right in his assertion that societal transformation is a "continuing revolution" (*jixu geming*). "Humanity left to its own devices does not necessarily reestablish capitalism," Mao said in his interview with Andre Malraux in 1965, a year before the Cultural Revolution was launched, "but it does reestablish inequality.... Khrushchev seemed to think that a revolution is done when a communist party has seized power—as if it were merely a question of national liberation."[89] There is general consensus that world order transition is a protracted, phased process. Both George Lakey and Johan Galtung have defined world order transition in five sequential phases: (1) conscientization; (2) building organization; (3) confrontation; (4) mass noncooperation (fight against dominance for Galtung); and (5) parallel government (self-reliance for Galtung).[90] Richard Falk proposes a sequential strategy for the transition from the present (S_1) to the preferred (S_2) system of world order in three phases: (1) political consciousness (i.e., orientations toward action); (2) political mobilization; and (3) institutional transformation.[91]

A nonviolent and noncataclysmic transition to a just world order is of necessity a cumulative, complex, sequential, and protracted process. Both traditional utopian and modern leftist approaches to system transformation suffer from a "Great Leap Forward" mentality. While the functionalist assumption of the separability of the political and the functional is untenable both normatively and empirically, the functionalists' organic, incremental community-building process, an approach that has been characterized as "peace by pieces,"[92] has much to recommend it for world order transition. The widely accepted notion that normative transformation is a necessary condition to system transformation is well captured in the Preamble to the UNESCO Constitution: "Since wars begin in the minds of men, it is in the minds of men that the defenses of peace must be constructed."

The Cultural Revolution in China may be treated as a microcosm, as an experimental case study from which certain lessons can be drawn for world order transition. Originally, Mao saw this "revolution" as a necessary and desirable risk in his attempt to deal with the problem of the superstructure in a fundamental way that had never been tried before: an ideological and structural transformation of the whole establishment in China. Mao admitted that such a cultural revolution to reassert a proletariat quest for social justice and equality, and once again "to touch the souls of people," can be taken two or three times at most in the course of one century. In short, Mao's quest for populist egalitarianism is fully in accord with our world order values.[93]

Clearly, all the turmoil, disruption, factionalism, and xenophobic nationalism which followed in the wake of the Cultural Revolution did not conform to Mao's theoretical expectations or normative visions. After having suffered from the self-inflicted wounds of internal convulsions and diplomatic isolation, Mao finally brought an end to the movement gone berserk, established "law and order," rejuvenated the Party, and inaugurated a new era in Chinese foreign policy. The new transition from revolutionary turmoil to pragmatic reconstruction is a veiled admission of the failure of the Cultural Revolution.

There are competing explanations for the failure of the Cultural Revolution.[94] As lessons for world order transition, however, only a few anomalies may suffice. First, Mao, an old revolutionary propelled by a sense of great alarm and urgency, telescoped all phases of societal transformation—normative, structural, and behavioral—into a convulsive, once-and-for-all transition, defying his own conception of "continuing revolution" as a protracted, phased struggle. Second, Mao's Machiavellian impulse—what matters most is correct line or ideology, not the means—reasserted itself during the Cultural Revolution, defying the means-ends complementarity in world order transition. Third, the unity between ideology and organization, which Franz Schurmann once considered as the most important factor explaining the success of the Maoist revolution,[95] was disconnected and ruptured. And fourth and finally, no attempt was made to identify the Cultural Revolution as part of global transformation. Instead, atavistic nationalism was allowed full play, and China's foreign policy was left largely unprotected from the disruptive spillovers of the domestic turmoil, adversely affecting Peking's diplomatic relations with friends and foes alike. In short, the Cultural Revolution failed not so much in the formulation of its normative visions as in transition strategy. Indeed, it is a vivid example of the disjuncture between a preferred future and a convulsive transition strategy, a telling epitaph to the monument of one of the most significant societal transformations of our time, miscarried in the transition process.

The Prospect of a Relevant Utopia

The search for a relevant utopia calls for constant balancing between desirable normative goals and feasible transition strategies. Normative forecasting helps us to see our stars. Exploratory forecasting helps us to see our limitations. Both normative and exploratory forecasting together can help us better appreciate and harness contradictory transformative forces of creativity and destruction dialectically contending in a struggle for human emancipation.

The prospect of a relevant utopia depends not only on *how* but also on *where* we look. There are many sources of despair, to be sure, but there are also two main sources of hope for mobilizing a global movement for system transformation. Humanity is becoming more literate, more urban, more mobile, and more demanding and more politicized. Humanity is also becoming less fatalistic, less passive, and less tolerant.

If the first "revolution of rising expectations" in the postwar period meant the fast mobilization of people's needs and demands, the second "revolution of rising expectations" is the fast mobilization of people's frustration and intolerance. We are just beginning to witness worldwide a rising threshold of intolerance for human deprivation and political oppression and the flickerings of a planetary consciousness. If the oppressed are no longer as fatalistic and passive as they used to be, the oppressors are no longer as strong and united as they used to be. More than ever before in human history, the defenders of the status quo are rapidly losing their authority and legitimacy because their secret opium weapon of social anesthesia is no longer working.[96] The conquest of the credo of inevitability is a *sine qua non* in world order transition to a relevant utopia. Herein lies one main source of hope for global transformation.

The potential for global transformation is also increasing because of the advanced system pathology. The system crisis whose symptoms are being manifest everywhere for everyone to see—and which have been discussed at some length in Part 2—is a great teacher of the reality principle. The Chinese word for crisis, which consists of two characters (*weiji*), one symbolizing "danger" (*weixian*) and the other "opportunity" (*jihui*), nicely captures and conveys two dimensions of the present human predicament. That is, the advanced system pathology represents another main source of hope for global transformation. As Alfred North Whitehead reminded us more than a half century ago, "the great ages have been unstable ages."[97]

Of course, it is not possible to prove whether such a dialectical conception of the human predicament is correct or whether world order transition can be initiated in time to avert cataclysmic system collapse. The journey to a future world without war, poverty, injustice, and ecocide is anchored in the belief that the future is not predestined and that we can still find our passage to the promised land if we lift our vision to follow the stars. In times of great turmoil and system crisis, it is easy to succumb to what Eric Fromm calls "pathology of normalcy."[98] We need constantly remind ourselves of the world order implications of what Shakespeare said in *Julius Caesar:*

The fault, dear Brutus, is not in our stars,
But in ourselves, that we are underlings.

Notes

Chapter 1

1. See "The Perversion of Science and Technology: An Indictment," in Richard A. Falk, Samuel S. Kim, and Saul H. Mendlovitz, eds., *Toward a Just World Order* (Boulder, Colo.: Westview Press, 1982), pp. 359–63. This statement was prepared by a transnational group of concerned scholars at the fourteenth meeting of the World Order Models Project in Poona, India, July 2-10, 1978.

2. See United Nations, *Report on the World Social Situation*, UN Publications, Sales No. E.82.IV.2 (New York: United Nations, 1982), Table 2, p. 181.

3. E. F. Schumacher, *Small Is Beautiful: Economics As If People Mattered* (New York: Harper & Row, 1973).

4. Roy Preiswerk, "Could We Study International Relations As If People Mattered?" in Falk, Kim, and Mendlovitz, *Toward a Just World Order* pp. 175–97. In August 1982, Roy Preiswerk died of cancer at a young age—a great loss to world order studies.

5. For a careful delineation of the major differences between traditional and world order approaches to the study of world affairs, see Burns H. Weston, "Contending with a Planet in Peril and Change: An Optimal Educational Response," *Alternatives* 5 (June 1979): 59–95.

6. Stephen Jay Gould, *The Mismeasure of Man* (New York: W. W. Norton & Co., 1981), p. 21.

7. The logical necessity of separating fact from value is elaborated in Arnold Brecht, *Political Theory, the Foundations of Twentieth Century Political Thought* (Princeton, N.J.: Princeton University Press, 1959).

8. John F. McCamant, "Social Science and Human Rights," *International Organization* 35 (Summer 1981): 534.

9. Preiswerk, "Could We Study International Relations As If People Mattered?" p. 178.

10. Eugene J. Meehan, *Value Judgment and Social Science* (Homewood, Ill.: Dorsey Press, 1969), p. 13. Emphasis added.

11. John Dewey, *Freedom and Culture* (New York: G. P. Putnam's Sons, 1939), p. 172.

12. J. R. Tedeschi, R. B. Smith, and R. C. Brown, "A Reinterpretation of Research on Aggression," *Psychological Bulletin* 81 (September 1974): 557–58.

13. R. T. Green and G. Santori, "A Cross Cultural Study of Hostility and Aggression," *Journal of Peace Research* 6, No. 1 (1969): 13–22.

14. Anatol Rapoport, *Strategy and Conscience* (New York: Schocken Books, 1964), p. 30.

15. The necessity of combining the normative and the empirical in international relations research is cogently argued and applied in Johan Galtung, "On the Future of the International System," *Journal of Peace Research* 4 (1967): 305–33; Johan Galtung, *Methodology and Ideology* (Copenhagen: Christian Ejlers, 1977); and Myres S. McDougal, Harold D. Lasswell, and Lung-Chu Chen, *Human Rights and World Public Order* (New Haven: Yale University Press, 1980).

16. Gould, *The Mismeasure of Man*, p. 22.

17. See Gunnar Myrdal, *An American Dilemma* (New York: Harper & Brothers Publishers, 1944), Vol. 2, Appendix 2, "A Methodological Note on Facts and Valuations in Social Science," pp. 1035–64; quote in the text on pp. 1057, 1064.

18. James N. Rosenau, "Muddling, Meddling and Modelling: Alternative Approaches to the Study of World Politics in an Era of Rapid Change," *Millennium: Journal of International Studies* 8 (Autumn 1979): 130.

19. John H. Herz, "Political Realism Revisited," *International Studies Quarterly* 25 (June 1981): 184, 192.

20. For an elaboration of this argument, see Herman E. Daly, *Steady-State Economics: The Economics of Biophysical Equilibrium and Moral Growth* (San Francisco: W. H. Freeman and Co., 1977), chap. 1.

21. See Barbara R. Bergmann, "The Failures of a Chair-Bound Science," *The New York Times*, December 12, 1982, p. F3.

22. Harold and Margaret Sprout, *Toward a Politics of the Planet Earth* (New York: Van Nostrand Reinhold Co., 1971), p. 13. Emphasis in original.

23. Yoshikazu Sakamoto, "The Rationale of the World Order Models Project," *American Journal of International Law* 66 (September 1972): 251. Emphasis in original.

24. Saul H. Mendlovitz, ed., *On the Creation of a Just World Order* (New York: Free Press, 1975), p. x.

25. Philip J. Meeks, "Interdisciplinary Analysis: Scientific Humanism in an Age of Specialization," in Gary K. Bertsch, ed., *Global Policy Studies* (Beverly Hills, Calif.: Sage Publications, 1982), p. 150.

26. Immanuel Wallerstein, *The Capitalist World-Economy* (New York: Cambridge University Press, 1979), pp. vii–xii; quote on p. xi.

27. Niccolo Machiavelli, *The Prince*, trans. Luigi Ricci (New York: Mentor Books, 1952), p. 89.

28. Karl W. Deutsch, *Politics and Government: How People Decide Their Fate*, 3d ed. (Boston: Houghton Mifflin Company, 1980), p. 77.

29. Hans J. Morgenthau, *Politics Among Nations: The Struggle for Power and Peace*, 5th ed. (New York: Alfred A. Knopf, 1973), p. 4.

30. Kenneth N. Waltz, *Theory of International Politics* (Reading, Mass.: Addison-Wesley Publishing Co., 1979), p. 109.

31. W. I. Thomas, *The Child in America* (New York: Knopf, 1928), p. 572. Robert Merton says that this statement of Thomas has now become "a theorem basic to the social sciences." See Robert K. Merton, *Social Theory and Social Structure: Toward the Codification of Theory and Research* (Glencoe, Ill.: Free Press, 1949), p. 179.

32. Leslie H. Gelb, "20 Years After Missile Crisis, Riddles Remain," *The New York Times*, October 23, 1982, pp. 1, 4; quote on p. 4.

33. Talcott Parsons, *The Social System* (Glencoe, Ill.: Free Press, 1951), p. 86. Emphasis in original.

34. Samuel P. Huntington, "The Change to Change," *Comparative Politics* 3 (April 1971): 284.

35. Ole R. Holsti, Randolph M. Siverson, and Alexander L. George, eds., *Change in the International System* (Boulder, Colo.: Westview Press, 1980); Richard L. Merritt,

ed., *Studies in Systems Transformation* inaugural issue, *International Political Science Review* 1 (January 1980).

36. *International Studies Quarterly* 25 (March 1981). Special issue. The larger version of this debate was published as *World System Structure: Continuity and Change*, ed. W. Ladd Hollist and James N. Rosenau (Beverly Hills, Calif.: Sage Publications, 1981).

37. Robert Gilpin, *War and Change in World Politics* (New York: Cambridge University Press, 1981).

38. Preiswerk, "Could We Study International Relations As If People Mattered?" p. 194.

Chapter 2

1. Karl Marx, *The 18th Brumaire of Louis Napoleon*, in Lewis Feuer, ed., *Basic Writings on Politics and Philosophy: Karl Marx and Friedrich Engels* (New York: Doubleday & Co., 1959), p. 320.

2. In a major work in progress over a decade, Manfred Halpern of Princeton University offers a theory of transformation "which links the transformation of inner being, of interpersonal relations, society, and cosmos." I am grateful to him for showing me the finished portions of this work (hereafter cited as Halpern, *Transformation*).

3. Capitalizations and italics in the original. James Legge, *The Chinese Classics*, Vol. I (London: Trubner, 1861), pp. 248–49. For further analysis of the traditional Chinese image of world order, see Samuel S. Kim, *China, the United Nations, and World Order* (Princeton, N.J.: Princeton University Press, 1979), pp. 19–48.

4. This formulation of a paradigm slightly differs from that of Thomas Kuhn, who had originally defined the paradigm concept for the study of scientific revolutions. In the second edition, Kuhn defines a paradigm as follows: "On the one hand, it [paradigm] stands for the entire constellation of beliefs, values, techniques, and so on shared by the members of a given community. On the other, it denotes one sort of element in that constellation, the concrete puzzle-solutions which, employed as models or examples, can replace explicit rules as a basis for the solution of the remaining puzzles of normal science." Thomas Kuhn, *The Structure of Scientific Revolutions*, 2d ed., (Chicago: University of Chicago Press, 1970), p. 175.

5. Lewis Mumford, *The Transformation of Man* (New York: Harper & Brothers, 1956), p. 231.

6. Cyril E. Black, *The Dynamics of Modernization: A Study in Comparative History* (New York: Harper & Row, 1966), p. 7.

7. For elaboration of this thesis, see Randolph M. Siverson, "War and Change in the International System," in Holsti, Siverson, and George, *Change in the International System*, pp. 211–29; and Gilpin, *War and Change in World Politics*.

8. For a most recent and thorough development of this argument, see Theda Skocpol, *States and Social Revolutions: A Comparative Analysis of France, Russia, and China* (New York: Cambridge University Press, 1979).

9. In anthropology the nature of human evolution has generated two contending theories. The traditional theory of evolutionary gradualism—the Darwinian theory of slow, gradual development through natural selection, also referred to as the "hypothesis of phyletic gradualism"—has recently been challenged by the sudden change theory or "the model of punctuated equilibrium." The latter theory holds that most species remained basically the same for long periods of time, then suddenly experienced discontinuities caused by shifts in environmental, behavioral, and

demographic variables. These theories differ on the mode of transformation (continuous or discrete), not on the major stages and time spans of hominid evolution through the Pliocene and Pleistocene. For elaboration of this debate, see John E. Cronin et al., "Tempo and Mode in Hominid Evolution," *Nature* 292 (July 9, 1981): 113–22; Stephen Jay Gould and Niles Eldredge, "Punctuated Equilibrium: The Tempo and Mode of Evolution Reconsidered," *Paleobiology* 3 (1977): 115–51.

10. Black, *The Dynamics of Modernization*, p. 4.

11. Quoted in Edward Cornish, *The Study of the Future* (Washington, D.C.: World Future Society, 1977), p. 1.

12. For the changes in the international system, see the following: Johan Galtung, "On the Future of the International System"; Holsti, Siverson, and George, *Change in the International System*; Morton A. Kaplan, *System and Process in International Politics* (New York: John Wiley & Sons, 1957); Evan Luard, *Types of International Society* (New York: Free Press, 1976); Edward L. Morse, *Modernization and the Transformation of International Relations* (New York: Free Press, 1976); and Richard N. Rosecrance, *Action and Reaction in World Politics* (Boston: Little, Brown and Co., 1963).

13. W. Arthur Lewis, *The Theory of Economic Growth* (New York: Harper & Row, 1970), pp. 17–18.

14. Halpern, *Transformation*, pp. 184–85.

15. For a careful critique of the literature on international systems along this line, see Dina A. Zinnes, "Prerequisites for the Study of System Transformation," in Holsti, Siverson, and George, *Change in the International System*, pp. 3–21.

16. See Rosecrance, *Action and Reaction in World Politics*, and Kaplan, *System and Process in International Politics*.

17. Note, for example, Rosecrance's definition of system change: "System-change occurs when the constituents of disruption and regulation undergo major change." Rosecrance, *Action and Reaction in World Politics*, p. 231. For further elaboration, see Richard A. Falk and Samuel S. Kim, eds., *The War System: An Interdisciplinary Approach* (Boulder, Colo.: Westview Press, 1980), pp. 531–81.

18. See Holsti, Siverson, and George, *Change in the International System*; Gilpin, *War and Change in World Politics*; and in the *International Political Science Review* 1 (1980): 23–33, Karl Deutsch, "Political Research in the Changing World System"; Charles F. Doran, "Modes, Mechanisms, and Turning Points: Perspectives on the Transformation of the International System," 35–61; and Richard L. Merritt, "On the Transformation of Systems," 13–22.

19. Wallerstein, *The Capitalist World-Economy*, p. 390.

20. Gilpin, *War and Change in World Politics*, p. 93.

21. This conception differs from that of Kenneth Boulding, who views transformation (or what he calls "the great transition") as "the long, continuous, and irreversible process" concerned "primarily with human learning and the process by which knowledge is acquired." Boulding is more concerned about the holistic transformation of civilization than about the transformation of world politics. See Kenneth E. Boulding, *The Meaning of the Twentieth Century* (New York: Harper Colophon Books, 1964), p. 27.

22. Hedley Bull, *the Anarchical Society: A Study of Order in World Politics* (New York: Columbia University Press, 1977), p. 13. Emphasis in original.

23. Milton Rokeach, *The Nature of Human Values* (New York: Free Press, 1973), p. 5.

24. For further elaboration, see ibid., pp. 11–12.

25. Chalmers Johnson, *Revolutionary Change*, 2d ed. (Stanford, Calif.: Stanford University Press, 1982), p. 21.

26. Quoted in ibid.

27. Robin M. Williams, Jr. "The Concept of Values," *International Encyclopedia of the Social Sciences* (New York: Free Press, 1968), Vol. 16, p. 284.

28. See Werner Levi, "The Relative Irrelevance of Moral Norms in International Politics," *Social Forces* 44 (1965): 226–33, and idem, *International Politics: Foundations of the System* (Minneapolis, Minn.: University of Minnesota Press, 1974).

29. Talcott Parsons, "Order and Community in the International Social System," in James N. Rosenau, ed., *International Politics and Foreign Policy* (New York: Free Press, 1961), p. 120.

30. Mao Tse-tung [Mao Zedong], *On the Correct Handling of Contradictions Among the People* (Peking: Foreign Languages Press, 1966; originally published in 1957), p. 37.

31. For a detailed analysis of the (normative) rules of the game in international politics, see Raymond Cohen, *International Politics: The Rules of the Game* (New York: Longman, 1981).

32. For an elaboration of "structural power" as used here, see Johan Galtung, *The True Worlds: A Transnational Perspective* (New York: Free Press, 1980), pp. 62–63.

33. C. Wright Mills, *The Sociological Imagination* (New York: Oxford University Press, 1959), p. 150.

34. See the special issue entitled "World System Debates," *International Studies Quarterly* 25 (March 1981), ed. W. Ladd Hollist and James N. Rosenau.

35. Immanuel Wallerstein, *The Modern World System: Capitalist Agriculture and the Origins of the European World-Economy in the Sixteenth Century* (New York: Academic Press, 1974). The most problematic feature of Wallerstein's approach lies in his reductionism. In his macrostructural conceptualization of the world system, political structures and processes are viewed as epiphenomena of economic structures and processes.

36. Skocpol, *States and Social Revolutions*.

37. See Johan Galtung, "A Structural Theory of Imperialism," *Journal of Peace Research* 8 (1971): 81–117.

38. Dieter Senghaas, "Conflict Formations in Contemporary International Society," *Journal of Peace Research* 10 (1973): 163–84.

39. Helge Hveem, "The Global Dominance System," *Journal of Peace Research* 10 (1973): 319–40. Note that the articles by Galtung, Senghaas, and Hveem were all published in the *Journal of Peace Research*, a house journal of the International Peace Research Institute, Oslo, Norway. Galtung is founder of this Scandinavian school of peace research.

40. Ralph Pettman, *State and Class: A Sociology of International Affairs* (New York: St. Martin's Press, 1979).

41. For more detailed analyses of the Peace of Westphalia, see the following: William D. Coplin, "International Law and Assumptions About the State System," *World Politics* 17 (July 1965): 615–34; Richard A. Falk, "The Interplay of Westphalia and Charter Conceptions of the International Legal Order," in Richard A. Falk and Cyril E. Black, eds., *The Future of the International Legal Order, Vol 1: Trends and Patterns* (Princeton, N.J.: Princeton University Press, 1969), pp. 32–70; idem, "A New Paradigm for International Legal Studies: Prospects and Proposals," *Yale Law Journal* 84 (April 1975): 969–1021; Leo Gross, "The Peace of Westphalia, 1648–1948," in Leo Gross, ed., *International Law in the Twentieth Century* (New York: Appleton-Century-Crofts, 1969), pp. 25–46; Morse, *Modernization and the Transfor-*

mation of International Relations, pp. 22–46; Arthur Nussbaum, *A Concise History of the Law of Nations*, rev. ed. (New York: Macmillan Co., 1961), pp. 115–85.

42. Falk, "A New Paradigm for International Legal Studies," p. 987.

43. I depart here from Brierly's oft-cited definition of international law or the law of nations as "the body of rules and principles of action which are binding upon civilized states in their relations with one another" because of the problematic use of the terms "civilized" and "binding." See J. L. Brierly, *The Law of Nations*, 5th ed. (London: Oxford University Press, 1955), p. 1.

44. Luiz Alberto Bahia, "The Concept of Sovereignty as a Form of Property," *Bulletin of Peace Proposals*, 2 (1971): 87. Emphasis in original.

45. Perry Anderson, *Lineages of the Absolutist State* (New York: Humanities Press, 1974), pp. 18–20.

46. See Falk, "A New Paradigm for International Legal Studies," p. 990, and Nussbaum, *A Concise History of the Law of Nations*, p. 162.

47. Charles de Secondat Montesquieu, *The Persian Letters* (Harmondsworth, England: Penguin Books, 1973), p. 176.

48. Nussbaum, *A Concise History of the Law of Nations*, p. 128.

49. Rosecrance, *Action and Reaction in World Politics*, p. 29.

50. Walter S. Dorn, *Competition for Empire* (New York: Harper & Row, 1963), p. 1.

51. Luard, *Types of International Society*, p. 215.

52. *New Cambridge Modern History*, 6 (1970): 169–70.

53. William Penn, *Essay Towards the Present and Future Peace of Europe by the Establishment of an European Diet, Parliament, or Estates* (1693); Abbe St. Pierre, *Project for Perpetual Peace* (1712); Jean Jacques Rousseau, *Lasting Peace Through the Federation of Europe* (1761); Jeremy Bentham, *Plan for an Universal and Perpetual Peace* (between 1786 and 1789); Immanuel Kant, *Thoughts on Perpetual Peace* (1795). For details, see F. H. Hinsley, *Power and the Pursuit of Peace* (New York: Cambridge University Press, 1967), chapters 2–4, and Louis Réne Beres, *People, States, and World Order* (Itasca, Ill.: F. E. Peacock Publishers, 1981), chap. 2.

54. For elaboration of this developmental interplay between "nation" and "state," see Mostafa Rejai and Cynthia H. Enloe, "Nation-States and State-Nations," *International Studies Quarterly* 13 (September 1969): 140–58.

55. For a detailed discussion of this issue, see McDougal, Lasswell, and Chen, *Human Rights and World Public Order*, pp. 653–89.

56. For the development of international efforts to abolish slavery and the slave trade, see a memorandum submitted by the Secretary-General entitled *The Suppression of Slavery*, UN Doc. St/SOA/4(1951).

57. Bittner, *Die Lehre von den völkerrechtlichen Vertragsurkunden* (1924), p. 13, cited in Nussbaum, *A Concise History of the Law of Nations*, pp. 196–97.

58. Donald J. Puchala and Raymond F. Hopkins, "International Regimes: Lessons from Inductive Analysis," *International Organization* 36 (Spring 1982): 254. See also Carlton J. H. Hayes, *The Historical Evolution of Modern Nationalism* (New York: Macmillan, 1948), p. 252.

59. Charles W. Kegley, Jr., "Measuring Transformation in the Global Legal System," in Nicholas G. Onuf, ed., *Law-Making in the Global Community* (Durham, N. C.: Carolina Academic Press, 1982), p. 188.

60. Like the economists, the positivists in international legal studies were infatuated with the scientific materialism of the nineteenth century, seeking a rigorous systemization of procedural methodology. The positivist school, in the judgment of one noted legal scholar, "came to strengthen, usually with no political

afterthought, an intransigent conception of sovereignty at the very moment when vast upheavals called for radical revision." See Charles de Visscher, *Theory and Reality in Public International Law*, trans. P. E. Corbett (Princeton, N.J.: Princeton University Press, 1957), pp. 51–52. In a similar vein, Coplin observed: "Almost every legal aspect of international relations from 1648 to 1914 reinforced and expressed the assumptions of the state system." See Coplin, "International Law and Assumptions About the State System," p. 619.

61. J. David Singer and Melvin Small, "The Composition and Status Ordering of the International System: 1815–1940," *World Politics* 18 (January 1966): 246.

62. The text of the *Règlement*, along with that of the subsequent *Protocol*, is found in *American Journal of International Law* 52 (January 1958): 185–87. The quotation in the text appears in the preamble to the *Règlement*.

63. Carlton J.H. Hayes, *A Generation of Materialism 1871–1900* (New York: Harper, 1941), p. 236.

64. Sun Yat-sen, *San Min Chu I: The Three Principles of the People*, trans. Frank W. Price (Shanghai: Commercial Press, 1932), p. 39.

65. Luard, *Types of International Society*, p. 221.

66. John K. Fairbank, Edwin O. Reischauer, and Albert M. Craig, *East Asia: The Modern Transformation* (Boston: Houghton Mifflin Co., 1965), p. 468.

67. The structure of German domestic politics prior to World War I is instructive in this connection: "Each group in Germany had a single enemy and would have liked to make peace with the others. . . . Tirpitz and his capitalist supporters wanted a naval conflict with Great Britain and deplored the hostility to France and Russia; the professional soldiers and their capitalist supporters wanted a continental war, especially against France, and deplored the naval rivalry with Great Britain; the mass parties—the social democrats and the Roman Catholic Centre—were friendly to both Great Britain and France and could be won only for the old radical programme of war against Russia. . . . The feeble rulers of Germany, William II and Bethmann, preferred a ring of foreign enemies to trouble at home." A.J.P. Taylor, *The Struggle for Mastery in Europe, 1848–1918* (Oxford: Clarendon Press, 1954), pp. 519–20.

68. These figures are derived from ibid., p. xxviii.

69. D. K. Fieldhouse, *Economics and Empires, 1830–1914* (Ithaca, N.Y.: Cornell University Press, 1973), p. 3.

70. See Luard, *Types of International Society*, pp. 330–32.

71. Cited in Louis Réne Beres, *People, States, and World Order*, p. 19.

72. As Vyshinsky put it: "Stalin's teaching is that the withering away of the state will come not through a weakening of the state authority but through its maximum intensification, which is necessary to finish off the remnants of the dying classes and to organize defense against capitalist encirclement, which is now far from being—and will not soon be—destroyed. Every other interpretation of the withering away of the state under present conditions is merely an attempt to disarm the proletariat, to weaken the authority of the proletarian state and the dictatorship of the proletariat—an attempt to justify the counterrevolutionary theory of the extinction of the class struggle." See Andrei Y. Vyshinsky, *The Law of the Soviet State*, trans. Hugh W. Babb (New York: Macmillan, 1948), p. 62. For an analysis of Stalin's state-building process and its consequences, see Robert C. Tucker, "Swollen State, Spent Society: Stalin's Legacy to Brezhnev's Russia," *Foreign Affairs* 60 (Winter 1981/1982): 414–35.

73. Quoted in Robert H. Ferrell, *American Diplomacy* (New York: W. W. Norton, 1959), p. 315.

74. Gilpin, *War and Change in World Politics*, p. 234.

75. For details, see "International Response" in Chapter 4.

76. E. H. Carr, *The Twenty Year's Crisis 1919–1939: An Introduction to the Study of International Relations* (New York: St. Martin Press, 1958).

77. Inis L. Claude, Jr., *Swords into Plowshares*, 4th ed. (New York: Random House, 1971), p. 43. Emphasis in original.

78. Cited in Stuart R. Schram, *The Political Thought of Mao Tse-Tung* (New York: Praeger, 1963), pp. 266–67. For additional references, see Jerome Alan Cohen and Hungdah Chiu, *People's China and International Law: A Documentary Study*, 2 vols. (Princeton, N.J.: Princeton University Press, 1974).

79. Between 1946 and October 1971 (when the PRC took up the China seat) the veto record of the Big Five was as follows: 1 by China (ROC); 1 by the United States (cast in 1970); 105 by the Soviet Union; 5 by the United Kingdom; and 4 by France. Note the dramatic shift in the veto record for the period October 1971 and April 1980: 21 by the United States; 12 by the United Kingdom; 9 by the Soviet Union; 7 by France; and 2 by China (PRC). A similar pattern of voting behavior is evident in the General Assembly. For more detailed quantitative data on the voting records of the Big Five in the General Assembly and the Security Council, see my *China, the United Nations, and World Order*, pp. 124, 190–91, 475, 518–21; and "Whither Post-Mao Chinese Global Policy?" *International Organization* 35 (Summer 1981): 442.

80. For a recent study advancing this thesis in stronger terms, see Stephen D. Krasner, "Transforming International Regimes," *International Studies Quarterly* 25 (March 1981): 119–48.

81. For an excellent analysis of the law-making significance of continually recited General Assembly resolutions that include this famous decolonization resolution, see Samuel A. Bleicher, "The Legal Significance of Re-Citation of General Assembly Resolutions," *American Journal of International Law* 62 (July 1969): 444–78.

82. Ad Hoc Judge van Wyk stated in the *South West Africa* cases that "applicants' contention involved the novel proposition that the organs of the United Nations possessed some sort of legislative competence whereby they could bind a dissenting minority." "It is clear from the provisions of the Charter," he went on to say, "that no such competence exists, and in my view it would be entirely wrong to import it under the guise of a novel and untenable interpretation of Article 38(1) (b) of the Statute of this Court." See *I.C.J. Reports 1966*, p. 170. It may also be noted in this connection that a proposal by the Philippine delegation at the United Nations Conference on International Organization at San Francisco to give legislative power to the General Assembly was overwhelmingly defeated.

83. See Obed Y. Asamoah, *The Legal Significance of the Declaration of the General Assembly of the United Nations* (the Hague: Martinus Nijhoff, 1966); Bleicher, "The Legal Significance of Re-Citation of General Assembly Resolutions," pp. 444–78; Jorge Castaneda, *Legal Effects of United Nations Resolutions*, trans. Alba Amoia (New York: Columbia University Press, 1969); Ingrid Detter, *Law Making by International Organizations* (Stockholm: Norstedt, 1965); Lino Di Qual, *Les effets des resolutions des Nations-Unis* (Paris: Pichon et Durand-Auzias, 1967); Richard A. Falk, "On the Quasi-Legislative Competence of the General Assembly," *American Journal of International Law* 60 (October 1966): 782–91; Rosalyn Higgins, *The Development of International Law Through the Political Organs of the United Nations* (London: Oxford University Press, 1963); "The United Nations and Lawmaking: The Political Organs," *Proceedings of the American Society of International Law at its Sixty-Fourth Annual Meeting* 64 (September 1970): 37–48; *A Memorandum by the Office of Legal Affairs*, UN Doc. E/CN.4/L.610(1962).

84. Bleicher, "The Legal Significance of Re-Citation of General Assembly Resolutions," pp. 456, 458–65, 470–75.

85. This thesis was most cogently stated by Judge Tanaka in his dissenting opinion in the *South West Africa* cases. See *I.C.J. Reports 1966*, p. 291. An argument along the same lines has also been advanced by a prominent international scholar regarding the establishment of international environmental law. See Louis Sohn, "The Stockholm Declaration on the Human Environment," *Harvard International Law Journal* 14 (Summer 1973): 514.

86. "International Law and Just World Order: An Interview with Burns H. Weston," *Macroscope*, No. 9 (Spring 1981): 8.

87. Bruce M. Russett, *Power and Community in World Politics* (San Francisco: W. H. Freeman and Co., 1974), p. 146.

88. See David P. Rapkin, William R. Thompson, and Jon A. Christopherson, "Bipolarity and Bipolarization in the Cold War Era," *Journal of Conflict Resolution* 23 (June 1979): 261–95.

89. For my further analysis, see Kim, "Whither Post-Mao Chinese Global Policy?"

90. See Charles W. Kegley, Jr. and Eugene R. Wittkopf, *World Politics: Trend and Transformation* (New York: St. Martin's Press, 1981), p. 79; Krasner, "Transforming International Regimes," pp. 126–27.

91. See K.K.S. Dadzie, "Economic Development," *Scientific American* 243 (September 1980): 65.

92. For a superb analysis of the global dominance system employing the concept of the 'technocapital' power, see Hveem, "The Global Dominance System." In a macrostructural analysis, Gernot Kohler has argued that "global apartheid" has become more unjust in terms of distribution of status, influence, power, and incidence of structural violence than the universally delegitimized system of South African apartheid. See his "Global Apartheid," *Alternatives* 4 (October 1978): 263–75.

93. Alex Inkeles, "The Emerging Social Structure of the World," *World Politics* 27 (July 1975): 479.

94. Of some 160 disputes having a significant likelihood of resulting in large-scale violence within fifteen years, a 1969 research team has concluded, nationalist and ethnic conflict accounted for about 70 percent of the cases. See Steven Rosen, ed., *A Survey of World Conflicts* (Pittsburgh, Pa.: University of Pittsburgh Center for International Studies Preliminary Paper, March 1969). For careful analyses of fragmentation as a dominant feature of global society, see K. J. Holsti, "Change in the International System: Interdependence, Integration, and Fragmentation," in Holsti, Siverson, and George, *Change in the International System*, pp. 23–53, and Arnfinn Jorgensen-Dahl, "Forces of Fragmentation in the International System: The Case of Ethno-nationalism," *Orbis* 19 (Summer 1975): 652–74.

95. Quoted in the *New York Times*, April 28, 1981, p. A10. Emphasis added.

96. Melvin Small and J. David Singer, "Patterns in International Warfare, 1816–1965," in Falk and Kim, *The War System*, p. 557.

97. Kegley, "Measuring Transformation in the Global Legal System," p. 205. For a similar argument about "the extended time-lag between past rule and present reality," see Wesley L. Gould and Michael Barkun, *International Law and the Social Sciences* (Princeton, N.J.: Princeton University Press, 1970), p. 183.

98. John H. Herz, "Rise and Demise of the Territorial State," *World Politics* 9 (July 1957): 489. Herz repeated this pronouncement of the demise of the territorial state in *International Politics in the Atomic Age* (New York: Columbia University Press, 1959), p. 107, but retracted it in "The Territorial State Revisited: Reflections on the Future of the Nation-State," *Policy* 1, No. 1(1968): 12–34.

99. Charles Kindleberger, *American Business Abroad* (New Haven: Yale University Press, 1969), p. 207.

100. For the nonstate actors approach to global politics described here, see Richard W. Mansbach, Yale H. Ferguson, and Donald E. Lampert, *The Web of World Politics: Nonstate Actors in the Global System* (Englewood Cliffs, N.J.: Prentice-Hall, 1976), and Richard W. Mansbach and John A. Vasquez, *In Search of Theory: A New Paradigm for Global Politics* (New York: Columbia University Press, 1981). The quoted passage in the text is found in Mansbach and Vasquez, *In Search of Theory*, p. 8.

101. For an elaboration of "world order realism" on the status of the state, see Falk, Kim, and Mendlovitz, *Toward a Just World Order*, pp. 55–59.

102. Compare the Common Heritage of Mankind Declaration—General Assembly 2749 (XXV) of December 17, 1970—and the text of the *United Nations Convention on the Law of the Sea*, UN Doc. A/CONF.62/122 (October 7, 1982).

103. For elaboration of this point, see J. David Singer and Michael Wallace, "Intergovernmental Organization and the Preservation of Peace, 1916–1964: Some Bivariate Relationships," *International Organization* 24 (Summer 1970): 520–47.

104. Martin Wight, "Why Is There No International Theory?" in Herbert Butterfield and Martin Wight, eds., *Diplomatic Investigations* (Cambridge, Mass.: Harvard University Press, 1968), p. 21.

105. A.F.K. Organski and Jacek Kugler, "Davids and Goliaths: Predicting the Outcomes of International Wars," *Comparative Political Studies* 11 (July 1978): 145.

106. *The New York Times*, March 13, 1983, p. 8.

Chapter 3

1. For a trenchant critique of "compulsive and mindless theorizing" in social science research, see Albert O. Hirschman, "The Search for Paradigms As a Hindrance to Understanding," *World Politics* 22 (April 1970): 329–43. For the wide gap between theory-building and policy-making, see Raymond Tanter and Richard H. Ullman, eds., *Theory and Policy in International Relations*, supplement, *World Politics* 24 (Spring 1972).

2. The seven contributors to the volume are Paul H. Nitze, Hans J. Morgenthau, William T. R. Fox, Kenneth N. Waltz, Charles P. Kindleberger, Arnold Wolfers, and Reinhold Niebuhr. The quote in the text appears in William T. R. Fox, ed., *Theoretical Aspects of International Relations* (Notre Dame, Ind.: University of Notre Dame Press, 1959), p. ix.

3. Both Dahl and Easton's "declarations" were issued during their presidential addresses at an annual meeting of the American Political Science Association and later published in the *American Political Science Review*. See Robert A. Dahl, "The Behavioral Approach in Political Science: Epitaph for a Monument to a Successful Protest," *American Political Science Review* 55 (December 1961): 763–72, and David Easton, "The New Revolution in Political Science," *American Political Science Review* 63 (December 1969): 1051–61.

4. Stanley J. Michalak, Jr., "Theoretical Perspectives for Understanding International Interdependence," *World Politics* 32 (October 1979): 150.

5. Stanley Hoffman, "An American Social Science: International Relations," *Daedalus* 106, No. 3 (Summer 1977): 51.

6. Rosenau, "Muddling, Meddling, and Modelling," p. 130.

7. See Morton A. Kaplan, *Towards Professionalism in International Theory: Macro-system Analysis* (New York: Free Press, 1979), and Kenneth N. Waltz, *Theory of International Politics*.

8. Short excerpts of the reviews by Kissinger, Hoffmann, and Morgenthau appear on the back of the book jacket. For Bull's review, see *Survival* 9, No. 11 (November 1967): 371.

9. Oran R. Young responded with a thoroughgoing and devastating critique of the book as "essentially a failure from the perspective of the criteria of theory." See his "Aron and the Whale: A Jonah in Theory," in Klaus Knorr and James N. Rosenau, eds., *Contending Approaches in International Politics* (Princeton, N.J.: Princeton University Press, 1969), p. 130.

10. This judgment is based on an unscientific sample of seven important recent works on international relations, divided as follows: two leading international relations texts; three trailblazing international relations monographs; one anthology with contributions from many leading scholars; and one special issue of *International Studies Quarterly* (the official journal of the International Studies Association) devoted exclusively to "world system debates." I have excluded the "world order literature" to minimize my own intellectual and normative biases. In none of the seven above-mentioned works is Aron's *Peace and War* ever cited or referred to. See K. J. Holsti, *International Politics: A Framework for Analysis*, 3d ed., (Englewood Cliffs, N.J.: Prentice-Hall, 1977); Kegley and Wittkopf, *World Politics*; Robert Jervis, *Perception and Misperception in International Politics* (Princeton, N.J.: Princeton University Press, 1976); Robert Keohane and Joseph S. Nye, *Power and Interdependence: World Politics in Transition* (Boston: Little Brown and Co., 1977); Glenn H. Snyder and Paul Diesing, *Conflict Among Nations* (Princeton, N.J.: Princeton University Press, 1977); Holsti, Siverson, and George, *Change in the International System*; and Hollist and Rosenau, *World System Debates*, a special issue of *International Studies Quarterly* 25 (March 1981).

11. Quoted in Abdul A. Said, ed., *Theory of International Relations: The Crisis of Relevance* (Englewood Cliffs, N.J.: Prentice-Hall, 1968), p. 1.

12. For further discussion on the instrumental view of a theory, see Fred M. Frohock, *the Nature of Political Inquiry* (Homewood, Ill.: Dorsey Press, 1967), pp. 7–10, and Alan C. Isaak, *Scope and Methods of Political Science* (Homewood, Ill.: Dorsey Press, 1969), pp. 140–41.

13. See Young, "Aron and the Whale," p. 135.

14. Kuhn, *The Structure of Scientific Revolutions*, p. 15.

15. See "Guiding Principle for Knowing and Changing the World—A Study of 'On Practice,'" *Peking Review*, No. 25 (June 18, 1971): 6–10.

16. *Selected Works of Mao Tse-tung*, Vol. 1 (Peking: Foreign Languages Press, 1965), p. 304. For further analysis of Mao's epistemology, see Kim, *China, the United Nations and World Order*, pp. 51–58.

17. Morgenthau, *Politics Among Nations*, p. 4.

18. Gilpin, *War and Change in World Politics*, p. 230.

19. Anatol Rapoport, "Various Meanings of 'Theory'" *American Political Science Review* 52 (December 1958): 982.

20. See Robert Keohane, "International Organization and the Crisis of Interdependence," *International Organization* 29 (Spring 1975): 357–65.

21. George Modelski, "The Long Cycle of Global Politics and the Nation-State," *Comparative Studies in Society and History* 20 (April 1978): 224.

22. "Address by President Carter to People of Other Nations," *Department of State Bulletin* 76 (February 14, 1977): 123.

23. For a criticism of world order studies along this line and my rebuttal, see the *Journal of Political and Military Sociology* 9 (Spring 1981): Guy Oakes and Kenneth Stunkel, "In Search of WOMP," pp. 83–99, and Samuel S. Kim, "The World Order Models Project and Its Strange Critics," pp. 109–15.

24. For typology and analysis along these lines, see Richard A. Falk, "Contending Approaches to World Order," in Falk, Kim, and Mendlovitz, *Toward a Just World Order*, pp. 146–74, and Antony J. Dolman, *Resources, Regimes, World Order* (New York: Pergamon Press, 1981), pp. 49–60. My analysis here draws upon, yet alters, these two studies.

25. See Holly Sklar, ed., *Trilateralism: The Trilateral and Elite Planning for World Management* (Boston: South End Press, 1980).

26. Daniel Bell, "The Future World Disorder: The Strutural Context of Crises," *Foreign Policy*, No. 27 (Summer 1977): 134. Emphasis added.

27. Bull, *The Anarchical Society*, pp. 86, 96–97, and "The State's Positive Role in World Affairs," *Daedalus* 108 (Fall 1979): 111–23.

28. Stanley Hoffmann, *Duties Beyond Borders: On the Limits and Possibilities of Ethical International Politics* (Syracuse, N.Y.: Syracuse University Press, 1981), pp. 191, 194.

29. See Stanley Hoffmann, "Muscle and Brains," *Foreign Policy*, No. 37 (Winter 1979–1980): 3–27, and *Duties Beyond Borders*, p. 193.

30. Karl Kaiser, et al., *Western Security: What Has Changed? What Should Be Done?*, A report prepared by the directors of Forschungsinstitut der Deutschen Gessellschaft für Auswartige Politik (Bonn), Council on Foreign Relations (New York), Institut Francais des Relations Internationales (Paris), and Royal Institute of International Affairs (London) (New York: Council on Foreign Relations, 1981), p. 11.

31. World Bank, *World Development Report 1981* (New York: Oxford University Press for the World Bank, 1981), p. 165.

32. See Jan Tinbergen (coordinator), *RIO: Reshaping the International Order*, a report to the Club of Rome (New York: E. P. Dutton & Co., 1976), and *North-South: A Program for Survival*, Report of the Independent Commission on International Development Issues under the Chairmanship of Willy Brandt (Cambridge, Mass.: MIT Press, 1980).

33. Ernst B. Haas, Mary Pat Williams, and Don Babai, *Scientists and World Order: The Uses of Technical Knowledge in International Organizations* (Berkeley, Calif.: University of California Press, 1977), p. 355.

34. See chapter 3 in ibid., pp. 36–57.

35. Keohane and Nye, *Power and Interdependence*, p. 242.

36. Tucker, "Swollen State, Spent,"p. 430.

37. Paul M. Sweezy, "A Crisis in Marxian Theory," *Monthly Review* 31 (June 1979): 23.

38. See Wallerstein, *The Capitalist World-Economy*, pp. 35–36.

39. Immanuel Wallerstein, "Friends and Foes," *Foreign Policy* No. 40 (Fall 1980): 119–31.

40. Kenneth N. Waltz, *Man, the State and War: A Theoretical Analysis* (New York: Columbia University Press, 1959), pp. 3, 21–28.

41. See Arnold Wolfers, *Discord and Collaboration* (Baltimore, Md.: Johns Hopkins University Press, 1962), pp. 83–84.

42. *Selected Works of Mao Tse-tung*, Vol. 1, p. 313.

43. Gould, *the Mismeasure of Man*, p. 21.

44. For my detailed critique along these lines, see Samuel S. Kim, "The Lorenzian Theory of Aggression and Peace Research: A Critque," *Journal of Peace Research* 13, No. 4 (1976): 253–76.

45. Edward O. Wilson, *Sociobiology* (Cambridge, Mass.: Harvard University Press, 1975), and *On Human Nature* (Cambridge, Mass.: Harvard University Press, 1978).

46. Wilson, *On Human Nature*, p. 99.

47. Gould, *The Mismeasure of Man*, pp. 330-31.

48. For a detailed analysis, see Merle Curti, *Human Nature in American Thought: A History* (Madison, Wis.: University of Wisconsin Press, 1980).

49. Cited in the *New York Times*, June 22, 1982, p. C2.

50. For details, see Gould, *The Mismeasure of Man*, pp. 192-233.

51. See Arthur R. Jensen, "How Much Can We Boost IQ and Scholastic Achievement?" *Harvard Educational Review* 39 (Winter 1969): 1-123, and Richard Herrnstein, "IQ," *Atlantic Monthly* (September 1971): 43-64.

52. D. D. Dorfman, "The Cyril Burt Question: New Findings," *Science* 201 (September 29, 1978): 1177-86; Gould, *The Mismeasure of Men*, pp. 234-320; Leon Kamin, *The Science and Politics of IQ* (Potomac, Md.: Lawrence Erlbaum Associates, 1974); and Peter Willmott, "Integrity in Social Science—the Upshot of a Scandal," *International Social Science Journal* 29 (1977): 333-36.

53. *New York Times*, May 25, 1982, p. A22; Laurie P. Cohen, "The Chinese: A Way with Mathematics," *New York Times* Section XII, January 9, 1983, p. 24.

54. For Ted Gurr, *Why Men Rebel* (Princeton, N.J.: Princeton University Press, 1970), and Ivo K. Feierabend and Rosalind L. Feierabend, "Aggressive Behaviors Within Politics, 1948-1962: A Cross-National Study," *Journal of Conflict Resolution* 10 (September 1966): 249-71.

55. John Dollard et al, *Frustration and Aggression* (New Haven: Yale University Press, 1939), p. 1.

56. Ibid., p. 25.

57. See Leonard Berkowitz, *Aggression: A Social Psychological Analysis* (New York: McGraw-Hill, 1962).

58. E.F.M. Durbin and John Bowlby, "Personal Aggressiveness and War," in Leon Bramson and George W. Goethals, eds., *War: Studies from Psychology, Sociology, Anthropology*, rev. ed. (New York: Basic Books, 1968), pp. 81-103.

59. See Albert Bandura, *Aggression: A Social Analysis* (Englewood Cliffs, N.J.: Prentice-Hall, 1973).

60. Bernard Berelson and Gary A. Steiner, *Human Behavior*, shorter ed. (New York: Harcourt, Brace & World, 1967), p. 199.

61. *Selected Works of Mao Tse-tung*, Vol. 1, p. 317. Emphasis added.

62. Abraham H. Maslow, "A Theory of Human Motivation," *Psychological Review* 50 (1943): 370-96; idem, *Toward a Psychology of Being* (Princeton, N.J.: D. Van Nostrand Co., 1962); and John McHale and Magda Cordell McHale, *Basic Human Needs: A Framework for Action* (New Brunswick, N.J.: Transaction Books, 1978).

63. Wallerstein, *The Capitalist World-Economy*, p. xi.

64. Meehan, *Value Judgment and Social Science*, p. 28.

65. For a lucid theoretical exposition of the actor-oriented and structure-oriented perspectives in world order studies, see Galtung, *The True Worlds*, pp. 41-79.

66. For a cogent analysis of three "traditional" theories of world order in terms of balance of power, collective security, and world government, see Inis L. Claude, Jr., *Power and International Relations* (New York: Random House, 1962), pp. 272-78.

67. Saul Mendlovitz, "On the Creation of a Just World Order: An Agenda for a Program of Inquiry and Praxis," *Alternatives* 7 (1981): 355-73.

68. Mendlovitz, *On the Creation of a Just World Order*, p. xiii.

69. See Eqbal Ahmad, "The Neo-Fascist State: Notes on the Pathology of Power in the Third World," in Falk, Kim, and Mendlovitz, *Toward a Just World Order*, pp. 74-83.

70. Rapoport, *Strategy and Conscience*, p. 30.

71. Kenneth E. Boulding, *The Image* (Ann Arbor: University of Michigan Press, 1956), pp. 6, 11.

72. Amilcar O. Herrerra et al., *Catastrophe or New Society? A Latin American World Model* (Ottawa, Canada: International Development Research Centre, 1976).

73. Fouad Ajami, "World Order: The Question of Ideology," *Alternatives* 6 (Winter 1980-1981): 483.

74. Harold D. Lasswell, "The Promise of the World Order Modelling Movement," *World Politics* 29 (April 1977): 427.

75. Grenville Clark and Louis Sohn, *World Peace Through World Law*, 3d ed. (Cambridge, Mass.: Harvard University Press, 1966).

76. See Richard A. Falk and Saul H. Mendlovitz, eds., *The Strategy of World Order*, Vol. 1: *Toward a Theory of War Prevention*; Vol. 2: *International Law*; Vol. 3: *The United Nations*; and Vol. 4: *Disarmament and Economic Development* (New York: World Law Fund, 1966).

77. Falk and Mendlovitz, *Toward a Theory of War Prevention*, p. vii.

78. Ajami, "World Order," p. 474.

79. In chronological order, the six books in the series are Rajni Kothari, *Footsteps into the Future: Diagnosis of the Present World and a Design for an Alternative* (New York: Free Press, 1974); Richard A. Falk, *A Study of Future Worlds* (New York: Free Press, 1975); Mendlovitz, *On the Creation of a Just World Order*; Ali A. Mazrui, *A World Federation of Cultures: An African Perspective* (New York: Free Press, 1976); Gustavo Lagos and Horacio H. Godoy, *Revolution of Being: A Latin American View of the Future* (New York: Free Press, 1977); and Galtung, *The True Worlds*.

80. For a comprehensive bibliography on the debates on WOMP, see Falk and Kim, *An Approach to World Order and the World System*.

81. Rajni Kothari, *Toward a Just World*, WOMP Working Paper No. 1 (New York: Institute for World Order, 1980).

82. See Falk, Kim, and Mendlovitz, *Studies on a Just World Order*, Vol 1: *Toward a Just World Order*; Richard A. Falk, Friedrich Kratochwil, and Saul H. Mendlovitz, eds., *Studies on a Just World Order*, Vol. 2: *International Law and a Just World Order* (Boulder, Colo.: Westview Press, 1983); and Richard A. Falk, Samuel S. Kim, and Saul H. Mendlovitz, eds., *Studies on a Just World Order*, Vol. 3: *The United Nations and a Just World Order* (Boulder, Colo.: Westview Press, forthcoming).

83. For a more comprehensive, though somewhat different, formulation of the cutting edge of world order inquiry, see Mendlovitz, "On the Creation of a Just World Order."

84. See Richard A. Falk, "On Invisible Oppression and World Order," in Falk, Kim, and Mendlovitz, *Toward a Just World Order*, pp. 43-46.

85. Harry R. Targ, "World Order and Futures Studies Reconsidered," *Alternatives* 5 (November 1979): 371, 381.

86. For further discussion about the linkage between regime research and world order studies, see Dolman, *Resources, Regimes, World Order*; and Samuel S. Kim, "International Regimes and World Order" (A paper presented at the 1981 International Studies Association Convention, Philadelphia, Pa., March 17-21, 1981).

87. Richard C. Snyder, Charles F. Hermann, and Harold D. Lasswell, "A Global Monitoring System: Appraising the Effects of Government on Human Dignity." *International Studies Quarterly* 20 (June 1976): 221-60.

88. See Kim, *China, the United Nations, and World Order*; Johansen, *The National Interest and the Human Interest: An Analysis of U.S. Foreign Policy*: (Princeton, N.J.:

Princeton University Press, 1980); and Richard A. Falk, ed., special issue on the World Order Models Project, *International Interactions* 8, Nos. 1–2 (1981).

89. For analysis of post-Mao Chinese foreign policy along these lines, see my "Whither Post-Mao Chinese Global Policy?" and "Normative Foreign Policy: The Chinese Case," *International Interactions* 8, Nos. 1–2 (1981): 51–77.

90. For the early results of transnational collaboration, see Richard A. Falk and Yoshikazu Sakamoto, eds., *Demilitarization I*, special issue, *Alternatives* 6 (March 1980) and *Demilitarization II*, special issue, *Alternatives* 6 (July 1980).

91. See Richard A. Falk, *Toward Security for the People*, World Policy Paper No. 26, (New York: World Policy Institute, 1983).

92. For various perspectives on the cultural frontier of world order, see Johan Galtung, "Western Civilization: Anatomy and Pathology," *Alternatives* 7 (Fall 1981): 145–69; Ali A. Mazrui, "The Moving Cultural Frontier of World Order: From Monotheism to North-South Relations," *Alternatives* 7 (Summer 1981): 1–20, and *A World Federation of Cultures*; and R.B.J. Walker, *Political Theory and the Transformation of World Politics*, World Order Studies Program Occasional Paper No. 8 (Princeton, N.J.: Center of International Studies, Princeton University, 1980), and "World Politics and Western Reason: Universalism, Pluralism, Hegemony," *Alternatives* 7 (Fall 1981): 195–227.

Chapter 4

1. In a narrow sense, epidemiology is a branch of medicine that investigates epidemic diseases. In a broad social science sense, it is "a branch of ecology that includes both the sum of what is known concerning the differential distribution of disease throughout a population and the techniques for collecting and analyzing data dealing with the prevalence and incidence of disease among different social groups." See Edward A. Suchman, "Epidemiology," in *International Encyclopedia of the Social Sciences*, Vol. 5 (New York: Free Press, 1968), p. 97. Francis A. Beer accepts this broad definition of epidemiology and applies an epidemiological model in his study of war and peace. See his "The Epidemiology of Peace and War," *International Studies Quarterly* 23 (March 1979): 45–86 and *Peace against War: The Ecology of International Violence* (San Francisco: W. H. Freeman and Co., 1981), chap. 1.

2. This definition is embodied in the preamble of the WHO Constitution. For complete text of the constitution, see *A Comprehensive Handbook of the United Nations*, Vol. 2, compiled and edited by Min-chaun Ku (New York: Monarch Press, 1979), pp. 96–108; quote on p. 96.

3. See WHO, *Global Strategy for Health for All by the Year 2000*, A34/5 Add. 1 (March 1981).

4. General Assembly Resolution 33/73 (December 15, 1978). Emphasis added.

5. See J. David Singer and Melvin Small, *The Wages of War 1816–1965: A Statistical Handbook* (New York: John Wiley & Sons, 1972).

6. The principal sources of empirical data and figures for global militarization are Stockholm International Peace Research Institute: *World Armaments and Disarmament: SIPRI Yearbook 1981* (Cambridge, Mass.: Oelgeschlager, Gunn & Hain, 1981) [hereafter cited as *SIPRI Yearbook 1981*], and *World Armaments and Disarmament: SIPRI Yearbook 1982* (London: Taylor & Francis, 1982) [hereafter cited as *SIPRI Yearbook 1982*]; Ruth Legar Sivard, *World Military and Social Expenditures 1981* (Leesburg, Va.: World Priorities, 1981) and *World Military and Social Expenditures 1982* (Leesburg, Va.: World Priorities, 1982).

7. For an elaboration of this argument, see the following: Stanley Diamond, *In Search of the Primitive* (New Brunswick, N.J.: Transaction Books, 1974); Marvin Harris, *Cannibals and Kings: the Origins of Cultures* (New York: Random House, 1977); Morton Fried, *The Evolution of Political Society* (New York: Random House, 1967); and Falk and Kim, *The War System*, pp. 159–226

8. Yoshikazu Sakamoto and Richard Falk, "World Demilitarized: A Basic Human Need," *Alternatives* 6 (March 1980): 4.

9. *SIPRI Yearbook 1981*, p. 41.

10. Leslie H. Gelb and Richard K. Betts, *The Irony of Vietnam: The System Worked* (Washington, D.C.: Brookings Institution, 1979), p. 2. Emphasis in original.

11. Zbigniew Brzezinski in an interview with Jonathan Power, *International Herald Tribune*, October 10, 1977, cited in Marek Thee, "The Arms Race, Armaments Dynamics, Military Research and Development, and Disarmament," *Bulletin of Peace Proposals* 9, No. 2 (1978): 109.

12. See Richard Halloran, "Pentagon Draws Up First Strategy for Fighting a Long Nuclear War," *New York Times*, May 30, 1982, pp. 1, 12. For Secretary of Defense Caspar W. Weinberger's acknowledgment, see the *New York Times*, June 4, 1982, p. A10.

13. B. Lambeth, "Selective Nuclear Operations and Soviet Strategy," in J. F. Holst and U. Nerlich, eds., *Beyond Nuclear Deterrence: New Aims, New Arms* (New York: Crane, Russak & CO., 1977), p. 87.

14. Cited in the *New York Times*, January 18, 1982, p. A3.

15. See Galtung, *The True Worlds*, Figure 1.6, p. 9.

16. Sivard, *World Military and Social Expenditures 1981*, p. 5.

17. See ibid., p. 7.

18. Peter Lock, "Armament Dynamics: An Issue in Development Strategies," *Alternatives* 6 (July 1980): 163.

19. Barry M. Blechman and Stephen S. Kaplan, *Force Without War: U.S. Armed Forces As a Political Instrument* (Washington, D.C.: Brookings Institution, 1978), pp. 522–23.

20. See Steve Chan, "The Consequences of Expensive Oil on Arms Transfers," *Journal of Peace Research* 17, No. 3 (1980): 235–46.

21. See Helge Hveem, "Militarization of Nature: Conflict and Control over Strategic Resources and Some Implications for Peace Policies," *Journal of Peace Research* 16, No. 1 (1979): 1–26.

22. A booklet entitled *Protection in the Nuclear Age*, produced by the Defense Civil Preparedness Agency of the U.S. Department of Defense, H-20 (February 1977), for example, provides a set of instructions and a checklist for supplies that citizens would need if nuclear war breaks out and cautions: "If you get caught in a traffic jam, turn off your engine, remain in your car, listen for official instructions, and be patient. Do not get out of the line to find an alternative route. All routes will be crowded." For further discussion on this point, see Louis René Beres, *Apocalypse: Nuclear Catastrophe in World Politics* (Chicago: University of Chicago Press, 1980), pp. 130–34.

23. See U.S. Arms Control and Disarmament Agency, *Worldwide Effects of Nuclear War . . . Some Perspectives* (Washington, D.C.: Arms Control and Disarmament Agency, 1975), pp. 4–5.

24. See *Long-Term Worldwide Effects of Multiple Nuclear-Weapons Detonations* (Washington, D.C.: National Academy of Sciences, 1975); and a Federation of American Scientists press release in *Bulletin of Peace Proposals* 7, No. 1 (1976): 50.

25. Quincy Wright, *A Study of War*, 2d ed. (Chicago: University of Chicago Press, 1965), p. 246.

26. See Beer, *Peace Against War*, pp. 34–38.

27. Robert Jay Lifton, *Death in Life: Survivors of Hiroshima* (New York: Vintage, 1967), p. 21. Emphasis in original.

28. The Committee for the Compilation of Materials on Damage Caused by the Atomic Bombs in Hiroshima and Nagasaki, *Hiroshima and Nagasaki: The Physical, Medical, and Social Effects of the Atomic Bombings*, trans. Eisei Ishikawa and David L. Swain (New York: Basic Books, 1981), pp. 113–14.

29. *Worldwide Effects of Nuclear War*, p. 14.

30. This issue, along with various studies and projections of the probability of nuclear war in the future, will be discussed in Chapter 8.

31. For further analysis of several paths to nuclear catastrophe, see Beres, *Apocalypse*, chapters 1–3.

32. United Nations, *Comprehensive Study on Nuclear Weapons*, UN Doc. A/35/392 (September 12, 1980), p. 91.

33. Sivard, *World Military and Social Expenditures 1982*, p. 15.

34. For different estimates, see Robert Woito, ed., *World Disarmament Kit* (Chicago: World Without War Publications, 1977), p. 12, and *La Lucarne* (Brussels) (October 1981), p. 2.

35. Istvan Kende, "Dynamics of Wars, of Arms Trade and of Military Expenditure in the 'Third World,' 1945–1976," *Instant Research on Peace and Violence* 7, No. 2 (Helsinki, 1977): 60.

36. Sivard, *World Military and Social Expenditures 1982*, p. 15.

37. Norman Alcock, "Peace, Justice, and Prosperity: Proposal for a Linkage Between Disarmament and Development," *Bulletin of Peace Proposals* 8, No. 4 (1977): 340. For an earlier statistical analysis from which this annual estimate of deaths resulting from structural violence is drawn, see Gernot Kohler and Norman Alcock, 'Empirical Table of Structural Violence," *Journal of Peace Research* 13, No. 4 (1976): 343–56.

38. Quoted in the *New York Times*, January 3, 1983, p. A3.

39. United Nations, *Study on the Relationship Between Disarmament and Development*, Report of the Secretary-General, UN Doc. A/36/356 (October 5, 1981), pp. 81, 92.

40. See Sivard, *World Military and Social Expenditures 1981*, p. 19 and *World Military and Social Expenditures 1982*, p. 23; and Hikaru Kerns, "Japan Wins–By a Mile," *Far Eastern Economic Review* (December 4, 1981): 97–98.

41. UN, *Study on the Relationship Between Disarmament and Development*, p. 90.

42. United Nations, *Economic and Social Consequences of the Arms Race and of Military Expenditures* Sales No. E.78.IX.1 (New York: United Nations, 1978), p. 45. In the House of Representatives debate on additional funding for the Clinch River breeder reactor in Oak Ridge, Tenn., to cite a more recent example, Representative Parren J. Mitchell observed that "if the breeder wound up costing $8.5 billion, and if it produced 8,000 jobs as the Administration has said, the Government would be spending $1 million to create one job." Following the debate the House voted for the first time to hold up additional funds for the reactor. See the *New York Times*, December 15, 1982, p. A28.

43. See UN, *Study on the Relationship Between Disarmament and Development*, pp. 47–50.

44. Mary Kaldor, *European Defense Industries—National and International Implications*, Monographs of the Institute for the Study of International Organization, first series, No. 8 (Brighton, England: University of Sussex, 1972), p. 9.

45. UN, *Report on the World Social Situation*, p. 195.

46. UN, *Economic and Social Consequences*, p. 27.

47. See UN, *Disarmament and Development*, ST/ECA/174, Sales No. E73.IX.1 (1973), pp. 33–37.

48. UN, *Economic and Social Consequences*, p. 31.

49. UNCTAD, *Trade and Development Report, 1982* (New York: United Nations, 1982), p. 118.

50. For an elaboration of this argument, see Lock, "Armaments Dynamics," pp. 157–78.

51. Michael Klare, *Supplying Repression: US Support for Authoritarian Regimes Abroad* (Washington, D.C.: Institute for Policy Studies, 1977), p. 8.

52. See Robin Luckham, "Armaments, Underdevelopment and Demilitarization in Africa," *Alternatives* 6 (July 1980): 179–245; quote on p. 243.

53. United Nations, *The State of the Environment: Selected Topics—1980*, UNEP/GC.8/3 (February 19, 1980), p. 34.

54. Ibid., p. 37.

55. See UN, *The United Nations Disarmament Yearbook*, Vol. 4: 1979 (New York: United Nations, 1980), p. 409.

56. UN, *Chemical and Bateriological (Biological) Weapons and the Effects of Their Possible Use* (New York: United Nations, 1969), p. 72.

57. See Arthur H. Westing, *Ecological Consequences of the Second Indo-China War* (Stockholm: Almqvist and Wiksell, 1976).

58. W. G. Magnuson, ed., *Weather Modification*, U.S. Senate, Committee on Commerce (Washington, D.C.: Government Printing Office, 1966), p. 33.

59. See SIPRI, *Weapons of Mass Destruction and the Environment* (London: Taylor & Francis, 1977), pp. 55–56.

60. Ibid., p. 59.

61. U.S. Arms Control and Disarmament Agency, *Worldwide Effects of Nuclear War*, p. 24.

62. In the wake of the controversy generated by the NAS study, another assessment was made by the Office of Technology Assessment in response to a request from the Senate Foreign Relations Committee. This study presents a much more sobering and realistic assessment of the effects of nuclear war. See U.S. Congress, Office of Technology Assessment, *The Effects of Nuclear War* (Washington, D.C.: Government Printing Office, 1979).

63. Stephen D. Krasner, "Structural Causes and Regime Consequences: Regimes as Intervening Variables," in Stephen D. Krasner, ed., *International Regimes, International Organization* 36, special issue (Spring 1982): 185.

64. Regime research is still largely confined to the global economic system, abandoning the dynamics of global militarization to military/strategic studies or peace/conflict resolution studies. A few exceptions where the concept of regime is included in the analysis of armament dynamics are: David C. Gompert et al., *Nuclear Weapons and World Politics: Alternatives for the Future* (New York: McGraw-Hill, Book Co. 1977); George H. Quester, ed., *Nuclear Proliferation: Breaking the Chain, International Organization* 35, special issue (Winter 1981).

65. Sivard, *World Military and Social Expenditures 1981*, p. 9.

66. See Robert C. Johansen, *Jimmy Carter's National Security Policy: A World Order Critique*, WOMP Working Paper No. 14 (New York: Institute for World Order, 1980), p. 18.

67. For further discussion of CAT talks, see Andrew J. Pierre, *The Global Politics of Arms Sales* (Princeton, N.J.: Princeton University Press, 1982), pp. 285–90.

68. For documentary references, see UN Docs. A/9669 (September 12, 1974); A/9669/Add. 1 (November 19, 1974); A/10195 (September 5, 1975); A/31/163 (August 18, 1976); A/31/163/Add. 1 (September 24, 1976); A/32/144 (August 15, 1977); and A/32/144/Add. 1 (September 26, 1977). For further discussion and analysis, see Richard R. Baxter, "Humanitarian Law or Humanitarian Politics? The 1974 Diplomatic Conference on Humanitarian Law," *Harvard International Law Journal* 16 (Winter 1975): 1–26; David P. Forsythe, "The 1974 Diplomatic Conference on Humanitarian Law: Some Observations," *American Journal of International Law* 69 (January 1975): 77–91; David Forsythe, "Three Sessions of Legislating Humanitarian Law: Forward March, Retreat, or Parade Rest?" *International Lawyer* 11 (Winter 1977): 131–42.

69. For details, see UN Doc. A/36/406 (September 9, 1981).

70. See UN Doc. A/C.1/33/PV.53 (November 29, 1978), pp. 36–38.

71. See Sivard, *World Military and Social Expenditures 1981*, pp. 15, 40–41, and *World Military and Social Expenditures 1982*, pp. 11, 42.

72. A careful and detailed analysis of the Soviet-American outer space arms race is contained in Mark C. Hallam, "The Arms Race in Outer Space," (A senior thesis presented to the Faculty of the Woodrow Wilson School of Public and International Affairs, Princeton University, April 16, 1981, 94 pp.). For the text of the Outer Space Treaty with a list of signatory states, see U.S. Arms Control and Disarmament Agency, *Arms Control and Disarmament Agreements: Texts and Histories of Negotiations* (Washington, D.C.: Arms Control and Disarmament Agency, 1982), pp. 51–58. For summary of various military uses of outer space, see *SIPRI Yearbook 1982*, pp. 291–316.

73. Cited in the *New York Times*, June 22, 1982, p. A19.

74. For a careful analysis along this line, see Robert C. Johansen, "SALT II: Illusion and Reality," *Alternatives* 5 (June 1979): 43–58.

75. General Assembly Official Records (GAOR), 22d Sess., First Committee, 1556th meeting (April 26, 1968), p. 11; see also GAOR, 22d Sess., First Committee, 1571st meeting (May 20, 1968), p. 3.

76. GAOR, 22d Sess., First Committee, 1556th meeting (April 26, 1968), p. 7.

77. For a list of signatory and nonsignatory states to the NPT, see *Disarmament Times*, August 21, 1980, p. 3.

78. *New York Times* editorial, June 9, 1981, p. A14.

79. *New York Times*, May 2, 1981, p. 2; see also November 6, 1977.

80. For details, see the *New York Times*, November 1, 1981, p. 14; September 25, 1982, pp. 1, 8; and November 17, 1982, p. A3.

81. Robert F. Goheen, "Problems of Proliferation: U.S. Policy and the Third World," *World Politics* 35 (January 1983): 200.

82. *New York Times*, February 21, 1983, p. A4.

83. See the testimony by two State Department officials before the Subcommittee on Asian and Pacific Affairs of the House Foreign Affairs Committee to this effect, in the *New York Times*, April 28, 1981, p. A10.

84. *New York Times*, December 8, 1982, p. A6.

85. See the *New York Times*, October 16, 1981, p. A3; November 20, 1981, p. A3; May 19, 1982, p. A7; and September 29, 1982, p. A26.

86. See Quester, *Nuclear Proliferation*, especially George H. Quester, "Introduction: In Defense of Some Optimism," pp. 1–14, and Joseph S. Nye, "Maintaining a Non-Proliferation Regime," pp. 15–38.

87. For world order critiques of the nonproliferation issue, see Richard A. Falk, "Nuclear Policy and World Order: Why Denuclearization?" *Alternatives* 3 (March

1978): 321–50; Johansen, "SALT II," and *Jimmy Carter's National Security Policy*; WOMP Declaration, "Denuclearization For a Just World: The Failure of Non-Proliferation," in *Alternatives* 6 (Winter 1980-1981): 491–96; and Ali Mazrui, "Changing the Guards from Hindus to Muslims: Collective Third World Security in a Cultural Perspective," *International Affairs* 57 (Winter 1980/1981): 1–20.

88. Mazrui, "Changing the Guards from Hindus to Muslims," p. 18.

89. For my analysis of the evolution of UN peacekeeping, see Kim, *China, the United Nations, and World Order*, pp. 179–94, 215–41.

90. In a sharp break from the annual reports of his predecessor, Secretary-General Javier Pérez de Cuéllar's first annual "state of the world" report concentrated almost exclusively on the dismal state of UN peacekeeping functions. For the text of the report, see UN Doc. A/37/1 (September 7, 1982).

91. For an account of institutional history, see *The United Nations Disarmament Yearbook*, Vol. 1: 1976 (New York: United Nations, 1977), pp. 98–100.

92. See *Report of the Committee on Disarmament*, GAOR, 35th Sess., Supplement No. 27 (A/35/27), p. 3.

93. Ibid., p. 15.

94. It is revealing to note in this connection how the Big Five voted on General Assembly Resolution 35/152J, adopted on December 12, 1980, by a recorded vote of 132:0:13. This resolution, in accepting the annual 1980 report of the Committee on Disarmament, notes, inter alia, the concern of the General Assembly about the lack of any progress in this new regime and the conviction that "the Committee on Disarmament, *as the single multilateral negotiating body on disarmament, should play the central role in substantive negotiations on priority questions of disarmament*" (emphasis added). France and China voted in favor of this resolution; the United States, the United Kingdom, and the Soviet Union abstained. The General Assembly on the same day passed another significant resolution (35/152D) by a recorded vote of 112:19:14, declaring, inter alia, that the use of nuclear weapons was "a crime against humanity" and it "should therefore be prohibited, pending nuclear disarmament." China voted in favor; France, the United States, and the United Kingdom against; and the Soviet Union abstained.

95. See the Preamble to the Biological Weapons Convention in U.S. Arms Control and Disarmament Agency, *Arms Control and Disarmament Agreements*, p. 124.

96. Quoted in Committee on Hiroshima and Nagasaki, *Hiroshima and Nagasaki*, p. xli.

97. *U.S. Foreign Policy for the 1970s: The Emerging Structure of Peace* Report to the Congress by Richard Nixon, President of the United States (February 9, 1972), p. 156.

98. See Lewis F. Richardson, *Arms and Insecurity: A Mathematical Study of the Causes and Origins of War*, ed. Nicolas Rashevsky and Ernesto Trucco (Pittsburgh: Boxwood Press, 1960).

99. For sociopsychological inquiries into the security problematique, see the following: Falk and Kim, *The War System*, pp. 227–308; Jerome D. Frank, *Sanity and Survival: Psychological Aspects of War and Peace* (New York: Vintage Books, 1968); Group for the Advancement of Psychiatry, *Psychiatric Aspects of the Prevention of Nuclear War* (New York: Group for the Advancement of Psychiatry, 1964); Lifton, *Death in Life*; Ralph K. White, *Nobody Wanted War* (New York: Anchor Books, 1970); and Robert Jay Lifton and Richard A. Falk, *Indefensible Weapons: The Political and Psychological Case Against Nuclearism* (New York: Basic Books, 1982).

100. Jonathan Schell, *The Fate of the Earth*: (New York: Avon Books, 1982), p. 8.

101. Lifton and Falk, *Indefensible Weapons*, p. ix.

102. Gordon W. Allport, *The Person in Psychology* (Boston: Beacon Press, 1968), p. 11.

103. Compare and contrast the Common Heritage of Mankind Declaration—General Assembly Resolution 2749 (XXV) of December 17, 1970—and the text of the UN Convention on the Law of the Sea.

104. Richard Darman, "The Law of the Sea: Rethinking U.S. Interests," *Foreign Affairs* 56 (January 1978): 376. Another former member of the U.S. Delegation to UNCLOS-III has made a passionate plea in support of the treaty, saying: "But perhaps most important to the United States is the protection of the freedom of navigation on and below the surface and of overflight and related uses that remain virtually inviolate throughout the treaty as a matter of cardinal importance to United States security and general maritime interests." See John Temple Swing, "The Law of the Sea," *Proceedings of the Academy of Political Science* 32 (1977): 140.

Chapter 5

1. Lester B. Pearson, *Partners in Development*, Report of the Commission on International Development (New York: Praeger, 1969); Tinbergen, *Reshaping the International Order*; and *North-South: A Program for Survival*.

2. Jeremy Rifkin, *Entropy: A New World View* (New York: Bantam Books, 1981), p. 6.

3. See Norman Podhoretz, "The Neo-Conservative Anguish Over Reagan's Foreign Policy," *New York Times Magazine* (May 2, 1982): 30–33, 88–89, 92, 96–7. There is nothing new or significant in this piece except its unexpected attack on the Reagan adminstration. For a more scholarly elaboration of the logic of global neo-conservatives, see Robert W. Tucker, *The Inequality of Nations* (New York: Basic Books, 1977).

4. See Keohane and Nye, *Power and Interdependence*; Wallerstein, *The Modern World-System* and *The Capitalist World-Economy*; and Dennis Pirages, *The New Context for International Relations: Global Ecopolitics* (North Scituate, Mass.: Duxbury Press, 1978).

5. Gunnar Adler-Karlsson, "Eliminating Absolute Poverty: An Approach to the Problem," in W. Howard Wriggins and Gunnar Adler-Karlsson, *Reducing Global Inequities* (New York: McGraw-Hill, 1978), p. 126.

6. For an extensive exposition on the PQLI, see Morris D. Morris, *Measuring the Condition of the World's Poor: The Physical Quality of Life Index* (New York: Pergamon Press for the Overseas Development Council, 1979).

7. See Roger D. Hansen et al., *U.S. Foreign Policy and the Third World: Agenda 1982* (New York: Praeger Publishers for the Overseas Development Council, 1982), pp. 158–71.

8. World Bank, *World Development Report 1980* (New York: Oxford University Press for the World Bank, 1980), p. 33.

9. WHO, *Global Strategy for Health*, p. 11.

10. ILO, *Employment, Growth and Basic Needs: A One-World Problem* (New York: Praeger Publishers, 1977), p. 23.

11. FAO, *Agriculture: Toward 2000* (Rome: FAO, 1981).

12. Wassily Leontief, Anne P. Carter, and Peter A. Petri, *The Future of the World Economy*, A United Nations Study (New York: Oxford University Press for the United Nations, 1977), pp. 10–11.

13. *The Global 2000 Report to the President*, Vol. 2: *The Technical Report* (Washington, D.C.: Government Printing Office, 1980), p. 77. Emphasis in original.

14. Raymond F. Hopkins, "Food As a Global Issue," in James E. Harf and B. Thomas Trout, eds., *Food in the Global Arena* (New York: Holt, Rinehart and Winston, 1982), p. 11.

15. Richard J. Barnet, *The Lean Years: Politics in the Age of Scarcity* (New York: Simon and Schuster, 1980), p. 175.

16. See the *New York Times*, October 5, 1981, p. D11; and United Nations Development Programme, *Development Issue Paper for the 1980s*, No. 11, "Food: The Obstacles to Feeding the Hungry," p. 2.

17. *Overcoming World Hunger: The Challenge Ahead*, Report of the Presidential Commission on World Hunger, (Washington, D.C.: Government Printing Office, 1980), p. 1.

18. See R. R. Puffer and C. V. Serrano, "Patterns of Mortality in Childhood," *Scientific Publication* No. 262 (Washington, D.C.: Pan-American Health Organization, 1973); and K. V. Bailey, "Malnutrition in the African Region," *WHO Chronicle*, No. 29 (1975): 354–64.

19. Roger Lewin, "Starved Brains," *Psychology Today* 9 (September 1975): 29–33. Likewise, Richard Barnet writes: "The most serious energy crisis in the world is the depletion of human energy because the brain receives too few calories or too few proteins to think and the body too few to act." See Barnet, *The Lean Years*, p. 161.

20. Robert P. Ambroggi, "Water," *Scientific American* 243 (September 1980): 103.

21. Barnet, *The Lean Years*, p. 193.

22. WHO, *Global Strategy for Health*, p. 16.

23. UN Doc. A/36/411 (August 26, 1981), p. 6.

24. UN, *Report on the World Social Situation*, p. 140.

25. Ibid.

26. "Housing in Africa: Problems and Prospects," *Planning and Administration* 4, No. 1 (1977).

27. Adler-Karlsson, "Eliminating Absolute Poverty," p. 140.

28. UN, *1978 Report on the World Social Situation*, Sales No. E.79.IV.1, p. 39.

29. UN, *Report on the World Social Situation*, p. 142.

30. UN, *World Housing Survey, 1974*, Sales No. E.75.IV.8, p. 40.

31. *New York Times*, June 30, 1982, p. A2.

32. Walter Goldstein, "Despair and the UN Development Decade," *Futures* 13 (June 1981): 207.

33. WHO, *Global Strategy for Health*, p. 16.

34. *World Vision* 26 (March 1982): 22.

35. See OECD, *Public Expenditure on Health*, Studies in Resource Allocation, No. 2 (Paris: OECD, 1977), pp. 43–48.

36. United Kingdom, Central Statistical Office, "Effects of Taxes and Benefits on Household Income, 1975," *Economic Trends* (December 1976).

37. See Official Records of the World Health Organization No. 226, *Twenty-Eighth World Health Assembly*, Geneva, May 13–30, 1975, Part I: Resolutions and Decisions and Annexes (Geneva: WHO, 1975); Official Records of the World Health Organization No. 229, *The Work of WHO 1975*, Annual Report of the Director-General to the World Health Assembly and to the United Nations (Geneva: WHO,

1976); *The Collection, Fractionation, Quality Control, and Uses of Blood and Blood Products* (Geneva: WHO, 1981).

38. See ILO, *Employment, Growth and Basic Needs*, Table 14, p. 130.

39. See A. Meijia and N. Pizurki, "World Migration of Health Manpower," *WHO Chronicle* 30 (1976): 455–460.

40. See Adler-Karlsson, "Eliminating Absolute Poverty," p. 146; and UN *1978 Report on the World Social Situation*, pp. 35–36; *Report on the World Social Situation*, pp. 114–116.

41. For details, see UN, *1978 Report on the World Social Situation*, pp. 33–34, 36; UN, *Report on the World Social Situation*, p. 103.

42. Gunnar Myrdal, *A World Anti-Poverty Program in Outline* (New York: Pantheon Books, 1970), p. 195.

43. See World Bank, *World Development Report, 1980*, pp. 48–50.

44. See ILO, *Employment, Growth and Basic Needs*, pp. 16–19.

45. *Development Forum* 10 (November 1982): 8.

46. *Development Forum* 10 (March 1982): 12.

47. UN, *Report on the World Social Situation*, p. 57.

48. World Bank, *World Development Report, 1981*, p. 51.

49. W. R. Bohming, *Future Demand for Migrant Workers in Western Europe* (Geneva: ILO 1976).

50. See General Assembly Resolution 2880 (XXVI) of December 21, 1971.

51. Charles Lipson, "The Transformation of Trade: The Sources and Effects of Regime Change," *International Organization* 36 (Spring 1982): 423.

52. UNCTAD, *Trade and Development Report, 1982* (New York: United Nations, 1982), p. 79.

53. For further analysis of this shift, see my "The Political Economy of Post-Mao China in Global Perspective," in Neville Maxwell and Bruce McFarlane, eds., *China's Changed Road to Development* (Oxford: Pergamon Press, 1983).

54. In 1970, the Third World's share of world trade was 5.8 percent for OPEC countries and 11.9 percent for non-OPEC developing market economies. By 1980, however, this ratio had changed considerably, with the former accounting for 14.7 percent and latter for only 12.1 percent. Roger Hansen et al., See *U.S. Foreign Policy and the Third World*, p. 201.

55. International Monetary Fund, *World Economic Outlook* (Washington, D.C.: IMF, June 1981), p. 7.

56. See Richard Blackhurst, Nicolas Marian, and Jan Tumlir, *Adjustment, Trade and Growth in Developed and Developing Countries*, Studies in International Trade, No. 6 (Geneva: GATT, 1978), p. 13.

57. For details, see *World Economic Outlook* (1981), p. 115.

58. See ibid., pp. 115, 118–119.

59. Jahangir Amuzegar, "Oil Wealth: A Very Mixed Blessing," *Foreign Affairs* 60 (Spring 1982): 815.

60. See *World Development Report, 1981*, pp. 21–22.

61. *World Economic Outlook* (1981), p. 52 and *World Economic Outlook* (Washington, D.C.: International Monetary Fund, April 1982), p. 150.

62. *North-South*, p. 145.

63. *UN Chronicle* 19 (October 1982): 39; *Development Forum* 10 (November 1982): 3.

64. Tinbergen, *Reshaping the International Order*, p. 34.

65. UNDP, *Development Issue Paper for the 1980s*, No. 2, "Commodities at a Crossroads: The Issues," p. 4.

66. "The Debt-Bomb Threat," *Time* (January 10, 1983): 42.

67. IMF, *World Economic Outlook* (1982), pp. 171, 173.

68. For details see Chandra Hardy, *Rescheduling Developing-Country Debts, 1956-1980: Lessons and Recommendations*, Overseas Development Council Working Paper No. 1 (Washington, D.C.: ODC, March 1981; revised February 1982).

69. See the *New York Times*, February 15, 1983, p. D9; March 3, 1983, p. D1; and March 8, 1983, p. D1. For a first-rate analysis of the increasing control of core corporations in the management of the global political economy, see Volker Bornschier, "The World Economy in the World-System: Structure, Dependence and Change," *International Social Science Journal* 34 (1982): 37-59.

70. See Bull, *The Anarchical Society*, p. 85, and Adda B. Bozeman, *The Future of Law in a Multicultural World* (Princeton, N.J.: Princeton University Press, 1971).

71. Rawls merely suggets at one point that it is possible to "extend the interpretation of the original position and think of the parties as representatives of different nations who must choose together the fundamental principles to adjudicate conflicting claims among states." Although there are a few illustrative examples concerning *jus ad bellum* and *jus in bello* in this connection, Rawls stops short of extending the argument to the distribution of wealth among states. See John Rawls, *A Theory of Justice* (Cambridge, Mass.: Belknap Press of Harvard University Press, 1971), pp. 378-79.

72. Ibid., p. 7.

73. Ibid., p. 60.

74. General Assembly Resolutions 3201 (S-VI) and 3202 (S-VI) of May 1, 1974, and General Assembly Resolution 3281 (XXIX) of December 12, 1974.

75. UNCTAD Resolution 93 (IV) was adopted without dissent at the 145th plenary meeting of May 30, 1976. See UN Doc. TD/217 (July 12, 1976), pp. 2-8. The phrase quoted in the text is taken from the first preambular paragraph of the resolution.

76. See General Assembly Resolution 3362 (S-VII) of September 16, 1975.

77. For an elaboration of this point, see my *China, the United Nations, and World Order*, pp. 253-81.

78. Cited in Dolman, *Resources, Regimes, World Order*, p. 86.

79. Roy Preiswerk, "Le nouvel ordre économique international est-il nouveau?" *Études Internationales* (Quebec) 8 (December 1977): 648-59.

80. Irma Adelman, "Development Economics—A Reassessment of Goals," *American Economic Review* 65 (May 1975): 302-9; quote on p. 302. See also Felix Paukert, "Income Distribution at Different Levels of Development: A Survey of Evidence," *International Labour Review* 168 (August-September 1973): 116-22; Irma Adelman and Cynthia Taft Morris, *Economic Growth and Social Equity in Developing Countries* (Stanford, Calif.: Stanford University Press, 1973), pp. 160, 179; a comprehensive six-part series of articles by André Fontaine, Marcel Niedergang, Eric Rouleau, Gérald Viratelle and Jacques Decornoy, Michel Boyer, and Pierre Drouin, "Croissance et Contrainte," *Le Monde* (Paris), February 22, 1977, pp. 1, 7; February 23, 1977, p. 6; February 24, 1977, p. 6; February 25, 1977, p. 8; February 26, 1977, p. 6; and February 27-28, 1977, p. 5.

81. Norman L. Hicks, "Growth vs. Basic Needs: Is There a Trade-Off?" *World Development* 7 (November-December 1979): 985-94; and World Bank, *World Development Report, 1980*, pp. 32-45; and *World Development Report, 1981*, pp. 1-7.

82. Ali A. Mazrui in Jagdish N. Bhagwatai, ed., *The New International Economic Order: The North-South Debate* (Cambridge, Mass.: MIT Press, 1977), p. 374.

83. Mahbub ul Haq, "Negotiating the Future," in *Toward a Just World Order*, p. 328.

84. The text of the declaration is contained in UN Doc. A/C.2/292 and is reprinted in *Alternatives* 1, Nos. 2–3 (June/September 1975): 396–406. The citations in the text are from the latter source.

85. *Alternatives* 1, Nos. 2–3 (June/September 1975): 399–400.

86. Ibid., p. 401.

87. *What Now—Another Development*. the 1975 Dag Hammarskjöld Report on Development and International Cooperation (Uppsala, Sweden: Dag Hammarskjöld Foundation, 1975), pp. 12–21.

88. Ibid., p. 28.

89. Herrera et al., *Castastrophe or New Society?* p. 25. Emphasis in original.

90. See ILO, *Employment, Growth and Basic Needs*, and ILO, World Employment Conference Document WEC/CW/E.1 (March 3, 1978). For debates on the BHN strategy, see various articles in *World Development* 6 (March 1978).

91. For a trenchant analysis along this line, see Johan Galtung, "The New International Economic Order and the Basic Needs Approach," *Alternatives* 4 (March 1979): 455–76.

92. Haq, "Negotiating the Future," p. 330.

93. Peter Bachrach and Morton S. Baratz, "Two Faces of Power," *American Political Science Review* 56 (December 1962): 948.

94. General Assembly Official Records (GAOR), 6th Special Sess., 2229th plenary meeting (May 1, 1974), para. 77.

95. See Irving Kristol, "The 'New Cold War'," *Wall Street Journal*, July 17, 1975, p. 18; *Wall Street Journal* editorial, "A Word to the Third World," July 17, 1975, p. 18; Daniel P. Moynihan, "The United States in Opposition," *Commentary* 59 (March 1975): 31–44; C. Fred Bergsten, "The Threat from the Third World," *Foreign Policy*, No. 11 (1973): 102–24; and Richard N. Cooper, Karl Kaiser, and Masataka Kosaka, *Towards a Renovated International System*, a report to the Trilateral Commission, Triangle Paper No. 14 (1977).

96. For a careful assessment of NIEO politics from its inception to mid-1980, see the final report of the Director-General for Development and International Economic Co-operation in UN Doc. A/S-11/5 (August 7, 1980).

97. Dolman, *Resources, Regimes, World Order*, p. 95.

98. See Hans-Henrik Holm, "The Game Is Up: The North-South Debate Seen Through Four Different Perspectives," Paper presented at the 23rd Annual Convention of the International Studies Association, March 24–27, 1982, Cincinnati, Ohio, pp. 8, 13.

99. OECD, *Facing the Future: Mastering the Probable and Managing the Unpredictable* (Paris: OECD, 1979), p. 281.

100. See, for example, the presentation of the representative of Czechoslovakia, speaking on behalf of Group D, in the Ad Hoc Committee of the 7th Special Session, in GAOR, 7th Special Sess., *Annexes*, Agenda Item 7, p. 15.

101. For a detailed analysis of the Soviet and East European countries' position on the NIEO, see E. Laszlo and J. Kurtzman, eds., *Eastern Europe and the New International Economic Order* (New York: Pergamon Press, 1980), and Toby Trister Gati, "The Soviet Union and the North-South Dialogue," *Orbis* 24 (Summer 1980): 241–70.

102. Cited in *Far Eastern Economic Review* (November 6, 1981): 110.

103. Bhagwati, *The New International Economic Order*, p. 1.

104. Cited in Holm, "The Game Is Up," p. 3.

105. Cited in Dolman, *Resources, Regimes, World Order*, p. 98.

106. For a detailed analysis of China's participation in the inaugural and implementation processes of the NIEO, see Kim, *China, the United Nations, and World Order*, Chaps. 5–6.

107. This section draws upon my "Whither Post-Mao Chinese Global Policy?" and "The Political Economy of Post-Mao China in Global Perspective."

108. Friedrich W. Wu, "Socialist Self-Reliant Development Within the Capitalist World Economy: The Chinese View in the Post-Mao Era," Paper presented at the 23d Annual Convention of the International Studies Association, March 24–27, 1982, Cincinnati, Ohio.

109. Edward Friedman, "On Maoist Conceptualizations of the Capitalist World System," *China Quarterly*, No. 80 (December 1979): 836–37.

110. U.S. Congress, Senate, Select Committee on Nutrition and Human Needs, *The United States, FAO and World Food Politics: U.S. Relations with an International Food Organization*, Staff Report, 94th Congress, 2d Sess. (Washington, D.C.: Government Printing Office, June 1976), pp. 11–13.

111. Cheryl Christensen, "The Right To Food: How to Guarantee," *Alternatives* 4 (October 1978): 198–99. Emphasis in original.

112. See Michael Lipton, *Why Poor People Stay Poor* (Cambridge, Mass.: Harvard University Press, 1977), p. 16, and Victor J. Elias, *Government Expenditure on Agriculture in Latin America*, Research Report No. 23 (Washington, D.C.: IFPRI, May 1981).

113. Francis Moore Lappé and Joseph Collins, *Food First* (New York: Ballantine Books, 1978). For another first-rate radical critique of the global political economy of food, see Susan George, *How the Other Half Dies: The Real Reasons for World Hunger* (Montclair, N.J.: Allanheld, Osmun & Co., 1977).

114. Christensen, "The Right to Food," p. 201.

115. Robert Paalberg, "A Food Security Approach for the 1980s: Righting the Balance," in Roger Hanson et al., *U.S. Foreign Policy and the Third World*, p. 83.

116. Thomas Nagel, "Poverty and Food: Why Charity is Not Enough," in Peter Brown and Henry Shue, eds., *Food Policy: The Responsibility of the U.S. in the Life and Death Choice* (New York: Free Press, 1977), p. 55.

117. Puchala and Hopkins, "International Regimes," pp. 263–65. For further analysis of the norms of the global food regime, see Donald J. Puchala and Raymond F. Hopkins, "Toward Innovation in the Global Food Regime," *International Organization* 32 (Summer 1978): 855–68 and Helge Bergesen, "A New Food Regime: Necessary but Impossible," *International Organization* 34 (Spring 1980): 285–302.

118. Paalberg, "A Food Security Approach for the 1980s," p. 73.

119. UN, *World Food Conference: Note by the Secretary-General*, UN Doc. No. E/5587 (November 22, 1974), p. 91.

120. See UN Doc. E/CONF.65/4, p. 236.

121. *Report of the World Food Conference, Rome, 5–16 November 1974*, UN Doc.E/CONF.65/20 (1975), p. 18.

122. See UN Doc. A/S-11/6 (July 25, 1980), Annex, p. 21.

123. Edouard Saouma, "New World Food Order," *Review of International Affairs* 31 (Belgrade, November 5, 1980): 1–5; the quote in the text on p. 2.

124. UN Doc. A/S-11/6 (July 25, 1980), Annex, p. 77.

125. *UN Chronicle* 20 (January 1983): 69.

126. See, for example, "Statement by Mr. Raul Prebisch, Secretary-General of the United Nations Conference on Trade and Development," *Proceedings of UNCTAD*, Geneva, 23 March–16 June 1964, Vol. 2: *Policy Statements*, pp. 76–77.

127. UN, *International Development Strategy for the Third United Nations Development Decade* (New York: United Nations, 1981), p. 9.

128. For analyses of the international trade regime upon this premise, see the following: Jock A. Finlayson and Mark W. Zacher, "The GATT and the Regulation of Trade Barriers: Regime Dynamics and Functions," *International Organization* 35 (Autumn 1981): 561–602; Robert Keohane, "The Theory of Hegemonic Stability and Changes in International Economic Regimes, 1967–1977," in Holsti, Siverson, and George, *Change in the International System*, pp. 131–62; Stephen D. Krasner, "The Tokyo Round: Particularistic Interests and Prospects for Stability in the Global Trading System," *International Studies Quarterly* 23 (December 1979): 491–531; Charles Lipson, "The Transformation of Trade: The Sources and Effects of Regime Change," *International Organization* 36 (Spring 1982): 417–55; and John G. Ruggie, "International Regimes, Transactions, and Change: Embedded Liberalism in the Postwar Economic Order," *International Organization* 36 (Spring 1982): 379–415.

129. "Address Delivered by Mr. Salvador Allende Gossens, President of Chile at the Inaugural Ceremony on 13 April 1972," *Proceedings of UNCTAD, Third Session*, Santiago de Chile, April 13 to May, 21, 1972, Vol 1: *Report and Annexes*, p. 354.

130. This figure is cited by Reubin Askew, U.S. Trade Representative, in his article, "Free Trade Benefits Everyone." *New York Times*, May 3, 1980, p. 23.

131. F. V. Meyer, *International Trade Policy* (New York: St. Martin's Press, 1978), p. 142.

132. Ibid., p. 141.

133. For an elaboration of this point, see Samuel S. Kim, "The Sino-American Collaboration and Cold War II," *Journal of Peace Research* 19, No. 1 (1982): 11–20.

134. U.S. Department of Commerce, *International Economic Indicators and Competitive Trends* 7 (June 1981), Table 28.

135. For a series of three articles on the threat of a farm-subsidy war among the Big Three, see the *New York Times*, February 21, 1983, pp. 1, D4; February 22, 1983, pp. 1, D11; and February 23, 1983, pp. 1, D11.

136. Quoted in the *New York Times*, November 25, 1982, p. D1.

137. Keohane, "The Theory of Hegemonic Stability," p. 139.

138. Lipson, "The Transformation of Trade," p. 439. Emphasis in original. John Ruggie has also concluded in his assessment of the international regimes for money and trade: "Much of the observed change has been at the level of instrument rather than norm." See Ruggie, "International Regimes, Transactions, and Change," p. 412.

139. *IMF Survey*, March 23, 1981, pp. 81, 89.

140. U.S. Department of State, *Bulletin* 81 (April 1981): 24.

141. UN, *International Development Stategy*, p. 10.

142. World Bank, *World Development Report, 1981*, p. 30.

143. See General Assembly Resolution 33/199 (January 29, 1979); General Assembly Resolution 34/199 (December 19, 1979); General Assembly Resolution 35/418 (December 5, 1980); and General Assembly Resolution 36/429 (December 16, 1981).

144. For excerpts from the ministerial declaration, see the *New York Times*, November 30, 1982, p. D25.

145. See UN, *Agreement Establishing the Common Fund for Commodities*, UN Doc. TD/IPC/CF/CONF/24 (July 29, 1980).

146. See IMF, *World Economic Outlook* (1982), pp. 137–38, 210.

147. UNDP, *Development Issue Paper for the 1980s*, No. 11, "Food: The Obstacles to Feeding the Hungry," p. 7.

148. *UN Chronicle* 20 (January 1983): 70.

149. Tucker, *The Inequality of Nations*, p. 161. Emphasis added.

150. Irving Kristol, as quoted in Noam Chomsky, *Peace in the Middle East* (New York: Vintage Books, 1974), p. 6.

151. Kenneth N. Waltz, "International Structure, National Force, and the Balance of World Power," *Journal of International Affairs* 21 (1967): 224.

152. See Bergsten, "The Threat from the Third World," and Tom J. Farer, "The United States and the Third World," *Foreign Affairs* 54 (October 1975): 79-97.

153. Joseph A. Camilleri, *Civilization in Crisis: Human Prospects in a Changing World* (New York: Cambridge University Press, 1976), p. 69.

154. See Ferando Henrique Cardoso, "Towards Another Development," in Falk, Kim, and Mendlovitz, *Toward a Just World Order*, pp. 343-58.

155. Walt W. Rostow, *The Stages of Economic Growth: A Non-Communist Manifesto* (New York: Cambridge University Press, 1960).

156. For elaboration of "pragmatic world order," see Haas, Williams, and Babai, *Scientists and World Order*, p. 53.

157. For example, the spokesman for the Group of 77 noted: "Developing countries have seen this work on restructuring as the first real opportunity they have had, as relative newcomers to membership in the United Nations, of participating in the shaping of the system in an area of fundamental importance to them." See UN Doc.A/32/PV.109, p. 14.

Chapter 6

1. Ali Shariati, "Reflections of a Concerned Muslim: On the Plight of Oppressed Peoples," in Falk, Kim, and Mendlovitz, *Toward a Just World Order*, p. 20.

2. Steve Biko, "Black Consciousness and the Quest for a True Humanity," in Falk, Kim, and Mendlovitz, *Toward a Just World Order*, p. 28.

3. Hedley Bull, "Order vs. Justice in International Society," *Political Studies* 19, No. 3 (September 1971): 279.

4. See Karel Vasak, "A 30-Year Struggle: The Sustained Efforts to Give Force of Law to the Universal Declaration of Human Rights," *UNESCO Courier* (November 1977): 29-32; and idem, "Colloquium on the Rights to Solidarity," *Bulletin of Peace Proposals* 11, No. 4 (1980): 405-7. For other scholars who have used and elaborated upon the concept of three generations, see the following: Philip Alston, "Peace as a Human Right," *Bulletin of Peace Proposals* 11, No. 4 (December 1980): 319-30; Stephen Marks, "The Peace-Human Rights-Development Dialectic," *Bulletin of Peace Proposals* 11, No. 4 (December 1980): 339-47; and idem, "Emerging Human Rights: A New Generation for the 1980s?" *Rutgers Law Review* 33 (Winter 1981): 435-52.

5. Cited in Marks, "Emerging Human Rights," p. 441.

6. Louis Henkin, *The Rights of Man Today* (Boulder Colo.: Westview Press, 1978), p. 5.

7. See Richard A. Falk, "What's Wrong with Henry Kissinger's Foreign Policy?" *Alternatives* 1, No. 1 (March 1975): 79-100, and *Human Rights and State Sovereignty* (New York: Holmes & Meir Publishers, 1981).

8. Henkin, *The Rights of Man Today*, pp. xii-xiii.

9. For the texts of the International Bill of Rights, see UN Docs. A/810 (1948) and A/6316 (1967). These texts are reproduced in Burns H. Weston, Richard A.

Falk, and Anthony A. D'Amato, eds., *Basic Documents in International Law and World Order* (St. Paul, Minn.: West Publishing Co., 1980), pp. 161–164, 196–211.

10. L. D. Easton amd K. H. Guddat, *Writings of the Young Marx on Philosophy and Science* (New York: Doubleday & Co., 1967), pp. 236–37. Emphasis added.

11. Kenneth E. Boulding, "Social Justice in Social Dynamics," in Richard B. Brandt, ed., *Social Justice* (Englewood Cliffs, N.J.: Prentice-Hall, 1962), p. 92.

12. Christian Bay, "Universal Human Rights Priorities: Toward a Rational Order," in Jack L. Nelson and Vera M. Green, eds., *International Human Rights: Contemporary Issues* (Standfordville, N.Y.: Human Rights Publishing Group, 1980), p. 17.

13. For an elaboration of this argument, see Charles E. Lindblom, *Politics and Markets* (New York: Basic Books, 1977).

14. Alpheus Thomas Mason and William B. Beaney, *American Constitutional Law*, 3d ed. (Englewood Cliffs, N.J.: Prentice-Hall, 1964), p. 32.

15. Rosalyn Higgins, "Conceptual Thinking About the Individual in International Law," *British Journal of International Studies* 4, No. 1 (April 1978): 12. It should also be noted in this connection that Prime Minister Margaret Thatcher declared during her official state visit to China in September 1982 that the treaties by which Britain acquired the colony (Hong Kong) from the Manchu Dynasty were valid under international law and that their abrogation would be "very serious indeed." At the same time, the New Nationality Act, which takes effect on January 1, 1983, would deprive most of the 2.6 million British passport-holders in Hong Kong of the automatic right to live in England. See the *New York Times*, September 22, 1982, p. A3; October 1, 1982, p. A3.

16. Rupert Emerson, "The Fate of Human Rights in the Third World," *World Politics* 27 (January 1975): 203.

17. Samuel P. Huntington, "Human Rights and American Power," *Commentary* 72 (September 1981): 38.

18. Quoted in the *New York Times*, December 4, 1982, p. 3.

19. Fouad Ajami, "Human Rights and World Order Politics," in Falk, Kim, and Mendlovitz, *Toward a Just World Order*, p. 377.

20. See Michel J. Crozier, Samuel P. Huntington, and Joji Watanuki, *The Crisis of Democracy: Report on the Governability of Democracies to the Trilateral Commission* (New York: New York University Press, 1975), p. 115; see also Alexander Solzhenitsyn, "The West Has Lost Its Courage," *Washington Post*, June 11, 1978, p. C1.

21. V. I. Lenin, in *Collected Works*, Vol. 21 (New York: International Publishers, 1932), p. 154. Emphasis in original.

22. Dollard, *Frustration and Aggression*, p. 25.

23. See Ahmad, "The Neo-Fascist State," pp. 74–83.

24. Martin Buber, *Paths in Utopia*, trans. R.F.C. Hull (London: Routledge & Kegan Paul, 1949), p. 13. Emphasis in original.

25. For various analyses of the Marxist/socialist perspective on human rights, see Helge Bergesen, "Human Rights—the Property of the Nation State or a Concern for the International Community?" *Cooperation and Conflict* 4 (1979): 239–54; Harold J. Berman, "American and Soviet Perspectives on Human Rights," *Worldview* 22 (November 1979): 15–21; I. P. Blishchenko, "The Impact of the New International Order on Human Rights in Developing Countries," *Bulletin of Peace Proposals* 11, No. 4 (1980): 375–86; V. Chkhidvadze, "Constitution of True Human Rights and Freedoms," *International Affairs* (Moscow, October 1980): 13–20; Richard A. Falk, "Comparative Protection of Human Rights in Capitalist and Socialist Third World Countries," *Universal Human Rights* 1, No. 2 (April-June 1979): 3–29; McDougal, Lasswell, and Chen, *Human Rights and World Public Order*, pp. 76–79; Susan Shirk,

"Human Rights: What About China?" *Foreign Policy*, No. 29 (Winter 1977-1978): 109-27; and Imre Szabo, "Fundamental Questions Concerning the Theory and History of Citizens," in Jozses Halasz, et al, eds., *Socialist Concept of Human Rights* (Budapest: Akademiai Kiado, 1966), pp. 2-81.

26. Falk, "Comparative Protection of Human Rights," pp. 13-14. It can be argued in this connection that the heavy "transition" costs apply to socialist/revolutionary regimes as well as capitalist/counterrevolutionary regimes during the initial phase of consolidating their political power.

27. Ibid., pp. 27-29.

28. Karel Vasak, cited in Marks, "Emerging Human Rights," p. 441. Emphasis in original.

29. See UNESCO Doc. SS-78/Conf.630/12 (1978).

30. Adam Lopatka, "The Right to Live in Peace as a Human Right," *Bulletin of Peace Proposals* 11, No. 4 (1980): 363, 365.

31. See Keba M'Baye, "Le droit au développement comme un droit de l'homme," *Revue des droits de l'homme* 5, Nos. 2-3 (Paris 1972): 503-34.

32. See UN, *The International Dimensions of the Right to Development as a Human Right. . . .* Report of the Secretary-General, UN Doc. E/CN.4/1334 (January 2, 1979) [hereafter cited as *The Secretary-General's Report on the Right to Development*].

33. For further analysis of the right to development, see Karel de Vey Mestdagh, "The Right to Development," *Netherlands International Law Review* 28, No. 1 (1981): 31-53; Asbjorn Eide, "Choosing the Path to Development," *Bulletin of Peace Proposals* 11, No. 4 (1980): 349-60; Stephen Marks, "Development and Human Rights," *Bulletin of Peace Proposals* 8, No. 3 (1977): 236-46, and "Emerging Human Rights"; and UN, *The Secretary-General's Report on the Right to Development*.

34. UN, *Report of the United Nations Conference on the Human Environment*, UN Doc. A/Conf. 48/14/Rev.1 (1973), p. 3. Emphasis added.

35. UN Docs. A/C.1/PV.15/5 (November 1, 1967) and A/C.1/PV.15/6 (November 1, 1967), pp. 1-3.

36. UN General Assembly Resolution 2749 (XXV) of December 17, 1970.

37. See UNESCO Doc. No. SS-80, Conf. 806/5 (1980), paras. 14-16.

38. Marks, "Emerging Human Rights," p. 448.

39. Legalistic biases have been more rampant in human rights scholarship. In taking stock of the human rights literature, one social scientist observed in 1981: "Heretofore nearly all writing on human rights had been done by international legal scholars. In the two-volume bibliography on international human rights compiled by the University of Notre Dame Law School, virtually all the entries are by legal scholars, with most of the articles published in law journals." See McCamant, "Social Science and Human Rights," p. 532. For another review of the human rights literature from a world order perspective, see Robert C. Johansen, "Human Rights in the 1980s: Revolutionary Growth or Unanticipated Erosion?" *World Politics* 35 (January 1983): 284-314.

40. See Jack Donnelly, "Human Rights and Human Dignity: An Analytic Critique of Non-Western Conceptions of Human Rights," *American Political Science Review* 76 (June 1982): 303-16.

41. Ajami, "Human Rights and World Order Politics," p. 377.

42. Johan Galtung and Anders Helge Wirak, "Human Needs and Human Rights— A Theoretical Approach," *Bulletin of Peace Proposals* 8, No. 3 (1977): 251.

43. See Oscar Schachter, "The Evolving International Law of Development," *Columbia Journal of Transnational Law* 15, No. 1 (1976): 1-16.

44. Maslow, *Toward a Psychology of Being*, p. 144.

45. See Hadley Cantril, *The Pattern of Human Concerns* (New Brunswick, N.J.: Rutgers University Press, 1965), especially pp. 301–322.

46. George H. Gallup, "Human Needs and Satisfactions: A Global Survey," *Public Opinion Quarterly* 40 (Winter 1976-1977): 463.

47. Christian Bay, "A Human Rights Approach to Transnational Politics," *Universal Human Rights* 1, No. 1 (January–March 1979): 29.

48. Maslow, *Toward a Psychology of Being*, p. 145. See also McDougal, Lasswell, and Chen, *Human Rights and World Public Order*, p. 4.

49. Bay, "Universal Human Rights Priorities," p. 10.

50. For a thoroughgoing discussion of the right to health as a human right, see the papers and discussion presented at an international workshop jointly sponsored by the Hague Academy of International Law and the UN University in July 1978 in *Le droit a la sante en tant que droit de l'homme* (Alphen aan den Rijn, the Netherlands: Sijthoff & Noordhoff, 1979).

51. WHO, *Global Strategy for Health*, p. 11.

52. Keba M'Baye, cited in ibid., p. 36.

53. A number of proposals have been advanced in recent years for establishing a more reliable system of measuring and monitoring the pattern and distribution of human rights abuses. See Snyder, Hermann, and Lasswell, "A Global Monitoring System," pp. 221–60; Jorge I. Dominguez, "Assessing Human Rights Conditions," in Jorge I. Dominguez et al., *Enhancing Global Human Rights* (New York: McGraw-Hill Book Co., 1979), p. 22; Nigel S. Rodley, "Monitoring Human Rights Violations in the 1980s," in ibid., p. 124. In spite of the recent entry of human rights issues into international relations research, however, leading international relations texts have yet to catch up. Not only "traditional" texts but also more modern and up-to-date texts have failed to assign a single chapter to global human rights problems. See the following: Gavin Boyd and Charles Pentland, eds., *Issues in Global Politics* (New York: Free Press, 1981); Holsti, *International Politics: A Framework for Analysis*; Walter S. Jones and Steven J. Rosen, *The Logic of International Relations*, 4th ed. (Boston: Little, Brown and Co., 1982); Kegley and Wittkopf, *World Politics: Trend and Transformation*; and Bruce Russett and Harvey Starr, *World Politics: The Menu for Choice* (San Francisco: W. H. Freeman and Co., 1981).

54. U.S. Department of State, *Country Reports on Human Rights Practices for 1981* (Washington, D.C.: Government Printing Office, 1982), pp. 2, 9. For the last annual report of the Carter administration, see U.S. Department of State, *Country Reports on Human Rights Practices* (Washington, D.C.: Government Printing Office, 1981), especially pp. 1–5.

55. For a text of the convention, see Weston, Falk, and D'Amato, *Basic Documents in International Law and World Order*, pp. 160–61. For a background analysis of the convention, see Leo Kuper, *Genocide: Its Political Use in the Twentieth Century* (New Haven, Conn.: Yale University Press, 1981), chap. 2.

56. Kuper, *Genocide*, p. 9.

57. For conflicting assessments of what had actually happened in Cambodia between 1975 and 1978, see the following: John Barron and Anthony Paul, *Murder of a Gentle Land* (New York: Thomas Y. Crowell, 1977); Noam Chomsky and Edward S. Herman, *The Political Economy of Human Rights*, Vol. 2: *After the Cataclysm: Postwar Indochina and the Reconstruction of Imperial Ideology* (Boston: South End Press, 1979), pp. 135–294; George C. Hildebrand and Gareth Porter, *Cambodia: Starvation and Revolution* (New York: Monthly Review Press, 1976); and Francois Ponchaud, *Cambodia: Year Zero*, trans. Nancy Amphoux (New York: Holt, Rinehart and

Winston, 1978). The figure cited in the text is drawn from *Amnesty International Report 1982* (London: Amnesty International Publications, 1982), p. 3.

58. See Brian Moynahan, "The Last Frontier," *Sunday Times* (London), June 18, 1978, and Darcy Ribeiro (a Brazilian anthropologist), cited in Shelton H. Davis, *Victims of the Miracle: Development and the Indians of Brazil* (New York: Cambridge University Press, 1977), p. 5.

59. Davis, *Victims of the Miracle*, p. 76.

60. See Chomsky and Herman, *The Political Economy of Human Rights*, Vol 1: *The Washington Connection and Third World Fascism*, and Vol. 2: *After the Cataclysm*.

61. Eric R. Wolf, "Killing the Achés," in Richard Arens, ed., *Genocide in Paraguay* (Philadelphia: Temple University Press, 1976), pp. 52–53.

62. Amnesty International, *Report on Torture* (London: Gerald Duckworth, 1973), p. 31.

63. See UN, *United Nations Action in the Field of Human Rights* (New York: United Nations, 1980), p. 158.

64. Cited in James Avery Joyce, *The New Politics of Human Rights* (New York: St. Martin's Press, 1978), p. 85.

65. Cited in ibid., p. 83.

66. *Amnesty International Report 1981* (London: Amnesty International Publications, 1981), p. 10.

67. Irving R. Kaufman, "A Legal Remedy for International Torture?" *New York Times Magazine* (November 9, 1980), p. 44.

68. For the major findings of various international investigation teams which generally point to the Israeli practice of torture in the occupied territories, see the following: Insight Team, "Israel and Torture," *Sunday Times* (London), June 19, 1977, p. 17; *New York Times*, August 2, 1977, p. 10; Ligue Suisse des Droit de L'Homme, *Violations des droits de l'homme en Cisjordanie* (Geneva: Ligue Suisse, September 30, 1977), p. 17; UN, Report of the Special Committee, UN Doc. A/ 32/284 (October 27, 1977), p. 40; Alexandra U. Johnson, "Israeli Torture of Palestinian Political Prisoners in Jerusalem and the West Bank: Three State Department Reports," *Palestine Human Rights Bulletin*, No. 17 (April 1979); *Christian Science Monitor*, April 4, 1979; and *UN Chronicle 19* (July 1982): 43–46. More recently and revealingly, Jacobo Timmerman responds to his son's query about life in prison: "Son, you can't compare an Argentine jail to an Israeli jail. In our jails, only Arabs are maltreated, and you are a member of the superior race. It's true that once we were the people chosen by God to be witnesses of his truth, but now that we have girded ourselves for the murder of another people, we are a superior race since, as our government says, nobody can defeat us. They won't torture you in jail." See Jacobo Timmerman, *The Longest War: Israel in Lebanon*, trans. Miguel Acoca (New York: Alfred A. Knopf, 1982), p. 166.

69. See U.S. Congress, *Abuse of Psychiatry for Political Oppression in the Soviet Union*, Hearing before the Subcommittee to Investigate the Administration of the Internal Security Act and Other Internal Security Laws of the Committee on the Judiciary, United States Senate, 92d Cong., 2d Sess. (Washington, D.C.: Government Printing Office, 1972).

70. Dominguez, "Assessing Human Rights Conditions," pp. 95–96.

71. See United Nations, *Maltreatment and Torture of Prisoners in South Africa*, UN Doc. ST/PSCA/SER.A/13 (1973).

72. For international law dimensions of the refugee problem, see McDougal, Lasswell, and Chen, *Human Rights and World Public Order*, pp. 935–40.

73. Weston, Falk, and D'Amato, *Basic Documents in International Law and World Order*, p. 172. The main effect of the 1967 Protocol is to broaden the temporal scope of Article 1 of the convention by deleting the clause, "As a result of events occurring before 1 January 1951."

74. For an explanation of a new way of reporting statistics on refugees, see United States Committee for Refugees, *1981 World Refugee Survey* (New York: U.S. Committee for Refugees, 1981), p. 33.

75. See U.S. Congressional Research Service, *World Refugee Crisis: The International Community's Response* (Washington, D.C.: Government Printing Office, 1979).

76. "International Protection," (editorial), *Refugees* (UNHCR), No. 1 (January 1982), p. 1.

77. Kathleen Newland, *Refugees: The New International Politics of Displacement*, Worldwatch Paper No. 43 (Washington, D.C.: Worldwatch Institute, March 1981), p. 13. The detention of the Haitian refugees in federal detention camps got drawn into a protracted legal battle in the United States. In the wake of a federal court decision ordering release of Haitian refugees an agreement between the U.S. government and refugee groups and voluntary assistance agencies was reached in July 1982. On July 23, 1982, the first batch of the Haitian refugees was released. See the *New York Times*, July 24, 1982, pp. 1, 7.

78. Emerson, "The Fate of Human Rights in the Third World," p. 217.

79. UN, *The Report of the United Nations High Commissioner for Refugees*, UN Doc. E/5306 (June 14, 1973), p. 13.

80. Newland, "Refugees," p. 17.

81. See "Boat People Shun Resettlement in Japan," (based on an article appearing in *Asahi Shimbun* of Tokyo), in *Refugees*, No. 1 (January 1982), p. 5, and John A. McKinstry and Carl E. Lutrin, "The Koreans of Japan: An Issue of Human Rights," *Journal of Contemporary Asia* 9, No. 4 (1979): 514–24.

82. Herman Kahn, *The Emerging Japanese Superstate* (Englewood Cliffs, N.J.: Prentice-Hall, 1970), pp. 72–73.

83. Erich Fromm, *The Anatomy of Human Destructiveness* (New York: Holt, Rinehart and Winston, 1973), pp. 96–97.

84. The data in this list are drawn from the recent issues of *Refugees*; U.S. Committee for Refugees, *1981 World Refugee Survey* and *World Refugee Survey 1982*; U.S. Congressional Research Service, *World Refugee Crisis*; and Newland, "Refugees."

85. Regime research has virtually ignored human rights issues. For a lone exception, see David P. Forsythe, "A New Human Rights Regime: What Significance?" Paper presented at the International Studies Association Convention, Philadelphia, Pa., March 1981.

86. In their monumental volume on the human rights/world public order nexus, McDougal, Lasswell, and Chen advance "a conception of human rights in terms of the shaping of values in community process and seek to locate such rights in their most comprehensive community context and in relation to all relevant processes of authoritative decision." See McDougal, Lasswell, and Chen, *Human Rights and World Public Order*, p. xvii.

87. For a list of declarations adopted during the period 1946–1977, see UN, *United Nations Action in the Field of Human Rights*, pp. 310–11. Only one declaration— the Declaration on the Elimination of All Forms of Intolerance and of Discrimination Based on Religion or Belief (1981)—has been added to this list to bring the discussion up to date (as of the end of 1981).

88. Economic and Social Council Official Records (ESCOR), 34th Sess., Supp. 8 (E/3616/Rev.1), para. 105.

89. C. Clyde Ferguson, "Global Human Rights: Challenges and Prospects," *Denver Journal of International Law and Policy* 8 (Spring 1979): 372.

90. See United Nations, *Human Rights: A Compilation of International Instruments*, UN Doc. ST/HR/1/Rev.1. (1978).

91. For a detailed analysis of China's treaty practice, see Samuel S. Kim, "The People's Republic of China and the Charter-Based International Legal Order," *American Journal of International Law* 62 (April 1978): 317–49.

92. Notice, for example, the resolute opposition of the Soviet Union to the new procedures initiated by Economic and Social Council (ECOSOC) Resolution 1503, apparently based on the belief that they represented a shift from standard-setting to implementation.

93. Theresa D. Gonzales, "The Political Sources of Procedural Debates in the United Nations: Structural Impediments to Implementation of Human Rights," *N.Y.U. Journal of International Law and Politics* 13 (Winter 1981): 439.

94. Cited in Ferguson, "Global Human Rights," p. 375.

95. See the *New York Times*, July 28, 1982, pp. A1, A4.

96. In a serious sense, however, the debate on the certification issue is misleading. It creates the illusion of U.S. concern for human rights in El Salvador while papering over the structural links of the IMF and the United States to the repressive rule in El Salvador. In July 1982 the IMF approved an $85 million loan to El Salvador, while the United States is busily engaged in training the Salvadoran soldiers for "a search-and-destroy" operation as well as giving private paramilitary training to Latin American exiles to overthrow leftist regimes in Nicaragua, Cuba, and Panama. For details, see the *New York Times*, December 24, 1981, p. A14; January 18, 1982, pp. A1, B6; June 13, 1982; p. 9; and July 17, 1982, p. 2.

97. See ECOSOC Resolution 1988 (LX) of May 11, 1976, in ECOSOR, Supp. 1, E/5850 (1976), p. 11.

98. GAOR, 32d Sess., Supp. 44, A/32/44 and Corr. 1, Annex IV.

99. See Dana D. Fischer, "Reporting Under the Covenant on Civil and Political Rights: The First Five Years of the Human Rights Committee," *American Journal of International Law* 76 (January 1982): 144–45.

100. For a description of the Canadian, Swedish, and Senegalese responses, see ibid., pp. 151–52.

101. See UN Doc. ST/HR/4/Rev.4, pp. 2–19.

102. For a detailed discussion about the working of the Commission on Human Rights under the 1503 procedure, see the following: Gonzales, "The Political Sources of Procedural Debates," pp. 427–72; Louis Sohn, "The Improvement of the UN Machinery on Human Rights," *International Studies Quarterly* 23 (June 1979): 201–6; Theo C. van Boven, "The United Nations and Human Rights: A Critical Appraisal," *Bulletin of Peace Proposals* 8, No. 3 (1977): 200–1.

103. UN Doc. E/CN.4/SR.1470 (March 1, 1978).

104. For details, see *Report of the Human Rights Committee*, GAOR, 34th Sess., Supp. No. 40, A/34/40.

105. In January 1977, 240 Czechoslovak intellectuals signed "Charter 77," a New Year's manifesto of human rights, the opening paragraph of which reads: "Law No. 120 of the Czechoslovak Collection of Laws, published October 13, 1976, includes the text of the International Covenant on Civil and Political Rights, and the International Covenant on Economic, Social and Cultural Rights, both signed on behalf of our Republic in 1968 and confirmed at the 1975 Helsinki Conference. These pacts went into effect in our country on March 23, 1976; *since that date our citizens have had the right, and the State has had the duty, to abide by them* [emphasis

added}." For the text of this manifesto, see Falk, Kim, and Mendlovitz, *Toward a Just World Order*, pp. 34–37; the quote is on p. 34. For a more detailed study, see H. Gordon Skilling, *Charter 77 and Human Rights in Czechoslavakia* (London: Allen & Unwin, 1981).

106. For NGO activities, see Forsythe, "A New Human Rights Regime"; Ved P. Nanda et al., *Global Human Rights: Public Policies, Comparative Measures, and NGO Strategies* (Boulder, Colo.: Westview Press, 1981); and Laurie Wiseberg and Harry Scoble, "Recent Trends in the Expanding Universe of Non-Governmental Organizations Dedicated to the Protection of Human Rights," *Denver Journal of International Law and Politics* 8 (special issue, 1979): 627–58.

107. Fischer, "Reporting Under the Covenant on Civil and Political Rights," p. 147.

108. See the statement Soviet representative Zorin made at the 1559th meeting of the Commission on Human Rights on February 27, 1980, in ECOSOR, 1980, Supp. No. 3A, E/1980/13 and Corr. 1-E/CN.4/1408 and Corr. 1, pp. 147–48.

109. *New York Times*, July 5, 1982, p. 3; see also the *New York Times*, February 11, 1982, p. A4.

110. For a sample of van Boven's writing, see: "The United Nations Commission on Human Rights and Violations of Human Rights and Fundamental Freedom," *Netherlands International Law Review* 15 (1968): 374–93; "Some Remarks and Special Problems Relating to Human Rights in Developing Countries," *Revue des droits de l'homme* 3 (1970): 383–96; "Partners in the Promotion and Protection of Human Rights," *Netherlands International Law Review* 24 (1977): 55–71; "The United Nations and Human Rights"; "United Nations Policies and Strategies: Global Perspectives," in B. Ramcharan, ed., *Human Rights: Thirty Years After the Universal Declaration* (The Hague: Martinus Nijhoff, 1979), pp. 83–92; and "The Role of the Commission on Human Rights in the International Community," *Human Rights Internet Newsletter* 5, Nos. 4–5 (December 1979/January 1980): 12–14.

111. David M. Paton, ed., *Breaking Barriers Nairobi 1975*, Office Report of the Fifth Assembly of the World Council of Churches (1976), Section 6, para. 9, p. 102.

112. Mazrui, "The Moving Cultural Frontier of World Order," pp. 1–2.

113. See Charles R. Beitz, *Political Theory and International Relations* (Princeton, N.J.: Princeton University Press, 1979), pp. 11–66.

114. Reinhold Niebuhr, *Moral Man and Immoral Society* (New York: Charles Scribner's Sons, 1960; originally published in 1932), p. xxiii.

115. See Hedley Bull, *the Anarchical Society*; "Human Rights and World Politics," in Ralph Pettman, ed., *Moral Claims in World Affairs* (New York: St. Martin's Press, 1979), pp. 79–91; Ernst Haas, "Human Rights: To Act or Not to Act?" in Kenneth A. Oye, Donald Rothchild, and Robert J. Lieber, eds., *Eagle Entangled: U.S. Foreign Policy in a Complex World* (New York: Longman, 1979), pp. 167–93; R. J. Vincent, "Western Conceptions of a Universal Moral Order," in Pettman, *Moral Claims in World Affairs*, pp. 52–78.

116. The Kantian image of world order as expressed in his *Perpetual Peace* lends itself to a variety of interpretations. For varying interpretations of *Perpetual Peace*, see the following: Bull, *The Anarchical Society*; Clark, *Reform and Resistance in the International Order*, pp. 31–54; Hinsley, *Power and the Pursuit of Peace*, pp. 62–80; and Waltz, *Man, the State, and War*, pp. 162–65.

117. See Kohler, "Global Apartheid," pp. 263–75.

118. In 1980, for example, the United States joined six other countries in voting against ECOSOC resolutions requesting determination and dissemination of "lists

of banks, transnational corporations, and other organizations giving assistance to the racist and colonial regime of South Africa." See *United Nations Chronicle* (July 1980): 30.

Chapter 7

1. Lester R. Brown, *World Without Borders* (New York: Vintage Books, 1973), p. 28.

2. Peter A. Corning, "The Biological Bases of Behavior and Some Implications for Political Science," *World Politics* 23 (1971): 355.

3. See Diamond, *In Search of the Primitive*.

4. Barry Commoner, *The Closing Circle: Nature, Man, and Technology* (New York: Alfred A. Knopf, 1971), pp. 33–48.

5. Harold Sprout and Margaret Sprout, *Toward a Politics of the Planet Earth*, p. 23. For other works by the same authors bearing on the ecological perspective in international relations research, see "Environmental Factors in the Study of International Politics," *Journal of Conflict Resolution* 1 (December 1957): 309–28; *The Ecological Perspective on Human Affairs, with Special Reference to International Politics* (Princeton, N.J.: Princeton University Press, 1965); *Multiple Vulnerabilities: The Context of Environmental Repair and Protection*, Research Monograph No. 40 (Princeton, N.J.: Center of International Studies, Princeton University, April 1974); and *The Context of Environmental Politics* (Lexington, Ky.: University Press of Kentucky, 1978).

6. William H. McNeill, *The Human Condition: An Ecological and Historical View* (Princeton, N.J.: Princeton University Press, 1980), p. 8.

7. Harold Sioli, director of the Max Planck Institute of Limnology, estimates that the Amazon rain forest is providing through its photosynthesis about "50 percent of the world's annual production of oxygen." See Barnet, *The Lean Years*, p. 75.

8. Richard A. Falk, *This Endangered Planet: Prospects and Proposals for Human Survival* (New York: Vintage Books, 1972), p. 25.

9. See Riley E. Dunlap, "Paradigmatic Change in Social Science," *American Behavioral Scientist* 24 (September/October 1980): 5–14, and Lynn White, Jr., "The Historical Roots of Our Ecologic Crisis," *Science* 155 (March 10, 1967): 1203–7.

10. Black, *The Dynamics of Modernization*, p. 7. Sociologist Marion Levy has defined modernization in terms of the ratio of inanimate to animate sources of energy, i.e., the higher the ratio, the higher the level of modernization. See Marion Levy, *Modernization and the Structure of Societies*, Vol. 1 (Princeton, N.J.: Princeton University Press, 1966), pp. 11–15.

11. White, "The Historical Roots of Our Ecological Crisis," p. 1203. Theodore Roszak also argues that science and technology are antithetical to the spiritual nature of man and have eroded his "transcendent energies" to the detriment of human creativity and awareness. Theodore Roszak, *Where the Wasteland Ends* (New York: Anchor, 1972), p. xxi.

12. See *The Global 2000 Report to the President*, Vol. 1: *Entering the Twenty-First Century*; Vol. 2: *The Technical Report*, and Vol. 3: *Documentation on the Government's Global Sectoral Models: The Government's "Global Model"* (Washington, D.C.: Government Printing Office, 1981).

13. Rajni Kothari, *Environment and Alternative Development*, WOMP Working Paper No. 15 (New York: Institute for World Order, 1981), p. 24.

14. For further analysis and elaboration, see my "Whither Post-Mao Chinese Global Policy?" and "The Political Economy of Post-Mao China in Global Perspective."

15. See Garrett Hardin, "The Tragedy of the Commons," *Science* 162 (December 1968): 1243–48; "The Survival of Nations and Civilization," editorial in *Science* 172 (June 25, 1971): 1297; "Lifeboat Ethics: The Case Against Helping the Poor," *Psychology Today* 8 (September 1974): 38–43, 123–26; "An Ecolate View of the Human Predicament"; "Limited World, Limited Rights," *Society* 17 (May-June 1980): 5–8; and Garrett Hardin and John Baden, eds., *Managing the Commons* (San Francisco: W. H. Freeman and Co., 1977).

16. For trenchant criticisms from three world-order scholars, see the following articles in *Alternatives* 7 (Winter 1981-1982): Rajni Kothari, "On Eco-Imperialism," pp. 385–94; Christian Bay, "On Ecolacy Sans Humanism," pp. 395–402; and Richard A. Falk, "On Advice to the Imperial Prince," pp. 403–8.

17. I owe this point to Canadian legal scholar/ecologist R. Michael M'Gonigle, as expressed in his personal communication to me in late 1982.

18. Commoner, *The Closing Circle*, p. 297.

19. See Robert L. Heilbroner, *An Inquiry into the Human Prospect* (New York: W. W. Norton & Co., 1974), chap. 5, and William Ophuls, *Ecology and the Politics of Scarcity* (San Francisco: W. H. Freeman and Co., 1977), chap. 8. These are among the most influential books published in the 1970s on ecological issues. Ophuls's book won the American Political Science Association's prize for the best book published in 1977 in American national policy, as well as the International Studies Association's prize for the best book of 1977 in international relations.

For an excellent analysis and critique of two extreme poles of ecologism—the ecological Leviathanism of Hardin, Heilbroner, and Ophuls and the soft decentralized path advocated by E. F. Schumacher, Amory Lovins, and others—and a cogent case for a third alternative path, see David W. Orr and Stuart Hill, "Leviathan, the Open Society, and the Crisis of Ecology," in David W. Orr and Marvin S. Soroos, eds., *The Global Predicament: Ecological Perspectives on World Order* (Chapel Hill, N.C.: University of North Carolina Press, 1979), pp. 308–26. Davis Bobrow has also argued persuasively that it is not always easy to distinguish a leviathan from a dinosaur. See Davis Bobrow, "The Politics of Coordinated Redistribution," in Dennis Pirages, ed., *The Sustainable Society* (New York: Praeger, 1977), pp. 197–219.

20. For the text of the Poona Declaration, see Falk, Kim, and Mendlovitz, *Toward a Just World Order*, pp. 359–63; the quote in the text is on p. 361.

21. For details, see *The Global 2000*, Vol. 2, pp. 182–84 and UN *The State of the World Environment 1972–1982*, Report of the Executive Director, UN Doc. UNEP/GC.10/3 (January 29, 1982), pp. 12–13.

22. Erik Eckholm, *Down to Earth: Environment and Human Needs* (New York: W. W. Norton & Co. 1982), p. 118.

23. See *The Global 2000*, Vol. 1, p. 36; *New York Times*, March 26, 1982, p. A12; and Eckholm, *Down to Earth*, p. 119.

24. National Academy of Sciences, *Atmosphere-Biosphere Interactions: Toward a Better Understanding of the Ecological Consequences of Fossil Fuel Combustion* (Washington, D.C.: National Academy of Sciences, 1981).

25. Thomas Crocker, cited in Eckholm, *Down to Earth*, p. 121.

26. *Environment and Health* (Washington, D.C.: Congressional Quarterly, 1981), p. 21.

27. UN, *The State of the World Environment 1972–1982*, p. 13.

28. See the *New York Times*, January 28, 1981, p. B5, and October 20, 1981, p. C1.

29. Geophysics Study Committee, *Energy and Climate* (Washington, D.C.: National Academy of Sciences, 1977), p. 4. See also UN, *The State of the World Environment 1972–1982*, p. 15.

30. See J. Hansen, D. Johnson, A. Lacis, S. Lebedeff, P. Lee, D. Rind, and G. Russell, "Climate Impact of Increasing Atmospheric Carbon Dioxide," *Science* 213 (August 28, 1981): 957–66.

31. Commoner, *The Closing Circle*, p. 79.

32. Heidi Steffens, "Nuclear Subs May be Dumped in the Deep," *Inter-Dependent* 8 (October/November 1982): 3.

33. *New York Times*, January 15, 1982, p. A8.

34. Lester R. Brown, "World Food Resources and Population: The Narrowing Margin," *Population Bulletin* 36 (September 1981): 13–15.

35. Edward D. Goldberg, *The Health of the Oceans* (Paris: UNESCO, 1976), pp. 79–97.

36. *The Global 2000*, Vol. 2, p. 315.

37. *New York Times*, November 7, 1982, p. 26.

38. Goldberg, *The Health of the Oceans*, p. 19.

39. Peter Thacher, "A Master Plan for the Watery Planet," *Uniterra* (January/ February 1981).

40. Lester R. Brown, *Building a Sustainable Society* (New York: W. W. Norton & Co., 1981), p. 13.

41. Brown, "World Food Resources and Population," p. 8.

42. For details, see Erik Eckholm and Lester R. Brown, *Spreading Deserts—The Hand of Man*, Worldwatch Paper No. 13 (Washington, D.C.: Worldwatch Institute, August 1977) and Lester R. Brown, *The Twenty-Ninth Day: Accommodating Human Needs and Numbers to the Earth's Resources* (New York: W. W. Norton & Co., 1978), pp. 27–33.

43. Eckholm, *Down to Earth*, pp. 143–44.

44. *New York Times*, August 28, 1977.

45. The United Nations Disarmament Yearbook: Vol. 4, p. 409.

46. See Michael F. Lofchie, "Political and Economic Origins of African Hunger," *Journal of Modern African Studies* 13, No. 4 (December 1975): 551–67.

47. *Interrelations: Resources, Environment, Population and Development*, Proceedings of a United Nations Symposium held at Stockholm, August 6–10, 1979 (New York: United Nations, 1980), p. 35, and Maurice Strong, "The International Community and the Environment," *Environmental Conservation* 4, No. 3 (Autumn 1977): 167.

48. See "The Green Wall of China," *Development Forum* 9 (July-August 1981); and *Forest Resources of Tropical Asia* (Rome: FAO, 1981).

49. *The Global 2000*, Vol. 1, p. 39.

50. For details, see Erik Eckholm, *The Other Energy Crisis: Firewood*, Worldwatch Paper No. 1 (Washington, D.C.: Worldwatch Institute, September 1975); *Planting for the Future: Forestry for Human Needs*, Worldwatch Paper No. 26 (Washington, D.C.: Worldwatch Institute, February 1979); *Down to Earth*, pp. 155–77; Norman Lewis, "The Rape of Amazonia," *Observer Magazine* (April 22, 1979); William Flanagan, "The Richest Man in America Walks to Work," *New York Magazine* (November 28, 1977); *New York Times*, January 20, 1981, p. A31; December 27, 1982, p. A10; and 'Daniel Ludwig's floating Factory,' *Time* (June 19, 1978).

51. UN Chronicle 20 (January 1983): 74.

52. *The Global 2000*, Vol. 2, p. 279.

53. See National Agricultural Lands Study, *Soil Degradation: Effects on Agricultural Productivity*, Interim Report No. 4 (Washington, D.C.: U.S. Department of Agriculture and the Council on Environmental Quality, November 1980).

54. *The Global 2000*, Vol. 2, p. 280.

55. The International Union for Conservation of Nature and Natural Resources, *World Conservation Strategy: Executive Summary* (Gland, Switzerland, 1980). This is an unpaginated document.

56. Ibid., p. 281. Emphasis in original.

57. See Barnet, *The Lean Years*, p. 162; Lester Brown, "World Food Resources and Population," pp. 10–11; *The Global 2000*, Vol 2, p. 282; Science Council of Canada, *Population, Technology and Resources* (Ottawa: July 1976); and David Pimentel, L. E. Hurd, A. C. Bellotti, M. J. Forster, I. N. Oka, O. D. Sholes, and R. J. Whitman, "Food Production and the Energy Crisis," *Science* 182 (November 2, 1973): 443–49.

58. Cited in *Environment and Health*, p. 35.

59. *New York Times*, May 2, 1982, Sec. 4, p. 22E.

60. For a detailed description of the land pollution problem in the United States, see *Environment and Health*, pp. 27–40.

61. See "State of World Population '82," *UN Chronicle* 19, No. 7 (July 1982): 77–82.

62. See UN, *World Population Situation in 1981*, Report of the Secretary-General, UN Doc. A/36/117 (March 6, 1981).

63. "State of World Population '82," p. 80.

64. For a cross-national study of energy policy, see Kenneth R. Stunkel, ed., *National Energy Profiles* (New York: Praeger Publishers, 1981).

65. Nathan Keyfitz, "World Resources and the World Middle Class," in Falk, Kim, and Mendlovitz, *Toward a Just World Order*, pp. 297–314.

66. Commoner, *The Closing Circle*, pp. 140–77.

67. *New York Times*, August 23, 1982, p. A13. Emphasis in original.

68. *New York Times*, December 12, 1980, p. A16.

69. For trenchant analysis and prescription, see Richard A. Falk, "Environmental Warfare and Ecocide;—Facts, Appraisal, and Proposals," *Bulletin of Peace Proposals* 4 (1973): 80–96.

70. Colin Norman, "Pentagon Admits Vietnam Rainmaking," *Nature* 249 (May 31, 1973): 402.

71. See Howard L. Rosenberg, *Atomic Soldiers: American Victims of Nuclear Experiments* (New York: Basic Books, 1980), and Thomas H. Saffer and Orville E. Kelly, *Countdown Zero* (New York: G. P. Putnam's Sons, 1982).

72. For a cogent argument to break the nuclear chain as prescriptions for nuclear weapons nonproliferation as well as for an alternative energy path, see Amory B. Lovins and L. Hunter Lovins, *Energy/War: Breaking the Nuclear Link* (New York: Harper Colophon Books, 1980).

73. For comparative and cross-national studies of environmental policies, see Cynthia H. Enloe, *The Politics of Pollution in a Comparative Perspective: Ecology and Power in Four Nations* (New York: David McKay, 1975); Donald R. Kelley, Kenneth R. Stunkel, and Richard R. Wescott, *The Economic Superpowers and the Environment: The United States, the Soviet Union, and Japan* (San Francisco: W. H. Freeman and Co., 1976); and Ophuls, *Ecology and the Politics of Scarcity*, pp. 200–8.

74. For an analysis of Chinese energy and environmental policy, see Samuel S. Kim, "The People's Republic of China," in Stunkel, *National Energy Profiles*, pp. 171–218.

75. For details, see the following: *Beijing Review*, No. 31 (August 3, 1981): 4–5; No. 39 (September 28, 1981): 19–22; *Renmin Ribao* (People's Daily), August 19, 1981, p. 1; August 24, 1981, p. 1; September 3, 1981, p. 2; September 5, 1981, p. 2; September 6, 1981, p. 5; September 8, 1981, p. 2; and September 10, 1981, p. 1.

76. For a careful analysis of the constraints in Japanese ecopolitics, see Kelley, Stunkel, and Wescott, *The Economic Superpowers*, pp. 180–96.

77. See "Protection Pays," *Development Forum* 9, No. 5 (June 1981): 8; and Eckholm, *Down to Earth*, p. 103.

78. This is based on my reading of numerous articles in the *New York Times*.

79. *New York Times*, November 22, 1982, p. D4.

80. Pierre Teilhard de Chardin, *The Future of Man*, trans. Norman Denny (New York: Harper & Row, 1964), p. 23.

81. For the proceedings of the Stockholm Conference including its Declaration and Action Plan, see UN, *Report of the United States on the Human Environment, Stockholm, 5–15 June 1972* (New York: United Nations Publication, Sales No. E.73.II.A.14,1973). For the Nairobi Declaration, see UN Doc. UNEP/GC (SSC)/4 (June 28, 1982), pp. 53–55.

82. For sharply contrasting interpretations from different perspectives, see Robert Gillette, "The News About Stockholm Isn't All Bad, State Officials Say," *Science* 175 (March 3, 1972): 969; F. H. Knelman, "What Happened at Stockholm," *International Journal* 28, No. 1 (Winter 1972-1973): 28–49; Sohn, "The Stockholm Declaration on the Human Environment," pp. 423–515; Maurice F. Strong, "One Year After Stockholm," *Foreign Affairs* 51, No. 4 (July 1973): 690–707; and Markus Timmler, "Die Umwelt-Konferenz in Stockholm," *Aussenpolitik* 23 (October 1972): 618–28.

83. Appropriately enough, a color photograph of the earth taken from the Apollo spacecraft is on the front cover of the paperback edition of Ophuls' prizewinning book, *Ecology and the Politics of Scarcity*.

84. See *Development and Environment*, report submitted by a panel of experts convened by the Secretary-General of the United Nations Conference on the Human Environment (Stockholm: Kungl. Boktryckeriet, 1971).

85. The name Dai Dong was derived from an ancient Chinese precept: "For a world in which not only a man's family is his family, not only his children are his children, but all the world is his family and all children are his."

86. See Knelman, "What Happened at Stockholm," pp. 48–49; quote on p. 46.

87. See the following UN publications: *Review of Major Achievements in the Implementation of the Action Plan for the Human Envioornment*, Report of the Executive Director, UN Doc. UNEP/GC(SCC)/INF.1 (January 26, 1982); *The State of the World Environment, 1972–1982; The Environment in 1982: Retrospect and Prospect*, UN Doc. UNEP/GC(SSC)/2 (January 29, 1982); and *Report of the Governing Council at Its Session of a Special Character*, UN Doc. UNEP/GC(SSC)/4 (June 28, 1982).

88. For a succinct analysis of the development of a collaborative research relationship between WMO and ICSU, see Kaare Langlo, "Impact of IMO and WMO on Meterological Research," *WMO Bulletin* 22 (January 1973): 3–6.

89. This account of MAB is drawn from John G. Ruggie, "On the Problem of 'The Global Problematique': What Roles for International Organizations?" *Alternatives* 5 (January 1980): 528–30.

90. See UN, *Review of Major Achievements*, p. 50.

91. UNEP, *Annual Review 1979* (Nairobi, Kenya: UNEP, 1980), p. 25.

92. This summary account is drawn from the following UNEP publications: UN, *The Environment Programme: Programme Performance Report*, Report of the

Executive Director, UN Doc. UNEP/GC.9/5 (February 25, 1981), pp. 8–12; *Annual Review 1979*, pp. 23–24; and *Review of Major Achievements*, pp. 48–49.

93. See the *New York Times*, June 8, 1982, p. C1; and *Atmosphere-Biosphere Interactions*. The insincerity of the Reagan administration was made clear in late 1982. While insisting that more research is needed before it would take any regulatory action to control acid rain, it ordered on December 1, 1982, that the money for the research project on acid rain (the Advanced Utility Simulation Model Program) be cut to $150,000 from $650,000 in the current fiscal year. See the *New York Times*, December 2, 1982, p. B17.

94. Sohn, "The Stockholm Declaration on the Human Environment," p. 440.

95. For further analysis of Chinese participation in the Stockholm Conference, see Kim, *China, the United Nations, and World Order*, pp. 487–91; Sohn, "The Stockholm Declaration on the Human Environment," pp. 423–515; and Timmler, "Die Umwelt-Konferenz in Stockholm," pp. 618–23. For the text of the "Ten Cardinal Principles on Amending 'Declaration on Human Envioronment,'" see *Peking Review*, No. 25 (June 23, 1972): 9–11.

96. See UN, *Interrelations: Resources, Environment, Population and Development*.

97. For a thoroughgoing analysis of the international legal order of the environment, see Michael M'Gonigle and Mark W. Zacher, *Pollution, Politics, and International Law* (Berkeley, Calif.: University of California Press, 1979); "New Perspectives on International Environmental Law," *The Yale Law Journal* 82, No. 8 (July 1973): 1659–80; and Jan Schneider, *World Public Order of the Environment: Towards an International Ecological Law and Organization* (Toronto: University of Toronto Press, 1979).

98. For details see UN, *Register of International Conventions and Protocols in the Field of the Environment*, UN Doc. UNEP/GC/INFORMATION/5/Supplement 5 (November 26, 1981). See also UN Docs. UNEP/GC.10/5/Add. 1 and Corr. 1 and UN Doc. UNEP/GC (SSC)/2 (January 29, 1982), pp. 51–52.

99. For a more detailed description and analysis, see M'Gonigle and Zacher, *Pollution, Politics, and International Law*, pp. 315–42.

100. The text of the Cocoyoc Declaration is reproduced in *Alternatives* 1, Nos. 2–3 (July–September 1975): 396–406; the quote in the text on p. 396.

101. This account of the reactions of the major global actors in UNEP is drawn from Ruggie, "On 'The Global Problematique,'" pp. 544–47.

102. General Assembly Resolution 35/7 of October 30, 1980, adopted without a vote. See General Assembly Resolution 36/6 of October 27, 1981. On October 28, 1982, the General Assembly adopted the World Charter for Nature. This action was taken in the form of a resolution by a recorded vote of 111-1-18 with the United States as the sole dissenter. See General Assembly Resolution 37/7 of October 28, 1982, and the accompanying Annex in *Resolutions and Decisions Adopted by the General Assembly During the First Part of Its Thirty-Seventh Session From 21 September to 21 December 1982*, Press Release GA/6787 (January 4, 1983), pp. 8–12.

103. UN, *International Development Strategy*, pp. 23–24.

104. UN Doc. UNEP/GC.10/INF.1, p.46.

105. For details, see General Assembly Resolution 2997 (XXVII) of December 15, 1972, adopted by a recorded vote of 116 in favor, none against, with 10 abstentions.

106. UN Doc. UNEP/GC.10/INF.1 (January 26, 1982), p. 69.

107. Deutsch, *Politics and Government*, p. 16.

108. For further elaboration, see UN Doc. UNEP/GC(SSC)/2 (January 29, 1982), pp. 70–72.

109. For the background and details, see the following: UN Doc. UNEP/GC.10/ INF.1 (January 26, 1982), pp. 16–17; *Earth*, No. 14 (September 1981): 2; J. L. McHugh, "Rise and Fall of World Whaling: The Tragedy of the Commons Illustrated," *Journal of International Affairs* 31, No. 1 (1977): 23–33; *Development Forum* 10 (September/October 1982): 7; *New York Times*, March 7, 1981, p. 3; June 17, 1981, p. A4; July 27, 1981, p. A3; July 24, 1982, pp. 1, 3.

110. *New York Times*, November 3, 1982, p. A10.

111. *New York Times*, Janaury 22, 1981, p. A3.

112. See UN Docs. UNEP/GC.10/INF. 1, p. 28; A/35/25, pp. 83–86; UNEP, *Annual Review 1979*, pp. 34–35.

113. M'Gonigle and Zacher, *Pollution, Politics, and International Law*, p. 313.

114. Heilbroner, *An Inquiry into the Human Prospect*, p. 132.

115. See Erwin Knoll and Judith Nies McFadden, eds., *War Crimes and the American Conscience* (New York: Holt, Rinehart and Winston, 1970), p. 71. Emphasis in original.

116. Falk, "Environmental Warfare and Ecocide," pp. 93–96.

117. Norman Cousins, "Who Owns the Ozone?" in Falk, Kim, and Mendlovitz, *Toward a Just World Order*, pp. 484–85.

118. OECD, *Environment Policies for the 1980s* (Paris: OECD, 1980), p. 12.

119. For a detailed cost-benefit analyses, see A. M. Freeman III, "The Benefits of Air and Water Pollution Control: A Review and Synthesis of Recent Estimates," report prepared for and published by the Council on Environmental Quality (Washington, D.C.: December 1979); Council on Environmental Quality, *Environmental Quality—1979* (Washington, D.C.: December 1979); "Protection Pays," *Development Forum* 9, No. 5 (June 1981): 8; Michael G. Royston, *Pollution Prevention Pays* (New York: Pergamon Press, 1979).

120. See Scott Overton and Larry Hunt, "A View of Current Forest Policy, with Questions Regarding the Future State of Forests and Criteria of Management," in *Transactions of the Thirty-Ninth North American Wildlife and Natural Resources Conference* (Washington, D.C.: Wildlife Management Institute, 1974), pp. 334–53.

121. For example, as part of the plan to cut domestic social spending, the Reagan administration has drastically reinterpreted the 1972 Clean Water Act to allow municipalities to seek exemptions allowing them to discharge sewage after removing as little as 25 percent, compared to the previous standard of 85 percent, of the biological material. Federal spending on the construction of sewage treatment facilities is reported to have declined under the Reagan administraton by nearly 43 percent, from $4.2 billion in the fiscal year 1979 to $2.4 billion in the fiscal year 1982. See the *New York Times*, September 13, 1982, pp. 1, B14.

122. Lewis Mumford, *The Myth of Machine* (New York: Harcourt Brace Jovanovich, 1970), p. 328.

123. John G. Cross and Melvin J. Guyer, *Social Traps* (Ann Arbor: University of Michigan Press, 1980), p. 4.

124. See Figure 1.1 in Deutsch, *Politics and Government*, p. 6.

125. Murray Edelman, *The Symbolic Uses of Politics* (Urbana: University of Illinois Press, 1964).

126. M'Gonigle and Zacher, *Pollution, Politics and International Law*, p. 348.

127. See Un Doc. A/36/532 (September 25, 1981).

Chapter 8

1. For the most comprehensive and up-to-date treatment of utopian thinking in the West, see Frank E. Manuel and Fritzie P. Manuel, *Utopian Thought in the*

Western World (Cambridge, Mass.: Harvard University Press, 1979). For critical review and analysis of utopian thinking from a world order perspective, see Louis René Beres and Harry R. Targ, *Constructing Alternative World Futures: Reordering the Planet* (Cambridge, Mass.: Schenkman Publishing Co., 1977), chap. 4, and Camilleri, *Civilization in Crisis*, chap. 9.

2. Carr, *The Twenty Years' Crisis 1919-1939*, p. 11.

3. A British author writes: "It is no extravagance to claim that the entire body of utopian fiction is little more than a series of variations on Plato. As the first in the field he was able to present—once and for all—the basic dilemma that puts power and passion into the dullest utopia—the eternal conflict between individual desires and public necessities, between the happiness of the citizen and the security of the state. From Plato the literary tradition runs straight to Sir Thomas More and on to the many visionaries, ideologues and propagandists of the last hundred years." See I. F. Clarke, "The Utility of Utopia," *Futures* 3 (December 1971): 396.

4. For details, see Beres and Targ, *Constructing Alternative World Futures*, pp. 63-91.

5. This is an official translation of the United Nations. See UN Press Release HQ/235 (April 26, 1968).

6. Karl Mannheim, *Ideology and Utopia* (New York: Harcourt, Brace & World, 1968), p. 206.

7. H. H. Gerth and C. Wright Mills, eds., *From Max Weber: Essays in Sociology* (New York: Oxford University Press, 1958), p. 128.

8. See B. F. Skinner, *Walden Two* (New York: Macmillan, 1948); Paul and Percival Goodman, *Communitas* (New York: Vintage Books, 1960); Theodore Roszak, *The Making of a Counter Culture* (Garden City, N.Y.: Anchor, 1969); de Chardin, *The Future of Man*, and W. Warren Wagar, *The City of Man* (Baltimore: Pelican, 1967).

9. Pope Paul VI, *Apostolic Letter to Cardinal Maurice Roy on the Occasion of the Eightieth Anniversary of the Encyclical "Rerum Norarum,"* Vatican, May 14, 1971.

10. *Writings of the Young Marx on Philosophy and Society*, edited and translated by Lloyd D. Easton and Kurt H. Guddat (Garden City, N.Y.: Anchor Books, 1967), p. 402.

11. A little-publicized incident involving a gift from "China" to the United Nations provides an apt illustration of contending images of world order. In April 1968 the Chinese Nationalist government presented a plaque engraved with the traditional concept of *datong* in Chinese (as shown in the English translation quoted above) with the declaration: "This is the kind of world order which mankind has strived for ages to build." In accepting the plaque, the Secretary-General of the United Nations said that "the principles of the Charter are not new; they are to be found even in the age-old civilization of China." However, the concept of *datong* was so offensive to the Chinese communist image of world order that the seemingly innocuous gift had to be removed from the UN building when the People's Republic of China replaced the Republic of China as the legitimate government of China in late 1971. See UN Press Release SG/SM/936 (April 26, 1968).

12. See Beres and Targ, *Constructing Alternative World Futures*, pp. 89-91.

13. The first report of the Commission on the Year 2000, formed in 1965 by the American Academy of Arts and Sciences and chaired by sociologist Daniel Bell (ed.), was entitled *Toward the Year 2000: Work in Progress* (Boston: Beacon Press, 1969). In 1967 Herman Kahn and Anthony Wiener published their trailblazing book, *The Year 2000: A Framework for Speculation on the Next Thirty-Three Years*, in the United States (New York: Macmillan, 1967). In the same year, the first world congress on futurism, officially called "First International Future Research

Conference," was held in Oslo, Norway, and two years later the conference papers were published under the umbrella title *Mankind 2000*.

The other important future projects that followed include: the "Poland 2000" Research and Forecasting Committee, set up in 1969 at the Polish Academy of Sciences; *Hawaii 2000* (1973); *Mankind and the Year 2000*, published in the Soviet Union in 1976; "Project 2000," initiated by the Department of Economic and Social Affairs of the United Nations Secretariat in the mid-1970s; *Images of the World in the Year 2000* (1976), a comprehensive comparative ten-nation study; three volumes of *The Global 2000 Report to the President* (1980–1981); and *Agriculture: Toward 2000*, a grand strategy for development of world agriculture to the end of the century, with particular reference to developing countries, proposed by FAO. See Robert Jungk and Johan Galtung, eds., *Mankind 2000* (London: Allen & Unwin, 1969); and Andrew Sicinski (Head, Division of Social Prognoses, Institute of Philosophy and Sociology, Polish Academy of Sciences), "The Main Trends of Contemporary Future Research," *Polsak 2000 Journal*, Spec. No. (1974), pp. 39–40; George Chaplin and Glenn D. Paige, eds., *Hawaii 2000: Continuing Experiment in Anticipatory Democracy* (Honolulu, Hawaii: University of Hawaii Press, 1973); V. Kosolapov, *Mankind and the Year 2000* (Moscow: Progress Publishers, 1976); H. Ornauer, et al., eds., *Images of the World in the Year 2000: A Comparative Ten Nation Study* (Atlantic Highlands, N.J.: Humanities Press, 1976); FAO, *Agriculture: Toward 2000* (Rome: FAO, 1981).

14. For major critiques of *The Limits to Growth* global models and alternative global models, see Johan Galtung, "The Limits to Growth and Class Politics," *Journal of Peace Research* 10 (1973): 101–14; H.S.D. Cole et al., *Models of Doom* (New York: Universe Books, 1973); Herrera, *Catastrophe or New Society?* and Christopher Freeman and Marie Jahoda, eds., *World Futures: The Great Debate* (New York: Universe Books, 1978).

15. See John A. Hannigan, "Fragmentation in Science: The Case of Futurology," *Sociological Review* 28 (May 1980): 317–32, and Erich Jantsch, *Technological Forecasting in Perspective* (Paris: OECD, 1967).

16. John McHale and Magda Cordell McHale, *Futures Studies: An International Survey*, Sales No. E.75.XV.FS/1 (New York: UNITAR, 1975), p. 17.

17. This 450-page study is classified secret, but the U.S. Air Force made an extract available to the press. See the *New York Times*, November 1, 1982, p. A13.

18. The commonly used terms include futures research, future studies, futuristics, futurology, prognostics, futurism, futuribles, forecasting, futures analysis, global modelling. Based on an international survey of future studies, John McHale and Magda Cordell McHale observe: *"Futuribles*, the word coined by de Jouvenel tends to be restricted to Western Europe. There is a preference for prognostics in Soviet and East European usage, with additional descriptors such as social, economic, political and so on. As the field has grown in respectability, *futures research and forecasting* tend to be preferred in more academic discussion." See McHale and McHale, *Futures Studies*, p. 3. Italics in original. It should also be noted in this connection that the *International Encyclopedia of the Social Sciences*, published in 1968, did not have a single entry under any of the above-mentioned terms of future studies.

19. For an elaboration, see Hannigan, "Fragmentation in Science."

20. Herman Kahn, William Brown, and Leon Martel, *The Next 200 Years: A Scenario for America and the World* (New York: William Morrow and Co., 1976), pp. 9–16.

21. Robert Gilpin, "Three Models of the Future," *International Organization* 29 (Winter 1975): 37–60.

22. Ian Miles, "Worldviews and Scenarios," in Freeman and Jahoda, *World Futures*, pp. 233–78.

23. See Elise Boulding, "Religion, Futurism, and Models of Social Change," in Robert Bundy, ed., *Images of the Future: The Twenty-First Century and Beyond* (Buffalo, N.Y.: Prometheus Books, 1976), pp. 168–81.

24. Richard A. Falk, "Toward a New World Order: Modest Methods and Drastic Visions," in Mendlovitz, *On the Creation of a Just World Order*, pp. 211–58.

25. Cited in McHale and McHale, *Futures Studies*, p. 10.

26. Elise Boulding, "Learning About the Future," *Bulletin of Peace Proposals* 12 (May 1981): 176.

27. Arthur C. Clarke, *Profiles of the Future* (New York: Harper & Row, 1962), p. 7.

28. Robert Boyd, "World Dynamics: A Note," *Science* 177 (August 11, 1972): 516–19.

29. Cited in Cornish, *The Study of the Future*, p. 18. Emphasis in original.

30. Gordon W. Allport, *The Person in Psychology* (Boston: Beacon Press, 1968), p. 191. For similar findings in other sociopsychological studies, see Kim, "The Lorenzian Theory of Aggression and Peace Research," pp. 253–76.

31. For details, see Cornish, *The Study of the Future*, pp. 214–15.

32. Kahn and Wiener, *The Year 2000*, p. 116.

33. See Herman Kahn and T. Mitchell Ford, "Don't Expect Doomsday," *New York Times*, October 3, 1980, p. A35. Emphasis added. See also Herman Kahn, *The Coming Boom* (New York: Simon & Schuster, 1982).

34. *The Global 2000 Report to the President*, Vol 1, p. 43.

35. Heilbroner, *An Inquiry into the Human Prospect*, pp. 22, 123.

36. Johan Galtung, "On the Future, Future Studies and Future Attitudes," in Ornauer, *Images of the World in the Year 2000*, p. 4.

37. Rene Dubos, "Reason for Optimism," *New York Times*, March 6, 1982, p. 23.

38. Willis W. Harman, "The Coming Transformation," *The Futurist* 11 (February 1977): 8.

39. Cornish, *The Study of the Future*, p. 20. Emphasis in original.

40. See Cantril, *The Pattern of Human Concerns*; Gallup, "Human Needs and Satisfaction"; and Ornauer, *Images of the World in the Year 2000*.

41. W. Warren Wagar, *The City of Man*, p. 15, and *Building the City of Man* (San Francisco: W. H. Freeman and Co., 1971), p. 52.

42. Harold D. Lasswell, *The Future of Political Science* (New York: Atherton Press, 1963), p. 242.

43. Nazli Choucri, "Key Issues in International Relations Forecasting," in Nazli Chouri and Thomas W. Robinson, eds., *Forecasting in International Relations: Theory, Methods, Problems, Prospects* (San Francisco: W. H. Freeman and Co., 1978), p. 4. Johan Galtung warned that "the researcher who wants to predict rather than to preview should lock up his findings rather than publish them." See his "On the Future of the International System," *Journal of Peace Research* 4 (1967): 305–33.

44. Ali Mazrui, "The Caste Factor in Social Forecasting: Predictability as a Brahminic and Bourgeois Value," in Choucri and Robinson, *Forecasting in International Relations*, pp. 373–83.

45. Charles Hampden-Turner, *Radical Man* (Cambridge, Mass.: Schenkman, 1970), pp. 305–6.

46. Quoted in Ralph Pettman, *Human Behavior and World Politics* (New York: St. Martin's Press, 1975), pp. 113–14.

47. These examples are all cited in Thomas W. Milburn, "Successful and Unsuccessful Forecasting in International Relations," in Choucri and Robinson, *Forecasting in International Relations*, p. 80. For further discussion on empirical and epistemological problems in international relations forecasting, see Robert H. Ament, "Comparison of Delphi Forecasting Studies in 1964 and 1969," in Franklin Tugwell, ed., *Search for Alternatives: Public Policy and the Study of the Future* (Cambridge, Mass.: Winthrop Publishers, 1973), pp. 164–75; John R. Freeman and Brian L. Job, "Scientific Forecasts in International Relations: Problems of Definition and Epistemology," *International Studies Quarterly* 23 (March 1979): 113–43; Galtung, "On the Future of the International System."

48. The obvious exceptions are civilian-military strategic planners—most notably Herman Kahn, whose detailed scenario construction and analysis of future nuclear warfare, beginning with *On Thermonuclear War* (Princeton, N.J.: Princeton University Press, 1960), is well known.

49. Sivard, *World Military and Social Expenditures 1982*, p. 6.

50. Ibid., p. 11.

51. UN, *Long-Term Trends in Economic Development: Report of the Secretary-General*, UN Doc. A/37/211 (May 26, 1982), p. 160.

52. Sivard, *World Military and Social Expenditures 1982*, p. 10.

53. See Frank Barnaby, "The Mounting Prospects of Nuclear War," *Bulletin of the Atomic Scientists* 33 (June 1977): 11; idem, "The Technological Explosion in Armaments," *Bulletin of Peace Proposals* 8 (1977): 347; Stockholm International Peace Research Institute, *SIPRI Yearbook 1981*, pp. xxvi–xxvii, 54–63; and the report of the Harvard–Massachusetts Institute of Technology Arms Control Seminar: Paul Doty et al., "Nuclear War by 1999?" *Harvard Magazine* 78 (November 1975): 19–25.

54. The Delphi technique, originally developed by Olaf Helmer and Norman Dalkey at the RAND Corporation, is a consensus forecasting method based on expert panels' estimations of certain future events or phenomena. It strives toward achieving an expert group opinion regarding possible future developments. For a detailed elaboration, see T. J. Gordon and Olaf Helmer, *Report on a Long-Range Forecasting Study*, Paper P2982 (Santa Monica, Calif.: RAND Corporation, September 1964), and Olaf Helmer, "The Use of Expert Opinion in International Relations Forecasting," in Choucri and Robinson, *Forecasting in International Relations*, pp. 116–23.

55. Sivard, *World Military and Social Expenditures 1982*, p. 15.

56. *The Global 2000 Report*, Vol. 1, p. 43.

57. *World Development Report 1982* (New York: Oxford University Press for the World Bank, 1982), chap. 4, pp. 31–37.

58. For a more recent and trenchant critque of the World Bank, see Cheryl Payer, *The World Bank: A Critical Analysis* (New York: Monthly Review Press, 1982), especially chapter 1.

59. UN, *Long-Term Trends in Economic Development*, p. 40.

60. Ibid., p. 45.

61. A. Michael Washburn and Thomas E. Jones, "Anchoring Futures in Preferences," in Choucri and Robinson, *Forecasting in International Relations*, p. 99.

62. Johan Galtung, Helmut Ornauer, and Hakan Wiberg, "The Future: Forgotten, and to Be Discovered," in Ornauer et al., *Images of the World in the Year 2000*, p. 581.

63. Arthur I. Waskow, "Looking Forward: 1999," in Tugwell, *Search for Alternatives*, pp. 177–84.

64. Wagar, *Building the City of Man*, p. 50.

65. Clark and Sohn, pp. xliii–xliv.

66. Ibid., p. liv.

67. Falk, *A Study of Future Worlds*, pp. 152–53.

68. For an elaboration of such an intermediate position, see Michael A. Washburn, "Outline for a Normative Forecasting/Planning Process," in Beres and Targ, *Planning Alternative World Futures*, pp. 60–90.

69. Sam Cole, "The Global Futures Debate 1965–1976," in Freeman and Jahoda, *World Futures*, pp. 48–49.

70. V. V. Zagladin and I. T. Frolov, "Global Problems As Areas of International Co-operation," *International Social Science Journal* 34, No. 1 (1982): 116. Emphasis added.

71. Cole, "The Global Futures Debate," pp. 43–45.

72. See Shigeko Fukai, "Japan's North-South Dialogue at the United Nations," *World Politics* 35 (October 1982): 73–105.

73. Yoshikazu Sakamoto and Hiroharu Seki, "Forecasting in Cross-National Perspective: Japan," in Choucri and Robinson, *Forecasting in International Relations*, p. 366.

74. OECD, *Facing the Future*, p. 414.

75. Herrerra et al., *Catastrophe or New Society?* p. 25.

76. See UN, *Long-Term Trends in Economic Development*, pp. 45–66.

77. Gene Sharp, *Social Power and Political Freedom* (Boston: Porter Sargent Publishers, 1980), p. 8.

78. Gene Sharp, *Exploring Nonviolent Alternatives* (Boston: Porter Sargent Publishers, 1971), pp. 31–32. See also Joan Bondurant, *Conquest of Violence: The Gandhian Philosophy of Conflict*, rev. ed. (Berkeley, Calif.: University of California Press, 1971); George Lakey, *Strategy for a Living Revolution* (San Francisco: W. H. Freeman and Co., 1973); and Gene Sharp, *Making the Abolition of War a Realistic Goal*, (New York: Institute for World Order, 1980).

79. For pioneering attempts to redefine world order in terms of human interests, see Robert C. Johansen, *The National Interest and the Human Interest*, and *Toward an Alternative Security System: Moving Beyond the Balance of Power in the Search for World Security*, World Policy Paper No. 24 (New York: World Policy Institute, 1983).

80. Johansen, *Toward an Alternative Security System*, p. 29.

81. This is a two-year "people's dialogue" project designed to establish links between intellectual theorists and activists as well as between various social groups and movements for social change in India. The world order scholar/activist Rajni Kothari has played an instrumental role in the conception and execution of the project. See the *New York Times*, June 15, 1982, p. A2.

82. Wilbert E. Moore, "Social Change," *International Encyclopedia of the Social Sciences*, Vols. 13–14, p. 370.

83. McDougal, Lasswell, and Chen, *Human Rights and World Public Order*, p. 63.

84. See Dankwart A. Rustow, "Communism and Change," in Chalmers Johnson, ed., *Change in Communist Systems* (Stanford, Calif.: Stanford University Press, 1970), pp. 343–58, and "Transitions to Democracy: Toward a Dynamic Model," *Comparative Politics* 2 (April 1970): 337–63.

85. Barrington Moore, Jr., *Injustice: The Social Bases of Obedience and Revolt* (White Plains, N.Y.: M. E. Sharpe, 1978).

86. See Robert Jay Lifton, "Imagining the Real," section 1 of Lifton and Falk, *Indefensible Weapons*.

87. Chadwick F. Alger, "Role of People in the Future Global Order," *Alternatives* 4 (October 1978): 233–62.

88. Kothari, *Toward a Just World.*

89. Andre Malraux, *Anti-Memoirs*, trans. Terence Kilmartin (New York: Holt, Rinehart and Winston, 1968), p. 373.

90. See George Lakey, "A Manifesto for Nonviolent Revolution," in Falk, Kim, and Mendlovitz, *Toward a Just World Order*, pp. 638–52, and Galtung, *The True Worlds*, p. 140.

91. Falk, *A Study of Future Worlds*, pp. 282–96.

92. Lyman C. White, "Peace by Pieces," *Free World* 11 (January 1946): 66–68.

93. For detailed analysis and documentation, see my *China, the United Nations, and World Order*, chap. 2.

94. See Byung-joon Ahn, *Chinese Politics and the Cultural Revolution* (Seattle, Wash.: University of Washington Press, 1976), and Hong Yung Lee, *The Politics of the Chinese Cultural Revolution* (Berkeley, Calif.: University of California Press, 1978).

95. Franz Schurmann, *Ideology and Organization in Communist China*, 2d ed. (Berkeley, Calif.: University of California Press, 1971).

96. For some empirical evidence of this, see Volker Bornschier, "The World Economy in the World-System: Structure, Dependence and Change," *International Social Science Journal* 34, No. 1 (1982): 37–59.

97. Alfred North Whitehead, *Science and the Modern World* (New York: Macmillan, 1925), p. 291.

98. Erich Fromm, *The Sane Society* (Greenwich, Conn.: Fawcett Publications, 1955), p. 23.

Bibliography

This bibliography includes the major works consulted in developing the central arguments of the book, but does not exactly coincide with the notes. Many newspaper articles and essays, some UN documents, and parts of books cited in the notes to support particular perspectives or points of view in the text are excluded here. The bibliography indicates the substance and range of reading upon which I have formed my ideas or lines of reasoning.

Adelman, Irma. "Development Economics–A Reassessment of Goals." *American Economic Review* 65 (May 1975): 302–9.

Adelman, Irma, and Cynthia Taft Morris. *Economic Growth and Social Equity in Developing Countries.* Stanford, Calif.: Stanford University Press, 1973.

Adler-Karlsson, Gunnar. "Eliminating Absolute Poverty: An Approach to the Problem." In *Reducing Global Inequities,* edited by W. Howard Wriggins and Gunnar Adler-Karlsson. New York: McGraw-Hill Book Co., 1978.

Ahmad, Eqbal. "The Neo-Fascist State: Notes on the Pathology of Power in the Third World." In *Toward a Just World Order,* edited by Richard A. Falk, Samuel S. Kim, and Saul H. Mendlovitz. Boulder, Colo.: Westview Press, 1982.

Ahn, Byung-joon. *Chinese Politics and the Cultural Revolution.* Seattle, Wash.: University of Washington Press, 1976.

Ajami, Fouad. "The Fate of Nonalignment." *Foreign Affairs* 59 (Winter 1980/1981): 366–85.

————. "World Order: The Question of Ideology." *Alternatives* 6 (Winter 1980-1981): 473–85.

————. "Human Rights and World Order Politics." In *Toward a Just World Order,* edited by Richard A. Falk, Samuel S. Kim, and Saul H. Mendlovitz. Boulder, Colo.: Westview Press, 1982.

Alger, Chadwick F. "Role of People in the Future Global Order." *Alternatives* 4 (October 1973): 233–62.

Alston, Philip. "Peace as a Human Right." *Bulletin of Peace Proposals* 11, No. 4 (December 1980): 319–30.

Alston, Philip, and Asbjorn Eide. "Peace, Human Rights and Development: Their Interrelationship." *Bulletin of Peace Proposals* 11 (December 1980): 315–18.

Ambroggi, Robert P. "Water." *Scientific American* 243 (September 1980): 101–16.

Amin, Samir. *Unequal Development.* New York: Monthly Review Press, 1976.

Amnesty International. *Report on Torture.* London: Gerald Duckworth, 1973.

————. *Amnesty International Report 1980.* London: Amnesty International Publications, 1980.

————. *Amnesty International Report 1981*. London: Amnesty International Publications, 1981.

————. *Amnesty International Report 1982*. London: Amnesty International Publications, 1982.

Amuzegar, Jahangir. "Oil Wealth: A Very Mixed Blessing." *Foreign Affairs* 60 (Spring 1982): 814–35.

Anderson, Perry. *Lineages of the Absolutist State*. New York: Humanities Press, 1974.

Angell, Robert C. *The Quest for World Order*. Ann Arbor: The University of Michigan Press, 1979.

Arens, Richard, ed. *Genocide in Paraguay*. Philadelphia: Temple University Press, 1976.

Aron, Raymond. *Peace and War: A Theory of International Relations*. Trans. Richard Howard and Annette Baker Fox. New York: Praeger, 1966.

Asamoah, Obed Y. *The Legal Significance of the Declaration of the General Assembly of the United Nations*. The Hague: Martinus Nijhoff, 1966.

Axelroad, Robert, and William Hamilton. "The Evolution of Cooperation." *Science* 211 (March 27, 1981): 1390–96.

Bachrach, Peter, and Morton S. Baratz. "Two Faces of Power." *American Political Science Review* 56 (December 1962): 947–52.

Bahia, Luiz Alberto. "The Concept of Sovereignty As a Form of Property." *Bulletin of Peace Proposals* 2 (1971): 87–91.

Bailey, K. V. "Malnutrition in the African Region." *WHO Chronicle*, No. 29 (1975): 354–64.

Bandura, Albert. *Aggression: A Social Analysis*. Englewood Cliffs, N.J.: Prentice-Hall, 1973.

Barkun, Michael. "International Norms: An Interdisciplinary Approach." *Background* 8 (August 1964): 121–29.

Barnaby, Frank. "The Mounting Prospects of Nuclear War." *Bulletin of the Atomic Scientists* 33 (June 1977): 10–19.

Barnet, Richard J. *The Lean Years: Politics in the Age of Scarcity*. New York: Simon and Schuster, 1980.

Barnett, A. Doak. *China's Economy in Global Perspective*. Washington, D.C.: Brookings Institution, 1981.

Baxter, Richard R. "Humanitarian Law or Humanitarian Politics? The 1974 Diplomatic Conference on Humanitarian Law." *Harvard International Law Journal* 16 (Winter 1975): 1–26.

Bay, Christian. "A Human Rights Approach to Transnational Politics." *Universal Human Rights* 1, No. 1 (January–March 1979): 19–42.

————. "Positive Peace and Rational Human Rights Priorities." *Bulletin of Peace Proposals* 10 (1979): 160–71.

————. "Universal Human Rights Priorities: Toward a Rational Order." In *International Human Rights: Contemporary Issues*, edited by Jack L. Nelson and Vera M. Green. Stanfordville, N.Y.: Human Rights Publishing Group, 1980.

————. *Strategies of Political Emancipation*. Notre Dame, Indiana: University of Notre Dame Press, 1981.

————. "On Ecolacy Sans Humanism." *Alternatives* 7 (Winter 1981-1982): 395–402.

Beebe, Gilbert, Hiroo Kato, and Charles E. Land. "Studies of the Mortality of A-Bomb Survivors." *Radiation Research* 75 (1978): 138–201.

Beer, Francis A. "The Epidemiology of Peace and War." *International Studies Quarterly* 23 (March 1979): 45–86.

_____ . *Peace Against War: The Ecology of International Violence.* San Francisco: W. H. Freeman and Co., 1981.

Beitz, Charles R. *Political Theory and International Relations.* Princeton, N.J.: Princeton University Press, 1979.

_____ . "Economic Rights and Distributive Justice in Developing Societies." *World Politics* 33 (April 1981): 321–46.

Belassa, Bela. "The Developing Countries and the Tokyo Round." *Journal of World Trade Law* 14 (March-April 1980): 93–118.

Bell, Daniel. "The Future World Disorder: The Structural Context of Crises." *Foreign Policy,* No. 27 (Summer 1977): 109–35.

Bell, Daniel, ed. *Toward the Year 2000: Work in Progress.* Boston: Beacon Press, 1969.

Berelson, Bernard, and Gary A. Steiner. *Human Behavior.* Shorter ed. New York: Harcourt, Brace & World, 1967.

Beres, Louis René. *Apocalypse: Nuclear Catastrophe in World Politics.* Chicago: University of Chicago Press, 1980.

_____ . *People, States, and World Order.* Itasca, Ill.: F. E. Peacock Publishers, 1981.

Beres, Louis René, and Harry R. Targ. "Perspectives on World Order: A Review." *Alternatives* 2 (June 1976): 177–98.

_____ . *Constructing Alternative World Futures: Reordering the Planet.* Cambridge, Mass.: Schenkman Publishing Co., 1977.

Beres, Louis René, and Harry R. Targ, eds. *Planning Alternative World Futures: Values, Methods, and Models.* New York: Praeger Publishers, 1975.

Bergesen, Albert, ed. *Studies of the Modern World-System.* New York: Academic Press, 1980.

Bergesen, Helge. "Human Rights—The Property of the Nation State or a Concern for the International Community?" *Cooperation and Conflict* 4 (1979): 239–54.

_____ . "A New Food Regime: Necessary but Impossible." *International Organization* 34 (Spring 1980): 285–302.

Bergsten, C. Fred. "The Threat from the Third World." *Foreign Policy,* No. 11 (1973): 102–24.

Berkowitz, Leonard. *Aggression: A Social Psychological Analysis.* New York: McGraw-Hill, 1962.

Berman, Harold J. "American and Soviet Perspectives on Human Rights." *Worldview* 22 (November 1979): 15–21.

Bertsch, Gary K, ed. *Global Policy Studies.* Beverly Hills, Calif.: Sage Publications, 1982.

Bhagwati, Jagdish N., ed. *Economics and World Order.* New York: Macmillan, 1972.

_____ . *The New International Economic Order: The North-South Debate.* Cambridge, Mass.: MIT Press, 1977.

Black, Cyril E. *The Dynamics of Modernization: A Study in Comparative History.* New York: Harper & Row, 1966.

Blackhurst, Richard, Nicolas Marian, and Jan Tumlir. *Adjustment, Trade and Growth in Developed and Developing Countries.* Studies in International Trade, No. 6. Geneva: GATT, 1978.

Blechman, Barry M., and Stephen S. Kaplan. *Force Without War: U.S. Armed Forces As a Political Instrument.* Washington, D.C.: Brookings Institution, 1978.

Bleicher, Samuel A. "The Legal Significance of Re-Citation of General Assembly Resolutions." *American Journal of International Law* 62 (July 1969): 444–78.

Blishchenko, I. P. "The Impact of the New International Order on Human Rights in Developing Countries." *Bulletin of Peace Proposals* 11, No. 4 (1980): 375–86.

"A Blueprint for Survival." *Ecologist* 2 (January 1972): 1–43.

Bohming, W. R. *Future Demand for Migrant Workers in Western Europe.* Geneva: International Labour Organization, 1976.

Bondurant, Joan. *Conquest of Violence: The Gandhian Philosophy of Conflict.* Rev. ed. Berkeley, Calif.: University of California Press, 1971.

Bornschier, Volker. "The World Economy in the World-System: Structure, Dependence and Change." *International Social Science Journal* 34, No. 1 (1982): 37–59.

Boulding, Elise. "Religion, Futurism, and Models of Social Change." In *Images of the Future,* edited by Robert Bundy. Buffalo, N.Y.: Prometheus Books, 1976.

————. "Learning to Learn: North's Response to the New International Economic Order." *Alternatives* 4 (March 1979): 429–54.

————. "Learning About the Future." *Bulletin of Peace Proposals* 12 (May 1981): 173–77.

Boulding, Kenneth E. *The Image.* Ann Arbor: University of Michigan Press, 1956.

————. *The Meaning of the Twentieth Century.* New York: Harper Colophon Books, 1964.

Bowen, Michael, Gary Freeman, and Kay Miller. *Passing By: The United States and Genocide in Burundi.* New York: Carnegie Endowment for International Peace, 1973.

Boyd, Gavin, and Charles Pentland, eds. *Issues in Global Politics.* New York: Free Press, 1981.

Bozeman, Adda B. *Politics and Culture in International History.* Princeton, N.J.: Princeton University Press, 1960.

————. *The Future of Law in a Multicultural World.* Princeton, N.J.: Princeton University Press, 1971.

Braybrooke, David. "The Relevance of Norms to Political Description." *American Political Science Review* 52 (December 1958): 989–1006.

Brecht, Arnold. *Political Theory, the Foundations of Twentieth Century Political Thought.* Princeton, N.J.: Princeton University Press, 1959.

Brierly, J. L. *The Law of Nations.* 5th ed. London: Oxford University Press, 1955.

Brown, Lester R. *World Without Borders.* New York: Vintage Books, 1973.

————. *Redefining National Security.* Worldwatch Paper No. 14. Washington, D.C.: Worldwatch Institute, 1977.

————. *The Twenty-Ninth Day: Accommodating Human Needs and Numbers to the Earth's Resources.* New York: W. W. Norton & Co., 1978.

————. "World Food Resources and Population: The Narrowing Margin." *Population Bulletin* 36 (September 1981): 3–43.

————. *Building a Sustainable Society.* New York: Norton, 1981.

Brown, Seyom, Nina W. Cornell, Larry L. Fabian, and Edith Brown Weiss. *Regimes for the Ocean, Outer Space, and Weather.* Washington, D.C.: Brookings Institution, 1977.

Brzezinski, Zbigniew. *Between Two Ages: America's Role in the Technotronic Era.* New York: Viking Press, 1970.

Buber, Martin. *Paths in Utopia.* Trans. R.F.C. Hull. London: Routledge & Kegan Paul, 1949.

Bull, Hedley. *The Anarchical Society: A Study of Order in World Politics.* New York: Columbia University Press, 1977.

————. "The State's Positive Role in World Affairs." *Daedalus* 108 (Fall 1979): 111–23.

————. "Human Rights and World Politics." In *Moral Claims in World Affairs,* edited by Ralph Pettman. New York: St. Martin's Press, 1979.

Bundy, Robert, ed. *Images of the Future: The Twenty-First Century and Beyond.* Buffalo, N.Y.: Prometheus Books, 1976.

Camilleri, Joseph A. *Civilization in Crisis: Human Prospects in a Changing World.* New York: Cambridge University Press, 1976.

Camps, Miriam. *Collective Management: The Reform of Global Economic Organizations.* New York: McGraw-Hill Book Co., 1981.

Cantril, Hadley. *The Patterns of Human Concerns.* New Brunswick, N.J.: Rutgers University Press, 1965.

Cardoso, Fernando Henrique. "Towards Another Development." In *Toward a Just World Order,* edited by Richard A. Falk, Samuel S. Kim, and Saul H. Mendlovitz. Boulder, Colo.: Westview Press, 1982.

Cardoso, Fernando Henrique, and Enzo Galetto. *Dependency and Development in Latin America.* Berkeley, Calif.: University of California Press, 1979.

Carneiro, Robert L. "A Theory of the Origin of the State." *Science* 169 (1970): 733–38.

Carr, E. H. *The Twenty Years' Crisis 1919–1939: An Introduction to the Study of International Relations.* New York: St. Martin's Press, 1958.

Castaneda, Jorge. *Legal Effects of United Nations Resolutions.* Trans. Alba Amoia. New York: Columbia University Press, 1969.

Chan, Steve. "The Consequences of Expensive Oil on Arms Transfers." *Journal of Peace Research* 17, No. 3 (1980): 235–46.

Chaplin, George, and Glenn Paige, eds. *Hawaii 2000: Continuing Experiment in Anticipatory Democracy.* Honolulu, Hawaii: University of Hawaii Press, 1973.

Chaudhuri, Kalyan. *Genocide in Bangladesh.* Bombay: Orient Longman, 1972.

Chkhidvadze, V. "Constitution of True Human Rights and Freedoms." *International Affairs* (Moscow, October 1980): 13–20.

Chomsky, Noam, and Edward S. Herman. *The Political Economy of Human Rights.* Vol. 1: *The Washington Connection and Third World Fascism;* Vol. 2: *After the Cataclysm: Postwar Indochina and the Reconstruction of Imperial Ideology.* Boston: South End Press, 1979.

Choucri, Nazli, and Robert C. North. *Nations in Conflict: National Growth and International Violence.* San Francisco: W. H. Freeman and Co., 1975.

Choucri, Nazli, and Thomas W. Robinson, eds. *Forecasting in International Relations: Theory, Methods, Problems, Prospects.* San Francisco: W. H. Freeman and Co., 1978.

Christensen, Cheryl. "The Right to Food: How To Guarantee." *Alternatives* 4 (October 1978): 182–220.

Clark, Grenville, and Louis Sohn. *World Peace Through World Law.* 3d ed. Cambridge, Mass.: Harvard University Press, 1966.

Clark, Ian. *Reform and Resistance in the International Order.* New York: Cambridge University Press, 1980.

Clarke, Arthur C. *Profiles of the Future.* New York: Harper & Row, 1962.

Claude, Inis L., Jr. *Power and International Relations.* New York: Random House, 1962.

―――――. *Swords into Plowshares.* 4th ed. New York: Random House, 1971.

Cohen, Jerome Alan, and Hungdah Chiu. *People's China and International Law: A Documentary Study.* 2 vols. Princeton, N.J.: Princeton University Press, 1974.

Cohen, Raymond. *International Politics: The Rules of the Game.* New York: Longman, 1981.

Cole, H.S.D., Christopher Freeman, Marie Jahoda, and K.L.R. Pavitt. *Models of Doom.* New York: Universe Books, 1973.

Cole, Sam. *Global Models and the International Economic Order.* New York: Pergamon Press for UNITAR, 1977.

Committee for the Compilation of Materials on Damage Caused by the Atomic Bombs in Hiroshima and Nagasaki. *Hiroshima and Nagasaki: The Physical, Medical, and Social Effects of the Atomic Bombings.* Trans. Eisei Ishikawa and David L. Swain. New York: Basic Books, 1981.

Committee to Study the Long-Term Worldwide Effects of Multiple Nuclear-Weapons Detonations. *Long-Term Worldwide Effects of Multiple Nuclear-Weapons Detonations.* Washington, D.C.: National Academy of Sciences, 1975.

Commoner, Barry. *The Closing Circle: Nature, Man, and Technology.* New York: Alfred A. Knopf, 1971.

Cooper, Richard N. "A New International Economic Order for Mutual Gain." *Foreign Policy,* No. 26 (Spring 1977): 66–120.

Cooper, Richard N., Karl Kaiser, and Masataka Kosaka. *Towards a Renovated International System.* A report to the Trilateral Commission. Triangle Paper No. 14 (1977).

Coplin, William D. "International Law and Assumptions About the State System." *World Politics* 17 (July 1965): 615–34.

Corning, Peter A. "The Biological Bases of Behavior and Some Implications for Political Science." *World Politics* 23 (April 1971): 321–70.

Cornish, Edward. *The Study of the Future.* Washington, D.C.: World Future Society, 1977.

Cox, Robert W. "On Thinking About Future World Order." *World Politics* 28 (January 1976): 175–96.

————. "Ideologies and the New International Economic Order." *International Organization* 33 (Spring 1979): 257–302.

————. "The Crisis of World Order and the Problem of International Organization in the 1980s." *International Journal* 35 (Spring 1980): 370–95.

Cronin, John E. et al. "Tempo and Mode in Hominid Evolution." *Nature* 292 (July 9, 1981): 113–22.

Cross, John G., and Melvin J. Guyer. *Social Traps.* Ann Arbor: University of Michigan Press, 1980.

Crozier, Michel J., Samuel P. Huntington, and Joji Watanuki. *The Crisis of Democracy: Report on the Governability of Democracies to the Trilateral Commission.* New York: New York University Press, 1975.

Curti, Merle. *Human Nature in American Thought: A History.* Madison, Wis.: University of Wisconsin Press, 1980.

Dadzie, K.K.S. "Economic Development." *Scientific American* 243 (September 1980): 59–77.

Dahl, Robert A. "The Behavioral Approach in Political Science: Epitaph for a Monument to a Successful Protest." *American Political Science Review* 55 (December 1961): 763–72.

Daly, Herman E. *Steady-State Economics: The Economics of Biophysical Equilibrium and Moral Growth.* San Francisco: W. H. Freeman and Co., 1977.

Darman, Richard. "The Law of the Sea: Rethinking U.S. Interests." *Foreign Affairs* 56 (January 1978): 373–95.

Davis, Shelton H. *Victims of the Miracle: Development and the Indians of Brazil.* New York: Cambridge University Press, 1977.

de Chardin, Pierre Teilhard. *The Future of Man.* Trans. Norman Denny. New York: Harper & Row, 1964.

de Jouvenel, Bertrand. *The Art of Conjecture.* New York: Basic Books, 1967.

Deutsch, Karl W. "Political Research in the Changing World System." *International Political Science Review* 1 (1980): 23–33.

————. *Politics and Government: How People Decide Their Fate.* 3d ed. Boston: Houghton Mifflin Co., 1980.

Deutsch, Karl W., ed. *Eco-Social Systems and Eco-Politics.* Paris: UNESCO, 1977.

de Visscher, Charles. *Theory and Reality in Public International Law.* Trans. P. E. Corbett. Princeton, N.J.: Princeton University Press, 1957.

Diamond, Stanley. *In Search of the Primitive.* New Brunswick, N.J.: Transaction Books, 1974.

Dollard, John, Neal E. Miller, Leonard W. Doob, O. H. Mowrer, and Robert R. Sears. *Frustration and Aggression.* New Haven: Yale University Press, 1939.

Dolman, Antony J. *Resources, Regimes, World Order.* New York: Pergamon Press, 1981.

Dominguez, Jorge I. "Assessing Human Rights Conditions." In *Enhancing Global Human Rights,* by Jorge I. Dominguez, Nigel S. Rodney, Bryce Wood, and Richard Falk. New York: McGraw-Hill Book Co., 1979.

Donnelly, Jack. "Human Rights and Human Dignity: An Analytic Critique of Non-Western Conceptions of Human Rights." *American Political Science Review* 76 (June 1982): 303–16.

Doran, Charles F. "Modes, Mechanisms, and Turning Points: Perspectives on the Transformation of the International System." *International Political Science Review* 1 (1980): 35–61.

Dorfman, D. D. "The Cyril Burt Question: New Findings." *Science* 201 (September 29, 1978): 1177–86.

Dorn, Walter S. *Competition for Empire.* New York: Harper & Row, 1963.

Doty, Paul, Richard Garwin, George Kistiakowsky, George Rathjens, and Thomas Schelling. "Nuclear War by 1999?" *Harvard Magazine* 78 (November 1975): 19–25.

Dunlap, Riley E. "Paradigmatic Change in Social Science." *American Behavioral Scientist* 24 (September/October 1980): 5–14.

Easton, David. "The New Revolution in Political Science." *American Political Science Review* 63 (December 1969): 1051–61.

Eckholm, Erik. *The Other Energy Crisis: Firewood.* Worldwatch Paper No. 1. Washington, D.C.: Worldwatch Institute, September 1975.

————. *Down To Earth: Environment and Human Needs.* New York: W.W. Norton & Co., 1982.

Eckholm, Erik, and Lester R. Brown. *Spreading Deserts—The Hand of Man.* Worldwatch Paper No. 13. Washington, D.C.: Worldwatch Institute, April 1977.

Edelman, Murray. *The Symbolic Uses of Politics.* Urbana, Ill.: University of Illinois Press, 1964.

Eide, Asbjorn. "A Value-Based Approach: Methods and Problems in Peace Research." *International Social Science Journal* 26 (1974): 119–33.

————. "The Right to Peace." *Bulletin of Peace Proposals* 10 (1979): 157–59.

————. "Choosing the Path to Development." *Bulletin of Peace Proposals* 11, No. 4 (1980): 349–60.

Elias, Victor J. *Government Expenditure on Agriculture in Latin America.* Research Report No. 23. Washington, D.C.: IFPRI, May 1981.

Emerson, Rupert. "The Fate of Human Rights in the Third World." *World Politics* 27 (January 1975): 201–26.

Enloe, Cynthia H. *The Politics of Pollution in a Comparative Perspective: Ecology and Power in Four Nations.* New York: David McKay, 1975.

Environment and Health. Washington, D.C.: Congressional Quarterly, 1981.

Falk, Richard A. "On the Quasi-Legislative Competence of the General Assembly." *American Journal of International Law* 60 (October 1966): 782-91.

————. "The Interplay of Westphalia and Charter Conceptions of the International Legal Order." In *The Future of the International Legal Order*, Vol. 1: *Trends and Patterns*, edited by Richard A. Falk and Cyril E. Black. Princeton, N.J.: Princeton University Press, 1969.

————. *This Endangered Planet: Prospects and Proposals for Human Survival*. New York: Vintage Books, 1972.

————. "Environmental Warfare and Ecocide—Facts, Appraisal, and Proposals." *Bulletin of Peace Proposals* 4 (1973): 80-96.

————. "A New Paradigm for International Legal Studies: Prospects and Proposals." *Yale Law Journal* 84 (April 1975): 969-1021.

————. *A Study of Future Worlds*. New York: Free Press, 1975.

————. "Nuclear Policy and World Order: Why Denuclearization?" *Alternatives* 3 (March 1978): 321-50.

————. "The World Order Models Project and Its Critics: A Reply." *International Organization* 32 (Spring 1978): 531-45.

————. "Comparative Protection of Human Rights in Capitalist and Socialist Third World Countries." *Universal Human Rights* 1, No. 2 (April–June 1979): 3-29.

————. "Some Thoughts on the Decline of International Law and Future Prospects." *Hofstra Law Review* 9 (Winter 1981): 399-409.

————. *Human Rights and State Sovereignty*. New York: Holmes & Meier Publishers, 1981.

————. "On Advice to the Imperial Prince." *Alternatives* 7 (Winter 1981-1982): 403-8.

————. "Contending Approaches to World Order." In *Toward a Just World Order*, edited by Richard A. Falk, Samuel S. Kim, and Saul H. Mendlovitz. Boulder, Colo.: Westview Press, 1982.

Falk, Richard A., and Samuel S. Kim. *An Approach to World Order Studies and the World System*. WOMP Working Paper No. 22. New York: Institute for World Order, 1982.

Falk, Richard A., and Saul H. Mendlovitz, eds. *The Strategy of World Order*. Vol. 1: *Toward a Theory of War Prevention*; Vol. 2: *International Law*; Vol. 3: *The United Nations*; Vol. 4: *Disarmament and Economic Development*. New York: World Law Fund, 1966.

Falk, Richard A., and Samuel S. Kim, eds. *The War System: An Interdisciplinary Approach*. Boulder, Colo.: Westview Press, 1980.

Falk, Richard A., and Yoshikazu Sakamoto, eds. *Demilitarization I*, special issue, *Alternatives* 6 (March 1980); *Demilitarization II*, special issue, *Alternatives* 6 (July 1980).

Falk, Richard A., Samuel S. Kim, and Saul H. Mendlovitz, eds. *Studies on a Just World Order*. Vol. 1: *Toward a Just World Order*. Boulder, Colo.: Westview Press, 1982.

Falk, Richard A., Friedrich Kratochwil, and Saul H. Mendlovitz, eds. *Studies on a Just World Order*. Vol. 2: *International Law and a Just World Order*. Boulder, Colo.: Westview Press, 1983.

Farer, Tom J. "The United States and the Third World." *Foreign Affairs* 54 (October 1975): 79-97.

_____. "The Greening of the Globe: A Preliminary Appraisal of the World Order Models Project (WOMP)." *International Organization* 31 (Winter 1977): 129–47.

Ferguson, C. Clyde. "Global Human Rights: Challenges and Prospects." *Denver Journal of International Law and Policy* 8 (Spring 1979): 367–77.

Fieldhouse, D. K. *Economics and Empires, 1830–1914.* Ithaca, N.Y.: Cornell University Press, 1973.

Finlayson, Jock A., and Mark W. Zacher. "The GATT and the Regulation of Trade Barriers: Regime Dynamics and Functions." *International Organization* 35 (Autumn 1981): 561–602.

Fischer, Dana D. "Reporting Under the Covenant on Civil and Political Rights: The First Five Years of the Human Rights Committee." *American Journal of International Law* 76 (January 1982): 142–53.

Food and Agricultural Organization of the United Nations (FAO). *Agriculture: Toward 2000.* Rome: FAO, 1981.

Forsythe, David P. "The 1974 Diplomatic Conference on Humanitarian Law: Some Observations." *American Journal of International Law* 69 (January 1975): 77–91.

_____. "A New Human Rights Regime: What Significance?" Paper presented at the Annual Meeting of the International Studies Association, Philadelphia, Pa., March 17–21, 1981.

Fox, William T. R., ed. *Theoretical Aspects of International Relations.* Notre Dame, Ind.: University of Notre Dame Press, 1959.

Frank, Andre Gunder. *Crisis in the World Economy and Crisis in the Third World.* New York: Holmes and Meier Publishers, 1981.

Frank, Jerome D. *Sanity and Survival: Psychological Aspects of War and Peace.* New York: Vintage Books, 1968.

Freeman, Christopher, and Marie Jahoda, eds. *World Futures: The Great Debate.* New York: Universe Books, 1978.

Freeman, John R., and Brian L. Job. "Scientific Forecasts in International Relations: Problems of Definition and Epistemology." *International Studies Quarterly* 23 (March 1979): 113–43.

Freire, Paulo. *Pedagogy of the Oppressed.* New York: Herder & Herder, 1970.

Friedman, Edward. "On Maoist Conceptualizations of the Capitalist World System." *China Quarterly,* No. 80 (December 1979): 806–37.

Frohock, Fred M. *The Nature of Political Inquiry.* Homewood, Ill.: Dorsey Press, 1967.

Fromm, Erich. *The Sane Society.* Greenwich, Conn.: Fawcett Publications, 1955.

_____. *The Anatomy of Human Destructiveness.* New York: Holt, Rinehart and Winston, 1973.

Fukai, Shigeko. "Japan's North-South Dialogue at the United Nations." *World Politics* 35 (October 1982): 73–105.

Gallup, George H. "Human Needs and Satisfactions: A Global Survey." *Public Opinion Quarterly* 40 (Winter 1976–1977): 459–67.

Galtung, Johan. "On the Future of the International System." *Journal of Peace Research* 4 (1967): 305–33.

_____. "Violence, Peace, and Peace Research." *Journal of Peace Research* 6 (1969): 167–91.

_____. "A Structural Theory of Imperialism." *Journal of Peace Research* 8 (1971): 81–117.

_____. "The Limits to Growth and Class Politics." *Journal of Peace Research* 10 (1973): 101–14.

————. "Measuring World Development." *Alternatives* 1 (1975): 523–55.

————. *Methodology and Ideology*. Copenhagen: Christian Ejlers, 1977.

————. "The New International Economic Order and the Basic Needs Approach." *Alternatives* 4 (March 1979): 455–76.

————. *The True Worlds: A Transnational Perspective*. New York: Free Press, 1980.

Galtung, Johan, and Anders Helge Wirak. "Human Needs and Human Rights—A Theoretical Approach." *Bulletin of Peace Proposals* 8, No. 3 (1977): 251–60.

Gati, Toby Trister. "The Soviet Union and the North-South Dialogue." *Orbis* 24 (Summer 1980): 241–70.

Gelb, Leslie H., and Richard K. Betts. *The Irony of Vietnam: The System Worked*. Washington, D.C.: Brookings Institution, 1979.

George, Susan. *How the Other Half Dies: The Real Reasons for World Hunger*. Montclair, N.J.: Allanheld, Osmun & Co., 1977.

The Global 2000 Report to the President. Vol. 1: *Entering the Twenty-First Century*; Vol. 2: *The Technical Report*; Vol. 3: *Documentation on the Government's Global Sectoral Models: The Government's "Global Model."* Washington, D.C.: Government Printing Office, 1980–1981.

Gilpin, Robert. "Three Models of the Future." *International Organization* 29 (Winter 1975): 37–60.

————. *War and Change in World Politics*. New York: Cambridge University Press, 1981.

Goheen, Robert F. "Problems of Proliferation: U.S. Policy and the Third World." *World Politics* 35 (January 1983): 194–215.

Goldberg, Edward D. *The Health of the Oceans*. Paris: UNESCO, 1976.

Goldstein, Walter. "Despair and the UN Development Decade." *Futures* 13 (June 1981): 206–16.

Gompert, David C., Michael Mandelbaum, Richard L. Garwin, and John H. Barton. *Nuclear Weapons and World Politics: Alternatives for the Future*. New York: McGraw-Hill Book Co., 1977.

Gonzales, Theresa D. "The Political Sources of Procedural Debates in the United Nations: Structural Impediments to Implementation of Human Rights." *N.Y.U. Journal of International Law and Politics* 13 (Winter 1981): 427–72.

Goodman, Kjell. "International Norms and Governmental Behaviour." *Cooperation and Conflict* 4 (1969): 162–204.

Goodman, Paul, and Percival Goodman. *Communitas*. New York: Vintage Books, 1960.

Goodwin, Geoffrey, and James Mayall, eds. *A New International Commodity Regime*. New York: St. Martin's Press, 1980.

Gordon, T. J., and Olaf Helmer. *Report on a Long-Range Forecasting Study*. Paper P2982. Santa Monica, Calif.: RAND Corporation, September 1964.

Gould, Jay Stephen. *The Mismeasure of Man*. New York: W. W. Norton & Co., 1981.

Gould, Jay Stephen, and Niles Eldredge. "Puctuated Equilibrium: The Tempo and Mode of Evolution Reconsidered." *Paleobiology* 3 (1977): 115–51.

Gould, Wesley L., and Michael Barkun. *International Law and the Social Sciences*. Princeton, N.J.: Princeton University Press, 1970.

Green, R. T., and G. Santori. "A Cross Cultural Study of Hostility and Aggression," *Journal of Peace Research* 6, No. 1 (1969): 13–22.

Griffin, Keith. *International Inequality and National Poverty*. New York: Macmillan, 1978.

Gross, Leo. "The Peace of Westphalia, 1648–1948." In *International Law in the Twentieth Century,* edited by Leo Gross. New York: Appleton-Century-Crofts, 1969.

Group for the Advancement of Psychiatry. *Psychiatric Aspects of the Prevention of Nuclear War.* New York: Group for the Advancement of Psychiatry, 1964.

Gurr, Ted. *Why Men Rebel.* Princeton, N.J.: Princeton University Press, 1970.

Haas, Ernst. *Beyond the Nation-State: Functionalism and International Organization.* Stanford, Calif.: Stanford University Press, 1964.

————. "Human Rights: To Act or Not To Act?" In *Eagle Entangled: U.S. Foreign Policy in a Complex World,* edited by Kenneth A. Oye, Donald Rothchild, and Robert J. Lieber. New York: Longman, 1979.

Haas, Ernst B., Mary Pat Williams, and Don Babai. *Scientists and World Order: The Uses of Technical Knowledge in International Organizations.* Berkeley, Calif.: University of California Press, 1977.

The Hague Academy of International Law and the UN University. *Le droit a la sante en tant que droit de l'homme.* Alphen aan den Rijn, the Netherlands: Sijthoff & Noordhoff, 1979.

Halasz, Jozses et al., eds. *Socialist Concept of Human Rights.* Budapest: Akademiai Kiado, 1966.

Hallam, Mark C. "The Arms Race in Outer Space." A senior thesis presented to the Faculty of the Woodrow Wilson School of Public and International Affairs, Princeton University, April 6, 1981, 94 pp.

Halpern, Manfred. *Transformation* (a book-length manuscript in progress).

Hannigan, John A. "Fragmentation in Science: The Case of Futurology." *Sociological Review* 28 (May 1980): 317–32.

Hansen, J., D. Johnson, A. Lacis, S. Lebedeff, P. Lee, D. Rind, and G. Russell. "Climate Impact of Increasing Atmospheric Carbon Dioxide." *Science* 213 (August 28, 1981): 957–66.

Hansen, Roger D. *Beyond the North-South Stalemate.* New York: McGraw-Hill Book Co., 1979.

Hansen, Roger D., Albert Fishlow, Robert Paarlberg, and John P. Lewis. *U.S. Foreign Policy and the Third World: Agenda 1982.* New York: Praeger Publishers for the Overseas Development Council, 1982.

Hardin, Garrett. "The Tragedy of the Commons." *Science* 162 (December 1968): 1243–48.

————. "The Survival of Nations and Civilization." *Science* 172 (June 25, 1971): 1297.

————. "Lifeboat Ethics: The Case Against Helping the Poor." *Psychology Today* 8 (September 1974): 38–43, 123–26.

————. *The Limits of Altruism: An Ecologist's View of Survival.* Bloomington, Ind.: Indiana University Press, 1977.

————. "An Ecolate View of the Human Predicament." *Alternatives* 7 (Fall 1981): 242–60.

Hardin, Garrett, and John Baden, eds. *Managing the Commons.* San Francisco: W. H. Freeman and Co., 1977.

Hardy, Chandra. *Rescheduling Developing-Country Debts, 1956–1980: Lessons and Recommendations.* Overseas Development Council Working Paper No. 1. Washington, D.C.: ODC, March 1981, revised February 1982.

Harman, Willis W. *An Incomplete Guide to the Future.* Stanford, Calif.: Stanford Alumni Association, 1976.

————. "The Coming Transformation." *The Futurist* 11 (February 1977): 5–12; 11 (April 1977): 106–12.

Harris, Marvin. *Cannibals and Kings: The Origins of Cultures.* New York: Random House, 1977.

Hayes, Carlton J. H. *The Historical Evolution of Modern Nationalism.* New York: Macmillan, 1948.

Heilbroner, Robert L. *An Inquiry into the Human Prospect.* New York: W.W. Norton & Co., 1974.

Held, Virginia, Sidney Morgenbesser, and Thomas Nagel, eds. *Philosophy, Morality, and International Affairs.* New York: Oxford University Press, 1974.

Henkin, Louis. *The Rights of Man Today.* Boulder, Colo.: Westview Press, 1978.

Herrerra, Amilcar O. et al. *Catastrophe or New Society? A Latin American World Model.* Ottawa, Canada: International Development Research Centre, 1976.

Herrnstein, Richard. "IQ." *Atlantic Monthly* (September 1971): 43–64.

Herz, John H. "Rise and Demise of the Territorial State." *World Politics* 9 (July 1957): 473–93.

————. "The Territorial State Revisited: Reflections on the Future of the Nation-State." *Polity* 1, No. 1 (1968): 12–34.

————. *The Nation-State and the Crisis of World Politics.* New York: David McKay, 1976.

————. "Political Realism Revisited." *International Studies Quarterly* 25 (June 1981): 182–97.

Hicks, Norman L. "Growth vs. Basic Needs: Is There a Trade-Off?" *World Development* 7 (November–December 1979): 985–94.

Higgins, Rosalyn. *The Development of International Law Through the Political Organs of the United Nations* (London: Oxford University Press, 1963).

————. "Conceptual Thinking About the Individual in International Law." *British Journal of International Studies* 4, No. 1 (April 1978): 1–19.

Hildebrand, George C., and Gareth Porter. *Cambodia: Starvation and Revolution.* New York: Monthly Review Press, 1976.

Hill, Stuart. "Leviathan, the Open Society, and the Crisis of Ecology." In *The Global Predicament: Ecological Perspectives on World Order,* edited by David W. Orr and Marvin S. Soroos. Chapel Hill, N.C.: University of North Carolina Press, 1979.

Hinsley, F. H. *Power and the Pursuit of Peace.* New York: Cambridge University Press, 1967.

Hirschman, Albert O. "The Search for Paradigms As a Hindrance to Understanding." *World Politics* 22 (April 1970): 329–43.

Hoffmann, Stanley. "Notes on the Elusiveness of Modern Power." *International Journal* 30 (Spring 1975): 183–206.

————. "An American Social Science: International Relations." *Daedalus* 106, No. 3 (Summer 1977): 41–60.

————. *Primacy or World Order.* New York: McGraw-Hill Book Co., 1978.

————. "Muscle and Brains." *Foreign Policy,* No. 37 (Winter 1979-1980): 3–27.

————. *Duties Beyond Borders: On the Limits and Possibilities of Ethical International Politics.* Syracuse, N.Y.: Syracuse University Press, 1981.

Hollist, W. Ladd, and James N. Rosenau, eds. *World System Structure: Continuity and Change.* Beverly Hills, Calif.: Sage Publications, 1981.

Holm, Hans-Henrik. "The Game Is Up: The North-South Debate Seen Through Four Different Perspectives." Paper presented at the 23rd Annual Convention of the International Studies Association, Cincinnati, Ohio, March 24–27, 1982.

Holsti, K. J. "Retreat from Utopia: International Relations Theory, 1945–70." *Canadian Journal of Political Science* 4 (June 1971): 165–77.

————. *International Politics: A Framework for Analysis.* 3d ed. Englewood Cliffs, N.J.: Prentice-Hall, 1977.

Holsti, Ole R., Randolph M. Siverson, and Alexander L. George, eds. *Change in the International System.* Boulder, Colo.: Westview Press, 1980.

Hopkins, Raymond F. "Food As a Global Issue." In *Food in the Global Arena,* edited by James E. Harf and B. Thomas Trout. New York: Holt, Rinehart and Winston, 1982.

Hsiung, James C., and Samuel S. Kim, eds. *China in the Global Community.* New York: Praeger Publishers, 1980.

Huntington, Samuel P. "The Change to Change." *Comparative Politics* 3 (April 1971): 283–322.

————. "Human Rights and American Power." *Commentary* 72 (September 1981): 37–43.

Hveem, Helge. "The Global Dominance System." *Journal of Peace Research* 10 (1973): 319–40.

————. "Militarization of Nature: Conflict and Control over Strategic Resources and Some Implications for Peace Policies." *Journal of Peace Research* 16, No. 1 (1979): 1–26.

Inkeles, Alex. "The Emerging Social Structure of the World." *World Politics* 27 (July 1975): 467–95.

International Labor Organization. *Employment, Growth and Basic Needs.* Geneva: ILO, 1976.

————. *The Basic Needs Approach to Development: Some Issues Regarding Concepts and Methodology.* Geneva: ILO, 1977.

International Monetary Fund. *World Economic Outlook.* Washington, D.C.: IMF, June 1981.

————. *World Economic Outlook.* Washington, D.C.: IMF, April 1982.

International Union for Conservation of Nature and Natural Resources (IUCN). *World Conservation Strategy.* Gland, Switzerland: IUCN, 1980.

Jacobson, Harold K. *Networks of Interdependence: International Organization and the Global Political System.* New York: Alfred A. Knopf, 1979.

————. "The Global System and the Realization of Human Dignity and Justice." *International Studies Quarterly* 26 (September 1982): 315–32.

James, Alan, ed. *The Bases of International Order.* London: Oxford University Press, 1973.

Jantsch, Erich. *Technological Forecasting in Perspective.* Paris: OECD, 1967.

Jensen, Arthur R. "How Much Can We Boost IQ and Scholastic Achievement?" *Harvard Educational Review* 39 (Winter 1969): 1–123.

Jervis, Robert. *Perception and Misperception in International Politics.* Princeton, N.J.: Princeton University Press, 1976.

Johansen, Robert C. *Toward a Dependable Peace: A Proposal for an Appropriate Security System.* WOMP Working Paper No. 8. New York: Institute for World Order, 1978.

————. "SALT II: Illusion and Reality." *Alternatives* 5 (June 1979): 43–58.

————. *Jimmy Carter's National Security Policy: A World Order Critique.* WOMP Working Paper No. 14. New York: Institute for World Order, 1980.

————. *The National Interest and the Human Interest: An Analysis of U.S. Foreign Policy.* Princeton, N.J.: Princeton University Press, 1980.

————. "Human Rights in the 1980s: Revolutionary Growth or Unanticipated Erosion?" *World Politics* 35 (January 1983): 286–314.

————. *Toward an Alternative Security System: Moving Beyond the Balance of Power in the Search for World Security.* World Policy Paper No. 24. New York: World Policy Institute, 1983.

Johnson, Chalmers. *Revolutionary Change.* 2nd ed. Stanford, Calif.: Stanford University Press, 1982.

Jorgensen-Dahl, Arnfinn. "Forces of Fragmentation in the International System: The Case of Ethno-nationalism." *Orbis* 19 (Summer 1975): 652–74.

Joyce, James Avery. *The New Politics of Human Rights.* New York: St. Martin's Press, 1978.

Jungk, Robert, and Johan Galtung, eds. *Mankind 2000.* London: Allen & Unwin, 1969.

Kahn, Herman. *On Thermonuclear War.* Princeton, N.J.: Princeton University Press, 1960.

————. *The Coming Boom.* New York: Simon & Schuster, 1982.

Kahn, Herman, and Anthony J. Wiener. *The Year 2000: A Framework for Speculation on the Next Thirty-Three Years.* New York: Macmillan, 1967.

Kahn, Herman, William Brown, and Leon Martel. *The Next 200 Years: A Scenario for America and the World.* New York: William Morrow and Co., 1976.

Kaiser, Karl, Winston Lord, Thierry de Montbrial, and David Watt. *Western Security: What Has Changed? What Should Be Done?* A report prepared by the directors of Forschungsinstitut der Deutschen Gessellschaft fur Auswartige Politik (Bonn), Council on Foreign Relations (New York), Institut Francaise des Relations Internationales (Paris), and Royal Institute of International Affairs (London). New York: Council on Foreign Relations, 1981.

Kaldor, Mary. *European Defense Industries—National and International Implications.* Monographs of the Institute for the Study of International Organization, first series, No. 8. Brighton, England: University of Sussex, 1972.

————. "The Military in Development." *World Development* 4 (1976): 459–82.

Kaldor, M., A. Eide, and S. Merrit. *World Military Order: The Impact of Military Technology in the Third World.* London: Macmillan, 1979.

Kamin, Leon. *The Science and Politics of IQ.* Potomac, Md.: Lawrence Erlbaum Associates, 1974.

Kaplan, Morton A. *System and Process in International Politics.* New York: John Wiley & Sons, 1957.

————. *Towards Professionalism in International Theory: Macrosystem Analysis.* New York: Free Press, 1979.

Kateb, George. "Utopianism." *International Encyclopedia of the Social Sciences,* Vol. 16. New York: Free Press, 1968, pp. 269–70.

Kegley, Charles W., Jr. "Measuring the Growth and Decay of Transnational Norms Relevant to the Control of Violence: A Prospectus for Research." *Denver Journal of International Law and Policy* 5 (Fall 1975): 425–39.

————. "Measuring Transformation in the Global Legal System." In *Law-Making in the Global Community,* edited by Nicholas G. Onuf. Durham, N.C.: Carolina Academic Press, 1982.

Kegley Charles W., Jr., and Eugene R. Wittkopf. *World Politics: Trend and Transformation.* New York: St. Martin's Press, 1981.

Kelley, Donald R., Kenneth R. Stunkel, and Richard R. Wescott. *The Economic Superpowers and the Environment: The United States, the Soviet Union, and Japan.* San Francisco: W. H. Freeman and Co., 1976.

Kelman, Herbert C. "Violence Without Moral Restraint: Reflections on the Dehumanization of Victims and Victimizers." *Journal of Social Issues* 29 (1973): 25-61.

————. "The Conditions, Criteria, and Dialectics of Human Dignity: A Transnational Perspective." *International Studies Quarterly* 21 (September 1977): 529-52.

Kelman, Herbert C., ed. *International Behavior: A Social-Psychological Analysis.* New York: Holt, Rinehart and Winston, 1965.

Kende, Istvan. "Twenty-Five Years of Local Wars." *Journal of Peace Research* 8 (1971): 5-22.

————. "Dynamics of Wars, of Arms Trade and of Military Expenditure in the 'Third World,' 1945-1976." *Instant Research on Peace and Violence* 7, No. 2 (Helsinki, 1977): 56-67.

————. "War of Ten Years (1967-1976)." *Journal of Peace Research* 15 (1978): 227-41.

Keohane, Robert. "International Organization and the Crisis of Interdependence." *International Organization* 29 (Spring 1975): 357-65.

————. "The Theory of Hegemonic Stability and Changes in International Economic Regimes, 1967-1977." In *Change in the International System,* edited by Ole Holsti, Randolph Siverson, and Alexander George. Boulder, Colo.: Westview Press, 1980.

Keohane, Robert, and Joseph S. Nye. *Power and Interdependence: World Politics in Transition.* Boston: Little, Brown and Co., 1977.

Keyfitz, Nathan. "World Resources and the World Middle Class." In *Toward a Just World Order,* edited by Richard A. Falk, Samuel S. Kim, and Saul H. Mendlovitz. Boulder, Colo.: Westview Press, 1982.

Kim, Samuel S. "The Lorenzian Theory of Aggression and Peace Research: A Critique." *Journal of Peace Research* 13, No. 4 (1976): 253-76.

————. "The People's Republic of China and the Charter-Based International Legal Order." *American Journal of International Law* 62 (April 1978): 317-49.

————. *China, the United Nations, and World Order.* Princeton, N.J.: Princeton University Press, 1979.

————. "International Regimes and World Order." Paper presented at the annual meeting of the International Studies Association, Philadelphia, Pa., March 17-21, 1981.

————. "Normative Foreign Policy: The Chinese Case." *International Interactions* 8, Nos. 1-2 (1981): 51-77.

————. "Whither Post-Mao Chinese Global Policy?" *International Organization* 35 (Summer 1981): 433-65.

————. "The World Order Models Project and Its Strange Critics." *Journal of Political and Military Sociology* 9 (Spring 1981): 109-15.

————. "The Sino-American Collaboration and Cold War II." *Journal of Peace Research* 19 No. 1 (1982): 11-20.

————. "The Political Economy of Post-Mao China in Global Perspective." In *China's Changed Road to Development,* edited by Neville Maxwell and Bruce McFarlane. Oxford: Pergamon Press, 1983.

Kim, Samuel S., ed. *Chinese Foreign Policy in the 1980s.* Boulder, Colo.: Westview Press, Forthcoming.

Kindleberger, Charles. *American Business Abroad.* New Haven: Yale University Press, 1969.

Kissinger, Henry. *White House Years.* Boston: Little, Brown and Co., 1979.

_____. *Years of Upheaval.* Boston: Little, Brown and Co., 1982.

Klare, Michael. *Supplying Repression: US Support for Authoritarian Regimes Abroad.* Washington, D.C.: Institute for Policy Studies, 1977.

Knelman, F. H. "What Happened at Stockholm." *International Journal* 28, No. 1 (Winter 1972-1973): 28–49.

Knorr, Klaus E. *On the Uses of Military Power in the Nuclear Age.* Princeton, N.J.: Princeton University Press, 1966.

Kohler, Gernot. "Global Apartheid." *Alternatives* 4 (October 1978): 263–75.

Kohler, Gernot, and Norman Alcock. "Empirical Table of Structural Violence." *Journal of Peace Research* 13 (1976): 343–56.

Kosolapov, V. *Mankind and the Year 2000.* Moscow: Progress Publishers, 1976.

Kothari, Rajni. *Footsteps into the Future: Diagnosis of the Present World and a Design for an Alternative.* New York: Free Press, 1974.

_____. *Toward a Just World.* WOMP Working Paper No. 11. New York: Institute for World Order, 1980.

_____. *Environment and Alternative Development.* WOMP Working Paper No. 15. New York: Institute for World Order, 1981.

_____. "On Eco-Imperialism." *Alternatives* 7 (Winter 1981-1982): 385–94.

Krasner, Stephen D. "The Tokyo Round: Particularistic Interests and Prospects for Stability in the Global Trading System." *International Studies Quarterly* 23 (December 1979): 491–531.

_____. "Transforming International Regimes." *International Studies Quarterly* 25 (March 1981): 119–48.

Krasner, Stephen D., ed. *International Regimes.* Special issue of *International Organization* 36 (Spring 1982).

Kratochwil, Friedrich V. *International Order and Foreign Policy.* Boulder, Colo.: Westview Press, 1978.

_____. *The Humean Perspective on International Relations.* World Order Studies Program Occasional Paper No. 9. Princeton, N.J.: Center of International Studies, Princeton University, 1981.

_____. "On the Notion of 'Interest' in International Relations." *International Organization* 36 (Winter 1982): 1–30.

Ku, Min-chuan, ed. *A Comprehensive Handbook of the United Nations.* 2 vols. New York: Monarch Press, 1979.

Kuhn, Thomas. *The Structure of Scientific Revolutions.* 2nd ed. Chicago: University of Chicago Press, 1970.

Kuper, Leo. *Genocide: Its Political Use in the Twentieth Century.* New Haven, Conn.: Yale University Press, 1981.

Lagos, Gustavo, and Horacio H. Godoy. *Revolution of Being: A Latin American View of the Future.* New York: Free Press, 1977.

Lakey, George. *Strategy for a Living Revolution.* San Francisco: W. H. Freeman and Co., 1973.

Lambeth, B. "Selective Nuclear Operations and Soviet Strategy." In *Beyond Nuclear Deterrence: New Aims, New Arms,* edited by J. F. Holst and U. Nerlich. New York: Crane, Russak & Co., 1977.

Lappé, Francis Moore, and Joseph Collins. *Food First.* New York: Ballantine Books, 1978.

Lasswell, Harold D. *The Future of Political Science.* New York: Atherton Press, 1963.

_____. "The Promise of the World Order Modelling Movement." *World Politics* 29 (April 1977): 425–37.

Laszlo, Ervin, and Judah Bierman, eds. *Goals in a Global Community.* New York: Pergamon Press, 1977.

Laszlo, E., and J. Kurtzman, eds. *Eastern Europe and the New International Economic Order.* New York: Pergamon Press, 1980.

Lean, Geoffrey. *Rich World, Poor World.* London: Allen & Unwin, 1978.

Lebedev, N. I. *A New Stage in International Relations.* New York: Pergamon Press, 1978.

Lee, Hong Yung. *The Politics of the Chinese Cultural Revolution.* Berkeley, Calif.: University of California Press, 1978.

Leontief, Wassily, Anne P. Carter, and Peter A. Petri. *The Future of the World Economy.* New York: Oxford University Press, 1977.

Letelier, Orlando, and Michael Moffitt. *The International Economic Order.* Transnational Institute Pamphlet No. 2. Washington, D.C.: Institute for Policy Studies, 1977.

Levi, Werner. "The Relative Irrelevance of Moral Norms in International Politics." *Social Forces* 44 (1965): 226–33.

_____. "International Law in a Multicultural World." *International Studies Quarterly* 18 (December 1974): 417–50.

_____. *International Politics: Foundations of the System.* Minneapolis, Minn.: University of Minnesota Press, 1974.

Lewin, Roger. "Starved Brains." *Psychology Today* 9 (September 1975): 29–33.

Lewis, W. Arthur. *The Theory of Economic Growth.* New York: Harper & Row, 1970.

_____. *The Evolution of the International Economic Order.* Princeton, N.J.: Princeton University Press, 1978.

Lifton, Robert Jay. *Death in Life: Survivors of Hiroshima.* New York: Vintage, 1967.

Lifton, Robert Jay, and Richard A. Falk. *Indefensible Weapons: The Political and Psychological Case Against Nuclearism.* New York: Basic Books, 1982.

Ligue Suisse des Droits de L'Homme. *Violations des droits de l'homme en Cisjordanie.* Geneva: Ligue Suisse, September 30, 1977.

Lindblom, Charles E. *Politics and Markets.* New York: Basic Books, 1977.

Lipson, Charles. "The Transformation of Trade: The Sources and Effects of Regime Change." *International Organization* 36 (Spring 1982): 417–55.

Lipton, Michael. *Why Poor People Stay Poor.* Cambridge, Mass.: Harvard University Press, 1977.

Lock, Peter. "Armament Dynamics: An Issue in Development Strategies." *Alternatives* 6 (July 1980): 157–78.

Lopatka, Adam. "The Right to Live in Peace As a Human Right." *Bulletin of Peace Proposals* 11, No. 4 (1980): 361–67.

Lovins, Amory B. *Soft Energy Paths.* New York: Ballinger, 1977.

Lovins, Amory B., and L. Hunter Lovins. *Energy/War: Breaking the Nuclear Link.* New York: Harper Colophon Books, 1980.

Luard, Evan. *Types of International Society.* New York: Free Press, 1976.

_____. "Human Rights and Foreign Policy." *International Affairs* 56 (Autumn 1980): 579–606.

Luckham, Robin. "Armaments, Underdevelopment, and Demilitarization in Africa." *Alternatives* 6 (July 1980): 179–245.

M'Baye, Keba. "Le droit au développement comme un droit de l'homme." *Revue des droits de l'homme* 5, Nos. 2–3 (Paris, 1972): 503–34.

McCamant, John F. "Social Science and Human Rights." *International Organization* 35 (Summer 1981): 531–52.

McDougal, Myres S., Harold D. Lasswell, and Lung-Chu Chen. *Human Rights and World Public Order*. New Haven: Yale University Press, 1980.

M'Gonigle, Michael, and Mark W. Zacher. *Pollution, Politics and International Law*. Berkeley, Calif.: University of California Press, 1979.

McHale, John, and Magda Cordell McHale. *Futures Studies: An International Survey*. Sales No. E.75.XV.FS/1. New York: UNITAR, 1975.

————. *Basic Human Needs: A Framework for Action*. New Brunswick, N.J.: Transaction Books, 1978.

Machiavelli, Niccolo. *The Prince*. Trans. Luigi Ricci. New York: Mentor Books, 1952.

McHugh, J. L. "Rise and Fall of World Whaling: The Tragedy of the Commons Illustrated." *Journal of International Affairs* 31, No. 1 (1977): 23–33.

McKinstry, John A., and Carl E. Lutrin. "The Koreans of Japan: An Issue of Human Rights." *Journal of Contemporary Asia* 9, No. 4 (1979): 514–24.

McNamara, Robert. "Population and International Security." *International Security* 2 (Fall 1977): 25–55.

McNeill, William H. *The Human Condition: An Ecological and Historical View*. Princeton, N.J.: Princeton University Press, 1980.

Magnuson, W. G., ed. *Weather Modification*. U.S. Senate, Committee on Commerce. Washington, D.C.: Government Printing Office, 1966.

Mannheim, Karl. *Ideology and Utopia*. New York: Harcourt, Brace & World, 1968.

Mansbach, Richard W., and John A. Vasquez. *In Search of Theory: A New Paradigm for Global Politics*. New York: Columbia University Press, 1981.

Mansbach, Richard W., Yale H. Ferguson, and Donald E. Lampert. *The Web of World Politics: Nonstate Actors in the Global System*. Englewood Cliffs, N.J.: Prentice-Hall, 1976.

Manuel, Frank E., and Fritzie P. Manuel. *Utopian Thought in the Western World*. Cambridge, Mass.: Harvard University Press, 1979.

Many Voices, One World. Report by the International Commission for the Study of Communication Problems. Paris: UNESCO, 1980.

Mao Tse-tung [Mao Zedong]. *On the Correct Handling of Contradictions Among the People*. Peking: Foreign Language Press, 1966. Originally published in 1957.

————. *Selected Works of Mao Tse-tung*. 5 vols. Peking: Foreign Languages Press, 1961, 1965, 1977.

Marks, Stephen. "Development and Human Rights." *Bulletin of Peace Proposals* 8, No. 3 (1977): 236–46.

————. "The Peace–Human Rights–Development Dialectic." *Bulletin of Peace Proposals* 11, No. 4 (December 1980): 339–47.

————. "Emerging Human Rights: A New Generation for the 1980s?" *Rutgers Law Review* 33 (Winter 1981): 435–52.

Maslow, Abraham. "A Theory of Human Motivation." *Psychological Review* 50 (1943): 370–96.

————. *Toward a Psychology of Being*. Princeton, N.J.: D. Van Nostrand Co., 1962.

Mazrui, Ali A. *A World Federation of Cultures: An African Perspective*. New York: Free Press, 1976.

————. "Changing the Guards from Hindus to Muslims: Collective Third World Security in a Cultural Perspective." *International Affairs* 57 (Winter 1980/1981): 1–20.

————. "The Moving Cultural Frontier of World Order: From Monotheism to North-South Relations." *Alternatives* 7 (Summer 1981): 1–20.

Meadows, Donella H., Dennis L. Meadows, Jorgan Randers, and William W. Behrens III. *The Limits to Growth*. 2d ed. New York: New American Library, 1974.

Meehan, Eugene J. *Value Judgment and Social Science.* Homewood, Ill.: Dorsey Press, 1969.

Meijia, A., and N. Pizurki. "World Migration of Health Manpower." *WHO Chronicle* 30 (1976): 455–60.

Mendlovitz, Saul H. "On the Creation of a Just World Order: An Agenda for a Program of Inquiry and Praxis." *Alternatives* 7 (1981): 355–73.

Mendlovitz, Saul H., ed. *On the Creation of a Just World Order.* New York: Free Press, 1975.

Merritt, Richard L. "On the Transformation of Systems." *International Political Science Review* 1 (1980): 13–22.

Merritt, Richard L., ed. *Studies in Systems Transformation.* In *International Political Science Review* 1 (January 1980).

Merton, Robert K. *Social Theory and Social Structure: Toward the Codification of Theory and Research.* Glencoe, Ill.: Free Press, 1949.

Mesarovic, Mihajlo, and Eduard Pestel. *Mankind at the Turning Point.* The Second Report to the Club of Rome. New York: Signet, 1976.

Mestdagh, Karel de Vey. "The Right to Development." *Netherlands International Law Review* 28, No. 1 (1981): 31–53.

Meyer, F. V. *International Trade Policy.* New York: St. Martin's Press, 1978.

Michalak, Stanley J., Jr. "Theoretical Perspectives for Understanding International Interdependence." *World Politics* 32 (October 1979): 136–50.

Mills, C. Wright. *The Sociological Imagination.* New York: Oxford University Press, 1959.

Mische, Gerald, and Patricia Mische. *Toward a Human World Order.* New York: Paulist Press, 1977.

Misra, K. P., and Richard Smith Beal, eds. *International Relations Theory: Western and Non-Western Perspectives.* New Delhi: Vikas Publishing House, 1979.

Modelski, George. "The Long Cycle of Global Politics and the Nation-State." *Comparative Studies in Society and History* 20 (April 1978): 214–35.

Modelski, George, ed. *Transnational Corporations and World Order.* San Francisco: W. H. Freeman and Co., 1979.

Moore, Barrington, Jr. *Reflections on the Causes of Human Misery and Upon Certain Proposals to Eliminate Them.* Boston: Beacon Press, 1972.

————. *Injustice: The Social Bases of Obedience and Revolt.* White Plains, N.Y.: M. E. Sharpe, 1978.

Moore, Wilbert E. "Social Change." *International Encyclopedia of the Social Sciences.* Vols. 13–14. New York: Free Press, 1968, pp. 365–74.

Morgenthau, Hans J. *Politics Among Nations: The Struggle for Power and Peace.* 5th ed. New York: Alfred A. Knopf, 1973.

Morris, Morris D. *Measuring the Condition of the World's Poor: The Physical Quality of Life Index.* New York: Pergamon Press for the Overseas Development Council, 1979.

Morse, Edward L. *Modernization and the Transformation of International Relations.* New York: Free Press, 1976.

Moynihan, Daniel P. "The United States in Opposition." *Commentary* 59 (March 1975): 31–44.

Mumford, Lewis. *The Transformation of Man.* New York: Harper & Brothers, 1956.

Myrdal, Alva. *The Game of Disarmament: How the U.S. & Russia Run the Arms Race.* New York: Pantheon Books, 1976.

Myrdal, Gunnar. *An American Dilemma.* 2 vols. New York: Harper & Brothers Publishers, 1944.

_____. *A World Anti-Poverty Program in Outline*. New York: Pantheon Books, 1970.

Nagel, Thomas. "Poverty and Food: Why Charity is Not Enough." In *Food Policy: The Responsibility of the U.S. in the Life and Death Choice*, edited by Peter Brown and Henry Shue. New York: Free Press, 1977.

Nanda, Ved P., James R. Scarritt, and George W. Shepherd, Jr., eds. *Global Human Rights: Public Policies, Comparative Measures, and NGO Strategies*. Boulder, Colo.: Westview Press, 1981.

Nelson, Jack L., and Vera M. Green, eds. *International Human Rights: Contemporary Issues*. Stanfordville, N.Y.: Human Rights Publishing Group, 1980.

Nerfin, Marc, ed. *Another Development*. Uppsala, Sweden: Hammarskjöld Foundation, 1977.

"New Perspectives on International Environmental Law." *Yale Law Journal* 82 (July 1973): 1659–80.

Newburg, Paula, ed. *U.S. Foreign Policy and Human Rights*. New York: New York University Press, 1981.

Newland, Kathleen. *Refugees: The New International Politics of Displacement*. Worldwatch Paper No. 43. Washington, D.C.: Worldwatch Institute, March 1981.

Niebuhr, Reinhold. *Moral Man and Immoral Society*. New York: Charles Scribner's Sons, 1960. Originally published in 1932.

North-South: A Program for Survival. Report of the Independent Commission on International Development Issues under the Chairmanship of Willy Brandt. Cambridge, Mass.: MIT Press, 1980.

Nussbaum, Arthur. *A Concise History of the Law of Nations*. Rev. ed. New York: Macmillan Co., 1961.

Oakes, Guy, and Kenneth Stunkel. "In Search of WOMP." *Journal of Political and Military Sociology* 9 (Spring 1981): 83–99.

Onuf, Nicholas G., ed. *Law-Making in the Global Community*. Durham, N.C.: Carolina Academic Press, 1982.

Ophuls, William. *Ecology and the Politics of Scarcity*. San Francisco: W. H. Freeman and Co., 1977.

Organization for Economic Cooperation and Development (OECD). *Public Expenditure on Health*. Studies in Resource Allocation, No. 2. Paris: OECD, 1977.

_____. *Facing the Future: Mastering the Probable and Managing the Unpredictable*. Paris: OECD, 1979.

_____. *Environment Policies for the 1980s*. Paris: OECD, 1980.

Organski, A.F.K., and Jacek Kugler. "Davids and Goliaths: Predicting the Outcomes of International Wars." *Comparative Political Studies* 11 (July 1978): 141–80.

Ornauer, H., H. Wiberg, A. Sicinski, and J. Galtung, eds. *Images of the World in the Year 2000: A Comparative Ten Nation Study*. Atlantic Highlands, N.J.: Humanities Press, 1976.

Orr, David W., and Marvin S. Soroos, eds. *The Global Predicament: Ecological Perspectives on World Order*. Chapel Hill, N.C.: University of North Carolina Press, 1979.

Overcoming World Hunger: The Challenge Ahead. Report of the Presidential Commission on World Hunger, an abridged version. Washington, D.C.: Government Printing Office, 1980.

Paalberg, Robert. "A Food Security Approach for the 1980s: Righting the Balance." In Hansen et al., *U.S. Foreign Policy and the Third World: Agenda 1982*. New York: Praeger Publishers for the Overseas Development Council, 1982.

Pardo, Arvid. *The Common Heritage: Selected Papers on Ocean and World Order, 1967–1974.* Occasional Paper No. 3. Malta: International Ocean Institute, 1975.

Pardo, Arvid, and Elizabeth Mann. *The New International Economic Order and the Law of the Sea.* Malta: International Ocean Institute, 1976.

Parsons, Talcott. *The Social System.* Glencoe, Ill.: Free Press, 1951.

_____. "Order and Community in the International Social System." In *International Politics and Foreign Policy,* edited by James N. Rosenau. New York: Free Press, 1961.

Parsons, Talcott, and Edward A. Shils, eds. *Toward a General Theory of Action.* Cambridge, Mass.: Harvard University Press, 1951.

Paukert, Felix. "Income Distribution at Different Levels of Development: A Survey of Evidence." *International Labour Review* 168 (August-September 1973): 116–22.

Payer, Cheryl. *The World Bank: A Critical Analysis.* New York: Monthly Review Press, 1982.

Pearson, Lester B. *Partners in Development.* Report of the Commission on International Development. New York: Praeger, 1969.

Peccei, Aurelio. *One Hundred Pages for the Future: Reflections of the President of the Club of Rome.* New York: Pergamon Press, 1981.

Pettman, Ralph. *Human Behavior and World Politics.* New York: St. Martin's Press, 1975.

_____. *State and Class: A Sociology of International Affairs.* New York: St. Martin's Press, 1979.

Pettman, Ralph, ed. *Moral Claims in World Affairs.* New York: St. Martin's Press, 1979.

Pierre, Andrew J. *The Global Politics of Arms Sales.* Princeton, N.J.: Princeton University Press, 1982.

Pirages, Dennis. *The New Context for International Relations: Global Ecopolitics.* North Scituate, Mass.: Duxbury Press, 1978.

Ponchaud, Francois. *Cambodia: Year Zero.* Trans. Nancy Amphoux. New York: Holt, Rinehart and Winston, 1978.

Preiswerk, Roy. "Le nouvel ordre économique international est-il nouveau?" *Études Internationales* (Quebec) 8 (December 1977): 648–59.

_____. "Could We Study International Relations As If People Mattered?" In *Toward a Just World Order,* edited by Richard A. Falk, Samuel S. Kim, and Saul H. Mendlovitz. Boulder, Colo.: Westview Press, 1982.

Puchala, Donald J., and Raymond F. Hopkins. "Toward Innovation in the Global Food Regime." *International Organization* 32 (Summer 1978): 855–68.

_____. "International Regimes: Lessons from Inductive Analysis." *International Organization* 36 (Spring 1982): 245–75.

Quester, George H., ed. *Nuclear Proliferation: Breaking the Chain.* A special issue of *International Organization* 35 (Winter 1981).

Ramcharan, B. G., ed. *Human Rights: Thirty Years After the Universal Declaration.* The Hague: Martinus Nijhoff, 1979.

Rapkin, David P., William R. Thompson, and Jon A. Christopherson. "Bipolarity and Bipolarization in the Cold War Era." *Journal of Conflict Resolution* 23 (June 1979): 261–95.

Rapoport, Anatol. "Various Meanings of 'Theory'." *American Political Science Review* 52 (December 1958): 972–88.

_____. *Strategy and Conscience.* New York: Schocken Books, 1964.

Rawls, John. "Two Concepts of Rules." *Philosophical Review* 64 (January 1955): 3–32.

————. *A Theory of Justice*. Cambridge, Mass.: Belknap Press of Harvard University Press, 1971.

Rejai, Mostafa, and Cynthia H. Enloe. "Nation-States and State-Nations." *International Studies Quarterly* 13 (September 1969): 140–58.

Richardson, Lewis F. *Arms and Insecurity: A Mathematical Study of the Causes and Origins of War*, edited by Nicholas Rashevsky and Ernesto Trucco. Pittsburgh: Boxwood Press, 1960.

————. *Statistics of Deadly Quarrels*, edited by Quincy Wright and C. C. Lienau. Pittsburgh: Boxwood Press, 1960.

Rifkin, Jeremy. *Entropy: A New World View*. New York: Bantam Books, 1981.

Rokeach, Milton. *The Nature of Human Values*. New York: Free Press, 1973.

Rosecrance, Richard N. *Action and Reaction in World Politics*. Boston: Little, Brown and Co., 1963.

Rosen, Steven, ed. *A Survey of World Conflicts*. Pittsburgh, Pa.: University of Pittsburgh Center for International Studies Preliminary Paper, March 1969.

Rosenau, James N. *International Politics and Foreign Policy*. Rev. ed. New York: Free Press, 1969.

————. "Muddling, Meddling and Modelling: Alternative Approaches to the Study of World Politics in an Era of Rapid Change." *Millenium: Journal of International Studies* 8 (Autumn 1979): 130–44.

————. *The Scientific Study of Foreign Policy*. Rev., enlarged ed. New York: Nichols Publishing Co., 1980.

Rosenberg, Howard L. *Atomic Soldiers: American Victims of Nuclear Experiments*. New York: Basic Books, 1980.

Rostow, Walt W. *The Stages of Economic Growth: A Non-Communist Manifesto*. New York: Cambridge University Press, 1960.

Rothstein, Robert L. *The Weak in the World of the Strong*. New York: Columbia University Press, 1977.

————. *Global Bargaining*. Princeton, N.J.: Princeton University Press, 1979.

Royston, Michael G. *Pollution Prevention Pays*. New York: Pergamon Press, 1979.

Ruggie, John G. "On the Problem of 'The Global Problematique': What Roles for International Organizations?" *Alternatives* 5 (January 1980): 517–50.

————. "International Regimes, Transactions, and Change: Embedded Liberalism in the Postwar Economic Order." *International Organization* 36 (Spring 1982): 379–415.

Russett, Bruce M. "The Ecology of Future International Politics." *International Studies Quarterly* 11 (March 1967): 12–31.

————. *Power and Community in World Politics*. San Francisco: W. H. Freeman and Co., 1974.

————. "The Marginal Utility of Income Transfers to the Third World." *International Organization* 32 (Autumn 1978): 913–28.

Rustow, Dankwart A. "Transitions to Democracy: Toward a Dynamic Model." *Comparative Politics* 2 (April 1970): 337–63.

Saffer, Thomas H., and Orville E. Kelly. *Countdown Zero*. New York: G. P. Putnam's Sons, 1982.

Said, Abdul A., ed. *Theory of International Relations: The Crisis of Relevance*. Englewood Cliffs, N.J.: Prentice-Hall, 1968.

Sakamoto, Yoshikazu. "The Rationale of the World Order Models Project." *American Journal of International Law* 66 (September 1972): 245–52.

Sakamoto, Yoshikazu, and Hiroharu Seki. "Forecasting in Cross-National Perspective: Japan." In *Forecasting in International Relations*, edited by Nazli Choucri and Thomas Robinson. San Francisco: W. H. Freeman and Co., 1978.

Sakamoto, Yoshikazu, and Richard Falk. "World Demilitarized: A Basic Human Need." *Alternatives* 6 (March 1980): 1-16.

Saouma, Edouard. "New World Food Order." *Review of International Affairs* 31 (Belgrade, November 5, 1980): 1-5.

Schachter, Oscar. "The Evolving International Law of Development." *Columbia Journal of Transnational Law* 15, No. 1 (1976): 1-16.

_____. "The Twilight Existence of Nonbinding International Agreements." *American Journal of International Law* 71 (April 1977): 296-304.

Schell, Jonathan. *The Fate of the Earth.* New York: Avon Books, 1982.

Schneider, Jan. *World Public Order of the Environment: Towards an International Ecological Law and Organization.* Toronto: University of Toronto Press, 1979.

Schram, Stuart R. *The Political Thought of Mao Tse-tung.* New York: Praeger, 1963.

Schumacher, E. F. *Small Is Beautiful: Economics As If People Mattered.* New York: Harper & Row, 1973.

Schurmann, Franz. *Ideology and Organization in Communist China.* 2d ed. Berkeley, Calif.: University of California Press, 1971.

Schwenninger, Sherle R. "The 1980s: New Doctrines of Intervention or New Norms of Nonintervention?" *Rutgers Law Review* 33 (Winter 1981): 423-34.

Senghaas, Dieter. "Conflict Formations in Contemporary International Society." *Journal of Peace Research* 10 (1973): 163-84.

Sewell, John W. and the staff of the ODC. *The United States and World Development: Agenda 1980.* New York: Praeger Publishers for the Overseas Development Council, 1980.

Shariati, Ali. "Reflections of a Concerned Muslim: On the Plight of Oppressed Peoples." In *Toward a Just World Order,* edited by Richard A. Falk, Samuel S. Kim, and Saul H. Mendlovitz. Boulder, Colo.: Westview Press, 1982.

Sharp, Gene. *Exploring Nonviolent Alternatives.* Boston: Porter Sargent Publishers, 1971.

_____. *Social Power and Political Freedom.* Boston: Porter Sargent Publishers, 1980.

_____. *Making the Abolition of War a Realistic Goal.* New York: Institute for World Order, 1980.

Shawcross, William. *Sideshow: Kissinger, Nixon and the Destruction of Cambodia.* New York: Simon and Schuster, 1979.

Shirk, Susan. "Human Rights: What About China?" *Foreign Policy,* No. 29 (Winter 1977-1978): 109-27.

Shue, Henry. *Basic Rights: Subsistence, Affluence and U.S. Foreign Policy.* Princeton, N.J.: Princeton University Press, 1980.

Singer, J. David, and Melvin Small. "The Composition and Status Ordering of the International System: 1815-1940." *World Politics* 18 (January 1966): 236-82.

_____. *The Wages of War 1816-1965: A Statistical Handbook.* New York: John Wiley & Sons, 1972.

Singer, J. David, and Michael Wallace. "Intergovernmental Organization and the Preservation of Peace, 1916-1964: Some Bivariate Relationships." *International Organization* 24 (Summer 1970): 520-47.

Sivard, Ruth Leger. *World Military and Social Expenditures 1981.* Leesburg, Va.: World Priorities, 1981.

_____. *World Military and Social Expenditures 1982.* Leesburg, Va.: World Priorities, 1982.

Siverson, Randolph M. "War and Change in the International System." In *Change in the International System,* edited by Ole Holsti, Randolph Siverson, and Alexander George. Boulder, Colo.: Westview Press, 1980.

Skinner, B. F. *Walden Two*. New York: Macmillan, 1948.

————. "Selection by Consequences." *Science* 213 (July 31, 1981): 501–4.

Skjelsbaek, Kjell. "Value Incompatibilities in the Global System." *Journal of Peace Research* 10 (1973): 341–54.

Sklar, Holly, ed. *Trilateralism: The Trilateral and Elite Planning for World Management*. Boston: South End Press, 1980.

Skocpol, Theda. *States and Social Revolutions: A Comparative Analysis of France, Russia, and China*. New York: Cambridge University Press, 1979.

Snyder, Glenn H., and Paul Diesing. *Conflict Among Nations*. Princeton, N.J.: Princeton University Press, 1977.

Snyder, Richard C., Charles F. Hermann, and Harold D. Lasswell. "A Global Monitoring System: Appraising the Effects of Government on Human Dignity." *International Studies Quarterly* 20 (June 1976): 221–60.

Sohn, Louis. "The Stockholm Declaration on the Human Environment." *Harvard International Law Journal* 14 (Summer 1973): 423–515.

————. "The Improvement of the UN Machinery on Human Rights." *International Studies Quarterly* 23 (June 1979): 186–215.

Sprout, Harold, and Margaret Sprout. "Environmental Factors in the Study of International Politics." *Journal of Conflict Resolution* 1 (December 1957): 309–28.

————. *The Ecological Perspectives on Human Affairs, with Special Reference to International Politics*. Princeton, N.J.: Princeton University Press, 1965.

————. *Toward a Politics of the Planet Earth*. New York: Van Nostrand Reinhold Co., 1971.

————. *Multiple Vulnerabilities: The Context of Environmental Repair and Protection*. Research Monograph No. 40. Princeton, N.J.: Center of International Studies, Princeton University, April 1974.

————. *The Context of Environmental Politics*. Lexington, Ky.: University Press of Kentucky, 1978.

Stanley, C. Maxwell. *Managing Global Problems*. Iowa City, Iowa: University of Iowa Press, 1979.

Steiner, Miriam. "Conceptions of the Individual in the World Order Models Project (WOMP) Literature." *International Interactions* 6 (1979): 27–41.

Stockholm International Peace Research Institute (SIPRI). *Weapons of Mass Destruction and the Environment*. London: Taylor & Francis, 1977.

————. *Arms Control: A Survey and Appraisal of Multilateral Agreement*. New York: Crane, Russak & Co., 1978.

————. *World Armaments and Disarmament: SIPRI Yearbook 1981*. Cambridge, Mass.: Oelgeschlager, Gunn & Hain, 1981.

————. *World Armaments and Disarmament: SIPRI Yearbook 1982*. London: Taylor & Francis, 1982.

Strange, Susan. "*Cave! hic dragones*: A Critique of Regime Analysis." *International Organization* 36 (Spring 1982): 479–96.

Strong, Maurice. "One Year After Stockholm." *Foreign Affairs* 51, No. 4 (July 1973): 690–707.

————. "The International Community and the Environment." *Environmental Conservation* 4, No. 3 (Autumn 1977): 165–72.

Stunkel, Kenneth R., ed. *National Energy Profiles*. New York: Praeger Publishers, 1981.

Suchman, Edward A. "Epidemiology." *International Encyclopedia of the Social Sciences*, vol 5. New York: Free Press, 1968, pp. 97–102.

Sun Yat-sen. *San Min Chu I: The Three Principles of the People.* Trans. Frank W. Price. Shanghai: Commercial Press, 1932.

Sweezy, Paul M. "A Crisis in Marxian Theory." *Monthly Review* 31 (June 1979): 20–24.

Swing, John Temple. "The Law of the Sea." *Proceedings of the Academy of Political Science* 32 (1977): 128–41.

Sylvester, Christine. "In Defense of the World Order Models Project: A Behavioralist's Response." *Journal of Political and Military Sociology* 9 (Spring 1981): 101–8.

Szabo, Imre. "Fundamental Questions Concerning the Theory and History of Citizens." In *Socialist Concept of Human Rights*, edited by Jozses Halasz. Budapest: Akademiai Kiado, 1966.

Tanter, Raymond, and Richard H. Ullman, eds. *Theory and Policy in International Relations.* Supplement, *World Politics* 24 (Spring 1972).

Targ, Harry R. "World Order and Futures Studies Reconsidered." *Alternatives* 5 (November 1979): 371–83.

Taylor, A.J.P. *The Stuggle for Mastery in Europe 1848–1918* (Oxford: Clarendon Press, 1954).

Taylor, Trevor, ed. *Approaches and Theory in International Relations.* London: Longman, 1978.

Tedeschi, J. R., R. B. Smith, and R. C. Brown. "A Reinterpretation of Research on Aggression." *Psychological Bulletin* 81 (September 1974): 540–62.

Thomas, W. I. *The Child in America.* New York: Knopf, 1928.

Thompson, Kenneth W. "Normative Theory in International Relations." *Journal of International Affairs* 21 (1967): 278–92.

Thompson, William I. *At the End of History: Speculations on the Transformation of Culture.* New York: Harper & Row, 1971.

Thompson, William R., ed. *Contending Approaches to World System Analysis.* Beverly Hills, Calif.: Sage Publications, 1983.

Timmerman, Jacobo. *The Longest War: Israel in Lebanon.* Trans. Miguel Acoca. New York: Alfred A. Knopf, 1982.

Tinbergen, Jan (coordinator). *RIO: Reshaping the International Order.* A report to the Club of Rome. New York: E. P. Dutton & Co., 1976.

Toffler, Alvin, ed. *The Futurists.* New York: Random House, 1972.

Tolstoy, Leo. *Tolstoy's Writings on Civil Disobedience and Nonviolence.* New York: Bergman Publishers, 1967.

Tucker, Robert C. "Swollen State, Spent Society: Stalin's Legacy to Brezhnev's Russia." *Foreign Affairs* 60 (Winter 1981/1982): 414–35.

Tucker, Robert W. *The Inequality of Nations.* New York: Basic Books, 1977.

Tugwell, Franklin, ed. *Search for Alternatives: Public Policy and the Study of the Future.* Cambridge, Mass.: Winthrop Publishers, 1973.

Turner-Hampden, Charles. *Radical Man.* Cambridge, Mass.: Schenkman, 1970.

United Nations. *The Suppression of Slavery.* UN Doc. ST/SOA/4 (1951).

————. *Chemical and Bacteriological (Biological) Weapons and the Effects of Their Possible Use.* New York: United Nations, 1969.

————. *Report of the United Nations Conference on the Human Environment.* UN Doc. A/Conf.48/14/Rev.1 (1973).

————. *Maltreatment and Torture of Prisoners in South Africa.* UN Doc. ST/PSCA/SER.A/13 (1973).

————. *World Food Conference: Note by the Secretary-General.* UN Doc. E/5587 (November 22, 1974).

————. *Report of the World Food Conference, Rome, 5–16 November 1974*. UN Doc. E/CONF.65/20 (1975).

————. *World Housing Survey 1974*. Sales No. E.75.IV.8 (1976).

————. *The United Nations Disarmament Yearbook*. Vol. 1: 1976. New York: United Nations, 1977.

————. *The United Nations Disarmament Yearbook*. Vol. 2: 1977. New York: United Nations, 1978.

————. *Economic and Social Consequences of the Arms Race and of Military Expenditures*. Sales No. E.78.IX.1 (1978).

————. *The United Nations Disarmament Yearbook*. Vol. 3: 1978. New York: United Nations, 1979.

————. *Report of the Human Rights Committee*. UN Doc. A/34/40 (1979).

————. *1978 Report on the World Social Situation*. UN Publication, Sales No. E.79.IV.1 (1979).

————. *The International Dimensions of the Right to Development as a Human Right in Relation with Other Human Rights Based on International Co-operation, Including the Right to Peace, Taking into Account the Requirements of the New International Economic Order and the Fundamental Human Needs*. Report of the Secretary-General. UN Doc. E/CN.4/1334 (January 2, 1979).

————. *The United Nations Disarmament Yearbook*. Vol. 4: 1979. New York: United Nations, 1980.

————. *Comprehensive Study on Nuclear Weapons*. Report of the Secretary-General. UN Doc. A/35/392 (September 12, 1980).

————. *The State of the Environment: Selected Topics—1980*, UNEP/GC.8/3 (February 19, 1980).

————. *Agreement Establishing the Common Fund for Commodities*. UN Doc. TD/IPC/CF/CONF/24 (July 29, 1980).

————. *United Nations Action in the Field of Human Rights*. New York: United Nations, 1980.

————. *Interrelations: Resources, Environment, Population and Development*. Proceedings of a United Nations Symposium held at Stockholm, August 6–10, 1979. New York: United Nations, 1980.

————. *International Development Strategy for the Third United Nations Development Decade*. New York: United Nations, 1981.

————. *Trade and Development Report, 1981*. UN Publication, Sales No. E.81.II.D9 (1981).

————. *The Environment Programme: Programme Performance Report*. Report of the Executive Director. UN Doc. UNEP/GC.9/5 (February 25, 1981).

————. *World Population Situation in 1981*. Report of the Secretary-General. UN Doc. A/36/117 (March 6, 1981).

————. *Study on the Relationship Between Disarmament and Development*. Report of the Secretary-General. UN Doc. A/36/356 (October 5, 1981).

————. *Register of International Conventions and Protocols in the Field of the Environment*. UN Doc. UNEP/GC/INFORMATION/5/Supplement 5 (November 26, 1981).

————. *The State of the World Environment 1972–1982*. Report of the Executive Director. UN Doc. UNEP/GC.10/3 (January 29, 1982).

————. *Review of Major Achievements in the Implementation of the Action Plan for the Human Environment*. Report of the Executive Director. UN Doc. UNEP/GC(SCC)/INF.1 (January 26, 1982).

————. *The Environment in 1982: Retrospect and Prospect*. UN Doc. UNEP/GC(SSC)/2 (January 29, 1982).

_____. *Long-Term Trends in Economic Development: Report of the Secretary-General.* UN Doc. A/37/211 (May 26, 1982).

_____. *Report of the Governing Council at Its Session of a Special Character.* UN Doc. UNEP/GC(SSC)/4 (June 28, 1982).

_____. *Trade and Development Report, 1982.* UN Publication, Sales No. E.82.II.D.12 (1982).

_____. *Human Rights International Instruments.* UN Doc. ST/HR/4/Rev.4 (1982).

_____. *Report on the World Social Situation.* UN Publication, Sales No. E.82.IV.2 (1982).

_____. *United Nations Convention on the Law of the Sea.* UN Doc. A/CONF.62/122 (October 7, 1982).

U.S. Arms Control and Disarmament Agency. *Worldwide Effects of Nuclear War . . . Some Perspectives.* Washington, D.C.: Arms Control and Disarmament Agency, 1975.

_____. *Arms Control and Disarmament Agreements: Texts and Histories of Negotiations.* Washington, D.C.: Arms Control and Disarmament Agency, 1982.

U.S. Committee for Refugees. *1981 World Refugee Survey.* New York: U.S. Committee for Refugees, 1981.

_____. *World Refugee Survey 1982.* New York: U.S. Committee for Refugees, 1982.

U.S. Congress. *Abuse of Psychiatry for Political Oppression in the Soviet Union.* Hearing before the Subcommittee to Investigate the Administration of the Internal Security Act and Other Internal Security Laws of the Committee on the Judiciary, Senate, 92d Cong., 2d Sess. Washington, D.C.: Government Printing Office, 1972.

_____. Office of Technology Assessment. *The Effects of Nuclear War.* Washington, D.C.: Government Printing Office, 1979.

U.S. Congressional Research Service. *World Refugee Crisis: The International Community's Response.* Washington, D.C.: Government Printing Office, 1979.

U.S. Department of State. *The Trade Debate.* Washington, D.C.: Department of State Publication 8942, 1978.

_____. *Country Reports on Human Rights Practices.* Washington, D.C.: Government Printing Office, 1981.

_____. *Country Reports on Human Rights Practices for 1981.* Washington, D.C.: Government Printing Office, 1982.

_____. *Country Reports on Human Rights Practices for 1982.* Washington, D.C.: Government Printing Office, 1983.

van Boven, Theo C. "The United Nations Commission on Human Rights and Violations of Human Rights and Fundamental Freedom." *Netherlands International Law Review* 15 (1968): 374–93.

_____. "Some Remarks and Special Problems Relating to Human Rights in Developing Countries." *Revue des droits de l'homme* 3 (Paris, 1970): 383–96.

_____. "Partners in the Promotion and Protection of Human Rights." *Netherlands International Law Review* 24 (1977): 55–71.

_____. "The United Nations and Human Rights: A Critical Appraisal." *Bulletin of Peace Proposals* 8, No. 3 (1977): 198–208.

_____. "United Nations Policies and Strategies: Global Perspectives." In *Human Rights: Thirty Years After the Universal Declaration,* edited by B. Ramcharan. The Hague: Martinus Nijhoff, 1979.

_____. "The Role of the Commission on Human Rights in the International Community." *Human Rights Internet Newsletter* 5, Nos. 4-5 (December 1979/January 1980): 12–14.

Vasak, Karel. "A 30-Year Struggle: The Sustained Efforts to Give Force of Law to the Universal Declaration of Human Rights." *UNESCO Courier* (November 1977): 29–32.

————. "Colloquium on the Rights to Solidarity." *Bulletin of Peace Proposals* 11, No. 4 (1980): 405–7.

Vincent, J. "Western Conceptions of a Universal Moral Order." In *Moral Claims in World Affairs*, edited by Ralph Pettman. New York: St. Martin's Press, 1979.

Vyshinsky, Andrei Y. *The Law of the Soviet State*. Trans. Hugh W. Babb. New York: Macmillan, 1948.

Wadsworth, Lawrence W. "On the Meaning of World Order." *World Affairs* 141 (Fall 1978): 130–38.

Wagar, W. Warren. *The City of Man*. Baltimore, Md.: Pelican, 1967.

————. *Building the City of Man*. San Francisco: W. H. Freeman and Co., 1971.

Wallerstein, Immanuel. *The Modern World System: Capitalist Agriculture and the Origins of the European World-Economy in the Sixteenth Century*. New York: Academic Press, 1974.

————. *The Capitalist World-Economy*. New York: Cambridge University Press, 1979.

————. "Friends and Foes." *Foreign Policy* No. 40 (Fall 1980): 119–31.

Walker, R.B.J. *Political Theory and the Transformation of World Politics*. World Order Studies Program Occasional Paper No. 8. Princeton, N.J.: Center of International Studies, Princeton University, 1980.

————. "World Politics and Western Reason: Universalism, Pluralism, Hegemony." *Alternatives* 7 (Fall 1981): 195–227.

Waltz, Kenneth N. *Man, the State and War: A Theoretical Analysis*. New York: Columbia University Press, 1959.

————. "International Structure, National Force, and the Balance of World Power." *Journal of International Affairs* 21 (1967): 215–31.

————. *Theory of International Politics*. Reading, Mass.: Addison-Wesley Publishing Co., 1979.

Walzer, Michael. *Just and Unjust Wars*. New York: Basic Books, 1977.

Washburn, A. Michael. "Outline for a Normative Forecasting/Planning Process." In *Planning Alternative World Futures*, edited by Louis Rene Beres and Harry R. Targ. New York: Praeger Publishers, 1975.

Washburn, A. Michael, and Thomas E. Jones. "Anchoring Futures in Preferences." In *Forecasting in International Relations*, edited by Nazli Choucri and Thomas Robinson. San Francisco: W. H. Freeman and Co., 1978.

Weltman, John J. "On the Obsolescence of War." *International Studies Quarterly* 18 (December 1974): 395–416.

Westing, Arthur H. *Ecological Consequences of the Second Indo-China War*. Stockholm: Almqvist and Wiksell, 1976.

Weston, Burns H. "Contending with a Planet in Peril and Change: An Optimal Educational Response." *Alternatives* 5 (June 1979): 59–95.

Weston, Burns H., Richard A. Falk, and Anthony A. D'Amato, eds. *Basic Documents in International Law and World Order*. St. Paul, Minn.: West Publishing Co., 1980.

What Now—Another Development. The 1975 Dag Hammarksjöld Report on Development and International Cooperation. Uppsala, Sweden: Dag Hammarskjöld Foundation, 1975.

White, Lynn, Jr. "The Historical Roots of Our Ecologic Crisis." *Science* 155 (March 10, 1967): 1203–7.

White, Ralph K. *Nobody Wanted War*. New York: Anchor Books, 1970.

Wight, Martin. "Why Is There No International Theory?" In *Diplomatic Investigations,* edited by Herbert Butterfield and Martin Wight. Cambridge, Mass.: Harvard University Press, 1968.

Wilkinson, David. "World Order Models Project: First Fruits." *Political Science Quarterly* 91 (Summer 1976): 329–35.

Willetts, Peter. *The Non-Aligned Movement: The Origins of a Third World Alliance.* New York: Nichols Publishing Co., 1978.

Willetts, Peter, ed. *The Nonaligned in Havana*. New York: St. Martin's Press, 1981.

Williams, Robin M., Jr. "The Concept of Values." *International Encyclopedia of the Social Sciences,* vol. 16. New York: Free Press, 1968, pp. 283–87.

Willmott, Peter. "Integrity in Social Science—The Upshot of a Scandal." *International Social Science Journal* 29 (1977): 333–36.

Wilson, Edward O. *Sociobiology*. Cambridge, Mass.: Harvard University Press, 1975.

————. *On Human Nature*. Cambridge, Mass.: Harvard University Press, 1978.

Wiseberg, Laurie, and Harry Scoble. "Recent Trends in the Expanding Universe of Non-Governmental Organizations Dedicated to the Protection of Human Rights." *Denver Journal of International Law and Politics* 8 (special issue, 1979): 627–58.

Wolf, Eric R. "Killing the Achés." In *Genocide in Paraguay,* edited by Richard Arens. Philadelphia: Temple University Press, 1976.

Wolfers, Arnold. *Discord and Collaboration*. Baltimore, Md.: Johns Hopkins University Press, 1962.

Wolin, Sheldon S. "Political Theory As a Vocation." *American Political Science Review* 63 (December 1969): 1062–82.

Woodard, Kim. *The International Energy Relations of China*. Stanford, Calif.: Stanford University Press, 1980.

World Bank. *Energy in the Developing Countries*. Washington, D.C.: World Bank, August 1980.

————. *World Development Report, 1980*. New York: Oxford University Press for the World Bank, 1980.

————. *World Development Report, 1981*. New York: Oxford University Press for the World Bank, 1981.

————. *World Development Report, 1982*. New York: Oxford University Press for the World Bank, 1982.

World Health Organization (WHO). *Twenty-Eighth World Health Assembly, Geneva, 13–30 May 1975. Part 1: Resolutions and Decisions, Annexes*. Geneva: WHO, 1975.

————. *The Work of WHO 1975*. Geneva: WHO, 1976.

————. *Primary Health Care: Report of the International Conference on Primary Health Care, Alma-Ata, USSR, 6–12 September 1978*. Geneva: WHO, 1978.

————. *The Collection, Fractionation, Quality Control, and Uses of Blood and Blood Products*. Geneva: WHO, 1981.

————. *Global Strategy for Health for All by the Year 2000*. A34/5 Add.1. Geneva: WHO, March 1981.

Wright, Quincy. *A Study of War*. 2d ed. Chicago: University of Chicago Press, 1965.

Young, Oran R. "Aron and the Whale: A Jonah in Theory." In *Contending Approaches to International Politics,* edited by Klaus Knorr and James N. Rosenau. Princeton, N.J.: Princeton University Press, 1969.

————. *Compliance and Public Authority: A Theory with International Application*. Baltimore, Md.: Johns Hopkins University Press, 1979.

————. "International Regimes: Problems of Concept Formation." *World Politics* 32 (April 1980): 331–56.

Zacher, Mark W. *International Conflicts and Collective Security, 1946–77*. New York: Praeger Publishers, 1979.

Zagladin, V. V., and I. T. Frolov. "Global Problems As Areas of International Co-operation." *International Social Science Journal* 34, No. 1 (1982): 113–32.

Zinnes, Dina A. "Prerequisites for the Study of System Transformation." In *Change in the International System*, edited by Ole R. Holsti, Randolph M. Siverson, and Alexander L. George. Boulder, Colo.: Westview Press, 1980.

Books Written Under the Auspices of the Center of International Studies Princeton University 1952–1982

Gabriel A. Almond, *The Appeals of Communism* (Princeton University Press 1954)

William W. Kaufmann, ed., *Military Policy and National Security* (Princeton University Press 1956)

Klaus Knorr, *The War Potential of Nations* (Princeton University Press 1956)

Lucian W. Pye, *Guerrilla Communism in Malaya* (Princeton University Press 1956)

Charles De Visscher, *Theory and Reality in Public International Law*, trans. by P. E. Corbett (Princeton University Press 1957; rev. ed. 1968)

Bernard C. Cohen, *The Political Process and Foreign Policy: The Making of the Japanese Peace Settlement* (Princeton University Press 1957)

Myron Weiner, *Party Politics in India: The Development of a Multi-Party System* (Princeton University Press 1957)

Percy E. Corbett, *Law in Diplomacy* (Princeton University Press 1959)

Rolf Sannwald and Jacques Stohler, *Economic Integration: Theoretical Assumptions and Consequences of European Unification*, trans. by Herman Karreman (Princeton University Press 1959)

Klaus Knorr, ed., *NATO and American Security* (Princeton University Press 1959)

Gabriel A. Almond and James C. Coleman, eds., *The Politics of the Developing Areas* (Princeton University Press 1960)

Herman Kahn, *On Thermonuclear War* (Princeton University Press 1960)

Sidney Verba, *Small Groups and Political Behavior: A Study of Leadership* (Princeton University Press 1961)

Robert J. C. Butow, *Tojo and the Coming of the War* (Princeton University Press 1961)

Glenn H. Snyder, *Deterrence and Defense: Toward a Theory of National Security* (Princeton University Press 1961)

Klaus Knorr and Sidney Verba, eds., *The International System: Theoretical Essays* (Princeton University Press 1961)

Peter Paret and John W. Shy, *Guerrillas in the 1960s* (Praeger 1962)

George Modelski, *A Theory of Foreign Policy* (Praeger 1962)

Klaus Knorr and Thornton Read, eds., *Limited Strategic War* (Praeger 1963)

Frederick S. Dunn, *Peace-Making and the Settlement with Japan* (Princeton University Press 1963)

Arthur L. Burns and Nina Heathcote, *Peace-Keeping by United Nations Forces* (Praeger 1963)

Richard A. Falk, *Law, Morality, and War in the Contemporary World* (Praeger 1963)

James N. Rosenau, *National Leadership and Foreign Policy: A Case Study in the Mobilization of Public Support* (Princeton University Press 1963)

Gabriel A. Almond and Sidney Verba, *The Civic Culture: Political Attitudes and Democracy in Five Nations* (Princeton University Press 1963)

Bernard C. Cohen, *The Press and Foreign Policy* (Princeton University Press 1963)

Richard L. Sklar, *Nigerian Political Parties: Power in an Emergent African Nation* (Princeton University Press 1963)

Peter Paret, *French Revolutionary Warfare from Indochina to Algeria: The Analysis of a Political and Military Doctrine* (Praeger 1964)

Harry Eckstein, ed., *Internal War: Problems and Approaches* (Free Press 1964)

Cyril E. Black and Thomas P. Thornton, eds., *Communism and Revolution: The Strategic Uses of Political Violence* (Princeton University Press 1964)

Miriam Camps, *Britain and the European Community 1955–1963* (Princeton University Press 1964)

Thomas P. Thornton, ed., *The Third World in Soviet Perspective: Studies by Soviet Writers on the Developing Areas* (Princeton University Press 1964)

James N. Rosenau, ed., *International Aspects of Civil Strife* (Princeton University Press 1964)

Sidney I. Ploss, *Conflict and Decision-Making in Soviet Russia: A Case Study of Agricultural Policy, 1953–1963* (Princeton University Press 1965)

Richard A. Falk and Richard J. Barnet, eds., *Security in Disarmament* (Princeton University Press 1965)

Karl von Vorys, *Political Development in Pakistan* (Princeton University Press 1965)

Harold and Margaret Sprout, *The Ecological Perspective on Human Affairs, With Special Reference to International Politics* (Princeton University Press 1965)

Klaus Knorr, *On the Uses of Military Power in the Nuclear Age* (Princeton University Press 1966)

Harry Eckstein, *Division and Cohesion in Democracy: A Study of Norway* (Princeton University Press 1966)

Cyril E. Black, *The Dynamics of Modernization: A Study in Comparative History* (Harper and Row 1966)

Peter Kunstadter, ed., *Southeast Asian Tribes, Minorities, and Nations* (Princeton University Press 1967)

E. Victor Wolfenstein, *The Revolutionary Personality: Lenin, Trotsky, Gandhi* (Princeton University Press 1967)

Leon Gordenker, *The UN Secretary-General and the Maintenance of Peace* (Columbia University Press 1967)

Oran R. Young, *The Intermediaries: Third Parties in International Crises* (Princeton University Press 1967)

James N. Rosenau, ed., *Domestic Sources of Foreign Policy* (Free Press 1967)

Richard F. Hamilton, *Affluence and the French Worker in the Fourth Republic* (Princeton University Press 1967)

Linda B. Miller, *World Order and Local Disorder: The United Nations and Internal Conflicts* (Princeton University Press 1967)

Henry Bienen, *Tanzania: Party Transformation and Economic Development* (Princeton University Press 1967)

Wolfram F. Hanrieder, *West German Foreign Policy, 1949–1963: International Pressures and Domestic Response* (Stanford University Press 1967)

Richard H. Ullman, *Britain and the Russian Civil War: November 1918–February 1920* (Princeton University Press 1968)

Robert Gilpin, *France in the Age of the Scientific State* (Princeton University Press 1968)

William B. Bader, *The United States and the Spread of Nuclear Weapons* (Pegasus 1968)

Richard A. Falk, *Legal Order in a Violent World* (Princeton University Press 1968)

Cyril E. Black, Richard A. Falk, Klaus Knorr and Oran R. Young, *Neutralization and World Politics* (Princeton University Press 1968)

Oran R. Young, *The Politics of Force: Bargaining During International Crises* (Princeton University Press 1969)

Klaus Knorr and James N. Rosenau, eds., *Contending Approaches to International Politics* (Princeton University Press 1969)

James N. Rosenau, ed., *Linkage Politics: Essays on the Convergence of National and International Systems* (Free Press 1969)

John T. McAlister, Jr., *Viet Nam: The Origins of Revolution* (Knopf 1969)

Jean Edward Smith, *Germany Beyond the Wall: People, Politics and Prosperity* (Little, Brown 1969)

James Barros, *Betrayal from Within: Joseph Avenol, Secretary-General of the League of Nations, 1933–1940* (Yale University Press 1969)

Charles Hermann, *Crises in Foreign Policy: A Simulation Analysis* (Bobbs-Merrill 1969)

Robert C. Tucker, *The Marxian Revolutionary Idea: Essays on Marxist Thought and Its Impact on Radical Movements* (W. W. Norton 1969)

Harvey Waterman, *Political Change in Contemporary France: The Politics of an Industrial Democracy* (Charles E. Merrill 1969)

Cyril E. Black and Richard A. Falk, eds., *The Future of the International Legal Order. Vol. I: Trends and Patterns* (Princeton University Press 1969)

Ted Robert Gurr, *Why Men Rebel* (Princeton University Press 1969)

C. Sylvester Whitaker, *The Politics of Tradition: Continuity and Change in Northern Nigeria 1946–1966* (Princeton University Press 1970)

Richard A. Falk, *The Status of Law in International Society* (Princeton University Press 1970)

John T. McAlister, Jr. and Paul Mus, *The Vietnamese and Their Revolution* (Harper & Row 1970)

Klaus Knorr, *Military Power and Potential* (D. C. Heath 1970)

Cyril E. Black and Richard A. Falk, eds., *The Future of the International Legal Order. Vol. II: Wealth and Resources* (Princeton University Press 1970)

Leon Gordenker, ed., *The United Nations in International Politics* (Princeton University Press 1971)

Cyril E. Black and Richard A. Falk, eds., *The Future of the International Legal Order. Vol. III: Conflict Management* (Princeton University Press 1971)

Francine R. Frankel, *India's Green Revolution: Economic Gains and Political Costs* (Princeton University Press 1971)

Harold and Margaret Sprout, *Toward a Politics of the Planet Earth* (Van Nostrand Reinhold Co. 1971)

Cyril E. Black and Richard A. Falk, eds., *The Future of the International Legal Order. Vol. IV: The Structure of the International Environment* (Princeton University Press 1972)

Gerald Garvey, *Energy, Ecology, Economy* (W. W. Norton 1972)

Richard H. Ullman, *The Anglo-Soviet Accord* (Princeton University Press 1973)

Klaus Knorr, *Power and Wealth: The Political Economy of International Power* (Basic Books 1973)

Anton Bebler, *Military Rule in Africa: Dahomey, Ghana, Sierra Leone, and Mali* (Praeger Publishers 1973)

Robert C. Tucker, *Stalin as Revolutionary 1879–1929: A Study in History and Personality* (W. W. Norton 1973)

Edward L. Morse, *Foreign Policy and Interdependence in Gaullist France* (Princeton University Press 1973)

Henry Bienen, *Kenya: The Politics of Participation and Control* (Princeton University Press 1974)

Gregory J. Massell, *The Surrogate Proletariat: Moslem Women and Revolutionary Strategies in Soviet Central Asia, 1919–1929* (Princeton University Press 1974)

James N. Rosenau, *Citzenship Between Elections: An Inquiry Into The Mobilizable American* (Free Press 1974)

Ervin Laszlo, *A Strategy for the Future: The Systems Approach to World Order* (George Braziller 1974)

R. J. Vincent, *Nonintervention and International Order* (Princeton University Press 1974)

Jan H. Kalicki, *The Patterns of Sino-American Crises: Political-Military Interactions in the 1950s* (Cambridge University Press 1975)

Klaus Knorr, *The Power of Nations: The Political Economy of International Relations* (Basic Books, Inc. 1975)

James P. Sewell, *UNESCO and World Politics: Engaging in International Relations* (Princeton University Press 1975)

Richard A. Falk, *A Global Approach to National Policy* (Harvard University Press 1975)

Harry Eckstein and Ted Robert Gurr, *Patterns of Authority: A Structural Basis for Political Inquiry* (John Wiley & Sons 1975)

Cyril E. Black, Marius B. Jansen, Herbert S. Levine, Marion J. Levy, Jr., Henry Rosovsky, Gilbert Rozman, Henry D. Smith, II, and S. Frederick Starr, *The Modernization of Japan and Russia* (Free Press 1975)

Leon Gordenker, *International Aid and National Decisions: Development Programs in Malawi, Tanzania, and Zambia* (Princeton University Press 1976)

Carl von Clausewitz, *On War*, edited and translated by Michael Howard and Peter Paret (Princeton University Press 1976)

Gerald Garvey and Lou Ann Garvey, *International Resource Flows* (D. C. Heath 1977)

Walter F. Murphy and Joseph Tanenhaus, *Comparative Constitutional Law: Cases and Commentaries* (St. Martin's Press 1977)

Gerald Garvey, *Nuclear Power and Social Planning: The City of the Second Sun* (D. C. Heath 1977)

Richard E. Bissell, *Apartheid and International Organizations* (Westview Press 1977)

David P. Forsythe, *Humanitarian Politics: The International Committee of the Red Cross* (Johns Hopkins University Press 1977)

Paul E. Sigmund, *The Overthrow of Allende and the Politics of Chile, 1964–1976* (University of Pittsburgh Press 1977)

Henry S. Bienen, *Armies and Parties in Africa* (Holmes and Meier 1978)

Harold and Margaret Sprout, *The Context of Environmental Politics: Unfinished Business for America's Third Century* (University Press of Kentucky 1978)

Samuel S. Kim, *China, the United Nations, and World Order* (Princeton University Press 1979)

S. Basheer Ahmed, *Nuclear Fuel and Energy Policy* (D. C. Heath 1979)

Robert C. Johansen, *The National Interest and the Human Interest: An Analysis of U.S. Foreign Policy* (Princeton University Press 1980)

Richard A. Falk and Samuel S. Kim, eds., *The War System: An Interdisciplinary Approach* (Westview Press 1980)

James H. Billington, *Fire in the Minds of Men: Origins of the Revolutionary Faith* (Basic Books, Inc. 1980)

Bennett Ramberg, *Destruction of Nuclear Energy Facilities in War: The Problem and the Implications* (D. C. Heath 1980)

Gregory T. Kruglak, *The Politics of United States Decision-Making in United Nations Specialized Agencies: The Case of the International Labor Organization* (University Press of America 1980)

W. P. Davison and Leon Gordenker, eds., *Resolving Nationality Conflicts: The Role of Public Opinion Research* (Praeger Publishers 1980)

James C. Hsiung and Samuel S. Kim, eds., *China in the Global Community* (Praeger Publishers 1980)

Douglas Kinnard, *The Secretary of Defense* (The University Press of Kentucky 1980)

Richard Falk, *Human Rights and State Sovereignty* (Holmes and Meier Publishers, Inc. 1981)

James H. Mittelman, *Underdevelopment and the Transition to Socialism: Mozambique and Tanzania* (Academic Press 1981)

Gilbert Rosman, ed., *The Modernization of China* (The Free Press 1981; paperback edition 1982)

Robert C. Tucker, *Politics as Leadership*. The Paul Anthony Brick Lectures. Eleventh Series (University of Missouri Press 1981)

Robert Gilpin, *War and Change in World Politics* (Cambridge University Press 1981)

Nicholas G. Onuf, ed., *Law-Making in the Global Community* (Carolina Academic Press 1982)

Ali E. Hillal Dessouki, ed., *Islamic Resurgence in the Arab World* (Praeger Publishers 1982)

Index